Betty Freidan (1921–2006)
The Feminine Mystique

Erving Goffman (1922–1982)
Presentation of Self in Everyday Life

Erving Goffman (1922–1982)
Gender Advertisements

Immanuel Wallerstein (1930–)
The Modern World System

Erving Goffman (1922–1982)
Forms of Talk

Margrit Eichler (1942–)
Non-Sexist Research Methods

Simone de Beauvoir (1908–1986)
The Second Sex

Wallace Clement
Canadian Corporate Elite and *Continental Corporate Power*

Dorothy Smith (1926–)

Jean Baudrillard (1929–2007)
Simulations

Park (1864–1944)
uction to the Science of Sociology

C. Wright Mills (1916–1962)
The Power Elite

Roland Barthes (1915–1980)
The Pleasure of the Text

2000

John Porter (1921–1979)
The Vertical Mosaic

Hubert Guindon (1929–2002)
Social Class and Québec's Bureaucratic Revolution

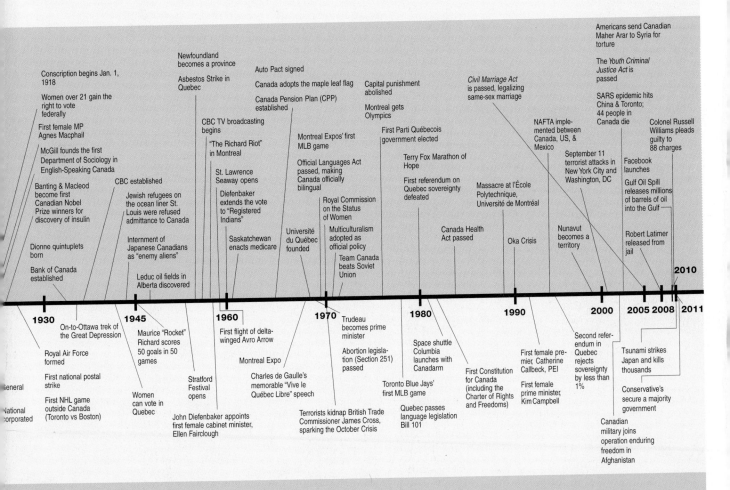

Conscription begins Jan. 1, 1918

Women over 21 gain the right to vote federally

First female MP Agnes Macphail

McGill founds the first Department of Sociology in English-Speaking Canada

Banting & Macleod become first Canadian Nobel Prize winners for discovery of insulin

Dionne quintuplets born

Bank of Canada established

CBC established

Jewish refugees on the ocean liner St. Louis were refused admittance to Canada

Internment of Japanese Canadians as "enemy aliens"

Leduc oil fields in Alberta discovered

Newfoundland becomes a province

Asbestos Strike in Quebec

CBC TV broadcasting begins

"The Richard Riot" in Montreal

St. Lawrence Seaway opens

Diefenbaker extends the vote to "Registered Indians"

Saskatchewan enacts medicare

Auto Pact signed

Canada adopts the maple leaf flag

Canada Pension Plan (CPP) established

Montreal Expos' first MLB game

Official Languages Act passed, making Canada officially bilingual

Royal Commission on the Status of Women

Multiculturalism adopted as official policy

Team Canada beats Soviet Union

Université du Québec founded

Capital punishment abolished

Montreal gets Olympics

First Parti Québecois government elected

Terry Fox Marathon of Hope

First referendum on Quebec sovereignty defeated

Canada Health Act passed

Civil Marriage Act is passed, legalizing same-sex marriage

Massacre at l'École Polytechnique, Université de Montréal

Oka Crisis

NAFTA implemented between Canada, US, & Mexico

September 11 terrorist attacks in New York City and Washington, DC

Nunavut becomes a territory

Americans send Canadian Maher Arar to Syria for torture

The *Youth Criminal Justice Act* is passed

SARS epidemic hits China & Toronto; 44 people in Canada die

Facebook launches

Gulf Oil Spill releases millions of barrels of oil into the Gulf

Robert Latimer released from jail

Colonel Russell Williams pleads guilty to 88 charges

2010

1930 **1945** **1960** **1970** **1980** **1990** **2000** **2005 2008** **2011**

On-to-Ottawa trek of the Great Depression

Royal Air Force formed

First national postal strike

First NHL game outside Canada (Toronto vs Boston)

eneral

National corporated

Maurice "Rocket" Richard scores 50 goals in 50 games

Women can vote in Quebec

First flight of delta-winged Avro Arrow

Montreal Expo

Stratford Festival opens

Charles de Gaulle's memorable "Vive le Québec Libre" speech

John Diefenbaker appoints first female cabinet minister, Ellen Fairclough

Trudeau becomes prime minister

Abortion legislation (Section 251) passed

Terrorists kidnap British Trade Commissioner James Cross, sparking the October Crisis

Space shuttle Columbia launches with Canadarm

Toronto Blue Jays' first MLB game

Quebec passes language legislation Bill 101

First Constitution for Canada (including the Charter of Rights and Freedoms)

First female premier, Catherine Callbeck, PEI

First female prime minister, Kim Campbell

Second referendum in Quebec rejects sovereignty by less than 1%

Canadian military joins operation enduring freedom in Afghanistan

Tsunami strikes Japan and kills thousands

Conservative's secure a majority government

SOCIOLOGY

A DOWN-TO-EARTH APPROACH

SIXTH CANADIAN EDITION

James M. Henslin, Southern Illinois University

Dan Glenday, Brock University

Norene Pupo, York University

Ann Duffy, Brock University

PEARSON

Toronto

Vice-President, Editorial Director: Gary Bennett
Editor-in-Chief: Michelle Sartor
Acquisitions Editor: Matthew Christian
Sponsoring Editor: Carolin Sweig
Marketing Manager: Lisa Gillis
Senior Developmental Editor: Patti Altridge
Project Manager: Andrea Falkenberg
Production Editor: Vasundhara Sawhney, Cenveo® Publisher Services
Copy Editor: Sally Glover
Proofreader: Lila Campbell and Nancy Caroll
Compositor: Cenveo Publisher Services
Photo and Permissions Researcher: Tara Smith
Art Director: Miguel Angel Acevedo
Cover and Interior Designer: Sandra Friesen
Cover Image: Fritz Brandtner
       City from a Night Train, No. 2, c. 1947
       Oil on canvas, 103.5 × 99.5 cm
       National Gallery of Canada, Ottawa
       Courtesy of Paul Kastel Gallery. Photo © NGC

10 9 8 7 6 5 4 3 2

Library and Archives Canada Cataloguing in Publication

     Sociology : a down-to-earth approach / James M. Henslin ... [et al.].—6th Canadian ed.

First Canadian ed. written by James M. Henslin, Adie Nelson.
Includes bibliographical references and indexes.
ISBN 978-0-205-84462-3

     1. Sociology—Textbooks. I. Henslin, James M

HM586.S63 2013   301   C2012-905475-5

ISBN 978-0-205-84462-3

BRIEF CONTENTS

CONTENTS

PART 2

THE INDIVIDUAL, SOCIAL GROUPS, AND GLOBALIZATION

PART 3

SOCIAL INEQUALITY

Chapter 6

SOCIAL INEQUALITY: THE CANADIAN EXPERIENCE IN A GLOBAL CONTEXT 111

PART 4

SOCIAL INSTITUTIONS

Chapter 13

THE FAMILY: DOORWAY TO SOCIETY 279

Chapter 14

EDUCATION AND RELIGION 307

Chapter 15

MEDICINE: HEALTH AND ILLNESS IN CANADA 342

PART 5

SOCIAL CHANGE

Chapter 16

CRIME AND SOCIAL DEVIANCE 359

Chapter 17

POPULATION, URBANIZATION, AND THE ENVIRONMENT 382

Chapter 18

SOCIAL MOVEMENTS AND SOCIAL CHANGE 405

LIST OF FEATURES

TO THE STUDENT

Welcome to sociology! I've loved sociology since I was in my teens, and I hope you enjoy it, too. Sociology is fascinating because it holds the key to so much understanding of social life.

If you like to watch people and try to figure out why they do what they do, you will like sociology. Sociology pries open the doors of society so you can see what goes on behind them. *Sociology: A Down-to-Earth Approach* stresses how profoundly our society and the groups to which we belong influence us. Social class, for example, sets us on a path in life. For some, the path leads to better health, more education, and higher income, but for others it leads to poverty, dropping out of school, and even a higher risk of illness and disease. These paths are so significant that they affect our chances of making it to our first birthday, as well as of getting in trouble with the police. They even influence how our marriage will work out, the number of children we will have—and whether or not we will read this book in the first place.

When I took my first course in sociology, I was "hooked." Seeing how marvelously my life had been affected by these larger social influences opened my eyes to a new world, one that has been fascinating to explore. I hope that this will be your experience also.

From how people become homeless to how they become presidents, from why people commit suicide to why women are discriminated against in every society around the world—all are part of sociology. This breadth, in fact, is what makes sociology so intriguing. We can place the sociological lens on broad features of society, such as social class, gender, and race-ethnicity, and then immediately turn our focus to the small-scale level. If we look at two people interacting—whether quarreling or kissing—we see how these broad features of society are being played out in their lives.

We aren't born with instincts. We don't come into this world with preconceived notions of what life should be like. At birth, we have no ideas of race-ethnicity, gender, age, or social class. We have no idea, for example, that people "ought" to act in certain ways because they are male or female. Yet we all learn such things as we grow up in our society. Uncovering the "hows" and "whys" of this process is also part of sociology's fascination.

One of sociology's many pleasures is that as we study life in groups (which can be taken as a definition of sociology), whether those groups be in some far-off part of the world or in some nearby corner of our own society, we constantly gain insights into our own selves. As we see how *their* customs affect *them*, effects of our own society on us become more visible.

This book, then, can be part of an intellectual adventure, for it can lead you to a new way of looking at your social world—and in the process, help you better understand both society and yourself.

I wish you the very best in college—and in your career afterward. It is my sincere hope that *Sociology: A Down-to-Earth Approach* contributes to that success.

James M. Henslin
Department of Sociology,
Southern Illinois University,
Edwardsville

PREFACE

To study sociology is to embark on a fascinating journey into a new world of perception and understanding. It is an exploration of other worlds and ideas far from your own—as well as a quest to understand your own world and ideas. Since this text is designed to help you on this journey, we'd like to show you how it is organized and review its themes and features.

The Organization of This Text

The text is organized into five parts. Each has a broad focus and is designed to help you acquire the sociological perspective. This will enable you to better analyze social relations—and the particular corner of life in which you find yourself.

Part I focuses on the sociological perspective, which we introduce in the first chapter; in Chapter 2 ("What Do Sociologists Do?"), we present the methods used by sociologists.

Part II builds on this foundation as we continue our sociological exploration of the significant influence that social groups have on our lives. We present an overview of culture, introduce socialization, and conclude with a chapter on globalization.

Part III focuses on social inequality, which has such a tremendous impact on our lives. Because social stratification is so significant—and to understand social life we need to know that it penetrates every crevice of our existence—we start with the Canadian experience and place it in the global context, which presents an overview of the principles of stratification; then we turn the sociological spotlight on social class. After establishing the broader context, we focus on gender, the most global of the social inequalities. Following this, we examine the inequalities of race, ethnicity, and age.

In Part IV, we turn to those engulfing social arrangements called social institutions. Social institutions are so significant that without understanding them we cannot understand life in society. First, we examine the impact of bureaucracy and formal organizations. Then we turn to an analysis of the overarching institutions of economy and politics, which exert an incredible amount of control over our lives. Following this, we look at four other social institutions that also play significant roles in the world—family, education, religion, and medicine.

In Part V, you will gain insight into why your world is changing so rapidly, as well as a glimpse of what is yet to come. This concluding part opens with social deviance and social control, which students often find to be among their favourite topics in sociology. The next chapter examines population, urbanization, and the environment, issues that impact us all. Lastly, we look at the fascinating areas of collective behaviour and social movements.

Themes and Features

Perhaps the single greatest goal of the introductory sociology course is to show the connection between the individual and society—to understand how social forces shape our behaviour. To help students reach this goal, this text has five central themes: down-to-earth sociology, cultural diversity and globalization, technology and society, critical thinking, and the growing influence of mass media on our lives.

Let's look at these themes in more detail.

Down-to-Earth Sociology

Why shouldn't sociology be presented in a manner that conveys its inherent excitement? Without any doubt, sociology is the most enticing of all the social sciences. Yet textbooks often make sociology seem dull, and thereby fail to reach students.

The choice of subtitle for this book, A Down-to-Earth Approach, is deliberate, for our goal is to share sociology's excitement as we embark on this fascinating journey. To note how the basic substance of sociology penetrates our everyday lives is to make visible the influence of the social on who we are. We know that you already have an awareness of the influence of the social on your life, and we hope to build on this awareness.

To stimulate your sociological imagination, we use examples that you can relate to. Threaded through the examples are the central insights provided by sociology's major perspectives. As we apply symbolic interactionism, for example, you will see how symbols create social life. As we examine functionalism, you will see how people's actions have both manifest and latent consequences. And you will have no difficulty seeing the far-reaching implications for your own life of the conflict perspective's view that groups compete for scarce resources. The inclusion of feminist theories complements the three major theoretical perspectives of the discipline, while postmodernism brings a fresh, new perspective to some of the issues raised.

Down-to-Earth Sociology boxes underscore this approach. They focus on such topics as Sociological Findings versus Common Sense (Chapter 1), Expressing Yourself Online (Chapter 3), Making the Invisible Visible: Gender Impacts Health (Chapter 7), Structures of Power and the Struggle to Survive (Chapter 10), The Higher Education–Jobs Conundrum (Chapter 14), and Youth Unemployment and Crime in Canada (Chapter 16).

We have attempted to reinforce the down-to-earth theme with a writing style that is also "down-to-earth"—that is, one that is accessible and inviting. We have tried, then, to avoid unnecessary jargon so you won't have to endure linguistic torture in order to grasp basic ideas. These ideas are of utmost importance in your sociological journey, and in introducing them we try to use concise explanations, clear (but not reductive) language, and relevant examples.

DOWN-TO-EARTH SOCIOLOGY

The New Shorthand: Expressing Yourself Online

Talking online has become a favourite activity of millions of people the world over. Teenagers, grandmothers, hobbyists, and businesspeople all appreciate the speed and ease of online communication.

Online communication doesn't allow its users to convey nuances that are transmitted during face-to-face talk. To make up for this, users have developed symbols to convey humour, disappointment, sarcasm, and other indications of mood or attitude. Common "text speak" symbols are listed below. (If you tilt your head to the left as you read, the symbols will be clearer.)

:-) Smile
:-)) Laugh
:-(Sad
:-((Very sad
:-X My lips are sealed
>:-) Feeling in a devilish mood
:-0 Wow! (What a surprise!)

Short forms are also common for online and cell phone communication. Can you translate the following text speak?

"my hart S n pieces n 1ly u put it bac 2gtha"

Answer: My HEART IS IN pieces AND ONLY YOU put it BACK TOGETHER.

Cultural Diversity and Globalization

Any attempt to explain Canadian society must pay keen attention to its diverse populations, for ours is truly a multicultural society. It must also explore the many implications of the globalization of the world's societies.

Discussions of diversity, such as the Perspectives box in Chapter 17 (Canada's Multicultural Cities) help you apply your growing sociological imagination to fundamental changes occurring in our society. They will also help you see connections among key sociological concepts, such as culture, socialization, norms, race, gender, and social class. As your sociological imagination

PERSPECTIVES

Over Half a Century of Citizenship

Most Canadians do not realize that our citizenship is a relatively new achievement. As late as 1946, Canadians were considered British subjects residing in Canada, not Canadian citizens.

It was not until 1947, with the passage of the first Citizenship Act, that the idea of a distinctly Canadian citizenship was introduced. The year 1997 saw the fiftieth anniversary of this step toward true nationhood for Canada.

The Citizenship Act came into being largely due to the efforts of Paul Martin, Sr., father of the former prime minister of Canada. It has been said that while visiting a military cemetery in France just after World War II, Paul Martin, Sr. was visibly shaken by the rows and rows of wooden crosses marking the graves of Canadians who had given their lives in the service of their country and for the peace and freedom that everyone now enjoys.

Martin was impressed by the various ethnic and religious backgrounds of the names on the graves. Despite their differences, these soldiers had come together in a struggle against the Nazi dictatorship and fascism and had died for what they believed in. When Martin returned to Canada, he set wheels in motion that led to the establishment of the Citizenship Act as a tribute to their memory. On January 1, 1947, Canada took a bold step toward independence when the Act came into being, and in so doing established a separate Canadian identity, new rights for Canadian women, and our own Canadian passport.

Source: Adapted from Citizenship and Immigration Canada website.

grows, you will better understand the social structure of our society—and your own place in it.

Global interconnections profoundly affect our lives. With this in mind, the text provides a separate chapter on globalization and its implications. For example, the dawn of a global economy—new to world history—influences the kinds of skills and knowledge you need to make a living, the types of work that will be available to you, and the variety and costs of the goods and services you consume. This global economy, which has married our fate with that of other nations, also determines other essential aspects of your life, such as whether you will experience war or peace. Of course, global changes are not simply or primarily economic. As McDonald's and KFC open up shop in Cairo and Beijing, there are profound cultural changes at hand.

Sociology and the New Technology

Sociology and the New Technology boxes explore an aspect of social life that has come to be central in our lives. We welcome new technological tools, for they help us to be more efficient at performing our daily tasks, from making a living to communicating with others—whether those people are nearby or on the other side of the globe. The significance of our new technology, however, extends far beyond the tools and the ease and efficiency they bring to our lives. The new technology is better envisioned as a social revolution that will leave few aspects of our lives untouched. Its effects are so profound that it even changes the ways we view life. Topics selected both for their relevance and timeliness include Global Village or Big Brother? (Chapter 3), Gender and Reproductive Technology (Chapter 7), High-Tech Reproduction and the Formation of Families (Chapter 13), and Internet University: No Walls, No Ivy, No Keg Parties (Chapter 14).

French sociologist Jacques Ellul feared that technology was destroying civilization, while Canadian Marshall McLuhan celebrated the "global village." The emerging sociological theory of technology, rather than regarding technology as an out-of-control force that drives culture and upon which all social change depends, emphasizes that individuals and groups—with all their values and special interests—shape technology. In addition to the impact of technology on our daily lives, this edition introduces the student to the growing influence of environmental sociology in Canada (Chapter 17).

Critical Thinking

Thinking Critically about Social Controversy boxes are another important feature of this text. These sections, which address pressing and often controversial social issues, underscore the significance of sociology for understanding the events that are challenging our ideas and changing our lives. They consider interesting issues, ranging from The Global Shame: Children in Poverty (Chapter 6) to Social Policy and Changes in the Family (Chapter 13). The Thinking Critically sections make excellent points of departure for class discussions, since they contrast several points of view or theoretical interpretations about areas of social

controversy. Critical thinking questions at the end of each chapter ask you to further apply such insights.

Mass Media and Social Life

These sections stress how the mass media affect our behaviour and permeate our thinking. We consider how they penetrate our consciousness to such a degree that they influence how we perceive our own bodies. As students consider this theme, they should begin to see mass media in a different light, which should further stimulate their sociological imagination.

The series of boxed features called Mass Media in Social Life make such issues more prominent for students. Among these are analyses of the worship of thinness—and how it affects our own body images (Chapter 1), the role of mass media in childhood socialization (Chapter 4), and Breastfeeding and Motherhood Anxieties (Chapter 13).

Additional In-Text Learning Aids

TALKING ABOUT THEORY

Theoretical Paradigms

	CLASSICAL PARADIGMS		
	Structural-Functional Paradigm	Social-Conflict Paradigm	Symbolic-Interaction Paradigm
What is the level of analysis?	Macro level	Macro level	Macro level
What is the importance of socialization for society?	Socialization is key to fitting the individual into society and its various institutions.	Socialization is key to understanding conformity in society and the role of specific institutions in providing social control. However, there must be an allowance for human agency.	Socialization provides us with the roles, techniques, and strategies that allow us to perform in specific social interactions.
Has socialization changed over time? How?	Somewhat. The primary function remains the same, but the specifics have changed. For example, the internet and mass media have provided new socializing agents.	Somewhat. The process of socialization has intensified in some instances (for example, prolonged education) and there are more extensive uses of socialization in social control. However, the overall process of socialization remains intact.	Somewhat. The process of socialization and the construction of social meanings remain intact, but the specific roles we acquire and learn to perform (for example, adolescence) have changed.

Applying Theory tables are provided in selected and relevant chapters to provide students with a quick overview of how the various theoretical perspectives consider the subject at hand.

Critical Thinking Questions encourage students to use MySearchLab (provided through MySocLab). This helps students develop their research skills and will bring them into contact with a wide scope of materials and resources.

CRITICAL THINKING QUESTIONS

1. Socialization is intended to turn us into conforming members of society. As a result, we are under considerable pressure to "do the right thing." Explain how socialization would also be useful in explaining the behaviour of the numerous individuals, from white-collar criminals to wife abusers, who deviate from social norms.
2. Some analysts fear that social media are taking over from traditional socialization agencies. Do you think, from your experience with Facebook, Twitter, Tumblr, and blogs, that youth socialization is being fundamentally altered by social media?
3. Socialization is presented as such a powerful social process that students sometimes have the impression that people are empty vessels filled with social messages—"this is what you should eat, wear, and say," for example. However, socialization theorists usually accept that each of us is actively involved in the social construction of the self. Consider the ways in which you, as a young child, were not simply a reflection of the socialization messages you received from parents, siblings, peers, and school.
4. Does traditional gender socialization and its resulting gender roles make it more difficult for North American men than women to connect emotionally to others? Access the Research Navigator through MySocLab and use keywords such as "masculinities," "homophobia," "sports," and "militarism" to locate relevant and recent scholarly and popular press publications to help you answer this question.

LEARNING OUTCOMES

After you have studied this chapter, you will be able to answer the following questions:

1. What is the sociological perspective? Is sociology a science?
2. When did sociology first appear as a separate discipline? What factors contributed to its emergence? What role did women play in the early development of sociology?
3. What universities were considered the historical centres of sociology in English-speaking Canada? How were they different?
4. What is a theory and what are the major theoretical perspectives?
5. What is the difference between pure (or basic) and applied sociology?

Learning Outcomes summarize what students will learn in each chapter.

INEQUALITIES OF GENDER

RECYCLING and reusing—these principles are now part of the modern Canadian household's standard practices. For most, these are simple tasks involve nothing more than tossing "garbage" into one bin or another. But for some, recycling and reusing—or waste picking—means survival. On the other side of the globe in Nairobi, about 6000 people, most of them women, make a daily trek to the Dandora city dump, 15 kilometres from the downtown core, where they pick through the rubbish for recyclables—glass, metal, plastics, and so on. For their work, they earn not more than $2.50 a day (Conrad, 2012). And they are not alone. The survival of millions of women around the world depends on things we throw away.

Spending long days in the hot sun doing back-breaking work, caring for children and elders, maintaining households, earning pitiful wages, and enduring the scorn of the middle classes—this is the story of many women around the globe. In many countries, women are not allowed to own property or inherit land. They endure honour killings, genital mutilation, trafficking, arranged marriages, and many other atrocities. They are denied equal access to health care, education, and employment, and, in some cases, they are not allowed to vote. Yet, despite these conditions, women manage to eke out a living, often jeopardizing their health and safety to support their children.

The world over, women run the majority of households and produce 75 to 90 percent of food crops (Shah, 2010). Yet women outrank men in numbers living in poverty and going to bed hungry. As food producers with limited mobility, they are tied to the land and their home bases. They are most vulnerable to environmental disasters, extreme weather conditions, and climate change. And when they face deteriorating conditions and the uncertainties

Opening Vignettes pique interest and alert students to key topics.

Focus Questions at strategic points in the chapters draw attention to important aspects of the topics and issues being discussed.

Focus Question
How did Marx and Weber differ in their views on rationality and how it came to permeate society?

In Sum boxes appear at various spots in the chapters to help review important points before going on to new materials.

IN SUM

As currently practised, capitalism is far from the classical laissez-faire model. Canada's economic system encourages the first two components of capitalism: private ownership of the means of production and the pursuit of profit. A vast system of government regulations both protects and restricts the third, market competition.

SUMMARY AND REVIEW

Engaging Chapter Summaries reinforce the important concepts and issues discussed in the chapters. A question-and-answer format enhances learning.

GAINING A SOCIOLOGICAL PERSPECTIVE ON CRIME AND SOCIAL DEVIANCE

How do psychological, biological, and sociological explanations of social deviance differ?
To explain why people deviate, psychologists and biologists look for reasons within the individual, such as **genetic predispositions** or **personality disorders**. Sociologists, in contrast, look for explanations *outside* the individual, in social relations. pp. 360–362.

HOW DO SYMBOLIC INTERACTIONISTS, FUNCTIONALISTS, CONFLICT THEORISTS, FEMINISTS AND POSTMODERNISTS EXPLAIN SOCIAL DEVIANCE?

The symbolic-interactionist perspective
Symbolic interactionists have developed several theories to explain social deviance such as **crime** (the violation of norms written into law). According to **differential association** theory, people learn to deviate from associating with others. **Labelling theory** focuses on how labels (names, reputations) help to propel people into or divert people away from social deviance. Many people commit socially deviant acts and still think of themselves as conformists. They apparently use five **techniques of neutralization**. Studies of prostitutes show three ways in which the self-concept is involved in socially deviant acts. In **primary social deviance**, the acts are fleeting and have little effect on the self-concept. In **secondary social deviance**, people incorporate their socially deviant acts into their self-concept. In **tertiary social deviance**, acts commonly considered socially deviant are relabelled as normal. Although most people resist being labelled socially deviant, some embrace social deviance. pp. 363–366.

The functionalist perspective
Functionalists point out that social deviance, including criminal acts, is functional for society. Functions include affirming norms and promoting social unity and social change. According to **strain theory**, societies socialize their members into desiring **cultural goals**, but many people are unable to achieve these goals in socially acceptable ways—by **institutionalized means**. Social deviants, then, are people who either give up on the goals or use socially deviant means to attain them. Merton identified five types of responses to cultural goals and institutionalized means: conformity, innovation, ritualism, retreatism, and rebellion. Illegitimate opportunity theory stresses that some people have easier access to illegal means of achieving goals. pp. 366–367.

The conflict perspective
Conflict theorists see power and social inequality as the primary characteristics of society. They stress that the state's machinery of social control, which includes the **criminal justice system**—the police, courts, and prisons that deal with the accused—represents the interests of the wealthy and powerful, a group that determines the basic laws essential to preserving its own power. pp. 370–371.

The feminist perspective
When it comes to male violence against women, virtually all feminists agree that men assault their female partners to maintain control over them, and, if they happen to live in a relationship, over their "domestic" situation. Control over women has been measured as (1) sexual fidelity, (2) obedience, (3) respect, (4) loyalty, (5) dependency, and (6) sexual access pp. 371–372.

The postmodern perspective
The postmodern approach emphasizes the need to "deconstruct" or decode the meaning of concepts such as "law and order" and the "criminal justice system." Postmodern theorists also argue that whether we are sitting at home, driving, or walking the streets, we are bombarded by information in the media about the risks we take—from air pollution and environmental hazards on and off the job to everyday choices about what we eat and drink pp. 372–373.

WHAT CAN BE DONE ABOUT MALE VIOLENCE AGAINST WOMEN?

Four strategies for coping with male violence against women are: (1) training the police to identify and charge offenders; (2) good job-creation strategies; (3) social services such as shelters and co-op housing; and (4) anti-sexist male collectives. DeKeseredy and Hinch,

Study on the Go provides students with additional resources by scanning the end-of-chapter barcode with their mobile device.

Learning new terms can be difficult. Key Terms are highlighted and introduced within a context that explains or illustrates them. They are listed together at the end of each chapter along with page numbers. To learn sociology, it is necessary to learn sociologists' basic vocabulary, and these terms provide working definitions of the most important sociological concepts.

At the end of each chapter a set of useful Weblinks helps you use the internet to explore ideas.

With complete and with clear definitions, the Comprehensive Glossary is designed to bring together the important concepts and terms introduced in the text, organizing them into a single, accessible format.

The Sixth Canadian Edition

The sixth Canadian edition is a substantial revision aimed at making content current relevant and of increased interest to Canadian students, particularly in the areas of globalization, feminism, postmodernism, social issues, social inequalities, and the mass media. By enhancing topic coverage in these areas while retaining the best features of the previous edition and drawing on the latest research and statistical reports, it also appeals to instructors who teach social action-oriented mainstream courses to university and college students.

Changes in the Sixth Canadian Edition

CHAPTER 1   THE SOCIOLOGICAL PERSPECTIVE

- **New**—Vignette on student debt as a worldwide phenomenon
- **New**—"Adonis Complex" on body obsession among young men and boys
- **New**—Student debt analyzed from different sociological theories

CHAPTER 2   WHAT DO SOCIOLOGISTS DO?

- **New**—Vignette on experiences of becoming a professional wrestler
- **New**—Career opportunities in sociology
- **New**—How to read a table: Parental Education and Student Debt

CHAPTER 3   CULTURE

- **New**—Vignette on a Canadian student's culture shock upon returning to Canada
- **New**—Noam Chomsky's views on language and thought
- **New**—Perspectives box: Endangered Languages in Canada
- **New**—Down-to-Earth Sociology box: Do Women and Men Use Language Differently?

- **Expanded coverage**—Value contradictions and multiculturalism in Canada

CHAPTER 4   SOCIALIZATION

- **New**—Vignette on an incident of Canadian intra-family homicide and its implications for cultural values
- **Updated**—The boundaries between biology and sociology
- **New**—Down-to-Earth Sociology box: Applying Socialization
- **Expanded**—Discussion on Pierre Bourdieu and cultural capital
- **Updated**—Smoking as global concern
- **Updated**—The role of mass media in gender socialization
- **Updated**—The role of video games in gender socialization and
- **New**—Inclusion of social media
- **New**—Down-to-Earth Sociology box: Challenging "Fat" Socialization
- **New**—Challenging the culture of the playground
- **New**—The information explosion: The role of mass media in childhood socialization.

CHAPTER 5   GLOBALIZATION

- Updated statistics on the top 10 countries with the largest number of international migrants

- **New**—Thinking Critically about Social Controversy box: Open Season: Children as Prey
- **New**—Anthony Giddens on how globalization is reshaping our lives
- **New**—Thinking Critically about Social Controversy box: Killing Little Girls: An Ancient and Thriving Practice

CHAPTER 6   SOCIAL INEQUALITY: THE CANADIAN EXPERIENCE IN A GLOBAL CONTEXT

- **New**—Vignette on the growing instability of the middle class in Canada and globally.
- **Updated**—The most recent statistics on individual and household wealth, income, and family income
- **Updated**—Revised information on the capitalist or upper class
- **Expanded coverage**—The relationship between income and physical and mental health, with a focus on Aboriginal populations
- **New**—Down-to-Earth Sociology box: Canadian Definitions of Low Income
- **New**—Thinking Critically about Social Controversy: The Global Shame: Children in Poverty

CHAPTER 7   INEQUALITIES OF GENDER

- **New**—Vignette on recycling in Nairobi and the inequality of women
- **New**—An examination of raising a genderless child in today's society
- **Revised**—Thinking Critically about Social Controversy box: Making "Herstory": Gender Challenges on the Track and the Runway
- **Updated**—Statistics Canada and global sources
- **New**—Down-to-Earth Sociology box: Making the Invisible Visible: Gender Impacts Health

CHAPTER 8   INEQUALITIES OF RACE AND ETHNICITY

- **New**—Vignette on Pikangikum, the northern Ontario community with the highest suicide rate in the world
- **New**—The projection of ethnic diversity in the Canadian population (2006–2031)

CHAPTER 9   INEQUALITIES OF AGE

- **New**—Vignette on the constructed meanings of age
- **New**—2011 Census data on the Canadian demographic profile
- **New**—Discussion of immigration and population aging in Canada
- **New**—Research on age stigma in Canada
- **New**—Down-to-Earth Sociology box: The Clueless Generation? The New Technology and Seniors

- **New**—Discussion of the pension crisis and generational conflict

CHAPTER 10   BUREAUCRACY AND THE CORPORATION

- **New**—Vignette on bureaucracy, home care, and the elderly
- **Expanded coverage**—New technologies and digitization
- **New**—Down-to-Earth Sociology box: Structures of Power and the Struggle to Survive
- **New**—Work-life balance
- **Revised**—Virtual organizations

CHAPTER 11   THE ECONOMY AND WORK

- **New**—Vignette a the middle-class family in Calgary
- **New**—Perspectives box: No Way to Treat a Guest Worker
- **Updated**—Statistics
- **New**—Cultural Diversity around the World box: The New Capitalism, Cars, and Social Status in China
- **New**—Canada's reliance on exporting natural resources and its impact on high paying jobs
- **New**—Down-to-Earth Sociology box: Women in Business: Maneuvering the Male Culture
- **New**—Perspectives box: Canada Income Inequality: Toronto's Cabbagetown
- **New**—Thinking Critically about Social Controversy: New Technology and the Restructuring of Work

CHAPTER 12   POLITICS: POWER AND AUTHORITY

- **New**—Vignette on Canada's political power shift to the west
- **Updated**—Information on the low rate of voter participation in Canada
- **New**—Perspectives box: Marriage, Divorce and Inheritance

CHAPTER 13   THE FAMILY: DOORWAY TO SOCIETY

- **New**—Vignette on work-family conflict in the immigrant family
- **New**—Down-to-Earth Sociology box: Finding Facts about Canadian Families
- **New**—Mass Media in Social Life: Breastfeeding and Motherhood Anxieties
- **Expanded**—Increased discussion on the impact of the economy on families
- **New**—Down-to-Earth Sociology: Social Meaning of "Unwed" Mothers
- **New**—Section on immigrant parenting

- **New**—Section on going it alone: opting out of marriage and family
- **Updated**—Research on family violence

CHAPTER 14 EDUCATION AND RELIGION

- **Updated**—Statistics
- **Expanded coverage**—The link between education and jobs or employability
- **Updated**—Discussion on whether education closes the gap between men and women in terms of pay equity and occupational attainment
- **Updated**—Discussion on spending on education and class differences among schools
- **Expanded coverage**—Bullying and student/peer culture
- **New**—Down-to-Earth Sociology box: The Higher Education–Jobs Conundrum
- **Expanded coverage**—Mainstreaming and students with disabilities
- **Revised**—Section on teachers expectations and marginalization
- **New**—Down-to-Earth Sociology box: Electronic Classrooms: A High-Tech Pedagogical Nightmare?

CHAPTER 15 MEDICINE: HEALTH AND ILLNESS IN CANADA

- **New**—Vignette on health and the fast food industry in Canada
- **New**—Down-to-Earth Sociology box: Women as Physicians
- **New**—Data on extra billing and international comparisons
- **New**—Thinking Critically about Social Controversy: Euthanasia in Canada
- **New**—Section on weight: How much is just enough?

- **Updated**—The globalization of disease
- **New**—Down-to-Earth Sociology box: Sociology, Stress, and the Canadian Workplace

CHAPTER 16 CRIME AND SOCIAL DEVIANCE

- **New**—Vignette on NHL player Sidney Crosby
- **New**—Discussion of the Vancouver hockey riots of 2011
- **New**—Canada's prostitution laws
- **New**—Daniel Wolfe's analysis of biker gangs in Canada
- **Updated**—Data on violent crime in Canada
- **New**—Perspectives box: Why Shouldn't Young Offenders Be Treated as Adult Criminals?
- **New**—Perspectives: Incarceration: Canada versus the United States

CHAPTER 17 POPULATION, URBANIZATION, AND THE ENVIRONMENT

- **New**—Vignette on the federal government's policing of Canadian scientists
- **New**—Perspectives box: Canada's Multicultural Cities
- **New**—Population growth in Canada shifts to the West
- **Updated**—Canada is the first country to withdraw from the Kyoto Protocol

CHAPTER 18 SOCIAL MOVEMENTS AND SOCIAL CHANGE

- **New**—Vignette on student protesters in Montreal
- **New**—Moral panics section includes Cohen's "folk devils"
- **New**—Urban legends section
- **New**—Perspectives box: Canada and the Occupy Wall Street Movement
- **New**—Sociology and the New Technology: Gay Porn at CHCH

Supplements for Students

MySocLab

Explore the topics covered in this chapter on MySocLab. Interactive resources include a study plan, cumulative exams, a multimedia library, MySocLab eReadings, and access to the MySocLab Video Series.

THE MOMENT YOU KNOW
Educators know it. Students know it. It's that inspired moment when something that was difficult to understand suddenly makes perfect sense. Our MyLab products have been designed and refined with a single purpose in mind—to help educators create that moment of understanding with their students.

MySocLab delivers **proven results** in helping individual students succeed. It provides **engaging experiences** that personalize, stimulate, and measure learning for each student. And, it comes from a **trusted partner** with educational expertise and an eye on the future.

MySocLab can be used by itself or linked to any learning management system. To learn more about how MySocLab combines proven learning applications with powerful assessment, visit www.mysoclab.com.

MySocLab—the moment you know.

Pearson eText

Pearson eText gives students access to the text whenever and wherever they have access to the Internet. eText pages look exactly like the printed text, offering powerful new functionality for students and instructors. Users can create notes, highlight text in different colours, create bookmarks, zoom, click hyperlinked words and phrases to view definitions, and view in single-page or two-page view. Pearson eText allows for quick navigation to key parts of the eText using a table of contents and provides full-text search. The eText may also offer links to associated media files, enabling users to access videos, animations, or other activities as they read the text.

Study on the Go

Featured at the end of each chapter, you will find a unique barcode providing access to Study on the Go, an unprecedented mobile integration between text and online content. Students link to Pearson's unique Study on the Go content directly from their smartphones, allowing them to study whenever and wherever they wish! Go to one of the sites below to see how you can download an app to your smartphone for free. Once the app is installed, your phone will scan the code and link to a website containing Pearson's Study on the Go content, including the popular study tools Glossary Flashcards, Student PowerPoints, and Quizzes, which can be accessed anytime.

SCANLIFE: http://getscanlife.com

NEOREADER: http://get.neoreader.com

QUICKMARK: http://www.quickmark.com.tw

CourseSmart

CourseSmart goes beyond traditional expectations—providing instant online access to the textbooks and course materials you need at an average savings of 60 percent. With instant access from any computer and the ability to search your text, you'll find the content you need quickly, no matter where you are. And with online tools like highlighting and note-taking, you can save time and study efficiently. See all the benefits at www.coursesmart.com/students.

Supplements for the Instructor

MYSOCLAB VIDEO SERIES: Pearson's MySocLab Video series features 37 video clips ranging from 8 to 12 minutes in length. Each clip has been edited from longer documentaries released within the past five years by the NFB and several independent film producers and focuses on key sociological topics covered in Introductory Sociology. An accompanying video guide outlines each clip's specific learning objective, a synopsis of the documentary, teaching notes, and discussion questions. Instructors can also assign auto-graded assessment, consisting of five multiple choice questions per clip, through MySocLab.

peerScholar

Firmly grounded in published research, peerScholar is a powerful online pedagogical tool that helps develop your students' critical and creative thinking skills. peerScholar facilitates this through the process of creation, evaluation, and reflection. Working in stages, students begin by submitting a written assignment. peerScholar then circulates their work for others to review, a process that can be anonymous or not depending on your preference. Students receive peer feedback and evaluations immediately, reinforcing their learning and driving the development of higher-order thinking skills. Students can then re-submit revised work, again depending on your preference. Contact your Pearson Representative to learn more about peerScholar and the research behind it.

The following instructor supplements are available for download from a password-protected section of Pearson Canada's online catalogue (http://catalogue.pearsoned.ca). Navigate to your book's catalogue page to view a list of supplements that are available. See your local sales representative for details and access.

INSTRUCTOR'S MANUAL This useful teaching aid provides chapter summaries, learning objectives, detailed lecture outlines, suggestions for introducing each chapter, discussion questions, class activities, student projects, and internet activities.

POWERPOINT PRESENTATION A PowerPoint presentation provides graphic and text images for complete multimedia presentations in the classroom.

IMAGE LIBRARY The image library provides electronic versions of the figures and tables that appear in the text.

TEST ITEM FILE The test item file contains more than 2000 questions in multiple-choice, true-false, short-answer, and essay formats, and is available in both Word and MyTest layouts.

MYTEST *FOR SOCIOLOGY: A Down-to-Earth Approach* from Pearson Education Canada is a powerful assessment generation program that helps instructors easily create and print quizzes, tests, exams, and homework or practice handouts. Questions and tests can all be authored online, allowing instructors ultimate flexibility and the ability to efficiently manage assessments at anytime, from anywhere.

CourseSmart

CourseSmart goes beyond traditional expectations—providing instant, online access to the textbooks and course materials you need at a lower cost for students. And even as students save money, you can save time and hassle with a digital eTextbook that allows you to search for the most relevant content at the very moment you need it. Whether it's evaluating textbooks or creating lecture notes to help students with difficult concepts, CourseSmart can make life a little easier. See how when you visit www.coursesmart.com/instructors.

TECHNOLOGY SPECIALISTS. Pearson's Technology Specialists work with faculty and campus course designers to ensure that Pearson technology products, assessment tools, and online course materials are tailored to meet your specific needs. This highly qualified team is dedicated to helping schools take full advantage of a wide range of educational resources by assisting in the integration of a variety of instructional materials and media formats. Your local Pearson Education sales representative can provide you with more details on this service program.

Pearson Custom Library

For enrollments of at least 25 students, you can create your own textbook by choosing the chapters that best suit your own course needs. To begin building your custom text, visit www.pearsoncustomlibrary.com. You may also work with a dedicated Pearson Custom editor to create your ideal text—publishing your own original content or mixing and matching Pearson content. Contact your local Pearson Representative to get started.

ACKNOWLEDGMENTS

The gratifying response to earlier editions of the text indicates that our efforts at making sociology down to earth have succeeded. The years that have gone into writing this book are a culmination of the many more years that preceded its writing—from graduate school to the equally demanding endeavour of classroom teaching. No text, of course, comes solely from its authors. Although we are responsible for the final words on the printed page, we have received excellent feedback from instructors and students who have used this book.

Numerous individuals at Pearson have provided invaluable support and assistance in the development of the Canadian edition. The most recent edition owes much to the efforts of Patti Altridge, Carolin Sweig, and Matthew Christian, who guided the authors through the complex process of revisions. It is difficult to heap too much praise on such fine and capable people. Their efforts, often going "beyond the call of duty" as we faced pressing deadlines, coalesced with ours in producing this text. Students, whom we constantly kept in mind as we prepared this edition, are the beneficiaries of this intricate teamwork.

Since this text is based on the contributions of many, we would count it a privilege if you would share your teaching experiences with this book, including any suggestions for improving the text. Both positive and negative comments are welcome. It is in this way that we learn.

We wish you the very best in your teaching. It is our sincere desire that *Sociology: A Down-to-Earth Approach* contributes to that success.

—JMH, DG, NP, AD.

It is often the case that an author acknowledges the "invaluable contribution" made by his/her spouse or partner. In this case, no such salutary statement will be made. Instead, the revisions to the original text were written during long periods of solitary confinement in my basement office. On numerous occasions, I was "liberated" from my work by Rick, my spousal partner. These interruptions may have caused some at Pearson Education to fret, but they prevented me from becoming a morose recluse.

—DG

To my family members, John, Jennifer, and Gregory Barkans—thank you for your ongoing support and patience during the long hours I spent at my desk.

—NP

I wish to thank Dusky, Mayra, and Hermana for their loving support through the years.

—AD

The Canadian authors would like to thank the following reviewers for their help in developing the sixth Canadian edition of *Sociology: A Down-to-Earth Approach*:

Luis Aguiar, University of British Columbia

William Boateng, University of Saskatchewan

Linda Cohen, Memorial University of Newfoundland

Stephen Decator, St. Clair College

Mike Sosteric, Athabasca University

ABOUT THE AUTHORS

James M. Henslin was born in Minnesota and graduated from high school and junior college in California and from college in Indiana. Awarded scholarships, he earned his master's and doctorate in sociology at Washington University in St. Louis, Missouri. He was awarded a postdoctoral fellowship from the National Institute of Mental Health and spent a year studying how people adjust to the suicide of a family member. His primary interests in sociology are the sociology of everyday life, deviance, and international relations. Among his more than a dozen books is *Down–to-Earth Sociology: Introductory Readings* (Free Press), now in its eleventh edition. This book of readings reflects some of his sociological interests. He has also published widely in sociology journals, including *Social Problems* and *American Journal of Sociology*.

While a graduate student, Jim Henslin taught at the University of Missouri at St. Louis. After completing his doctorate, he joined the faculty at Southern Illinois University, Edwardsville, where he is Professor Emeritus of Sociology. He says, "I've always found the introductory course enjoyable to teach. I love to see students' faces light up when they first glimpse the sociological perspective and begin to see how society has become an essential part of how they view the world."

Henslin enjoys spending time with his wife, reading, and fishing. His two favourite activities are writing and travelling. He especially enjoys living in other cultures, which brings him face to face with behaviours that he cannot take for granted, experiences that "make sociological principles come alive."

Dan Glenday was educated in Quebec, where he earned a BA with Distinction from Sir George Williams University—now Concordia University—and an MA from McGill University, and was awarded a PhD from Carleton University in Ontario. He has taught at the University of Toronto, Queen's University, and Eastern Michigan University, and is now at Brock University, where he is a full professor of Sociology and founder and director of the Centre for Labour Studies. His present research had led him into the work world of professional wrestlers. His most recent books include *The Shifting Landscape of Work: Surviving and Prospering in the New Economy* (with Ann Duffy and Norene Pupo), *Canadian Society: Meeting the Challenges of the Twenty-first Century* (with Ann Duffy), and *Good Jobs, Bad Jobs, No Jobs: The Transformation of Work in the 21st Century* (with Ann Duffy and Norene Pupo).

Ann Doris Duffy was educated in Ontario (BA, MA, and PhD at McMaster University). She is currently a full professor in the Department of Sociology at Brock University, where she is cross-appointed to the Labour Studies program and is active in the Women's Studies and Master's Program in Social Justice and Equity Studies programs. She is currently active in the development of an MA program in critical sociology at Brock. In 1995, she received the Ontario College and University Faculty Associations' Teaching Award. Her research interests include women's employment, family violence, and aging. She has co-authored and co-edited a number of books, including *Few Choices: Women, Work and Family*; *The Part-Time Paradox*; *Good Jobs, Bad Jobs, No Jobs: The Transformation of Work in the 21st Century*; *Family Violence: A Canadian Introduction*; and *Canadian Families: Diversity, Conflict and Change*. In 2008, she co-authored *Connection, Compromise, and Control: Canadian Women Discuss Midlife*.

Norene Pupo (PhD at McMaster University) teaches in the Department of Sociology at York University. Professor Pupo has researched and published in the areas of women and work, part-time employment, women and social policy, call centres, and unions and economic restructuring. She co-authored *The Part-time Paradox and Few Choices: Women, Work and Family*, and co-edited *Good Jobs, Bad Jobs, No Jobs: The Transformation of Work in the 21st Century*. She recently co-edited two books on work issues: *Interrogating the New Economy*, with Professor Mark Thomas, and *The Shifting Landscape of Work*, with Professors Duffy and Glenday.

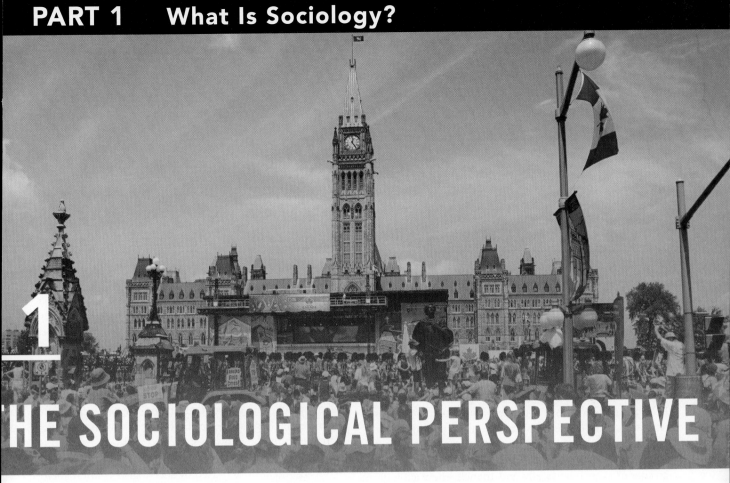

1

THE SOCIOLOGICAL PERSPECTIVE

LEARNING OUTCOMES

After you have studied this chapter, you will be able to answer the following questions:

1. What is the sociological perspective? Is sociology a science?
2. When did sociology first appear as a separate discipline? What factors contributed to its emergence? What role did women play in the early development of sociology?
3. What universities were considered the historical centres of sociology in English-speaking Canada? How were they different?
4. What is a theory and what are the major theoretical perspectives?
5. What is the difference between pure (or basic) and applied sociology?

"**AS** a single mother nearing the end of my studies in early childhood education, I've joined today's occupation to demand that the Ontario government reverse their decision to increase tuition fees next fall," said Cindy Brownlee of George Brown College. Cindy, along with several hundred other Ontario students, was protesting the increasing debt load faced by students in Ontario. The federal government estimated that student debt would climb above $15 billion in 2011—$9 billion of which will belong to Ontario students.

Student protests against high student debt are not unique to Ontario. Spring 2012 saw seemingly never-ending student protests in Quebec, and at New York City's "Kiss-In,"' students demonstrated that the United States must also "kiss student debt goodbye." As far away as Chile and New Zealand, more students are protesting their ever-growing debt loads.

Do you have a student loan? Are you worried about how much money you will owe after you graduate? Did you know that if you declare bankruptcy, your student debt remains intact? Your financial situation may be personal, but it is one shared by other students, not only in Canada but around the world. Sociology, as a social science, can help you understand how this very personal circumstance can be understood as a social problem. That is to say, sociology can help you understand how your particular circumstance fits into a much larger public, and even global, issue. Welcome to the sociological imagination.

✹ **Explore** "Invitation to Sociology" by Peter Berger on **MySocLab.**

The Sociological Perspective

Taking out a student loan every year to help pay the costs of higher education has become a normal course of action for most Canadian students. Some students see this debt as something that comes with university education. Others believe the debt load is too high and the government should step in to help financially strapped students. However you hope to pay your student debt, your particular situation is not unique: it is shared by thousands of students across Canada and hundreds of thousands more in the United States, Great Britain, and elsewhere in the world. Sociology possesses the singular perspective to help you understand your private issue as part of a larger social problem. Moreover, sociological understanding is advanced when we can compare the social circumstances of one group with another.

For example, in contrast to student debt, we can examine the circumstances facing the homeless in Canada. Christopher Hauch's important (1985) study of skid row in Winnipeg in 1984 dealt with the experience of homelessness. Hauch listed silence as a method of surviving on the street. Why do you think not speaking to someone waiting in line for shelter or food might be better or safer than talking to them? How would you feel about living with homeless men and women if you knew you could leave at any time and return to the comforts of your home and family?

As you read this text, you will find yourself looking at your own world in a different light. As you observe other groups or your own family and friends, the sociological perspective (or imagination) might open a window into unfamiliar worlds or offer a fresh look at well-known surroundings. In fact, this is what many find appealing about sociology.

The sociological perspective has been a motivating force in the lives of the authors of this text. Since we embarked on our first introductory courses in sociology, we have thoroughly enjoyed exploring how and why individuals interact with one another under different circumstances and questioning our own assumptions about life. We sincerely hope the same happens to you.

Seeing the Broader Social Context

The **sociological perspective** stresses the social contexts in which people live and how these contexts influence their lives. At the core of this perspective is the sociological imagination, a term coined by C. Wright Mills (1959). The **sociological imagination** is a sociological vision—a way of looking at the world that allows links between the apparently private problems of the individual and important social issues. At the centre of the sociological perspective is the question of how people are influenced by their **society**—the group of people with whom they share a culture and territory.

To find out why people do what they do, sociologists look at **social location** by considering their occupation, income, education, gender, age, and ethnicity. Think about, for example, how growing up identified as a member of a group called females or a group called males affects our ideas of what we should attain in life. Growing up as a male or a female influences not only our aspirations, but also how we feel about ourselves and how we relate to others in dating and establishing households and at work.

Levels of Sociological Analysis

Macrosociology and Microsociology

Macrosociology focuses on the broad features of society. Sociologists who use this approach analyze such things as social class and patriarchy. If macrosociologists were to analyze student debt, for example, they would stress that university students come from different classes in the social system. Students from low status families will experience greater difficulties in finding good jobs to help pay for their debt than students coming from the middle and upper classes. This is partly due to their relative lack of "cultural capital" (see Pierre Bourdieu, Chapter 3).

Conflict theory, functionalism, and feminism focus on the broader picture and are examples of the macrosociological approach. The goal of these theories is to examine and interpret the large-scale social forces that influence people's conduct in public and private spaces and our reactions to their behaviours.

A second approach used by sociologists is **microsociology**. Here, the emphasis is placed on **social interaction**, or what people do when they come together. Microsociologists are likely to focus on how groups of university students who come from different social class backgrounds handle the resources they have; their relationships with girlfriends or boyfriends or same-sex partners, family, and friends; where they spend their time and what they do there; their language, pecking order, and so on. Symbolic interactionism, queer theory, postmodernism, and feminism that emphasizes the social construction of gender are examples of microsociological approaches. While the macrosociological approach stresses the broad features of society, the microsociological approach has a narrower focus, placing its emphasis on face-to-face social interaction, language and discourse, or what people do when they are in each other's presence.

Sociologist C. Wright Mills (1959: 2) said of sociology: "The sociological imagination or perspective enables us to grasp the connection between history and biography."

Watch various speakers discuss the work of C. Wright Mills on **MySocLab.**

Explore the sociological perspective by taking a sociological tour through cyberspace on **MySocLab.**

Explore C. Wright Mills' "The Promise" on **MySocLab.**

You Can't Be Thin Enough: Body Images and the Mass Media

When you stand before a mirror, do you like what you see? To make your body more attractive, do you watch your weight or work out? You have ideas about what you should look like. Where did you get them?

Television and magazine ads keep pounding home the message that our bodies aren't good enough, that we've got to improve them. Female movie stars effortlessly go through tough workouts without breaking a sweat. Muscular hunks show off machines that magically produce steel abs and incredible biceps—in just a few minutes a day! Women and men are led to believe that attractive members of the opposite sex will flock to them if they purchase that wonder-working exercise machine.

Although we try to shrug off such messages, knowing they are designed to sell products, they still get our attention. They penetrate our thinking and feeling, helping to shape ideal images of how we "ought" to look. Could those models sashaying down the runway in beautiful clothes be any thinner? For women, the message is clear: you can't be thin enough. The message for men is also apparent: you can't be strong enough.

Woman or man, your body isn't good enough. It sags where it should be firm. It bulges where it should be smooth. It sticks out where it shouldn't and doesn't stick out enough where it should. And—no matter what your weight—it's too much. You've got to be thinner.

Exercise takes time and getting in shape can be painful. Once you get there, if you slack off, it seems to take only a few days for your body to return to its former drab appearance. You can't let up, you can't exercise enough, and you can't diet enough.

But who can continue at such a torrid pace? A few people, of course, but not many. Liposuction becomes appealing: just lie there, put up with a little discomfort, and the doctor will suck the fat right out of you. Surgeons can transform flat chests into super breasts overnight. They can lower receding hairlines and smooth furrowed brows. They can remove lumps with magical tummy tucks and reverse a decade with rejuvenating skin peels and face lifts.

The bosomy girls paraded on the reality show *The Bachelor Canada* and the impossibly shaped models in Victoria's Secret ads set the standard to which women hold themselves. Even teens call on plastic surgeons.

The thinness craze has moved to the East, too. Glossy magazines in Japan and China are filled with skinny models and ads touting diet pills and diet teas. In China, where famine used to abound, a bit of extra padding was once valued as a sign of good health. Today, the obsession is thinness (Rosenthal, 1999). Not-so-subtle ads scream that fat is bad. Some teas come with a package of diet pills. Weight-loss machines, complete with electrodes to be attached to acupuncture pressure points, not only reduce fat but also build breasts—or so the advertisers claim. Not limited by the same rules adhered to in North America, advertisers in Japan and China push soap that supposedly "sucks up fat through the skin's pores" (Marshall, 1995:B1). What a dream product! After all, even though television models smile as they go through their paces, those exercise machines look like a lot of hard work.

Then there is the other bottom line: attractiveness pays off. Human resource studies have examined physical

We often contrast the reality we see when we look in the mirror with our culture's ideal body types. The woman on the left represents an ideal body type that has developed in some parts of Western culture. Cultural ideals can make it difficult for larger people to maintain positive self-images. These women in Florida have struggled against cultural stereotypes.

attractiveness and earnings and found that "good-looking" men and women earn the most (Hosoda, et al., 2003; Hamermesh & Biddle, 1994). Consider obese women: their net worth is less than half that of their slimmer sisters (Fonda et al., 2000). Attractive women have another cash advantage—they attract and marry higher-earning men.

For Your Consideration

What image do you have of your body? How do cultural expectations of "ideal" bodies underlie your image? Can you recall any advertisement or television program that has affected your self-image?

Most advertising and television programs that focus on weight are directed at women. Women are more concerned than men about weight, more likely to have eating disorders, and more likely to express dissatisfaction with their bodies (Honeycutt, 1995; Stinson, 2001). However, today, men are increasingly the target of marketing for waxing, facials, and other cosmetic remedies and surgeries. The negative consequence of the pressure for men to attain bigger muscles is called the "Adonis Complex" (Pope, Phillips, & Olivardia, 2000). Do you think that advertising creates these disordered attitudes and behaviours? Or would these attitudes and behaviours exist without the ads? Why?

As a result of history, each society has certain broad characteristics—such as its ideas of the proper roles of men and women or the role of sociology as an academic discipline. In using the term *biography*, Mills is referring to the individual's specific experiences at a particular moment in time.

One of your authors was an undergraduate student in sociology during the latter half of the 1960s in Montreal, Quebec. His experiences were radically different from those of an undergraduate student attending university today in Regina, Saskatchewan. This is an important concept to grasp: people don't do what they do because of inherited characteristics such as instinct. Rather, external influences—such as where and when we live—fashion our personal experiences and become part of our thinking and motivations. A sociology student must develop a sociological imagination if she or he is to understand the extent to which her or his "personal troubles" are linked to broader "public issues" arising from changing views of social inequalities from generation to generation. When and where we grow up—whether in Vancouver or Quebec City, Red Deer or Campbellton, 50 years ago or today—influences our sociological understanding of behaviour.

People around the globe take their particular worlds for granted. Something inside Canadians tells us that hamburgers are delicious; small families are attractive; and an iPad, cellphone, and designer clothing are desirable. And something inside some Sinai Desert Arab tribes used to tell them that warm, fresh camel's blood made a fine drink and that everyone should have a large family and wear flowing robes (Murray, 1935; McCabe & Ellis, 1990). That "something" certainly isn't an instinct: as sociologist Peter Berger (1963:93) put it, that "something" is "society within us."

This brings us to you—to how your social groups have shaped your ideas and desires. Over and over in this text, you will see that the way you look at the world is the result of your exposure to specific social groups and your ignorance of others. We think you will enjoy the process of self-discovery offered by sociology.

Sociologists have a particular interest in the social consequences of material goods, group structure, and belief systems, as well as how people communicate with one another.

The Growing Global Context

As is evident to all of us—from the labels on our clothing to the components in our cars—our world is becoming a global marketplace. Communications used to be so slow that, in the War of 1812, the Battle of New Orleans continued to be fought for two weeks after the United States and Great Britain had signed a peace treaty. The armed forces had not yet received word that the war was over (Volti, 1995).

Today, we use the internet to communicate with our friends, our neighbours, and people all over the planet. Economic agreements and organizations, such as the North American Free Trade Agreement (NAFTA) and the World Trade Organization (WTO), connect Canada not only with the United States and Mexico, but also with France, Japan, Korea, and China. Yet we continue to occupy small corners of life marked by a particular social space and differences in family background, religion, occupation, gender, ethnicity, and social class. It is from the vantage of these corners that we learn our distinctive ways of viewing the world.

One of the beautiful—and fascinating—aspects of sociology is that it is able to analyze the two parts of our reality: the changes that incorporate us into a global network and our unique experiences in our small corners of life. In this text, we examine both of these vital aspects of the contemporary experience.

Sociology and The Other Sciences

To satisfy our basic curiosity about the world, humans gradually developed **science**—systematic methods of studying the social and natural worlds and the knowledge obtained by those methods. Sociology, the scientific study of society and human behaviour, is one of the sciences developed by modern civilization.

A useful way of comparing the sciences—and of gaining a better understanding of sociology's place—is to first divide them into the natural and the social sciences.

The Natural Sciences

The **natural sciences** are the intellectual and academic disciplines designed to comprehend, explain, and predict events in our natural environment. The natural sciences are divided into specialized fields of research according to subject matter, such as biology, geology, chemistry, and physics. These are further subdivided into even more highly specialized areas, with a further narrowing of content. Biology is divided into botany and zoology, geology into mineralogy and geomorphology, chemistry into its inorganic and organic branches, and physics into biophysics and quantum mechanics. Each area of investigation examines a particular "slice" of nature (Henslin, 1997a).

The Social Sciences

In the pursuit of a more adequate understanding of life, the social sciences emerged in Western Europe around the mid nineteenth century. Just as the natural sciences attempt to understand the world of nature, the **social sciences** attempt to understand the social world, and just as the world of nature contains ordered (or lawful) relationships that are not obvious but must be discovered through theoretical advances and controlled observation, the ordered relationships of the human or social world are not obvious and require study. However, unlike nature, humans create and re-create their second nature—their particular society. Fortunately—or unfortunately, for some—there are several theoretical perspectives that help us understand ourselves, our society, and the countries and nations around us. Each theory is based on observations derived from specific methods. (See Chapter 2 for detailed descriptions of these methods.)

Like the natural sciences, the social sciences are divided into specialized fields on the basis of their subject matter. These divisions are political science, economics, anthropology, psychology, and sociology.

POLITICAL SCIENCE *Political science* focuses on how people govern themselves: the various forms of government, their structures, and their relationships to other institutions in society. In studying a constitutional democracy such as Canada's, political scientists also analyze voting behaviour.

ECONOMICS *Economics* is the social science that deals with the theory and management of the production, distribution, and consumption of goods.

ANTHROPOLOGY *Anthropology* —with the exception of physical anthropology, which studies anatomy and biology— examines the origins of human migration and the development of tools, techniques, kinships, value systems, and social relationships. Anthropological fieldwork or ethnography is a specific form of inquiry involving long-term exposure to the daily life of the people being studied. Well-known anthropologists include Margaret Mead, famous for her work in Samoan and New Guinea cultures, and Jane Goodall, who has made significant discoveries about primate societies, especially those of chimpanzees. (See the website of the Department of Anthropology at the University of Winnipeg, available at www.uwinnipeg.ca/index/anthropology-index.)

PSYCHOLOGY The focus of *psychology* is processes that occur within the individual. Psychologists are primarily concerned with mental processes: intelligence, emotion, perception, and memory.

SOCIOLOGY Simply put, **sociology** is the disciplined study of human social behaviour, especially the investigation of the origins, classifications, institutions, and development of human society on a global level. Sociology ranges from understanding passing encounters between individuals on the street to understanding global social processes.

An Updated Version of the Old Elephant Story

It is said that in the recent past, five wise men and women, all blindfolded, were led to an elephant and asked to explain what they "saw." The first, a psychologist, feeling the top of the head, said, "This is the only thing that counts. All feeling and thinking take place inside here. To understand this beast, we need study only this."

The second, a political scientist, feeling the gigantic ears, said, "This is the power centre. What goes in here controls the entire beast. Concentrate your studies here."

The third, an economist, feeling the mouth, said, "This is what counts. What goes in here is distributed throughout the body. Concentrate your studies on this."

The fourth, an anthropologist, tenderly touching the top of the head, the ears, the mouth, the trunk, and the tusks, said, "I am interested in understanding the meaning behind these different attributes. I will concentrate on these and possibly other aspects of the animal by spending more time with it."

Then came the sociologist (of course!), who, after feeling the entire body, said, "You can't understand the beast by concentrating on only one part. Each is but part of the whole. The head, the trunk and tusks, the ears, the mouth—all are important. But so are the parts of the beast that you haven't even mentioned. We must remove our blindfolds so we can see the larger picture. We have to see how everything works together to form the entire animal."

Pausing for emphasis, the sociologist added, "And we also need to understand how this creature interacts with similar creatures. How does their life in groups influence their behaviours?"

We wish we could conclude this fable by saying that the psychologist, anthropologist, political scientist, and economist threw away their blindfolds and, joining together, began to examine the larger picture. But, on hearing this sage advice, all stubbornly bound their blindfolds even tighter to concentrate all the more on the single parts. And if you listened very carefully you could even hear them mutter, "The top of the head is mine—stay away from it." "Don't touch the tusks." "Take your hand off the ears." "Stay away from the mouth—that's my area."

Unlike political scientists and economists, sociologists do not concentrate on a single social institution. And unlike psychologists, sociologists stress factors *external* to the individual to determine what influences people. The Down-to-Earth Sociology box below revisits an old fable about how members of different disciplines perceive the same subject matter.

Focus Question
Why is sociology different from the other social sciences?

The Goals of Science

The first goal of each science is to *describe* and *explain* why something happens. The second goal is to make generalizations—that is, to go beyond the individual case and make statements that apply to a broader group or situation. For example, a sociologist wants to explain not only why Mary went to university or became a renowned astrophysicist, but also why people with her characteristics are more likely than others to go to university or become astrophysicists. To achieve generalizations, sociologists look for patterns, recurring characteristics or events. The third scientific goal is to *predict*—to specify what will happen in the future in light of current knowledge.

To attain these goals, scientists need to examine evidence with an open mind so that their work can be checked and repeated by other trained scientists. Secrecy, prejudice, faith, and other biases are contrary to scientific inquiry.

Sociologists and other scientists move beyond common sense, or beyond those ideas that prevail in a society that "everyone knows" are true. "Everyone" can be mistaken today just as easily as when common sense dictated that the world was flat or that no human would ever walk on the moon. Sometimes the explorations of sociologists lead them to study

Enjoying a Sociology Quiz—Sociological Findings versus Common Sense

Some findings of sociology support common-sense understandings of social life, while others contradict them. Can you tell the difference? To fully enjoy this quiz, complete all the questions before looking at the next Down-to-Earth Sociology box to check your answers.

1. **True/False** The earnings of Canadian women have just about caught up with those of Canadian men.

2. **True/False** When faced with natural disasters such as floods and earthquakes, people panic and social organization disintegrates.

3. **True/False** Revolutions are more likely to occur when conditions remain poor than when they are improving.

4. **True/False** Most people on welfare are lazy and looking for a handout. They could work if they wanted to.

5. **True/False** Compared with men, women touch each other more often when talking.

6. **True/False** Compared with women, men maintain more eye contact when conversing.

7. **True/False** How long people live depends on their genetic or biological makeup and therefore is not strongly influenced by any social differences.

8. **True/False** Not long ago the family was a stable unit, but today we face an explosion of broken and dysfunctional families.

9. **True/False** Today, because women face more stress and anxiety at work and in the home, more women than men commit suicide.

10. **True/False** Wars have been fought throughout history because humans have aggressive instincts.

things that people would prefer remain unexplored. For example, a sociologist might study how some people decide to commit a crime, engage in switching (wife/spouse swapping), or work for Greenpeace. With all realms of human life considered legitimate avenues of exploration by sociologists, their findings sometimes challenge cherished ideas. To test your own "common sense," read the Down-to-Earth Sociology box above.

It seems that every organization or group nourishes a pet image that it presents to the public. Sociologists are interested in knowing what is really going on behind the scenes, however, so they peer beneath the surface to get past such sugar-coated imagery (Berger, 1963). This approach sometimes brings sociologists into conflict with people who feel threatened by that information, usually those holding powerful economic and political positions—which is all part of the adventure—and risk—of being a sociologist.

Focus Question
What makes sociology a science?

The Origins of Sociology

How did sociology begin? It emerged at about the middle of the nineteenth century, when European social observers began to use scientific methods to test their ideas. Three factors combined to lead to its development.

The first was the Industrial Revolution. By the middle of the nineteenth century, Europe was evolving from an agriculture-based society to one dependent on factory production. Masses of people were forced from their land. They moved to cities, where they were greeted by horrible working conditions: low pay; long, exhausting hours; dangerous work; foul smoke; and much noise. To survive, families were forced to send their children to work in these conditions, some of whom were even chained to factory machines to make certain they did not run away.

Such negative changes in people's lives sparked transformations in what they believed to be true and false, good and evil. In the realm of ideas, Enlightenment philosophers such as Jean Jacques Rousseau (1712–1778, French) and John Locke (1632–1704, English) pointed out that human growth and development of society occurs when tradition gives way to reason. Reason and science, in turn, contribute to the ability of people to comprehend, change, and perhaps control not only their society but also the world as a whole. Enlightenment philosophers foresaw a world free from religious dogma, within human control, and leading ultimately to emancipation for all humankind (Sydie, 1987; Zeitlin, 1990). The Enlightenment's scientific ideas for the application of reason and rationality to the physical and social world and human progress swept through Europe and North America. In the realm of politics and the economy, these philosophers encouraged the idea that individuals could possess land, property, and inalienable rights.

The second factor that stimulated the development of sociology was imperialism. The new European colonial

Sociological Findings versus Common Sense—Answers to the Sociology Quiz

1. **False.** Over the years, the income gap has narrowed, but only slightly. On average, full-time working women earn only about 65 percent of what full-time working men earn. This low figure is actually an improvement; in the 1970s, women's incomes averaged about 60 percent of men's.

2. **False.** Following such disasters, people develop greater cohesion, co-operation, and social organization to deal with the catastrophe.

3. **False.** Just the opposite is true. When conditions are consistently bad, people are more likely to be resigned to their fate. Rapid improvement causes their aspirations to outpace their circumstances, which can increase frustration and incite revolution.

4. **False.** Most people on welfare are children, elderly, sick, mentally or physically handicapped, or young mothers with few skills. Less than 2 percent meet the common stereotype of a lazy able-bodied male. See also "Stereotyping the Poor" in Chapter 6.

5. **False.** Men touch each other more during conversation (Whyte, 1989).

6. **False.** Female speakers maintain considerably more eye contact (Henley, Hamilton, & Thorne, 1985).

7. **False.** The poor are less healthy on average than the rich because their diets are worse and their work lives are more physically demanding.

8. **False.** The proportion of children living with single parents was probably as high 200 years ago as it is today because many more people died at a young age. This was the result of the premature death of one parent (usually the mother) due to inadequate health care. Today, it is the result of separation and divorce.

9. **False.** In Canada, suicide rates for males have been at least three times higher than for females since the 1950s, with the difference increasing to four times higher in the 1990s and remaining there by 2008. (See www.statcan.gc.ca/tables-tableaux/sum-som/l01/cst01/hlth66a-eng.htm.

10. **False.** Humans do not have instincts—that is, fixed and inherited patterns of behaviour (Berger, 1963).

empires, stretching from Asia through Africa to North America, exposed colonists to radically different cultures. Startled by these contrasting ways of life, Europeans began to ask why cultures differed. Anthropology concentrated on providing insight into the colonies of the Western European empires, while sociology slowly took on the task of understanding the social changes happening in the burgeoning cities of England, Europe, and, later, North America.

The third impetus for the development of sociology was the success of the natural sciences. At the time that the Industrial Revolution and imperialism moved people to question fundamental aspects of their social worlds, the **scientific method**—objective, systematic procedures used to acquire knowledge based on empirical evidence—practised in chemistry and physics, uncovered truths about the physical world. Given these successes, it seemed logical to apply this method to questions being raised about the social world.

Auguste Comte

Auguste Comte (1798–1857) was the founder of French positivism. **Positivism** was a theory of knowledge based on experience alone and not on metaphysical speculation or ungrounded philosophical concepts. Knowledge, to be positive, must also be situated in its proper historical context.

Comte argued that human understanding of the world was initially religious, defined by the significance of supernatural forces. It then advanced to a metaphysical stage of abstract principles, and finally proceeded to positive or scientific knowledge based on an empirical grasp of the relations between observable phenomena.

Auguste Comte (1798–1857), considered the founder of sociology, began to analyze the bases of social order. Although he stressed that the scientific method should be applied to the study of society, he did not apply it himself.

With the French Revolution fresh in his mind, Comte left the small, conservative town of Montpellier, where he had grown up, and moved to Paris. The changes he experienced led to his interest in the twin problems of social order and social change (which he called "social statics" and "social dynamics"). What holds society together? he wondered. Why is there social order instead of anarchy or chaos? And once society becomes set on a particular course, what causes it to change? Why doesn't it always continue in the direction it began? Comte concluded that the right way to answer his questions about social order and social change was to apply positivism to social life. This new approach would not only uncover society's fundamental laws, but it would also apply them to social reform. Comte is often credited as being the founder of the discipline because he called this new science sociology—"the study of society" (from the Greek *logos*, "study of," and the Latin *socius*, "being with others").

Karl Marx

Karl Marx (1818–1883) not only influenced sociology but also left his mark on world history. Marx's influence has been so great that the *Wall Street Journal* called him one of the three greatest modern thinkers (the other two being Sigmund Freud and Albert Einstein).

Marx believed that the engine of human history is **class conflict** and that capitalism is the highest stage of human development. He said that the *bourgeoisie* (the controlling class of *capitalists*, or those who own the means to produce wealth—capital, land, factories, and machines) are locked in conflict with the *proletariat* (the exploited class—the mass of workers who do not own the means of production). According to Marx, this bitter struggle can end only when members of the working class unite in revolution and throw off their chains of bondage, resulting in a classless society, one free of exploitation (Marx & Engels, 1848/1967).

Marxism is not the same as communism. Although Marx stood firmly behind revolution as the only way for workers to gain control of society, he did not develop the political system called communism. Indeed, Marx himself felt disgusted when he heard debates about his insights into social life. After listening to some of the positions attributed to him, he even declared, "I am not a Marxist" (Dobriner, 1969: 222; Gitlin, 1997: 89).

Unlike Comte, Marx did not think of himself as a sociologist. He spent years studying in the library of the British Museum in London, where he wrote widely on history, philosophy, and, of course, economics and political science. Because of his insights into the relationship between the social classes, especially the class struggle between the "haves" and the "have-nots," many sociologists today claim Marx as a significant early sociologist. He also introduced one of the major perspectives in sociology: conflict theory, which is discussed later in this chapter.

Émile Durkheim

Émile Durkheim (1858–1917) grew up in eastern France and was educated there and in Germany. At the beginning of his academic career, sociology was viewed within the university as an offshoot of history and economics (Coser, 1977). Durkheim sought recognition for sociology as a separate academic discipline and achieved his goal when, in 1887, he received the first academic appointment in sociology in France, at the University of Bordeaux.

Durkheim also had two other major goals (Giddens, 1978). One was to study how individual behaviour is shaped by social forces. In one of his most enduring studies, he compared the suicide rates of several European countries. Durkheim (1897/1966) found that each country's suicide rate was different and that it remained remarkably stable year after year. He also found that different groups within a country had different suicide rates. For example, unmarried Protestant males killed themselves at a higher rate than Catholics, Jews, females, and married people. From his research findings, Durkheim drew the highly insightful conclusion that suicide is not simply a matter of individuals here and there deciding to take their lives for personal reasons; instead, social factors underlie the act.

Karl Marx (1818–1883) believed that the roots of human misery lie in the exploitation of the proletariat, or propertyless working classes, by the capitalist class—those who own the means of production. Social change, in the form of the overthrow of the capitalists by the proletariat, was inevitable from Marx's perspective. Although Marx did not consider himself a sociologist, his ideas have profoundly influenced many in the discipline, particularly conflict theorists.

French sociologist Émile Durkheim (1858–1917) contributed many important concepts to sociology. When he compared the suicide rates of several countries, he discovered an underlying social factor: people are more likely to commit suicide if their ties to others in their communities are weak. Durkheim's identification of the key role of social integration in social life remains central to sociology today.

Durkheim identified social integration, or the degree to which people are tied to their social group, as a key factor in suicide. He concluded that people with weaker social ties are more likely to commit suicide. This factor, he said, explained why unmarried Protestant males have higher suicide rates. Durkheim argued that Protestantism encourages greater freedom of thought and action, males are more independent than females, and unmarried people lack the ties and responsibilities of marriage. However, this freedom comes at a cost—the loss of social anchors inhibiting the individual from taking his life. In other words, because their social integration is weaker, people with these characteristics have fewer social ties that keep them from committing suicide. Durkheim called this *egoistic suicide*. It is prevalent in industrial societies dominated by large cities and ideas such as reason, science, and individualism.

Although strong social bonds help protect people from suicide, Durkheim noted that in some instances they actually encourage it. This type of suicide, which Durkheim termed *altruistic suicide*, can occur when some people kill themselves following the death of a dearly loved spouse. Their own feelings are so integrated with those of their mate that they choose death rather than life without that person.

Durkheim singled out a third type of suicide—*anomic suicide*—also characteristic of industrial capitalist societies. For Durkheim, capitalism was an economic system based on greed and the unattainable goal of material wealth for almost everyone. When aspirations of wealth become unfulfilled, such as during a severe economic depression, some individuals may feel so passionately about their "loss" that they contemplate suicide.

Because of its scientific rigor and excellent theoretical interpretations, Durkheim's study is still quoted over a hundred years later. His research was so thorough that the principle he uncovered still applies: people who are less socially integrated have higher rates of suicide.

Durkheim's third concern was that social research be practical. He concluded, for example, that the new individualism or selfishness emerging during the nineteenth century was a characteristic of capitalism and not pathological; it was an expected outcome of a changing society. When individualism goes too far, however, it then poses the danger of what Durkheim called *anomie*—a breaking down of the controlling influences of society. Under such conditions, individuals become detached from society and are left with too little moral guidance. This is dangerous, as their desires are no longer regulated by social norms (Coser, 1977). Durkheim suggested that sociologists intervene: to prevent anomie, they should promote the creation of new social groups to stand between family and the state. These groups, such as professional associations and even trade unions, would help meet the need for a sense of belonging that was being eroded by the new, impersonal industrial society.

In sum, Durkheim achieved his three goals. First, he made sociology an accepted academic discipline in France, and then elsewhere in the world. Second, he showed how social forces shape individual behaviours. Suicide, for example, appears to be such an intensely individual act that we might expect psychologists, rather than sociologists, to examine it. Yet, as Durkheim illustrated, if we look at suicide only in individualistic or psychological terms, we miss its social basis. Finally, he showed how to make social research practical.

Max Weber

Max Weber (1864–1920), a German sociologist and a contemporary of Durkheim, also held professorships in the new academic discipline of sociology. Weber is one of the most influential sociologists; you will encounter his writings and theories numerous times in the coming chapters.

One of Weber's most important contributions to sociology was his study of the rise of capitalism. How, he asked,

Durkheim believed that modern societies produce feelings of isolation, mainly from the division of labour. In contrast, members of traditional societies who work alongside family and neighbours and participate in similar activities experience a high degree of social integration. The Malian women in the photo on the right are pounding millet into flour.

Max Weber (1864–1920) was another early sociologist who left a profound impression on the discipline. He used cross-cultural and historical materials to help us understand modern bureaucracies, charismatic leaders, and theories of domination.

did capitalism come about—and why did some countries adopt it with enthusiasm while others lagged behind? Weber suspected that religion might be the key. As background, we need to understand that the typical approach to life before the development of capitalism was not to strive "to get ahead," but to work only enough to maintain one's usual way of life. Weber (1904–1905/1958) theorized that all religions except Protestantism encouraged their followers to cling to this traditional way of life, while the Protestant belief system, and especially Calvinism, encouraged people to embrace change. Protestantism pushed people to work hard, to save money, and to invest it. Weber called this religious doctrine the **Protestant Ethic**. He termed the readiness to invest capital to make more money the **spirit of capitalism**. Thus, Weber theorized, Protestantism included the set of ideas that were sufficient to jump-start capitalism.

To test his theory, Weber compared Roman Catholic and Protestant countries and found that Protestant countries were much more likely to embrace the new economic system called capitalism. This theory was controversial when Weber developed it, and it continues to be debated today (Dickson & McLachlan, 1989; Zou, 1994).

The Role of Values In Social Research

Weber raised another issue that remains controversial among sociologists when he declared that sociology should be **value-free**. By this he meant that a sociologist's values—personal beliefs about what is good or worthwhile in life and about the way the world ought to be—should not affect his or her research. Weber wanted **objectivity** to be the hallmark of sociological work.

All sociologists agree that objectivity is an important goal in the sense that sociologists should not distort data to make it fit preconceived ideas or personal values, and that research reports must accurately reflect actual, not desired, findings. On the other hand, sociologists are members of a particular society at a given point in history and their values inevitably play a role in their research. For example, values

may be in part responsible for why one sociologist chooses to research the Mafia while another turns a sociological eye on kindergarten students or professional wrestlers. As a way of uncovering any unintended distortions in original research, sociologists stress the need for **replication**—that is, repeating a study to compare secondary results with initial findings. If values have unwittingly influenced research findings, replication by other sociologists should uncover this problem and correct it.

Another related problem faced by sociologists centres on the proper purpose and use of sociological research (Seubert, 1991; Hewa, 1993). Some sociologists believe that the proper role of sociology is to advance understanding. Others are convinced that sociologists have a responsibility to explore harmful social arrangements in society—to investigate what causes poverty, crime, war, and other forms of human exploitation (see Figure 1.1).

Regarding the uses of sociology, those who assert that understanding is sociology's proper goal take the position that the knowledge gained by social research belongs to the scientific community and the world. Accordingly, sociologists should not be concerned with how their research is funded because it can be used by anyone for any purpose. In contrast, those who say that the goal of sociology should be to explore harmful social arrangements believe that sociologists should use their studies to alleviate human suffering and make society a better place to live. Sociologist John Galliher (1991) perhaps best expresses today's majority position when he says:

> A value-free and nonjudgmental social science has no place in a world that has experienced the Holocaust, in a world having had slavery, in a world with the ever-present threat of rape and other sexual assault, in a world with frequent, unpunished crimes in high places, including the production of products known by their manufacturers to cause death and injury as has been true of asbestos products and continues to be true of the cigarette industry, and in a world dying from environmental pollution by these same large multinational corporations.

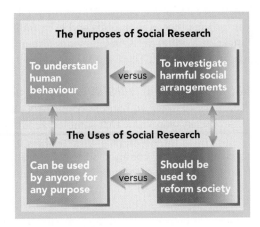

FIGURE 1.1 The Debate Over Values in Sociological Research

Verstehen and Social Facts

Weber and *Verstehen*

Weber stressed that one cannot understand human behaviour simply by looking at statistics, because numbers must be interpreted. To understand people, he said, we should use **Verstehen**—a German word meaning "to understand." By emphasizing *Verstehen*, Weber meant that we must pay attention to what are called **subjective meanings**—the ways in which people interpret their own behaviour. We can't understand what people do, Weber insisted, unless we look at how people view and explain their own behaviour.

To better understand this term, let's return to the student debt example from the opening vignette. Why did Cindy protest? We know that students around the world face similar escalating debt problems. Many feel a sense of despair; their future employment prospects look bleak.

By applying *Verstehen*—your own understanding of what it means to face this particular situation in life and trying to relate to how others are coping with rising student debt—you gain a better understanding of other people's behaviour.

Durkheim and Social Facts

In contrast, Durkheim stressed what he called **social facts**—the patterns of behaviour that characterize a social group, community, or nation. (Note that Weber did not disagree about the significance of social facts, for they are the basis of his conclusions about Protestantism and capitalism.) Examples of social facts in Canada include June to August being the most popular months for weddings, July 1 being the most popular date for moving in Montreal, suicide being higher among Native peoples and, more recently, Quebec teenagers, and more births occurring between Tuesdays and Thursdays than any other days of the week.

People all over the country don't just coincidentally decide to do similar things, be it getting married or committing suicide. If that were the case, in some years middle-aged people would be most likely to kill themselves; in other years, young people, and so on. Patterns that hold true year after year indicate that as thousands and even millions of people make individual decisions, they are responding to conditions in their society. These are social facts.

How Social Facts and *Verstehen* Fit Together

Social facts and *Verstehen* go hand in hand. As a member of Canadian society, you know that summer weddings are related to the end of the school year and how these months, now locked in tradition, common sentiment, and advertising, carry their own momentum. As for suicide among Canada's Native peoples or the recent burst in the suicide rate among Quebec's teenagers, you probably already have a sense of the greater isolation or anomie that many Native peoples and some teenagers feel about living in their communities.

Sexism In Early Sociology

Attitudes of the Time

As you may have noticed, all the sociologists we have discussed so far are male. In the 1800s, sex roles were rigidly defined, with women assigned the roles of wife and mother. In the classic German phrase, women were expected to devote themselves to the four Ks: "*Kirche, Küchen, Kinder, und Kleider*" (church, cooking, children, and clothes). To dare to break out of this mould was to risk severe social disapproval.

Most women received no education beyond basic reading and writing, and many not even that. A few women from wealthy families, however, insisted on pursuing higher education, which at the time was reserved almost exclusively for men. A few managed to study sociology, although deeply entrenched sexism in universities stopped them from obtaining advanced degrees or becoming professors. In line with the times, their research was almost entirely ignored.

Harriet Martineau

When Martineau, who had been born into a wealthy English family, first began to analyze social life, she hid her writing beneath her sewing when visitors arrived, for "writing was 'masculine' and sewing 'feminine'" (Gilman, 1911/1971: 88).

An active advocate for the abolition of slavery, she toured the United States in 1834 and wrote two volumes based on her travels, entitled *Society in America* and *Retrospect of Western Travel*, and a methodological treatise called *How to Observe Manners and Morals* (Hoecker-Drysdale, 1992). *Society in America* was published in 1837, two or three decades before Durkheim and Weber were born, and criticized America's failure to live up to its democratic principles. Among her suggestions in the book, Martineau argued for improvement in women's education so that "marriage need not be their only object in life." (Simkin, n.d.). At the end of her life, she defended the right to unionize and strike. Martineau is primarily known for her 1853 translation into English of Auguste Comte's *Cours de philosophie positive* rather than her pioneering work on culture and

Interested in social reform, Harriet Martineau (1802–1876) studied sociology and discovered the writings of Comte. She became an advocate for the abolition of slavery, travelled widely, and wrote extensive analyses of social life.

methodology. Her translation allowed Comte's ideas of positivism to be circulated in the English-speaking world.

Sociology In Quebec, Canada, and The United States

Sociology in Quebec

The establishment of sociology as an academic discipline in Canada followed a different course than the history of sociology in the United States. Sociology in Canada is the story of the "Two Solitudes" (MacLennan, 1946), or Quebec sociology and sociology in the rest of Canada.

Quebec sociology owes its early development in the late nineteenth and early twentieth centuries to conservative European (mainly French) developments. Gaudrée Boilleau, a student of the conservative French sociologist Frédéric LePlay, conducted the first known study of a Quebec family in 1886. The sociology of Leon Gérin, the pre-eminent Quebec sociologist of the early twentieth century, was deeply influenced by LePlay's sociology of the family. Gérin spent his "career" as a sociologist studying rural family life in Quebec (Glenday & McMullan, 1970). Until the arrival of Everett Hughes at McGill University in the early 1940s, sociology in the province concentrated on the microcosm of the individual and family in rural Quebec society.

FROM THE QUIET REVOLUTION TO THE PRESENT Until his untimely death in 2002, the contributions of Hubert Guindon (1964, 1967, 1978, 1988) made it easier for English-speaking sociologists, political scientists, and policymakers in Canada to better understand the social roots of not only the Quiet Revolution, but the seemingly inexplicable rise of the nationalist and separatist movement in Quebec. Guindon was the first social scientist to identify the Quiet Revolution as state modernization; that is, the expansion of the province's health, education, and welfare bureaucracies. The burgeoning public sector during the 1960s meant well-paying careers for the growing number of well-educated, French-speaking Quebecois professionals. The private sector, however, remained firmly in English-speaking hands. For Guindon, a good part of the explanation for the rise of nationalist, and even separatist, sentiment during the 1960s and beyond rested with the struggle over "opening up" the linguistic barrier in the private sector in Quebec to qualified French-speaking Quebecois. Certainly, there were also other sources of discontent expressed by Quebec nationalists, both then and now.

However, Hubert Guindon was a rare Canadian sociologist. His genius was his ability to communicate to both sides in this deeply divisive debate in Canada. This was achieved through a combination of his engaging prose and his personal charm and convivial wit. All who read and met him agreed that his work helped bridge the gap of misunderstanding separating Quebecois from anglophone sociologists, political scientists, and public policymakers.

Today, unfortunately, there are few willing or able to communicate across the linguistic and cultural duality that is at the core of Canadian society. A case in point is the year-long commission into "reasonable accommodation" in Quebec. Headed by Charles Taylor (political scientist and philosopher) and Gerard Bouchard (sociologist) and entitled "Building the Future: A Time for Reconciliation," (2008) the report deals with major issues such as freedom of religion and gender equality and the hierarchical ordering of rights facing not only Quebec society but Canadian society at large.

What little is known about this contentious issue in English-speaking Canada is the hyperbole reported in the media. Instead of addressing, for example, the lack of debate and discussion over similar issues facing the rest of Canada, Montreal's English-language newspaper *The Gazette* would accentuate the "we versus them" distinction in Quebec with headlines such as, "Language debate creeps into Quebec hearings on cultural accommodation" (September 27, 2007) and "leaked portions" of the report allegedly stating "Quebec francophones [must] open their minds, get informed and learn more English" (May 20, 2008), as if to suggest that the anglophone minority stands above ethnic and racial conflict.

Sociology in Quebec carries on its connection to statebuilding in the province. Granted, there remain sociologists committed to some form of political independence, but many are now tackling issues as diverse as teenage suicide, immigration and multiculturalism, workplace health and safety, and criminology.

Sociology in English-Speaking Canada

British and American traditions influenced the development of sociology in English-speaking Canada. The British tradition was centred at the University of Toronto, while the U.S. influence was positioned at McGill University. Most historians of sociology credit University of Chicago–trained sociologist Carl Dawson with introducing the discipline to an English-speaking audience in Canada. Even though sociology courses had been offered at the University of Manitoba and in the Maritimes, Canada's first major program in sociology began in 1922 at McGill University under Dawson's leadership. During the period known as the "Chicago connection" (1920s to mid-1950s), Dawson brought many Chicago sociologists and anthropologists to McGill, with Everett Hughes considered the most notable in terms of the development of sociology in Quebec and Canada. Until the early 1960s, Dawson's work on rural settlements in western Canada helped to establish the prevalence of community studies in early Canadian sociology.

Unlike French or American influences, the British tradition outside Quebec did not involve a separate department of sociology among the social sciences. On the contrary, until the 1960s, when an independent department of sociology was established at the University of Toronto, any sociology done was through the auspices of the Department of Political Economy.

For several years, Harold A. Innis headed the Department of Political Economy at the University of Toronto. Innis was an economic historian who created the model of economic development known as the staples theory of international trade. Historically, Canada's usefulness, first to the French and later to Great Britain and the United States, was its abundance of natural resources. Staples such as furs, fish, timber, mineral ores, oil, and so on were, for the most part, exploited by "foreign" rather than Canadian capitalists.

According to Innis, these staple exports created the conditions for a particular pattern of Canadian economic development. For example, companies involved in the building of Canada's railways and canals were needed in order to cheaply ship exports out of the country. In other words, the conditions for the development of a more complex Canadian society were dependent on the number and kind of staple exports. Today, for example, the oil-rich province of Alberta has the lowest unemployment rate in the country (in 2012 Alberta's unemployment rate was 4.6 percent compared to 7.2 percent in Canada as a whole; see www.statcan.gc.ca/tables-tableaux/sum-som/101/cst01/lfss01c-eng.htm).

Samuel D. Clark, an M.A. graduate of the Department of Sociology at McGill University who worked alongside Harold Innis, became the lead sociologist among a group of social scientists working at the University of Toronto during the late 1930s and 1940s. Clark built on the work of Innis by showing how the staples approach helped shape our society over the past 250 years—from the French Regime to the mid-twentieth century. It is especially interesting to note the parallel development of distinctive sociologies in English and French Canada during this period, a phenomenon exemplified by S.D. Clark's important study entitled *The Social Development of Canada* (1942), which was published at about the same time as Everett Hughes's *French Canada in Transition* (1943).

The 1960s, however, witnessed a large influx of American-trained sociologists into universities across Canada. Their interest in the discipline did not rest either in the development of a distinctive sociology in Canada or in community studies or historical sociology; instead, their interest lay in social problems and in rigorous research methods, especially statistical research methods. As a result of their training in the United States, these sociologists did very little research on the changing dynamics of Canadian society. There were few courses taught in which either the content or course descriptions dealt with Canadian topics.

THE CANADIANIZATION MOVEMENT While Quebec sociologists were enmeshed in the province's political struggles in the 1960s and 1970s, Canadian English-speaking sociologists were faced with their own dilemma. The expanding university system in Canada meant an increase in undergraduate and graduate student enrollments. However, many feared there would be few career openings to Canadian-trained PhD graduates. In 1975, the Commission on Canadian Studies of the Association of Universities and Colleges issued a report entitled "To Know Ourselves"—otherwise known as the Symons Report. Among its recommendations, the report called on the Canadian government and policymakers to increase knowledge of Canadian society through research, publications, and the hiring of Canadian-trained faculty.

SOCIOLOGY IN PRESENT-DAY ENGLISH-SPEAKING CANADA Unlike sociology in Quebec, sociology in English-speaking Canada is not concerned with nation building. According to Robert Brym and Céline St. Pierre (1997), one of the defining features of English-speaking sociology is its Leftist nature.

Building on the 1960s connection with political economy, sociologists such as Wallace Clement and William Carroll have written about Canada's corporate structure and role in globalization. In addition to political economy, the impact of feminist scholarship—and, to a lesser extent, postmodernism—has contributed to the perception of sociology's activist nature in English-speaking Canada. Among feminist scholars, Margrit Eichler and Dorothy Smith stand out as exceptional contributors to their field. Margrit Eichler (1988b) is widely recognized for her work in nonsexist research methods, while Dorothy Smith (1987, 1999) is best known for her studies of feminist theory, especially her work on the everyday world of women and men. We will have more to say about feminist theories in the next section of this chapter (see the Down-to-Earth Sociology box: Early Women Sociologists in Canada).

John Porter (1921–1979) was one of the leading sociologists in Canada during the post–World War II period. His book *The Vertical Mosaic* is considered a benchmark in scholarship and practical public policies. John Porter is discussed in Chapters 8 and 12.

Wallace Clement (b. 1952) is considered by many to be Canada's pre-eminent sociologist. His books include *The Canadian Corporate Elite*, *Continental Corporate Power*, and *Relations of Ruling: Class and Gender in Postindustrial Societies* (with John Myles). Wallace Clement is discussed in Chapters 8 and 12.

Early Women Sociologists in Canada

Aileen Ross (1902–1995)

In addition to her pioneering work on philanthropy, Aileen Ross pursued fieldwork in India and published two very different books in one year (1961): *The Hindu Family in its Urban Setting* and *Becoming a Nurse*. Several years later she followed her first book on India with her second, entitled *Student Unrest in India: A Comparative Approach.*

Kathleen "Kay" Herman (b. 1920)

First appointed assistant professor of sociology in the Department of Political Science at Queen's University in 1966, "Kay" Herman became one of the founding members of the new Department of Sociology in 1969, where she taught until her retirement in 1989.

Annie Marion MacLean (1870–1934)

Chicago-trained sociologist Annie Marion MacLean was born on Prince Edward Island. She taught for almost 30 years at Adelphi College, where she championed women's rights in the workplace. She is considered one of the pioneers, if not the "mother," of modern ethnographic research.

Sociology in the United States

THE BEGINNINGS At first, sociology in the United States was dominated by the department at the University of Chicago, founded by Albion Small (1854–1926), who started the *American Journal of Sociology* and was its editor from 1895 to 1925. George Herbert Mead (1863–1931), who developed the symbolic interactionist perspective examined later, was an early member of the same department.

EARLY WOMEN SOCIOLOGISTS The position of women in North America was similar to that of European women, and their contributions to sociology met a similar fate. Denied faculty appointments in the discipline, many turned to working with the poor and became social activists (Young, 1995). Among the early women sociologists in the United States were Jane Addams, Alice Hamilton, Florence Kelley, Elsie Clews Parsons, and Alice Paul.

George Herbert Mead (1863–1931) is one of the founders of symbolic interactionism, an important theoretical perspective in sociology. His lectures at the University of Chicago were very popular. Though he wrote very little, after his death his students compiled his lectures into an influential book, *Mind, Self and Society* (1934).

Dorothy Smith, born in England in 1926, has taught at OISE in Toronto since 1977. In 1999, she was awarded the Distinguished Scholarship Award by the American Sociological Association (ASA). Among her more notable publications is *The Everyday World as Problematic: A Feminist Sociology* (1987).

Jane Addams (1860–1935), a recipient of the Nobel Peace Prize, tirelessly worked on behalf of poor immigrants. With Ellen G. Starr, she founded Hull-House, a centre to help immigrants in Chicago. She was also a leader in women's rights (women's suffrage) and in the peace movement.

JANE ADDAMS Jane Addams (1860–1935), like Harriet Martineau, came from a background of wealth and privilege.

Addams worked tirelessly for social justice (Addams, 1910/1981). She founded Hull-House in Chicago's notorious slums, which was open to any person needing refuge—immigrants, the sick, the elderly, the poor. At her invitation, sociologists from the nearby University of Chicago were frequent visitors at Hull-House. Her efforts at social reform were so outstanding and so effective that in 1931 she was a co-winner of the Nobel Peace Prize, the only sociologist ever to win this coveted award.

W.E.B. DU BOIS With the racism of this period, African-American professionals also found life difficult. The most notable example is provided by W.E.B. Du Bois (1868–1963) (Lemert, 1994).

Du Bois's writings, numbering almost 2000, preserve a picture of race relations of that period. Frustrated at the lack of improvement in the issue, he turned to social action. Along with Jane Addams, Florence Kelley, and others from Hull-House, he founded the National Association for the Advancement of Colored People (NAACP) (Deegan, 1988). Combating racism both as a sociologist and a journalist, Du Bois eventually embraced revolutionary Marxism. Dismayed that so little improvement had been made in race relations, at the age of 93 he moved to Ghana, where he was eventually buried (R. Stark, 1989).

SOCIAL REFORM VERSUS SOCIAL THEORY Like Du Bois, many early American sociologists combined the role of sociologist with that of social reformer. During the 1920s and 1930s, for example, Robert Park and Ernest Burgess not only studied prostitution, crime, drug addiction, and juvenile delinquency, but also offered suggestions for how to alleviate these social problems.

During the post–World War II period, sociology in the United States took a different direction. Its rise as the dominant force in the capitalist world did not go unchallenged. The Soviet Union was viewed as the communist threat to its influence in the developed European nations

and less-developed world. In this milieu of U.S. supremacy, great emphasis was given to earning academic respect for sociology, and the focus shifted from social reform to serving the interests of U.S. global capitalism. Talcott Parsons (1902–1979), for example, developed abstract models of society known as structural functionalism that exerted great influence on sociology and political science. These models of how parts of society work harmoniously together did little to stimulate social activism among its adherents either at home or abroad. Consequently, Parsons had critics, including C. Wright Mills.

C. Wright Mills (1916–1962) deplored the theoretical abstractions of the period, which he said were accompanied by empty research methods. Mills (1956) urged sociologists to return to social reform, seeing imminent danger to freedom from the coalescing of interests of the powerful elite—the wealthy, politicians, and the military. After his death, turbulence in U.S. and Canadian universities during the 1960s and 1970s fuelled by the Vietnam War also shook the dominance of structural functionalism. As U.S. supremacy in the world weakened, interest in social activism was revived, and Mills's ideas became popular among a new generation of sociologists.

Robert Merton (1910–2003) stressed the need for sociologists to develop **middle-range theories**—explanations that tie together many research findings but avoid sweeping generalizations that attempt to account for everything. Such ideas, he claimed, are preferable because they can be tested. Merton's

C. Wright Mills was a controversial figure in sociology because of his analysis of the role of the elite in U.S. society. Today, his work is taken for granted by many sociologists and members of the public.

theories (1949/1968) contend that U.S. society's emphasis on attaining material wealth encourages crime and delinquency.

THE PRESENT Since the 1970s, U.S. sociology has not been dominated by any one theoretical orientation. Some sociologists are content to study various aspects of social life, interpret their findings, and publish them in sociology journals (for example, the *American Journal of Sociology*). Others direct their research toward social change and actively participate in community affairs to help bring about a vision of a more just society (see *Social Problems*, the journal of the Society for the Study of Social Problems).

What Do Sociologists in Canada and the United States Do Now?

Over the past two decades, the activities of sociologists have broadened. Early PhD graduates in sociology had difficulty finding work beyond university teaching. Although many in the field still teach, the government has become the second-largest employer of sociologists. Many others work for private firms in management and planning positions. Still others work in criminology and demography, in social work, and as counsellors. Sociologists put their training to use in such diverse efforts as tracking the spread of AIDS and helping teenage prostitutes pursue other lifestyles. Later we will look more closely at some of the careers open to sociology graduates. At this point, however, let's concentrate on a better understanding of sociological theory.

Theoretical Perspectives In Sociology

Facts never interpret themselves. A number is just a number; a statistic is simply a statistic. In everyday life, we interpret what we observe by using common sense. That is, to understand our experiences (our "facts"), we situate them in a framework of more-or-less-related ideas. Sociologists place their observations into a conceptual framework called a theory. A **theory** is a general statement about how some parts of the world fit together and how they work. It is an explanation of how two or more facts are related to one another. By providing a framework for observations, a theory interprets social reality in a distinct way.

Sociologists in Canada use five major and two emerging theories: symbolic interactionism, functional analysis, conflict theory, feminist theories, postmodernism, critical race, and queer theory. Let's examine the main elements of each of these theories (see Table 1.1).

Symbolic Interactionism

Unlike functionalism or conflict theory, which focus on organizations, institutions, or national societies, **symbolic interactionism** studies specific behaviours of interacting individuals caught in identifiable face-to-face social settings or encounters. We can trace the origins of symbolic interactionism to the Scottish moral philosophers of the eighteenth

century, who noted that people evaluate their own conduct by comparing themselves with others (Stryker, 1990). This micro-theoretical perspective was developed by sociologists Charles Horton Cooley (1864–1929), William I. Thomas (1863–1947), and George Herbert Mead (1863–1931). We will discuss in more detail how symbols form the basis of our individual self-concept in Chapter 4.

Symbolic interactionists view *symbols*—things to which we attach meaning—as the basis of social life. Without symbols, we would have no mechanism for perceiving others in terms of relationships (aunts and uncles, employers and teachers, and so on). Symbols define what such interpersona relationships mean to us. For example, if you think of someone as an aunt or uncle, you behave in certain ways, but if you think of that person as a boyfriend or girlfriend, you behave quite differently. And without symbols, we could not coordinate our actions with others. If we lacked the ability to specify time, materials, sizes, or goals, we could not build bridges and highways. Without symbols, there would be no books, movies, or musical instruments. We would not have schools or hospitals, government or religion. In short, symbols make social life possible.

IN SUM

Symbolic interactionists explain order and personal stability using the symbols we share with others in our community and define change in terms of the changing symbols (or meanings) associated with particular institutions, such as family, the economy, or universities.

Functional Analysis

Functional analysis, also known as *functionalism* and *structural functionalism*, is a macrosociological theory that views society as a unit made up of interrelated parts that work together (Turner, 1978). When all the parts of a society fulfill their functions, that society is in a "normal" state. If they do not fulfill their functions, the society is in an "abnormal" or "pathological" state. To understand society, then, functionalists contend that we must look at both *structure* (how the parts of a society fit together to make a whole) and *function* (what each part does and how it contributes to society).

Continuing the work of Durkheim, Robert K. Merton used the term *functions* to refer to the beneficial consequences of people's actions that help keep a group (society or social system) in equilibrium. In contrast, *dysfunctions* are consequences that undermine a system's equilibrium.

Functions can often be both manifest and latent. If an action is intended to help some part of a system, it is a *manifest function*. For example, suppose the tuition at your university is doubled. The intention, or manifest function, of such an increase may be to raise faculty salaries and thus recruit better staff. Merton pointed out that actions can also have *latent positive functions*, or unintended consequences that help a system adapt. Suppose the tuition increase

TABLE 1.1 Major Theoretical Perspectives in Sociology

Perspective	Usual Level of Analysis	Focus of Analysis	Key Terms
Symbolic interactionism	Microsociological—examines small-scale patterns of social interaction	Face-to-face interaction; how people use symbols to create social life	Social act Dramaturgy Social object Generalized other
Functional analysis (also called functionalism and structural functionalism)	Macrosociological—examines large-scale patterns of society	Relationships among the parts of society; how these parts are functional (have beneficial consequences) or dysfunctional (have negative consequences)	Objective social factors Scientific research Functions (manifest and latent) Equilibrium
Conflict theory	Macrosociological—examines large-scale patterns of society	The struggle for scarce resources by groups in a society; how dominant elites use power to control the less powerful	Rational self-interest Progress Conflict Control Domination Exploitation
Feminist theories	Microsociological—individual and small groups Macrosociological—patterns of patriarchy	Individuals in face-to-face interaction, predominately women	Patriarchy Sexism Coercive structures Gender division of labour
Postmodernism	Macrosociological—language and culture Microsociological—describing the socially constructed postmodern individual	Texts—documents, film, photos, video, collages, and so on	Spectacle Free-floating signifiers Simulation Sign/image
Queer theory (emergent: from the 1990s onward)	Microsociological—individual sexual identities	Texts, films, photography	Heterosexual identity Subversions Bodies LGBT (lesbian, gay, bisexual, transgendered) Drag queens Homophobia
Critical race theory (emergent: from the 1970s onward)	Macrosociological—discrimination and the law	Texts, fieldwork	Racism Critical legal studies Discrimination

Source: Various, including Kenneth Allan, *Contemporary Social and Sociological Theory*, London: Pine Forge Press, 2006; and David Harvey, *The Condition of Postmodernity*, Oxford, England; New York: Blackwell, 1989 (p. 43).

worked and the quality of the faculty improved and significantly increased the university's position in the *Maclean's* ranking of universities across Canada. As a result, the school was flooded with new student applicants and was able to expand its programs and its campus. The expansion contributed to the growth and stability of your university, but it was an unintended positive consequence of the tuition increase.

Sometimes actions have the opposite effect, of course, and hurt or weaken the social system. Because such consequences are usually unintended, Merton called them *latent*

✱ **Explore** "The Looking-Glass Self" by Charles Horton Cooley on **MySocLab.**

✱ **Explore** Herbert Blumer's "The Nature of Symbolic Interactionism" on **MySocLab.**

dysfunctions. Let's assume that doubling the tuition backfired, and that half the student body couldn't afford the increase and dropped out. With this loss of income, the university had to reduce salaries and lost ranking in the *Maclean's* annual poll. Because these results were not intended and resulted in harm, they represent a latent dysfunction of the tuition increase.

Finally, structural functionalism contends that individuals living in a normally functioning social system will share a number of *values*—beliefs about what is right and wrong—that help hold a society together. Values help maintain a state of social equilibrium. The process of socialization, to be discussed in Chapter 4, contributes to the social integration of individuals in society.

IN SUM

From the perspective of functional analysis, society is a functioning unit, with each part related to the whole. Whenever we examine a smaller part, we need to look for its functions and dysfunctions to see how it is related to the larger unit. This basic approach can be applied to any social group—an entire society, a university or college, or even a group as small as a family.

Conflict Theory

Conflict theory provides a third perspective on social life. Karl Marx witnessed the Industrial Revolution that transformed Europe. He saw that peasants who left the land to seek work in urbanizing areas were forced to work for wages that barely provided enough to eat. The average worker died at age 30, and the wealthy lived to 50 (Edgerton, 1992:87). Shocked by this suffering and exploitation, Marx developed **conflict theory**, concluding that class struggle is the key to all human history. In each society, one small group controls the means of production and exploits those who do not. In industrialized societies, the struggle is between the **bourgeoisie**, the small group of capitalists who own the means to produce wealth, and the **proletariat**, the mass of workers they exploit. The capitalists also control politics, so that when workers rebel, they are able to call on the power of the state for control (Angell, 1965).

When Marx made his observations, capitalism was in its infancy and workers were at the mercy of their employers. Workers had none of what we take for granted today—the right to strike (for unionized workers), minimum wages, eight-hour days, coffee breaks, five-day workweeks, paid vacations and holidays, medical benefits, sick leave, unemployment compensation, and government pension plans. His analysis reminds us that these benefits came not from generous hearts, but from workers who forced such concessions from their employers.

Some current conflict sociologists use conflict theory in a much broader sense. Ralf Dahrendorf (b. 1929) sees conflict as inherent in all relations that have authority. He points out that **authority**, or power that people consider legitimate, runs through all layers of society—in small groups, a community, or an entire society. People in positions of authority try to enforce conformity, which in turn creates resentment and resistance. The result is a "contested terrain" over who has authority over what within business organizations, political bureaucracies, and even families (Turner, 1978).

Another sociologist, Lewis Coser (b. 1913), asserts that conflict is especially likely to develop among people who are in close relationships. Such people are connected by a network of responsibilities, power, and rewards, and changing something can easily upset carefully worked out arrangements. Consequently, we can think of even close relationships as a balancing act—of maintaining and reworking a particular distribution of responsibilities, power, and rewards.

IN SUM

Unlike functionalists, conflict theorists see society as composed of groups competing for scarce resources. Although alliances or co-operation may prevail on the surface, a struggle for power lies beneath. Marx focused on struggles between the bourgeoisie and proletariat, but today's conflict theorists have expanded this perspective to include smaller groups and even basic relationships such as the family and its kinship networks (see Chapter 13, The Family).

Feminist Theories

There are, at present, at least three variants of **feminist theories**: Marxist feminist theories, liberal feminist theories, and non-Marxist radical feminist theories. While they differ in important ways from one another, especially when it comes to their programs for changing society, they share a few common characteristics, which we will outline after briefly describing each approach.

MARXIST FEMINIST THEORIES Marxist feminists share the view of Marxists that social class is more fundamental than gender in explaining inequality. Like Marxists, they assert that women's position in society is a consequence of the property relations of capitalism. Both women and men are viewed as property, but the exploitation of women includes their objectification in roles that serve men's interests. Marxist feminists argue that revolutionary changes in the world economy are the only way to change both men's and women's exploitation by capitalism. Modern-day Marxist feminists see one of their goals as combating the "false consciousness" of women's groups such as Real Women, who dignify women's traditional role of subservience and exploitation in the traditional family.

⊙ **Watch** how a functionalist would interpret "Dress Western Day" in Denver, Colorado, on **MySocLab**.

LIBERAL FEMINIST THEORIES Liberal feminists claim that legal restraints and customs are at the root of women's subservient role in society. While they recognize the importance of class, ethnicity, and race as valid criteria in understanding women's inequality, our society's laws and customs stand out as the principal factors. Liberal feminism has been criticized for being exclusionary—preserving middle-class women's position in universities and society at the expense of women of colour or women from poor backgrounds. Moreover, liberal feminists have attracted controversy over their opposition to prostitution and soft pornography as exploitative. On the other hand, liberal feminists have been at the forefront of changes that have tackled sexist privileges in the existing structure—changes such as pay equity, provision of day care for working mothers, better education for women, and opening nontraditional career options to women.

RADICAL FEMINIST THEORIES Radical feminists believe patriarchy oppresses women. Patriarchy is characterized by power, dominance, hierarchy, and competition. Not only must patriarchy's legal structures and gender socialization be changed, but society's cultural and social institutions that keep women "in their place" must be transformed. Institutions such as the traditional family, the church, and academia are often singled out for restructuring. While many radical feminists point to women's biology (e.g., childbearing) as a critical factor in their relegation to second-class status, they endeavour to support those initiatives that can overcome whatever socially-constructed negative effects biology may have on both men and women.

Recent developments in feminist theory include lesbian feminism, men's feminism, and postmodern feminism. Lesbian feminism argues that if heterosexual relationships are exploitative by nature, then women should build a separate culture for themselves. Men's feminism applies feminist theories to the study of men and masculinity. Postmodern feminism undermines previous theories based on an optimistic belief in progress (Lorber, 1998:174).

WHAT IS COMMON TO FEMINIST THEORIES? These three feminist theories share a number of commonalities:

1. Biological sex differences account for differing genitalia (although this is not a perfect relationship, as transgendered individuals will attest) and physical strength between the sexes, but gender differences are not simply derived from biology; they are a product of complex social, historical, and cultural factors.
2. The gender division of labour is hierarchical, with men's roles dominant and better rewarded and women's roles subordinate and less valued.
3. Relations between the genders are so intertwined that changes in one area affect many other aspects of social life. Social issues such as abortion or homosexuality are related to the "liberation of women" from the structures of subservience in society. Gains or losses in the struggle

for women's rights influence the direction of change in other areas, such as gay and lesbian rights.

4. The knowledge of science, ourselves, and society has been largely derived from an androcentric bias—that is, men's experiences—because men have held positions of authority in academia. The contributions made by women and other "invisible" minorities must be uncovered and communicated for the benefit of all.

IN SUM

The three variants of feminist theory are Marxist, liberal, and non-Marxist radical. All feminist theories share at least four characteristics.

Postmodernism

Postmodernism in present-day society could be viewed as the logical rejection of modernity. Modernity, as a sociological concept, was first employed by Max Weber to describe the society or civilization that had emerged from feudalism, otherwise known as industrial capitalism. It was a society based on the Enlightenment ideas of reason, science, and freedom. Modernity meant that change was possible because humans could act collectively. In addition, science could make society materially better while reason promised to unmask prejudices based on religious or other irrational ideas and lead all humanity toward personal freedom.

C. Wright Mills was the first sociologist to argue that we are living in a "postmodern period," by which he meant a society where "the ideas of freedom and of reason have become moot; that increased rationality may not be assumed to make for increased freedom" (1959:167). The advent of two world wars, nuclear weapons, the Cold War, and so on meant that personal freedom was not automatically linked to progress, reason, science, capitalism, or communism—quite the contrary. Many horrors against humanity were and continue to be visited in the name of these ideas.

Postmodernism, as a theory of present-day society, recognizes diversity where modernity pushes sameness. Postmodernism recognizes cultural and sexual differences while modernity looks for uniformity of tastes and habits. In other words, the culturally homogenized world promised by modernity with the spread of capitalism is being replaced with a view of present-day society as a cultural collage where people can live in their own cultural and social space as free individuals. For some analysts, such as David Harvey (1989), postmodernity as a theory of diversity in an otherwise culturally homogeneous capitalist world is made possible as a result of the computer revolution. Computers and other information technologies contribute to the economic viability of small businesses based in culturally distinct communities. Instead of assimilation or marginalization, information technologies make cultural diversity a reality. In an age of conglomerates, it is increasingly possible to make a comfortable living working from home or starting a small business, in part because the internet links us to the world market.

The computer is a place where image is dominant and the symbol supreme. Jean Baudrillard (1983, 1993, 1995), a French theorist of postmodernity, is noted for his developmental theory of the symbol. In preindustrial societies, signs or symbols are passed on in festivals, rites of passage, and rituals, and are often expressed in the exchange of gifts. In industrial capitalist societies—which Baudrillard labels "productionist"—signs and symbols and the real world are the same. Statements such as "The clothes make the man/woman" capture the essence of a link between signs and the real world; that is, the clothes someone wears confer his or her status in society. The rise of postmodernity breaks the link between symbols and the real world. Signs and symbols become autonomous. In cyberspace, for example, image is more important than the real world. Young people today play video games in realms of their own choosing. For postmodern theorists, image, symbols, and signs are steadily encroaching on modernity.

Postmodernism can also be viewed as both macrosociology and microsociology. The link between macro- and microsociology begins with language as the primary social bond in contemporary society. Postmodernists call their emphasis on language *discourse analysis*. Language and culture form the structures within which individuals become social beings. Lyotard (1984) defines the postmodern condition as skepticism toward all universal or absolute truths that have been used to legitimize political and scientific projects such as communism (Marx) or the dominance of the unconscious mind (Freud). Modern information and communications technologies (ICTs) have brought about the postmodern condition. To some postmodernists, the plight of student debt embodies one of the tragic fallouts of modernism. Today's world has no need for past or future; it is made up of two "presents"—one that is based in the virtual reality of new ICTs and media, and the other "real" present that appears to many as elusive or even borderline. To escape the angst of the "real-world" present, a postmodern person might enjoy cybersex with Lulu, the first porn star of virtual reality, for example. Or, with the advent of the "teledildonic" suit, made up of a head piece with video and audio inputs connected to a suit that stimulates the erogenous zones, a player can take on any idealized persona and enjoy distant, uncommitted, and safe sex (Appignanesi & Garratt, 2000).

The major criticisms of postmodernism centre on its preoccupation with surface reality. In addition, postmodern theorists often view society as a closed system in which events happen but seemingly under no one's control. Why some images, symbols, or signs are more important than others is a question of power that is usually left unasked by postmodern theorists.

IN SUM

Postmodernism emphasizes cultural diversity in opposition to the cultural homogeneity promised by modernism. Information and communications technologies help make cultural diversity a reality. The concept of power, however, is absent from most postmodern theories.

Queer Theory (from the 1990s onward)

Queer theory is an emerging theory that has become associated with gay and lesbian studies—a recent academic achievement spanning the social sciences and humanities. However, queer theory owes its origins to the pioneering work of several researchers and theorists. Only two will be discussed here. In her 1990 book *Gender Troubles*, Judith Butler, a professor of comparative literature and rhetoric at the University of California, Berkeley, rejects the feminist argument that "women" are a group with common characteristics and interests. In place of a binary view of gender and sexuality, Butler points to the significance of the human body in defining the parameters of a person and his or her personality in her later book, *Bodies That Matter* (1993). Today, the fluidity of gender identities is understood in Freudian terms, and especially Oedipal law.

Gayle Rubin, in her widely cited essay "Thinking Sex" (1984), discusses the oppressions that fall upon groups of lesbians and gay men in the context of a more general intolerance of sexual difference and a fear of (or at least a distaste for) sex itself. She sees intolerance of gays and lesbians as part of a broader "moral panic" (see Chapter 18) that targets pornography, sadomasochism, leather, prostitution, birth control, divorce, and even masturbation, especially among the young. Morality crusaders attack obscene literature, nude paintings, abortion, birth control information, and "sexual" public dancing. On the other hand, Rubin claims that sexual norms are constantly being challenged and contested. As a result, social dynamics constitute the substance of queer theory.

Queer theory deliberately challenges all notions of fixed identity. Therefore, instead of viewing sex, gender, and desire as a continuum, queer theory smashes any link between them. Gender and desire/pleasure become more free-floating and based on individual attraction—regardless of the sex of the other person.

Critical Race Theory (from the 1970s onward)

Critical race theory—another emerging theory—is linked to the development of African-American legal thought in the post–civil rights era (Tate, 1996). For some civil rights scholars, the pace of legal reform during the 1960s and 1970s slowed appreciably. Derrick Bell, a lawyer who served as the executive director of the NAACP in the 1970s, is considered to be the first activist scholar to fashion arguments that were designed to expand the reformation of existing laws in the United States (Bell, 1993).

Today, **critical race theory** encompasses the disciplines of anthropology, sociology, history, philosophy, and politics. Notions of the social construction of race and race identity and the reality of discrimination are ever-present in the writings of contemporary critical race theorists.

Focus Question
What are the major sociological theories and the two emerging ones?

Levels of Analysis: Macro and Micro

A major difference between the theoretical orientations described above is their level of analysis. Functionalists, conflict theorists, and critical race theorists focus on **macro-level analysis**; that is, they examine large-scale patterns of society. In contrast, symbolic interactionists, postmodernists, and queer theorists usually focus on **micro-level analysis**—they analyze social interaction, or what people do when they are in one another's presence. Feminist theories engage in both levels of analysis (see Table 1.1).

Let's return to the example of student debt to make the distinction between micro and macro analysis levels clearer. In studying student debt, symbolic interactionists would focus on, for example, what students say they are doing to minimize their debt by taking part-time jobs, sharing the costs of accommodation and food, and relying more on their families. Symbolic interactionists might also be interested in students' strategies for paying their student loans after graduation, when—and if—they find jobs or start careers. The observations about the despair some students might express about how to pay their debt load would be an area of interest to symbolic interactionists—as well as to critical race theorists (e.g., ethnic differences in how debt is managed), postmodernists, and queer theorists.

Analysis at the micro level would be of no interest to functionalists and conflict theorists. They would focus instead on the macro level. Functionalists would examine how changes in the cost of higher education function to socialize students to adapt to a more competitive labour market. They might look at how changing relationships in the family unit (e.g., size, divorce rate) and economic conditions (e.g., higher housing costs, inflation, fewer skilled jobs, loss of jobs overseas) cause students to select programs of study they believe will give them a competitive advantage. Conflict theorists stress that the struggle between the social classes ensures that children of the elite will maintain the status of their family, and that the middle and lower classes will be sufficiently indoctrinated to worry about their precarious futures in this labour market. High student debt becomes one way to keep university graduates on the defensive about their future employment prospects.

Conflict theorists point out that employers routinely use education as a means of career selection. Careers with a high social status, such as corporate executives, Bay Street lawyers, and politicians at the national level, are almost exclusively recruited from elite universities. Employers looking for middle management and other white-collar workers require certain levels of education that indicate sufficient motivation and social experience. This assures employers that the individual has at least received the social training to be a good employee. The technical skills taught in schools are of little or no significance in the eyes of many conflict theorists (Collins, 1971). Feminists are capable of understanding how gender impacts what programs women choose, the disparities in debt load by gender, and the competitive disadvantage some women face in the labour market. Most feminists would attribute any continued disadvantages experienced by women in Canada today to patriarchy.

Putting the Theoretical Perspectives Together

Which theoretical perspective should we use to study human behaviour? Which level of analysis is correct? As you have seen, each theoretical perspective provides a different and often sharply contrasting picture of the world. No theory or level of analysis encompasses all reality. Rather, by focusing on different aspects of social life, each provides a distinctive interpretation. Consequently, it is necessary to use all seven theoretical lenses to analyze human behaviour. By putting the contributions of each perspective and level of analysis together, we gain a more comprehensive picture of social life.

Applied and Clinical Sociology

Sociologists Paul Lazarsfeld and Jeffrey Reitz (1989) divide sociology into three phases. As we have already learned, sociology was initially indistinguishable from attempts to reform society. The primary concern of early sociologists was making the world a better place—in other words, analyzing social conditions to improve social life.

During the discipline's second phase of development, the goal of sociologists was to establish sociology as a respected field of knowledge. To this end, sociologists sought to develop **pure** or **basic sociology**—that is, research and theory aimed at making discoveries about life in human groups. During sociology's third phase, there has been an attempt to merge sociological knowledge and practical work. Dissatisfied with "knowledge for the sake of knowledge," many sociologists use their sociological skills to bring about social change—to make a difference in social life.

Efforts to blend sociological knowledge with practical applications are known as **applied sociology**. Today's applied sociologists work in a variety of settings, recommending practical changes that can be implemented. A business firm may hire a sociologist to solve a problem in the workplace; sociologists may do research for government commissions or agencies investigating social problems such

Careers in Sociology: What Sociologists Do with Their Degrees

Contrary to popular belief, sociologists use their skills in a variety of settings, not just in universities. They can be found counselling children, consulting with businesses and governments, and improving relationships in the workplace.

Pat Eklund graduated with an undergraduate degree in sociology and several hundred hours of "time" spent as an intern in a local correctional facility. According to Pat, "that time and those experiences in prison [as an intern] have been the springboard for my career in criminal justice." Underlying these experiences was his sociological perspective: "I am always looking for why things happen, what is underneath someone's behaviour. This is where my degree in sociology has proved invaluable."

Mary's interest in sociology included writing a departmental honours thesis. While practical applications intrigued her, Mary was passionate about abstract modelling. Because of extenuating circumstances, Mary was unable to pursue her studies in graduate school. Instead, she worked at a variety of jobs, one of which involved conducting training seminars on abuse

for police officers. She used her sociological training to develop models for identifying abusive situations. Without the models, the police officers might not have recognized the potential for abuse in certain situations. According to Mary, "The problem is that people experience so much of their lives as a kind of chaos. They don't really see how the things that happen are interconnected. . . . If you are going to have a real effect on people's lives, then making them aware of the larger picture—the model—is a real gift."

Dave Blume and Bob Chase both earned undergraduate degrees in business. Each also earned a second degree in sociology. According to Dave, "The competition in the business world can be very intense. You have to give potential employers a reason to select you over other candidates who have the same business degree that you do. Sociology, with its focus on groups, organizations, and human interaction, is a natural complement to business. And, it is a degree which is increasingly well received in the business world." Bob adds, "Sociology prepares you for understanding change and anticipating it. The degree is a real asset."

Donna decided to pursue sociology because in many ways it defined her own life: "It seemed that my whole life has been spent working with people in groups—my work, my children, and their groups like Girl Scouts and other organizations. I have had to learn how to get along with many different people in many different settings." Donna focused her course work on the sociology of politics and power and started a career as an independent consultant and trainer. Donna's consultations and training sessions often take the form of workshops that cover a wide variety of topics, including cultural diversity, women, organizational creativity, and power and organization.

For some, this kind of work can be difficult to grasp. Donna suggests that "workshops like I do are an ongoing part of the business and government worlds. Simply because you haven't heard about them doesn't mean that they do not exist. You could begin by contacting convention bureaus and getting a list of industry conventions or annual meetings which have come to your city. Then ask for convention schedules. You will see for yourself the array of workshops offered. But this is only a start."

as pornography, crime, violence, or environmental pollution. The Down-to-Earth Sociology box on the next page describes several careers in sociology.

Clinical sociologists deal with specific problems for particular organizations. Examples include those who work with drug addicts and ex-convicts, or others who work with families to change basic relationships between husbands and wives or children and parents. Figure 1.2 contrasts basic and applied sociology.

THE FUTURE Sociology has come full circle. From an initial concern with improving society, sociologists switched their focus to developing abstract knowledge. Today, sociologists are again seeking ways to apply their findings. These efforts have gained momentum in recent years. Many departments

of sociology offer courses in specialties such as gender, workplace issues, criminology, and family violence, and some offer co-op programs and internships at graduate and undergraduate levels.

The evolution of sociology has allowed renewed contact with the discipline's roots, with invigorating changes that challenge us to grasp a vision of what society can become—and what sociology's role will be in that process of change.

Focus Question
What can you do with a degree in sociology?

👁 **Watch** the video "Sociologists at Work" on **MySocLab.**

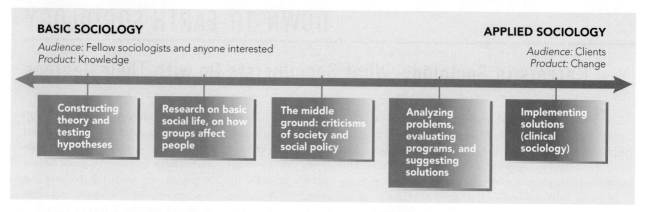

FIGURE 1.2 Comparing Basic and Applied Sociology

Source: Based on "Basic and Applied Sociological Work: Divergence, Convergence, or Peaceful Co-existence?" by J.R. DeMartini, 1982, *The Journal of Applied Behavioral Science*, 18, 2, pp. 203–215.

THE SOCIOLOGICAL PERSPECTIVE

What is the sociological perspective? Is sociology a science?

The sociological perspective stresses that people's social experiences—the groups to which they belong and their particular experiences within these groups—underlie their behaviour. C. Wright Mills referred to this as the intersection of biography (the individual) and history (time-limited social factors acting on the individual). Sociology is a social science. Science is the application of systematic methods to obtain knowledge. Science is divided into the natural sciences, which seek to comprehend, explain, and predict events in the natural environment, and the social sciences, which seek to understand the social world objectively by means of controlled and repeated observations. Sociology is the scientific study of society and human behaviour. pp. 2–7.

THE ORIGINS OF SOCIOLOGY

When did sociology first appear as a separate discipline? What factors contributed to its emergence? What role did women play in the early development of sociology?

Sociology emerged as a separate discipline in the mid-1800s in Western Europe during the onset of the Industrial Revolution. Industrialization brought social changes so sweeping that they affected all aspects of human existence—where people lived, the nature of their work, and interpersonal relationships. Early sociologists who focused on these social changes include Auguste Comte, Karl Marx, Harriet Martineau, Émile Durkheim, and Max Weber. pp. 7–11. Only a few wealthy women received advanced education, and their writings were largely ignored. Harriet Martineau is an example from the United States, while Aileen Ross and Kay Herman were early Canadian pioneer women sociologists. pp. 12–13.

SOCIOLOGY IN QUEBEC, CANADA, AND THE UNITED STATES

What universities were considered the historical centres of sociology in English-speaking Canada? How were they different?

Sociology in English-speaking Canada was influenced by two traditions, the British and the American. The British influence was centred at the University of Toronto, while the U.S. influence emerged at McGill University.

Canada's first major program in sociology began in 1922 at McGill University under the leadership of Carl Dawson. Dawson used the program at the University of Chicago, the leading centre of U.S. sociology in this period, as a model for establishing sociology at McGill. He was instrumental in bringing several Chicago-trained sociologists to the university.

The British tradition treated sociology as a branch of political economy. Unlike at McGill, an independent department of sociology was not established at the University of Toronto until the 1960s. There was a healthy disdain for the U.S. brand of sociology among the sociologists, political economists, and historians who dominated the Department of Political Economy at the University of Toronto. Their main criticisms were that U.S. sociology was practised as little more than the study of social problems such as poverty and delinquency and that it lacked research and theoretical rigour. pp. 13–17.

THEORETICAL PERSPECTIVES IN SOCIOLOGY

What is a theory and what are the major theoretical perspectives?

A theory is a general statement about how sets of facts are related to one another. A theory provides a conceptual framework within which facts are interpreted.

According to Weber, to understand why people act as they do, sociologists must try to put themselves in their shoes. He used the German term *Verstehen*, "to grasp by insight," to describe this essentially subjective approach. Émile Durkheim, although not denying the importance of *Verstehen*, emphasized the importance of uncovering "social facts" that influence human actions. Social facts are objective social conditions that influence how people behave. Contemporary sociology uses both approaches to understand human behaviour. p. 12.

Sociologists make use of five primary theoretical frameworks to interpret social life. Symbolic interactionism examines how people use symbols to develop and share their views of the world. Symbolic interactionists usually focus on the micro level—on small-scale patterns of human interaction. Functional analysis, in contrast, focuses on the macro level—on large-scale patterns of society. Functional theorists stress that a social system is made up of various parts. When working properly, each part contributes to the stability of the whole, fulfilling a function that contributes to a system's equilibrium. Conflict theory also focuses on large-scale patterns of society. Conflict theorists stress that society is composed of competing groups struggling for scarce resources.

Feminist theories focus on both microsociological and macrosociological analysis. All three variants of feminist theory stress the importance of biology and patriarchy in determining the position of both women and men in society.

Postmodernism concentrates on both macrosociological and microsociological levels of analysis. Postmodern theorists are concerned with analyzing the importance of symbols, signs, and images in present-day society.

Queer theory and critical race theory are two emerging theories. The former owes much to developments in feminist and postmodern scholarship, while the latter is a more distinctly U.S.-based multidisciplinary theory.

Because no single theory encompasses all of reality, at different times sociologists may use any or all of the seven theoretical lenses. With each perspective focusing on certain features of social life and each providing its own interpretation, their combined insights yield a more comprehensive picture of social life. pp. 17–22.

APPLIED AND CLINICAL SOCIOLOGY

What is the difference between pure (or basic) and applied sociology?

Pure (or basic) sociology is sociological research whose only purpose is to make discoveries. In contrast, applied sociology is the use of sociology to solve problems. pp. 22–24.

KEY TERMS

applied sociology   22
authority   19
basic sociology   22
bourgeoisie   19
class conflict   9
conflict theory   19
critical race theory   22
feminist theories   19
functional analysis   17
macro-level analysis   22

macrosociology   2
micro-level analysis   22
microsociology   2
middle-range theories   16
natural sciences   5
objectivity   11
positivism   8
postmodernism   20
proletariat   19
Protestant Ethic   11

pure sociology   22
queer theory   21
replication   11
science   5
scientific method   8
social facts   12
social interaction   2
social location   2
social sciences   5
society   2

sociological imagination   2
sociological perspective   2
sociology   5
spirit of capitalism   11
subjective meanings   12
symbolic
   interactionism   17
theory   17
value-free   11
Verstehen   12

WEBLINKS

All URLs listed are current as of the printing of this text.

Canadian Sociological Association
www.csa-scs.ca
The Canadian Sociological Association is the national professional non-profit association of Canadian sociologists that promotes the research, publication, and teaching of sociology.

Canadian Journal of Sociology Online
www.cjsonline.ca
The Canadian Journal of Sociology Online provides access to selected articles and book reviews. It is an excellent resource for students.

Social Science Departments in Canada
www.sociosite.net/socdeps/canada.php
This site contains a complete listing of sociology departments in Canada.

1. Do all sociological theories espouse progress—that is, the view that all societies advance from one stage of civilization to the next?
2. Why are symbolic interactionism and queer theory regarded as microsociology?
3. Why are functionalism, conflict theory, and critical race theory considered to be macrosociology?
4. Why are feminist theories and postmodernism both microsociological and macrosociological?
5. Considering the macro and micro approaches in sociology, which one do you think best explains social life? Access the Research Navigator through MySocLab and use keywords such as "micro," "macro," and "social life" to locate relevant and recent scholarly and popular press publications to help you answer this question.

MySocLab

Explore the topics covered in this chapter on MySocLab. Interactive resources include a study plan, cumulative exams, a multimedia library, MySocLab eReadings, and access to the MySocLab Video Series.

2

WHAT DO SOCIOLOGISTS DO?

LEARNING OUTCOMES

After you have studied this chapter, you will be able to answer the following questions:

1. What is a valid sociological topic?
2. Why isn't common sense adequate?
3. How do sociologists choose a particular research method?
4. What are the eight basic steps of scientific research?
5. How important are ethics in sociological research?
6. What is the relationship between theory and research?

OVER a period of roughly a year and a half, from May 2008 to November 2009, at the age of 61, I trained to become a professional wrestler. At first, until September 2008, I trained one-on-one with a former WWF (now WWE) professional wrestler. When it rained, we trained in a barn; otherwise, we worked in a professional wrestling ring in an open field. This phase was followed by formal training at a professional wrestling school, where I was the oldest novice. During my time spent at the school, there were six much younger wrestlers, ranging in age from their mid teens to their early twenties)—five males and a female. Both training periods were videotaped.

The process of learning to become a professional wrestler required me to understand the logic of a professional wrestling match while acquiring the skills needed to safely execute certain basic manoeuvres. These included "rollovers" and taking a "bump." Only once I had mastered these fundamental skills did I begin to develop a repertoire of wrestling holds. At my advanced age, I was interested in learning how to "chain wrestle." I left the high flying moves, the punches (although I learned how to take and "sell" punches), and the chest slaps to the younger trainees. As is the case with any subculture (see Chapter 3), I also learned the unique language of professional wrestling. For example, to "do a job" in professional wrestling means to lose a match.

My experience preparing for my first professional wrestling match was more than a personal journey: my time spent in the field, along with the training I had acquired over several decades, was part of a qualitative research strategy called *participant observation*. It was one of several methods I used to study professional wrestling as a qualitative sociological research project. My first professional match was filmed as part of a documentary entitled *Théatre*

What Is a Valid Sociological Topic?

Sociologists conduct research on nearly every aspect of human behaviour. At the macro level, we study such broad matters as the military (Moscos & Butler, 1997), race relations (Wilson, 1996), and transnational corporations (Kanter, Wiersema, & Kao, 1997). At the micro level, we study individualistic matters, such as pelvic examinations (Henslin & Biggs, 1997), how people interact on street corners (Whyte, 1989, 1997), and how people find time for individual innovation and creativity while working in large organizations (Glenday, 2011a). In fact, no human behaviour is ineligible for sociological scrutiny, whether routine or unusual, respectable or reprehensible.

You might have been surprised to learn in the chapter opening vignette that professional wrestling is not only an enormously popular cross-cultural phenomenon, it is also a valid topic of sociological research.

Common Sense and the Need for Sociological Research

Why do we need sociological research? Why can't we depend on common sense—on what "everyone knows"? As discussed in Chapter 1, common-sense ideas may or may not be true. For example, common sense would lead us to believe that strangers are responsible for most violence against women and children. Nothing could be further from the truth (see Chapter 13). Common sense also tells us that if a woman or man is abused, she or he should leave the abusive partner. Research shows, however, that the reality of abuse is much more complicated. Some women and gay men leave right away, but for a variety of reasons—primarily

Because all human behaviour is open to be researched by sociologists, studies range from the unusual to the routines of everyday life. Sociologists might look at broad-scale social change, such as the globalization of capitalism, or the practices and rituals around tattooing, piercing, and body painting. Shown here is a tattooed and pierced woman at an international tattoo exposition in London, England.

because they feel trapped and can't see viable alternatives—many put up with abuse for years.

Sociological research helps explain why some put up with abuse and others don't. We may also want to know something entirely different, such as why men are more likely to inflict abuse or why some people abuse persons they say they love.

Regardless of the research question, we must look beyond guesswork and common sense to find out what is really going on. For accurate answers, we need sociological research.

Six Research Methods

Sociologists use six **research methods** (or **research designs**) for gathering data: surveys, participant observation,

Dan Glenday's opponent is caught in a punishing professional wrestling hold and is forced to tap out.

👁 **Watch** how sociologist Dr. Michael Atkinson interprets "Flesh Wounds: Marked Bodies in the Civilising Process" on **MySocLab.**

Three Ways to Measure Average

The term average seems clear enough. However, sociologists use three statistics to summarize data by describing the average score in a distribution of outcomes. This is called the *three measures of central tendency*. Consider the following results from seven sociology exams:

35 52 65 78 78 82 95

1. Mean: The mean is the average of a group and is most often used as the starting point in the calculation of more advanced statistics. Add together the results from each exam, then divide by the number of exam results. The mean in this case is 69 (485/7).

2. Median: The median is the middle score in a distribution. List the exam results from lowest to highest (as shown) and find the middle one. The median is 78. This measure divides the exams into two categories: "highs" and "lows."

3. Mode: The mode is the most frequently occurring result in a distribution. The mode of the exam results is 78. It is the only score that appears more than once. This measure can be used to find the most common score and is the only measure that can be used with nominal level data, such as sex (male or female) and ethnicity or race.

---

qualitative interviews, secondary analysis, documents, and unobtrusive measures. To under stand these strategies better, note how the choice of method depends on the questions we want to answer.

Surveys

Let's assume that your resources allow you to investigate alcohol and marijuana consumption at your university. Let's also suppose that your university's enrollment is large, making it impractical to **survey**, or question, every student. You

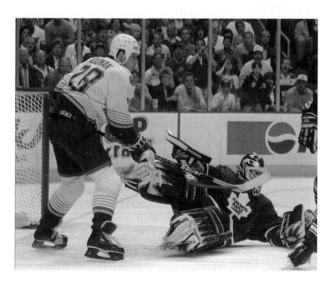

Because sociologists usually cannot interview or observe every member of the group they wish to study, such as the spectators at this hockey game, they must select a sample that will let them generalize to the entire group. The text explains how samples are selected.

must select a **sample** of individuals from among your target **population**. The population of your study is the total number of students at the university. How you choose a sample is critical, for the choice will affect the results of your study.

A survey of only first-year students, only seniors, only those enrolled in introductory sociology courses, or only those in advanced physics classes will produce unrepresentative results in each case. To be able to generalize your findings to the entire campus, you must select a sample that is representative of the campus (called a "representative sample").

The best representative sample is a **random sample**. *In a random sample, everyone in the population has the same chance of being included in the study.* In this case, since the population is every student enrolled in your university, every student, whether first-year, male or female, full-time, part-time, or graduate, must have the same chance of being included in the sample.

How would you get a random sample in this case? You'd need a list of all the students enrolled in your university. You could assign a number to each name on the list and, using a table of random numbers, determine which students would become part of your sample. (Random numbers are available in tables in statistics books or can be generated by a computer.)

❋ **Explore** "Sense and Nonsense about Surveys" by Howard Shuman on **MySocLab**.

◉ **Watch** how different sociologists decide which type of method to employ in their research on **MySocLab**.

- physical or sexual abuse, which accounts for almost three out of four young people who are homeless
- severe mental illness or addiction, which are the significant cause(s) of homelessness among single adults
- distinct problems of the one in seven street homeless who are Aboriginal

The "typical" homeless person is no longer a single, alcoholic adult male. Youth under the age of 18 and families with children are the fastest-growing groups of homeless persons. Together, these groups accounted for almost half the people using hostels in Toronto in 1996.

Homelessness in Other Canadian Cities

While members of the task force did not have a comprehensive knowledge of homelessness in other Canadian cities, they did analyze the causes of and responses to homelessness in the larger metropolitan areas and discovered that Toronto is not unique. In Calgary, the homeless population includes employed and unemployed people. In Montreal and Vancouver, homeless youth are a major problem. The root causes of homelessness in all big Canadian cities are the same: poverty, a lack of affordable housing, abuse, mental illness, and addiction. Experts in major Canadian cities reported that the federal government's withdrawal of funding from social housing was a primary cause of the rise in homelessness in the five years preceding the study.

There was widespread consensus on what is needed to combat the problem. First and foremost, there must be programs to preserve the existing stock of low-cost housing while increasing its supply in all major Canadian cities.

---

analysis is especially useful for data gathered by participant observation and in-depth interviews. That is, sociologists classify statements people have made in qualitative interviews to identify the main themes. This process can also be used by queer theorists and postmodernists to uncover themes in movies, music videos, television programs, newspapers, or any visual or written document. The goal is to faithfully reproduce the world of the people being studied. In Henslin's (1967, 1993) research on cab drivers, for example, he tried to picture the world as cabbies see it, so that anyone reading the analysis would understand not just what cabbies do, but also why they do it.

Quantitative analysis involves statistically analyzing relationships between variables, sometimes known as number-crunching (see Table 2.1). Quantitative analysis is especially useful in testing hypotheses. The computer has become an especially powerful tool for quantitative analysis because statistical packages such as MicroCase and the Statistical Package for the Social Sciences (SPSS) can analyze huge amounts of information and identify basic patterns in an instant.

8. **Sharing the Results** In this step, researchers write a report to share their findings with the scientific community. The report includes a review of the preceding steps to help others evaluate the research. It also shows how the findings are related to the literature—the published results of other research on the topic. When research is published, usually in a scientific journal or a book, it then "belongs" to the scientific community. Table 2.1 illustrates how published research is often displayed. These findings are available for **replication**; that is, others can repeat the study to see if they come up with similar results.

Ethics In Sociological Research

In addition to choosing an appropriate research method, sociologists must also consider ethics. Their research must meet the profession's ethical criteria, which centre on basic assumptions of science and morality (Canadian Sociology and Anthropology Association, 1995). Research ethics require openness (sharing findings with the scientific community), honesty, and truth. Ethics clearly forbid the falsification of results, as well as *plagiarism*—stealing someone else's work. Another basic ethical guideline is that research subjects should not be harmed by the research. Sociologists are required to protect the identity of people who provide information, which can sometimes be intimate, potentially embarrassing, or otherwise harmful to them. Finally, although not all sociologists are in agreement about this, it is generally considered unethical for researchers to misrepresent themselves.

Conducting sociological research also involves the issue of funding: Where will the money come from and are there any "strings attached"? Virtually all research foundations in Canada, such as the Donner Foundation, or "think-tanks," like The Fraser Institute, have a political agenda. What ethical questions are raised when spokespersons for these organizations stipulate the general orientation a research initiative should take? Unfortunately, this question is being asked less frequently. Instead, the majority of questions on ethics in sociological research deal with the responsibility of individual sociologists. The examples that follow represent some of the ethical considerations individual sociologists can be confronted with when doing their research. To illustrate the extent to which researchers will go to protect their respondents, consider the following research conducted by two U.S. sociologists, Mario Brajuha and Rik Scarce.

The Brajuha Research

Mario Brajuha, a graduate student at the State University of New York at Stony Brook, conducted participant observation of restaurant work (Brajuha & Hallowell, 1986). He had lost his job as a waiter when the restaurant where he was working burned down. The fire turned out to be of "suspicious origin," and during their investigation detectives learned that Brajuha had taken field notes. They

TABLE 2.1 How to Read a Table

Highest Level of Parental Education	Parental Education and Student Debt					
	Have Debt		Do Not Have Debt		Total	
	N	%	N	%	N	%
High School	476	77%	123	23%	599	100%
College	623	64%	286	36%	909	100%
University	899	59%	848	41%	1,747	100%
Not Reported	177	45%	204	55%	381	100%

A table is a concise way of presenting information. Because sociological findings are often presented in tabular form, it is important to understand how to read a table. Tables contain five elements: a title, headings, columns, rows, and a source. When you understand how these elements work together, you know how to read a table.

1. The title states the topic of a table, and is usually located at the top. What is the title of this table? Please determine your response before looking at the correct answer below.
2. The headings tell what kind of information is contained in the table. Are there any headings in this table?
3. The columns present information arranged vertically. What does the first column tell you?
4. The rows present information arranged horizontally. Read rows 2 and 4. Are there any differences between the level of the parents' education (one indicator of socio-economic status) and whether their children have or do not have debt?
5. The "source" of a table, usually given at the bottom, provides information on where the data shown in the table originated. Often, as in this instance, the information is specific enough for you to consult the original source. What is the source for this table?
6. This table indicates the number of survey participants by level of parental education. How many had parents whose highest level of education was high school? How many had parents with university education?

Answers

1. The title is "Parental Education and Student Debt."
2. Yes. The headings are "Highest Level of Parental Education," "Have Debt," "Do Not Have Debt," and "Total."
3. The first column indicates the highest level of parental education.
4. Yes, children from lower socio-economic status were more likely to have debt.
5. Canadian Student Survey: Next Steps: Upper-Year Canadian PSE Students' Future Plans and Debt, Canadian Alliance of Student Associations, March 2010, p. 29.
6. The total number of parents whose highest level of education was high school was 599, while 1747 parents had received university education.

Source: Canadian Student Survey: Next Steps: Upper-Year Canadian PSE Students' Future Plans and Debt, Canadian Alliance of Student Associations, March 2010, p. 29.

Ethics in social research are of vital concern to all sociologists. As discussed in the text, sociologists may disagree on some of the issue's finer points, but none would approve of slipping LSD to unsuspecting subjects "just to see what would happen," as was done to U.S. servicemen in the 1960s under the guise of legitimate testing.

asked to see them. When Brajuha refused, the district attorney subpoenaed the notes. Brajuha still refused to hand them over. The district attorney then threatened to send Brajuha to jail. By this time, Brajuha's notes had become rather famous, and unsavoury characters, perhaps those who had set the fire, also began to wonder what was in them. They, too, demanded to see them—accompanying their demands with threats of a different nature. Brajuha unexpectedly found himself in a very disturbing double bind.

Brajuha refused to hand over his notes for two years, even though he had to appear at numerous court hearings, and he became filled with anxiety. Finally, the district attorney dropped the subpoena. When the two men under investigation for setting the fire died, so did the threats to Brajuha, his wife, and his children.

The Scarce Research

In 1991, a group calling itself the Animal Liberation Front broke into a research facility at Washington State University, released animals, and damaged computers and files. Rik Scarce, a doctoral student in sociology at the university who was doing research on radical environmental groups, was summoned

before a federal grand jury investigating the break-in. Scarce was not a suspect, but law enforcement officers thought that during his research, Scarce might have come across information that would help lead them to the guilty parties.

Scarce answered scores of questions about himself and topics related to the raid, but refused to answer questions that would violate his agreements of confidentiality with research subjects.

A federal judge did not agree with Scarce's ethics and put him in the Spokane County Jail for contempt of court. Although he could have obtained his freedom at any time simply by testifying, he maintained his laudable ethical stance and continued to refuse, in his words, "to be bludgeoned into becoming an agent of the state." Scarce served 159 days in jail. The longest any previous U.S. scholar had been held in contempt was one week (Scarce, 1993a, 1993b, 1994).

The Humphreys Research

Sociologists agree on the necessity of protecting respondents, and applaud the professional manner in which Brajuha and Scarce handled themselves. Let's look at the Humphreys case, which forced sociologists to rethink and refine their ethical stance.

Humour in sociology is rare. Here a student gives us all a chance to recall Peter Berger's sage advice about the role of humour in creating sociological insights (Berger, 1963:165).

Laud Humphreys, a classmate of Henslin at Washington University in St. Louis, was an Episcopal priest who was training to become a sociologist. For his PhD dissertation, Humphreys (1970, 1971, 1975) decided to study social interaction in "tearooms," public restrooms where some men go for quick, anonymous oral sex with other men.

Humphreys found that some restrooms in Forest Park, across from the campus, were tearooms. He first conducted participant observation by hanging around the restrooms. He found that in addition to two men having sex, a third person—called a "watchqueen"—served as a lookout for police and other unwelcome strangers. Humphreys took the role of watchqueen, not only watching for strangers but also observing what the men did. He systematically recorded these encounters, which became part of his dissertation.

Humphreys became curious about the regular lives of these men. Impersonal sex in tearooms was a fleeting encounter, and the men clearly spent most of their time doing other things. What things? And with whom? What was the significance of the wedding rings worn by many of the men? Humphreys hit on an ingenious technique: after observing an encounter, he would leave the restroom and record the licence plate number of the subject's car. With the help of a friend in the St. Louis police department, Humphreys then obtained each man's address. About a year later, he arranged for these men to be included in a medical survey conducted by some of the sociologists on the Washington University faculty. Disguising himself with a different hairstyle and clothing, and driving a different car, he visited these men at their homes. He conducted interviews, supposedly for the medical study.

Humphreys said that no one recognized him, and he obtained the information he was looking for: family background, education, income, health, religion, and even details about the men's relationships with their wives and children. He found that most of the men were in their mid-thirties and had at least some college education. Surprisingly, the majority were married, and a higher proportion than in the general population turned out to be Roman Catholic. Moreover, these men led very conventional lives. They voted, mowed their lawns, and took their kids to Little League games.

Humphreys also found that although most of the men were committed to their wives and families, their sex lives were far from satisfactory. Many reported that their wives were not aroused sexually or were afraid of getting pregnant because their religion did not allow them to use birth control. Humphreys concluded that these were heterosexual men who were using the tearooms for an alternative form of sex, which, unlike affairs, was quick (taking no time away from their families), inexpensive (zero cost), and nonthreatening (the encounter required no emotional involvement to compete with their wives). If a wife had discovered her husband's secret sex life, she would have been devastated. However, Humphrey's research findings have done much to dispel the myth that only gay men engage in such behaviours in public washrooms.

This study stirred controversy among both sociologists and non-sociologists (Goodwin, Horowitz, & Nardi, 1991). Humphreys was severely criticized by many sociologists, and a national columnist wrote a scathing denunciation of "sociological snoopers" (Von Hoffman, 1970). Concerned about protecting the identity of his respondents, Humphreys placed his master list in a safety deposit box. As the controversy grew more heated, however, he feared that the names might be subpoenaed (a court case was threatened), and he had the list destroyed. Humphreys had a contract to remain at Washington University as an assistant professor but was fired before he could begin teaching. (Although other reasons were involved, his research was a central issue. There was even an attempt by one professor to have his doctorate revoked.)

Was this research ethical? That question is not easily decided. Although many sociologists sided with Humphreys, and his book reporting the research won the highly acclaimed ASA C. Wright Mills Award, criticisms mounted. At first, Humphreys vigorously defended his position but, five years later, in a second edition of his book (1975), he stated that he should have identified himself as a researcher.

Several years later, Frederick Desroches (1990) replicated Laud Humphrey's study in Canada. Desroches, however, worked with the police in five cities across the country. In total, Desroches found 190 men who had been arrested by police. Consistent with Humphrey's observations, the majority of the men were married and primarily heterosexual. Like their U.S. counterparts, most Canadian tearoom participants (a) communicated through nonverbal gestures and seldom spoke, (b) did not attempt to learn one another's identity or exchange biographical information, and (c) did not use force or coercion or attempt to involve youths or children. There were two differences between the findings: there were no watchqueens or lookouts, in Canada, and these acts were more likely to take place in a shopping mall than in public parks. However, the men's behaviour in both studies showed significant consistency across time and place.

How Research and Theory Work Together

As previously discussed, sociological research is based on a sociologist's personal interests, access to subjects, appropriate methods, and ethical considerations. But the value of research is related to sociological theory. On one hand, as sociologist C. Wright Mills (1959) forcefully argued, research without theory is of little value and is simply a collection of unrelated "facts." On the other hand, theory unconnected to research is abstract and empty, unlikely to represent the way life really is.

Research and theory are both essential for sociology. As such, theory stimulates research. And as sociologists conduct research, they often come up with surprising

THINKING CRITICALLY ABOUT SOCIAL CONTROVERSY

Are Sex Offenders Sick? A Close-Up View of Research

Two sociologists, Diana Scully and Joseph Marolla, were not satisfied with the typical explanation that rapists are "sick," psychologically disturbed, or different from other men. They developed the hypothesis that rape, like most behaviour, is learned through interaction with others. That is, some men learn to think of rape as appropriate behaviour.

When presented with the opportunity to interview convicted rapists in prison, Scully and Marolla jumped at it. They sent 3500 letters to men serving time in seven prisons in Virginia, the state where they were teaching. About 25 percent of the prisoners agreed to be interviewed. They matched these men on the basis of age, education, race, severity of offence, and previous criminal record, resulting in a sample of 98 prisoners who had been convicted of rape.

Scully and Marolla discovered something that goes against common sense: most rapists are not sick and are not overwhelmed by uncontrollable urges. They found that the psychological histories of rapists and nonrapists were similar. Rapists, they concluded, are emotionally average men who have learned to view rape as appropriate in various situations. Some rape spontaneously, while others plan their attacks. Others use rape as a form of revenge, to get even with someone, not necessarily the victim.

The researchers also found support for what feminists had been pointing out for years—that power is a major element in rape. According to one subject:

Rape gave me the power to do what I wanted to do without feeling I had to please a partner or respond to a partner. I felt in control, dominant. Rape was the ability to have sex without caring about the woman's response. I was totally dominant.

The discovery that most rape is calculated behaviour, that rapists are not "sick," that the motivating force is power rather than passion—the criminal pursuit of pleasure rather than mental illness—is extremely significant.

Connecting Research and Theory
Such findings go far beyond simply adding to our storehouse of "facts." As indicated in Figure 2.3, research stimulates both the development of theory and the need for more research.

Sources: Scully & Marolla (1984, 1985); Marolla & Scully (1986); Scully (1990); Foley, Evancic, Karnik, King, & Parks (1995).

---

findings—findings that, in turn, stimulate the development of theory to explain them.

The Real World: When the Ideal Meets the Real

Although one can list the ideals of research, real-life situations often force sociologists to settle for something that falls short of the ideal. Consider the research presented in the 'Thinking Critically about Social Controversy box below' for a look at how two sociologists confronted the ideal and the real.

Sociology needs more imaginative and sometimes daring research conducted in an imperfect world under less-than-ideal conditions. This is really what the discipline is all about. Sociologists study what people do, whether those behaviours are conforming or nonconforming, or whether they are pleasing to others or disgust them and arouse intense anger. No matter what the behaviour studied, systematic research methods, together with the application of social theory, take us beyond common sense. They allow us to penetrate surface realities to allow a better understanding of human behaviour and, in the ideal case, to make changes to help improve social life.

WHAT IS A VALID SOCIOLOGICAL TOPIC?

What is a valid sociological topic?
Any human behaviour is a valid sociological topic, even disreputable behaviour. Spousal abuse is an example. Sociological research is based on a sociologist's interests, access to subjects, appropriate methods, and ethical considerations. p. 28.

COMMON SENSE AND THE NEED FOR SOCIOLOGICAL RESEARCH

Why isn't common sense adequate?
Common sense does not provide reliable knowledge. When subjected to scientific research methods, common-sense ideas are often found to be very limited or false. p. 28.

SIX RESEARCH METHODS

How do sociologists choose a particular research method?

Sociologists choose their research method on the basis of the research questions to be answered, their access to potential subjects, the resources available, their training, and ethical considerations. p. 28.

Sociologists use six research methods (or research designs) for gathering data: surveys, participant observation, qualitative interviews, secondary analysis, documents, and unobtrusive measures. pp. 28–34.

A RESEARCH MODEL

What are the eight basic steps of scientific research?

1. Selecting a topic
2. Defining the problem
3. Reviewing the literature
4. Formulating a hypothesis or research question
5. Choosing a research method
6. Collecting the data
7. Analyzing the results
8. Sharing the results pp. 35–38.

ETHICS IN SOCIOLOGICAL RESEARCH

How important are ethics in sociological research?

Ethics are of fundamental concern to sociologists, who are committed to openness, honesty, truth, and protecting their subjects from harm. In addition, most research foundations and think-tanks in Canada have political agendas that can seriously undermine the ethical neutrality of sociological research. The Brajuha research on restaurants, the Scarce research on the environmental movement, and the Humphreys research on tearooms were cited to illustrate ethical issues and the personal responsibility expected of sociologists. p. 38.

HOW RESEARCH AND THEORY WORK TOGETHER

What is the relationship between theory and research?

Theory and research are interdependent. Sociologists must use theory to interpret the data they gather. Theory without research is not likely to represent real life, while research without theory is merely a collection of unconnected facts. p. 41. As illustrated by the Scully–Marolla research on rapists in prison, real-life situations often force sociologists to conduct research under real-life conditions. Although conducted in the natural social world, social research stimulates sociological theory, more research, and the potential of improving human life. pp. 41–42.

 Explore "From Summer Camps to Glass Ceilings: The Power of Experiments" to see the connection between research, theory, and developing strategies to deal with social problems on **MySocLab.**

KEY TERMS

WEBLINKS

All URLs listed are current as of the printing of this book.

Data Liberation Initiative (DLI)
www.statcan.gc.ca/dli-idd/dli-idd-eng.htm
Visit the DLI website and locate your university's DLI contact person(s).

The Canadian Sociological Association
www.csaa.ca
Visit the CSA website and locate the Professional Code of Ethics. What does the code say about an organization's ethical responsibilities to its researchers and research participants?

Statistics Canada
www.statcan.gc.ca/start-debut-eng.html
Canada's national statistical agency profiling Canada's business, economics, and society.

Courses in Applied Social Surveys
www.s3ri.soton.ac.uk/cass
CASS is an Economic and Social Research Council (ESRC) resource centre run jointly by the National Centre for Social Research, the University of Southampton, and the University of Surrey. It provides short courses in survey methods and is developing a survey question bank for use by social scientists and social researchers in the academic world, governments, market researchers, and the independent and voluntary sectors.

Canadian Journal of Sociology Resources Online
www.ualberta.ca/~cjscopy/resource.html
Online resources for Canadian students doing research on Canadian sociology topics.

CRITICAL THINKING QUESTIONS

1. Can someone who is heterosexual study homosexuals? Describe the steps you would take before developing your research hypothesis or research question.
2. Why would anyone want to study the personal records of dead people?
3. Can you generalize from a case study? If not, why do sociologists continue to employ this research technique?

4. When is it appropriate to lie to a research subject? Access the Research Navigator through MySocLab and use keywords such as "deception," "ethics," and "research" to locate relevant and recent scholarly and popular press publications to help you answer this question.

MySocLab

Explore the topics covered in this chapter on MySocLab. Interactive resources include a study plan, cumulative exams, a multimedia library, MySocLab eReadings, and access to the MySocLab Video Series.

3

CULTURE

LEARNING OUTCOMES

After you have studied this chapter, you will be able to answer the following questions:

1. What is culture?
2. Why is language so significant to culture?
3. How do values, norms, folkways, mores, and sanctions reflect nonmaterial culture?
4. How do subcultures and countercultures differ?
5. What are cultural relativism and ethnocentrism?
6. Are the values of Canadian and Quebec societies different?
7. Do animals have culture?
8. How is technology changing culture?

AFTER studying as an exchange student in Australia for a year, a Canadian student, Ian Bethune, recounted, in a recent article in *Maclean's*, what it was like for him to return to Canada. Getting ready to leave Adelaide, Bethune (2012) wrote, "I . . . developed the laughable idea that going home would be—new Australian phrase I learned—"a piece of piss.'" We might be asking ourselves why it *wouldn't* be easy to return to Canada after a year studying abroad. Canada and Australia are quite alike, aren't they? After all, the two countries share a common link with Great Britain, the same language, and a vast geography.

Ironically, the similarities between the two countries struck Ian the most. As he put it, "Coming back was harder than I imagined. And not just because my parents were suddenly 15 000 km closer again. Part of it was precisely because Australia is so similar to Canada in so many ways. That made the things I liked best there more painful to do without here. If Adelaide can organize a reasonable transfer system for its public transit, why can't Toronto? For that matter, why can't Canadian cities have as much green space as drought-prone Australian cities? . . . [E]veryone expects to feel like a stranger in a strange land, while no one is prepared to feel like that at home."

Exposure for an extended period of time to a different national culture, even one we believe to be similar to our own, requires learning what people take for granted in their day-to-day lives. We come to know the other culture's likes, dislikes, habits, gestures, and colloquial speech. Invariably, it seems "natural" to adopt many of these attitudes and behaviours because we believe we are so similar. However, upon returning home, we are often confronted with conflicting aspects of the two countries' nonmaterial cultures.

What Is Culture?

What is culture? The concept is sometimes easier to grasp by description than by definition. Suppose you meet a young woman who has just arrived in Canada from India. That her culture is different from yours is immediately evident: you can see it in her clothing, jewellery, makeup, and hairstyle. You can also hear it in her language and see it in her gestures. Later, you may hear her express unfamiliar beliefs about the world and different opinions about what is valuable in life. All these characteristics are indicative of **culture**, the language, beliefs, values, norms, behaviours, and even material objects that are *passed from one generation to the next*. Culture, then, focuses on attributes people acquire not through biological inheritance but by growing up in a distinct community, at a particular moment in time, and bounded by a specific social class.

In North Africa, a Canadian would be surrounded by a culture quite alien to her or his own. Evidence would be everywhere. The **material culture**—jewellery, art, buildings, weapons, machines, and even eating utensils, hairstyles, and clothing—would provide a sharp contrast to what a Canadian would be used to. There is nothing inherently "natural" about material culture. That is, it is no more natural (or unnatural) to wear gowns on the street than it is to wear jeans.

There exist contrasting **nonmaterial cultures**—ways of thinking (beliefs, values, and other assumptions about the world) and doing (common patterns of behaviour, including language, gestures, and other forms of interaction). Here again, no particular custom is "right." As you saw in the opening vignette, even in a country like Australia, which has many similar values to our own, Ian felt somewhat estranged when he returned to Canada after spending a year as an exchange student in Adelaide.

IN SUM

To avoid losing track of the ideas under discussion, let's pause for a moment to summarize, and in some instances clarify, the principles covered so far.

1. There is nothing "natural" about material culture. Visiting the Art Gallery of Ontario (AGO) or the H.R. MacMillan Space Centre in Vancouver feels like a natural thing to do for a Canadian tourist, but so does visiting the Vatican for a devout Catholic or making a pilgrimage to Saintes-Maries-de-la-Mer, France, for dutiful gypsies.
2. There is nothing "natural" about nonmaterial culture; it is just as arbitrary to stand in line as it is to push and shove.

Components of Symbolic Culture

Sociologists sometimes refer to nonmaterial culture as **symbolic culture** because one of its central components is the symbols that people use to communicate. That is, cultural learning depends on the human capacity to use symbols that have no necessary connection to the things they

Technology is central to social life. From this photo, we can see how technology limits or expands human activities, and, ultimately, how it plays a significant role in the types of societies we develop.

signify. My pet animal that barks is no more naturally a "dog" than it is a *Hund*, *chien*, or *perro*—in German, French, and Spanish, respectively. A **symbol** is anything to which people attach meaning and then use to communicate. Symbols can be gestures, language, values, norms, sanctions, folkways, or mores.

Gestures

Gestures, the use of one's body to communicate with others, are useful shorthand ways of giving messages without using words. While people in every culture use gestures, their meaning may change completely from one culture to another. Canadians and Americans, for example, communicate a succinct message by raising the middle finger in a short, upward stabbing motion. We wish to stress this gesture's use by Canadians and Americans, for it does not convey the same message in South America or most other parts of the world.

In Mexico, the rudest gesture—placing the hand under the armpit and moving the upper arm up and down—means "Your mother is a whore"—absolutely the worst possible insult in that culture.

Gestures thus not only facilitate communication but can also lead to misunderstandings, embarrassment, and, more often than we care to admit, interpersonal conflict. In Mexico, raising your hand to a certain height to indicate how tall a child is may result in laughter. Mexicans use several hand gestures to indicate height, and there are separate ones for people, animals, and plants (see Figure 3.1).

To get along in another culture, it is important to learn that culture's gestures. In many cultures, for example, you would provoke deep offence if you were to offer food or a gift with your left hand, because the left hand is reserved for dirty tasks such as wiping after going to the bathroom. Left-handed Canadians visiting countries such as Morocco and Bangladesh should be careful not to provoke locals into thinking they are filthy barbarians.

> **IN SUM**
>
> 1. Culture penetrates deep into the recesses of our thinking and affects the way we see the world and obtain our perception of reality.
> 2. Culture provides implicit instructions that tell us what we ought to do in various situations. For example, all people have to eat, but our particular culture teaches us what, when, and how to do so.
> 3. Culture also provides a "moral imperative"; that is, by internalizing a culture, people learn ideas of right and wrong. (For example, Canadians believe it is unacceptable to push and shove to get ahead of others in a line.)

Language

The primary means of communication for people is **language**—a system of symbols that can be strung together in an infinite number of ways for the purpose of communicating abstract thought. The significance of language for human life is difficult to overstate. Language itself is universal in the sense that all human groups possess it, but there is nothing universal about the meanings given to particular sounds. Thus, as with gestures, in different cultures the same sound may mean something entirely different or may have no

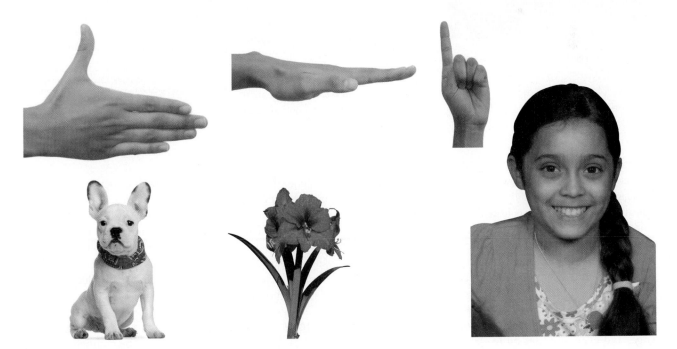

FIGURE 3.1 Gestures to Indicate Height, Southern Mexico

The New Shorthand: Expressing Yourself Online

Talking online has become a favourite activity of millions of people the world over. Teenagers, grandmothers, hobbyists, and businesspeople all appreciate the speed and ease of online communication.

Online communication doesn't allow its users to convey nuances that are transmitted during face-to-face talk. To make up for this, users have developed symbols to convey humour, disappointment, sarcasm, and other indications of mood or attitude. Common "text speak" symbols are listed below. (If you tilt your head to the left as you read, the symbols will be clearer.)

:-) Smile
:-)) Laugh
:-(Sad
:-((Very sad
:-X My lips are sealed

>:-) Feeling in a devilish mood
:-0 Wow! (What a surprise!)

Short forms are also common for online and cell phone communication. Can you translate the following text speak?

"my hart S n pieces n 1ly u put it bac 2gtha"

Answer: My HEART IS IN pieces AND ONLY YOU put it BACK TOGETHER.

Endangered Languages in Canada

Northwest Pacific Plateau (British Columbia coastline)

Every 14 days, a language is lost in the world. *National Geographic's* Enduring Voices Project, conducted in collaboration with the Living Tongues Institute for Endangered Languages, strives to preserve endangered languages by identifying language hotspots—places on the planet with the most unique, poorly understood, or threatened indigenous languages—and documenting the languages and cultures within them.

Why Is It Important?

Studying languages increases our understanding of how humans communicate and store knowledge. Every time a language dies, we lose part of the picture of what our brains can do.

Why Do Languages Die?

The languages of powerful groups have spread through official language policies or through the allure that the high prestige of speaking an imperial language can bring.

Source: National Geographic Enduring Voices Project: Documenting the Planet's Endangered Languages. http://travel.nationalgeographic.com/travel/enduring-voices

meaning at all. As the first Down-to-Earth Sociology box illustrates, symbols can take on unique meanings within a unique culture—in this case, the culture of online communication. The second Down-to-Earth Sociology box (see page 50) points out differences between French-speaking Quebecois and English-speaking Canadians that exist in many areas of social life, including mores around teenagers and sex at home.

LANGUAGE ALLOWS HUMAN EXPERIENCE TO BE CUMULATIVE Through language, we pass ideas, knowledge, and even attitudes on to the next generation. This allows young people to build on experiences they may not undergo themselves. Hence the central sociological significance of language: *language allows culture to develop by freeing people to move beyond their immediate experiences.*

Without language, human culture would be little more advanced than that of the lower primates. You could grunt and gesture that you want a drink of water, but in the absence of language, how would you share ideas and feelings concerning past or future events?

LANGUAGE PROVIDES A SOCIAL OR SHARED PAST AND FUTURE Using language, events can be codified—that is, attached to words and then recalled so they can be discussed

Teenagers and Sex at Home: Two Distinct Views

For more than 20 years, *Maclean's* polls have shown that Canadians are generally tolerant and liberal.

But what about parents, teens, and sex? Would Canadian parents permit their 18-year-old son with a steady girlfriend to have sex in their home? Two out of three Canadians say no. One province stood out as an exception, however. In Quebec, 57 percent—almost three times the result of any other province—say they would allow their 18-year-old to have sex at home. Additionally, 42 percent of Quebecers would allow their 18-year-old gay son with a steady boyfriend to have sex at home—a rate between three and six times higher than that of any other province in the nation (B.C.= 7 percent yes; Ontario= 13 percent yes).

Consider explanations from two sets of parents.

Pierre and his wife Céline (both fictitious names) have raised two children: a daughter, 21, and a son, 18. The family talks openly about sex. Both kids have been allowed to have sex at home with their steady partners since they were 17.

Their children say most of their friends enjoy the same policy at home. Their son doesn't have a girlfriend now, but when he did, she would stay the night. "During the day we're around the house with my parents, but at night, we go into my bedroom and close the door," says the son.

For Pierre and Céline, the freedom they allow their teenagers sends a strong message: the house belongs to all of them . . . and it's a safe haven from the chaotic world of teenage life. Céline says: "School, work, and friends demand so much from my kids. They are faced with all kinds of rules and limitations. When they're at home, I want them to feel safe, secure, and natural."

It's a different story for a family in southwestern Ontario, where the teenage daughters are younger: 13 and 15. Both their father, John, and his wife, Ann (again, fictitious names), answered no when asked if their girls were 18, would they be allowed to have sex in the house?

The older sibling says many of her friends are having sex, but she's not

ready. And when the time does come, she agrees with the house rules: "I wouldn't feel comfortable having sex in my parents' house, especially when they are home. It has to do with the whole respect thing my parents talk about."

On other matters of sex and teenagers, Ann says: "I would encourage my daughters to talk to me if they ever decide to have sex with someone. I would want to talk to them about birth control."

On the issue of teenagers and sex in the home, many French-speaking Quebecers are more tolerant than most Canadians (see Figure 3.2). Why? In Quebec, the family is seen as a refuge against a hostile world, while in Ontario, the family offers other compensations. (For a discussion of the nature of the family in Quebec, see Gerin, 1928. For a broader view of the role of the family in the social and political life of society, see Hart, 1995.)

Source: Adapted from The National Magazine/ *Maclean's* Poll, 1998. Retrieved September 25, 2002 from www.tv.cbc.ca/national/ pgminfo/ poll/index.html.

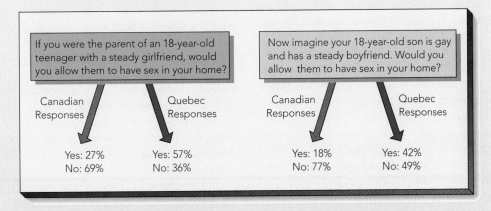

FIGURE 3.2 Differences between Quebec and the Rest of Canada on Matters of Parenting, Sex, and Teens

in the present. Talking allows people to arrive at the shared understandings that form the essence of social life.

Language also extends our time horizons forward. When people talk about past events, they share meanings that allow them to decide how they will or should act in similar circumstances in the future. Because language enables people to agree with one another concerning times, dates, and places, it also allows them to plan activities together.

Think of the difficulty—perhaps impossibility—of conveying even a slight change in the response: "I can't make it tomorrow."

LANGUAGE ALLOWS COMPLEX, SHARED, GOAL-DIRECTED BEHAVIOUR Common understandings enable people to establish a purpose for getting together. Suppose you want to go on a picnic. You use speech not only to plan the picnic (who will drive; who will bring the hamburgers, potato chips, and drinks; where you will meet; and so on), but also to decide on reasons for the picnic, which may range from "because it's a nice day that shouldn't be wasted studying" to "because it's my birthday." Only with language can you participate in such a common yet complex event.

LANGUAGE AND PERCEPTION: THE SAPIR-WHORF HYPOTHESIS In the 1930s, anthropologists Edward Sapir and Benjamin Whorf became intrigued when they noted that the language of the Hopi Indians of the southwestern United States had no words to distinguish between the past, the present, and the future. In contrast, English, German, French, Spanish, and so on can carefully specify when something takes place. From their observation, Sapir and Whorf concluded that language is embedded with ways of looking at the world. Therefore, when we learn a language, we learn not only words, but also a certain way of thinking and perceiving. The French have a unique phrase to convey this meaning: "*prise de conscience.*" The Germans say "*Weltanschauung.*" There is no similar phrase in English (Sapir, 1949a, 1949b; Whorf, 1956).

The implications of the **Sapir-Whorf hypothesis** alert us as to how extensively we are affected by language. The hypothesis reverses common sense: it suggests that rather than objects and events forcing themselves into our consciousness, our language determines our consciousness, and hence our perceptions of objects and events. Inuit, for example, have many words for snow. As Inuit children learn their language, they learn distinctions between types of snowfalls that are imperceptible to non-Inuit speakers. Other Canadians might learn to see heavy and light snowfalls, wet and dry snowfalls, and so on, but not having words for "fine powdery," "thicker powdery," and "more granular" snowfalls actually prevents us from perceiving snow in the same way as Inuit do.

Although Sapir and Whorf's observation that the Hopi do not have tenses was incorrect (Edgerton, 1992:27),

Language is the basis of human culture. The past decade has seen a major development in communication—the ease and speed with which we can "speak" to people across the globe. This development is destined to have vital effects on culture.

we must still take their conclusion seriously. Sociologist Eviatar Zerubavel (1991) presents a different example. Hebrew, his native language, does not differentiate between jam and jelly. Only when Zerubavel learned English could he "see" this difference, which is "obvious" to native English speakers. Similarly, if you learn to classify students as "jocks," "emos," "baby bats" (young Goths), and "indies," you will perceive them in an entirely different way than someone who does not know these classifications.

Noam Chomsky, a well-known linguist, takes a different approach to the relation between language and thought. He argues that the human brain contains a common structural basis made up of a limited set of rules for organizing

✱ **Explore** "Sex and Temperament in Three Tribes" by Margaret Mead on **MySocLab.**

language. The fact that people can learn foreign languages and that words and ideas can be made sense of from one language to another tends to support Chomsky's view that all humans have similar linguistic abilities and thought processes.

IN SUM

The sociological significance of language is that it frees us from the present by giving us the capacity to share understandings about the past and to develop common perceptions about the future. Consequently, as in the case of a picnic, each individual is able to perform a small part of a larger activity, aware that others are carrying out related parts. In this way, a series of separate activities becomes united into a larger whole.

Focus Question
Why is language so important to human culture?

Values, Norms, and Sanctions

To learn a culture is to learn people's **values**, their ideas of what is desirable in life. When we uncover people's values, we learn a great deal about them, for values are the standards by which people define good and bad, beautiful and ugly.

Sociologists use the term **norms** to describe the expectations, or rules of behaviour, that develop out of a group's values. They use the term **sanctions** to refer to positive or negative reactions to the ways people follow norms. **Positive sanction** refers to an expression of approval given for following a norm, while **negative sanction** denotes disapproval for breaking a norm. Positive sanctions can be material, such as a money reward, prize, or trophy, but in everyday life, they usually consist of hugs, smiles, a pat on the back, soothing words, or even handshakes. Negative sanctions can also be material—a fine, for example—but they, too, are more likely to consist of gestures, such as frowns, stares, harsh words, or raised fists. The North American middle-finger gesture described earlier is a negative sanction.

Folkways and Mores

Norms that are not strictly enforced are called **folkways**. We expect people to comply with folkways, but we are likely to shrug our shoulders and not make a big deal about it if they don't. If someone insists on passing you on the left side of the sidewalk, for example, you are unlikely to take corrective action. However, if the sidewalk is crowded and you must move out of the way, you might give the person a dirty look.

Other norms, however, are taken much more seriously. We think of them as essential to our core values, and we insist on conformity. These are called **mores** (MORE-rays). A person who steals, rapes, or kills has violated some of society's most important mores, which results in formal sanctions otherwise identified as the criminal justice system (see Chapter 16). As sociologist Ian Robertson (1987:62) explained,

> A man who walks down a street wearing nothing on the upper half of his body is violating a folkway; a man who walks down the street wearing nothing on the lower half of his body is violating [a] mores, the requirement that people cover their genitals and buttocks in public.

It should also be noted that one group's folkways may be another group's mores. For example, to walk down a sidewalk in a nudist camp with the entire body uncovered would be conforming to that subculture's folkways.

A **taboo** refers to a norm so strongly engrained that even the thought of its violation is greeted with revulsion. Eating human flesh and having sex with one's parents are examples of such behaviours (Benales, 1973; Read, 1974; Henslin, 1997b).

Pierre Bourdieu and Cultural Capital

French sociologist Pierre Bourdieu developed the concept of *cultural capital* in the early 1960s to help address the fact that "economic obstacles are not sufficient to explain" disparities in the educational attainment of children from different social classes (Bourdieu & Passeron 1979:8). He noted that certain "cultural habits and . . . dispositions" inherited from family are fundamentally important to school success (Bourdieu & Passeron 1979:14). According to Bourdieu, children from the middle and upper classes possess cultural capital, or a set of "habits and dispositions" that give them advantages over children from the working class.

In proposing his theory, Bourdieu broke sharply with traditional sociological conceptions of culture, which tended to view it primarily as a source of *shared norms and values*. Instead, Bourdieu maintained that culture shares many of the properties that are characteristic of economic capital. In particular, he maintained that certain cultural "habits and dispositions" comprise a resource capable of generating "profits." They are cultural competencies or skills that become part of an individual's identity and can be continuously "cashed-in" when called upon or needed. Those without cultural capital are left behind. Moreover, under appropriate conditions, these skills can be *transmitted* from one generation to the next (Lareau & Weininger, 2003).

Bourdieu's concept of cultural capital contributes to our understanding of how wealth, privilege, and poverty can be transmitted (see Chapter 14, Education).

Watch "Individual rights versus the Common Good" on **MySocLab**.

Watch "Organizational Culture: Norms and Values" on **MySocLab**.

Watch the video "Fashion as a Folkway" on **MySocLab**.

Watch "Organizational Culture: Rules and Conformity" on **MySocLab**.

Olympic wrestlers are a close-knit subculture. Dedicated wrestlers spend years of their lives training and competing around the world.

Subcultures and Countercultures

A **subculture** consists of people whose experiences have led them to a distinctive way of looking at life. Canadian society contains thousands of subcultures. Some are as broad as the way of life we associate with teenagers, others as narrow as those we associate with wrestlers or philosophers. Ethnic groups also form subcultures: their values, norms, and foods set them apart. So might their religion, language, and clothing. Occupational groups form subcultures, as anyone who has hung out with cab drivers (F. Davis, 1959; Henslin, 1993), the police (Pepinsky, 1980), factory workers (Halle, 1984), artists (McCall, 1980), or construction workers (Haas, 1972) can attest. Even sociologists form a subculture, and, as you are learning, they use a unique language for carving up the world.

Subcultures have a specialized set of terms and distinctions that are particularly important to members of that group. Table 3.1 defines some terms used by professional wrestlers.

The values and norms of most subcultures are compatible with the larger society to which they belong. In some cases, however, a group's values and norms place it in opposition to the dominant culture. Sociologists use the term **counterculture** to refer to these groups. Heavy-metal adherents who glorify Satanism, hatred, cruelty, sexism, violence, and death are an example of a counterculture. Note that motorcycle enthusiasts who emphasize personal freedom and speed and affirm cultural values of success are members of a subculture. In contrast, the members of an outlaw motorcycle gang who also stress freedom and speed but add the values of despising women and selling drugs and prostitution form part of a counterculture (Watson, 1988).

Countercultures do not have to express negative values but can encourage over-conformity to some of society's mainstream values. Fundamentalist Christian groups in the United States and Canada who seek to impress their view of the world onto others are another example of a

TABLE 3.1 Professional Wrestling Terms

Professional Wrestling Terms	Insiders' Meaning
Face	Heroes (can be good or have attitude)
Chemistry	Two wrestlers work well together and by so doing effectively tell a story to the audience
Spot Monkey	A wrestler who focuses heavily on cramming many acrobatic moves (high spots) into a single match without regard for the in-ring story
Ring Rust	An out-of-practice wrestler
Sell	A wrestler's reaction to an opponent's attack in a manner that suggests the hold or punch is being applied at full force.

((•● **Listen** to "Building a Town on Sign Language"—a story about a community trying to create a subculture on **MySocLab.**

counterculture. Skinheads who are members of Skinheads Against Racial Prejudice (SHARP), Anti Racist Action/ Alliance (ARA), or Queer Skinhead Brotherhood (QSB) counter the negative image presented by neo-Nazi skinhead groups in Canada, such as Western Guard and Heritage Front, and are more correctly seen as a subculture. Each of the three groups is international, with chapters in North America and Europe. Unfortunately, neo-Nazi groups are given more press and media coverage than SHARP.

Culture and Taken-for-Granted Orientations to Life

To develop a sociological imagination, it is essential to understand how culture affects people's lives. While meeting someone from a different culture may make us aware of culture's pervasive influence, attaining the same level of awareness regarding our own culture is quite another matter. *Our* speech, *our* gestures, *our* beliefs, and *our* customs are usually taken for granted. We assume that they are "normal" or "natural," and we almost always follow them without question. As anthropologist Ralph Linton (1936) said, "The last thing a fish would ever notice would be water." Except in unusual circumstances, the effects of our own culture generally remain imperceptible to us.

Yet culture's significance is profound; it touches on almost every aspect of who and what we are. We came into this life without language, values, or morality, and with no ideas about religion, war, money, love, use of space, and so on. Yet at this point in our lives, we all have them. Sociologists call this "culture within us." *Culture becomes the lens through which we perceive and evaluate what is going on around us.* The rare instances in which these assumptions are challenged, however, can be upsetting. Our Canadian values and norms, or our nonmaterial culture, can fail us and leave us feeling embarrassed or out of place. For example, if you are travelling and participating in the cultural life of Southeast Asia, there will be many occasions when you will be introduced to new ways of handling your experiences with food, dress, polite conversation, and interactions with other people. You will feel uneasy when, for example, someone is talking to you no more than five centimetres from your face. Not only that, you can smell his breath and it's not pleasant! But you feel you can't move away; you are somehow locked in this social encounter. When this happens—when your nonmaterial culture fails to make sense of your surroundings—the disconnection you experience is known as *culture shock*. Additionally, the relationships between men and women, men and men—otherwise known as "male bonding"—and women and women vary greatly from culture to culture.

An important consequence of culture within us is **ethnocentrism**, a tendency to use our own group's ways of doing things as a yardstick for judging others. All of us learn that the ways of our own group are good, right, proper, and even superior to other ways of life. As sociologist William Sumner (1906), who developed this concept, said, "One's own group is the center of everything, and all others are scaled and rated with reference to it." Ethnocentrism has both positive and negative consequences. On the positive side, it creates in-group loyalties. On the negative side, ethnocentrism can lead to harmful discrimination against people whose ways differ from ours, such as those of Muslim, Caribbean, and other non-white immigrants.

The effects of culture on our lives fascinate sociologists. By examining more explicitly just how profoundly culture affects everything we are, this chapter will serve as a basis from which you can start to analyze your previously unquestioned assumptions of reality and thus gain a different perspective on social life and your role in it.

Practising Cultural Relativism

To counter our tendency to use our own culture as a standard to judge other cultures, we can practise **cultural relativism** by trying to understand a culture on its own terms.

For example, many Canadians may appear to have strong feelings against raising bulls for the sole purpose of stabbing them to death in front of shouting crowds. According to cultural relativism, however, bullfighting must be viewed strictly within the context of the culture in which it takes place—its history, its folklore, its ideas of bravery, and its ideas of gender roles.

As a Canadian, you may still regard bullfighting as wrong because our culture has no history of the activity. We all possess culturally specific ideas about cruelty to animals, ideas that have evolved slowly and match other elements of our culture. Consequently, practices that once were common in some areas—cock-fighting, dog-fighting, and so on—have been gradually weeded out (Bryant, 1993). Cultural relativism, however, is an attempt to refocus our cultural lens and thereby appreciate other ways of life rather than simply asserting that "our way is the right way."

Although cultural relativism is a worthwhile goal and helps us avoid cultural smugness, this view has come under attack. In a provocative book, *Sick Societies*, anthropologist Robert Edgerton (1992) points out that some cultures endanger their people's health, happiness, or survival. He suggests that we should develop a scale to evaluate cultures on their "quality of life." He also asks why we should consider cultures that practise female genital mutilation, gang rape, or wife beating, or sell daughters into prostitution, as morally equivalent to those that do not. Cultural values that result in exploitation, he says, are inferior to those that enhance people's lives.

✱ **Explore** the MySocLab eReading "Ultimate Ticket: How Extreme Fighting Captures a Generation—and Its Money" and think about how ultimate fighting has become an acceptable part of our culture on **MySocLab.**

◉ **Watch** Sam Dunn discuss the role of heavy metal music on **MySocLab.**

Edgerton's sharp questions and incisive examples bring us to a point that will come up repeatedly in this text—disagreements arise between scholars as they confront changing views of reality. It is such questioning of assumptions that keeps sociology interesting.

Values In Canadian Society

An Overview of Canadian Values

As you know, Canada is a **pluralistic society**, made up of many different religious, racial, and ethnic groups, as well as countless interest groups centring on such divergent activities as collecting Barbie dolls and hunting deer. The study of national cultural values is of interest to many sociologists, not just in Canada, but in the United States, Europe, and many other countries (see Hofstede, 1980 for an interesting examination of masculine and feminine characteristics of many national cultures).

Some recent Canadian analysts, such as Hiller (1996) and literary icon Margaret Atwood (1972, cited in Lipset, 1986:124), point to our vast geography to account for the existence of a national set of values based on "survival" in an inhospitable environment. However, John Porter (1965), English Canada's pre-eminent sociologist, was the first to point to Canada's geography as a unifying principle in our national political culture. That is why the call for more provincial autonomy, whether it comes from Alberta or Newfoundland, or the occasional stirrings of Quebec nationalism otherwise known as "separatism," evokes such strong emotions over national unity in the rest of the country. We need look no further than the paintings of the Group of Seven or to note that Canada's national motto—*A mari usque ad mare*, from sea to sea—is stamped on all our paper currency to reinforce the importance of geography in Canada's history. That said, is that all there is to Canadian culture?

A more serious analysis goes deeper. Seymour Martin Lipset (1986, 1990), for example, contrasts the "revolutionary" national values of the United States with the "counterrevolutionary" main beliefs of the dominant anglophone culture throughout the nineteenth and well into the twentieth century. He locates this contrasting set of values in the historical experiences of both countries. The United States "broke away" from Great Britain in the "successful"

Many Canadians outside Quebec perceive *la fête nationale du Quebec* with suspicion. To most French-speaking Quebecois and those who have inherited Quebec culture, *la fête nationale du Quebec* is a colourful and joyous time for family and friends. Cultural relativism requires the suspension of our own perspectives in order to grasp the perspectives of others, which is sometimes much easier said than done.

revolution of 1776 and established a unique constitution that promoted individual rights, personal freedoms, and the pursuit of happiness through profit or capitalism. Canada, however, maintained its colonial status within the British Empire. For Lipset, this means Canadian identity is caught up in our "successful" counterrevolution. As such, Lipset concluded that anglophone Canadians are more elitist; that is, we are more deferential to authority than Americans. In addition, Canadian political and economic culture is more collectivist than that in the United States. This fact, Lipset argues, helps explain the existence in Canada of a social democratic party on the traditional left (the NDP), much like the Labour Party in Great Britain or the Socialist Party in France. The collectivist tradition leads Canadians to accept, more than Americans, government intervention in the economy. We are also more likely to accept the social status we were born into. In a word, there is no equivalent in Canadian economic cultural history to the Horatio Alger myth—the notion that anyone could achieve material success with enough hard work.

It was not until 1982, when Pierre E. Trudeau, then prime minister, repatriated the constitution from Great Britain and

The study of national cultural values has become much more interesting for sociologists as Canadian society has grown in complexity and created a mosaic that envelopes its two-founding-nations status.

enshrined into law Canada's *Charter of Rights and Freedoms*, that we matured as a nation. Therefore, as Canadians, we have often defined ourselves by what we are not—namely, Americans. Table 3.2 (see page 56) provides evidence of our perceptions of cultural distance from American culture throughout recent history. What is startling about this data is the dramatic break shown for 2006, when the responses for "Essentially Different" from American culture were halved from 31 percent in 2004 to only 17 percent in just two years. Note that for Quebec, this was not as significant an issue as it was for the rest of Canada. Let's examine Quebec culture and what makes it different from the rest of Canada.

QUEBEC AS A DISTINCT SOCIETY Throughout the nineteenth century, until the beginning of the Quiet Revolution in 1959/60, Quebec was viewed by social scientists as a rural peasant society controlled by the Roman Catholic Church (Glenday & McMullan, 1970; Miner, 1964; for dissenting views, see Garigue, 1964). A set of collective values that upheld clericalism, agriculturalism, and anti-industrialism was said to dominate French-speaking Quebec society (Taylor, 1964). The Quiet Revolution dramatically changed all that. Hubert Guindon called this societal transformation and its accompanying secularization of Quebec society "state modernization" (see Chapter 10 for a discussion of bureaucracy). That is, the modernization of Quebec society witnessed not only the creation of a new middle class of professionals with well-established careers in the provincial government bureaucracies of health, education, and welfare (Guindon, 1964, 1978, 1988), it also meant the dramatic decline of the role of the Catholic Church in the lives of most French-speaking Quebecois.

What replaced the societal values of clericalism, agriculturalism, and anti-industrialism? Hubert Guindon has suggested that an important societal and political value for most

Quebecers is the belief that the establishment of Canada as a nation in 1867 was constituted by "two founding peoples"— the French and the English—or what John Porter referred to as the "two charter groups." (See Chapter 12 for a discussion of this political value and its significance for Canadian society.) When it comes to personal value clusters, the secularization of Quebec society has meant the almost complete disappearance of Catholic morals. We will examine this concept further after we discuss some of the similarities among Canadians on matters of sexual mores.

Quebecers differ from other Canadians on the following issue. Refer back to Figure 3.2 (see page 49), which shows the differences between Quebec and the rest of the country on matters of parenting, sex, and teens. Quebec is much more accepting of teenagers, whether gay or straight, having sex at home with a steady partner than any other province or region. Why? In the Down-to-Earth Sociology box on page 49, two different explanations were provided, representing marked differences in the perception of the character of the home in Quebec and the rest of Canada.

When it comes to other differences in values and beliefs, Quebec is a paradox. There are values that Quebecers share with the rest of Canada and there are those they do not. This should not be surprising. Quebec's history is bound to French language and culture and, until recently, with agriculturalism and Catholicism. Quebecers live within a language frontier that generates a sense of collective belonging. Moreover, Quebec has its own media and star system. The data in Table 3.2 reveal an interesting paradox. On one hand, Quebecers report greater concern over social problems than do individuals in the rest of Canada. However, when it comes to the personal values of compassion and social conscience, Quebecers score lower than other Canadians.

Allan Gregg, a well-known Canadian pollster, once stated that when he asked Canadians whether they agreed

TABLE 3.2 Social Problems (2006), Personal Values (2006), and International Issues (2002): Quebec and the Rest of Canada

Social Problem*	Quebec	Rest of Canada
Poverty	48%	28%
Child Abuse	53%	32%
Suicide	42%	14%
Violence	39%	28%
Racism	21%	11%
Terrorism	35%	24%
Personal Values**		
Friendliness	53%	78%
Courtesy	64%	83%
Forgiveness	60%	80%
Generosity	45%	58%
Politeness	66%	77%
Honesty	87%	94%
International Issues (2002)		
More Likely to Support		
Canada re-evaluating its Israeli–Palestinian policies	63%	49%
Less Likely to Support		
Canadian involvement in Afghanistan	65%	83%
More funding for the Canadian military	48%	74%
Giving up some freedoms to combat terrorism	47%	63%

* Percentage of respondents who were "Very Serious" when asked how concerned they were about the issues above

** Percentage of respondents who indicated that the personal values above were "Very Important" to them

Sources: For 2006 data, see Cameron Ainsworth-Vincze, "Values lost in translation," *Maclean's* Vol 119, July 3, 2006, Issue 27/28. For 2002 data, see "Where solitudes meet," by Benoit Aubin, *Maclean's*, Vol 114, December 31–January 7, 2001–2002, p. 32.

or disagreed with the statement: "eat, drink, and be merry, for tomorrow you may die," 77 percent of Quebec teenagers agreed, compared with only 17 percent of teens in British Columbia (Aubin, 2001–2002). He coined the term "hedonist-individualist" to characterize the response of Quebec teenagers. For Gregg, this dramatic shift in values represented more than a simple break with Catholic morals. It represented a break from the traditional values of agriculturalism and clericalism toward a new postmodern value for this generation of Quebecers. The results reported in Table 3.2 speak to this dramatic shift in values. Leslie Laczko, a sociology professor at the University of Ottawa, may have a more salient answer, which is that Quebec has a much higher proportion of people who are single and who live in common-law relationships than the rest of Canada.

"That itself is a significant part of this big puzzle that social scientists are trying to solve," he says, because single people are more likely to feel bored and isolated than married couples.

Just as interesting is the fact that when Quebecers look outside their province, they tend to "skip" Canada and adopt a continental or global view. According to Table 3.2, Quebecers are less likely to give up personal freedom to combat terrorism, indicating that they are more guarded of their personal liberties than the average Canadian.

Focus Question

In what ways do Canadians outside of Quebec differ from Quebecers, and in what ways are they similar?

Do Men and Women Use Language Differently?

Deborah Tannen's (2007) research shows that men and women communicate differently. Tannen uses the terms "rapport" and "report" to contrast women's and men's linguistic styles. *Rapport* refers to the use of language and body movements to establish social connections with others. *Report*, on the other hand, involves reciting information that serves to establish hierarchical position. Conversation with other men, then, becomes the means by which men attempt to determine social rank.

For your consideration

Save emails from your friends and family members. Are there gender differences that could be catalogued as either "rapport" (building social connections) or "report" (reciting information)? Does the use of emoticons, for example, vary, both in manner (joking or serious, reassuring or negative) and in number? Can the differences be put in a table with women's approach on one side and men's on the other?

Native Peoples in Canada

The multicultural aspect of recent Canadian history is often viewed as positive. Many ethnic groups celebrate their differences and similarities as Canadians at numerous festivals, carnivals, and celebrations every year across the country. Native Canadians, however, have very little reason to rejoice and make merry. Their present status as Canadians was enshrined in the *Indian Act* of 1876. Today, the Minister of Indian Affairs and Northern Development administers the *Indian Act* at the federal level. As shown in Table 3.3, the *Indian Act* has served to isolate Natives from mainstream Canadian society by keeping them on reserves. More importantly, and in many ways because the federal government controls their social life, Native peoples in Canada are afforded few opportunities for meaningful employment or for starting business ventures that respect their diverse cultures.

Neither are the living conditions on many reserves healthy. Nor are there opportunities for young people to explore their place in the Native way of life. The combination of adverse social, psychological, and economic conditions serves to heighten susceptibility to illness and poor health. It is little wonder, then, that Native peoples report the highest incidences of death due to respiratory disease, accidents, violence, and poisoning (Jarvis & Boldt, 1983; Department of Indian Affairs and Northern Development, 2001).

Value Contradictions and Multiculturalism in Canada

Not all values fall into neat, integrated packages. Some contradict one another. The **value contradiction** of national or group superiority violates freedom, democracy, and equality. There simply cannot be full expressions of freedom, democracy, and equality alongside homophobia, racism, and sexism. Something has to give. One way Canadians sidestepped this contradiction in the past was to say that the values of freedom, democracy, and equality applied only to certain groups. The contradiction surfaced, however, with the internment of the Japanese during World War II and the women's liberation

TABLE 3.3 Highlights from the History of the *Indian Act*

1.	1876	The first *Indian Act* was passed by Parliament.

a. The concept of enfranchisement was a key provision of the act. This meant and still means the total assimilation of the First Nations population in Canada.

b. The *Indian Act* gave substantial powers to the federal government to control First Nations people living on reserves. It explicitly forbade the selling or leasing of any reserve land unless it was first surrendered or leased to the federal government.

c. It also distinguished between Status and non-Status Indians. (Status Indians are those who are registered with the federal government as Indians according to the terms of the *Indian Act*. Non-Status Indians are those who are not registered.)

d. The *Indian Act* of 1876 also made provision for the election of First Nations chiefs. Essentially, chiefs functioned as agents of the federal government, exercising limited power within federal supervision. The act was so limiting that First Nations band members could not leave reserves without a special pass, and their children were taken away to residential schools to be assimilated.

After returning from fighting for Canada in World War II, Aboriginal men fought against the injustices of the *Indian Act*. In the 1940s, Aboriginal leaders began to emerge as champions of Native rights.

2.	1951	The *Indian Act* was revised, but Indian status and enfranchisement clauses were retained. The law banning Indian ceremonies was repealed and First Nations members were given the right to enter public bars.
3.	1960	First Nations were allowed to vote in federal elections.
4.	1973	Native leaders reclaimed their right to educate their children through their culture, and church-operated or residential schools soon disappeared.
5.	1975/78	The first modern land claims settlement was signed by the Cree and the Quebec government in 1975 and the Naskapi and Quebec in 1978. A total of $225 million was awarded as compensation to the James Bay Cree and the Inuit of Northern Quebec.
6.	1988	The federal government amended the *Indian Act*, enabling First Nations to pass bylaws to levy property taxes on reserve lands that they would lease.
7.	1996	The 13 First Nations and the Department of Indian Affairs signed the Framework Agreement on First Nations Land Management in February 1996, which allows First Nations to pass their own laws to develop, conserve, protect, manage, and use their lands. The 13 First Nations are Westbank, Musqueam, Lheit-Lit'en, N'Quatqua, Squamish, Siksika, Muskoday, Cowessess, Opaskwayak Cree, Nipissing, Mississaugas of Scugog Island, Chippewas of Georgina Island, and Chippewas of Mnjikaning.
8.	1999	Nunavut ("our land") was created as the largest and newest territory in Canada with a population of approximately 29 500. The federal government agreed to pay Nunavut $1.2 billion over a period ending in 2007.

Source: Adapted from The First Nations Governance Act, by Linda Ward, June 14, 2002, CBC News Online. Accessed at www.cbc.ca/news/features/indian_act.html and www.ainc-inac.gc.ca/pr/info/info14_e.html.

movement during the 1960s and 1970s. Most Canadians who live and work with many different subcultural groups continue to extend the values of freedom and equality and, as we saw earlier when discussing values in Canadian society, tolerance to more and more groups. As a result, we are reducing the emphasis on a single national group superiority.

Multiculturalism in Canada is a case in point. The debates arguing ghettoization versus integration barely changed over the past 35 years. However, new evidence suggests that multiculturalism plays a positive role in the process of immigrant and minority integration and is a more effective practice in Canada than in other Western countries. Integration includes economic integration into the labour market, political participation in the electoral process, and social integration via informal networks and membership in formal organizations (Statistics Canada, 2010a).

Value Clusters

Values are not independent units. Instead, some come together to form a larger whole, or **value cluster**. As previously discussed, "hedonistic individualism" represents a recent Quebec value cluster, while Seymour Martin Lipset distinguished "counterrevolution" as a value cluster for the anglophones that have dominated Canadian history.

EMERGING VALUE CLUSTERS A value cluster of four interrelated core values—leisure, self-fulfillment, physical fitness, and youth—appears to be emerging in Canada and the United States. A fifth—concern for the environment—has established itself on a global scale.

1. *Leisure.* The emergence of leisure as a value is reflected in the rapid growth of a huge recreation industry—from computer games, boats, and motor homes to sports arenas, vacation homes, and a gigantic travel and vacation industry.
2. *Self-fulfillment.* This value is reflected in the "human potential" movement, a concern with "becoming all one can be," "self-help," "relating," and "personal development."
3. *Physical fitness.* There is much greater emphasis being placed today on both men and women to appear attractive. For men, the standard is Los Angeles Galaxy soccer player David Beckham, or, for the sophisticated urban man, what Mark Simpson (1994) called the "Metrosexual Male." This trend can be seen in the mushrooming of health clubs and physical fitness centres, the "natural" foods craze, and brew bars, and in obsessive concerns about weight and diet.
4. *Youth.* While valuing youth and disparaging old age is not new, some sociologists note a new sense of urgency. Aging baby boomers are targeted by advertisers to buy products that are said to fight the normal physical changes that happen with growing older. Advertising, to be sure, fuels cosmetic makeovers, but so do so-called experts, one of whom recently claimed that "aging is not a normal life event, but a disease" (Cowley, 1996). It is not surprising that techniques of youth enhancement—from cosmetics to surgery—have become popular.

   These first four items in the cluster are a response to needs and interests resulting from fundamental changes in Canadian and American society. Not long ago, Canadians were preoccupied with forging a nation and fighting for economic survival. Today, advertisers push an increasing variety of wares and services, not only to mass markets but especially to emerging, age-specific "niche" markets such as kids, teenage boys and girls, and young adults.
5. *Concern for the environment.* Throughout most of Canadian history, the environment was seen as a challenge—a wilderness to be settled, forests to be chopped down, rivers and lakes to be fished, and animals to be hunted for their furs. Today, most Canadians have developed a genuine and long-term concern for the environment because we now recognize our dependence on natural resources. In fact, the environment is increasingly linked to health and is associated with judgments about our quality of life and economic success (Reil, 2001).

When Values Clash

Core values do not change without meeting strong resistance from traditionalists—those who hold them dear. Consequently, many people are upset at the changes swirling around them, seeing their way of life challenged and their future growing insecure. Efforts to change gender roles, for example, arouse intense controversy, as do support of alternative family forms and changes in sexual behaviour. Alarmed at such onslaughts to their values, traditionalists fiercely defend idealized family relationships and gender roles. The majority of Canadians, unlike many of their American neighbours, are embracing the changing moral values of tolerance and respect for other cultures and ways of life, including gay and lesbian lifestyles.

The Americanization of Canadian Values?

As John Porter (1965) remarked over three decades ago, Canadians, unlike Americans, lack a unifying ideology. Canadians are not brought up with a set of beliefs and values that tell us who we are and what we should strive for in order to make our lives meaningful and fulfilling. At the same time, we have been preoccupied with who we are as a nation. Many of us have been known, on frequent occasion, to ask the proverbial question, "What is the Canadian identity?" Many social scientists, Canadian and non-Canadian, have sought answers to this perplexing national question.

Could it be that we are losing what distinctiveness we possess as Canadians as we become more closely tied economically with the United States—that is, as our trade, capital, and people move north and south? As shown in Table 3.4, it seems we want to see ourselves as essentially different from Americans even though the latest data suggests a shift in perception. However, what constitutes truly Canadian values remains elusive to us. American filmmaker Michael Moore underlined some similarities between Canadian and American societies in his film *Bowling for Columbine*, in which he asked the question, "What is responsible for the exceptionally high level of killing in America?" Not a large number of guns, Moore answered, because other countries, including Canada, have proportionally as many guns. Neither is it poverty, unemployment, ethnic diversity, or a love of violent movies and video games, because Canada has as much ethnic diversity and more unemployment. Two things, according to Moore, are primary causes: the U.S. media, which, as he shows, constantly encourages fear among the American populace; and the government in Washington, which solves problems by bombing people somewhere in the world. According to Moore's argument,

TABLE 3.4 Canada–United States: Are We Getting Closer Culturally?*

Response	1999 (%)	2002 (%)	2004 (%)	2006 (%)	2006 Quebec (%)
Essentially the same	8	7	12	6	3
Mainly the same	44	34	32	44	27
Mainly different	23	29	23	32	47
Essentially different	24	28	31	17	22

* Survey question asked of Canadians, "Would you describe Canadians and Americans as essentially the same, mainly the same but with small differences, mainly different but with small similarities, or essentially different?"

Source: "The Nation's Mood," *Maclean's*, December 27, 2004. www.macleans.ca/topstories/polls/article.jsp?content=20041220_145019_3484.

perhaps the Canadian media differs in some respects from that in the United States—and certainly the Canadian government exercises much less military power than the U.S. government does. What do you think? Are there unique Canadian values worth preserving?

Cultural Universals

With the amazing variety of human cultures around the world, are there any **cultural universals**—values, norms, or other cultural traits that are found everywhere?

Human being possess certain distinct biological universals: a long period of infant dependency; year round, not seasonal, sexuality; and a complex brain enabling the use of language and tools. Anthropologists point to social universals such as living in groups and living in some kind of family (Brown, 1991). However, there are no cultural universals such as a common language like English or a common family type like the nuclear family.

Humans have no biological imperative that results in one particular form of behaviour throughout the world.

Focus Question
Is there a universally accepted way of conducting basic human activities such as cooking, marriage, and so on?

Animals and Culture

Let us digress for a moment to follow a fascinating and related issue: Do animals have culture? Do they have language?

Do Animals Have Culture?
According to our definition of culture as a learned way of life passed on to others, it would seem that animals could not have culture. The basic sociological question is this: Are there any behaviours that animals learn and then pass on to others?

We begin with Jane Goodall, who extensively studied chimpanzees in Tanzania, Africa (Van Lawick-Goodall, 1971).

When the chimps became accustomed to Goodall and allowed her to join them, she slowly figured out how they communicate. Eventually she was even able to participate in their gestures, hoots, and facial expressions. For 30 years, Goodall lived in the remote jungle (Walters, 1990). She observed that wild chimps make and use **tools**; that is, they modify objects and use them for specific purposes. Until her observation, it was assumed that only humans use tools. The chimps would pick a blade of grass, then strip off its leaves, and lick one end. Next they would poke the sticky end into a nest of termites. After waiting a bit, they would pull it out covered with termites, then savour the taste as they licked off the stick. In 1977, Goodall founded the Jane Goodall Institute for Wildlife Research, Education and Conservation to provide ongoing support for field research on wild chimpanzees. Today, she is on a globe-spanning crusade to promote conservation and improve conditions for captive chimps (Miller, 1995). In 2003, Queen Elizabeth II named Dr. Goodall a Dame of the British Empire.

A related question that has intrigued both scientists and non-scientists is whether animals have language. Animal sounds appear to be close in meaning to a baby's cries. A cry of distress, even though it brings a parent running, is not language. The cry is merely a biological response to pain, similar to reflexes. Anthropologists characterize the natural communications systems of other primates such as apes and monkeys as *call systems*. That is, these animals make a limited number of sounds—calls—when they encounter particular environmental challenges (Kottak, 2012).

Focus Question
What makes humans different from all other animals?

Technology In the Global Village

New Technologies
In addition to symbolic or nonmaterial culture, there is also a material aspect—a group's things, ranging from houses to toys. Central to a group's material culture is its **technology**; that is, the skills or procedures necessary to make and use tools.

We can use the term **new technology** to refer to emerging technologies, such as computers, satellites, and various forms of microelectronics-based media.

The sociological significance of technology is that *the type of technology a group has sets the framework for its nonmaterial culture*. Technology influences the way people think and how they relate to one another, a focus of the box on Sociology and the New Technology on page 62. Consider gender relations. Through the centuries and throughout the world, it has been the common custom (a group's nonmaterial culture) for men to dominate women. Today, with instantaneous communications (the material culture), this custom has become much more difficult to maintain. For example, when women from many nations gathered in Beijing for the UN Conference on Women in 1995, satellites instantly transmitted their grievances around the globe. Such communications may create discontent, or sometimes a feeling of sisterhood, and taken together women will agitate for social change (see Chapters 7 and 18). In addition, the internet has facilitated an explosion of small businesses in Canada and the United States owned by entrepreneurial women. It is much easier to offer online payments to customers for products through companies such as PayPal or CCNow, for example, than it is for a woman to get a merchant's account from one of Canada's chartered banks.

Cultural Lag and Cultural Change

A couple of generations ago, sociologist William Ogburn (1922) coined the term **cultural lag**. By this, Ogburn meant that not all parts of a culture change at the same pace. Ogburn pointed out that a group's material culture usually changes first, with the nonmaterial culture lagging behind, playing a game of catch-up. For example, when we get sick, we can type our symptoms into a computer and get an immediate printout of our diagnosis and best course

This Barbie doll, sold in Japan, is dressed in the stage costume of a Japanese singer. As objects diffuse from one culture to another, they are modified to meet the tastes of the adoptive culture. In this instance, the modification has been done intentionally as part of the globalization of capitalism.

"COOL! A KEYBOARD THAT WRITES WITHOUT A PRINTER."

Technological advances have become so rapid that the technology of one generation is practically unrecognizable by the next.

of treatment. In fact, in some tests, computers outperform physicians (Waldholz, 1991). Yet our customs have not caught up with technology, and we continue to visit doctors' offices.

Technology and Cultural Levelling

Except in rare instances, humans have always had some contact with other groups. In this process, called **cultural diffusion**, groups are eager, for example, to adopt superior weapons and tools. During these contacts, people learned from one another, adapting some part of the other's way of life. In remote areas of South America, one can find metal cooking pots, steel axes, and even bits of clothing spun in mills in North America. Although the direction of cultural diffusion today is primarily from the West to other parts of the world, cultural diffusion is not a one-way street, which can be seen in architectural designs, food (bagels, falafel, Thai, and so on), and leisure items such as the hammock.

Not long ago, a trip from Canada to Africa was so unusual that only a few hardy people made it, and newspapers would herald their feat. With today's technology in

Information and Communications Technologies (ICTs): Global Village or Big Brother?

A sign over a photocopy machine:

> WARNING! This machine is subject to breakdowns during periods of critical need . . . Threatening the machine with violence only aggravates the situation. Keep cool and say nice things to the machine. Nothing else seems to work. Never let the machine know you are in a hurry.

All over the country, users of copiers have laughed at some version of this attempt to turn frustration into humour. This sign comes close to a point of view called **technological determinism**, the idea that technology is the single greatest force shaping our lives (Chandler, 1995).

Two Canadian analysts from the University of Toronto, Harold Innis and Marshall McLuhan, examined the effects of technological revolutions on our culture. For Innis, oral cultures were limited to the size of small communities. However, the ability to write made human geographical expansion possible because a literate group could keep in touch through writing. In Innis's mind, bureaucratic empires became possible when people could check records and develop standards of judgment.

Marshall McLuhan built on Innis by portraying communications technologies as extensions of the human body. Just as a pole increases the reach of your arm, the new and varied ways we communicate with one another today extend the power of our senses. But not all senses share equally in their extension. Literacy may amplify one's eyes, McLuhan observed figuratively, but shrink one's ears. A computer, for example, extends the power of our brain and ears with the use of computer games and access to new music over the web, but not our sense of touch or smell. The more we use a cellphone, computer, or MP3 player, the smaller our world becomes. We are living in what McLuhan coined "The Global Village."

Sherry Turkle (1984/2005; 1995) takes McLuhan several steps further by arguing that ICTs, when incorporated into toys, video games, and internet games, help create separate virtual realities that play on our fantasies, both sexual and nonsexual.

For Your Consideration

Technological determinists highlight a significant issue: Are we in control of

Marshall McLuhan.

technology, or is technology in control of us?

In today's world, the long-accepted idea that it is proper to withhold rights because a person is a women or gay no longer holds. What is usually invisible in such a revolutionary change is the role of technology in joining the world's nations into a global communications network. Can you explain how it is possible for global information technologies to bring about the expansion of human rights?

---

travel and communications, cultural diffusion is occurring rapidly. Air travel has made it possible to journey around the globe in a matter of hours. Hundreds of thousands now make the trip every year.

The changes in communication are no less vast. Today's electronic communications transmit messages across the globe in a matter of seconds. In fact, travel and communication unite us. One result is **cultural levelling**, a process in which cultures become similar to one another as expanding industrialization brings not only technology, but also Western culture to the rest of the world.

Cultural levelling, occurring rapidly around the world, is apparent to any traveller. The golden arches of McDonald's

welcome today's visitors in Tokyo, Paris, London, Madrid, and even Moscow, Beijing, and Hong Kong. In Mexico, the most popular piñatas are no longer of donkeys but of Mickey Mouse and Fred Flintstone (Beckett, 1996). "Thanks to MTV," says an Indian girl in Calcutta, "I can wear a miniskirt to a disco" (Brauchli, 1993).

Some would argue globalization facilitated the spread of U.S. popular culture around the world. In addition to the pervasive influence of U.S. television, movies, and magazines, sports such as basketball, football, and baseball are played in many countries. A much maligned but fascinating form of sports entertainment, the World Wrestling Entertainment franchise, has followers in almost every

Sociology of Professional Wrestling at Brock University

Professional wrestling draws the attention of millions of men, women, and children from diverse backgrounds and ages. It is not just a North American trend; professional wrestling is a worldwide cultural phenomenon.

Recently, professional wrestling has been on the receiving end of academic criticism for its misogyny, homophobia, and violence. Is this an accurate representation of what happens in the "squared circle"? Or is there more to professional wrestling than the exclusively negative messages some academics see in the ring?

Professional wrestling in North America is but one variant in the world of professional wrestling. Other examples include the Mexican *lucha libre*, the Japanese *puroresu*, and the Bolivian *cholita* styles of professional wrestling.

Until now, there has been little sociological research on professional wrestling as a worldwide cultural phenomenon. One of the authors of this text, Dan Glenday, is completing a long-term research project on professional wrestling as a cross-cultural phenomenon. Today, students at Brock University in St. Catherines, Ontario, are able to study the sociology of professional wrestling in a course offered through the Department of Sociology.

Each year, Brock University's student pub hosts a professional wrestling card where students can witness the sport firsthand and write a report based on the interaction between the athletes and their audience.

corner of the world. Professional wrestling, with its soap opera antics, staged violence, and comedic rituals, fascinates an increasingly large number of young men and women (see the Perspectives box on Pro Wrestling on page 63).

The bridging of geography and culture by electronic signals does not in itself mark the end of traditional cultures. Japan, for example, has adapted not only Western economic production but also Western forms of dress and music. These changes, superimposed on Japanese culture, have turned Japan into a blend of Western and Eastern cultures.

Globalization, a topic to be discussed in Chapter 5, is a process of transnational economic activity that has contributed to the resurgence of religious and ethnic nationalism in various parts of the world.

SUMMARY AND REVIEW

WHAT IS CULTURE?

What is culture?
All human groups possess culture—language, beliefs, values, norms, and material objects passed from one generation to the next. Material culture consists of objects (art, buildings, clothing, and tools). Nonmaterial (or symbolic) culture is a group's way of thinking and patterns of behaviour. The central component is symbols—anything to which people attach meaning and use to communicate with others. Universally, the symbols of nonmaterial culture are gestures, language, values, norms, sanctions, folkways, and mores. p. 46. Anthropologists point to social universals such as living in groups and living in some kind of family However, cultural universals are values, norms, or other cultural traits found in all cultures. Although all human groups have customs concerning cooking, funerals, weddings, and so on, because the specific forms of these customs vary from one culture to another, there are no cultural universals. pp. 46–54.

COMPONENTS OF SYMBOLIC CULTURE

Why is language so significant to culture?
Language allows human experience to be goal-directed, co-operative, and cumulative. It also lets humans move beyond the present to share a past, future, and other common perspectives. According to the Sapir-Whorf hypothesis, language even shapes our thoughts and perceptions. pp. 46–54.

How do values, norms, folkways, mores, and sanctions reflect nonmaterial culture?
All groups have values, standards by which they define what is desirable or undesirable, and norms, rules or expectations about behaviour. Groups use positive sanctions to show approval of those who follow their norms, and negative sanctions to show disapproval of those who do not. Norms that are not strictly enforced are called folkways, while mores are norms to which groups demand conformity because they reflect core values. p. 51.

How do subcultures and countercultures differ?

A subculture is a group whose values and related behaviours distinguish its members from the general culture. A counterculture holds values that in some way stand in opposition to those of the dominant culture. pp. 52–53.

What are cultural relativism and ethnocentrism?

People are naturally ethnocentric; that is, they use their own culture as a yardstick for judging the ways of others. In contrast, those who embrace cultural relativism try to understand other cultures on those cultures' own terms. pp. 52–53.

VALUES IN CANADIAN SOCIETY

Are the values of Canadian and Quebec societies different?

Although Canada is a pluralistic, multicultural society made up of many groups—each with its own set of values—tolerance and liberal moral values dominate. There are differences in values between Quebecers and the rest of Canada. p. 55.

Some values come together (value clusters) to form a larger whole. Value contradictions (such as equality and racism) indicate areas of social tension, which are likely points of social change. Changes in a society's fundamental values are opposed by people who hold strongly to traditional values. pp. 54–60.

ANIMALS AND CULTURE

Do animals have culture?

To the extent that some animals teach their young certain behaviours, such as using tools, animals also have a rudimentary culture. Some primates have a call system, but only humans speak. p. 60.

TECHNOLOGY IN THE GLOBAL VILLAGE

How is technology changing culture?

Ogburn coined the term *cultural lag* to refer to a group's nonmaterial culture lagging behind its changing technology. With today's technological advances in travel and communications, cultural diffusion is occurring rapidly. This leads to cultural levelling, whereby many groups are adopting Western culture in place of their own customs. Much of the richness of the world's diverse cultures is being lost in the process. pp. 60–62.

KEY TERMS

counterculture 52
cultural diffusion 61
cultural lag 61
cultural levelling 62
cultural relativism 53
cultural universals 60
culture 46
ethnocentrism 53

folkways 51
gestures 47
language 47
material culture 46
mores 51
negative sanction 51
new technology 61
nonmaterial cultures 46

norms 51
pluralistic society 54
positive sanction 51
sanctions 51
Sapir-Whorf hypothesis 50
subculture 52
symbol 47
symbolic culture 46

taboo 51
technological
    determinism 62
technology 60
tools 60
value cluster 59
value contradiction 57
values 51

WEBLINKS

All URLs listed are current as of the printing of this text.

Maclean's Poll
www.macleans.ca/article.
jsp?content=20060701_130104_130104
Since 1983, *Maclean's* magazine has polled Canadians on topics from taxes to sex, politics, and morality. Here, you can see the results from the 2006 poll.

The Canadian Graduate Student Journal of Folklore and Ethnology
www.ucs.mun.ca/~culture
Canada's longest-running bilingual folklore journal, published for nearly 20 years in French and English, it is currently run by graduate students in folklore at Memorial University of Newfoundland. Topics covered include the traditional arts, music, cuisine, architecture, beliefs, cultural

psychology, and sociological structure of regional ethnic, religious, and industrial groups in Canada.

Citizenship and Immigration Canada
**www.cic.gc.ca/english/resources/publications/
multi-state/section1.asp**
In 1971, Canada became the first country in the world to adopt multiculturalism as an official policy. The 1971 Multiculturalism Policy of Canada also confirmed the rights of Aboriginal peoples and the status of Canada's two

official languages. This website provides the latest evidence on multiculturalism and integration in Canada.

Disappearing Languages
**http://travel.nationalgeographic.com/travel/
enduring-voices**
National Geographic's Enduring Voices Project (conducted in collaboration with the Living Tongues Institute for Endangered Languages) strives to preserve endangered languages.

CRITICAL THINKING QUESTIONS

1. Are all cultures equally valid? Can you think of a culture (e.g., Nazism) that you would find unacceptable? Why do you feel the way you do?
2. Does the media influence our culture, or does the expanding cultural diversity in our society influence the changes we find expressed in the media?
3. Is sexual orientation simply the product of a person's cultural upbringing? What role does biology play in our sexual preferences?

4. Why do many teenagers rebel against authority? Access the Research Navigator through MySocLab and use keywords such as "teenage" and "authority" to locate relevant and recent scholarly and popular press publications to help you answer this question.

MySocLab

Explore the topics covered in this chapter on MySocLab. Interactive resources include a study plan, cumulative exams, a multimedia library, MySocLab eReadings, and access to the MySocLab Video Series.

4

SOCIALIZATION

IN the early months of 2012, a saga surrounding an epic family tragedy reached its culmination. Mohammad Shafia, the younger of his two wives, and his son were convicted of orchestrating the 2009 murder of three of his daughters, ages 19, 17, and 13, as well as his childless older wife. Their bodies were discovered in a car submerged in a canal in Kingston, Ontario. According to court testimony, the Montreal-based family had been torn apart by the rebellious behaviour of the three daughters, who wore "revealing clothing to school," took up with boys the family did not approve of, ran away from home, and complained to public authorities about their ill-treatment at home. The trial, which drew international media coverage, was seen by some to speak to the problems of immigrant families struggling to adopt the values of their new country, while others pointed to a monstrous misconception of family honour (DiManno, 2011). Leaders of the Afghani and Muslim communities were quick to disavow any cultural or religious explanation for this heinous behaviour. Indeed, Canadian Muslim leaders issued a *fatwa* against violence against women to publically memorialize their rejection of this behaviour. In the wake of the murder conviction, we must struggle to rationalize how a mother, father, and brother could end the lives of girls with whom they had shared such a profound social and biological connection. In this, as in many other instances, we are left to wonder about the roots and parameters of human behaviour.

What does it mean to be a human being? What is our "nature," and why and how do we differ from other animals? Many people assume that humans will show empathy for those who are smaller and weaker and not mindlessly inflict pain and death. According to this popular viewpoint, while non-human animals are amoral and may kill their own young, humans are different. For years, scientists pointed to the "fact" that animals do not use tools, do not employ symbols, and do not communicate with spoken language as evidence of our distinctly human category. Recent scientific research indicating that animals do use tools, are capable of using symbols, and, in fact, can be taught limited spoken language has dramatically blurred the lines between humans and other animals, and the question of what it means to be human and where "human nature" is located remains more troubling than ever.

Biology, Sociobiology, or Socialization?

For generations, one of the major issues every sociology student has been introduced to is an exploration of the "nature versus nurture" debate. Two competing perspectives have long struggled against one another. Are people's fates, likes and dislikes, and behaviours dictated by biologically inborn characteristics—in other words, genetic material—or are our lives the product of our exposure to the culture, historical period, family, and friendship groups we happen to belong to? Was Steve Jobs, whose work transformed personal computing, animated movies, phones, digital publishing, tablet computing, and music, a "born" genius who was destined to impact the course of human history? Or did his legacy owe as much to his lucky friendship with Steve Wozniak as to his abilities (Isaacson, 2011)?

The "human nature" explanations are essentially biological, or genetic: people act in specific ways because of their biological makeup. If human behaviour is the result of "human nature," then this conclusion has profound implications. After all, if your "bad" acts are the result of genetics, how can we blame you and how can we hope to change your behaviour? Similarly, if certain races or genders are "genetically inferior," then their social subordination is simply "natural."

In the nineteenth and early twentieth centuries, many researchers embraced the idea of **biological determinism**—the belief much of our behaviour reflects in-built biological traits such as the need to reproduce, the need to survive, and so on. Strongly influenced by the then-emerging field of modern biology and its new theory of evolution, many analysts pointed to aspects of human biology—such as "instincts" (the mothering instinct, for example) and biological differences (especially "racial" differences)—as the root causes of human actions. These beliefs later informed Nazi eugenics policies. After all, if some people and some races are "naturally" inferior, they should be eradicated so that the superior ones can flourish. As sociology emerged as a discipline at the turn of the twentieth century, it was influenced by this debate, and North American sociologists vigorously challenged this kind of "born in the bone" thinking. They argued that human behaviour is in large measure a reflection of societal and cultural forces. In other words, through the process of **socialization**, our beliefs, values, attitudes,

and even our emotions are sculpted throughout our lives by our contact with parents, siblings, peers, schools, religion, media, and a wide variety of major societal institutions (Gerth & Mills, 1958).

Today, the debate over whether human behaviour is fundamentally social or biological is far from resolved. People often explain human actions in terms of "human nature," and popular culture still provides support for biological determinism. We all are familiar with comments such as "that's just like a man" or "that's just like a woman." These phrases implicitly attribute behaviour to biological gender differences. Equally troubling are commonplace "racial" explanations, such as "Asians make bad drivers" or "Blacks are good at sports." These biological stereotypes support both prejudice and active discrimination against others. Further, these "racial" explanations ignore the fact that scientists overwhelmingly reject the concept of "racial difference" on the grounds that it is inaccurate, lacks consistency, and has no basis in scientific reality (Sorenson, 2003:37). Despite any differences in appearance between members of different "races," there are enough biological similarities across "races" and enough differences within a "race" to render the construct unusable (Wente, 2008).

Nonetheless, enthusiasm for biology remains alive and well, including among some sociologists who term themselves *sociobiologists* and argue that much human social behaviour can and should be explained in terms of our evolutionary heritage and resultant biological makeup. For example, in a recent article, social analysts argued that the complex human behaviour implied by "becoming an entrepreneur" is at least partly genetic. Without going so far as to suggest that genes determine occupation, they concluded that genetic factors predispose some people to certain careers (Nicolaou & Shane, 2010). Similarly, Canadian researcher Scott Forbes (2005) suggests that family life, notably parental investment in children, should be explored in terms of parents' evolutionary impulse to perpetuate their genetic image. In order to ensure that their genes are successfully reproduced in some of their children, they will even engage in anti-social acts, such as infanticide and fratricide. In a recent article, Daniel Vining (2011) calls for a revival of sociobiology. As he points out, evolutionary logic would suggest that women are eager to mate with males who are "successful," since they are able to provide for offspring. In this way, both the male and female would be able to satisfy the evolutionary imperative to successfully reproduce their genetic material. However, in modern society, the very wealthy do not translate their wealth into many children. According to Vining, this is a central social issue that must be confronted by sociobiology.

That said, consider the implications of explaining who you are in terms of, as suggested by a leading primatologist, your "inner ape." Are you in a significant way simply a reflection of humans' evolutionary past and our primate genes (De Waal, 2005)? Similarly, what are the implications of accepting a "sociobiological" explanation of male violence? Should we simply acknowledge, as suggested by a leading Canadian criminologist, that men are "hard wired" to respond with violence (Boyd, 2000)?

Blurring Boundaries Between Biology and Sociology

More and more the debate about biological and cultural influences is being reframed. While biology and social environment continue as two major players, another element has been recognized. This new field, *epigenetics*, refers to a third factor that may function as a bridge between the environment and genes or may "operate on its own to shape who we are" (Miller, 2012:47). This new paradigm emerged from on-going research involving twins.

After all, identical twins seem to provide a common biological base onto which environmental differences are inscribed. This is even more intriguing when, as in the Minnesota Study of Twins Reared Apart (ended in 2000), twins have been separated by adoption and raised in different social environments. Research from the Minnesota project attests to the significance of genetics. For example, findings indicated that 75 percent of IQ scores, criminality, and religious fervour are shaped by genes. Similarly, certain disorders, such as reading disability, autism, alcoholism, and Alzheimer's disease, are strongly affected by biological inheritance (as cited in Miller, 2012:58). While a loving, supportive family certainly impacts how these biological pluses and minuses are experienced, the Minnesota study made it clear that biology matters.

Twin research reveals the complexities of nature versus nurture. Today, the focus of twin research is on identical twins raised in the same family who are, in at least some ways, very different (as cited in Miller, 2012). Despite the constants of biological and environmental input, some twins grow up to be significantly dissimilar; for example, in terms of body weight, Alzheimer's disease, and autism. This research on twins has helped to reveal the role of epigenetic tags: chemical mechanisms attached to genes that, as a result of outside influences such as stress or nutrition (or, sometimes, with no known outside influence) activate or suppress specific genes to varying degrees. If, as suggested by Miller (2012), our genes are visualized as keys on a gigantic piano, the epigenetic processes determine when and how each key may be played. The result is that even identical twins may develop quite differently. Some analysts suggest a pen and pencil analogy—genes are biology written in pen, while epigenetics is biology written in pencil. The long-term hope is that epigenetics—an intermediary between genes and the environment—may at some point allow for fixes to disorders such as autism (Miller, 2012).

Many Chinese girls have been adopted into North American families in the past decade, and a number of adopted Chinese twins have been contacted by researchers. These twins are often reared apart by different adoptive families. For the first time, researchers will be able to undertake prospective research on twins—following them through the life course, noting differences as well as similarities, and, hopefully, identifying some of the environmental factors that influence epigenetics (Segal, Stohs, & Evans, 2011).

As a result of diverse scientific advances, contemporary discussion of the nature versus nurture debate articulates a subtler vision of human behaviour: humans are both free-willed and driven by biology and culture. Human genes both "set" the paths of human behaviour and also absorb and respond to human experiences (Ridley, 2003). Within this highly complex and interactive vision of the relationship between nature and nurture, it seems accurate to conclude that that human biology establishes some general parameters for human development, but that environmental and social experiences are pivotal to human behaviour.

Research with children deprived of almost all human contact suggests, for example, that our biological makeup sets time limits on our abilities to acquire language and make connections to others. In recent years, there have been reports of children who have been severely deprived of normal socialization—confined to basements, dog kennels, or cribs throughout their formative years. For example, for seven years, three Austrian girls were imprisoned in their home by their mentally ill mother. They were kept in complete

An orphanage in Kaliyampoondi, India. The treatment of these children is likely to affect their ability to reason and to function as adults.

✹ **Explore** the MySocLab eReading "Can't Stand Putting Your Money at Risk? Blame DNA" by Susan Pinker on **MySocLab**.

darkness and never allowed to leave the home. Rescued by police in 2005, the girls have been in specialized therapy ever since. Reflecting research in other cases, it is believed that they will never fully recover (Pancevski, 2007). In contrast, Elizabeth Smart, a 14-year-old girl from Utah who was kidnapped and held captive for nine months, and Jaycee Dugar, who was kidnapped at age 11 and held for 18 years, have apparently been able to return to "normal" lives. Despite extreme isolation, brutalization, sexual assault—and, in Dugar's case, multiple pregnancies—their sense of personal identity and foundational human skills (especially language) were sufficiently well developed to survive the subsequent abuse (Nelson, 2012; *Mail Online*, 2011).

Focus Question

In what ways does epigenetics introduce increased complexity into the nature versus nurture debate?

IN SUM

Scientific research has shown that the relationship between biology and environment in the development of human beings is complex and nuanced. Babies raised in isolation from human contact would likely mature into full-size adults, but would not develop into "human beings" as we understand them. Without the use of language or other symbol systems, humans reared in isolation would not experience or grasp relationships between people, would not be able to share the knowledge of others, and would be unable to chronicle their own history. Once this early foundation is established, however, humans appear to be capable of withstanding incredible deprivation and social isolation. It would seem that biology, in the form of genetics, provides the basic framework, epigenetics allows for interplay between the environment (and other factors) and the expression of genetic information, and the social and physical environment generates enormous variability in human experience

The Social Development of the Self, Mind, and Emotions

At birth, we have no idea that we are separate beings. Babies will cry in anguish when they pull on their own toes. How do we develop a **self**—the picture we have of how others see us, our view of who we are? The overall process by which we learn the ways of society (or of particular groups) is called *socialization*. This is what sociologists have in mind when they say, "Society makes us human."

Cooley and the Looking-Glass Self

In the 1800s, Charles Horton Cooley (1864–1929), pioneering sociologist at the University of Michigan, theorized about the emergence of human identity. In contrast to the biological explanations of his day, he argued that the unique aspect of "humanness" called the "self" is *socially created*; that is, our sense of self develops from interaction with others. He was suggesting that to become human beings we must *interact* with one another, and this interaction is premised on a shared set of **symbols** (typically, language). Only in this context do we develop a sense of our "self" as a separate and manageable entity. For example, parents teach their children symbols—certain sounds ("Mama") that stand for certain objects. Once the child makes this profound discovery, it is possible to learn the next fundamental lesson: that the child herself is an object that can also be referred to by a sound (her name). The door opens to complex interaction with others and with our "selves." Cooley (1902) coined the term **looking-glass self** to describe the process by which a sense of self develops, which he summarized in the following couplet:

> Each to each a looking-glass
>
> Reflects the other that doth pass.

The looking-glass self entails three ingredients. First, we imagine how we appear to others around us. Second, we interpret their reactions. And third, based on our interpretations of the reactions of others, we develop feelings and ideas about ourselves.

Mead and Role-Taking

Another influential analyst, George Herbert Mead (1863–1931), who taught at the University of Chicago, suggested that play is also a critical element in the development of a self. In play, children learn **taking the role of the other**—that is, putting themselves in someone else's shoes to understand how someone else feels and thinks and anticipating how that person will act. Mead's ideas provided the foundation for symbolic interactionism. This popular sociological theory emerged in the first 20 years of the twentieth century, assumed considerable popularity as an opposition to structural functionalism in the 1960s, and, most recently, has grown through offshoots into postmodernism, feminism, and cultural theory.

According to Mead and the symbolic interactionists, understanding human behaviour requires a focus on the ways in which "meanings" emerge through social interaction. In particular, by learning to take the role of the other (to view the world through the meanings ascribed by the other), young children take an important step toward becoming a full-fledged member of a group and of society. At first, we are able to take the role only of **significant others**—individuals who significantly influence our lives, such as parents or siblings. "Mommy (significant other) will

✸ **Explore** the reading "Final Note on a Case of Extreme Isolation" by Kingsley Davis on **MySocLab**.

✸ **Explore** the reading "Socialization: The Internalization of Reality" by Peter L. Berger and Thomas Luckman on **MySocLab**.

To help his students understand what the term *generalized other* means, Mead used baseball as an illustration. The text explains why team sports and organized games are excellent examples of this concept.

be mad (ascribed meaning) if I touch the stove (interactive behaviour)." Later, we develop the capacity to take the role of the **generalized other**—we can imagine how people in general might react to our behaviour. "It is wrong (meaning ascribed to generalized other) to hurt animals (interactive behaviour)." This second step is essential not only for extended co-operation, but also for controlling antisocial desires (Mead, 1934; Coser, 1977).

Prominent Canadian sociologist Marlene Mackie used Mead's analogy of the three stages of learning to take the role of the other in order to explain how we learn our **gender roles**—the behaviour that is socially defined as appropriate to boys or girls (1987:124–127).

1. *Imitation/preparatory stage.* Children under three can only mimic others. They do not yet have a sense of self as separate from others. This stage is not actually role-taking, but it prepares the child for it. Gradually, the child learns that there are symbols and that they are often distinguished by gender. The gender difference is socially defined as very important (unlike, for example, eye colour), since the child witnesses that boys and girls are treated differently, wear different clothes, play with different toys, and so on.

2. *Play stage.* During the second stage, from the age of about three to five or six, children tend to take on the roles of specific people. Girls will play at being mother or teacher, while boys pretend to be hockey players or action heroes. They still often have an imperfect understanding of gender roles—thinking that hair length or urination posture determines gender, for example.

Mead analyzed *taking the role of the other* as an essential part of learning to be a full-fledged member of society. At first, we are able to take the role only of *significant others*, as this child is doing. Later we develop the capacity to take the role of the *generalized other*, which is essential not only for cooperation but also for the control of antisocial desires.

Applying Socialization

Analysts who stress the significance of the socialization perspective draw particular attention to the practical implications of their work. For example, research reveals that kindergartners who have poor attention skills are likely to grow into adults with relatively poor workplace skills. Linda Pagani, of the University of Montreal and Centre Hospitalier Universitaire Sainte-Justine, followed 1369 kindergarten students from 1997 to 2004. The children were assessed for their ability to work autonomously as well as with classmates. Pagani found that those children with low classroom engagement were more likely to stay disengaged through to Grade 6. Pointing to other research indicating that these traits are related to employment earnings as adults, she urges that kindergarten curricula put more emphasis on attention skills rather than simply cognitive skills if schools are to fulfill their mandate to create adults who function well in the paid labour force (Menon, 2012).

Similarly, Rosalind Barnett and Caryl Rivers's recent book, *The Truth About Boys and Girls: Challenging Toxic Stereotypes About Our Children* (2011), underlines the concrete ramifications of gender socialization research. The authors point out that parents' acceptance of gender stereotypes often results in limiting children even when they are infants. For example, mothers of infant girls, when asked to adjust the angle of a carpeted ramp to show the angle their babies were capable of crawling down, underestimated their daughters' abilities. Other research indicates that mothers engage in more conversation with their little girls and expect more responsiveness from them than from boys. Barnett and Rivers strongly recommend that parents recognize and question the role of restrictive gender stereotypes in their parenting practices. By acknowledging, for example, that their infant daughters may be daring, and by engaging in more emotionally rich conversation with their young sons, parents may communicate that gender need not limit the children's horizons (Douglas, 2011; Barnett & Rivers, 2011).

Caregivers, parents, and peers directly and indirectly convey the message that boys and girls are profoundly and permanently different.

3. *Game stage.* This third stage, involving organized play or team games, begins roughly at age seven and lasts through puberty. The significance for the development of the self is that to play games, an individual must be able to take on multiple roles. Mead used the analogy of a baseball game. To play baseball, it is important to know not only what to do when you go up to bat but also what to expect from the other players in the game. Without knowledge of the entire game and these diverse roles, it is impossible to really participate. Similarly, the role of "being a girl" hinges on some other (physically present or imaginary), who will act the role of boy and who understands the overall "game."

Needless to say, the processes of gender socialization at each stage of development are very subtle and complex. In recent years, some feminist sociologists have increasingly explored these complexities through the work of Pierre Bourdieu (1930–2002), who was one of the most eminent French sociologists in the later part of the twentieth century. Bourdieu argued for a complex vision of socialization, including gender socialization, in which social learning is often unconscious and/or symbolic. Gender socialization extends into adulthood, and women, for example, may learn to function in an institutional context (a university or corporation) that is implicitly premised on masculine dominance. In being socialized into this institutional arrangement, the dominant power arrangements are culturally reproduced and the dominated (in this instance, women) come to accept as legitimate their own condition of domination (a process termed "symbolic violence" by Bourdieu).

Bourdieu was particularly interested in the ways in which structurally based social inequalities are socialized into the individual. He introduced the notion of *cultural capital* to refer to the ideas, tastes, preferences, and symbols that may be acquired through socialization and that may be deployed in social action to establish one's social position. For example, upper-middle-class parents provide access to aspects of language and culture that are then employed by their children to secure success at university and beyond. Children of privilege may have travelled, may have read the classics, or may have the appropriate accent and language fluency that immediately (though indirectly) identifies them as members of their class. The result is what Bourdieu termed **habitus**—a socialized proclivity to think, act, and feel in a particular manner that becomes embodied in the individual. These automatic responses or habits (for example, smiling appropriately or not laughing too loudly) become one more way in which children are socialized, at the deepest levels, to reflect their position in the social structure.

Parents may also, according to Bourdieu, transfer social capital through early socialization; that is, children are introduced to individuals and families who will facilitate their successful negotiation of the social hierarchy. From joining an elite golf club to obtaining a personal employment reference, these contacts may later become concrete social resources for advancement (Scott & Marshall, 2005). Although individuals may not be directly conscious of these social processes unless their attention is drawn specifically to them, they fulfill the socialization mandate of fitting the individual into his or her niche in society.

Focus Question

In what ways might the *habitus*—the proclivity to think, act, and feel in a particular manner—of a young working-class male differ from that of a upper-middle-class male when they present themselves at a job interview?

Freud, the Development of Personality, and Civilizing the "Id"

Along with the development of the mind and the self comes the development of personality. Let's look at a theory that has profoundly influenced the Western world.

Physician Sigmund Freud (1856–1939) founded psychoanalysis, a technique for treating emotional problems through long-term, intensive exploration of the subconscious mind.

Freud proposed that personality consists of three elements. Every child is born with an **id**, Freud's term for inborn drives for self-gratification—the avoidance of discomfort and the desire for pleasure. The id of the newborn is evident in cries of hunger or pain. The pleasure-seeking id (which, according to Freud, operates throughout our lives), demands the immediate fulfillment of our needs: attention, safety, food, sexual gratification, and so on.

The id's drive for immediate and complete satisfaction often runs directly counter to the needs of other people. As children come up against norms and other constraints—usually represented by parents—they must adapt to survive. For example, parents may have responsibilities and distractions that make it impossible to immediately satisfy a child's hunger pangs. To adapt to the constraints that inevitably block the immediate fulfillment of our desires, a second component of the personality emerges, which Freud called the **ego**. The ego is the balancing force between the id and the demands of society that suppress it. The third component in personality is the **superego**. Commonly referred to as the *conscience*, the superego represents *culture within us*—the norms and values we internalize from our social groups. As the *moral* component of the personality, the superego gives us feelings of guilt or shame when we break social rules, or pride and self-satisfaction when we follow them. To summarize, the ego navigates between our desires for immediate gratification (the id) and our recognition of the social rules and responsibilities that structure our lives

(the superego). Freud (1930) argued that civilization must, by necessity, repress impulses from the id. If we were freed from the repressions of society, life would become so chaotic that culture would be impossible.

By the mid-twentieth century, many of Freud's ideas had been rejected, especially by feminist theorists, who vehemently challenged some of his central assertions. His suggestion that women have a deep-seated desire for a penis—a longing that, according to Freud, is only resolved by the birth of a child—and his refusal to publicly acknowledge his suspicions that many of his female patients were victims of child sexual abuse have been criticized as evidence of his patriarchal biases. Nonetheless, Freud's ideas contributed profoundly to our understanding of the complexities of our social experiences. In particular, his notion of "unconscious aspects" of the human psyche played an important role in Bourdieu's theorizing. Today, Freud's theories continue to have a significant impact on sociological research, particularly in Europe (Uriely, Ram, & Malach-Pines, 2011; Thurer, 2005). Social analysts today believe that the psychoanalytic framework provides an important access point into aspects of our unconscious lives, notably our motivations, perceptions, and imagination (Clarke, 2006).

Goffman and the Presentation of the Self

Goffman's emphasis on symbolic meanings—even in terms of how we dress, stand, and gesture—was crucial to fleshing out how we "play" our particular scripts and how we learn specific ways to embody them. In his fascinating book, *Stigma* (1963), Goffman applied his approach to the ways individuals present and manage identities that are, in some sense, damaged or spoiled. From physical deformities to criminal records, we often have to find a way to "put on a good face." Further, Goffman's analysis of **total institutions** (as discussed later in the chapter) proved key to exploring the limits of social control and resocialization.

Goffman's work continues to influence research on topics as varied as feminist perspectives on sexuality and the emotional labour of hairstylists (Sheane, 2012; Jackson & Scott, 2010).

Focus Question

Although we like to think of ourselves as individuals, as a result of socialization experiences we tend to share certain dreams and motivations. What dreams and motivations might be shared by typical undergraduate students in Canada?

IN SUM

Prominent social theorists have attempted to explain how we develop a sense of self, the capacity to reason, and emotions. Their analyses suggest that our fundamental sense of self—what we desire, who we love, how we experience sadness—is rooted in socialization (Settersten & Owens, 2002).

Socialization Into Gender

One of the key ways that Canadian society channels behaviour is through gender. By expecting different attitudes and behaviours depending on whether we identify as male or female, the social group nudges boys and girls in separate directions. This foundation of contrasting behaviour is so thorough that, as adults, most of us simply take gendered behaviour for granted. Since gender socialization is a universal experience in Canadian society, let's briefly consider the gender messages we receive from family and the media.

Gender Messages in the Family

Our parents are usually the first significant others in our lives and typically teach us our part in the gender division of society. Often they do so implicitly, perhaps by enrolling a daughter in ballet classes or dressing her in frilly garments. Gender messages from parents may also be explicit and direct. For example, in many cultures, parental rules specifically allow boys more freedom and independence than girls and at an earlier age—"because they are boys." Most significantly, boys are often expressly discouraged from "acting like girls" (Blakemore & Hill, 2008).

As we mature, gender lessons from parents become more complex. Research suggests that mothers and fathers often hold gender-stereotypic views about their sons' and daughters' abilities: one prevailing assumption is that boys are better than girls at science and computers. Not surprisingly, parents' interactions with their children unwittingly reflect and reinforce these gendered views (Tenenbaum & Leaper, 2003).

Many parents, consciously and unconsciously, push young men and women along a narrow gendered path. Whether young people accept or reject this path, they cannot help but struggle with its subtle and not-so-subtle pressures. For example, the estimated 10 percent of the population who are LGBTQ (lesbian, gay, bisexual, transgender, transsexual, two-spirit, queer, or questioning) likely spend some portion of their childhood feeling, at best, uncomfortable when confronted by traditional gender norms (Taylor & Ristock, 2011). By the time a child enters the formal education system, the family—along with the media, toys, sports, and so on—has reflected the hegemonic gender discourse. Whether comfortably or not, boys and girls understand the behaviours and attitudes considered appropriate for each sex, and they know where they fit in the gender schema.

The role of parents in early childhood gender socialization is complex and varied. As reflected in the popular television program *Toddlers & Tiaras*, some parents embrace a deeply gendered and sexualized identity for their daughters. In contrast, numerous parents are lesbian, gay, and/or feminist (Arnup, 2005; Taylor & Ristock, 2011). When parents explicitly reject traditional gender roles and lead lives in contradiction to those roles, the impact on their children is likely to be important.

For example, single-mother families socialize adolescent boys to do significantly more household work. While single mothers model a nontraditional structure to their children, they tend to need their sons' day-to-day contributions to keep the household running. The net result is male socialization that encourages boys to grow up to be "good partners" who are capable of taking on household responsibilities. Since boys typically take pride in their abilities, it is likely that their socialization experience helps lay the foundation for future relationships with an egalitarian division of household work (Berridge & Romich, 2011).

The complex relationship between parenting, children, and gender roles is underscored in research with parents and children who are part of the LGBTQ community. Although likely a significant underestimation, the latest Canadian Census (2006) found that 6 out of every 1000 couples are same-sex, and one in six female same-sex couples has children under 25 living in the home (Taylor & Ristock, 2011:133). Lesbian parents tend to be liberal with regard to children's gendered behaviours and are more likely to share an egalitarian spousal relationship. If parents act out their roles as parents in an egalitarian fashion—whether they share parenting and/or paid labour responsibilities—they are likely to influence their children's acceptance or rejection of gender stereotypic beliefs (Fulcher, Sutfin, & Patterson, 2008). In other words, if lesbian parents live an egalitarian lifestyle, this appears to directly impact their children's gender beliefs and attitudes (Blakemore & Hill, 2008).

Gender Messages in the Mass Media

No matter how conscientiously parents try to insulate their children from the gendered social context, the social environment will nonetheless mediate any messages they instill in their children (Sutfin, Fulcher, Bowles, & Patterson, 2008). The **mass media**—forms of communication directed to large audiences—are a particularly prominent element in contemporary gender socialization and play a pivotal role in both creating and reinforcing cultural expectations of gender. For example, as Canadian filmmaker Sophie Bissonnette explains in her documentary, *Sexy Inc.*, various elements of the mass media, including television advertisements, music videos, and major motion pictures, promote the hypersexualization of young girls (2007). The message that girls who wear sizes 6 to 14 should present themselves as sexual beings is communicated, for example, through Walmart advertisements for girls' underwear bearing the slogan "Who needs credit cards . . . when you've got Santa." By marketing sexualized products such as thong underwear or "cute butt sweatpants," the culture encourages teens and preteens to view themselves as objects to be admired and to evaluate their bodies according to "narrow standards of (often sexualized) attractiveness" (Goodin et al., 2011:1; Bragg et al., 2011).

👁 **Watch** the video "Gender Socialization" on **MySocLab.**

THINKING CRITICALLY ABOUT SOCIAL CONTROVERSY

Global Socialization: The Social Creation and Eradication of Smokers

Cigarettes provide a useful example of the power and complexity of socialization and resocialization. There is no evidence that people have any inborn drive to inhale tobacco smoke—although, of course, nicotine is highly physically addictive. Nonetheless, we live on a planet where growing numbers of people engage in smoking, even though an enormous body of scientific evidence documents that it may harm your health, shorten your life, and negatively affect the lives of those around you. The World Health Organization (WHO) estimated that, globally, 6 million deaths resulted from tobacco use in 2011, 1 billion deaths will be attributable to tobacco use during the twenty-first century, and 100 million people died as a result of this behaviour in the past century (Sinha, 2011; Picard, 2008).

Enormous effort and expense have been put toward educating the public about these risks. In Canada, resocialization efforts such as graphic health warnings on cigarette packs, restrictions on cigarette advertisements, anti-smoking health education in schools, and bans on the public display of cigarettes in some jurisdictions appear to have had a significant impact. Along with more effective strategies for addressing tobacco addiction, these initiatives have dramatically changed tobacco consumption patterns. In 1965, half of all Canadians aged 15 and older were smokers, with 61 percent of men and 38 percent of women smoking. In 2010, only 17 percent of Canadians described themselves as smokers, with only 20 percent of men and 14 percent of women still indulging (Canadian Cancer Society, 2012). Interestingly, resocialization efforts have been particularly effective with beginner smokers:

only 9 percent of adolescents now smoke, down from 12 percent in 2009 (Ogilvie, 2011)

While these successes speak to the potency of resocialization, the question remains: Why does smoking persist in spite of clear health warnings, and how are some individuals socialized into this behaviour?

It appears that gender remains one important ingredient. Historically, smoking was a male-dominated behaviour—a symbol of masculinity—and women who smoked were likely to be defined as lower-class or deviant. Men bought into smoking as a way of presenting a tough, male image. However, in the early twentieth century, the tobacco industry dramatically expanded its market focus and promoted the product to women. This legitimization of women's smoking was accomplished by way of a long-running media campaign. Popular magazines, through images of celebrity and upper-class women smoking in advertisements, modelled smoking as a glamorous, "modern," and even rebellious behaviour (Tinkler, 2001). Product placement in popular movies, where female heroes were often portrayed smoking, also served to legitimate smoking as a mechanism for representing oneself as attractive, sexy, and "classy" (Sargent et al., 2007). By the 1920s, cigarette manufacturers were marketing smoking as a mechanism for weight loss: "Reach for a cigarette instead of a sweet" (Cordileone, 2011).

Today, many Canadians continue to be exposed to smoking socialization premised on gender. Parents and peers who smoke may model the behaviour, and they may also help perpetuate rationales for smoking such as mood regulation and weight

control—a particularly significant motivator for female smokers (Villanti, Boulay, Juon, 2011). In this process, gendered identities are constructed around smoking. Male smokers are seen by both men and women as "manly, relaxed, and in control," while female smokers convey edginess and nonconformity (Nademin et al., 2010). In particular, women are targeted with "bitch sticks"—extra long, skinny cigarettes that resemble lipstick tubes packaged in elegant boxes and tagged as "super slim" and "smooth." This marketing conveys the message that cigarette smoking is a means for women to be "cool" and "slim" (Cordileone, 2011).

Despite extensive laws restricting the sale and marketing of cigarettes, contemporary films continue to portray actors smoking cigarettes. Research indicates that exposure to such images increases smoking behaviour among young smokers (Shmueli, Prochaska, Glantz, 2010). Along with movies, YouTube has created a whole new component in smoking socialization. Research reveals that smoking fetish videos—videos rated PG-13 or R in which there is explicit smoking by sexy, young, healthy females—are "prevalent and accessible to adolescents on the website" (Kim, Paek, Lynn, 2010). Suggestion, even when made implicitly by a link between sexuality and cigarette smoking, provides a powerful reinforcement for the behaviour and perpetuates smoking socialization.

Of course, smoking is far from strictly a North American preoccupation. The tobacco industry has been subject to increasing regulation in the Global North, and as a result has shifted focus toward the global market. However, the socialization of smoking varies depending on the cultural context. Contemporary China, the largest consumer of tobacco in the world, was home to an estimated 301 million smokers (28 percent of the population) in 2010. There, smoking appears to be identified with masculinity. More than half (52.9 percent) of Chinese men smoked in 2010, but only 2.4 percent of women did so. Heavy smoking was the norm, with 85.6 percent of smokers smoking daily and averaging 14.2 cigarettes per day. Smoking was also associated with middle age, with one-third of those aged 45 to 64 smoking and only 17.9 percent of those aged 15 to 24 doing so (Tiu, 2011). This pattern suggests that smoking is not as symbolic of youthful rebellion as it has been in North America and Europe.

There is another explosion in tobacco smoking in India. The WHO estimates that one-quarter of males and 2.9 percent of females smoke. Although youth are less likely to smoke (only 19 percent of young males), it is clearly popular among young females, 8.3 percent of whom smoke. These statistics suggest that, while smoking in India was once associated with masculinity, it has grown in popularity among young women. However, smokeless tobacco, or snuff, is even more popular than cigarettes, with one-third of males and almost one-fifth of females using the product. The relative cheapness of smokeless tobacco in India may explain its popularity as a stimulant, and the expense of cigarettes may suggest that smoking conveys an important social class distinction (Sinha, 2011).

The continued global popularity of smoking, despite concerted campaigns to make the health costs explicit and to render smoking a difficult and costly practice, suggests that the act of smoking remains, at least in its initial stages, socially significant. This behaviour is still believed to communicate an important and, in some way, positive message about the smoker, particularly with regard to gender. Once socialization results in addiction, the struggle to end smoking becomes profoundly more difficult.

Focus Question

In Canada, what elements socialize males and females to take up smoking? In what ways is smoking linked to gender identity?

In this manner, the mass media help to set up girls for body dissatisfaction and self-esteem issues.

TELEVISION Sixty years ago, televisions entered Canadian homes and, in a relatively short time, transformed our private and public lives. Today, almost three-quarters of

Canadians watch nearly three hours of television a day, or 21 hours per week. Television plays an important role in the ongoing socialization of most North Americans ("Canadians' Television," 2012) (Statistics Canada, 2011d).

As children mature, television remains a constant source of social information. A recent study of television use among

Even parents who read to their children may be inadvertently supporting gender stereotypes. Illustrations in award-winning children's books published between 1999 and 2009 tend to represent female characters as working inside the home and male characters as working outside (Crabb & Marciano, 2011).

Ontario adolescents found that boys aged 12 to 14 spend approximately 2.5 hours on Sundays and 1.3 hours on school days watching television and videos, while girls of the same age watch slightly less than 1.25 hours each day (Hillbrecht, Zuzanek, & Mannell, 2008:349–350). Various other studies also indicate that boys watch more television than girls.

What are children learning from these hours of "entertainment"? Of particular concern to feminists is the tendency of television programming to reinforce traditional gender stereotypes and social patterns in which women play subordinate or supportive roles. Although things have changed since the days of *Bewitched* and *Happy Days*, and women are now often portrayed as leading independent lives and pursuing successful careers, gendered stereotypes still persist.

Sometimes, embedded gender messages are quite subtle. A recent examination of patterns of physical affection displayed between family members in television programs revealed that male family members "received, on average, significantly more affection than female members." Specifically, sons received more affection than daughters (Callister & Robinson, 2010). As Callister and Robinson point out, children learn about cultural standards in part by watching television. Patterns typically presented in mainstream programs imply that female family members play a secondary role.

Gendered reality may take on more momentous implications as children age. An examination of the impact of television viewing on adolescent body satisfaction found that girls who watch television frequently and indiscriminately "reported the most severe drop in body satisfaction" (Schooler & Trinh, 2011). It would seem that programs such as *Keeping Up with the Kardashians* and *The Real Housewives of Vancouver*, which focus on voluptuous, toned women, leave many young girls feeling profoundly inadequate and unattractive. This pattern is also supported through research into the gendered discourses of music videos. The message communicated is that female artists, much more than male artists, are presented to the audience as sexual objects who demonstrate "sexy" behaviour and conform to strict standards of appearance (Aubrey & Frisby, 2011). Given the cultural prominence of these women, they likely serve as role models for many young women and further encourage body image concerns.

Much popular prime time television tends to prioritize male characters and establish men as "leaders"—such as in *CSI* and its offshoots, for example. Similarly, "serious" television—concerning politics and recent events—typically involves a male host, and evening news programs have hardly been enthusiastic in their employment of female anchors. Implied in this pattern is one of the key gendered messages in the media: only certain types of women are visible on television—young, slender, and physically attractive. Further, their appearance is their primary identity, rather than their intellect or sense of humour. The implicit media message is that women's primary value is in relation to men: youthful, attractive women have a place in the idealized media reality, while older, heavier, or unattractive women are rendered invisible (Cruikshank, 2003).

Women are not alone in facing a media-generated gender script. While women may be confronted by media representations of unrealistic standards of appearance, men have long faced demands to be strong, emotionally controlled, successful, and fiercely competent. From *Gunsmoke* to *Mission: Impossible* to *Survivor*, "real" men have confronted a strict, even rigid, gender script on television. To the degree that men embrace this model of masculinity and fail, for example, to emotionally express themselves, particularly with intimate partners, their successful gender performance may place them at risk for depression, substance abuse, violence, and non–help-seeking behaviours. Further, recent media research suggests that the popularization of unrealistic images of male bodies—buff, strong, six-pack abs—may contribute to body image problems among men (Agliata & Tantleff-Dunn, 2004).

The argument could be made that not only does television viewing support traditional gender discourses, it may also complicate and expand conceptions of gender roles. Programs such as *Sex and the City,* for example, may suggest the possibility of a new, empowered female role. Carrie, Miranda, Charlotte, and Samantha are portrayed as leading adventurous, independent lives in a manner that is in sharp contrast to early embodiments of single women on television, such as in *The Mary Tyler Moore Show*. However, it is important to remember that these gender messages are typically embedded in fairly traditional notions of heterosocialization and female sexuality (Lorie, 2011). After all, Carrie ends up married to Mr. Big.

VIDEO GAMES, SOCIAL MEDIA, AND GENDER MESSAGES

While television viewing remains a fairly ubiquitous experience and an important contributor to gender socialization, it is clear that our media consumption habits are changing. Although Canadians who watch television are watching approximately the same amount as they did in previous years, fewer Canadians report watching TV at all. In 1998, the average daily television consumption was almost a whole hour more per day than it was in 2005. We are either watching less television, or we are combining this activity with other media, such as listening to MP3 players and communicating on the internet. In particular, recent research suggests that there is an emerging demographic of young, well-educated Canadians who have tuned out TV (watching on average only 2.2 hours per week) and instead spend almost 25 percent more time on the internet than the average TV viewer (Oliveira, 2012). This shift

✳ **Explore** the reading "Condemning Our Kids to Life on Mars or Venus" and think about how the media constructs gender differences on **MySocLab**.

Young people who spend a lot of time playing video games are subjected to many disturbing and skewed gender messages from the games' characters.

to computer-based activities is supported by the growing proportion of Canadians who use computers for non-paid work such as email, social interaction, and information searches. This segment of the population grew by nearly 500 percent (from 5 percent to 24 percent) between 1998 and 2010 (Statistics Canada, 2011). Computer users spend, on average, almost 1.5 hours a day on the computer. Not surprisingly, almost a third of Canadians aged 15 to 24 years are computer users, and they spend about an hour and 41 minutes a day on their computers. In a very short period, Facebook, Twitter, Tumblr, blogging, and other social media sites have transformed personal space and identity.

Researchers are beginning to explore the socialization implications of this communication revolution. After all, the meanings of community and friends have been transformed by Facebook and personal blogs (Davis, 2010). There is every reason to believe that important socialization messages about beliefs, values, norms, and mores are being established and communicated through social media (McLaughlin & Vitak, 2011). In particular, social information about identities that were once marginalized and difficult to explore is increasingly easy to access (Lombardo, 2012).

Video games are a booming segment of the new interactive media. On a typical day in 2010, 6 percent of Canadians played video games—double the number from 1998—and spent almost 2.5 hours gaming per day, up from 1.75 hours (Statistics Canada, 2011d). In these many hours of activity, extending through childhood and into adulthood, what kinds of messages about gender are being communicated?

Initial research suggested that video games took up where television left off in the perpetuation of sexist depictions of male and female roles—portrayals in which women are not only different to men, but inferior to them. From this early work, it seemed, for example, that boys were much more likely than girls to participate in video gaming and that the content of video games tended to mirror gender stereotypes (for example, male action heroes engaging in violent aggression, while females serve as sexual objects). In this way, gaming seemed to have become one more method of marginalizing females from the rapidly expanding world of technology (Miller & Summers, 2007; Burgess, Stermer & Burgess, 2007; Dill & Thill, 2007).

Recent research suggests a more gender-nuanced reality. A Canadian study examined the play practices of girls and boys aged 12 to 14 as well as those of young men and women aged 22 to 24 to determine the implications of game-playing in same-sex and mixed-sex groups. Certainly, the researchers found evidence of gendered patterns at the outset. Few boys opted to play with girls, and all boys reported playing with other boys. All the girls played with boys, but played infrequently with other girls. The mechanism that allowed girls to play video games with boys was often family relations (boyfriends, cousins, brothers, and fathers).

Over the three-year study, as girls participated in both same-sex and mixed-sex gaming groups, there appeared to be a "levelling up" between girls and boys as girls gained greater access, support, and a "girls' gamer model." In particular, the results suggest that providing girls with initial girls-only groups was important in securing these changes

◉ **Watch** "Play Again" and think about how video games and social media are changing how we live our lives on **MySocLab.**

THINKING CRITICALLY ABOUT SOCIAL CONTROVERSY

Fat Stigma Grows and Goes Global—Socialization and our Bodies

Perhaps one thing we all confront as a biological fact is our body. Our facial characteristics, eye colour, height, and so on are fixed realities. As has become increasingly apparent, however, societal values about the ideal shape have resulted in an amazing array of products and services intended to change our bodies. The market for cosmetic surgery, non-surgical procedures, and cosmetics is a billion-dollar industry that continually grows. Purchases of some of these products have become an important signifier of social class.

Through most of human history, for the overwhelming majority of people, simply having access to enough nutritious food was a daily, lifelong struggle. Obesity or being overweight was a problem only for a miniscule portion of the population. Beginning in the nineteenth century, certain sized bodies were portrayed, notably by modern clinical medicine, as deviant and pathological. Further, this pathologization of fat bodies followed specific, gendered patterns (Hardy, 2012). As discussed below, parents, peers, and the media today consistently perpetuate the socialization message that being overweight is bad. It has particularly dire implications for girls and women (Anschutz et al., 2011).

The result is several generations of people socialized to be preoccupied with monitoring and managing their weight. Their strategies may be socially legitimate—going to a gym, joining a weight loss organization, or dieting—but a significant minority engage in socially deviant behaviour such as anorexia and bulimia. While "Ana (anorexia)" and "Mia (bulimia)" may be commonplace in youth cultures, they are understood by the general society to be activities that jeopardize physical well-being.

In Canada, an estimated 2 million women suffer from eating disorders (Gollom, 2012). A recent Ontario study reported that among adolescents aged 10 to 14, almost a third (29.3 percent) are actively

trying to lose weight. About one in five Canadian female teenagers is on a diet, and as many as two-thirds have attempted to lose weight at some point in their lives. In many instances, teenage girls seeking weight loss may not be classified as having eating disorders, but their eating may be considered "disordered" since it involves fasting, skipping meals, excessive exercise, or extreme dieting (Canadian Paediatric Society, 2004; McVey, Tweed, & Blackmore, 2004). In the United States, a recent poll reported that more than three-quarters of adults are not at their desired weight, and 59 percent of women want to lose 10 to 20 pounds (UPI, 2012).

Further, there is every indication that this is an increasingly global phenomenon. Research in mainland China indicates that adolescent body dissatisfaction is prevalent, and girls more than boys report feeling pressure from the media to lose weight (Xu et al., 2010). Multi-ethnic and lifespan research comparing the United States and China suggests that ethnic and age differences among women produce only small differences in body dissatisfaction. Regardless of age, country of origin, and ethnic background, women are surprisingly consistent in their dislike for some aspect of their bodies, especially their weight (Frederick, Forbes, Grigorian, & Jarcho, 2007; Forbes & Frederick, 2008; Bessenoff & Del Priore, 2007). Alarmingly, a recent survey of the "fat stigma" found that in 10 countries around the globe—including such areas as Samoa, which "historically held more positive views of larger bodies"—all cultures are embracing a prejudice against those deemed overweight (Parker-Pope, 2011).

Although dissatisfaction with body image is a complex issue and may involve psychoanalytic and psychological dimensions, the historical shifts and documented global dimensions suggest a significant role for cultural factors. A

growing body of research suggests that contemporary Western mass media and consumerism—especially appearance-related advertisements in magazines, on television, and elsewhere—play a key role in disseminating specific body dissatisfactions around the world. Popular magazines that ridicule celebrity cellulite, television programs such as *The Biggest Loser* that reward weight loss, and fashion magazines that glorify skinny, prepubescent girls all help communicate that being slim is a social necessity. The pervasive message that being fat is bad can be turned inward to create body dissatisfaction and used to stigmatize others. A recent study of Toronto preschoolers aged two to six found that even very young children are likely to assume that the mean rather than nice characters in a story are the fatter ones (Daubs, 2012).

In sum, prevailing cultural messages encourage fat stigmatization. This results not only in negative self-criticism and self-monitoring, but also provides a foundation for bullying, discrimination, and social ostracism.

Analyzing the impact of socialization on our bodies and how we treat them is important in a variety of ways. First, it underscores that biology is subject to social pressures. Second, it is clear that history and culture have an important place in our understanding of socialization. In the historic and cultural context, body weight became socially relevant for the majority of people, for example. Third, socialization reflects and reaffirms the major patterns of social inequality in society—in this instance, gender. Fourth, socialization makes use of a variety of mechanisms and, in modern consumer society, the mass media have become increasingly significant socializers. Finally, the process of socialization may not be benign. Socialization pressures may function to undermine women's and men's well-being and even jeopardize their lives.

Challenging "Fat" Socialization

Social agencies are drawing on the insights provided by socialization research to mobilize positive body-image programs at the community level. A recent initiative in a public school in Eastern Ontario targeted pre-adolescents with a one-week resocialization course. Students were provided with a variety of exercises that encouraged them to think critically about media messages and "beauty" standards as well as to employ social support systems, coping techniques, and communication skills to respond to body image issues. When re-tested post-program, both boys and girls expressed higher levels of self-esteem and more positive body images (Norwood, Murray, Nolan, & Bowker, 2011). A similar program was directed to students enrolled in three Canadian universities. Once again, interventions emphasizing media literacy, self-esteem, stress management, and relationship skills resulted in significantly less internationalization of media stereotypes and in improvements in body satisfaction (McVey et al., 2010). Each of these efforts confirms the possibility of challenging fat stigmatization and reducing its social costs.

(Jenson & de Castel, 2011). By the third year of the study, the girls were becoming explicitly competitive in their approach to play; now, like the boys, they were keeping and comparing game scores. Boys and girls wanted to play together in their final session, and, for the first time, boys asked girls to join their teams. Significantly, the girls then played rather than watching or "helping" (Jenson & de Castell, 2011). This research suggests that the presumed relationship between video games and gender socialization is more complex than originally thought.

Focus Question

What gender messages might a teenage boy and girl learn from watching the most popular television shows and from belonging to Facebook?

The Contradictions of Socialization: Masculinity in Flux

With the popularization of feminism in the 1970s and 1980s, analysts increasingly approached masculinity from a critical perspective. As a result of this work, today many analysts argue that the traditional male role in Western countries is unclear and in transition. Traditionally, boys were confronted by a rather rigid and strict gender role—one that emphasized strength, aggression, autonomy, competitiveness, success, and emotional control. To the degree to which this remains true (it is less the case in more "feminine" countries such as Spain and Italy), boys confront a demanding and unforgiving gender agenda (Calvo-Salguero, Garcia-Martinez, & Monteoliva, 2008). After all, boys are much more likely to be charged with juvenile crime, less likely to graduate from high school, less likely to be university students, and four times as likely to commit suicide (Frenette & Zeman, 2007). Researchers argue that old-fashioned masculine socialization—as conveyed by the media, sports, religion, peers, and teachers—placed many boys at a disadvantage in education, employment, and social life in general (White, 2011; Levitt, Swanger, & Butler, 2008). Emulating the high-risk behaviour of male role-model celebrities—drugs, alcohol abuse, fast cars, guns, smoking—continues to put young men at increased risk for personal injury, addiction, and other health problems (Nelson, 2010; Pappas, McKenry, & Skilken Catlett, 2004). Research indicates, for example, that men may feel so intimidated by height standards that they over-report their own height in order to fit in to the ideal tall physique (Bogaert & McCreary, 2011). While this may seem like a minor thing, it speaks to the insecurities that can be inculcated along with traditional masculinity. Gendered pressures may be further compounded if a young man is a Native Canadian, a visible minority, gay, disabled, a recent immigrant, poor or working-class, and so on (Roper & Halloran, 2007; Sparkes & Smith, 2002).

At the same time, there is growing evidence that traditional masculinity is being challenged by new approaches to the male role. Notably, research suggests that men are increasingly involved in actively parenting their children—through pregnancy, in the delivery room, and with parental leave (Beaupre, Dryburgh, & Wendt, 2010). Such transitions are far from easy. The economy continues to be structured around a male "breadwinner," and many men experience severe role strain as they seek to navigate between traditional models of a father who "brings home the bacon" and new calls for involved and physically present dads (Cribb, 2012; Doucet, 2012).

Focus Question

What does it mean to be a "good" father today? Does this role conflict with men's activities at work?

The gender roles we learn during childhood become part of our basic orientations to life. We refine these roles as we grow older; as seniors, gender becomes a less prominent determinant of social roles and relationship patterns.

Socialization Into Groups

Sociologists often make a direct connection between social groups and the socialization process. In most instances, socialization teaches us to fit into **social groups**; that is, people who regularly and consciously interact with one another over an extended period of time.

Groups in Society

Some social groups are involuntary, such as the family or gender group into which we are born, and some are voluntary, including the clubs and sports teams we join. The family is a key example of what Charles Horton Cooley termed a **primary group**—a group characterized by intimate face-to-face association and co-operation. In these kinds of groups, such as with close friends, we develop a sense of belonging and feelings of self-esteem. However, much of our life is spent in **secondary groups**—ones that are larger, more anonymous and temporary, and more formal and impersonal, such as a workplace or university class.

Sometimes groups are organized into **in-groups** (groups we feel loyal to) and **out-groups** (groups we feel antagonistic toward). In-groups are somewhat similar to **cliques**—close-knit clusters of individuals or factions within groups that tend to set themselves off from the rest of the group.

In-groups built around ethnic or racial distinctions may be important in the development of **ethnocentrism**—the belief that our group is superior to another. In certain social situations, in-group/out-group conflicts may create **xenophobia**—a fear of strangers.

Groups may also take the form of **reference groups**—groups we use as standards to evaluate ourselves. For example, if you want to become a politician, you might start dressing like Stephen Harper, reading *The Economist*, and watching parliamentary debates.

Sometimes, our groups encourage us to conform to behaviours we are not personally comfortable with. Famous experiments by Stanley Milgram (1963, 1965) and Solomon Asch (1952) reveal the tremendous influence of groupthink. Groups can cultivate tunnel vision about social reality and members may become blind to the nature and consequences of their actions. Using Goffman's approach, a group may come to define a situation and by doing so may create social reality. Consider, for example, some contemporary reactions to the "terrorist threat": certain groups defined anyone who was "different" (a Sikh wearing a turban) as a potential threat and acted upon this reality by assaulting or imprisoning innocent Canadian citizens. These acts reflect sociologist W. I. Thomas's classic theorem (Thomas & Thomas, 1928), "If people define situations as real, they are real in their consequences."

Groups may coalesce to provide a sense of community—these are the groups we feel we belong to and can identify with. In recent years, the internet has provided an entirely new medium for the creation and maintenance of community. Electronic communities (e-communities) allow people worldwide to connect, and in some instances, their interaction online leads to a sense of belonging. The impact of these new communities on society provides a rich source for future social research.

Agents of Socialization

Socialization is a pervasive and lifelong series of processes. Every time we enter a new social environment—get a new job, go to a new school, move to a new neighbourhood, take retirement, are diagnosed as cancer patients, become a mother or father—we go through a socialization process. Directly or indirectly, formally or informally, we learn what to say, what to do, who has power and who doesn't, what to wear, and where and when to talk, along with all the other complex information that is needed to function in the new social context. The social institutions, organizations, groups, and individual people who socialize us are **agents of socialization**, and through their intervention, our self-concept, emotions, attitudes, and behaviours may be profoundly changed.

The Family

Around the world, the first group to have a major impact on almost all humans is the family. Unlike some animals, we cannot survive by ourselves, and as babies we are utterly dependent on our caregivers. Our family experiences are so intense that, as Freud and others have pointed out, they have a lifelong impact on us (Putney & Bengston, 2002). They lay down our basic sense of self, establishing our initial motivations, values, and beliefs. The family gives us ideas about who we are and what we deserve out of life.

As Goffman puts it, the family is a "socialization depot" (1977, 314). This is where our journey begins and where we pick up most of our baggage. Around the globe and in contemporary Canadian society, we generally assume that a person's family is key to the development of "productive and responsible" adults (Heath, 2004). While our families are only part of the picture, as a culture, we recognize that they are a crucial early socializing agent.

We also recognize that "dysfunctional" families may contribute to social problems (Momirov & Duffy, 2011). Structural functionalist Talcott Parsons identified socialization in the family unit as a key social process in ensuring that children fit neatly into the social order. However, family life is much messier and more diverse than implied by the widely discredited structural-functional model. Parson's ideal typical family—with a loving dad who "earns" the bacon and a dutiful mother who cooks it, and a flock of happy, obedient children—was more a creation of 1950s television than a reflection of real life.

In Canada today, most mothers, even of very young children, work for pay outside the home, more children grow up as only children, children are more likely to spend part of each day in formal or informal day care, more families are common-law unions, more married families are divided by divorce, more families are headed by single mothers, more gay and lesbian families are visible in Canadian communities, and peer groups appear to be increasingly important in young people's lives. Discussing present-day family socialization means addressing a much more complex and diverse process—one that acknowledges these major structural shifts (Milan, Keown, & Urquijo, 2011; Mandell, 2011).

Focus Question

How are Canadian families changing? What do these changes mean for childhood socialization?

Religion: A Declining Influence?

Some social commentators suggest that Canada is increasingly a secularized society. Noted Canadian sociologist Reginald Bibby suggests that about one-third of Canadians continue to value religious faith and incorporate it in their lives; one-third are uninvolved; and one-third comprise the "ambivalent middle," who identify with a religious group but are not actively involved in it. Bibby projects that this pattern is likely to persist in the future, with ebbs and flows as religiosity increases and decreases, but without eradication of religion from Canadian life altogether (Bibby, 2012).

It is too soon to count out religion as a socializing agent. While Canadian involvement in formal religion has declined over the past 50 years, religious activities persist. Significantly, while only 14 percent of young Canadians aged 20 to 29 surveyed in 1986 described themselves as having no religion, in 2010 more than one-third of young Canadians did so (Marshall, 2011). Whether these young people will remain secular or embrace religion as they marry and have children is an open question. At present, the aging Canadian population, along with the continuing inflow of immigrants (who tend to have a higher degree of religiosity than native-born Canadians), will likely mean that religion will remain somewhat prominent on the social landscape (Clark & Schellenberg, 2006).

As long as religion remains a significant social institution, and as long as religious beliefs and values are reflected in major social issues, religion will be an important ingredient in the socialization of many Canadian children. Organized religions and specific beliefs are central to personal positions on gay rights, capital punishment, gay marriage, abortion, and the status of women. Religion has been at the centre of a variety of recent public debates, including the rights of girls to wear religious head coverings while attending Quebec schools, the rights of Catholic schools to ban gay and lesbian student groups, and the rights of non-Catholic religious schools to receive state funding. Canada and its influential neighbour to the south are far

✓● **Practise** by taking the quiz "Spanking" and determine to what extent spanking is considered an acceptable form of discipline on **MySocLab.**

from secular at this point in history, and religion must be understood as an important element of childhood socialization (Ecklund, 2008).

Day Care: The New Normal

According to a recent government report, there has been a dramatic increase in the proportion of Canadian children growing up in some form of childcare. By 2002–2003, 54 percent of Canadian children aged six months to five years were in some form of non-parental childcare—an increase of 42 percent in eight years. The majority of Canadian children spend an average of 29 hours a week in one of the following: day care, the care of a non-relative, or the care of relatives inside or outside the home. Each of these options accounts for about 30 percent of children in childcare. A small minority of children are cared for by a nanny or are in some form of nursery school (Statistics Canada, 2006a).

This growing participation in childcare reflects changes in Canadian families—and in particular the growth of dual-income families and increases in single-parent (typically mother-headed) families. Put simply, much of this change is the result of a dramatic increase in the number of employed mothers. In 2009, 67 percent of mothers of children under age six, and 64 percent of mothers of children under age three, were employed—a sharp rise from the approximately 30 percent who held paid employment in 1976 (Ferrao, 2010: 9).

Changes in childcare have been particularly marked in Quebec. In 1997, Quebec introduced $7-a-day childcare (along with other supports for families with children), and, predictably, by 2002–2003, 67 percent of Quebec children aged six months to five years were in some form of care, with 52 percent in a daycare centre (a 100-percent increase from eight years previous). As a result, the employment rate for Quebec mothers, traditionally lower than for mothers in the rest of Canada, grew to be 3.4 percent higher than for other provinces in 2012.

Despite the Quebec initiatives, the remainder of Canada lags behind much of the Global North in the area of childcare. A 1970 recommendation from the Report of the Royal Commission on the Status of Women for a national policy to provide high quality, affordable childcare remains unanswered. Tellingly, a recent UNICEF report (2010) ranked Canada at the very bottom of 25 developed countries in terms of the quality, access, financing, and policies of early childhood education (Bourque & St. Amour, 2011; Albanese, 2012).

Nonetheless more and more children are spending some portion of their childhood in the care of others. However, the nature of that care may be dramatically different from family to family. On one hand, the children of immigrants may be cared for in the home by their grandmother, while children of lower-income families may be cared for in a daycare centre staffed by a diversity of licensed individuals. Regardless of the quality of the experience, it is likely that these socialization experiences will have an impact. In addition, children may be exposed to parental frustration and concern as they juggle unreliable and/or costly care alternatives.

Given the dramatic shift in child-rearing patterns, it is not surprising that day care remains a contentious issue. Some condemn the trend to day care as a reflection of our growing materialism and the loss of family values (Shaw, 2003). Others counter that parents have little choice but to take paid work and that day care benefits many children by providing them with a stimulating environment and the opportunity to socialize with other children. But while day care may be a necessity, what effect does it have on our children?

Various research into the impact of non-parental childcare on children points to the same conclusion: it depends. It depends on the child (and his or her temperament), on the parents (and their strengths or weaknesses as parents), and on the quality of the child-care arrangements themselves. Some children who are coming from overburdened, deprived, or abusive backgrounds may benefit enormously from a safe, well-staffed daycare centre (Wrigley & Dreby, 2006). Similarly, children who attend a daycare centre that allows them to explore their specific cultural background (for example, Aboriginal daycare centres) may experience important growth in self-esteem. Further, if parents provide high-quality parenting in the hours that they do spend with their children, many problems may be minimized.

Generally, if childcare is well-funded and facilitated by qualified and dedicated staff, it is more likely to have a positive impact on the child and also on the parents (Gagne, 2003; Canadian Council on Learning, 2006; University of Waterloo, 2006; Albanese, 2006). Recent developments—notably the lack of progress toward a national child-care strategy and the increased role of corporations in for-profit day care (so-called "big box" day care)—may further muddy the water. An Australian corporation called Groves created a $2.2-billion "kiddie care kingdom," operating 2400 ABC Learning Centres on three continents. This type of development may spell significant changes in the typical daycare experience for children (Cribb & Brazao, 2007). As childhood socialization continues to change, it is particularly important that research keep up with thoughtful examinations of its implications for children and families.

Focus Question

Viewed from the perspective of a four-year-old, what might be the costs and benefits of being placed in a licensed daycare centre?

The School: Extended Years of Socialization

One of the most important sites of socialization is school. Not only do we learn to "do student," but we acquire the specific knowledge and skills needed to function in the social order (Prus, 2007). If asked how schools socialize students, you might stress the formal knowledge and skills they transmit, such as reading, writing, and arithmetic. From a structural-functionalist perspective, the **manifest functions**, or intended purpose, of formal education in transmitting such skills is certainly part of socialization. Our schools' **latent functions**, the unintended or hidden consequences that help the social system, are also significant.

Sociologists have identified a *hidden curriculum* in our schools. This term refers to the latent function of education—namely, the inculcation of values that, though not explicitly taught, form an inherent part of a school's "message." One of the unspoken but prominent tasks of schools is to produce graduates that are "polite, well-dressed and on time" (Raby, 2007). In addition, there are indirect lessons in the stories and examples used to teach math, English grammar, or Canadian history—messages that may bring with them lessons in gender or racial inequality and help to create, for example, a "chilly climate" for girls and Native Canadians (Nelson, 2010; Restoule, 2005).

This socialization perspective is key to understanding the introduction of an Africentric Alternative School in Toronto. Concerned that traditional schools tend to render African culture invisible—or worse, irrelevant—in their curricula, social activists launched a black-focused school in September 2009. The black perspective is incorporated and normalized in every aspect of day-to-day school interactions. Math questions are framed, for example, in terms of African geometric art, and the school is staffed overwhelmingly by people of colour. This strategy was so effective in encouraging black student engagement and reducing the 40 percent dropout rate among black students that an Africentric high school has been approved for fall 2012 or 2013 (CBC News, 2009a; CBC News, 2011a; Chen, 2012).

Specialized approaches to education have long been embraced by the wealthy. In many societies, upper-class groups explicitly use the educational process to secure their position of power and privilege. Elite private schools are typically structured to provide the personal friendships, manners, and social values that are key to establishing the upper-class credentials of students, encouraging intra-group friendships and marriages, and providing access to prestigious post-secondary institutions (Maxwell & Maxwell, 1971; Gabler & Kaufman, 2006).

Lastly, the process of educational socialization in contemporary Canadian universities and community colleges also indirectly communicates a strong corporate agenda. Today, the daily experiences of most post-secondary students are embedded in a corporate landscape where everything from buildings and classrooms to elevators and stadiums hold plaques thanking corporate sponsors. Campuses are inundated with brand-name product placement (Turk, 2008). As we participate in education, we not only learn facts and figures, we also assimilate important messages about acceptable behaviour, gender arrangements, social status, and corporate branding.

Changing the Culture of the Playground

Much bullying and taunting takes place at school during recess. Recognizing that it is possible to redefine the playground as a social space, Brock University researcher, Lauren McNamara, launched the Niagara Recess Project. By deploying university student volunteers to three St. Catharines schools, the program set about turning "recess into summer camp." The university students recruited and trained Grade 7 and 8 students to be junior leaders, to serve as positive role models, and to assist in positive conflict resolution. Older children learned to be skilled leaders and younger children were taught to play fair and to include everyone in their games. The Niagara program, along with others in Canada and the United States, seeks to reduce the bullying and misery that has haunted too many childhoods (Porter, 2012).

Peer Groups: Bullying and Popularity

Almost every social behaviour, from success at school to drug and pornography use, has been associated with the influence of **peer groups**. Considerable research has focused on the ways in which peers reinforce gender norms. It is thanks to the social pressures mobilized by peers in "teenage tribes," for example, that certain girls are labelled "sluts" and become the object of derision and avoidance (White, 2002). Often, appearance—socially constructed by clothing as well as biological factors such as weight, height, and figure—is used by peer groups to establish social hierarchies among girls (Pomerantz, 2006). In popular parlance, those who are being marginalized by such hierarchies are being bullied. The role of peer groups in taunting and harassing certain groups of individuals has attracted increasing attention in recent years as it becomes evident that such activities may, on occasion, result in serious consequences, including suicide. Certainly, research has documented that bullying is a much more ubiquitous experience than was once assumed. A U.S. poll found that 56 percent of youth in their teens and early twenties had been the target of some form of online bullying (Cass & Anderson, 2011).

Peer groups can also form around and support "deviant" sets of values. The trend toward increasing female youth violence and "girl gangs" may be seen as one example of such group influence. There is evidence suggesting that girls are now more likely to engage in violent attacks on other girls and that this behaviour is reinforced by peer group values. However, it is important to keep in mind that minority racial status, poverty, inner-city residence, and residence on a rural reserve are all related to the likelihood that a girl will be charged with a criminal offence, engage in violence, or be the victim of violence (Duffy, 1996; Hussain et al. 2006; Jiwani, 2006).

Peers may play a crucial role in providing the social support that allows for individual survival and even the courage to challenge societal constraints. Among Aboriginal girls engaged in prostitution—usually victims of sexual abuse, racism, family breakdown, or economic marginalization—peers provide the sense of community and self-worth that allows for not only survival but the possibility of personal transcendence (Downe, 2006). A recent study of Alberta homeless youth aged 12 to 17 underscores that for this particular population, peers may be an especially invaluable resource. Homeless boys and girls relied heavily on their peers as a source of community and spent most of their days "hanging out" with friends. As the researchers noted, "they often described friends as family." More than the adult homeless, these young people appeared to need the support and companionship of their peers (Miller, Donahue, Este, & Hofer, 2004).

Sports: Hidden Lessons

Since the ancient Greeks, sports participation has been considered a powerful socializing process. Sports teach not only physical skills but also values and self-esteem. About half (49.5 percent) of Canadian children aged 5 to 14 regularly took part in some organized sport activity in 2005—55 percent of boys and 44 percent of girls. Soccer was most popular, followed by ice hockey, swimming, and baseball (Statistics Canada, 2008). If we include watching sports events and supporting sports teams, there are a tremendous number of Canadians engaged in sports. What are they learning?

Canadians may be learning that sports participation is primarily a facet of youth: sports involvement is highest among young people (while 59 percent of teenagers aged 15 to 18 were active in sports in 2005, research indicates that 28 percent of all Canadians in 2010 were engaged in active sports for an average of 39 minutes per day [Statistics Canada, 2011]). Active individuals are not only more likely to be physically fit, but they are also more likely to occupy institutional contexts (high schools, for example) that explicitly encourage organized sports activities. As Canadians age, they often face pressure to focus their attention on other pursuits. Among Canadians aged 25 to 34, 45 percent indicated in 2005 that they lacked the time to be regularly involved in a sport.

Sports involvement tends to reaffirm class differences among Canadian adults and children. Only 43 percent of children from lower income families (less than $40 000 annual income) were active in sports in 2005, in contrast to 65 percent of children from higher income families ($80 000 or more annual income) (Statistics Canada, 2008i).

Sports are very much implicated in gender socialization (Pappas, McKenry, & Skilken Catlett, 2004). Until the second half of the twentieth century, most Canadian sports were generally constructed as male activities. Even in 1998, 43 percent of men, compared with only 26 percent of women, were regularly active in a sport. While the difference narrowed in 2005 to 36 percent for men and 21 percent for women, and there were more female coaches (up 400 percent since 1992), referees, officials, and umpires, it is clear that a gender discrepancy persists (Statistics Canada, 2008i; Cunningham, 2008; Statistics Canada, 2011d).

Sports may also play a crucial role in fitting Canadians into an increasingly organized, urbanized, and corporatized society. In the past, sports activities were often unorganized and spontaneous. Neighbourhood boys played baseball in empty fields; a frozen pond was an invitation to a hockey game. As our culture changed—as communities became more intensely urbanized and suburbanized, families became increasingly time-pressured, and organized sports became more like business enterprises—the experience of sports was transformed. Boys and girls enrolled in soccer leagues are learning very different lessons about life than their counterparts who played soccer spontaneously and without adult supervision.

The Mass Media: The Information Explosion

While we discussed the relationship between gender socialization and the mass media earlier in the chapter, it is important to underline that we live in an historical moment when the mass media have been transformed. Technological advances—e-books, digitized music players, cellphones, tablets, laptops, and net books—have permeated our social spaces and allowed for the transmission of information on a 24/7 basis. Parenting books in the 1960s, for example, were measured against one book—Dr. Spock's *Baby and Child Care*. Today, the number of parenting books and magazines has increased exponentially, with a wide variety of niche products available and accessible in a range of formats. While this certainly benefits parents of children with disabilities, who can access media that addresses their specific concerns, there is increased pressure on parents to keep up with this burgeoning mass of information. One message tends to predominate in the media—you must prepare your child for academic success—but its complexity has attained remarkable proportions (Quirke, 2012). Whether or not parenting has improved—the primary emphasis on academic success seems problematic—it is now far removed from any notion that it is "natural."

One interesting element in the new parenting paradigm is the promulgation of media as a socializing resource for infants. The emergence of "baby media" has meant that even infants are increasingly exposed to videos, cable television, and computer software targeted directly to them. Baby Einstein's release in 1997 was followed by a host of alternatives, including *Teletubbies*, Brainy Baby, Baby Mozart, and BabyFirst TV. Predictably, since these products are marketed as an important supplement to parenting of very young children, huge numbers of infants and toddlers now engage with screen media. Research suggests that 61 percent of children aged one year or younger, and 88 percent of two- and three-year-olds, spend approximately one to two hours of each day with TV, videos, computers, or video games (Wartella, Richert, & Robb, 2010). In this amazing process, not only are infants—particularly those in well-to-do households—being exposed to a new pattern of socialization, parents have been resocialized, too.

A crucial element in the new mass media is its intersection with consumerism. From the internet to DVDs, marketing is embedded in the new media experience. As a result, not only are children exposed to media messages, they are deeply immersed in the marketing of a wide range of products and services. In this process, boys and girls are routinely the target of advertising—from snack foods and breakfast cereals to computer games and clothing. Not only are children socialized to construct their identities around specific products, they are enlisted to socialize their parents into specific consumer behaviours. Some analysts are very critical of this process, since marketing is generally premised on the creation of both need and dissatisfaction (Soron, 2012). Canadian media analyst Jennifer Ann Hill (2011) argues that the pressure from consumerism for children to construct their identities around "faux values"—such as running shoe brands—and an "insatiable desire to transform the self" through consumption have led to increasingly negative self-esteem and poor psychological and physical health. For example, the marketing of games and toys has eroded opportunities for children to engage in autonomous, creative play, while the expansion of corporate branding into schools has removed any non-commercial space in their lives. Through these processes, Hill suggests that childhood itself is endangered.

The Workplace: Adult Socialization

Socialization—learning how to think and behave according to the norms and values of a specific social location—is a lifelong process. In the course of life, most Canadians will learn how to fit into a workplace and function as an employee.

Focus Question

What important socialization lessons are learned through part-time work at a fast food restaurant?

Our socialization into the workplace begins very early in life. The ubiquitous question "What do you want to be when you grow up?" is almost always construed as a question about future paid work. The significance attached to this question and its routine use in adult–child interactions speaks to the importance attached to work identities. By our teens, almost everyone has engaged in some kind of employment and in the process navigated through a variety of important socialization messages. These include not only the traditional work axioms—show up on time, follow instructions, and so forth—but also more subtle lessons. It's all right to help yourself to a pop, a pen, or an extra doughnut as long as the manager isn't around; behind the scenes—in the kitchen, in the backroom—humour and license may be permitted so long as the appropriate performance as server, retail clerk, or camp counsellor is presented out front.

In the midst of these general socialization experiences, most of us, especially youth from the middle class and above, begin to think of our future in terms of a specific employment trajectory—teacher, lawyer, social worker, and so on. Although we may not find our "dream job," we will likely start to engage in **anticipatory socialization**, or learning to play a role before entering it—a sort of mental rehearsal for some future activity. We may read books or watch movies about people who work in our hoped-for career, talk to them, or take a summer internship. This allows us to gradually identify with the role, to become aware of some of its expectations and rewards, and, perhaps, to reject it as a career choice.

An interesting aspect of work as a socializing agent is that the more you participate in a line of work, the more the work becomes a part of your self-concept, such as saying, "I am a teacher, personal chef, or lawyer," for example.

Acquiring certain professional identities—such as becoming a doctor or police officer—entails particularly powerful socialization processes. Several classic American and Canadian sociological studies focused on the training of medical students (Merton, Reader, & Kendall, 1957; Becker et al., 1961; Haas & Shaffir, 1987). A recent Canadian examination of the process of becoming a doctor indicates that the socialization process into the career is remarkably unchanged (Beagan, 2012). Medical students must focus on constructing a professional appearance; adopting appropriate ("doctorly") patterns of language, thinking, and communicating; learning (and deferring to) the complex hierarchy within medicine; and negotiating the patient–doctor relationship. Despite changes in the medical profession—in particular, the dramatic increase in the number of female doctors and medical students—many of the problematic aspects of medical socialization persist—notably, the messages to pretend competence and confidence, to establish emotional distance with patients, to work oppressively long hours, and to sacrifice family, friends, and outside interests in order to pursue a medical career (Beagan, 2012).

As this example reveals, the workplace as an agent of socialization may have contradictory or even negative impacts on an individual's identity. Traditional police academy socialization may encourage, for example, a paramilitary as opposed to a community-based approach to law enforcement (Chappell & Lanza-Kaduce, 2010). The negative consequences of this kind of work socialization are not randomly scattered throughout the population. A considerable body of research suggests that learning to fit in to certain professions and jobs often brings with it patterns of exclusion and structured inequality. Women, racialized groups, the disabled, gays and lesbians, seniors, and others may find that learning to "fit in" at work (if even possible) means accepting a restricted or troublesome sense of self (see, for example, Galabuzi, 2006).

IN SUM

Many agents of socialization affect us throughout our lives. From the moment of birth until our death, we are encouraged to act, think, and feel in a socially specified fashion. The most intimate components of our identity—how we feel love and joy, how we experience grief and despair—are moulded by our interactions with family members, with religion, with day care and education, with peers and sports, with the mass media, and within our workplaces. Some agents of socialization are particularly powerful in demanding conformity and punishing deviance. The socialization process and its agents are powerful determinants of who we are and who we wish to become.

Resocialization

As with smoking, body image, and bullying, socializing agents may seek to change or redirect socialization messages. The process of **resocialization**—which may take many different forms—involves learning new norms, values, attitudes, and behaviours. In its most common form, resocialization occurs every time we learn something contrary to our previous experiences. Most resocialization is mild, with only a slight modification of things already learned. Resocialization can be intense, however. Drug rehabilitation programs or psychotherapy, for example, may not only change an individual's behaviour, but she or he may learn a fundamentally different way of looking at life.

The Case of Total Institutions

Relatively few of us experience the most powerful expressions of socialization that Goffman (1961) called the *total institution*. He coined this term to refer to a place where people are cut off from the rest of society and come under almost total control of those who run the place. Boot camps, prisons, concentration camps, group homes for juvenile offenders, convents, some religious cults, and some elite boarding schools are examples of total institutions.

Sociologists study total institutions because they provide insight into the complexities and contradictions of social control and underscore the enormous impact of socialization.

A person entering a total institution is typically greeted with a **degradation ceremony** (Garfinkel, 1956; Santos, 2006), or an attempt to remake the self by stripping away the

Resocialization is often a gentle process, as we are gradually exposed to different ways of thinking and doing. Sometimes, however, resocialization can be swift and brutal, as it is for Canadians incarcerated in the federal prison system.

Sociologists point out that children look up to and emulate role models. However, who is seen as a suitable role model may change dramatically through the course of historical events.

individual's current identity and stamping a new one in its place. This unwelcome greeting may involve fingerprinting, photographing, shaving the head, and banning the person's **personal identity kit** (items such as jewellery, hairstyle, clothing, and other body decorations used to express individuality). Newcomers may be ordered to strip, be examined (often in humiliating, semipublic settings), and then be given a uniform to designate their new status. (For prisoners, the public reading of a verdict and being led away in handcuffs by armed police also form part of the degradation ceremony.) As evidenced in recent pictures of inmates at Abu Ghraib and in practices at the detention centre in Guantanamo Bay, total institutions continue to follow this kind of regimen.

Total institutions are extremely effective in stripping away people's personal freedom. They are isolated from the larger society (walls, bars, and geographic isolation not only keep inmates in, but they also keep outsiders from interfering). They suppress pre-existing statuses (prison inmates, for example, learn that their previous roles—such as spouse, parent, worker, or student—mean nothing, and that the only thing that counts is their current role). Total institutions suppress the norms of "the outside world," replacing them with their own rules, values, and interpretation of life. They also closely supervise the entire lives of the residents—eating, sleeping, showering, and recreation are all standardized. Information flow is also controlled, which helps the institution shape the individuals' ideas and "picture" of

the world. Finally, they control rewards and punishments. (Under conditions of deprivation, simple rewards for compliance, such as sleep, a television program, a letter from home, extra food, or even a cigarette, are powerful incentives in controlling behaviour.) The institution also holds the power to punish rule-breaking—often severely: for example, in prisons by solitary confinement or acceptance of inmate violence and assaults (Kupers, 1999).

IN SUM

Resocialization is an important aspect of the socialization process. When individuals are identified by others or identify themselves as being improperly socialized, various agencies may step in to replace earlier socialization messages with more appropriate ones. In some instances, resocialization efforts are voluntary (as in drug rehabilitation programs); in others, a state or other social agent may deploy its own resources (as in prisons and jails) not only to punish inappropriate behaviour but to inculcate more socially acceptable actions.

Socialization Through the Life Course

In recent decades, sociologists have increasingly employed a life-course approach to socialization processes. Although there is tremendous diversity in our experiences and the sequences of our lives, there is often a series of socially constructed stages—childhood, adolescence, relationship formation, parenting, middle age, retirement, early and late old age—that comprise our existence and our understanding of life (Giele & Elder, 1998; Hunt, 2005; Hostetler, Sweet, & Moen, 2007). A life-course approach does not assume that events and roles inevitably proceed in a particular sequence or that all stages occur in all lives. Indeed, in terms of current general trends, there is evidence of increased **individuation**—a growing diversity of individual paths through the life course.

The life-course approach accepts that historical events and ongoing social interaction interplay with established patterns of biological and psychological development to produce diverse and changing outcomes from childhood to death. For example, when children grow up, their views on gender roles are not simply a reflection of gender messages in their parents' home. After all, many female lawyers, househusbands, female governors-general, and male nurses grew up in traditional male breadwinner–female homemaker families. Furthermore, as we go through our lifespan, our gender beliefs and attitudes often change; for example, in old age, men are much more likely to identify with both masculine and feminine personality traits than younger and adolescent males (Strough et al., 2007). Below, we examine some of the major stages in the life course, discuss their current means, and consider how their social construction has shifted through the course of history.

Childhood (Birth to About Age 12)

What a child "is" differs from one culture to another and from one historical period to the next (Goelman, Marshall, & Ross, 2004). To understand this point, consider how different your childhood would have been if you had grown up during the Middle Ages or in contemporary Myanmar.

When historian Philippe Ariès (1962) examined European paintings from the Middle Ages, he noticed that children were always dressed in adult clothing. If they were not stiffly posed for a family portrait, children were depicted as engaging in adult activities. Ariès concluded that at that time and place, childhood was not regarded as a particularly special time of life. Rather, Europeans considered children miniature adults.

Childhood was harsh during other periods in history. Lloyd DeMause (1975) documented the nightmare of childhood in ages past. Beating children used to be the norm. Parents who did not beat their children were considered neglectful of their social duty to keep them off the road to hell. Even teachers were expected to beat their students, and one nineteenth-century German schoolteacher methodically recorded every beating he administered.

Physically harsh realities of childhood persist in both poor and rich nations. Visitors to emerging nations are often struck by the fact that children are expected to work side-by-side with adults, helping to support the family, but this reality also exists in impoverished and marginalized neighbourhoods in the most affluent countries (Heesterman, 2005). Nonetheless, in more well-to-do regions around the globe, economic development has meant that most children have been afforded the leisure to go to school. Reflecting this shift, children have increasingly come to be thought of as tender and innocent, in need of adult care, comfort, and supervision. Starting with the children of the affluent, and gradually trickling down to all children, the prevailing perception is that children are by nature innocent, gentle, and good.

Historically and cross-culturally, ideas of childhood vary. For instance, from paintings such as this 1642 British piece by the Le Nain brothers, *A Woman and Five Children*, some historians conclude that Europeans once viewed children as miniature adults who assumed adult roles at the earliest opportunity. Today this view is received with considerable skepticism.

As society continues to change, so does our conception of childhood. Contemporary social analysts have repeatedly questioned whether modern childhood is being eroded. Children today are not only spending more of their lives connected to computers, televisions, and video games, but the dramatic increase in the use of psychiatric drugs on young children—including Ritalin and antidepressants—and the numerous examples of young celebrities whose sexualized appearance, illicit drug use, and sexual behaviour is role-modelled by young people, have raised concerns. Some analysts suggest that the increased generalized pressures on young people are creating an experience of childhood that "sucks the joy" out of being a kid (Honore, 2008). Others argue that the new post-industrial experience of childhood is in crisis and demands new forms of selfhood and socialization (Block, 2005). As parents juggle double and triple days and children confront unclear but demanding educational and personal agendas, together they rush from one activity to the next with little if any chance to "enjoy the moment" (McDonnell, 2002). Viewed from this perspective, any golden era of childhood may have come and gone.

Adolescence and Youth (About Age 13 to 17)

In earlier centuries, societies did not mark adolescence as a distinct time of life. People simply moved from childhood into young adulthood with no stopover in between. The Industrial Revolution, over time, reduced the need for child labour but increased the need for skilled labour and thus the demand for education. The convergence of these two forces in industrialized societies created a gap between childhood and adulthood—hence the "discovery" of adolescence in the early twentieth century (Hall, 1904).

The experience of adolescence has changed dramatically in the past hundred years. Youth culture is now much more likely to be reflected in music, television, movies, and computer technology. A significant segment of the consumer market is devoted to this demographic and often makes explicit connections between youth identity and resistance to the larger social order. A recent study of raves in southern Ontario suggests that rave culture provides youth with "an escape from and a reaction against a mainstream culture where people are intolerant of one another and are poor communicators, and where day-to-day life is so intense that 'letting go' is almost impossible" (Wilson & Jette, 2005: 79).

The framing of adolescence as "rebellious" is apparent in the emerging stereotype of youth as the "whatever" generation. Although individual adolescents—depending on gender, sexual orientation, disability, race, and so on—have varying experiences, sociologists are concerned that pressures on adolescents are so intense that they are destructive. In his aptly titled book, *The Road to Whatever*, Elliott Currie (2004) argues that the harsh "winner/loser" world of middle-class adolescence—where there is little in the way of compassionate help to deal with educational, social, and economic pressures, and where there is an increasingly punitive

approach to adolescent misbehaviour—is producing a life stage that is experienced by many as desperate and painful.

Young Adulthood (About Age 18 to 29)

Historian Kenneth Keniston (1971) suggests that industrialized societies seem to be adding a period of prolonged youth to the life course—a period in which young adults are no longer adolescents but are not yet sociological adults. As education, particularly for middle and higher classes, extends increasingly into college, university, and graduate or professional school, the attributes of adulthood—marriage, home ownership, parenthood—are often delayed. For example, between 1986 and 2009, the probability that an individual whose parents did not graduate from university would earn a university degree almost doubled (Turcotte, 2011). While in the past high school graduates could hope to land well-paid and secure manufacturing jobs, those opportunities have all but vanished. Prolonged education is emerging as the only path to economic security.

As a result of longer educational commitments, along with decreased employment opportunities, many youth are postponing life decisions. The shift in patterns of young adulthood is also striking in terms of the once-momentous step of "moving out." It appears that many young Canadians either do not move out at all or become **boomerang kids**—young adults who move out of their parents' home but move back in at a later date. When surveyed in 2010, 51 percent of Canadian youth aged 20 to 29 were living with their parents, in contrast to 31 percent of the same age group in 1998. Not surprisingly, many have postponed family formation. In 2010, 19 percent of youth had children, compared to 29 percent of youth surveyed in 1986. Even serious relationships appear to be postponed—only 33 percent of youth in 2011 were married or living common-law, in contrast to 48 percent of those surveyed in 1986 (Marshall, 2011).

The Middle Years (About Age 30 to 65)

Today, it is during the early middle years (age 30 to 49) that most people enter more firmly into adult status. At this stage, many men and women undertake conjugal unions and become parents. In 2008, the average age at first marriage for men was 31.6 years and for women 29.6 years—in sharp contrast to 1972 when women were marrying for the first time at around age 23 and men at around age 25. The average age of first birth for mothers was 28.1 years in 2008 (Milan, Keown, & Urquijo, 2011). The number of births to teens has been declining for the past 31 years. The net result is that for many Canadians, their thirties and forties is a period for formalizing long-term relationships and entering into parenthood.

Both of these new identities—spouse and parent—typically involve intense socialization and may entail problematic outcomes, such as divorce. In 2008, slightly more than 40 percent of marriages could be expected to end

⊙ **Watch** Professor Bill McCarthy's "Youth, Sex, and Crime" lectures on **MySocLab.**

in divorce (before the thirtieth year of marriage), and almost half of divorces involved marriages that had lasted less than 10 years. The average age at divorce was 44 for men and 41 for women (Milan, Keown, & Urquijo, 2011). These sometimes tumultuous middle years are often discussed in terms of *mid-life crises*, as individuals struggle to establish a personally satisfying sense of themselves as adults.

Resocialization of the self to accommodate such ruptures in expectation and self-conceptualization may be a years-long process. Even stable relationships may entail painful adjustments in an economy where there is tremendous pressure to consume, coupled with sometimes inadequate support systems. Single parents and adults who must juggle care for their children and extensive paid employment may feel trapped by conflicting pressures and lack of time. These difficulties may be further compounded if they find themselves part of the **sandwich generation**, who are not only caring for their own children but also providing assistance and support to their aging parents. Even though they are now fully-fledged adults, men and women during these years may be constantly adjusting their sense of self to accommodate personal and societal demands.

The Older Years (About Age 66 Onward)

In industrialized societies, the older years begin around the sixties. This, too, is recent; in preindustrial societies, when most people died early, old age was thought to begin at around age 40. Today, being over 65 is often experienced not as old age but as "mid life." Indeed, the recent elimination of mandatory retirement and the postponement of pension benefits to age 67 in many countries, including Canada, suggest that many will experience their sixties as another period of paid employment. Continuing to work depends on health and the ability to stay socially active. Growing old varies depending on social class, gender, and other significant social markers (Mandell, Wilson, & Duffy, 2008).

As with the preceding periods of life (except the first), there is no precise beginning point to the last stage—the later older years. For some, the seventy-fifth birthday may mark entry into this period. For others, that marker may be the eightieth or even the eighty-fifth birthday. For many, this stage is marked by growing frailty and illness, and for all who reach this stage, by impending death. Physical decline may be slow, and increasing numbers of people now manage to see their hundredth birthdays (although for many centenarians, quality of life is compromised by cognitive and/or physical disabilities). Increasing numbers of Canadians will experience a period of socialization in which they must redefine themselves as elderly and, possibly, dependent (see, for example, Martin-Matthews, 2011).

Focus Question
What specific steps might be taken by Canadian society to socialize seniors to be healthier and more socially productive in their old age?

Focus Question
In what ways are your own experiences of the life course different from those of your parents and your grandparents?

IN SUM

According to life-course analysis, our lives often involve a series of stages: childhood, adolescence, young adulthood, the middle years, and the older years. However, how we experience these stages depends on a complex interplay of factors—in particular, historical location and culture. In all stages of life, our social location, as determined by the intertwining influences of social class, gender, and race, is typically highly significant. Within these complexities, patterns of human life tend to establish the general boundaries at each stage. As a result, we can speak of "boomerang kids," "mid-life crises," or "the sandwich generation" and strike a chord with many Canadians at those particular stages.

The Limitations of Socialization

Socialization is an extremely appealing explanation for human behaviour. It makes a great deal of sense to look to the influence of father, mother, friends, media, school, and career in order to understand who we are, what we value, and how we act. However, even the framers of socialization theory understood its limitations. George Herbert Mead emphasized the powerful impact of social forces on our lives; he even argued that *the human mind is a social product*. According to Mead, we need symbols to be able to think, and these symbols come from society when we learn our language. If society did not provide the symbols, we would not be able to think and would not possess what we call the mind.

Despite Mead's strong endorsement of a socialization perspective, he also wanted to allow for human freedom in his framework. He was not prepared to argue that we are simply the sum total of societal inputs. He introduced the concepts of the "I" and the "me." The "I" is *the self as subject*, the active, spontaneous, creative part of the self, as in "I throw the ball." In contrast, the "me" is *the self as object*, made up of attitudes internalized from our interactions with others, as in "They made *me* do it." Mead stressed that the individual is not only a "me," like a computerized robot passively absorbing patterns from others. Rather, the "I" actively makes sense of those responses and then acts. With this inclusion in his theory, Mead made provision not only for **human agency** (the ability to individually or collectively resist social pressures and provide for social change) but also for human responsibility. We are the products of socialization, but we also make choices.

BIOLOGY, SOCIOBIOLOGY, OR SOCIALIZATION?

What is the latest thinking on the roots of human behaviour and, specifically, on the contributions of biology?

In the past, the roots of human behaviour were debated in terms of nature versus nurture. Sociologists tended to support the view that our behaviour is rooted in social processes such as socialization, along with the impact of societal institutions and shifting historical forces. From this perspective, biology simply provided the page on which society wrote the message. However, recent biological research on genetics has made enormous strides in proving that a "blank slate" approach to the human infant is inaccurate. Particularly through advances in genetic research and through twin studies, researchers have been able to reveal a complex intersection between human biological potentiality and the influence of environmental (including social) forces. pp. 67–69.

THE SOCIAL DEVELOPMENT OF THE SELF, MIND, AND EMOTIONS

In what ways does social experience create and structure our human existence, including our beliefs, values, goals, and perceptions?

In every way, how we feel, what we value, what we want to achieve, what we believe, and even what we see is influenced by our social environment. If you imagine a typical day in your life, virtually every act, from brushing your teeth with your favourite toothpaste to worrying about gaining weight over breakfast, is a socially constructed activity. We act in particular ways and value or enjoy those actions because we have been directly or indirectly taught that these are things we should do and should value. Through our experience in social relationships, our basic identity is constructed. In the absence of such human contact, it is likely that not only our beliefs, values, and goals would be absent, but our basic perceptions would be altered. What would we make of a car if we had never heard the word or seen the object before? It is the processes of social interaction, starting at birth, that construct who we are, what we want, and what we perceive. pp. 69–72.

SOCIALIZATION INTO GENDER

How is gender identity created through gender socialization and how does this process relate to larger changes in society?

Gender socialization commences before birth, since it is rooted in the gender socialization of our parents. As soon as we are born, our parents are likely to provide direct and indirect messages about gender (appropriate names, for example). These gender messages then permeate our childhood and adolescence and are reflected in almost every aspect of our social existence. The mass media and education play an important part in affirming the importance of gender differences. Even seemingly unrelated activities such as buying clothes become gendered when girls are targeted with "sexy" advertisements. Some gender socialization is profoundly indirect and we are often unaware of it. For example, young men and women have different responsibilities in terms of household work; males tend to have more "free" time. Both men and women are likely to be unaware that the temporal structures of their lives are gendered. Gender socialization may have profoundly negative or profoundly different outcomes for males and females. Young women are more likely to engage in self-destructive behaviours, such as eating disorders, while young men are more likely to be risk-takers (such as with alcohol use, for example).

Further, gender socialization is far from a static process; it must respond to larger societal shifts. Consider, for example, the socialization practices that were appropriate to producing the typical full-time homemaker in the 1950s, and contrast them with the contemporary economic pressures that produce women who work much of their lives in the paid labour force. These larger changes in society need not be as momentous as women's liberation and the movement of women into paid labour. They also include the proliferation of information technology, the changing role of social media, and the growing emphasis on image as reflected in the "fat stigma." pp. 78–79.

RESOCIALIZATION

Why might the changing of socialization messages through resocialization be a powerful instrument of control?

Specific instruments of resocialization—prisons, drug rehabilitation centres—may intentionally seek to alter our socialization. Here, different sets of beliefs, values, and attendant behaviours may be rewarded while prior patterns are challenged or rejected. Many societies contain resocialization organizations to maintain social control and eradicate what they define as inappropriate patterns of behaviour or attitudes. pp. 86–87.

SOCIALIZATION THROUGH THE LIFE COURSE

What are the stages of human socialization? What kinds of transitions do we experience as we proceed through the life course?

The stages of human socialization include childhood, adolescence, relationship formation, parenting, middle age, retirement, and early and late old age. Not everyone goes through all of these stages, and they do not necessarily follow a particular order. The transitions we experience as we move from one stage to another may be easy or tumultuous depending on a variety of social factors. For example, becoming a young adult may be particularly difficult in modern society as young people find limited employment opportunities along with an escalating cost of living. As a result, their transition may be bumpy and far from straightforward; they may move out on their own only to return to their parents' home as boomerang kids. Similarly, seniors may experience the transition to dependency and frailty an intimidating and difficult process.pp. 87–90.

THE LIMITATIONS OF SOCIALIZATION

What are the limitations of socialization as an explanation of human behaviour?

Socialization may become a blanket explanation. Why do we drive on the right side of the road in Canada? Because we are socialized to do so. While it is important to recognize that we are tremendously influenced by the beliefs, values, and norms we are taught in a particular social context, and that we often unconsciously follow societal rules, we are not simply the end result of various socialization inputs. This is certainly revealed by advances in genetic research, but it is also embedded in sociological theory. Leading socialization theorists allow for the possibility that individuals will reject or resist socialization pressures. Even in total institutions, inmates may find ways to express their individuality or "get around" the rules. Sometimes members of society contradict socialization messages and arrive at their own path for navigating life. Socialization reveals the pressures to act in a particular manner, but it does not imply that we necessarily capitulate to those social forces. p. 90.

Theoretical Paradigms

CLASSICAL PARADIGMS		
Structural-Functional Paradigm	**Social-Conflict Paradigm**	**Symbolic-Interaction Paradigm**
What is the level of analysis? Macro level	Macro level	Macro level
What is the importance of socialization for society? Socialization is key to fitting the individual into society and its various institutions.	Socialization is key to understanding conformity in society and the role of specific institutions in providing social control. However, there must be an allowance for human agency.	Socialization provides us with the roles, techniques, and strategies that allow us to perform in specific social interactions.
Has socialization changed over time? How? Somewhat. The primary function remains the same, but the specifics have changed. For example, the internet and mass media have provided new socializing agents.	Somewhat. The process of socialization has intensified in some instances (for example, prolonged education) and there are more extensive uses of socialization in social control. However, the overall process of socialization remains intact.	Somewhat. The process of socialization and the construction of social meanings remain intact, but the specific roles we acquire and learn to perform (for example, adolescence) have changed.

agents of socialization 81
anticipatory socialization 85
biological determinism 67
boomerang kids 89
cliques 80
degradation ceremony 86
ego 72
ethnocentrism 80
gender roles 70
generalized other 70

habitus 71
human agency 90
id 72
individuation 88
in-groups 80
latent functions 83
looking-glass self 69
manifest functions 83
mass media 73
out-groups 80

peer groups 83
personal identity kit 87
primary group 80
reference groups 80
resocialization 86
sandwich generation 90
secondary groups 80
self 69
significant others 69
social groups 80

socialization 67
superego 72
symbols 69
taking the role of the
    other 69
total institutions 72
xenophobia 80

All URLs listed are current as of the printing of this text.

National Longitudinal Study of Children and Youth
www23.statcan.gc.ca/imdb/p2SV.pl?Function=getSurvey&SDDS=4450&lang=en&db=imdb&adm=8&dis=2
A long-term study of Canadian children that follows their development from birth to early adulthood.

Men For Change
www.chebucto.ns.ca/CommunitySupport/Men4Change
The website of Men For Change, a pro-feminist group interested in promoting gender equality and ending sexism.

Socialization
www.delmar.edu/socsci/rlong/intro/social.htm
Part of Russell Long's academic page on sociology, presented to support various courses and to encourage students to use the internet.

Niagara Recess Project
www.unitedwaysc.ca/community_recess.php
The website of the Niagara Recess Project, which seeks to change the informal socialization practices on school playgrounds.

Sexy Inc.
http://topdocumentaryfilms.com/sexy-inc-our-children-under-influence
This website contains information on Sophie Bissonnette's documentary film *Sexy Inc.*

1. Socialization is intended to turn us into conforming members of society. As a result, we are under considerable pressure to "do the right thing." Explain how socialization would also be useful in explaining the behaviour of the numerous individuals, from white-collar criminals to wife abusers, who deviate from social norms.

2. Some analysts fear that social media are taking over from traditional socialization agencies. Do you think, from your experience with Facebook, Twitter, Tumblr, and blogs, that youth socialization is being fundamentally altered by social media?

3. Socialization is presented as such a powerful social process that students sometimes have the impression that people are empty vessels filled with social messages—"this is what you should eat, wear, and say," for example. However, socialization theorists usually accept that each of us is actively involved in the social construction of the self. Consider the ways in which you, as a young child, were not simply a reflection of the socialization messages you received from parents, siblings, peers, and school.

4. Does traditional gender socialization and its resulting gender roles make it more difficult for North American men than women to connect emotionally to others? Access the Research Navigator through MySocLab and use keywords such as "masculinities," "homophobia," "sports," and "militarism" to locate relevant and recent scholarly and popular press publications to help you answer this question.

MySocLab

Explore the topics covered in this chapter on MySocLab. Interactive resources include a study plan, cumulative exams, a multimedia library, MySocLab eReadings, and access to the MySocLab Video Series.

5

GLOBALIZATION

LET'S consider two "average" families from different parts of the world:

For Getu Mulleta, 33, and his wife, Zenebu, 28, of rural Ethiopia, life is a constant struggle to keep themselves and their seven children from starving. They live in a 320-square-foot (30 m²) manure-plastered hut with no electricity, gas, or running water. They have a radio, but the battery is dead. Surviving on $130 a year, the family farms teff, a cereal grain.

The Mulletas' poverty is not the result of a lack of hard work. Getu works about 80 hours a week, while Zenebu works even more. "Housework" for Zenebu includes fetching water, making fuel pellets out of cow dung for the open fire over which she cooks the family's food, and cleaning animal stables. Like other Ethiopian women, she eats after the men.

In Ethiopia, the average male can expect to live to 48, and the average female to 50.

The Mulletas' most valuable possession is their oxen. Their wishes for the future? More animals, better seed, and a second set of clothing.

Kitchener, Ontario, is home to the Kellys—Rick, 36, Patti, 34, Julie, 14, and Michael, 10. The Kellys live in a four-bedroom, 2100-square-foot (195 m²), carpeted, ranch-style house, with central heating and air conditioning, a basement, and a two-car garage. Their home is equipped with a refrigerator, washing machine, clothes dryer, dishwasher, garbage disposal, vacuum

Sources: Menzel (1994); Population Reference Bureau (1995); "Statistical Abstract," (2011): Tables 102, 686, 695, 966; Statistics Canada (2001); Statistics Canada (2005e).

of women work in less skilled jobs in the garm
while in the public and not-for-profit sectors
the largest share of health care professionals su
and home care and personal support workers.

The textile and garment industries were an
to be globalized. United Colors of Benetton, or
Group, an Italian family-run clothing multina
operations in the mid-1960s. Today, the compa
not only for its images of beautiful faces and
around the world, but also for its ability to c
through music, theatre, photography, publish
internet. Benetton is the precursor to compa
Gap and Old Navy.

The garment industry in Canada—be it al
Avenue in Toronto or in the Chabanel District c
experienced massive changes under the force
tion. Consider the Exchange District in Wini
designated historic site, or the rapid demise
Vancouver, and the dramatic effects of globaliza
ous. The existing industry in Montreal and 1
hard times in a global economic world. Emplo
clothing sector in Quebec fell from 57 000 in 2(
in 2005—a massive change in a short period of
those affected were women; many were recent

Offshore textile and garment manufacturir
global in scope. In many Asian countries, yo
lured to tax-free "factory cities," called **expor
zones**, on the promise of good jobs manufactu
for export. Among the hazards they are confro
forced overtime, stifling hot factories with poc
forced pregnancy tests, sexual violence, and u
ing water.

Job loss in Canada and hazardous offshore
ditions tell only half the story. What happens
return home? Who does the housework? Wh
their husband or partner loses his or her jot
recent Asian economic crisis, the Korean gover
upon women to "get your husband energized"
his job, and to help offset the impact of the ec
on men who, as government ads pointed out,
to depression and possible suicide.

Education is critical in order for women ii
the rest of the world to compete as equals in th
world and earn a decent income. However, in
dent debt has skyrocketed. On average, fem
earn less than their male counterparts, result
debt repayment periods. Those without a ur
cation are particularly disadvantaged. When
government eliminated the *National Training*
which included training programs geared tov
good paying jobs for women in nontradit
became even harder to get.

University education and skills developme
nificant factors for achieving equity in the wo
in Canada and elsewhere.

"Worlds Apart" would be an appropriate caption for these photos, which illustrate how life chances depend on globalization. On the left is an Ethiopian girl fetching water for her family. Due to draught, children have to walk for over an hour to retrieve water. On the right are North American teenagers with cellphones and headphones.

cleaner, food processor, microwave, and stovetop and convection oven. They also own cellphones, colour televisions, digital cameras, an iPod, computers with DVD players, a printer-scanner-fax machine, blow dryers, a juicer, an espresso coffee maker, a pickup truck, and an SUV.

Rick works 40 hours a week as an electrical power line and cable worker for the provincial power company. Patti is an elementary school teacher. Together they make $73 000* a year, plus benefits. The Kellys can choose from among dozens of super-stocked supermarkets. They spend $7046 on food for their home, and another $3520 eating at restaurants—a total of nearly 15 percent of their annual income.

In Canada, the average life expectancy is 78 for males, and 82 for females.

*This figure represents the median income for a Canadian family in 2006.

On the Kellys' wish list are a new hybrid car with satellite radio, a 500-gigabyte laptop with Bluetooth wi-fi, a 50-inch plasma TV with surround sound, a boat, a motor home, an ATV, and—one day—a vacation cabin.

What is Globalization?

Globalization is the latest stage in a process characterized by the spread and intensification of capitalism across the globe (see Figure 5.1). Today, globalization involves the interaction and integration of increasing numbers of people through international trade and investment, travel and tourism, and information technology and the mass media. Let's look at how globalization impacts the movement of people around the world.

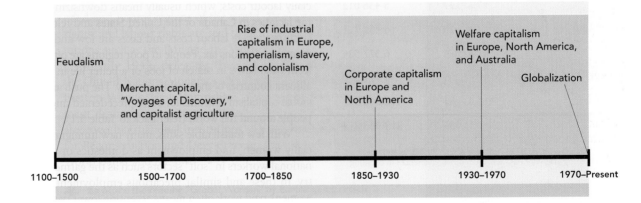

FIGURE 5.1 Stages of Capitalism, Expansion, and Intensification

Globalization and Patterns of Movement of People

Immigration

International migration has mushroomed In 2010, 214 million people migrated to di the world. The United States had the high with Canada placing sixth after France and Table 5.1). Together, the countries with th rates in 2010 accounted for over 51 per migration. What is behind this upsurg movement? Partly, migration can be attrib search for a better life in the richer coun Another factor, according to Anny Hefti (1 ization of communications technology. Th mass communication, including televisio music, has reinforced dreams of an "easy contends that fax machines and cellpho snail mail communications and that relatic grant communities abroad and home comr facilitated by these new communications result, migration has become very attractiv

TABLE 5.1 Top 10 Countries with the of International Migrants (2005, 2010)

	Number of Immigrants
	2005
United States	38 354 709
Russian Federation	12 079 626
Germany	10 143 626
France	6 471 029
Saudi Arabia	6 360 730
Canada	6 105 722
India	5 700 147
United Kingdom	5 408 118
Spain	4 790 074
Australia	4 097 204
Top 10 Total	99 510 985
World	190 633 564

Note: As countries collect statistics on immigrants in often difficult to harmonize data across countries; diff deeply affect rank orders.

Source: United Nations, Trends in Total Migrant Stock: data in digital form, 2006, 2012. Available at http://esa. index.asp?panel=1

WORLD BANK With considerable financial power, the World Bank shapes development policies across Africa, Latin America, Asia, and Eastern Europe. Its self-proclaimed primary objective is to eradicate poverty, yet evidence suggests that World Bank programs often increase social inequalities and cause environmental destruction.

IMF The IMF was founded in 1944 as a result of the financial turmoil of the Great Depression of the 1930s and the devastation caused by World War II. The organization provided financial stability in the decades following the Second World War in order to increase world trade. Today, the IMF has a membership of 184 countries and has intervened in such financial crises as the 1995 crash of the Mexican peso and the 1997/98 East Asian financial crisis. IMF policies have been criticized for increasing poverty and suffering among ordinary citizens while shielding multinational corporations and their backers in wealthy countries.

WTO Growing out of the Uruguay Round of GATT trade talks (1986 to 1994), the WTO was founded in January 1995 as an international body of 146 member countries whose purpose, like the GATT, is to promote free trade. Unlike the GATT, WTO decisions are absolute and every member must abide by its rulings. As such, it has become closely associated with globalization.

GATT The GATT was first signed in 1947 as a United Nations treaty, rather than an organization. The agreement was designed to provide an international forum to encourage free trade between member states.

Globalization, Inequality, and Development

Until recently, a simple model consisting of *First*, *Second*, and *Third Worlds* was used to depict global stratification. "First World" referred to industrialized capitalist nations, "Second World" to communist nations, and "Third World" to any nation that did not fit into the first two categories. After the collapse of the Soviet Union in 1989, these terms became outdated. In addition, although "first," "second," and "third" did not mean "best," "second best," and "worst," they sounded like it. An alternative classification now in use—*developed*, *developing*, and *undeveloped nations*—has the same drawback. By referring to ourselves as "developed," it sounds as though we are mature and the "undeveloped" nations lack our desirable traits. Consequently, we employ more neutral descriptive terms: *most industrialized*, *industrializing*, and *least industrialized nations*.

Such descriptions are used to depict, on a global level, three primary dimensions: property, power, and prestige. The most industrialized nations have greater property (wealth), power (they get their way in international relations), and prestige (rightly or wrongly, they are looked up to as world leaders with something to contribute to humanity). As illustrated in

Figure 5.2, internationally, more than 1.2 billion people—or one in five—survive on less than U.S.$1 a day (United Nations, 2003:5). The past few decades have seen some improvements in the least industrialized countries: life expectancy increased by eight years and literacy rates improved dramatically (United Nations, 2003:2). However, during the 1990s, average per capita income growth was less than 3 percent in 125 countries, and actually declined in 54 of them (United Nations, 2003:3). The poorest countries face critical, life-threatening crises: increasing poverty, food shortages, and increased rates of hunger.

To further understand the tremendous differences between the richest and poorest people in the world, consider income share. In the first years of the twentieth century, the richest 1 percent of people received income equal to 57 percent of the world's poorest people. Further, the income of the world's richest 10 percent of the population was 127.7 times that of the poorest 10 percent (Centre for Social Justice, 2001; United Nations, 2001). The two families sketched in the chapter's opening vignette provide insight into the far-reaching effects of globalization on citizens around the world, as does the Thinking Critically about Social Controversy box on Children as Prey.

Over the past two centuries, the gap between the richest and poorest countries has grown tremendously. In 1820, the richest countries were roughly three times richer than the poorest, based on gross domestic product (GDP) per capita. This ratio rose to 15 times by 1950 and to 19 times by 1998 (Lee, 2002). And the world's richest people's share of total GDP has skyrocketed over the past 40 years (see Table 5.2). GDP measures the dollar value of all final goods and services produced within the borders of a country, such as Canada or the United States, in a given year. GDP must be

TABLE 5.2 Share of the Total GDP of the World's People: Richest 20 Percent versus Poorest 20 Percent

Year	Share of Top 20% Compared to Bottom 20%
1960	30x
1970	32x
1980	45x
1989	59x
1997	74x
2007	83x

Note: In 2007, the top 20 percent received 83 times the income of the bottom 20 percent.

Source: Based on "The Global Divide: Inequality in the World Economy" by Marc Lee, 2002, *Behind the Numbers: Economic Facts, Figures and Analysis*, 4, No. 2. Ottawa: Canadian Centre for Policy Alternatives. Reproduced from United National Development Program, Human Development Report 1999. New York: Oxford University Press, pp. 36–37. For 2007, see Isabel Ortiz. 2011. *Global Inequality: Beyond the Bottom Billion*, New York: UNICEF.

THINKING CRITICALLY ABOUT SOCIAL CONTROVERSY

Open Season: Children as Prey

In Phnom Penh, Cambodia, the city dump is home to many people, and a highly developed social organization has emerged. Pictured here, after garbage has been delivered by truck, people stream around it, struggling to be the first to discover something of value. Workers use metal picks, like the one this child is holding, to sift through the trash. Note that children work alongside adults.

What is childhood like in the industrializing nations? The answer depends on who your parents are. If you are the son or daughter of rich parents, childhood can be pleasant—a world filled with luxuries and even servants. If you are born into poverty but live in a rural area where there is plenty to eat, life can still be good—although there may be no books or television and little education. If you are born into poverty and live in a slum, however, life can be horrible—worse even than in the slums of the most industrialized nations (Barbassa, 2010). Let's take a glance at a notorious slum in Brazil.

Not enough food, along with wife abuse, broken homes, alcoholism, drug abuse, and a lot of crime: from your knowledge of slums in the most industrialized nations, you would expect these things. What you may not expect, however, are the brutal conditions in which Brazilian slum (*favela*) children live. Sociologist Martha Huggins (Huggins et al., 2002) reports that poverty is so deep that children and adults swarm through garbage dumps to try to find enough decaying food to keep themselves alive. You might also be surprised to learn that the owners of some of these dumps hire armed guards to keep the poor out—so that they can sell the garbage for pig food. And you will likely be shocked to learn that some shop owners hire hit men, auctioning designated victims to the *lowest* bidder! Life is cheap in the poor nations—but death squads for children? To understand, we must first note that Brazil has a long history of violence. Brazil also has a high rate of poverty, has only a tiny middle class, and is controlled by a small group of families who, under a veneer of democracy, make the country's major decisions. Hordes of homeless children, with no schools or jobs, roam the streets. To survive, they wash windshields, shine shoes, beg, and steal (Huggins & Rodrigues, 2004). The "respectable" classes see these children as nothing but trouble. They hurt businesses, as customers feel intimidated when they see begging children—especially teenaged boys—clustered in front of stores. Some shoplift. Others break and enter. With no effective social institutions to care for these children, one solution is to kill them. As Huggins notes, murder sends a clear message—especially if it is accompanied by ritual torture: gouging out the eyes, ripping open the chest, cutting off the genitals, raping the girls, and burning the victims' bodies.

Not all life is bad in the industrializing nations, but this is about as bad as it gets.

For Your Consideration
Death squads for children also operate in the slums of the Philippines ("Death Squads . . . ", 2008). Do you think there is anything the most industrialized nations can do about this situation? Or is it just an "internal"—though unfortunate—affair that should be left to the individual nation to handle as it wishes? Police in these regions are known assassinate rapists and drug dealers ("Death to . . . ", 2009). What do you think about this activity?

distinguished from GNP, or gross national product, which does not include goods and services manufactured by foreign producers but does include the dollar value of goods and services produced by all Canadian-owned firms operating in foreign countries. GDP is the preferred measure of whether an economy is expanding or contracting used by economists and other social scientists.

According to the U.S. Institute for Policy Studies, there were 497 billionaires worldwide in 2001, with a combined wealth of $1.54 trillion, a figure that exceeded the combined GNPs of all the nations of sub-Saharan Africa or those of the oil-rich regions of the Middle East or North Africa. Moreover, the billionaires' combined wealth was "greater than the combined incomes of the poorest half of all of humanity" (IPS, as cited in Mokhiber & Weissman, 2002).

Modifying the Model
The classification of nations into the most industrialized, industrializing, and least industrialized is helpful in that it pinpoints gross differences among them. But it also

👁 **Watch** the video "Slum Futures" on **MySocLab.**

The Most Industrialized Nations

	Nation	Income per Person
1	Luxembourg	$77,600
2	Norway	$59,300
3	Singapore	$50,300
4	United States	$46,400
5	Hong Kong	$42,700
6	Switzerland	$41,600
7	Iceland	$39,800
8	Austria	$39,400
9	Netherlands	$39,000
10	Canada	$38,400
11	Sweden	$36,800
12	Australia	$38,500
13	Belgium	$36,600
14	Denmark	$36,200
15	United Kingdom	$35,400
16	Finland	$34,900
17	Germany	$34,200
18	France	$32,800
19	Japan	$32,600
20	Italy	$30,200
21	Taiwan	$30,200
22	Israel	$28,400
23	Slovenia	$28,200
24	New Zealand	$27,700
25	Korea, South	$27,700
26	Czech Republic	$25,100

The Industrializing Nations

	Nation	Income per Person
27	Ireland	$42,200
28	Spain	$33,700
29	Greece	$32,100
30	Portugal	$21,700
31	Slovakia	$21,100
32	Greenland	$20,000
33	Estonia	$18,800
34	Hungary	$18,800
35	Poland	$17,800
36	Croatia	$17,600
37	Russia	$15,200
38	Lithuania	$15,000
39	Malaysia	$14,700
40	Chile	$14,700
41	Libya	$14,600
42	Latvia	$14,500
43	Argentina	$13,800
44	Gabon	$13,700
45	Venezuela	$13,200
46	Mexico	$13,200
47	Bulgaria	$12,600
48	Mauritius	$12,400
49	Romania	$11,500
50	Costa Rica	$11,300
51	Turkey	$11,200
52	Brazil	$10,200
53	South Africa	$10,000
54	Cuba	$9,700
55	China	$6,500

The Least Industrialized Nations

	Nation	Income per Person		Nation	Income per Person
56	Uruguay	$12,600	72	Tunisia	$8,000
57	Botswana[2]	$12,100	73	Ecuador	$7,300
58	Panama	$11,900	74	Algeria	$7,100
59	Belarus	$11,600	75	Turkmenistan	$6,700
60	Lebanon	$11,500	76	Ukraine	$6,400
61	Kazakhstan	$11,400	77	Namibia	$6,400
62	Azerbaijan	$9,900	78	Bosnia	$6,300
63	Colombia	$9,200	79	Albania	$6,200
64	Macedonia	$9,000	80	Bhutan	$6,200
65	Suriname	$8,800	81	El Salvador	$6,000
66	Angola	$8,800	82	Egypt	$6,000
67	Peru	$8,600	83	Armenia	$5,900
68	Jamaica	$8,300	84	Jordan	$5,300
69	Belize	$8,200	85	Guatemala	$5,200
70	Dominican Republic	$8,200	86	Syria	$4,700
71	Thailand	$8,100	87	Bolivia	$4,600
			88	Morocco	$4,600

FIGURE 5.2 Global Stratification: Income of the World's Nations

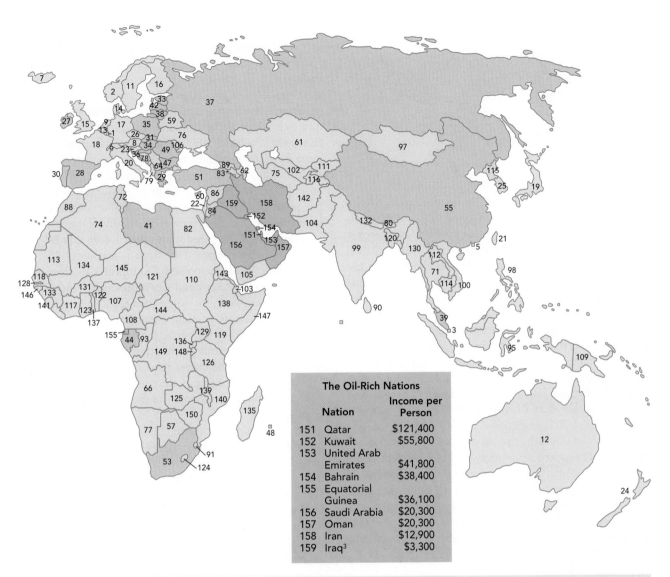

The Oil-Rich Nations

	Nation	Income per Person
151	Qatar	$121,400
152	Kuwait	$55,800
153	United Arab Emirates	$41,800
154	Bahrain	$38,400
155	Equatorial Guinea	$36,100
156	Saudi Arabia	$20,300
157	Oman	$20,300
158	Iran	$12,900
159	Iraq[3]	$3,300

The Least Industrialized Nations

	Nation	Income per Person		Nation	Income per Person		Nation	Income per Person		Nation	Income per Person
89	Georgia	$4,500	106	Moldova	$2,400	122	Benin	$1,500	138	Ethiopia	$900
90	Sri Lanka	$4,500	107	Nigeria	$2,400	123	Ghana	$1,500	139	Malawi	$900
91	Swaziland	$4,400	108	Cameroon	$2,300	124	Lesotho	$1,500	140	Mozambique	$900
92	Honduras	$4,200	109	Papua-New Guinea	$2,300	125	Zambia	$1,500	141	Sierra Leone	$900
93	Congo	$4,200	110	Sudan	$2,300	126	Tanzania	$1,400	142	Afghanistan	$800
94	Paraguay	$4,100	111	Krygyzstan	$2,100	127	Haiti	$1,300	143	Eritrea	$700
95	Indonesia	$4,000	112	Laos	$2,100	128	Gambia	$1,300	144	Central African Republic	$700
96	Guyana	$3,900	113	Mauritania	$2,100	129	Uganda	$1,300	145	Niger	$700
97	Mongolia	$3,400	114	Cambodia	$1,900	130	Burma (Myanmar)	$1,200	146	Guinea-Bissau	$600
98	Philippines	$3,300	115	Korea, North	$1,800	131	Burkina Faso	$1,200	147	Somalia	$600
99	India	$3,100	116	Tajikistan	$1,800	132	Nepal	$1,200	148	Burundi	$300
100	Vietnam	$2,900	117	Cote d'Ivoire	$1,700	133	Guinea	$1,100	149	Congo, Dem. Rep.	$300
101	Nicaragua	$2,800	118	Senegal	$1,700	134	Mali	$1,100	150	Zimbabwe	$200
102	Uzbekistan	$2,800	119	Kenya	$1,600	135	Madagascar	$1,000			
103	Djibouti	$2,800	120	Bangladesh	$1,600	136	Rwanda	$1,000			
104	Pakistan	$2,600	121	Chad	$1,500	137	Togo	$900			
105	Yemen	$2,500									

[1]Income is a country's purchasing power parity based on its per capita gross domestic product measured in U.S. dollars. Since some totals vary widely from year to year, they must be taken as approximate. [2]Botswana's relative wealth is based on its diamond mines. [3]Iraq's oil has been disrupted by war.

Sources: By the author. Based on *Statistical Abstract of the United States* 2007: Table 1324, with a few missing countries taken from the CIA's latest *World Factbook*.

TABLE 5.3 An Alternative Model of the Global Economy

Four Worlds of Development
1. Most industrialized nations
2. Industrializing nations
3. Least industrialized nations
4. Oil-rich, non-industrialized nations

presents problems. How much industrialization does a nation require in order to be classified as "most industrialized" or "industrializing"? Several nations have become "postindustrial." Does this new stage require a separate classification? The oil-rich nations of the Middle East are not industrialized, but by providing the oil and gasoline that fuel the machinery of the most industrialized nations, they have become immensely wealthy. Consequently, to classify them simply as "least industrialized" glosses over significant distinctions, such as their modern hospitals, extensive prenatal care, pure water systems, abundant food and shelter, high literacy, and computerized banking. Kuwait, on whose behalf the United States and other most industrialized nations fought Iraq in the First Gulf War, is an excellent example of the difficulties posed by this classification system. Kuwait is so wealthy that almost none of its citizens are employed. The government simply pays each resident a generous annual salary. Migrant workers from poor nations do most of the onerous chores of daily life, while highly skilled workers from the most industrialized nations run the specialized systems that keep Kuwait's economy going—and, on occasion, fight its wars. Table 5.3 reflects this significant distinction.

Sociological Theories of Global and Social Economic Development

How did the world come to be divided into such distinct stages of development? The obvious answer is that the poorer nations have fewer resources than the richer ones. As with so many other "obvious" answers, however, this one, too, falls short, for many of the industrializing and least industrialized nations are rich in natural resources, while one of the most industrialized nations, Japan, has few. Four competing theories explain how some countries developed faster than others and how globalization came about.

Imperialism and Colonization

The first theory suggests that the first European nations to industrialize got a jump on the rest of the world. Beginning in Great Britain around 1750, industrialization spread throughout Western Europe. Powerful new technology produced great wealth, resulting in surplus capital. According to economist John Hobson (1858–1940), the industrialized

nations lacked enough consumers to make it profitable to invest all excess capital at home. Consequently, business leaders persuaded their governments to embark on **imperialism** to take over other countries so they could expand their markets and gain access to cheap raw materials.

Backed by the powerful armaments developed by their new technology, the industrialized nations found easy prey elsewhere (Harrison, 1993). The result was **colonization**—more powerful nations made colonies out of weaker ones. After invading and subduing a country, colonizers left a controlling force to exploit its labour and natural resources. At one point, there was virtually a free-for-all among European industrialized nations as they rushed to divide the continent of Africa. As Europe sliced it into pieces, even tiny Belgium got in the act and acquired the Congo—a country 75 times its own size. While the powerful European nations planted national flags in a colony and sent representatives to directly run the government, the United States, after it industrialized, usually chose to plant corporate flags in a colony and let corporations dominate the territory's government. Central and South America are prime examples of U.S. *economic imperialism*. No matter the form, whether benevolent or harsh, the purpose was the same—to exploit another nation's people and resources for the benefit of a "mother" country.

Western imperialism and colonization shaped the least industrialized nations (Martin, 1994). In some instances, the most industrialized nations were so powerful that to divide their spoils, they drew lines across a map, creating new states without regard for tribal or cultural considerations (Kennedy, 1993). Britain and France followed this policy in North Africa and parts of the Middle East, which explains why the national boundaries of Libya, Saudi Arabia, Kuwait, and other nations are so straight.

World System Theory

Sociologist Immanuel Wallerstein (1974, 1979, 1984, 1990) proposed a **world system theory**. Since the 1500s, Wallerstein argued, economic, political, social, and cultural interactions have grown between nations. Today, these links are so great that they tie most of the world's countries together. At the beginning of the expansion of capitalism from its European origins, Wallerstein identified four groups of interconnected nations. The first group is comprised of the *core nations*, those that first embraced capitalism. These regions (Britain, France, Holland, and later Germany) grew rich and powerful. The second group—the nations around the Mediterranean—Wallerstein called the **semiperiphery**. Their economies stagnated as a result of their dependence on trade with the core nations. The third group, the **periphery**, or fringe, consists of the Eastern European countries. Because they were primarily limited to selling cash crops to the core nations, their economies developed even less. The fourth group, the *external area*, includes most of Africa and Asia. These nations were left out of the development

Inside a maquiladora in Matamoros, Mexico. The steering wheels are for North American auto makers.

EDAE0194124   Matamoros, Mexico: April, 2006. Steering wheel manufacturing at Delphi Delco Electronica de Mexico, a maquiladora plant across the U.S. border that makes parts for General Motors cars. Delphi has about 11,000 Mexican workers in seven factories near Matamoros. ©Bob Daemmrich / The Image Works

of capitalism and had few economic connections with the core nations.

Capitalism's relentless expansion gave birth to a **capitalist world economy**, dominated by the most industrialized nations. This economy is so all-encompassing that today no single region is outside the reach of global capitalism. All the nations of the world can be classified as core, semiperiphery, or periphery.

CANADA AS A SEMIPERIPHERAL COUNTRY At a time when most sociologists and political economists argued that Canada was a developed core nation, one of the authors of this text, a graduate student of Immanuel Wallerstein in the mid 1970s, tackled the question of whether this was true or whether Canada displayed the characteristics of a semiperipheral country. In an article entitled "Rich but Semiperipheral: Canada's Ambiguous Position in the World Economy," Dan Glenday (1989) presented evidence for Canada as a semiperipheral nation. Canada's major economic sectors, with the exception of banking, insurance, and transportation, are heavily foreign owned and/or controlled. Canada ships its natural resources to the United States, Japan, and China, but operates its own direct investment outlets in the Caribbean and in other peripheral countries of the world economy.

Why was this important? Semiperipheral countries, according to Wallerstein, possess unique characteristics. First, they act like core countries when trading with the periphery, but appear to behave as peripheral nations when engaged in economic relations with core regions. Semiperipheral nations also display direct and immediate interest in the control of the market at both internal and international levels (Glenday, 1989:238). Clearly, from the point of view of global economic relations, Canada behaved and still behaves like a semiperipheral country.

Glenday argued that Canada's state policies, such as the Free Trade Agreement and, later, the North American Free Trade Agreement, were critical in defining our status in the world economy. Would these initiatives raise Canada's status in the world economy and thereby increase economic and social advantages for all Canadians? Or would they push Canada down, distancing it from the core countries, and, as a result, negatively impacting our economic and social future?

Recently, Glenday (2011b) undertook an assessment of how these and other state policies affect Canada's position in the world economy. While Canada remains defined as a rich nation, it is sliding downward economically.

Focus Question

How does Canada's descent impact the kind of job opportunities available to young Canadians, the social choices we can make, and the life chances for this and future generations?

Developed core countries offer their citizens access to many economic, social, medical, and cultural advantages, especially when compared to poorer peripheral countries. In relation to semiperipheral countries such as Canada, core countries such as France, Germany, Great Britain, and Japan are better off economically, socially, and culturally. Canada's good fortune lies in our rich endowment of natural resources, from oil and gas to gold and diamonds. Our natural resources are exported to other countries, where they are processed and re-sold in the global marketplace, expanding employment, social choices, and life chances in those regions. Today, Canadians in Alberta and Saskatchewan benefit from the export of oil and natural gas. Tomorrow, Canadians in Newfoundland and Nova Scotia will likely benefit from the discovery and exploitation of offshore natural resources. Instead of unifying the country, the uneven distribution of natural resources is transforming Canada into a patchwork of natural resource "sheikdoms." How long will our good fortune last? On what other industries is our economy being built? These questions must be addressed.

INFORMATION TECHNOLOGY AND THE NEWS As noted at the beginning of the chapter, the extensive movement of capital, technology, people, and ideas between nations that was ushered in by the expansion of capitalism is called **globalization** (Kanter, 1997). Although globalization has been under way for several hundred years, today's new forms of communication and transportation have greatly intensified the process.

Our extensive interconnection has been made possible in part by the existence of cable news. Satellite, fibre-optic, and other technologies bring events that are happening in remote parts of the world into our living rooms. Communications technology has made the world smaller, with international outlets such as CNN, Fox News, the BBC, and Al Jazeera creating a "global news village" in which those with the means to can watch stories from around the world. People can now claim certain commonalities on which to base a shared experience even though they live in very different cultures.

Conversely, much technology is owned and controlled by a small group of companies and, as a result, has made the world more divisive—the heavy influence of "Americanized" news underscores the disparity between the United States and the rest of the world. Instead of serving to unite the global news village, the news often inserts a wedge between civilizations. Deep divisions about how to interpret what is happening in the world are reproduced in news presentations worldwide. All societies today, no matter where they are, are part of a global social system with built-in contradictions.

Dependency Theory

The third theory is sometimes difficult to distinguish from world system theory. **Dependency theory** stresses how the least industrialized nations became dependent on the most industrialized nations (Cardoso, 1972; Furtado, 1984). According to dependency theory, the first nations to industrialize turned other nations into plantations and mines, harvesting or extracting whatever they needed to meet their growing appetite for raw materials and exotic foods. As a result, many of the least industrialized nations began to specialize in single cash crops. Brazil became a coffee plantation for the most industrialized nations. Nicaragua and other Central American countries specialized in bananas (hence the term "banana republic"). Chile became the primary source of tin, and Zaire (then the Belgian Congo) was transformed into a rubber plantation. Nations in the Middle East were turned into gigantic oil wells. A major point of dependency theory is that the domination of the least industrialized nations rendered them unable to develop independent economies. There is substantial evidence that as capital has moved around the world, poverty has increased and quality of life for millions of people has deteriorated. The process of globalization has accelerated economic competition among countries. To compete with one another in world markets, many nations have lowered wages, eliminated worker support programs and environmental protection, decreased social spending, and dismantled public

health care and other essential services (Brecher & Costello, 1998; McNally, 2002). Sociologists such as James Petras and Henry Veltmeyer (2001) argue that globalization is a modern form of imperialism that advances the interests of the powerful and privileged and neither enhances quality of life nor extends social justice to ordinary people.

Anthony Giddens's "Runaway World: How Globalization Is Reshaping our Lives"

In a series of the BBC Reith Lectures given in 1999, Anthony Giddens outlined his argument about how the process of globalization, with its ever-increasing reliance on what he called "decontextualized knowledge"—expert systems built on data derived from information and communications technologies and transported via the internet—deepens the questioning of traditional views. These views, bounded by local knowledge and religious precepts, influence our interpersonal relationships.

On an individual level, Giddens argued that the loosening of traditional values by globalization continues the Enlightenment's project of secularization by expanding people's capacity to live as independent, self-directed persons. However, globalization as we now experience it tears away all previously held, sacred beliefs about the family, marriage, and sexuality, and substitutes what Giddens called the "pure relationship." A pure relationship is based upon communication; that is, "talk or dialogue is the basis of making the relationship work" (2010:62). Couples today have recourse to "experts" to help them raise children, resolve marriage difficulties, or assist in the making of "correct" financial decisions for retirement. These experts are modelled after the expert systems governing today's processes of globalization. When communication breaks down, couples are free to break up and search for new partners. Giddens also argued that "gays rather than heterosexuals have been pioneers in discovering the new world of relationships and exploring its possibilities" (2010:64). On the negative side, he acknowledged the potential increase in personal anxieties caused by losing what he termed "ontological security"—"a sense of continuity and order in the events of an individual's life" (Giddens, 1991:243)

Culture of Poverty

An entirely different explanation of global poverty was proposed by economist John Kenneth Galbraith (1979), who contends that the least industrialized nations were held back by their own cultures. Building on the ideas of anthropologist Oscar Lewis (1966a, 1966b), Galbraith argued that some nations are crippled by a **culture of poverty**, a way of life that perpetuates poverty from one generation to the next. Most of the world's poor live in rural areas, where they barely eke out a living from the land. Their marginal life offers little room for error or risk, so they tend to stick closely to tried-and-true,

✳ Explore the reading "The Uses of Global Poverty: How Economic Inequality Benefits the West" on **MySocLab**.

traditional ways, according to Galbraith. Experimenting with new farming or manufacturing techniques is threatening, because if they fail, the result could be hunger or death. Their religion also reinforces traditionalism, for it teaches fatalism, the acceptance of one's lot in life as God's will.

Evaluating the Theories

Most sociologists prefer imperialism, world system theory, and dependency theory to Galbraith's culture of poverty theory, given that the latter places blame on the victim—the poor nations themselves. It faults the characteristics of poor nations rather than international arrangements that benefit the most industrialized nations at their expense. But even taken together, these theories yield only part of the picture, as becomes evident from the example of Japan. After World War II, with a religion that stressed fatalism and two major cities destroyed by atomic bombs, Japan—through stripped of its colonies—became an economic powerhouse that turned the Western world on its head. Looking at detailed socio-historical national studies examining the way in which culture, political structure, and class relations affect global economic positioning may provide us with the clearest understanding of globalization, inequality, and development. On the other hand, Giddens points sociologists in a different direction by focusing attention on globalization's impact on interpersonal relationships in the most industrialized nations.

Focus Question

Which theory or theories do you think most adequately explain globalization?

The Structures of Globalization

Regardless of how globalization developed, why do the same countries remain rich year after year, while the rest stay poor? Let's look at how world inequality is maintained by some of the structures of globalization.

Neocolonialism

Sociologist Michael Harrington (1977) argued that nineteenth-century colonialism was replaced by twentieth-century **neocolonialism**. When World War II changed public sentiment about sending soldiers and colonists to weaker countries, the most industrialized nations turned to international markets as a way of controlling the least industrialized nations. These powerful nations determine how much they will pay for tin from Bolivia, copper from Peru, coffee from Brazil, and so forth. They also move hazardous industries into the least industrialized nations.

As many of us learn, falling behind on a debt often means that we find ourselves dangling at the end of a string pulled by our creditor. The same is true for neocolonialism. Selling weapons and other manufactured goods to the least industrialized nations on credit turns those countries into eternal debtors. The capital they need to develop their own industries goes instead to debt, ever bloated with mounting interest. As debtors, these nations are also vulnerable to trading terms dictated by the agents of globalization, such as the IMF and World Bank (Tordoff, 1992; Carrington, 1993).

Thus, although the least industrialized nations have their own governments—whether elected or dictatorships—they remain almost as dependent on the most industrialized nations as they were when those nations occupied them.

Transnational Corporations

Transnational or **multinational corporations**, companies that operate across many national boundaries, also help maintain the global dominance of the most industrialized nations. In some cases, multinational corporations directly exploit the least industrialized nations. A prime example is the United Fruit Company, which controlled national and local politics in Central America for decades, running these nations as fiefdoms for the company's own profit while the U.S. Marines waited in the wings in case the company's interests needed to be backed up. Most commonly, however, transnational corporations help maintain globalization simply by doing business. A single transnational may do mining in several countries, do manufacturing in many others, and run transportation and marketing networks around the globe. No matter where profits are made or where they are reinvested, the primary beneficiaries are the most industrialized nations, and especially the one in which the multinational corporation has its world headquarters. As Michael Harrington (1977) stressed, the real profits are made in processing the products and in controlling their distribution—profits that are withheld from the least industrialized nations. For more on multinational corporations, see Chapter 11.

Transnational corporations try to work closely with the elite of the least industrialized nations (Lipton, 1979; Waldman, 1995; Sklair, 2001). Those elite, who live a sophisticated upper-class life in the major cities of their home countries, send their children to Oxford, the Sorbonne, McGill, or Harvard to be educated. Multinational corporations funnel investments to this small circle of power, whose members favour projects such as building laboratories and computer centres in capital cities, projects that do not help the vast majority of people living in poor, remote villages eking out a meagre living on small plots of land.

The end result is an informal partnership between transnational corporations and the elite of the least industrialized nations. The elite benefit by receiving subsidies (or payoffs); the corporations gain access to the countries' raw materials, labour, and market. Both benefit through political stability, which is necessary to keep the partnership alive.

This is not the full story, however. Transnational corporations also play a role in changing the process of development in some countries, such as in India and China. This is an unintentional by-product of their worldwide search for cheap resources and labour. By moving manufacturing from the most industrialized nations with high labour costs to the least industrialized nations with low labour costs, they not only exploit cheap labour, but, in some cases, also bring prosperity to certain regions within those nations. Although workers in the least industrialized nations are paid a pittance, it is more than they can earn elsewhere. With new factories come opportunities to develop new skills and a capital base. This does not occur in all nations, but the Pacific Rim nations, nicknamed the "Asian tigers," are remarkable. They have developed such a strong capital base that they have begun to rival the older capitalist nations.

Technology and the Maintenance of Global Domination

The race between the most and least industrialized nations to develop and apply new information technologies can be compared to a marathon runner competing against a one-legged man. The vast profits amassed by multinational corporations allow the most industrialized nations to invest huge sums in the latest technology. Walmart, along with a few restaurant chains, controls 54 percent of the direct sales market in Mexico, with 687 stores in 71 cities (Ribeiro, 2005). Multinationals often use technologies to track their customers' purchases and streamline production processes in order to shave what sometimes amounts to only a fraction of a cent off costs. Gillette spent $100 million to adjust its output "on an hourly basis" (Zachary, 1995). Many least industrialized nations would greatly benefit from a $100 million investment in their national economy, much less to fine-tune production in a single organization. In short, new technologies accrue even more advantages for the most industrialized nations.

Anti-Globalization

José Bové is considered by many to be an important representative of the anti-globalization movement. He is widely known for campaigning against genetically modified crops and has led protests in Brazil and France. His most publicized protest was directed at the cheese used by McDonald's restaurants, which he viewed as the most effective way to protest U.S. trade restrictions against locally made Rocquefort cheese. On August 12, 1999, Bové led a group known as the Peasant Confederation to vandalize a McDonald's restaurant in Millau, France. He was sentenced to three months in prison and, together with nine others, became known as the Millau 10. ("Bové Loses," BBC, March 22, 2001).

Targeting the negative practices of transnational corporations is one major strategy of the anti-globalization movement. Such protests usually focus on corporations that do the following:

- aim for the maximization of profits
- locate where the salaries are lowest
- employ children and women in factories
- destroy the environment through production
- obliterate cultural identities
- amass greater power than many nation states

Eight-year-old Mahashury is a bonded laborer who was exchanged by her parents for a 2000 rupee loan (about $14). To repay the loan, Mahashury must do construction work for a year. She will receive one meal a day and a single set of clothing for the year. Because this centuries-old practice is now illegal, the master bribes Indian officials who inform him when they are going to inspect the construction site.

A second target of anti-globalization protestors is international organizations such as the World Bank, the International Monetary Fund, and the World Trade Organization, whose objective is to promote policies of free trade and balanced state budgets. According to the movement, such policies put an intolerable weight on the shoulders of the poor countries by increasing debt loads and pushing for reductions in social expenditures. Often, protesters request that rich countries "forgive" the debts owed to them by poorer nations.

World Social Forum

Founded in 2001 in Porto Alegre, Brazil, the World Social Forum (WSF) is not an organization or formal group; rather, it uses the internet as an "open space" to bring together social movements, organizations, NGOs, and individuals to discuss alternatives to globalization. In its own words, the WSF seeks to bring together all those who oppose "neo-liberal globalization" and "imperialism in all its forms." It meets in January of every year in order to counterbalance the discussions of the World Economic Forum, which is a

Geneva-based foundation whose annual meetings in Davos, Switzerland bring together leaders of the most powerful economic organizations (companies with annual earnings over $1 billion), national political leaders (presidents, prime ministers, and others), and selected intellectuals.

Globalization, Forced Child Labour, and Slavery

Before attending university, many young Canadians work part-time. However, in all provinces and territories, there are several laws prohibiting employers from hiring a young person for full-time work (see Chapter 11 for a description of the Canadian labour market and labour laws). The most important restriction is compulsory school attendance. In every province, a young person must attend school until graduation from high school or until she or he reaches the age of 18 (Minimum age for employment, October 15, 2006). At least five Canadian provinces allow children under the age of 14 to work with permission from their parents and the Director of Employment Standards (www.cbc.ca/news/background/child-labour/childlabour-canada.html).

The International Labour Organization, a United Nations agency, has established conventions regarding child labour. Convention 138 deals with the minimum age of working and recommends a minimum age of 15 for employment of any kind. Convention 182 deals with dangerous work environments for children. On June 22, 2008, Canada signed Convention 182 but not Convention 138 (http://webfusion.ilo.org/public/db/standards/normes/appl/appl-ratif8conv.cfm?Lang=EN).

The rich nations have not rushed forward to resolve the global inequalities. The IMF is a specialized United Nations agency with 182 member countries. It was created in 1944 to help maintain the world monetary system. The World Bank was set up as a lender of last resort to the least industrialized nations. The WTO (which is a successor to other international trade organizations) is intended to bring countries together to improve international trade and, indirectly, encourage global standards in environmental protections, worker protections, and so on. The history of the various global governing agencies is complex, but their roles remain hotly debated and global inequality is a growing concern.

Even more direct efforts at assisting developing countries through the provision of foreign aid have had limited results and elicited only limited enthusiasm on the part of richer nations. Only Denmark, the Netherlands, Sweden, Norway, and Luxembourg have met the United Nations target of contributing 0.7 percent of their GDP to foreign aid. Canada contributes a scant 0.25 percent, behind much smaller economies such as Portugal and New Zealand. Indeed, Canadian foreign aid contributions in 2008 were at their lowest level in 30 years. Interestingly, at the bottom of the pack of 22 wealthy nations providing developmental aid to foreign countries is the United States, contributing 0.10 percent of its GDP ("Saturday Special," 2002:A25).

Currently, about one in three of the world's 6 billion people lives in a state of extreme poverty, and inhabitants in 21 countries are subsisting on average incomes of less than U.S.$1000 a year, while at the wealthy end of the scale, citizens of 17 wealthy nations average U.S.$20 000 a year. As widely publicized by Live Aid and other anti-poverty groups, if less than 1 percent of the income of the wealthiest countries was redirected to the poorest, almost everyone on the globe would have enough to eat as well as adequate health and education (Williams, 2004). However, the future for global poverty appears bleak. The global population is expected to grow by another 2 billion people over the next 25 years, 97 percent of whom will live in poorer countries (Rees, 2002; Crane, 2000).

Certainly, if the growing strains of global and local inequalities are not addressed, the negative consequences will likely impact both the rich and poor (Laxer, 1998). Globalization—with its world trade and world travel in the midst of a world economy—ensures that we all share the outcomes. Ultimately, while the wealthy nations have attempted to create "gated communities," disease and environmental destruction cannot be kept out. If poor countries continue to plunder their natural resources in order to survive and in the process disregard environmental consequences, everyone on the planet will bear the results.

While the restrictions vary between provinces and Canada has yet to sign Convention 138, the exploitation of child labour in Canada is not knowingly tolerated. Child labour exists in many other parts of the globe, however. Globalization exposes the poorest people to some of the harshest working conditions. Consider chocolate, for example. Many Canadians and Americans were shocked to learn in early 2000 that some of their favourite candies might have been produced by child labourers in West Africa. In 2000, the U.S. State Department, Knight Ridder, and the BBC reported that roughly 15 000 children worked in conditions of forced labour picking beans in Ghana and Ivory Coast. Trafficked from extremely poor countries such as Mali and Burkina Faso, the children worked on some of the 1.5 million small cocoa farms in West Africa. These farms produce more than half the world's cacao, used to make candy, cookies, or cocoa butter for cosmetics. Attempts have been made to curb child labour on the cocoa plantations. One recent result is the Cocoa Protocol, a partnership of the major chocolate companies, government officials, and others. It called for a deadline of July 1, 2005, to ensure that all cocoa bean products would be grown and processed without violating internationally-accepted labour standards. Unfortunately, child labour still thrives on cocoa plantations even amid efforts by activists and others who have filed suits against Nestlé, ADM, and Cargill for their violations of international child labour laws.

All forms of slavery have not been eliminated. Child slavery in the form of the trafficking of young girls for the sex trade affects all parts of the globe, even Canada (see Chapter 6 for a more in-depth discussion of slavery).

Killing Little Girls: An Ancient and Thriving Practice

"The Mysterious Case of the Missing Girls" could have been the title of this box. Around the globe, for every 100 girl births, about 105 boys are born. In China, however, for every 100 baby girls, the total jumps to 120 baby boys. Given China's huge population, this means that China has about *30 million* more males than females under the age of 20 (Yardley, 2010). Why aren't there 30 million girls?

The answer is *female infanticide*, the killing of baby girls. When a Chinese woman goes into labour, the village midwife sometimes grabs a bucket of water. If the newborn is a girl, she is plunged into the water before she can draw her first breath.

At the root of China's sexist infanticide is economics. The people are poor, and they have no pensions. When parents can no longer work, sons support them. In contrast, a daughter must be married off, at great expense, and at that point her obligations transfer to her husband and his family.

"Raising a girl is like watering someone else's plant," they say in India, where female infanticide is also common.

In China, the past few years have brought even larger percentages of boy babies. The reason, again, is economics, but this time with a new twist. When China adopted capitalism, opportunities for travel and trade opened up—but primarily to men, for it is not thought appropriate for women to travel alone. With men finding themselves in a better position to bring money home, parents have one more reason to want boys.

The gender ratio is so lopsided that for Chinese

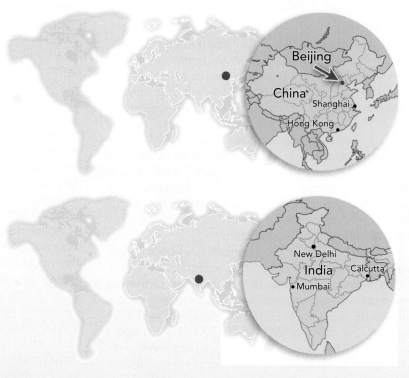

in their twenties, there are six bachelors for every five potential brides. Politicians

The sign above this couple waiting in a New Delhi doctor's office reminds patients that they should not abort fetuses just because they are female, that girls are also desirable children.

fear that the men who cannot marry— "bare branches," as they call them—will become disgruntled. Lacking the stabilizing influences of marriage and children, these bare branches might become a breeding ground for political dissent. To head this off, officials have begun a campaign to stop the drowning of girl babies and the abortion of female fetuses.

For Your Consideration

What is it about China's culture that encourages female infanticide? Do you think China's female infanticide will stop before women hold as much power as men? What do you think can be done to reduce its incidence? Why do you think this issue receives so little publicity and is not a priority with world leaders?

Sources: Jordan, 2000; Dugger, 2001; Eckholm, 2002; French, 2004; Riley, 2004; Sang-Hun, 2007; Yardley, 2007.

A Concluding Note

Consider again the two families in the opening vignette. Remember that they represent two worlds of development—that is, globalization and inequality. Their life chances—from access to material possessions to their opportunities for education and even the likely age at which they will die—are profoundly affected by globalization and its consequences. The division of the globe into interconnected units of nations with more or less wealth and more or less power and prestige is much more than a matter of theoretical interest. In fact, it is your life we are talking about.

WHAT IS GLOBALIZATION?

What is globalization?
Globalization involves the interaction and integration of increasing numbers of people in the world through international trade and investment, travel and tourism, and information technology and the mass media. p. 95.

GLOBALIZATION AND PATTERNS OF MOVEMENT OF PEOPLE

How does globalization impact the movement of people?
The globalization of communications technology, the pervasiveness of mass communication—including television, film, videos, and music—and cheap air travel open the world to more people through increased tourism and immigration. p. 96.

How does globablization impact the paid and unpaid work of women?
Globalization involves cutting costs, especially labour costs. This means factories and offices are closed in developed countries and transplanted to less developed countries, where labour—and women's labour in particular—is cheap. In the developed world, globalization means depressing wages and benefits for workers, especially vulnerable workers such as immigrant women. pp. 96–97.

GLOBALIZATION: THE ISSUES

What are the main arguments for and against globalization?
Proponents of globalization argue that poor countries and their citizens benefit economically from increased employment opportunities and rising standards of living. Opponents of globalization point to the increased wealth, power, and privilege enjoyed by the developed and rich parts of the world that come at the expense of the less developed and poorer regions of the globe. Democracy, human rights, and labour rights are said to be undermined by institutions such as the IMF and the World Bank. pp. 97–98.

SOCIOLOGICAL THEORIES OF GLOBAL AND SOCIAL ECONOMIC DEVELOPMENT

What are the main sociological theories of economic and social development?
The main sociological theories that seek to account for global stratification are imperialism and colonization, world system theory, dependency theory, and the culture of poverty. p. 102. The model favoured by the authors of this text divides the world's nations into three groups: most industrialized, industrializing, and least industrialized. This layering represents relative property, power, and prestige. The oil-rich nations are an exception. pp. 102–103.

What makes Canada a semiperipheral country and why is this important to know?
Canada's major economic sectors, with the exception of banking, insurance, and transportation, are heavily foreign-owned or controlled. Canada ships its natural resources primarily to core countries but has direct investment outlets in the Caribbean and in other peripheral countries of the world economy. Canada's state policies, such as the FTA and NAFTA, which make us "open for business" to globalization, have consequences for Canadian employment and social and life choices. p. 103.

capitalist world
   economy   103
colonization   102
culture of poverty   104
dependency theory   104

export processing
   zones   97
globalization   104
imperialism   102

multinational
   corporations   105
neocolonialism   105
periphery   102

semiperiphery   102
transnational
   corporations   105
world system theory   102

All URLs listed are current as of the printing of this text.

Planeta.com
www.planeta.com
Planeta.com is the first website focusing on ecotourism, conservation, and tourism's effects on local communities.

The Stephen Lewis Foundation
www.stephenlewisfoundation.org
The Stephen Lewis Foundation website provides information on the AIDS pandemic in Africa and the need for greater action from Western countries. Stephen Lewis, a prominent Canadian, is the United Nations special envoy for HIV/AIDS in Africa.

Runaway World: A BBC 1999 Lecture Series
by Anthony Giddens
http://news.bbc.co.uk/hi/english/static/events/reith_99
This website is a useful resource for students interested in learning more about globalization. It provides access to text, audio, and video lectures given by Anthony Giddens, who plainly and succinctly dissects the links between globalization and its impact on tradition, the family, and democracy.

Globalization and the Student Loan Crisis
www.globalization101.org/
globalization-and-the-student-loan-crisis
Sponsored by The Levin Institute (a graduate institute of the State University of New York), this website provides a useful overview of globalization and the student loan crisis.

Anti-Globalization
www.anti-marketing.com/anti-globalization.html
An introduction to anti-globalization, including links to anti-globalization and pro-globalization organizations.

World Social Forum 2012
http://english.pravda.ru/society/stories/22-01-2012/
120295-World_Social_Forum_2012-0
The main webpage of the World Social Forum for 2012.

1. Do you think that the low wage factories of multinational corporations, located in such countries as Mexico or China, represent exploitation or opportunity? Why?
2. Think of something you use every day—such as a cellphone or iPod, or Starbucks or Tim Horton's coffee—and find out where it was manufactured and assembled, marketed, and sold. How easy was it to find out? What did your journey of discovery teach you about globalization?

MySocLab

Explore the topics covered in this chapter on MySocLab. Interactive resources include a study plan, cumulative exams, a multimedia library, MySocLab eReadings, and access to the MySocLab Video Series.

6

SOCIAL INEQUALITY
THE CANADIAN EXPERIENCE IN A GLOBAL CONTEXT

LEARNING OUTCOMES

After you have studied this chapter, you will be able to answer the following questions:

1. What is social class, and how do sociologists measure it?
2. How do nations maintain social stratification?
3. How does social class affect people?
4. What are the three types of social mobility?
5. Who becomes poor and why?
6. Why is poverty in Canada and around the world so frequently ignored?

OMAR leaned back in his chair and stared at the computer screen. It was a bit of a ritual to end the day by going on Facebook and catching up with friends. And today had been a great day. He had just attended his graduation for his four-year degree in sociology and would be heading up to his girlfriend's Muskoka cottage for the weekend. He felt as though he was at the beginning of his real life.

There had been times he'd thought he'd never get here. When his parents had split up 10 years earlier, things had been really tough. His mother had only been able to find part-time work and his dad had been laid off. For six months, they had to get welfare. He remembered his mother sitting in the dark crying and the sting of humiliation he'd felt when the case worker had come to check out their apartment. He let out a long, slow breath. That was all behind him.

Omar clicked on the screen and light filled the room. He thought about his friend Bailey, whom he'd met through a gamers' website. Omar smiled to himself; even though Bailey was Mexican-American, his mom had chosen to name him "Bailey." Bailey was one of the brightest, most creative people Omar had ever met, and yet there he was, stuck working nights at some fast-food place. He was supposed to be studying toward a practical nursing degree and was getting government assistance to pay his tuition and books, but he had to have a job to pay for rent, food, and a bus pass. His family could not help, since his mother and her new boyfriend had moved to Juarez with Omar's younger siblings.

Omar suddenly felt deeply sad as he remembered Bailey's delight at getting a second-hand bike so he could cycle to school instead of paying for the bus. Cycling in the Arizona heat was a whole other reality. Omar glanced

Education is often used as a mechanism for social mobility.

Obtaining and retaining a job position are key to class location.

through an email. Great! Now there were bed bugs in Bailey's apartment complex and he was sleeping in the bathtub.

Omar's computer beeped and a message popped up from Miguel in Barcelona. They had met when Miguel had come to Canada as a university exchange student. Miguel was crazy and fun and his family wanted him to be a doctor. But there hadn't been much talk about medical school recently. The recession had rocked Miguel's parents; both had lost their government jobs and had been forced to move in with Miguel's grandparents, who at least were getting pension income. Judging by his texts, Miguel was spending most of his time hanging out in the streets just to get away from the crowded apartment.

Omar turned off his screen and let darkness fill the room once again. For a moment, he felt overwhelmed. What was going happen to his friends? Not just Bailey and Miguel, but also Neeva, who'd sent out hundreds of résumés but hadn't found a job, or his older brother, Kalil, who had just accepted a six-month unpaid internship with a software development firm so he could get some work experience.

The screen glowed back to life as Omar opened his You-Tube favourites. The Fonz appeared. Sometimes, TV was the best way to take his mind off things.

What Is Social Stratification?

Ask any Canadian on the street about the distribution of resources in this country and she or he will say there are wealthy Canadians, poor Canadians, and some in between. The layering of groups of people within a nation is called *social stratification*. It is one of the most significant topics discussed in this text, for it affects not only how we see ourselves and others around us, but also our chances—for a good career, home ownership, partnerships, and even the age at which we die.

Social stratification also affects our orientations to life and the way we see the world. If you relied on a homeless shelter in Vancouver for survival, you would expect hunger to be part of life and not be too surprised when people died around you. If you lived life as Justin Bieber or Carly Rae Jepsen, you would have quite a different view of the world.

It is important to emphasize that social stratification does not refer to individuals. *It is a way of ranking large groups of people into a hierarchy that shows their relative privileges.* **Social stratification** is a system in which people are divided into layers according to their relative power, property, and prestige.

Let's examine how social inequalities profoundly affect everyone's chances in life. But first we'll review the major systems of social stratification.

Systems of Social Stratification

Every society stratifies its members in some form. Some, such as agricultural societies, draw firm lines that separate group from group, while others, such as hunting and gathering societies, show much greater equality. Regardless of its forms, however, the existence of social stratification is universal. There are four major systems of social stratification: slavery, caste, clan, and class.

Slavery

Slavery, with its essential characteristic of *ownership of some people by others*, has been common throughout world history. The Israelites of the Old Testament kept slaves, as did the ancient Africans. In classical Greece and Rome, slaves worked while free citizens engaged in politics and the arts. Slavery was least common among nomads, especially hunters and gatherers, and most common in agricultural societies (Landtman, 1938/1968).

> **Watch** what Professor Susan Ostrander says about what sociologists mean when they talk about social class on **MySocLab.**

Contrary to popular assumption, slavery was not always based on racism, but on one of three other factors. The first was debt. In some cultures, an individual who could not pay a debt could be enslaved by the creditor. The second was a violation of the law. Instead of being killed, a murderer or thief might be enslaved by the family of the victim as compensation for their loss. The third was war and conquest. When one group of people conquered another, it was often convenient to enslave at least some of the vanquished (Starna & Watkins, 1991). Historian Gerda Lerner (1986) notes that through this practice the first slaves were women. When men raided a village or camp, they killed the men, raped the women, and then brought the women back as slaves. Women were valued for sexual purposes, reproduction, and extra labour. Slavery, then, was a sign of defeat in battle, of crime, or of debt, and not the sign of an inherently inferior status.

Indentured service, or bonded labour, represents a fuzzy line between a contract and slavery (Main, 1965; Elkins, 1968). Many people who desired to start a new life in early British North America were unable to pay their passage. Ship captains would carry them on credit, depending on someone to "buy their paper" when they arrived. This arrangement provided passage for the penniless, payment for the ships' captains, and servants for wealthier colonists for a set number of years. During that specified period, servants had to serve their master—and could be captured and forcibly returned if they ran away. At the end of the period of indenture, servants became full citizens, able to live where they chose and free to sell their labour.

Between 1869 and the early-1930s, over 100 000 "home children" were sent to Canada from the overcrowded cities of Great Britain. Most worked as indentured servants on farms in Ontario until they were 18 years old.

When colonists found that there were not enough indentured servants to meet their growing need for labour, they tried to enslave Native peoples. This attempt failed miserably, however. Among other reasons, when Native peoples escaped they knew how to survive in the wilderness and were able to make their way back to their tribes. The American colonists then turned to Africans, who were being brought to U.S. colonies and South America by the Dutch, English, Portuguese, and Spanish.

Finding it profitable to make people slaves for life, slave owners developed an **ideology**, a system of beliefs that justifies social arrangements. Essential to an ideology that would justify lifelong slavery was the view that slaves were inferior. Some said that they were locked in a helpless, childlike state, which meant that they needed to be taken care of by superior people—white colonists, of course. Others even contended that slaves were not fully human. With such views, colonists developed elaborate justifications for slavery on the presumed superiority of their own race.

During the French colonial period in Canada (1628–1759), a total of 1132 slaves were transported to New France. During the British colonial era, most slaves were family servants living in urban areas. Slavery never took root in Canada largely because of the short growing season and the high cost of housing and feeding slaves over the winter months. The *British Imperial Act* of 1833/1834 effectively abolished slavery in the British Empire (see www.osblackhistory.com/history.php).

Although slavery was abolished in the United States as a result of the Civil War, patterns of legal discrimination were still prevalent. Until 1954, for example, the United States operated two separate school systems. Even until the 1950s, to keep races from "mixing," it was illegal in Mississippi for a white and an African-American to sit together on the same seat of a car. To allow for African-American chauffeurs, there was no outright ban on both races being in the same car.

SLAVERY TODAY Slavery—also known as human trafficking—has surfaced in current times in Sudan, Mauritania, Niger, and Ivory Coast (Appiah & Bunzl, 2007; Henslin, 2012). This region of Africa has a long history of slavery, and the practice was not officially abolished until 1980 in Mauritania, 1987 in Sudan (Ayittey, 1998), and 2004 in Niger (Andersson, 2005). Although officially abolished, slavery continues to exist.

Caste

The second system of social stratification is caste. Broadly speaking, a **caste system** is a process of placing people in occupational groups. It has pervaded several aspects of

British immigrant children from Dr. Barnardo's Homes at landing stage in Saint John, New Brunswick.

((• **Listen** to documentary photographer Gigi Cohen's report on a form of child slavery taking place in Haiti in "Haiti's Dark Secret" on **MySocLab.**

These photographs, taken at the end of the nineteenth century, illustrate the different worlds social classes produce within the same society. The boys on the left worked full-time when they could get work. They did not go to school, and they had no home. The children on the right, Cornelius and Gladys Vanderbilt, are shown in front of their parents' estate. They went to school and did not work. You can see how the life situations illustrated in these photos would have produced different orientations to the world—and, therefore, politics, ideas, and so on—the stuff of which life is made.

Indian society for centuries. Rooted in religion and based on a division of labour, the caste system, among other things, dictates the type of occupations persons can pursue and the social interactions that they may have. In a caste system, status is determined by birth and is lifelong. Castes are an aspect of Hindu religion. Other religions in India do not follow this system. In sociological terms the basis of a caste system is ascribed status. Societies with this form of stratification try to make certain that the boundaries between castes remain firm. They practise **endogamy**, marriage within their own group, and prohibit intermarriage. To prevent contact between castes, they even develop elaborate rules about ritual pollution, teaching that contact with inferior castes contaminates the superior caste.

INDIA India provides the best example of a caste system. Based on religion rather than race, the caste system has existed in India for almost 3000 years (Chandra, 1993a, 1993b; Jaffrelot, 2006). India has four main castes, or *varnas*. These are subdivided into thousands of specialized subcastes, or *jati*, with each *jati* working in a specific occupation. For example, knife-sharpening is done only by members of a particular subcaste.

The *Harijan*, the lowest group, is actually so low that it is beneath the caste system altogether. *Harijans*, along with some *Shudras*, make up India's "untouchables." The most obvious problem with this system was that under its rigidity, the lower castes were prevented from aspiring to climb higher, and therefore social mobility was restricted. Today, the government is sensitive to this historic injustice by reserving seats in colleges and providing job opportunities for these disadvantaged groups.

Although the Indian government abolished the caste system in 1949, the force of centuries-old practices cannot be easily eliminated, and the caste system remains part of everyday life in India (Sharma, 1994). The ceremonies followed at births, marriages, and deaths, for example, are still dictated by caste (Chandra, 1993a). As a result of globalization and in urban India, however, this system is breaking down as people of all castes meet socially or for business. Discriminating against anyone because of their caste for things like club memberships and so on is against the law.

Clan

The **clan system** was once common in agricultural societies. In this system, every individual is linked to a large network of relatives called a **clan**. A clan is like a greatly extended family. Just as in a family, if a clan has a high status, so do individual members. Like a family, allegiance to a clan is a lifelong obligation. The most common form of clan today is the Scottish clan (from Gaelic *clann*, "progeny"). They provide a sense of identity and shared descent to people in Scotland and to their relations throughout the world.

Most clans have their own tartan patterns, usually dating from the nineteenth century, and members of a clan may wear kilts, plaids, sashes, ties, scarves, or other items made of the appropriate tartan as a badge of membership and as a uniform, where appropriate.

Unlike castes, marriages can cross clan lines. In fact, marriages may be used to forge alliances between clans, for the obligations that a marriage establishes between in-laws can bind clans together (Erturk, 1994).

Just as globalization is eroding the lines that separate the castes of India, it also makes clans more fluid, eventually replacing them with social classes.

Class

A **class system**, in contrast to slavery, caste, and clan systems, is much more open, since it is based primarily on money or material possessions. It, too, begins at birth, when an individual is ascribed the status of his or her parents, but, unlike slavery, caste, and clan, one's social class may change as a result of what one achieves (or fails to achieve) in life. However, because of the power of early childhood socialization, we carry some of the subtle "marks" of class, known as *cultural capital*, even after changes in status. In addition, there are no laws that specify occupation on the basis of birth or that prohibit marriage between classes.

A major characteristic of this fourth system, then, is its relatively fluid boundaries. A class system allows for the possibility of **social mobility**—that is, movement up or down the class ladder. The potential for improving one's social circumstances or class is one of the major forces that drives people to go far in school and to work hard. However, the family background inherited by an individual at birth may bestow such obstacles that a child has little chance of climbing very far—or it may provide such privileges that it is almost impossible to fall very far down the class ladder.

Global Stratification and the Status of Women

In *every* society of the world, gender is a basis for social stratification. In no society is gender the sole basis for stratifying people, but gender cuts across *all* systems of social stratification (Huber, 1990). In all systems, on the basis of their gender, people are sorted into categories and given different access to the good things available in their society.

Apparently such distinctions always favour males. It is remarkable, for example, that in *every* society of the world, men's earnings are higher than women's. Men's dominance is even more evident when we consider forms of violence committed against women, including rituals such as female circumcision. That most of the world's illiterate are female also drives home women's relative position in society. Of the several hundred million adults who cannot read, about two-thirds are women (UNESCO, 2011b). Because gender affects so much of what happens to us in life, it is the focus of Chapter 7.

What Determines Social Class?

In the early days of sociology, a disagreement arose about the meaning of social class in industrialized societies. Let's compare how Marx and Weber viewed the matter.

Karl Marx: The Means of Production

As discussed in Chapter 1, when the feudal system broke down, masses of peasants were displaced from their traditional lands and occupations. Fleeing to cities, they competed for few available jobs. Offered only a pittance for their labour, they dressed in rags, went hungry, and slept under bridges and in shacks. In contrast, factory owners built mansions, hired servants, and lived in the lap of luxury. Seeing this great disparity between owners and workers,

Karl Marx (1818–1883) concluded that social class depends on a single factor: people's relationship to the **means of production**—the tools, factories, land, and investment capital used to produce wealth (Marx, 1844/1964; Marx & Engels, 1848/1967).

Marx argued that the distinctions people often make between themselves—such as clothing, speech, education, or relative salary—are superficial matters. They camouflage the only real significant dividing line. People either own the means of production (the **bourgeoisie**) or they work for those who do (the **proletariat**). According to Marx, this is the only distinction that counts, and these two classes make up modern society. In short, people's relationship to the means of production determines their social class.

Marx recognized that other groups were part of industrial society: farmers and peasants; a *lumpenproletariat* (marginal people such as migrant workers, beggars, vagrants, and criminals); and a middle class (self-employed professionals). Marx did not consider these groups social classes, however, for they lacked **class consciousness**—a common identity based on their position in the means of production. They did not see themselves as exploited workers whose plight could be solved only by collective action. Consequently, Marx thought of these groups as insignificant in the coming workers' revolution that was destined to overthrow capitalism.

Capital becomes concentrated, Marx said, which makes capitalists and workers increasingly hostile toward one another. When workers recognize capitalists as the source of their oppression, they unite and throw off the chains of their oppressors. In a bloody revolution, they seize the means of production and usher in a classless society, where the few will no longer grow rich at the expense of the many. What holds back the workers' unity and their revolution is **false consciousness**—workers mistakenly identifying with capitalists and their interests. For example, workers with a few dollars in the bank often forget that they are workers and instead see themselves as investors or as capitalists who are about to launch a successful business.

The only distinction worth mentioning, then, is whether a person is an owner or a worker. This decides everything else, Marx stressed, since property determines people's lifestyles, shapes their ideas, and establishes their relationships with one another.

Max Weber: Property, Prestige, and Power

Max Weber (1864–1920) became an outspoken critic of Marx. He asserted that property is only part of the picture. Social class, he said, is actually made up of three components—*property*, *prestige*, and *power* (Gerth & Mills, 1958; Weber, 1922/1968). Some call these the three Ps of social class. (Although Weber used the terms "class," "status," and "power," some sociologists find "property," "prestige," and "power" to be clearer terms. To make them even clearer, some substitute wealth for "property.")

The text describes the many relationships among Weber's three components of social class: property, prestige, and power. What mix of the three do you think apply to John A. Macdonald and Governor General David Johnston?

Property (or wealth), said Weber, is certainly significant in determining a person's standing in society: on that he agreed with Marx. But, added Weber, ownership is not the only significant aspect of property. For example, some powerful people, such as managers of corporations, control the means of production even though they do not own them. If managers can control property for their own benefit—awarding themselves huge bonuses and magnificent perks—it makes no practical difference that they do not own the property they so generously use for their own benefit.

Prestige, the second element in Weber's analysis, is often derived from property, since people tend to look up to the wealthy. Prestige, however, can also be based on other factors. Olympic gold medalists, for example, may not own property, yet they have very high prestige. Some are even able to exchange their prestige for property—such as being paid to say that they start their day with a particular breakfast cereal or for endorsing a brand of sportswear. In other words, property and prestige are not one-way streets: although property can bring prestige, prestige can also bring property.

Power, the third element of Weber's social class, is the ability to control others, even over their objections. Weber agreed with Marx that property is a major source of power, but added that it is not the only source. Prestige can be turned into power. For example, actor Arnold Schwarzenegger became governor of California, and previously, another actor, Ronald Reagan, was president of the United States. For other interrelationships of property, prestige, and power, see Figure 6.1.

Focus Question

What are some of the differences between Marx's and Weber's approaches to social class?

IN SUM

For Marx, social class was based solely on a person's position in relation to the means of production—as a member of either the bourgeoisie or the proletariat—while Weber argued that social class is a combination of property, prestige, and power.

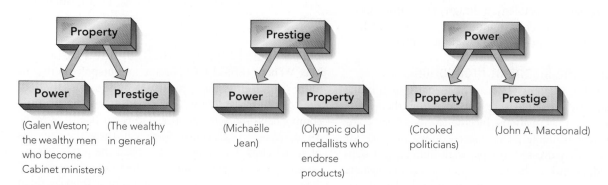

FIGURE 6.1 Weber's Three Components of Social Class and the Interrelationships between Them

Complexities of Inequality

In this chapter, we closely examine social class as a dimension of inequality. However, inequalities are highly complex, and in order to unravel that complexity we must question the interrelationships among various inequalities. We refer to this as **intersectionality**, and feminists and other sociologists who adopt a critical perspective approach studies of inequality by considering the ways in which class, gender, and race intersect (McCall, 2001). In other words, from this perspective, we are not only interested in how each of these dimensions may affect a person's life experiences, but we suggest that it is important to consider class, race, and gender simultaneously, since we may uncover inequalities in the interconnections of these dimensions.

Defining Social Class

"There are the poor and the rich—and then there are you and I, neither poor nor rich." That is about as far as most Canadians' consciousness of social class goes. Let's try to flesh this out.

Our task is made somewhat difficult because sociologists have no clear-cut, agreed-upon definition of social class. As noted above, conflict sociologists (of the Marxist orientation) see only two social classes: those who own the means of production and those who do not. A problem with this view, say most sociologists, is that it lumps too many people together. Physicians and corporate executives with incomes of $250 000 a year are lumped together with hamburger flippers working at McDonald's for $10 000 a year.

Most sociologists agree with Weber that there are more components of social class than a person's relationship to the means of production. Consequently, most sociologists use the components Weber identified and define **social class** as a large group of people who rank closely to one another in wealth, power, and prestige. These three elements separate people into different lifestyles, give them different chances in life, and provide them with distinct ways of looking at the self and the world.

Measuring Social Class

We will examine wealth, power, and prestige in the next section, but first let's look at three different ways of measuring social class.

1. *Subjective method.* The **subjective method** involves asking people what their social class is. Although simple and direct, this approach is filled with problems. First, people may deny that they belong to any class, claiming, instead, that everyone is equal. Second, people may classify themselves according to their aspirations—where they would like to be—rather than where they actually are. Third, when asked which class they belong to, most Canadians identify themselves as middle-class, as do most citizens of industrialized nations (Kelley & Evans, 1995;

Forcese, 1997). This perception removes the usefulness of the subjective method for most purposes.

2. *Reputational method.* In the **reputational method**, people are asked what class others belong to on the basis of their reputations. Social anthropologist W. Lloyd Warner (Warner & Hunt, 1941; Warner, Hunt, Meeker, & Eels, 1949) pioneered this method in a study of a community he called "Yankee City." Its use is limited to smaller communities, where people are familiar with one another's reputation.

   Three of Warner's colleagues used the reputational method to study "Old City," a small southern town in the United States (Davis, Gardner, & Gardner, 1941). They found that just as people at each class level see life differently, so too do they carry around different pictures of society's classes. People see finer divisions at their own class level, but tend to lump people together as one social class as they recede from them. Thus, people at the top see several groups of people at the top, but tend to lump the bottom into a single unit ("the poor"), while people at the bottom see several distinctions among the poor but tend to see just "the rich" at the top.

3. *Objective method.* In the **objective method**, researchers rank people according to objective criteria such as wealth, power, and prestige. This method has the advantage of letting others know exactly what measurements were made, so that they can test them.

Given the three methods of determining social class, sociologists primarily use the objective method. The studies reported in this chapter are examples of the objective approach.

The Components of Social Class

Let's look at how sociologists measure the three components of social class: wealth, power, and prestige.

Wealth

The primary dimension of social class is **wealth**. Wealth consists of property and income. Property comes in many forms, such as buildings, land, animals, machinery, cars, stocks, bonds, businesses, and bank accounts. Income is money received as wages, rents, interest, royalties, or the proceeds from a business.

PROPERTY Overall, Canadians are worth a hefty sum. Most of this wealth is in the form of real estate, corporate stocks, bonds, and business assets and is highly concentrated. If we consider wealth distribution, in 1984, families in the top 10 percent held 52 percent of aggregate household wealth, while the bottom 50 percent held only 5 percent. This concentration of wealth increased from 1984 to 1999 and again from 1999 to 2005. By 2005, the top 10 percent increased their share of Canadians' net worth to 58 percent, and, in fact, it was only those in the

THINKING CRITICALLY ABOUT SOCIAL CONTROVERSY

Canada's Rich and Poor: Miles Apart

Each year on January 3, about the time most Canadians begin a new year of work, Canada's 100 top-paid CEOs will already be having a good year. They'll pocket the equivalent of the national average wage ($44 366 in 2010) by noon that day. They will continue to earn the average Canadian wage every nine hours and 33 minutes for the rest of the year. That's what happens when your income is $8.38 million, the average annual earnings of Canada's 100 best-paid CEOs in 2010. These individuals make more than 155 times someone working full-time for a full year on the average Canadian annual wage. For Canadians making minimum wage, the gap is even more astounding. In the wee hours of New Year's Day, the top-paid CEOs will pocket what will take a minimum-wage worker the entire year to earn. Every four hours and four minutes, they will keep pocketing the annual income of a full-time, full-year minimum-wage worker (Mackenzie, 2007; 2012).

Are those at the top of the income ladder really worth that much? And are those at the bottom worth that little?

Power and wealth are very concentrated within Canadian society. Table 6.1 provides a list of Canada's 10 wealthiest individuals or families and their major corporate fields. The web of ownership, wealth, power, and property weaves a complex network, making it very difficult to indicate precisely the nature of this concentration, although sociologists such as Porter (1965) and Clement (1975), along with journalists Peter Newman (1979) and Diane Francis (1986), have all demonstrated it (Forcese, 1997). Earlier estimates suggest that, for example, a third of all corporate assets in Canada are controlled by only 12 families and five conglomerates, while about 80 percent of the Toronto Stock Exchange's list of 300 companies are controlled by eight conglomerates (Allahar & Coté, 1998).

TABLE 6.1 Canada's Super-Rich Top 10

	Billions of Canadian Dollars
1. Thomson family (media)	$21.34
2. Galen Weston (groceries)	$8.0
3. James (J.K.) Arthur and the estate of John (Jack) Irving	$7.8
4. Rogers Family (media)	$5.9
5. James (Jimmy) Pattison (diversified)	$5.73
6. Saputo family (dairy)	$4.34
7. Paul Desmarais, Sr. (power corporation)	$4.27
8. Jeff Skoll (eBay)	$3.75
9. Fred and Ron Mannix diversified)	$3.44
10. Bernard (Barry) Sherman (pharmaceuticals)	$3.31

Source: *Canadian Business* (October 2011).

top 10 percent who increased their share of total wealth between 1984 and 2005 (Morissette & Zhang, 2006:6). Another way to describe the pattern is that during this period the poorest fifth of Canadian families experienced a negative net worth, while the wealth of the richest fifth grew by 64 percent. This group, the wealthiest 20 percent of families, holds 75 percent of Canada's personal wealth (Morissette & Zhang, 2006; Dunphy, 2006).

When compared with other countries, and with the United States in particular, Canada has a small percentage of the world's wealthiest, or the super-rich. According to estimates, in 2001, 315 000 Canadians held over $1 million in investable assets, excluding real estate. In 1988, the top 100 CEOs were paid 105 times the average wage. Since then, that ratio has generally moved up. But the number of Canadians who are at the top of this elite group is relatively small. Only 26 out of 1226 billionaires are Canadian. In other words, Canada could claim only 2 percent of the world's billionaires in 2011 (*Forbes*, 2012).

Family dynasties hold a prominent place among the wealthy and powerful of Canada. Some family names, including Weston, Black, Desmarais, Irving, Thomson, and Bronfman, have appeared on lists of the richest people for years. Most Canadians are unaware of such levels of concentration of wealth and power, but nevertheless are touched by it as they go about their daily routines and activities. As Diane Francis (1986) notes, "Everything from your glass of orange juice in the morning, to the clothes you put on, to the office where you work, to the department store and mall where you shop, to that after-work beer and a night at the ball game—are likely to be produced by these families and conglomerates."

The distribution of wealth is more unequal than that of income, and the distribution of inherited wealth is much more unequal than that of wealth in general (Davies, 1999). While income has to be declared for taxation purposes, it is unclear how much wealth there is in Canada. The majority of the population will never inherit significant wealth, and a small minority receives outrageous amounts. This extreme concentration makes inheritance an important determinant of wealth inequality (Davies, 1999).

INCOME How is income distributed in Canada? Very unequally, it turns out. Income distribution can be configured into a pyramid shape, with a small percentage of Canadians (1 percent) at the top with very high incomes and the majority residing near the bottom. Economist Paul Samuelson (Samuelson & Nordhaus, 1989) put it this way: "If we made an income pyramid out of a child's blocks, with each layer portraying $500 of income, the peak would be far higher than Mount Everest, but most people would be within a few feet of the ground" (1989:644).

Evidence suggests that there is a growing disparity in income, and this mirrors a growing disparity in the distribution of wealth (Valpy, 2008). As with wealth, the disparity between the highest and lowest income earners in Canada has grown over the past two decades. For example, in 1982, the top 5 percent of individual incomes equalled 322 percent of the median income that year, but by 2004, this had increased to 364 percent (Murphy, Roberts, & Wolfson, 2007:7). The gain among the super-rich was even more dramatic. In 1982, the income threshold for individuals in the top 1 percent was 55 times larger than the median, but by 2004, it was over 115 times larger (Murphy, Roberts, & Wolfson, 2007:7).

In 2010, the median income of Canadian families of two or more people was just over $65 500; for two-parent families with children under 18, it was about $78 800. The median income for female lone parent families was $38 700, and for families headed by a senior, the median income was $46 800 (Statistics Canada, 2012g). The vast inequalities of Canadian income are indicated pictorially in Figure 6.2: compared with the "Mount Everest" incomes of a select few, the earnings of the typical Canadian family would bring it only three metres off the ground. The fact that some Canadians enjoy the peaks of Mount Everest while most make it only a few metres up the slope presents a striking image of income inequality in Canada. The share of wealth

Some Canadians: Higher than Mount Everest

If a 4-centimetre child's block equals $500 of income, the average Canadian is only 2 metres off the ground, and the average family just over 3 metres, while the income of some families propels them past the top of Mount Everest.

2 metres
Average Canadian

Just over 3 metres
Average Canadian Family

FIGURE 6.2 Inequality of Canadian Income

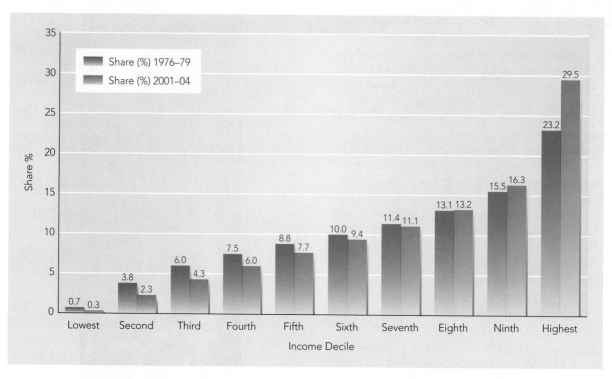

FIGURE 6.3 Share of Earnings of Families with Children by Income Percentile, 1976–79 and 2001–04

Source: Yalnizyan, *The Rich and the Rest of Us*. 2007, p. 12.

for the top 1 percent of individuals in Canada has grown from 9 percent of total income in 1970 to 13.3 percent in 2007. We will elaborate on this idea further in Chapter 11 (see Table 11.1).

Another way to present the contrasts in income is to visualize the following: "If the average CEO is perched atop the CN Tower, Canadians making the average wage are merely two steps up a six-foot ladder. Comparatively, the minimum wage worker is standing in a three-foot deep hole" (Mackenzie, 2007:5; Mackenzie, 2012).

Another picture emerges if we consider the percentage of Canadian families distributed within high- and low-income groups. If we divide all families into 10 groups based on their income levels that we refer to as "deciles," with each group representing 10 percent of the total number of families, we uncover vast inequalities among Canadian families. In 2004, the after-tax income of families in the top decile averaged $135 810, and the combined income of these families totalled over 29 percent of the income of all Canadian families (Yalnizyan, 2007:8,12). In contrast, families at the other end—in the bottom decile—had incomes below $23 300, and the combined total income of these families was about 1 percent of the total Canadian family income (Statistics Canada, 2009b) (see Figure 6.3).

Two features of the data on incomes are outstanding. First, income inequality has remained remarkably consistent through the years. Second, the changes that do occur indicate growing inequality. Since the 1940s, the richest 20 percent of Canadian families have grown richer, while the poorest 20 percent have grown poorer. In spite of numerous social welfare programs, the poorest 20 percent of Canadians receive less of the nation's income today than they did in the 1940s. The richest 20 percent, in contrast, receive more than ever. In 2004, about 3.5 million Canadians were in low-income jobs, earning less than $20 000 (Statistics Canada, 2006c). Nearly 3.2 million Canadians had low incomes in 2009 (Statistics Canada, 2012e). Earning $20 000 a year for full-time work means working for $10 an hour for 50 weeks a year at a rate of 40 hours each week. Women, recent immigrants, lone parents, and young workers are overrepresented among low-wage workers and are falling further behind the wealthiest workers. Impacting heavily upon those falling behind is a labour market increasingly characterized by low-paid, insecure, entry-level jobs. Table 6.2 makes clear that earnings grow more quickly for the top 20 percent compared to the bottom 20 percent. In all cases, those in the top quintile earned more than five times those in the bottom quintile.

Over the border, in the United States, former Microsoft CEO Bill Gates has more wealth than the bottom 45 percent of American households. In 1997, his wealth surpassed the total GNP of Central America (including Guatemala,

TABLE 6.2 Average After-Tax Income by Quintile, 2005–2009*

	2005	2006	2007	2008	2009
Lowest quintile	14 100	14 800	15 500	15 500	15 400
Second quintile	25 400	25 800	27 000	27 300	27 200
Third quintile	34 700	35 300	36 500	37 300	37 500
Fourth quintile	46 100	46 900	48 300	49 400	49 600
Highest quintile	76 600	78 800	81 700	83 800	83 500

*in constant 2009 dollars

Source: Statistics Canada. (2012e). *Income in Canada: Analysis.* June 13. Accessed at www.statcan.gc.ca/pub/75-202-x/2009000/analysis-analyses-eng.htm#a8.

El Salvador, Costa Rica, Panama, Honduras, Nicaragua, and Belize). The following year, Gates's wealth grew to $60 billion, more than the GNPs of Central America plus Jamaica and Bolivia (Mokhiber & Weissman, 1999). Gates now ranks second among the world's top billionaires (*Forbes*, 2012).

Gates has met his match in the family of the late Sam Walton. Along with their mother, Sam Walton's widow, the four Walton "boys" control 38 percent of the shares of Walmart, one of the most powerful economies in the world. Four members of the Walton family are on the list of the world's top 20 billionaires (*Forbes*, 2012). Yet, despite the Waltons' massive wealth, the annual income of full-time, hourly paid Walmart workers in the United States in 2007 was below the poverty line for a family of four (Greenhouse, 2009:139).

Imagine how you could live on a seven-figure income. For most people, it is difficult to even dream about living with such wealth. Beyond the cold numbers lies a dynamic reality that profoundly affects people's lives. The difference in wealth between those at the top and the bottom of the Canadian class structure means vastly different lifestyles for each. For example, a colleague of one of the authors, who was teaching at an exclusive eastern university in the United States, piqued his students' curiosity when he lectured on poverty in Latin America. That weekend, one of his students borrowed his parents' corporate jet and pilot, and in Monday's class the student and his friends reported on their personal observations of the problem. Others, in contrast, must choose whether to spend the little they have at the laundromat or on milk for their baby. In short, divisions of wealth represent not mere numbers, but choices that make real differences in people's lives.

Power

Like many people, you may have said to yourself, "Sure, I can vote, but somehow the big decisions are always made in spite of what I might think. Certainly, I don't make the decision to raise taxes. It isn't I who decides to change welfare benefits."

Another part of you might say, "But I do it through my representatives in Parliament." True enough—as far as it goes. The trouble is, it just doesn't go far enough. Such views of being a participant in the nation's "big" decisions are a playback of the ideology we learn at an early age—an ideology that Marx said is put forward by the elites to both legitimize and perpetuate their power. Sociologists Daniel Hellinger and Dennis Judd (1991) call this the "democratic façade" that conceals the real source of power in society.

In the 1950s, sociologist C. Wright Mills (1956) was criticized for insisting that **power**—the ability to carry out your will in spite of resistance—was concentrated in the hands of the few, for his analysis contradicted an almost sacred ideology of equality. As discussed in Chapter 1, Mills coined the term **power elite** to refer to those who make the big decisions in society.

Mills and others have stressed how wealth and power coalesce in a group of like-minded individuals who share ideologies and values. They belong to the same private clubs, vacation at the same exclusive resorts, and even hire the same bands for their daughters' debutante balls. These shared backgrounds and vested interests all serve to reinforce their view of the world and of their special place in it (Domhoff, 1978, 1997). The elite wield extraordinary power in Canadian society. Although there are exceptions, most prime ministers and Cabinet ministers come from this group—rich white males from families with "old money" (Baltzell & Schneiderman, 1988).

Continuing in the tradition of Mills, sociologist William Domhoff (1990, 1996) argues that this group is so powerful that no major government decision is made without its approval. He analyzed how the group works behind the scenes with elected officials to set both the nation's foreign and domestic policies—from establishing taxes to determining trade tariffs. Although Domhoff's conclusions are controversial—and alarming—they certainly follow

Displays of prestige and social position vary over time and from one culture to another.

logically from the principle that wealth brings power, and extreme wealth brings extreme power.

Prestige

OCCUPATIONS AND PRESTIGE What would you like to do with the rest of your life? Chances are you don't have the option of relaxing under palm trees at the beach. Almost all of us have to choose an occupation and go to work.

Why do people give some jobs more **prestige**—respect or regard—than others? Generally, the most prestigious jobs share four elements:

1. They pay more.
2. They require more education.
3. They entail more abstract thought.
4. They offer greater autonomy (freedom or self-direction).

If we reverse this idea, it means that people give less prestige to jobs that are low-paying, require less preparation or education, involve more physical labour, and are closely supervised. In short, the professions and some white-collar jobs are ranked at the top with respect to prestige, while blue-collar (and pink-collar) jobs are at the bottom.

One of the more interesting aspects of ranking occupations by prestige is how consistent they are across countries and over time. For example, people in every country rank university professors higher than nurses, nurses higher than social workers, and social workers higher than janitors.

Similarly, the occupations that were ranked high in the 1970s are still ranked high today.

DISPLAYING PRESTIGE In times past, only emperors and their families could wear purple in some countries. In France, only the nobility could wear lace. In England, no one could sit while the king was on his throne. Some kings and queens required subjects to walk backward as they left a room—so that no one would "turn his (or her) back" on the "royal presence."

Concern with the display of prestige has not let up—and for some, it is almost an obsession. Western kings and queens expect curtsies and bows, while their Eastern counterparts demand that their subjects touch their faces to the ground. The prime minister enters a room only after others are present—to show that he isn't the one waiting for them. Military officers surround themselves with elaborate rules about who must salute whom, while bailiffs, sometimes armed, make certain everyone stands when a judge enters a courtroom.

The display of prestige permeates society. Addresses in Vancouver's Shaughnessy, Toronto's Rosedale, Calgary's Upper Mount Royal, or Montreal's Westmount are well recognized as among the most prestigious places to live in Canada. Many willingly pay more for clothing that bears a "designer" label. Prestige can be a primary factor in deciding which university to attend. Everyone knows that the prestige of a degree from the University of Toronto compares with a degree from Harvard, Princeton, Yale, or Stanford.

The Big Win: Life After the Lottery

Many Canadians dream about winning the lottery, thinking that with a win, life will be good and problems will disappear. Approximately one in four Canadians plays the lottery. Canadian households shelled out an average of $520 in 2008 on lotteries and games of chance (Marshall, 2010:13) with the glimmering hope that they might hit it big.

Most are lucky to win $10 or another scratch-and-win ticket, but sometimes there are big hits. What happens to these winners? Do they live worry-free in the lap of luxury?

According to sociologist H. Roy Kaplan, who surveyed hundreds of lottery winners in Canada and the United States, for some people winning becomes a disruption in their lives, heightening their anxieties and changing their attitudes (Brean, 2008). Kaplan's conclusions were confirmed by Professor Richard Tunney, who studied big winners in Britain, and Professor Mark Lutter of the Max Planck Institute in Germany, whose research found that winning may even decrease one's happiness. Lutter notes that suddenly acquiring wealth changes the balance in life and that such an abrupt change in affluence may contribute to deviant behaviours, including suicide (Brean, 2006).

Why does this happen? Our connections with others provide the basis for our orientations in life and how we feel about the world. Sudden wealth can rip these moorings apart, and the resulting status inconsistency can lead to a condition sociologists refer to as **anomie**.

Shock is generally the first emotion after a big win, and is accompanied by reporters asking about plans for the new-found wealth. Then come the calls. Some callers offer sincere congratulations, but long-forgotten friends and distant relatives often suddenly remember how close they are to you—and, strangely enough, they all have emergencies that your money can solve. You may even get calls from strangers with ailing mothers, terminally sick kids, sick dogs, and so on . . . Winners often have to unplug their phones or get unlisted numbers.

Some lottery winners are flooded with marriage proposals. These individuals surely didn't become more attractive or sexy overnight—or did they? Maybe money makes people sexy.

Some winners have trouble trusting people, not knowing what their real motives are. The normal becomes the abnormal. Winning big has resulted in numerous court battles over questions of who owns the winning ticket, how the winnings should be split, and what agreements had been made prior to the draw. And the battles are nasty, often with family members, co-workers, or long-time friends throwing accusations at one another.

Many winners who don't make sudden changes in their lifestyle or behaviour have been able to avoid the negative consequences of quick money. They maintain their old friendships, routines, and other anchors in life that give them identity and a sense of belonging. Some even keep their old jobs—not for the money, but because working affords them an identity with which they are familiar and comfortable. To a certain degree, most Canadians relate to this behaviour. In a recent poll by Ipsos Reid of over 2000 workers, the majority—65 percent—said they would not quit their jobs or retire permanently if they won the lottery (Morrissy, 2008).

Sudden wealth, in other words, may pose a threat that must be guarded against. Of course, as we check our numbers in the weekly draws, most of us say we are willing to accept any risks that winning big may bring.

Status symbols vary with social class. Clearly, only the wealthy can afford certain items, such as a Maybauch sedan, a Milguss watch, or Schlumberger jewellery. But beyond affordability lies a class-based preference in status symbols. For example, the "nouveau riche" are quick to flaunt labels and other material symbols to show they have "arrived," while those with old money, more secure in their status, often prefer to flaunt their own status symbols, such as the "right" address.

Status Inconsistency

Ordinarily, a person has a similar rank in all three dimensions of social class—wealth, power, and prestige. Such people show **status consistency**. Sometimes individuals have a mixture of high and low ranks, a condition called **status inconsistency**. This leads to some interesting situations.

Sociologist Gerhard Lenski (1954, 1966) observed that each of us tries to maximize our **status**, or social ranking. Individuals who rank high on one dimension of social class but lower on others expect people to judge them on the basis of their highest status. Sometimes, however, people hoping to maximize their own position may respond on the basis of people's lowest status.

A classic study of status inconsistency was conducted by sociologist Ray Gold (1952). He found that after apartment-house janitors unionized, they made more money than some of the people whose garbage they carried out. Tenants became upset when they saw their janitors driving more expensive cars than they did. Some attempted to "put the janitor in his place" by making "snotty" remarks. Similarly, during a strike by outside workers (including garbage collectors) in 2009 in the city of Toronto, several media commentaries questioned the rights and motives of garbage collectors to strike for higher wages and job security. Interestingly, as the stench of rotting garbage in the summer heat rose and as serious health concerns issued by public officials escalated, few acknowledged the essential contribution of these workers to our communities, our safety, and our well-being.

Instant wealth, the topic of the Down-to-Earth Sociology box above, provides an interesting case of status inconsistency.

Individuals with status inconsistency, then, are likely to confront one frustrating situation after another. They claim the higher status, but are handed the lower. The sociological significance of this condition, said Lenski, is that such people tend to be more politically radical. An example is university professors: their prestige is high, but their incomes are relatively low. Hardly anyone in Canadian society is better educated, yet university professors don't come close to the top of the income pyramid. In line with Lenski's prediction, the political beliefs of many professors are left of centre.

Focus Question

What are some of the ways we define or measure social class?

Why Is Social Stratification Universal?

What is it about social life that makes all societies stratified? We shall first consider the explanation proposed by functionalists, which has aroused much controversy in sociology, followed by criticisms of this position. We then explore theories proposed by conflict theorists.

The Functionalist or Conservative View

Functionalists take the position that the patterns of behaviour that characterize a society exist because they are functional for that society. They contend that because social inequality is universal, inequality must help societies survive. Using this principle, sociologists Kingsley Davis and Wilbert Moore (1945, 1953) concluded that stratification is inevitable for the following reasons:

1. Society must make certain that its positions are filled.
2. Some positions are more important than others.
3. The more important positions must be filled by the more qualified people.

4. To motivate the more qualified people to fill these positions, society must offer them greater rewards.

Let's look at some examples to flesh out the functionalist argument. The position of a university president is deemed much more important for society than that of a student, because the president's decisions affect many more people. Any mistakes he or she makes carry implications for a large number of people, including many students. The decisions of university presidents affect careers, paycheques, and, in some cases, even life and death.

Positions with greater responsibility also require greater accountability. University presidents are accountable to boards of trustees for how they perform. How can society motivate highly qualified people to enter such high-pressure positions? What keeps people from avoiding them and seeking less demanding jobs?

The answer, according to functionalists, is that society offers greater rewards for its more responsible, demanding, and accountable positions. If higher salaries, benefits, and greater prestige were not offered, why would anyone strive for these positions? Thus, a salary of $2 million, a country-club membership, a private jet, and a chauffeured limousine may be necessary to motivate the most highly qualified people to compete with one another for a certain position, while a $40 000 salary without fringe benefits is enough to get hundreds of people to compete for a less demanding position. Similarly, higher rewards are necessary to recruit people to positions that require rigorous training. Why suffer through taking tests and writing papers in university or graduate school if you can get the same pay and prestige with a high-school education?

The functionalist argument is simple and clear. Society works better if its most qualified people hold its most important positions. For example, to motivate highly talented people to become surgeons—to undergo many years of rigorous training and cope with life-and-death situations on a daily basis—requires a high payoff.

The Conflict Approach: A Critical Response

The functionalist view makes many sociologists uncomfortable, for they see it as coming close to justifying the inequalities of society.

Melvin Tumin (1953) was the first sociologist to point out what he saw as major flaws in the functionalist position. He developed four major arguments.

First, how is the importance of a position measured? It can't be measured by the rewards a position carries, for that argument is circular. An independent measure of

✳ **Explore** the reading "Some Principles of Stratification" by Davis and Moore on **MySocLab**.

✳ **Explore** the reading "Some Principles of Stratification: A Critical Analysis" by Melvin Tumin on **MySocLab**.

importance must exist to test whether the more important positions actually carry higher rewards. For example, is a surgeon really more important to society than a garbage collector, since the garbage collector helps prevent contagious diseases?

Second, if stratification worked according to functionalist theory, society would be a **meritocracy**; that is, all positions would be awarded on the basis of merit. Ability, then, should predict who goes to university. Instead, the best predictor of university entrance is family income—the more a family earns, the more likely their children are to go to university, as we will see in Chapter 14. Similarly, while some people get ahead through ability and hard work, others simply inherit wealth and the opportunities that go with it. Moreover, if a stratification system places most men above most women, it does not live up to the argument that talent and ability are the bases for holding important positions. In short, factors far beyond merit give people their relative positions in society.

Third, the functionalist view places too much emphasis on money and fringe benefits. These aren't the only reasons people take jobs. For example, if money were the main motivator for professors, why would they spend four years in university, plus another six or seven pursuing a PhD—only to earn wages that are far behind those of physicians, lawyers, and other highly educated professionals? Obviously, university teaching offers more than monetary rewards: high prestige, autonomy (university professors have considerable discretion about how they do their job), rewarding social interaction (much of the job consists of talking to people), security (when given tenure, professors have lifetime employment), and leisure and the opportunity to travel (many professors work short days, enjoy several weeks of vacation during the school year, and have the entire summer to do research on subjects that interest them).

Fourth, if social stratification is functional, it ought to benefit almost everyone. In reality, however, social stratification is *dysfunctional* to many. Think of the people who could have made invaluable contributions to society if they were not members of a visible minority or if they had not been born into poverty and forced to drop out of school, taking menial jobs to help support their families; or the many who, born female, are passed over for promotions or are paid wages unequal to those of their male colleagues, as we will discuss further in Chapters 7 and 8. In other words, the functionalist perspective of social stratification does not explain why women and members of visible minority groups are vastly underrepresented among those most highly paid in Canada.

The Conflict Perspective and Competition for Scarce Resources

Conflict theorists sharply disagree with the functionalist position. They stress that conflict, not function, is the basis of social stratification. Sociologists such as William Domhoff (1990, 1997), C. Wright Mills (1956), and Irving Louis Horowitz (1966) assert that in every society, groups struggle with one another to gain a larger share of their society's limited resources. Whenever a group gains power, it uses that power to extract what it can from the groups beneath it. It also uses social institutions to keep other groups weak and itself in power. Class conflict, according to conflict theorists, is the key to understanding social stratification, since society is far from being a harmonious system that benevolently distributes greater resources to its supposedly more qualified members.

All ruling groups—from slave masters to modern elites—develop an ideology to justify their position at the top. This ideology often seduces the oppressed into believing that their welfare depends on keeping society stable. Consequently, the oppressed may support laws against their own interests and even sacrifice their children as soldiers in wars designed to enrich the bourgeoisie.

The day will come, Marx believed, when class consciousness will overcome bourgeois ideology and the force of the bourgeoisie, who control the police, the military, and even education (where false consciousness is implanted in the minds of workers' children). At first, the struggle for control of the means of production may be covert, taking the form of work slowdowns or industrial sabotage, but it will ultimately break out into open resistance.

Some sociologists have refocused conflict theory. C. Wright Mills (1956), Ralf Dahrendorf (1959), and Randall Collins (1974, 1988), for example, stress that groups within the same class also compete for scarce resources—power, wealth, education, housing, and even prestige—whatever benefits society has to offer. The result is conflict not only between labour unions and corporations, but also between the young and the old, between women and men, and among racial and ethnic groups. Unlike functionalists, conflict theorists hold that just beneath the surface of what may appear to be a tranquil society lies overt conflict—only uneasily held in check, usually by political concessions such as minimum wage laws, workplace safety legislation, employment equity regulations, and so on.

Feminist and Anti-Racist Approaches

Critical thinkers drawing from feminist and anti-racist perspectives believe that people should be valued equally and seek explanations for unequal treatment and inequalities of wealth and power within Canadian and other societies. They argue that classic analyses of inequality from functionalist and conflict perspectives do not account for the relative lack of power, resources, and wealth experienced by women and racialized minorities. In their analyses, they argue that gender and race are socially constructed and form the bases for limitations to equality of condition and opportunity. These critical approaches consider the ways in which women and racialized minorities, including some men, have been oppressed within patriarchy and the capitalist economy. They consider how people come to be exploited and dominated by others, and the characteristics of those exploited as opposed to those who dominate.

In particular, feminists argue that underlying women's oppression and inability to achieve equality with men are their roles in social reproduction; that is, in unpaid household and family labour. As we will discuss in Chapter 7, women's unpaid work at home has an effect on their wages and ability to achieve equality with men in the labour force.

In addition to the questions raised by feminists about gender inequality, anti-racist theorists also consider structural aspects of inequality and the ways in which categories of race and ethnicity affect life chances, opportunities, and social class position. In examining inequalities within the labour market, for example, they will consider the ways in which inequalities of gender, race, and class are intertwined and argue that the labour market is split along these divisions. An anti-racist theorist might contend that these multi-layered inequalities are complexly woven by unequal structures of power and are based on assumptions regarding the different characteristics people bring to the structures of opportunity.

How Do Elites Maintain Social Inequality?

Suppose you are part of the ruling elite of your society. What can you do to maintain your privileged position? The key lies in controlling ideas and information, in social networks, and, least effectively, in the use of force.

Ideology versus Force

Medieval Europe provides a good example of the power of ideology. During medieval times, land was owned by only a small group of people called the "aristocracy" and was the primary source of wealth. With the exception of the clergy and some craftsmen, most citizens were peasants working for this small group of powerful landowners. Peasants farmed the land, took care of cattle, and built roads and bridges. Every year, they had to turn over a designated portion of their crops to their feudal lord and the church. For centuries, this system of wealth creation and distribution persisted.

CONTROLLING IDEAS Why didn't the peasants rebel? There were many reasons, not the least of which being that the army was controlled by the aristocracy. Coercion, however, only goes so far, for it breeds hostility and nourishes rebellion. It is much more effective to convince people to want to do what the ruling elite desires. This is where *ideology* comes into play, and medieval aristocracies and the church used it to great effect. They developed an ideology known as the **divine right of kings**—the idea that the king's authority came directly from God—and could be traced back several

The divine right of kings was an ideology that made the king God's direct representative on Earth—to administer justice and punish evildoers. This theological-political concept was supported by the Roman Catholic Church, whose representatives crowned the king. Shown here is Pope Clement IV crowning Charles Anjou as king of Sicily in 1226.

thousand years to the Old Testament. The king could delegate authority to nobles, who, as God's representatives, also had to be obeyed. To disobey was to commit a sin against God; to rebel meant physical punishment on Earth and a sentence to suffer in eternal hell.

The control of ideas, then, can be remarkably more effective than brute force. Although this particular ideology no longer governs people's minds today, the elite in every society develop ideologies to justify their position at the top. For example, schools around the world teach that their country's form of government—*whatever form of government that may be*—is the best. Each nation's schools also stress the virtues—rather than the vices—of governments past and present. Religion also teaches that we owe obedience to an authority, and that laws are to be obeyed. To the degree that the elites' ideologies are accepted by the masses, both economic and political arrangements are stable.

CONTROLLING INFORMATION To maintain their positions of power, elites also try to control information (Carroll & Hackett, 2006). In dictatorships, this is accomplished through the threat of force. Dictators can—and do—imprison editors and journalists for publishing reports that are critical of them, and sometimes for simply publishing unflattering information (Timerman, 1981). The ruling elites of democracies accomplish the same purpose by manipulating the media through the selective release of information, withholding whatever they desire "in the interest of national security." But just as coercion has its limits, so does the control of information—especially given its new forms (satellite communications, email, and the internet), which pay no respect to international borders (Jackson, Nielsen, & Hsu, 2011).

SOCIAL NETWORKS Also critical in maintaining stratification are *social networks*—the social ties that link people (Higley, Hoffmann-Lange, Kadushin, & Moore, 1991). These networks, expanding outward from an individual to gradually encompass more and more people, supply valuable information and tend to perpetuate social inequality. Sociologists William Domhoff (1983, 1990), John Porter (1965), Wallace Clement (1975), and Bill Carroll (2004) have documented how members of the elite move in a circle of power that multiplies their opportunities. Contacts with people of similar backgrounds, interests, and goals allow the elite to pass privileges from one generation to the next. In contrast, the social networks of the poor perpetuate poverty and powerlessness.

TECHNOLOGY The desire of elites to preserve their position is aided by recent developments in technology, especially monitoring devices. These devices—from "hot telephones" (taps that transform a telephone into a microphone even when off the hook) to security cameras on streets and university campuses and devices that can read the entire contents of a computer without leaving a trace—help the elite, through the police and other government agencies such as CSIS, monitor citizens' activities without their knowledge. Dictatorships have few checks on how such technology can be employed, but in democracies, checks and balances, such as Canada's *Charter of Rights and Freedoms* and the necessity of court orders, although limited by Canada's *Anti-Terrorism Act*, at least partially curb their use.

> **IN SUM**
>
> Underlying the maintenance of the system of social inequality is control of a society's institutions. In a dictatorship, the elite make the laws. In a democracy, the elite influence law. In both systems, laws are enforced by the legal establishment. The elite also command the police and military and can give orders to crush a rebellion—or even to run a post office or air traffic control unit if workers go on strike. As noted, force has its limits, and a nation's elite generally finds it preferable to maintain its stratification system by peaceful means, especially by influencing the thinking of its citizens.

Applying Sociological Models of Social Class

The question of how many social classes exist is a matter of debate. Sociologists have proposed various models, but none has gained universal support. There are two main models: one based on Marx, the other on Weber.

Applying Marx

Marx argued that there are two classes—capitalists and workers—with membership based solely on a person's relationship to the means of production. Sociologists have criticized these categories as too broad. For example, executives, managers, and supervisors are technically workers because they do not own the means of production. But what do they have in common with assembly-line workers? Similarly, the category of "capitalist" takes in too many types; the decisions of someone who employs a thousand workers directly affect a thousand families, for example. Compare this with a man the authors know in Calgary, Alberta. Working on cars in his own backyard, he gained a following, quit his regular job, and in a few years put up a building with an office and five bays. This mechanic is now a capitalist who employs five or six other mechanics and owns the tools and building (the "means of production"). But what does he have in common with a factory owner who controls the lives of a thousand workers? Not only is his work different, but so are his lifestyle and the way he looks at the world.

Sociologist Erik Wright (1985) resolved this problem by regarding some people as members of more than one class at the same time. They have what he called **contradictory class locations**. By this, Wright meant that people's position in the class structure can generate contradictory interests. For example, the automobile-mechanic-turned-business-owner may want his mechanics to have higher wages, since he, too, has experienced their working conditions. At the same time, his current interests—making profits and remaining competitive with other repair shops—may lead him to resist pressures to raise wages.

Because of such contradictory class locations, Wright modified Marx's model. As summarized in Table 6.3, Wright identified four classes: (1) *capitalists*, business owners who employ many workers; (2) *petty bourgeoisie*, small business owners; (3) *managers*, who sell their own labour but also exercise authority over other employees; and (4) *workers*, who simply sell their labour to others. As you can see, this model allows finer divisions than the one Marx proposed, yet maintains the primary distinction between employer and worker. The question of how many social classes exist and how they relate to one another is highly complex. Even with Wright's modifications to Marx's model, problems persist. How do we categorize university professors who employ research assistants with their research grants, for example? As you know, there are huge differences in the power and resources of managers. An executive at General Motors, for

TABLE 6.3 Social Class and the Means of Production

Marx's Class Model (based on the means of production)
1. Capitalist (bourgeoisie)
2. Workers (proletariat)

Wright's Modification of Marx's Class Model (to account for contradictory class locations)
1. Capitalists
2. Petty bourgeoisie
3. Managers
4. Workers

example, may be responsible for a thousand workers, while a shift manager at the local McDonald's may oversee only a handful. They, too, have little in common.

Updating Weber

Sociologists Dennis Gilbert and Joseph Kahl (1998; Gilbert, 2008) developed a six-class model to portray the class structure of the United States and other capitalist countries. Think of their model, illustrated in Figure 6.4, as a ladder. Our discussion will start with the highest rung and move downward. In line with Weber, on each lower rung there is less wealth, less power, and less prestige. Note that in this model education is a primary criterion of class.

THE CAPITALIST CLASS OR UPPER CLASS The super-rich, who occupy the top rung of the class ladder in Canada, comprise only about 1.1 percent of the population. In Canada, the top 1 percent includes about 246 000 people, who each earn about $405 000 annually (Yalnizyan, 2010). This group accounted for almost a third (32 percent) of income growth for the 10-year period between 1997 and 2007, a time of rapidly increasing incomes (Yalnizyan, 2010). This 1.1 percent is so wealthy that its members are worth more than the entire bottom 90 percent of the nation. Their power is so great that their decisions open or close jobs for hundreds of thousands of people. Through their ownership of newspapers, magazines, telecommunications, and radio and television stations, and their access to politicians, this elite class even helps shape public consciousness. Its members perpetuate themselves by passing

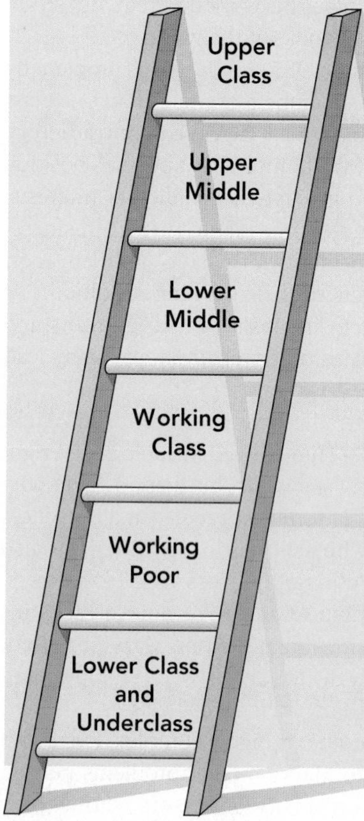

Social Class	Education	Occupation	Income	Percentage of Population
Upper Class	Prestigious university	Investors and heirs, a few top executives	$1 000 000	1.1%
Upper Middle	College or university, often with postgraduate study	Professionals, upper managers	$125 000	26.5%
Lower Middle	At least high school; perhaps some college or apprenticeship	Semiprofessionals and lower managers, craftspeople, forepersons	About $60 000	
Working Class	High school	Factory workers, clerical workers, low-paid retail sales and craftspeople	About $36 000	63.7%
Working Poor	Some high school	Labourers, service workers, low-paid salespeople	About $20 000	
Lower Class and Underclass	Some high school	Unemployed and part-time, on welfare	About $12 000	8.7%

FIGURE 6.4 The Canadian Social Class Ladder

Source: Statistics Canada. (2007). "The Role of Family and Government Financial Supports in Helping Canadian Workers Avoid Poverty.". http://www.hrsdc.gc.ca/eng/publications_resources/research/categories/inclusion/2007/sp_678_04_07/sp_678_04_07e.pdf

The Bronfmans are among Canada's oldest wealthy families. Old-money capitalists wield vast power and have numerous political, social, and economic connections that they draw on in order to protect their huge economic empires.

on to their children their assets and influential social networks.

The capitalist class can be divided into "old" and "new" money (Aldrich, 1989). In general, the longer wealth has been in a family, the more it adds to the family's prestige. Many people entering the capitalist class have found it necessary to cut moral corners, at least occasionally. This "taint" to the money disappears with time, however, and the later generations of Kennedys, Rockefellers, Vanderbilts, Mellons, Du Ponts, Chryslers, and Fords in the United States; and of Eatons, Molsons, and Bronfmans in Canada are considered to have "clean" money simply by virtue of the passage of time. Old-money families in Canada such as the Thompsons, Irvings, and Westons preserve their privileged positions via trust funds, making certain that subsequent generations attend prestigious prep schools and universities. They also encourage their heirs, especially males, to enter law. These old-money capitalists wield vast power and use their extensive political connections to protect their huge economic empires (Sklair, 2001; Domhoff, 1990, 1997, 2006; Clement, 1975; & Newman, 1979, 2004). Some members of the capitalist class who possess vast sums of money and power are referred to as the *nouveau riche* because their money is "new." Although such people may have made fortunes in business, the stock market, inventions, entertainment, or sports, they don't necessarily share the social networks that come with old money. Donald Trump, for example, is a member of this group. The children of new-monied families can ascend into the upper part of the capitalist class if they attend the right schools and marry into old money.

THE UPPER-MIDDLE CLASS Of all the classes, the upper-middle is the one most shaped by education. Almost all members of this class have at least a bachelor's degree, and many have postgraduate degrees in business, management, law, or medicine. These people manage the corporations owned by the capitalist class or operate their own businesses or professions. As Gilbert and Kahl (1982) say, these positions

> may not grant prestige equivalent to a title of nobility in the Germany of Max Weber, but they certainly represent the sign of having "made it" in contemporary America . . . Their income is sufficient to purchase houses and cars and travel that become public symbols for all to see and for advertisers to portray with words and pictures that connote success, glamour, and high style.

Consequently, parents and teachers push children to prepare them for upper-middle-class jobs.

THE LOWER-MIDDLE CLASS Members of the lower-middle class follow orders given by those who have upper-middle-class credentials. Their technical and lower-level management positions earn them a decent living—albeit one constantly threatened by rising taxes and inflation—and they generally enjoy a comfortable, mainstream lifestyle. They usually feel secure in their positions and anticipate moving up the social class ladder.

The distinctions between lower-middle class and working class on the next lower rung are more blurred than those between other classes, and it may be that, as the economy changes and more full-time, relatively well-paid unionized and secure jobs are replaced by part-time or temporary and less-secure jobs, there will be no discernible distinction

more likely to be premature than those born to mothers living in more affluent areas (Lewis, 2007:A10). Overall, health researchers have established a link between low incomes and higher risks of babies born prematurely or with low birth weights, even at full term (Urquia, Frank, Glazier, & Moineddin, 2007).

In old age—whether 70 or 90—the poor are more likely to die of illness and disease. In Canada, the highest life expectancies are found in large metropolitan and urban centres where education levels are high, while people in remote northern communities, where a large percentage of the population is Aboriginal and where income and education levels are low, have the lowest life expectancies (Shields & Tremblay, 2002; Statistics Canada, 2005b; Allard, Wilkins, & Berthelot, 2004). A recent study of life expectancy in Inuit-inhabited areas of Canada found that the life expectancy of the Inuit population was 12 to 15 years less than the figures for Canada as a whole (Wilkins et al., 2008; Statistics Canada, 2010b).

From a comparative global perspective, Canadians enjoy relatively healthy and long lives. A recent ranking placed Canada twelfth on a new life expectancy measure. This means that, on average, Canadians will live into their seventies free of disease or disability, while total life expectancy is over 81 years. In Monaco, the top-ranked country for life expectancy, people might live to almost their ninetieth birthday; in contrast, people living in Afghanistan, or in African countries such as Swaziland, South Africa, or Chad, may not live to celebrate their fiftieth birthdays. Interestingly, the United States, the most prosperous nation in the world, ranks fiftieth on the life-expectancy scale (CIA, 2009). This relatively poor ranking is explained by the tremendous gap between rich and poor in the United States, where Native Americans, rural blacks, and the inner-city poor enjoy far fewer years free of health problems than others (Philp, 2000).

One study found that air pollution along one of the major NAFTA trucking routes at Ciudad Juarez in Mexico is contributing to increased sickness and death among children living near this border crossing. However, when data from other border crossings were compared, the increased mortality at Ciudad Juarez was clearly linked to lower incomes and poverty (Bueckert, 2003). In Canada, a study by the Montreal Public Health Department found that people in poor areas were more likely to be injured in a traffic accident than their wealthier neighbours, and kids in poor neighbourhoods were 7.3 times more likely to face injuries as pedestrians. Generally, in low-income areas, people are more likely to walk and they tend to live on busier and more crowded streets than those who live in wealthier parts of the city (Canadian Press, 2012b).

During both childhood and adulthood, the poor are also more likely to be killed by accidents, fires, and homicide. Children under the age of nine living in poor neighbourhoods are more likely to be hospitalized for injuries related to accidents, poisoning, fire, drowning, or suffocation compared to those living in higher-income neighbourhoods (Statistics Canada, 2010e). Underlying the different death and accident rates are the living conditions those in poverty endure—unsafe neighbourhoods, poorer quality housing, and unequal access to medical care and nutrition.

Despite Canada's government-funded health care system, the higher classes receive better medical treatment. A recent study found that lower-income women were much more likely to develop Type 2 diabetes as compared to their higher-income counterparts (Statistics Canada, 2010f). Another study found that cancer patients from lower-income backgrounds faced poorer outcomes than those from higher income brackets (Tobin, 2010). A study in Ontario of 535 000 birth records concluded that there is a strong relationship between poverty and the rate of teenage pregnancy at both neighbourhood and community levels (Pecoskie & Buist, 2011). Poor people tend to be less educated about nutrition, and their meals tend to be heavy in fats and sugars, neither of which are healthy. Children living in poor neighbourhoods and low-income families are at greater risk of being overweight or obese because the foods available to them are of lower nutritional value and they have fewer opportunities to be physically active (Statistics Canada, 2005c).

Social class also affects mental health. From the 1930s until now, sociologists have found that the mental health of the lower classes is worse than that of the higher classes (Faris & Dunham, 1939; Srole et al., 1978; Brown & Gary, 1988; Lundberg, 1991; Burman, 1996; Capponi, 1997). This difference reflects the greater stresses experienced by those in the lower classes, such as unpaid bills, unemployment, dirty and dangerous work, the threat of eviction, unhappy marriages, and broken homes. People higher up the social class ladder also experience stress in daily life, of course, but their stresses are generally less and their coping resources greater. Not only can they afford vacations, psychiatrists, and counsellors, but their class position gives them greater control over their lives, a key to good mental health.

The Reach of Social Class

Social class plays a significant role in all aspects of life. How social class affects various aspects of life, including our personal lives—such as family life or choice of marital partner—and our public lives, such as which school we will attend and for how long, are examined throughout the chapters of this text. Below are some examples of the consequences of social class.

- *Choice of Husband or Wife.* The capitalist class strongly emphasizes family tradition and continuity, stressing the importance of ancestry, history, and even a sense of purpose or destiny in life (Baltzell, 1979; Aldrich,

1989). Children of this class learn that their choice of husband or wife affects not just themselves but the whole family unit, and that their spouse will have an impact on the "family line." Consequently, their field of "eligibles" is much narrower than it is for the children of any other social class. In effect, parents in this class play a greater role in their children's mate selection. Marriage has even become a class indicator—"an important class divider" (Wente, 2007, A25). Women with more education are not only more likely to marry, but are more likely to stay married and raise children with their biological father. When marriage breaks down, there is a greater likelihood that the children will grow up in a household where their mothers struggle to make ends meet.

- *Divorce.* The more difficult daily life of the lower social classes, especially the many tensions that come from insecure employment and inadequate incomes, leads to more marital friction and a greater likelihood of both spouse and alcohol abuse. Consequently, the marriages of the poor are more likely to fail and their children are more likely to grow up in broken homes.

- *Child-Rearing.* Sociologist Melvin Kohn (1977) finds significant class differences in child-rearing. Lower-class parents are more concerned that their children conform to conventional norms and obey authority figures. Middle-class parents, in contrast, encourage their children to be more creative and independent and tolerate a wider range of behaviours (except in speech, where they are less tolerant of bad grammar and curse words).

- *Education.* As was shown in Figure 6.4, education increases as one goes up the social class ladder. It is not just the amount of education that changes, but also the type. Children of the upper class bypass public schools entirely in favour of exclusive private schools, where they are trained to take a commanding role in society. Prep schools such as Upper Canada College teach upper-class values and prepare students for prestigious universities (Beeghley, 1996).

- *Religion.* Classes tend to cluster in different denominations. Anglicans, for example, are much more likely to recruit from the middle and upper classes, Baptists draw heavily from the lower classes, and Methodists are more middle-class. Patterns of worship also follow class lines: those that attract the lower classes have more spontaneous worship services and louder music, while the middle and upper classes prefer more "subdued" worship.

- *Politics.* As has been stressed throughout this text, symbolic interactionists emphasize that people see events from their own corner in life. Political views are no exception to this principle, and the rich and poor walk different political paths. The working class, which feels much more strongly than the classes above it that government should intervene in the economy to make citizens financially secure, is more likely to vote New Democrat, while those in higher classes are more likely to vote Conservative. The Liberal Party is the party of the centre. However, voting patterns and party allegiance are mixed. There is no clear class majority supporting any one party (Forcese, 1997). Today the working and middle classes tend to lean to the right on *economic* issues (i.e., they favour reducing taxes and government spending). People toward the bottom of the class structure are less likely to become politically active—to campaign for candidates or even vote (Gans, 1991; Gilbert & Kahl, 1993; Curtis, Grabb, & Guppy, 1999).

- *Crime and the Criminal Justice System.* Justice certainly is not blind when it comes to one's chances of being arrested (Henslin, 2008). In Chapter 16, we will discuss the different styles of crime the upper and lower social classes engage in. The white-collar crimes of the more privileged classes are more likely to be dealt with outside the criminal justice system, while the street crimes of the lower classes are dealt with by the police. One consequence of this class standard is that poor people, especially non-white poor people, are far more likely to be on probation, on parole, or in jail (National Council of Welfare, 2000; Reiman, 2001). In addition, since people tend to commit crimes in or near their own neighbourhoods, the lower classes are more likely to be robbed, burglarized, or murdered.

Focus Question

In everyday life, what are some of the ways in which social class differences may be observed?

Social Mobility

No aspect of life, then—from marriage to politics—goes untouched by social class. Because life seems much more satisfying for the more privileged classes, people strive for upward social mobility. What affects people's chances of climbing the class ladder?

Three Types of Social Mobility

There are three basic types of social mobility: intergenerational, structural, and exchange mobility. **Intergenerational mobility** refers to adult children ending up on a different rung of the social class ladder than their parents—a change that occurs between generations. For example, if the child of someone who sells used cars goes to university and eventually buys a Toyota dealership, that person experiences **upward social mobility**. Conversely, if the child of the dealership owner parties too much, drops out of university, and ends up selling cars, he or she experiences **downward social mobility**.

Today, in a period of economic upheaval, government austerity plans, and growing social inequality, many of the old debates have resurfaced. In particular, neoliberalism and individualism are being promoted by those who maintain that Canadians who are struggling economically should rely foremost on their own efforts and the support of their families and not turn to the state. Further, the amount of assistance provided should be kept to a minimum, since it merely encourages dependence on an already overburdened social welfare system.

In contrast to these positions, in the 1950s and 1960s, Canada embraced collectivist solutions and created a social welfare state based on legislative provisions that sought to ensure that every Canadian enjoyed basic economic well-being. Indeed, even in the late-1990s, politicians of all stripes supported Campaign 2000, which was intended to end child poverty by the year 2000. Today, the collectivist, societal responsibility approach is under attack, and many have embraced the view that we cannot or should not continue to provide as much support for those who are economically marginalized.

As a result of this political debate, the definition of poverty is as hotly contested today as ever. Of course, ruling political parties do not want to see newspaper headlines such as "Ontario poverty rate up since last election," "Life 'impossible' on $610 a month," or "Record 46.2 million Americans in poverty" (Monsebraaten, 2011b:A14; Fong, 2012:A6; Lee, 2011:A23). In purely fiscal terms, political leaders do not want to see large numbers of citizens qualifying for social assistance (ranging from welfare to employment insurance benefits).

Here, definitions and statistics play a crucial part. If poverty and eligibility for social assistance can be redefined, there are clear political benefits. India (where 455 million citizens live on less than $1.25 a day) provides a revealing example. The Indian government recently decided that only citizens receiving less than 68 cents a day (in urban areas) would qualify for poverty benefits (Westhead, 2011:A5). With the stroke of a keyboard, poverty rates dropped and public finances improved.

In Canada, there have been hotly contested changes to employment insurance eligibility, resulting in the exclusion of 60 percent of jobless workers, as well as legislation, effective in 2013, that will redefine the meanings of both "a reasonable job search" and "a suitable job" (Goar, 2012:A13; Harper, 2012:A1, A6). Fewer individuals qualifying for and relying on employment insurance creates good political optics (and a healthy surplus). The recent federal government decision to axe the National Council of Welfare (founded in 1962) has been seen by many as an effort to eliminate one of the key national bodies reporting on poverty and welfare rates (Goar, 2012). In the absence of national statistics on welfare rates, the dimensions and implications of poverty become murkier.

Focus Question

What are some of the popular stereotypes about the poor, and why is this misinformation widely believed?

Who Are the Poor?

GEOGRAPHY Reflecting differences in local economies (and, as a result, opportunities for employment), long-term poverty rates by 2007 ranged from a high of about 8 percent in British Columbia [LICO] to a low of 2 percent in Alberta [LICO] (Murphy, Zhang, & Dionne, 2012:78). We know relatively little about the Yukon, the Northwest Territories, or Nunavut, since Statistics Canada does not include them in its income surveys. However, high rates of Aboriginal poverty suggest that impoverishment is a very significant issue in these areas (Liodakis, 2012). The strongest predictor of whether Canadians are poor is not geography, but rather race/ethnicity, education, age, disability, and gender of the head of household.

RACE/ETHNICITY AND IMMIGRATION Despite Canada's official agenda of multiculturalism, being a visible minority, a recent immigrant, or an Aboriginal Canadian carries with it an increased risk of poverty (Wallis & Kwok, 2008). According to the latest census data (2006), racialized persons in Canada experienced a 22 percent poverty rate in 2006, while the overall poverty rate was 11 percent. The national poverty rate among visible minorities is about twice that of other groups, and, in specific provinces such as Newfoundland and Nova Scotia, visible minorities are more likely than other Canadians to be poor (Morissette & Zhang, 2001:26).

Predictably, immigrants, and especially recent immigrants, are also disadvantaged (National Council of Welfare, 2012a). Between 1980 and 2005, the employment income of recent immigrants slipped further below their Canadian-born counterparts. In 1980, while both male and female recent immigrants received 85 cents for each dollar earned by Canadian-born men, by 2005, the numbers fell to 63 cents for recent immigrant men and 56 cents for recent immigrant women (National Council of Welfare, 2012a:6). For immigrant families in which the major income earner came to Canada after 1989, the poverty rate was 29.8 percent, while for families in which the income earner was born in Canada, the rate was 9.8 percent (National Council of Welfare, 2006a, 2006b). Even highly educated recent immigrants often find themselves stuck in low-skill, low-income jobs as their educational credentials are not recognized or are downgraded by employers (Zuberi & Ptashnick, 2011; Galarneau & Morissette, 2004).

Not surprisingly, Aboriginal peoples are at economic risk. In several provinces, their poverty rate is more than twice that of non-Aboriginals, and in 2000 in Saskatchewan and Manitoba, more than half of all Aboriginals were living in poverty (CCSD, 2000). The 2008 recession had a

DOWN-TO-EARTH SOCIOLOGY

Social Assistance and Poverty

In 2009, a lone-parent with one child received the following welfare income in Ontario: basic social assistance $10 937, federal child benefit $4574, provincial child benefit $850, GST provincial tax credit $392—a total income of $17 323, or $1444 a month. The after-tax LICO for a lone parent in Ontario with one child in 2009 was $22 420. The poverty gap between government support and "poverty" was $5048 (National Council of Welfare, 2010:A6,A14)s. Living on social assistance is not living the good life.

particularly devastating impact on off-reserve Aboriginals, pushing the 2010 jobless rate to 12.3 percent, compared to 6.8 percent for non-Aboriginals (Grant, 2011:A16). The Aboriginal disadvantage is also evident in food bank use, where across Canada, 10 percent of users self-identify as First Nations, Métis, or Inuit. In some areas, the majority of food-bank users (62 percent) are Aboriginal (Food Banks Canada, 2011).

EDUCATION As discussed earlier, education is a vital factor in poverty. Unattached persons with eight years of education or less have an astounding poverty rate of 57 percent, while for those with a bachelor's degree, the rate is 21.7 percent (National Council of Welfare, 2006b:48). This disparity is also reflected in earning patterns. Compared to their counterparts without a high school diploma, for example, young men between the ages of 25 and 34 who had a trade or apprenticeship in 2006 earned $8000 more per year (Frenette et al., 2008:17). Ironically, while education may serve as a way out of low-income situations for many, rising tuition costs and mushrooming student-loan debt may stand in the way.

By 2013, the federal government expects to surpass $15 billion in outstanding student debt held in its Canada Student Loans Program ("Student Loans," 2011).Needless to say, the dramatically increased cost of education and the prospects for indebtedness are particularly daunting for poor families. In 1990 a poor family would have had to divert 981 days of income to pay for a child's tuition, textbooks, and living expenses (taking into consideration tax breaks). In 2011, the same family had to spend 1268 days of income (Taylor, 2011:A3.)

Education is not a guarantee against bad economic times. Indeed, in 2003, 50 percent of all poor, two-parent family, major income earners had education beyond the high school level (National Council of Welfare, 2006b:51). In 2005, 27.4 percent of food-bank users in the Greater Toronto Area had completed college or university, and 53.3 percent of immigrant users of food banks had some college or university education (Lightman, Mitchell, & Herd, 2008:16,18). Particularly after the 2008 recession,

it is apparent that poverty may be as much a result of absent or inadequate employment opportunities as too little education.

AGE As discussed in Chapter 9, the reduction of poverty among seniors is one of the great poverty success stories. Poverty rates among Canadians 65 and older dropped from 33.9 percent in 1980 to 16.8 percent in 2001. Despite small increases, the poverty rate for Canadians 65 and older remained at a historically low rate of 5.3 percent in 2010 (Murphy, Zhang, & Dionne, 2012:7; Statistics Canada, 2012k). This dramatic improvement is largely the result of significant increases in government support programs for seniors. Recent income security policies, such as Old Age Security, the guaranteed income supplement, and spouse's allowance, have significantly improved the lives of many seniors.

However, seniors are far from poverty-free. Single senior women, in particular, remain at risk, with poverty rates above those of comparable men. In 2010, 15.6 percent (roughly one in seven) of unattached women 65 and older were living below the LICO (Statistics Canada, 2012k). Similarly, aged seniors appear to be at a disadvantage. Among older seniors (85 and older), 28.6 percent of women are living in poverty regardless of marital status (National Council of Welfare, 2006b:41). In short, a substantial number of very old seniors, especially those not sharing expenses with a partner, are struggling with low income.

Recent economic events are jeopardizing the future financial well-being of many seniors. For example, many government employees have seen their pension plans experience losses in value of up to 20 percent. The stock market crash in 2008 meant that many pension plans, both governmental and private, lost billions of dollars, and making up these losses will likely take years. While these new economic realities prompted legislation to extend the retirement age to 67, it has also led to calls to reduce pension benefits (Wallace, 2012:A8; Young, 2011).

✱ Explore the reading "Report Urges 100 Fixes to Stop Native Teen Suicides" on MySocLab.

Poverty as a social issue is far from straightforward. Determining who "qualifies" as poor is complex. Particular categories of individuals—notably women, seniors, members of racial and ethnic minorities, recent immigrants, the disabled, and children whose primary caregivers belong to these categories—are much more likely to be poor. Even though legislation exists at both the federal and provincial levels to address poverty, it has remained a persistent social problem.

Focus Question

Which social characteristics "set up" certain Canadians for high rates of impoverishment?

The Dynamics of Poverty

In the 1960s, Michael Harrington (1962) and Oscar Lewis (1966a) suggested that the poor tend to become trapped in a **culture of poverty**. They assumed that the values and behaviours of the poor "make them fundamentally different . . . and that these factors are largely responsible for their continued long-term poverty" (Ruggles, 1989:7). This perspective is closely linked to the notions of deserving and undeserving poor discussed earlier in the chapter. Implied by this "culture of poverty" approach is the idea that many poor people are lazy and bring poverty on themselves through their acceptance of certain beliefs and values. Is a self-perpetuating culture, transmitted across generations, that locks poor people into poverty the basic reason for its existence?

Until recently, we knew little about how long Canadians spend in poverty and how they move in and out of it. In the early-1990s, Statistics Canada began tracking individuals over six-year stretches, and as a result, we now have longitudinal information on the financial lives of Canadians. These data suggest, first, that while many Canadians do experience a period of low income, these periods are largely transitory and many Canadians move in and out of poverty in a short space of time. For example, between 2002 and 2007, 20 to 24 percent of Canadians experienced a period of low income, but the yearly rates (according to all three poverty measures) ranged from only 9 to 13 percent of Canadians.

Second, relatively few people experience low income for extended periods of time. From 2002 to 2007, only 2.1 percent of Canadians experienced low income every year (using LICO measures). Third, the severity of poverty (the gap between a poor person's actual income and the low income cut-offs) increased through the mid- to late-1990s and then decreased until 2008, when it appears to have started to intensify. Specific sectors of the population—unattached non-elderly persons and lone-parent families—are particularly vulnerable to persistent low income. In particular, between 13 and 17 percent (depending on low-income measure) of unattached non-elderly people were low-income earners for all six years between 2002 and 2007. Lone parents, despite the high rates (48 percent under the LICO) of short-term low income, experienced a reduced vulnerability to persistent low income between 1993 and 2007. It is important to keep in mind, however, that this data does not capture the consequences of the 2008 recession. It is reasonable to believe that low-income rates have trended upward since 2009 (Murphy, Zhang, & Dionne, 2012:23–25,61–68).

✔• **Practise comparing your ideas of the poor with the myths outlined in "Exploring Myths about the Poor" on MySocLab.**

SUMMARY AND REVIEW

COMPLEXITIES OF INEQUALITY

What is social class, and how do sociologists measure it?

Most sociologists have adopted Weber's definition of social class as a large group of people who rank closely to one another in wealth, power, and prestige. There are three ways to measure social class. In the subjective method, people assign themselves to their own social class. In the reputational method, people identify the social class of others on the basis of knowledge of their circumstances. In the objective method, researchers assign subjects to a social class on the basis of objective criteria such as wealth, power, and prestige. pp. 117.

HOW DO ELITES MAINTAIN SOCIAL INEQUALITY?

How do nations maintain social stratification?

To maintain social stratification within a nation, the ruling class uses an **ideology** that justifies current arrangements. It also controls information, and, when all else fails, depends on brute force. The social networks of the rich and poor also perpetuate social inequality. pp. 126–127.

CONSEQUENCES OF SOCIAL CLASS

How does social class affect people?

Social class leaves no aspect of life untouched. It affects people's chances of benefiting from new technology, dying early, becoming ill, receiving good health care, and getting divorced. Class membership also affects child-rearing, educational attainment, religious affiliation, political participation, and contact with the criminal justice system. pp. 131–133.

SOCIAL MOBILITY

What are the three types of social mobility?

The term **intergenerational mobility** refers to changes in social class from one generation to the next. *Exchange mobility* is the movement of large numbers of people from one class to another, with the net result that the relative proportions of population in each class remain about the same. The term **structural mobility** refers to social changes that affect the social class membership of large numbers of people. pp. 133–136.

POVERTY

Who becomes poor and why?

Poverty is unequally distributed in Canada. Women, members of racial and ethnic minorities, the disabled, recent immigrants, and children whose primary parents are members of these categories are much more likely to be poor. p. 137.

Some popular analysts argue that characteristics of individuals, such as the lack of a "work ethic" or the desire for immediate gratification, cause poverty. While "blaming the victim" is easy, it ignores many of the complexities of poverty. Sociologists examine structural features of society, such as the lack of employment opportunities, to find the causes of poverty. Sociologists generally conclude that life orientations are a consequence, not the cause, of people's position in the social class structure. pp. 137–140.

Why is poverty in Canada and around the world so frequently ignored?

Poverty is a complex and depressing topic. Despite government and community efforts, few long-term improvements have been made. In addition, the global recession of 2008 has exacerbated the numbers of poor and their plight both in Canada and around the world. In the face of poverty's intractability, there is a tendency to turn away rather than come to terms with the personal and social costs of ignoring social inequality. p. 141.

TALKING ABOUT THEORY

Theoretical Paradigms

	CLASSICAL PARADIGMS		RECENT PARADIGMS
	Structural-Functional Paradigm	Social-Conflict Paradigm	Feminist and Anti-Racist Paradugm
What is the level of analysis?	Macro level	Macro level	Micro and macro levels
How are social stratification and inequality explained?	The most qualified people are rewarded with high-ranking positions, decision-making power, and high income.	Conflict between social classes for resources—power, wealth, status—is the basis of social stratification.	Gender and race are the basis by which people are limited from equality of condition or opportunity.
How is the gap between rich and poor explained?	People are rewarded on the basis of merit and members of the wealthy and powerful classes have proven themselves through their achievements.	Class system reproduces itself, and within the structure of capitalist society, there are many limitations—low wages, poor benefits, high cost of housing—that keep the classes separate.	The labour market and opportunities for mobility are split along race, ethnicity, gender, and class lines.

KEY TERMS

patriarchy. In the economy, women's low wages and inferior, low-paid, low-status jobs relate to their unpaid work in the home. That women are responsible for the lion's share of unpaid domestic work and child/family care devalues their work in the paid labour market. These feminists call for equality rights for women, and argue that this would be possible within a socialist economic framework.

Radical feminism calls for the end of patriarchy, arguing that men's power over women is the root of women's oppression (Firestone, 1970). Because men occupy positions of power within the broader society, their decisions and the institutions they govern, including the media, maintain women's subordination. The way to change, say radical feminists, is through the development of alternative women-centred organizations and institutional arrangements that meet women's needs.

QUEER THEORY By the early 1980s, disagreements among feminists broke out around questions of sexuality. In particular, debate erupted between lesbians identifying themselves as cultural feminists who embraced more "traditional" sexual practices and lesbian feminists who embraced more radical sexual practices. Essentially, new practices of lesbianism broke down the old notions that there were two forms of women's sexuality—heterosexual and lesbian—because the disagreements gave rise to the understanding that there are multiple expressions of sexuality (Martindale, 2001). The discussion around sexual practices helped initiate the emerging disciplines of lesbian and gay studies and their theories of sexuality, known as *queer theory*. Queer theory attempts to break down the binary gay–straight categorization of people and their sexuality. Queer theorists give meaning and understanding to gay and lesbian cultures and the deep forms of oppression, including the silencing, experienced by gays and lesbians. However, recently, some argue that queer theory may ignore multiple diversities and oppressions and thereby call for greater inclusiveness in understanding sexual marginalization (Martindale, 2001).

POSTMODERNISM Interrelated to theories of feminism, the postmodern approach starts with the understanding of gender as socially constructed and interrelated with race, class, and sexual orientation, all of which are also socially constructed (Elliott & Mandell, 2001). Postmodernists ask us to question our categorizing and conceptualizations of "others," emphasizing the importance of understanding identities from the individual's viewpoint, rather than through universal assumptions about gender, oppression, and patriarchy by categorizing women as a group and assuming that they share common values, beliefs, and histories. Postmodernists caution against generalizing about others, asking researchers to avoid drawing conclusions based on "hard and fast" definitions or characterizations of people based on objective, scientific methods that may obscure individuals' experience of their own complex identities.

Gender Inequality In Canada

Inequality is not some accidental, hit-or-miss affair; the institutions of every society work together to maintain its particular forms. Custom, venerated by history, both justifies and maintains arrangements of gender inequality. Although men have resisted sharing their privileged positions with women, changes are occurring.

Fighting Back: The Rise of Feminism

To see how far we have come, it is useful to see where we used to be. In early Canadian society, the second-class status of women was taken for granted. A husband and wife were legally one person—him (Chafetz & Dworkin, 1986). Women who worked for wages could not even collect their own paycheques—single women were often required to hand them over to their fathers; married women, to their husbands. Women could not serve on juries; nor could they vote, make legal contracts, or hold property in their own name. These conditions were generally seen as part of the proper relations of the sexes. How could times have changed so much that such conditions sound like fiction?

A central lesson of conflict theory is that power yields tremendous privilege; that, like a magnet, it draws to the elite the best resources available. Because men held on tenaciously to their privileges and used social institutions to maintain their position, basic rights for women came only through prolonged and bitter struggle (Offen, 1990).

Feminism, the view that biology is not destiny, and that, therefore, stratification by gender is wrong and should be resisted, met strong opposition—both by men who had privilege to lose and by many women who accepted their status as morally correct. In Great Britain and the United States, for example, women had to directly confront men, who first denied them the right to speak and then ridiculed them when they persisted in speaking in public. Leaders of the feminist movement, then known as suffragists, chained themselves to posts and to the iron grillwork of public buildings—and then went on protesting while police sawed them loose. When imprisoned, they continued to protest by going on hunger strikes. Threatened by such determination

Unlike its counterparts in Britain and the United States, where suffragists adopted militant tactics, the "first wave" of the Canadian women's movement was regarded as a war of words. One of the most outspoken suffragists was Nellie McClung, whose passionate statements were strong and compelling.

and confrontations, men spat on demonstrators for daring to question their place, slapped their faces, tripped them, pelted them with burning cigar stubs, and hurled obscenities at them (Cowley, 1969).

Although heavily influenced by developments in the United States and Britain, the Canadian women's movement may be characterized as a war of words. The militant tactics of British and American suffragists were not adopted by Canadian feminists, who instead employed a relatively peaceful approach. The Canadian movement upheld Nellie McClung's motto: "Never retract, never explain, never apologize, get the thing done and let them howl" (cited in Wilson, 1991). These words were strong and compelling, yet moderate. While they may have offended some aspects of the prevailing social etiquette prescribed for women, they were not suggestive of a radical departure from conventional social norms.

This "first wave" of the women's movement had a conservative branch that concentrated on winning the vote for women and a radical branch that wanted to reform all the institutions of society (Chafetz & Dworkin, 1986). Both groups worked toward winning the right to vote, but after the vote was won in 1917 in Canada (and in 1920 in the United States), many declared that the movement had achieved its ultimate purpose, and some argued that this victory left the movement with no unifying goal. However, women continued to struggle for change, by working to establish their voice and presence in trade unions, in the workplace, within the political process, through the courts, and in educational institutions. Women also carried the message of equality into their homes and families—the private sphere—where they worked to establish more equitable divisions of domestic work and to have a say in the household's decisions. Every victory was hailed, but feminists realized that barriers to women's social and economic equality, including attitudes and beliefs about women's status and rights, would not be easily changed.

The "second wave" began in the 1960s. Sociologist Janet Chafetz (1990) points out that, up to this time, most women thought of work as a temporary activity to fill the time between completing school and getting married. When larger numbers of women began to enter the labour force, however, they began to compare their working conditions with those of men. This shift in reference group created a different view of working conditions, launching a second wave of protest and struggle against gender inequalities. Women from all walks of life asserted themselves in public as well as in their own homes. The goals of this second wave are broad—from changing work roles to changing policies on violence against women.

The second wave is also broken into liberal and conservative factions. Although each holds a different picture of what gender equality should look like, they share several goals, including non-discrimination in job opportunities and pay. Through ongoing discussions, which sometimes include divergent views, the women's movement will continue to take shape and affect public policy.

Although women enjoy fundamental rights today, gender inequality continues to play a central role in social life. In some instances, it can even be a life-and-death matter, as with the medical situations discussed in the Down-to-Earth Sociology box that follows.

Let's now look at gender relations in education and everyday life, and then, in greater detail, at discrimination in the world of work.

Gender Inequality in Education

In education, too, a glimpse at the past sheds light on the present. About a century ago, leading educators claimed that women's wombs dominated their minds. This made higher education a burden on women's frail capacities. Dr. Edward Clarke, of Harvard University's medical faculty, expressed the dominant (nineteenth century) sentiment this way:

> A girl upon whom Nature, for a limited period and for a definite purpose, imposes so great a physiological task, will not have as much power left for the tasks of school, as the boy of whom Nature requires less at the corresponding epoch. (Cited in Andersen, 1988)

Because women were seen as so much weaker, Clarke urged them to spend only a third of the amount of time that young men spent studying—and not to study at all during menstruation.

Over 200 years ago, in 1792, Mary Wollstonecraft, a well-known early feminist, published *A Vindication of the Rights of Woman*, in which she discussed male power as the underlying cause of society's problems (Mackie, 1991:252). She believed that education was the key to liberating both men and women. Although she was heavily criticized as a man-hating crusader, her ideas on the importance of education in contributing to women's equality were not only subsequently echoed by John Stuart Mill and other historical thinkers, but also became part of the foundation of the suffrage movements.

According to Marlene Mackie (1991), the problem of access to higher education was the spark that initiated the Canadian suffrage movement. In the 1860s, schoolteacher Emily Stowe found herself supporting her disabled husband and their three children. Although she managed to save enough money to study medicine, Canadian medical schools denied her admission because of her gender. Eventually she was admitted to an American medical school, and, upon her return, became Canada's first female physician. She continued to struggle with others for the acceptance of women in the professions. As a result, the University of Toronto began to admit women in 1886.

Over the years, the situation gradually improved, but discrimination persisted. Through the 1960s, for example, girls were not welcome in shop classes, which were reserved for boys. Instead, they were routed to home economics,

Making the Invisible Visible: Gender Impacts Health

Gender differences and unequal access to money, wealth, resources, and power affect health and can even have deadly consequences. In Africa, for example, women in the throes of childbirth are often turned away from clinics and hospitals because of their inability to pay for the supplies required for their treatment or to pay bribes to the staff in exchange for care (York, 2011:A27). As a result, the United Nations and the World Health Organization report alarming statistics: in Mali, for every 1000 live births, nine birthing mothers die; mothers' risk of dying during childbirth is 300 times greater in Africa than in Canada (York, 2011:A27; WHO, 2012).

In the early 1990s, reports indicated that women, who live longer than men, were twice as likely to die after coronary bypass surgery. This prompted researchers at numerous sites across the United States, Canada, and elsewhere to consider why these differences were occurring. Medical researchers first turned to an answer based on biology. In coronary bypass surgery, a blood vessel is taken from one part of the body and stitched to a coronary artery on the surface of the heart. Perhaps this operation was more difficult to perform on women because of their smaller coronary arteries. To find out, researchers measured the amount of time surgeons kept patients on the heart-lung machine while they operated. They were surprised to learn that women spent less time on the machine than men, indicating that the operation was not more difficult to perform on women. As the researchers probed, a surprising answer unfolded—unintended sexual discrimination. Referring physicians had not taken the chest pains of their women patients as seriously as those of their men patients. Physicians, it turned out, were 10 times more likely to give men exercise stress tests and radioactive heart scans. They also sent men to surgery on the basis of abnormal stress tests but waited until women showed clear-cut symptoms of coronary heart disease before sending them to surgery. Being referred for surgery after the disease has progressed decreases the chances of survival. In another study, researchers found that women who are hospitalized for heart attacks are less likely than men to be referred to rehabilitation programs, which have the potential to decrease the risk of death by 25 percent (Yelaja, 2002). Overall, the majority of Canadians with cardiac conditions are not referred for rehabilitation; along with gender, income may be a critical barrier.

While the differential treatment women may receive in cardiac care may have deadly consequences, in other areas of medicine, treating women differently may negatively impact quality of life, pain management, and lifestyle. For example, despite the similarity in the presenting condition of moderate knee osteoarthritis, researchers in Toronto recently found that women were less likely to be recommended for knee-replacement surgery than males (Pearce, 2008:L1). How is this difference explained? The lead researcher, Dr. Borkhoff, suggests that there may be a number of answers, but the most likely is the "subconscious bias" held by doctors, both male and female, who may not recognize women's symptoms as being equally as serious as those of their male patients. Some doctors are under the false assumption that female patients do not benefit as much as males from this type of surgery. However, the findings point out that women are more likely to be recommended for surgery when their condition is at a more advanced stage. Generally, when surgery is performed at a earlier stage, it is more likely to be successful (Pearce, 2008:L4).

Some researchers wondered if the sex of the physician matters when it comes to ordering Pap smears and mammography. They examined the records of 98 000 patients and found that it does make a difference—women physicians are much more likely to order these screening tests. However, in her study of knee replacements and gender bias, Dr. Borkhoff suggests that the social stereotyping that affects doctors' decisions may be as widely held by female physicians as it is by males (Pearce, 2008:L4).

For Your Consideration

In short, gender bias is so pervasive that it operates beneath our level of awareness and is so severe that it can even be a matter of life or death. Health Canada now recognizes that sex and gender do affect health conditions and their treatments. Even the effectiveness of commonly prescribed drugs is impacted by gender (Health Canada, 2010). It is important to note that the doctors are unaware that they are discriminating. They have no intention of doing so. In what ways does gender bias affect your own perceptions and behaviour?

Sources: York (2011); Yelaja (2002); Pearce (2008); Health Canada (2010).

TABLE 7.1 Public Postsecondary Enrollments (University and College) by Sex and Field of Study, 2009–2010

Public Postsecondary Enrollments by Sex and Field of Study (Males), 2009–2010	
Total, instructional programs	817 938
Personal improvement and leisure	9027
Education	24 087
Visual and performing arts and communications technologies	29 976
Humanities	143 346
Social and behavioural sciences and law	77 667
Business, management, and public administration	149 880
Physical and life sciences and technologies	45 042
Mathematics, computer, and information sciences	42 627
Architecture, engineering, and related technologies	146 241
Agriculture, natural resources, and conservation	13 275
Health, parks, recreation, and fitness	52 353
Personal, protective, and transportation services	24 387
Other instructional programs	60 033

Source: www.statcan.gc.ca/tables-tableaux/sum-som/l01/cst01/educ72b-eng.htm

considered appropriate for their station in life. (Even today, whenever I attend Toronto Raptors basketball games, I still see an organized group of women, at times scantily clad in short, brightly coloured outfits, wildly cheering from the sidelines. There is no such group of young men leading organized cheers in the WNBA.)

The situation has so changed from what it used to be, however, that some measures of education make it look as though discrimination may be directed against males. For example, more women than men are enrolled in Canadian universities, and in 2006, accounted for 58 percent of students in all bachelor degree programs. This represents a dramatic increase from the 1970s, when about one in three full-time students was female. Just over half (51.8 percent) of master's degrees and over 40 percent (42.9) of PhD degrees were earned by women in 2009 (Canadian Council on Learning, 2009:54). Graduation rates for women are climbing, whereas rates for men are declining (Canadian Council on Learning, 2009:54).

Probing below the surface, however, reveals that degrees follow gender, thus reinforcing male–female distinctions. Extremes at the bachelor's level highlight gender tracking: in 2008, men earned over 77 percent of bachelor's degrees in engineering and 69 percent of degrees in mathematics—which are considered "masculine" fields—while women were awarded 73 percent of bachelor's degrees in health professions and occupations, over 76 percent of degrees in

education, and 66 percent of degrees in visual and performing arts and communications technologies—traditionally "feminine" fields (Statistics Canada, 2010g). While business, management, and public administration were popular fields of study among both men and women, the top fields for men and women otherwise differ widely. Table 7.1 lists postsecondary enrollments by sex and field of study for 2009–2010.

Because gender socialization gives men and women different orientations to life, they enter postsecondary education with gender-linked aspirations. It is this socialization—rather than any presumed innate characteristics—that channels them into different educational paths.

If we trace the steps of those who earn doctoral degrees back into colleges and universities, we find gender stratification in both prestige and income. Overall, women hold about 27 percent of all earned PhDs in Canada, but again they are vastly underrepresented in fields traditionally dominated by men, including science and engineering, physics, computer and physical sciences, and mathematics (McKenzie, 2007:27). A study conducted in 2007 based on a survey and interviews with 2500 workers concluded that women leave science, technology, and engineering professions in disproportionate numbers, despite their advances in education in these fields, because of the "hard hat," "lab coat," and "geek" cultures, all of which are unaccommodating and intimidating to women (Belkin, 2008:A13). Some suggest that the "hard sciences" are the most difficult environments for women because of firmly rooted beliefs that women are not as good at math and science as men are.

In universities throughout Canada, women are less likely to be full professors, the highest, most prestigious rank. It is important also to note that full professors are paid more than the lower ranks (instructor, assistant professor, and associate professor) and enjoy greater status. In 2011, about 38 percent of university professors in Canada were women (Service Canada, 2012), but men outnumbered women in the ranks of full professor (Perkel, 2007). The level of Full Professor carries the most status in the university and often takes years to achieve and women's underrepresentation in this group is far greater than in the ranks of Associate and Assistant Professor. To see the extent of the inequality, we can note that even when women are full professors, they average less pay than men who are full professors. At all ranks, the median salary of female professors is lower than that of their male colleagues. Sociologists Janice Drakich and Penni Stewart argue that although the situation for female professors has improved tremendously since the 1990s, it is still the case that "systemic discrimination is alive and well in the academy" (as cited in Perkel, 2007).

Some encouraging changes are taking place in higher education. Although we are still a long way from equality, the proportion of professional degrees earned by women has increased sharply. In Canada today, women constitute almost half of all graduates in medical studies and research, and are studying dentistry in increasing numbers. In addition, women are now the majority among graduates in two previously male-dominated professional fields—pharmacy and veterinary medicine—outnumbering their male counterparts by almost two to one.

Gender Inequality in Everyday Life

Gender discrimination pervades everyday life. Let's consider the general devaluation of femininity and inequalities in social interaction.

In general, women's capacities, interests, attitudes, and contributions are not taken as seriously as those of men. Masculinity is valued as representing success and strength. In contrast, femininity is devalued; it is perceived as representing weakness and lack of accomplishment (Schur, 1984). Often people are unaware of discriminatory assumptions and evaluations, but by listening and watching carefully, it is easy to observe them in everyday interactions.

During World War II, sociologist Samuel Stouffer noted the general devaluation of femininity. In his classic study of combat soldiers, *The American Soldier*, Stouffer reported that officers used feminine terms as insults to motivate troops (Stouffer et al., 1949). To show less-than-expected courage or endurance was to risk the charge of not being a man. An officer might say, "Whatsa matter, Bud—got lace on your drawers?" A generation later, to prepare soldiers to fight in Vietnam, accusations of femininity were still used as

motivating insults. Drill sergeants would mock their troops by saying, "Can't hack it, little girls?" (Eisenhart, 1975). The practice continues today.

The same phenomenon occurs in sports. Sociologist Douglas Foley (1997) notes that football coaches insult boys who don't play well by saying that they are "wearing skirts," and sociologists Jean Stockard and Miriam Johnson (1980), who observed boys playing basketball, heard boys who missed a basket called a "woman." This pattern continues in professional sports, and hockey players who are not rough enough on the ice are called "girls" (Gallmeier, 1988:227). So commonplace is the mocking of boys in feminine terms that it has prompted women athletes to sport T-shirts, popular in women's locker rooms, retorting: "You only wish" (front) . . . "you played like a girl" (back).

Such name-calling is sociologically significant because the insults embody a generalized devaluation of females and there is no comparable phenomenon among women (Stockard & Johnson, 1980:12). Girls' coaches do not ridicule them by calling them "boys." Quite the contrary. In some athletic circles, such as in rowing, which demands rigorous strength training, pumping iron and pulling "like a man" is laudable.

Social interaction is rife with gender inequalities. Take conversation, for example: gender inequality shows up in everyday talk. Men are more likely to interrupt a conversation and to control changes in topic, thereby making conversation between a man and a woman often more like talk between an employer and an employee than between social equals (West & Garcia, 1988; Smith-Lovin & Brody, 1989; Tannen, 2007). At school, men interrupt their instructors more often than do women, especially if the instructor is a woman (Brooks, 1982). In short, conversations between men and women mirror their relative positions of power in society.

Derogatory terms and conversation represent only the tip of the iceberg, however. Underlying these aspects of everyday life is a structural inequality based on gender that runs throughout society. Let's examine that structural feature in the workplace.

Gender Relations In the Workplace

To examine the work setting is to make visible basic relations between men and women. Let's consider changes in the labour force, the pay gap, and opportunities for women.

Women's Participation in the Labour Force

While women have always worked, over the past 40 years there has been a massive movement of women, including those with young children, into the paid labour force. Women's high level of involvement in paid work has prompted sociologists to examine the ways women's employment differs from that of men. This includes comparisons between men's and women's jobs, wages, patterns of employment, and opportunities for promotion, and how women's paid work experiences are affected by familial responsibilities and expectations.

These protestors are lobbying for pay equity at Bell Canada. In 1992, the Canadian Human Rights Commission ruled that former female Bell Canada operators had suffered from pay discrimination. The case was in court for 10 years, with demands that Bell pay its male and female operators equitably, and that the company pay some 800 former female employees $400 million in pay equity money. The case was settled in 2002 for $178 million.

The *labour force participation rate* is the proportion of men and women 16 years and older who are in the labour force, working full- or part-time. In 2009, 53.8 percent or 8.1 million Canadian women, more than double the number in 1976, were employed (Statistics Canada, 2012k). A century ago, almost all married women were full-time housewives. While married women often worked in the informal economy (e.g., sewing at home or taking in laundry or boarders), they did not usually participate formally in the labour force. In 1891, two-fifths of employed women were servants or were working at jobs that mirrored their domestic roles. Eventually the range of occupations open to women widened somewhat and certain jobs became regarded as "women's work." In 1901, about 25 percent of clerical workers were women, but by 1921 more than 40 percent were women (cited in Duffy & Pupo, 1992:15–17). Today, retail sales work is the most prevalent occupational category for women (Statistics Canada, 2012k).

With the increased demand for workers during and immediately following the world wars, women's labour force participation grew from 17 percent in 1921 to 20 percent in 1931 and from 24.4 percent in 1939 to 33.5 percent in 1944 (cited in Duffy & Pupo, 1992:17). After a decline following World War II, when millions of women left factories and offices to return home as full-time wives and mothers, women's labour force participation steadily climbed from the mid-1950s on. Today, almost 60 percent of all women aged 15 and over and 82 percent of women between the ages of 25 and 54 work for pay (Statistics Canada, 2012k:26). Differences among women, however, persist.

Female recent immigrants, for example, experience lower work-force participation rates than males who immigrated at the same time, as well as compared to Canadian-born women (Statistics Canada, 2012k).

The Pay Gap

Mark your calendars—your long, long-range calendars. Now circle the year 2593. That's when Canadian law professor Kathleen Lahey determined that women will finally be celebrating Women's Equality Day (Brennan, 2012:A3). Taking into account a number of factors, including women's participation in paid and unpaid work; budgetary changes in taxation, health care, and the retirement income system, along with other considerations, women's equality is certainly not in view within our lifetimes. While the gains women were making in earlier decades, particularly between 1977 and 1993, seemed to hold promise, recessions and other factors combined to slow or even reverse progress. There has been no progress toward equality with men in Canada since 1997 (Brennan, 2012:A3).

Most of us would like to earn an extra $800 000 from work. But to do this, we would have to earn, on average, an extra $20 000 a year between the ages of 25 and 65. Is this hard to do? Not if you are a man. Comparing workers who have bachelor's degrees, $800 000 is precisely how much more the average man will earn compared to the average woman. Hardly any single factor pinpoints gender discrimination better than this total. A gender gap in earnings shows up at all levels of education and exists in all industrialized nations.

The gender gap in wages is pervasive. In 2009, the average annual earnings of men working full-year, full-time was $62 200, while women working full-year, full-time averaged $46 400. In other words, women (full-time, full-year) were paid an average of 74.5 cents for every dollar their male counterparts earned. For those working full-time, full-year with a university degree, the gap was wider—women earned 67.5 percent of their male counterparts' wages (Statistics Canada, 2009b). While the gap today represents huge gains from the late 1960s, when Canadian women were only earning 58 cents for every dollar earned by males, it is persistent, and there is some indication it may be widening among younger workers.

What logic can underlie the gender pay gap? Earlier we saw that university degrees are gender-linked, so perhaps this gap is due to career paths. Maybe women tend to work at lower-paying jobs, such as primary school teaching, whereas men are more likely to go into better-paying fields, such as business and engineering. Actually, researchers have found that less than half the pay gap can be attributed to such factors. The balance, however, is due to workplace characteristics, such as high performance systems, degree of foreign ownership, and the rate of part-time work, and to gender discrimination (Drolet, 2002; Iyer, 2002; Jackson, 2005; Canadian Labour Congress, 2008a). A key factor contributing to the gender pay gap is the "child penalty"— women missing out on work experience and opportunities while they care for children. In other words, women are placed on the "mommy track" rather than the "career track," and it is presumed that they are not as committed to their paid work as their male colleagues. Depending on your sex, then, you are likely either to benefit from gender discrimination—or to be its victim.

Because the pay gap will be important in your own work life, let's consider women's presence in corporate Canada. According to statistics for 2010, women accounted for only 17.7 percent of the senior officers of Canada's 500 largest corporations (Catalyst, 2012). Further, a 2011 study by the Canadian Centre for Policy Alternatives found no women among the ranks of the hundred highest earning CEOs heading publically traded Canadian corporations in 2009 (Mackenzie, 2011).

Your best chance to reach the top is to be named— in this order—John, Robert, James, William, or Charles. Edward, Lawrence, and Richard are also advantageous. Amber, Candace, Leticia, and María, however, apparently draw a severe penalty.

Struggling for pay equity has paid off for many Canadian women. A settlement of female civil servants in Ontario in 2001 provided each woman about $45 000 in retroactive pay, and a few years ago, a settlement with Bell Canada brought female operators' pay in line with that of their male counterparts. These two decisions, both favourable toward mending the gap, will pay off for thousands of others waiting to have their cases heard.

Focus Question
How can the pay gap between men and women be explained?

Women in Manufacturing and IT

Gaining equity in the workplace for women has been an uphill climb. Overall, women's jobs tend to be lower-paying, with fewer benefits and lower rates of unionization, often part-time and located in the service sector. What happens when we look at a work sphere traditionally associated with males? Are women's job prospects any better? In contrast to service sector jobs (the so-called McJobs), those in manufacturing usually offer a better deal—higher wages; more benefits, including pension plans; and higher rates of unionization. For example, the average hourly wage in manufacturing is over $19 compared to just over $15 in retail (Statistics Canada, 2012a). However, over the past five years, Canadians have experienced significant job loss in the manufacturing sector, largely due to plant closures, work relocation overseas, corporate downsizing, and other factors, and these changes have impacted women's (and men's) access to and ability to hang on to manufacturing jobs.

There have been over 300 000 manufacturing jobs lost in Canada in the past five years (Bernard, 2009). According to the Canadian Labour Congress, women's losses in manufacturing are greater relative to those of men—9 percent of women faced job loss, compared to 7 percent of men (2008b). When women lose their manufacturing positions in industries such as auto, auto parts, aerospace, and food and fish processing, the jobs available to them are frequently insecure McJobs.

Will new developments in technology and other highly skilled fields make a difference for women? Recent figures indicate that women hold just over 41 percent of jobs in professional, scientific, and technical services (Statistics Canada, 2012d). A study by Krista Scott-Dixon (2004) traced women's paths in developing careers in IT. The women she studied worked in high-tech industries, applying technological, scientific, and engineering skills and knowledge in their jobs. Yet despite their knowledge and skills, women in a variety of technological occupations continue to face barriers preventing them from reaching their full potential.

The Glass Ceiling or the Glass Escalator?

THE GLASS CEILING What keeps women from breaking through the "glass ceiling," the mostly invisible barrier that keeps women from reaching the executive suite? Researchers have identified a "pipeline" that leads to the top—marketing, sales, and production—positions that

 Explore the table "Gender Pay Gap" on **MySocLab.**

directly add to the corporate bottom line (Hymowitz 2004). Stereotyped as better at "support," women are often steered into human resources or public relations. There, successful projects are not appreciated as much as those that bring in corporate profits—and bonuses for their managers.

Another reason the glass ceiling is so powerful is that women lack mentors—successful executives who take an interest in them and show them the ropes. Some men executives fear gossip and sexual harassment charges if they get close to a woman in a subordinate position. Others don't mentor women because of stereotypes of women as less qualified or lacking the necessary commitment to the job. To lack a mentor is no trivial matter, especially since women often experience a "chilly climate" in executive boardrooms or decision-making chambers.

The glass ceiling is cracking, however slowly, as more women reach the executive suite (Flavelle, 2006:A16). However, estimates suggest that it will be over 150 years before men and women share equal numbers among the ranks of middle management (CBC News, 2011b). A look at women above the glass ceiling reveals highly motivated women with a fierce competitive spirit who are highly committed to their work and career. Often they play by "men's rules," developing a style that makes men comfortable. In order to "play the game" successfully, these women establish a support system with their partners or through paid help for household and family work.

THE GLASS ESCALATOR Sociologist Christine Williams (1995) interviewed men and women who worked as nurses, elementary school teachers, librarians, and social workers. She found that the men in these traditionally women's occupations, instead of bumping into a glass ceiling, had climbed aboard a glass escalator. That is, compared with women, the men were accelerated into more desirable work assignments, higher-level positions, and larger salaries. The motor that drives the glass escalator is the stereotype that, because someone is male, he is more capable.

Evidence today suggests that the number of men entering fields that have been traditionally dominated by women is growing by leaps and bounds (Dewan & Gebeloff, 2012). One reason is that traditional female occupations have been growing, whereas traditional male strongholds, such as heavy manufacturing, have been in decline. But are men displacing women? Most analysts say that's not the case, although it's still too early to draw definite conclusions. What we do know, however, is that men, and white men in particular, are still riding the glass escalator with early promotions and higher salaries compared to their female co-workers (Dewan & Gebeloff, 2012).

Conflict theorists argue that capitalists exploit gender divisions among workers in order to control them—the "divide and rule" principle. Their method is not overt, but rather owners and managers divide workers in subtle ways. For example, a manufacturing firm in the Silicon Valley, California, specifies the colour of the smocks that it requires workers to wear. The colour of the men's smocks depends on the particular job they do, but all the women wear the same colour, regardless of their jobs.

Why should management have such a policy? According to sociologist Karen Hossfeld (2000), who studied these workers, the underlying message is: no matter what your job is, you are primarily a woman. Encouraging the women to think of themselves not as workers, but as women workers, makes them easier to control. Hossfeld found that when their bosses flirted with them, the women were not inclined to file grievances.

The same company has a "Ladies' Corner" in its newsletter. The subtle message: it is a men's newsletter with a little corner devoted to women. In other words, men are the real workers, but women are there, too.

Women, Family, and Inequality

Women are more likely than their partners to be the caretakers of the family, to nurture it through the hard times. Women usually take greater responsibility for caring roles—with children, elders, and disabled family members—and for maintaining family ties (such as sending greeting cards). They also spend considerably more time doing housework. Recent figures indicate that women on average spend an hour and thirteen minutes daily more than men on unpaid activities (Statistics Canada, 2011d). Consequently, most employed women face greater role conflict than do their partners.

The greatest constraint limiting women's labour-force participation or their career advancement is the pressure they face from their family-related roles, expectations, and responsibilities. The burdens of reconciling family and work fall particularly heavily on the shoulders of mothers with small children whose personal costs (the guilt they feel, not having time for themselves, not living up to the image of the "good mother") for working outside the home are tremendously high. Even when both partners work full-time, there is a substantial difference between males and females in the hours they spend on housework and care-giving. A case study by Luxton and Corman (2001) of working-class men and women in Hamilton, Ontario, confirms this pattern. Most women in the labour force work a *double day*—that is, a shift of unpaid work at home following or before their shift in the workplace. Not surprisingly, most women at some point face the likelihood of leaving their paid jobs in order to undertake their domestic responsibilities, including care-giving to senior, young, or disabled family members, on a full-time basis.

When researchers compared men and women at the same age across generations, there are indications that Canadian couples may be sharing more equally in household work. When baby boomer women were in their twenties, they averaged 1.2 hours more per day on housework compared to men. But during their twenties, Generation Y

Mother and Sally

Mother can sew.
Jane can sew.

"I will help," said Dick.
"I will help you with the pigs."

Father

FIGURE 7.1 Teaching Gender

women spent 0.4 hours more than men in the same age group on housework. In other words, younger generations are increasingly establishing more equitable divisions of domestic responsibilities. According to researchers, this more equitable balance reflects women's increased paid work along with men's greater involvement in household work (Statistics Canada, 2011d).

To resolve the conflict over inequitable division of domestic work and the costs it entails for women in paid work, a number of years ago, Felice Schwartz (1989) suggested that corporations offer women a choice of two parallel career paths. The "fast track" consists of high-powered, demanding positions that may require 60 or 70 hours of work per week—regular responsibilities, emergencies, out-of-town meetings, and a briefcase jammed with work at night and on weekends. Or, instead, women may choose a "mommy track," which would allow for a lower commitment to the firm, freeing time for a higher commitment to family.

What is wrong with this proposal is that a "mommy track" would encourage women to be satisfied with lower aspirations and fewer promotions, and confirm men's stereotypes of women executives. Because there is no "daddy track," it also assumes that child-rearing is primarily women's work (Starrels, 1992). To encourage women to slow down in the race to climb the corporate ladder would perpetuate, or even increase, the pay gap. The "mommy track," conclude critics, would keep men in executive power and relegate women to an inferior position in corporate life.

Critics suggest that a better way to confront the conflict between work and family is for partners to take greater responsibility at home and for workplaces to provide on-site day care, flexible work schedules, and parental leave without loss of benefits (Auerbach, 1990; Galinsky & Stein, 1990; Duffy & Pupo, 1996). Others maintain that the choice between family and career is artificial, that there are ample role models of family-oriented, highly successful

women, from Hilary Weston, former lieutenant-governor of Ontario, to judges Rosalie Abella and Louise Arbour and CEO Christine Magee.

Interestingly, gender stereotypes regarding men's and women's domestic, and particularly childcare, roles persist. Canadian teens still see women's primary role as the caretaker of their families and their homes, and men are expected to be "tough" and primary breadwinners (Baluja, 2011:A3). While many teens today broadly embrace notions of gender equality, like previous generations, they are holding on to traditional notions regarding gender roles and are unclear about how these stereotypes might conflict with gender equality.

Parenting and work often bring conflict, some of which we will examine in Chapter 13. The next Sociology and the New Technology box presents a controversy surrounding motherhood that has been ushered in by technology.

Sexual Harassment

Until the 1970s, women considered it a personal matter when they experienced unwanted sexual comments, touches, looks, or pressure to have sex. The term **sexual harassment**, which refers to these activities, especially in occupational or school settings, was unknown. In 1979, Catharine MacKinnon, an activist lawyer, published *Sexual Harassment of Working Women: A Case of Sex Discrimination*. MacKinnon stressed that such unwanted sexual advances are a *structural* problem; that is, they are built into the social structure. It is not a case of a man here and a man there doing obnoxious things because they are attracted to a woman; rather, it is a case of men abusing their positions of authority to force unwanted sexual activities on women.

 Explore the chart "Two-Paycheque Marriages" on MySocLab.

Rent-a-Uterus: Gender and Reproductive Technology

Breakthroughs in reproductive technology have led to a cultural lag. That is, our technology allows forms of reproduction that have outpaced our norms, our standards of right and wrong. Let's look at some real-life examples.

Consider surrogate motherhood:

Mary Beth Whitehead of New Jersey signed a contract for which she was paid to be artificially inseminated with the semen of Bill Stern, whose wife was ill. During pregnancy, Whitehead became emotionally attached to her developing child and decided to keep the baby.

Stern sued Whitehead to enforce the contract. The controversy, known as the "Baby M case," captivated the nation. Should the contract be enforced, or did a "mother's right" supersede the contract? Stern won, not on the basis of the contract, which was ruled illegal, but on the basis of his fathering the baby.

Consider the growth of commercial surrogacy:

In the city of Anand in western India, 15 pregnant women, cared for by a team of maids, cooks, and doctors, live at a clinic at Kaival Hospital, preparing to give birth to children for infertile couples from around the world. Here, surrogate motherhood, or "outsourced pregnancy," has become an enterprise. Couples provide the egg and sperm and sign a contract, guaranteeing payment of medical expenses and the surrogate's fee. The surrogate mother also signs a contract, promising to hand over the baby after birth. Surrogate motherhood pays the young women well—what would take about 15 years to earn at a regular job. Is this arrangement exploitative of young poor women, who endure the pain and possible complications of pregnancy for relatively low rates of pay? ("Wombs for Rent", 2007:A6)

Consider artificial insemination for the purpose of abortion:

Rae Leith loved her father, who was suffering the ravages of Alzheimer's disease. She wanted to be inseminated with her father's sperm in order to have an abortion, and then have the brains of the fetus, which would match her father's tissue, transplanted into her father's brain. Her father said no.

Consider postmortem ventilation (PMV), in which a brain-dead body is kept alive by artificial means:

Brain-dead pregnant women have been kept in a ventilated state for several months in order to allow their fetuses to have a better chance to survive. In one case, the man who claimed to be the father of a fetus requested PMV, but the husband objected. The court ruled that since the woman was dead, the state had the right to make the decision, which it did, ruling in favour of PMV. Seven weeks later, the baby died after a Caesarean delivery.

For Your Consideration

What should be the relative roles of men and women in technological conception? In the first case described, should contracts for surrogate motherhood be legally enforceable—and placed higher than a woman's right to motherhood? In the second case, what are the ethics of commercial surrogacy and how are exploitation and globalization together impacting young women's lives and their reproductive health? In the third case, should a woman have an absolute right to do whatever she wishes with her uterus—regardless of whose sperm is used? In the fourth case, should the state be able to determine what happens to a woman's womb and fetus if she is brain-dead? Is this the rightful saving of a child's life, or the state's wrongful control over a woman's womb? Finally, on the basis of this last case, since brain-dead women have no legal rights, could they be used as incubators for the embryos of others—something that is totally within our technological capacity?

Sources: Overvold (1988); Rothman (1989); Raymond (1993); "Wombs for Rent" (2007).

Although the targets of sexual harassment are usually women, the number of male victims has been increasing as women have moved into positions of power. Male victims are less likely than female victims to receive a sympathetic ear. Like women victims, however, these men report that they feel powerless and used. Social norms and symbolic perceptions, we assume, will eventually catch up to this emerging reality of women abusing power and men as victims. With most authority and power vested in men, the majority of sexual harassers are still men.

As symbolic interactionists stress, labels affect our perception. Today the term *sexual harassment* sheds a different light on unwanted sexual attention as compared to the understanding of this behaviour by earlier generations. The meaning of sexual harassment continues to be redefined as court cases change what the term does and does not include.

The Simpsons' Take on Issues of Gender

Spawning a myriad of toys, posters, and other pop culture paraphernalia, *The Simpsons*, one of the longest-running television shows in North America, is familiar to most Canadian households. Woven through the hundreds of episodes are a number of recurring themes, gently poking at traditional values, structures, and institutions and exposing absurdities in American society. Producer Matt Groening's sarcasm, satire, and wit have extended to schools, policing, local politics, the environment, the church, and the values and practices of capitalism. Through feisty Lisa, with her intelligence and strong sense of justice, and Marge, housewife and mother, with her quiet commentary, strong moral convictions, fairness, and willingness to engage in local politics, women's places in family and community are exposed and questioned.

In one notable episode, Lisa's concerns over phrases such as "Let's make cookies for the boys," uttered by the popular talking doll, Malibu Stacy (a doll styled with great similarity to Mattel's Barbie), led her to the executive boardroom. There, Malibu Stacy's creator, who was recently bought out by a giant competitor, listens to Lisa's concerns over the sexist doll and, with Lisa's help, recreates the doll with intelligence. Not surprisingly, the new doll is a bomb.

Along with candid commentary on gender socialization and sexism in the marketplace, gender tensions are featured throughout the series: when Marge gets a job as a policewoman, she is assigned the toughest tasks to prove that she should be there; when Marge is employed at the nuclear plant, Mr. Burns tries to fire her because she is married; Bart's daring antics are chalked up to the notion that "boys will be boys"; Marge's unpaid household work is unnoticed by Homer and other family members until she is hospitalized with a broken leg. Often the message is that change is difficult and many give up trying. Lisa's enthusiasm for achievement is met with lukewarm welcome, and Marge's ventures into the paid labour force or into local politics are dismal failures.

Underlying many episodes are serious questions about gender relations, opportunities, and roles. Within our society, poking fun at women and trivializing their concerns and contributions to family and society is highly entertaining. While we are also entertained by Homer's stupidity and obsession with food and Bart's boyish pranks, the humour is bounded by different sets of expectations based on gender and position in the family.

How are the issues of gender relations and roles infused in our sense of humour and in entertainment in Canadian culture?

Latvia, Norway, Finland, Switzerland, South Korea, Liberia, Mozambique, and Bangladesh, among others.

Today, women constitute just over 24 percent of all elected politicians in federal, provincial, and territorial governments in Canada (Parliament of Canada, 2012). Three out of ten provincial premiers and one of the three territorial leaders are women (McCarthy, 2011). Worldwide, Canada ranks forty-first (out of 150) in terms of women's representation in government (Inter-Parliamentary Union, 2012). Why don't women, who outnumber men, take political control of the nation? The fact is, in spite of the political gains women have made in recent elections, they are greatly outnumbered by men in political office.

The reasons for women's underrepresentation? First, they are still underrepresented in law and business, the careers from which most politicians come. Further, many women do not identify themselves as belonging to a class of people who need bloc political action in order to overcome domination. Feminist activists and theorists ask us to look beyond the ways in which women (and other disadvantaged groups) are victimized or further oppressed and examine **agency**, or the ways in which women are responding positively to change their circumstances. When we analyze women's political activities, we see that women are making a difference locally and internationally. Many women are engaged in the politics of their local communities, pressing environmental, educational, health-related, and social justice issues. Postmodern theorists refer to the actions of a number of women who have made tremendous gains within their unions, a forum from which they struggle for change, both within their workplaces and in the broader society.

The irregular hours needed to run for any type of political office are incompatible with women's role as mothers. Fathers, in contrast, whose ordinary roles are more likely to take them away from home, often do not feel this conflict as intensely. Women may also be less likely to have a supportive partner willing to play an unassuming background role while providing solace, encouragement, childcare, and voter appeal. Finally, preferring to hold on tightly to their positions of power, men have been reluctant to incorporate women into centres of decision-making or to present them as viable candidates.

These factors are changing, however, and we can expect more women to seek and gain political office. More are going into law, where they are doing more travelling and making provincial and national contacts. Increasingly, childcare is seen as a mutual responsibility of mothers and fathers. And in some areas, party leaders are searching for qualified candidates ("people with voter appeal and without skeletons in their closets"), regardless of gender. The primary concern in at least some areas today is not gender, but whether a candidate can win. This generation, then, is likely to mark a fundamental change in women's political participation, and it appears it will be only a matter of time until a woman once again occupies 24 Sussex Drive.

Arenas, Gyms, and Courts: Women in Sports

While they were once almost exclusively spectators, cheering for their brothers and boyfriends from the stands, Canadian women have developed a notable presence in sports communities across the country—in professional, amateur, and school-sponsored activities of all types and at all levels. Hockey, our national sport, is now the domain of both women and men, owing largely to the hard work and success of the Canadian women's ice hockey team, gold medal winners at the 2002, 2006, and 2010 Winter Olympics, and the establishment of girls' leagues across the country. Many Canadians have followed the triumphs and defeats of athletes such as Silken Laumann, Joanne Malar, Cassie Campbell, and dozens of other women who are role models for novice competitors.

Challenges continue to present themselves, however. Women are still excluded from membership at prestigious golf clubs, known as havens for elite players and very wealthy enthusiasts (Nicholson, 2012:A15). Women's sports are still underfunded and often marginalized compared to men's (Doren & Jones, 2000). Athletes contend with ill-fitting, made-for-males equipment and sometimes raucous and jeering crowds. With the exception of those in certain sports, such as figure skating and gymnastics, female athletes are often assumed to be lesbians or tough, out-of-character women, and are treated as such. The image of lean, muscular bodies and a fiercely competitive spirit, for many, does not fit with the likeness of femininity and motherhood.

Such challenges are not keeping young women out of the action. Women's basketball, for example, has been growing by leaps and (re)bounds, particularly since the introduction of a women's professional league, the WNBA, in 1997. On the horizon for these young women may be a growing number of university scholarships, a place in coaching and mentoring, and recognition earned by exceptional achievement.

Changing Roles of Men

This chapter has provided an introduction to gender dynamics and the social production of gender differences through a feminine lens. From a feminist perspective, sociologists are concerned with finding explanations for gender inequality and with uncovering the ways gender difference and discrimination are embedded in our institutions, laws, customs, behaviours, and practices. We have discussed some of the ways women's social world is changing in response to their historical and ongoing struggles for recognition, rights, access, and equality.

But what has the women's movement meant for men? Has the women's movement raised issues regarding masculinity and the structure of men's gendered lives as well (Connell, 2000)? Is the world of men and boys changing as women's roles shift?

Jackson Katz's video *Tough Guise: Violence, Media and the Crisis in Masculinity* examines the social construction of masculine identities and argues that the media creates violent (machismo) masculinity as a cultural norm. On one hand, they are pushed to distinguish themselves, although this sometimes means standing out from the rest, often at a price. Men are socialized to avoid emotions (Doyle, 1995). On the other hand, they are pulled to oblivion, to blend with whatever group—skateboarders, jocks, preppies, computer nerds and geeks, druggies—they are most attracted to or that pull them the hardest.

Is the world of boys and men changing? As women have confronted fresh challenges and taken on a wider variety of roles, and as their achievements have become socially recognized, men's world is adapting. On a personal level, over the past few decades there has been a great deal of discussion about the development of men's affective side ("Yes, it's okay—real men do cry"). Today, it is more socially acceptable for men to share their intimate feelings and to participate in their children's lives more fully. In the television series *Modern Family*, the dads in both the nuclear family and the same-sex couple are involved "father figures." Yet, at the same time, our image of dads as uncomfortable or incapable of their roles as caretakers is reinforced by popular shows such as *Family Guy* and *The Simpsons*.

On a structural level, more men are finding themselves not working outside the home and having to undertake unpaid domestic work as "househusbands" in ways that only women had formerly done. Is it by choice or by circumstance? While there are numerous stories about fathers who quit their jobs and opt to stay home with their children (there are many chat lines, websites, and support programs available for stay-at-home dads), it is important to distinguish between those who make a decision to stay at home and those who are reluctant stay-at-homes—thrust into the realms of un- or underemployment in an unrelenting economy.

"Troubled by an unattainable ideal, boys are learning what girls have long known: it isn't easy living in a . . . [body-beautiful] world" (Hall, 1999). Research that concluded that tall men are sexually more active and more attractive to women drew loud complaints from short men, who countered with evidence of their own sexual prowess.

The media flurry around this and other similar stories underscores men's deep-seated concern with body image and size. The boom in the men's cosmetics industry, the promotion and advertising of skin and hair care products and services for men, and the growth in men's clothing lines are signs of change (NBC News, 2010). Previous generations of men, haunted by a fear of being regarded as sensitive—a euphemism for weak or feminine—prided themselves on their apparent lack of interest in their image.

In her book, *Stiffed: The Betrayal of the American Man*, author Susan Faludi (1999) moves away from the conventional explanations of men's behaviour as resulting from a combination of social expectations, biology, reactions to the women's movement, and other structural changes to consider the ways men have been pushed and profoundly betrayed by the very institutions (corporate and political worlds, communities, and families) that promised power, success, recognition, and, ultimately, fulfillment.

Faludi, along with others, is convinced that men should abandon their "illusions of control" and question the trappings of traditional notions of masculinity. Is there a crisis in masculinity? Do we see a "new man" emerging? While exploring this issue falls outside the purview of this text, many authors discuss changing masculinities as a complex and dynamic process, unfolding as men's experiences and opportunities are challenged and affected by changes in women's lives (Laker, 2012; Whitehead & Barrett, 2001).

Glimpsing the Future—With Hope

Playing a fuller role in the decision-making processes of our social institutions, women are breaking the stereotypes and role models that lock males into exclusively male activities and push females into roles considered feminine. As structural barriers fall and more activities become degenderized, both males and females will be free to pursue activities more compatible with their abilities and desires as *individuals*.

At present, structural obstacles, accompanied by supporting socialization and stereotypes, cast most males and females into fairly rigid moulds along lines dictated by culture. To overcome these obstacles and abandon traditional stereotypes is to give males and females new perceptions of themselves and one another. Both females and males will then be free to feel and to express needs and emotions denied to them by present social arrangements. Females are likely to perceive themselves as having greater access to power and control over their environment. Males are likely to feel and to express more emotional sensitivity—to be warmer, more affectionate and tender, and to give greater expression to anxieties and stresses that their gender now forces them to suppress. In the future, we may discover that such "greater wholeness" of males and females entails many other dimensions of the human personality.

As men and women develop new consciousness of themselves and of their own potential, relationships between the sexes will change. Certainly, distinctions between males and females will not disappear. There is no reason, however, for biological differences to be translated into social inequalities. An understanding and appreciation of gender differences along with structural changes and the provision of opportunities for women may lead to a society in which, as sociologist Alison Jaggar (1990) noted, gender equality can become less a goal and more a background condition for living in society.

ISSUES OF SEX AND GENDER

What is gender stratification?

The term gender inequality refers to unequal access to power, prestige, and property on the basis of sex. Every society establishes a structure that, on the basis of sex and gender, opens and closes access to the group's privileges. p. 146.

How do sex and gender differ and why do the behaviours of males and females differ?

Sex refers to biological distinctions between males and females. It consists of both primary and secondary sex characteristics. Gender, in contrast, is what a society considers proper behaviours and attitudes for its male and female members. Sex physically distinguishes males from females; gender defines what is "masculine" and "feminine." pp. 155–157.

In the "nature versus nurture" debate—whether differences between the behaviours of males and females are caused by inherited (biological) or learned (cultural) characteristics—almost all sociologists take the side of nurture. In recent years, however, the door to biology has opened somewhat. pp. 146–147.

GENDER INEQUALITY IN A GLOBAL PERSPECTIVE

Is gender inequality universal?

George Murdock surveyed information on premodern societies and found not only that all of them have sex-linked activities, but also that all of them give greater prestige to male activities. Patriarchy, or male dominance, appears to be universal. Besides work, other areas of discrimination include education, politics, and violence. pp. 149–151.

GENDER INEQUALITY IN CANADA

Is the feminist movement new?

In what is called the "first wave," feminists made political demands for change in the early 1900s—and were met with much hostility, even violence. The "second wave" of feminism began in the 1960s and continues today. pp. 154–155.

Is there gender inequality in education, in the workplace, and in everyday life?

Although more women than men now attend university, each tends to select "feminine" or "masculine" fields. In addition, men outnumber women in most scientific disciplines. Change is indicated by the growing numbers of women in such fields as law and medicine. pp. 155–158.

Over the past century, women have comprised an increasing proportion of the workforce. Nonetheless, a gender gap in pay characterizes all occupations. For university graduates, the lifetime pay gap runs tens of thousands of dollars in favour of men. Sexual harassment also continues to be a reality in the workplace. pp. 162–164.

Two indications of gender inequality in everyday life are the general devaluation of femininity and the male dominance of conversation. pp. 158–161.

GENDER AND VIOLENCE

What forms does violence against women take?

The victims of battering, sexual assault, incest, and spousal murder overwhelmingly are females. Conflict theorists point out that men use violence to maintain their power. pp. 164–165.

GLIMPSING THE FUTURE—WITH HOPE

What progress has been made in reducing gender inequality?

In Canada, women are playing a fuller role in the decision-making processes of our social institutions. Men, too, are re-examining their traditional roles. The ultimate possibility of gender equality is a new conception of the human personality, one that allows both males and females to pursue their individual interests unfettered by gender. p. 168.

TALKING ABOUT THEORY

Theoretical Paradigms

	CLASSICAL PARADIGMS			RECENT PARADIGMS
	Structural-Functional Paradigm	Social-Conflict Paradigm	Feminist Paradigm	Postmodernist Paradigm
What is the level of analysis?	Macro level	Macro level	Micro and macro levels	Micro levels
How is gender inequality explained?	Biological, or inborn differences, explain different behaviours, emotions, temperaments.	Factors of socialization, social structure, and social control—not biological factors—explain different behaviours and expectations.	Drawing on conflict theory, feminism argues that patriarchy—men's power and control over property—explains gender inequality.	Gender differences are socially constructed and gender identities should be analyzed from an individual point of view because not all women share similar identities and experiences.

KEY TERMS

agency 166
feminism 153
gender 146

gender inequality 146
minority group 150

patriarchy 152
sex 146

sex-typed 150
sexual harassment 162

All URLs listed are current as of the printing of this text.

York University Centre for Feminist Research
www.cfr.info.yorku.ca
The Centre for Feminist Research at York University engages in research and education in feminist studies. It links with the Women's Studies program at York and with women's research networks in Canada and internationally.

Backlash and the Fact of Battered Husbands
www.dadsrights.org/articles/backlash_and_battered_husbands.shtml
"One way to trivialize and dismiss a point of view is to claim it is part of a backlash. That is the contemptuous and derogatory characterization often applied when the topic of men's issues arises. Domestic violence is a case in point."

Deceptions of a "Gender-Equal Society"
www.fathermag.com/9607/Leacock
Eleanor Leacock, an anthropologist, published claims of societies that were supposedly egalitarian in regard to both wealth and sex. In her essay "Women In Egalitarian Societies," one of her principal examples was the Montagnais-Naskapi of the Labrador peninsula. The authors argue that it is now clear that the gender equality of that society has no basis in fact.

CRITICAL THINKING QUESTIONS

1. As some forms of work become increasingly "faceless" due to advances in technology (internet businesses, for example), will gender inequalities among workers be minimized?

2. What evidence is there that the women's world is beginning to mirror the men's world? What factors most significantly contribute to gender inequality?

3. The pay gap is one indicator of gender inequalities in the workplace. Access the Research Navigator through MySocLab, and use it to find five recent articles on gender inequality at work. Based on these articles, would you conclude that women's position in the workplace has improved over the past few decades?

MySocLab

Explore the topics covered in this chapter on MySocLab. Interactive resources include a study plan, cumulative exams, a multimedia library, MySocLab eReadings, and access to the MySocLab Video Series.

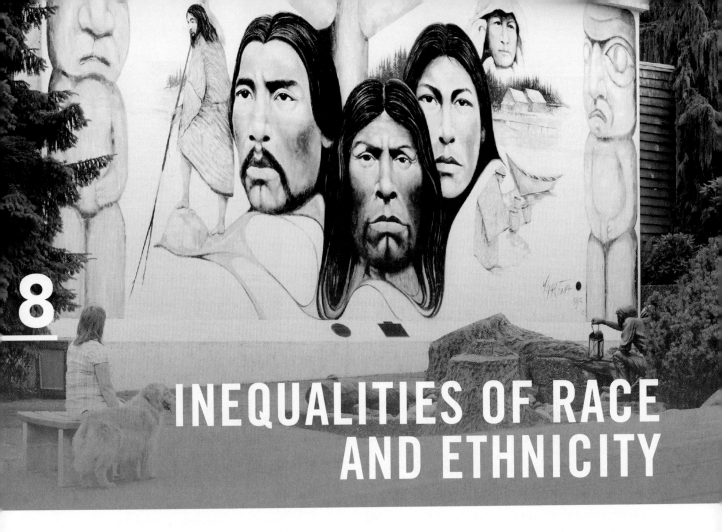

8

INEQUALITIES OF RACE AND ETHNICITY

LEARNING OUTCOMES

After you have studied this chapter, you will be able to answer the following questions:

1. How do race and ethnicity differ?
2. What are minority and dominant groups?
3. Are prejudice and discrimination the same thing?
4. How do individual and institutional discrimination differ?
5. What are the major ethnic groups in Canada?
6. Why don't all Native peoples in Canada support the *Charter of Rights and Freedoms*?
7. What was the Quiet Revolution in Quebec?

SUICIDE Capital of the World! reads the headline of a recent *MacLean's* magazine article. In 2011, Pikangikum, a northern Ontario community of roughly 2400 people, had a suicide rate equivalent to 250 per 100 000—nearly 20 times that of Canada, and the highest in the world. Pikangikum has held this dubious distinction for nearly 20 years.

As in Attawapiskat, which captivated the news media for several months from October to December 2011, some would say the life chances are bleak for Ojibwa First Nations residents of Pikangikum. Eighty percent of Pikangikum's housing is without sewage, and there were 3600 lockups in the community and nearly 5000 calls for service from the police in 2011. Attawapiskat and Pikangikum are fly-in First Nations communities separated by 500 kilometres.

Was it always this way? In 1954, there was one recorded drunken assault in Pikangikum. A study of the reserve published five years later noted its "low incidence of violence." During the second half of the 1950s, the outpost store began carrying items beyond staples such as flour and lard, and started advancing credit. Welfare also came in. Today, the Northern Store cashes welfare cheques, and residents can buy food and clothing and eat at Pizza Hut and Kentucky Fried Chicken, the reserve's only restaurants.

Gas sniffing is ubiquitous, especially among young people, replacing getting drunk as a teenage rite of passage. According to Martin Patriquin, "during the day about the only sign of gas sniffers are the foot trails darting off Pikangikum's roads, and the knotted, leaking bags of gasoline they leave

Adapted from: Patriquin (2012).

behind . . . can often hear them at night, howling at the sky. They are the reason many park their trucks with the fuel cap as close to their houses as possible."

After 14 years of negotiations, Whitefeather, a Canadian First Nations–owned company based in Pikangikum, will receive a licence to harvest the roughly 1.3 million hectares of the area's surrounding forest—the first such project of its kind. The local community will directly benefit from the exploitation of this natural resource. In the suicide capital of the world, Whitefeather is Pikangikum's source of hope.

Contrary to Prime Minister Stephen Harper's 2009 G20 statement that "Canada has no history of colonialism," the history of Canada's indigenous peoples tells us otherwise. The *Indian Act* and residential schools are but two institutional examples. Ironically, it was Prime Minister Stephen Harper who made an official government apology for the residential school system—the aim of which was to eradicate First Nations culture and identity.

Laying the Sociological Foundation

The plight of Canada's First Nations has been well documented and is generally well known to Canadians. Yet, except on rare occasions, in our society, newspaper headlines and evening newscasts keep other issues constantly before us. Why haven't successive Canadian governments tackled the poverty and destitution of Canada's indigenous peoples? Why hasn't the media been more vigilant? What prejudices do Canadians express about Canada's First Nations, including other ethnic and visible minorities? Sociological findings on the topic can contribute greatly to a better understanding of this aspect of social life. To begin, we will consider to what extent the concept of race is a myth.

Race: Myth and Reality

With 6.5 billion people (United Nations, 2005), the world is home to a diverse range of human shapes and colours. Eyes come in various shades of blue, brown, and green. Lips are thick and thin. Hair can be straight, curly, kinky, black, white, or red—and, of course, all hues of brown.

As humans spread throughout the world, their adaptations to diverse climates and other living conditions resulted in a profusion of complexions, colours, and shapes. In this sense, the concept of **race**, a group with inherited physical characteristics that distinguish it from another group, is a reality. Humans do, indeed, come in a variety of colours and shapes.

COMMON SENSE VERSUS SOCIOLOGY According to common sense, our racial classifications represent biological differences between people. Sociologists, however, stress that what we call "races" are social classifications, not biological categories.

The racial categories common in Canada, for example, constitute merely one of numerous ways that people around

Humans show remarkable diversity. Shown here is just one example—He Pingping, from China, who, at two feet four inches, is the world's shortest man; and Svetlana Pankratova, from Russia, who, according to the *Guinness Book of World Records*, is the woman with the longest legs. Race-ethnicity shows similar diversity.

the world classify physical appearances. Although different groups use different categories, each group assumes that its categories are natural—merely a response to visible biology.

What about that biology? Biological differences are real, regardless of how we categorize them, aren't they? It is true that humans have numerous physical differences. But if biology is the main element, then biologists, of all people, should agree on the numbers and characteristics of human races.

However, modern geneticists conclude that there is only *one* racial category (genotype) of humans: *Homo sapiens*!

RACIAL SUPERIORITY People are inclined to think that their own "race" is superior to others, regardless of the logical

✳ **Explore** the article "The Nation; And There Was Light, and It Was Good?" on **MySocLab.**

◉ **Watch** the video "Multiracial Identity" to see how race is socially constructed on **MySocLab.**

These photos were selected to illustrate how seriously we must take all preaching of hatred and racial supremacy, even though it may seem to come from harmless or even humorous sources. The result in this instance was the Holocaust, the systematic slaughter of Jews and others deemed "racially inferior" in Nazi Germany. In the photo on the left, Adolf Hitler is wearing lederhosen, traditional clothing of Bavaria, Germany. He caused the horrific scene depicted in the image on the right, which reflects conditions in the concentration camp in Buchenwald, Germany, where thousands of people died of starvation and diseases amid piles of rotting bodies awaiting burial.

arguments just recounted. The idea of racial superiority haunts humanity.

That race is an arbitrary classification makes little difference to common thinking. "I know what I see, and you can't tell me any different" seems to be a frequent response. "I know what *they* are like. *They* are (fill in the cultural stereotype)." For the race in question, the description becomes reality.

Sociologist W.I. Thomas observed, "If people define situations as real, they are real in their consequences" (Thomas & Thomas, 1928:572). What people *believe* affects social life, for *people act on beliefs, not facts.* As a result, the ideas of race that are firmly embedded in our culture—rather than scientific fact—influence attitudes and behaviour. As you read this chapter, you will examine some of the racial ideas you learned as you were socialized in your culture.

IN SUM

Race, then, is in the eye of the beholder. Humans show such diversity in physical characteristics—skin colour, hair texture, nose shape, head shape, eye colour, and so on—that there is no inevitable, much less universal, way to classify our many biological differences. Because racial classifications are arbitrary, the categories we use change over time.

Ethnic Groups

Whereas people use the term *race* to refer to the supposed biological characteristics that distinguish one group from another, **ethnicity** and **ethnic** apply to cultural characteristics. Derived from the Greek *ethnos*, meaning "people" or "nation," these terms refer to people who identify with one another on the basis of common ancestry and cultural heritage. Their sense of belonging often centres on nation of origin, distinctive foods, dress, family names and relationships, language, music, religion, and other customs.

People often confuse the terms *race* and *ethnic group*. For example, many people, including many Jews, consider the Jews a race. Jews, however, are more properly considered an ethnic group; it is their cultural characteristics, especially religion, that bind them together.

Some of us have a greater sense of ethnicity than others. We can use the term **ethnic work** to refer to the way people construct their ethnicity. For people who have a strong ethnic identity, *ethnic work* refers to how they enhance and maintain their group's distinctions—from clothing, food, and language to religious practices and holidays. For people whose ethnic identity is not as firm, the term refers to attempts to recover their ethnic heritage, such as trying to trace family lines or visiting the country or region of their family's origins.

Focus Question
What is the difference between a race and an ethnic group?

Minority Groups and Dominant Groups

Sociologist Louis Wirth (1945) defined a **minority group** as people who are singled out for unequal treatment *and* who regard themselves as objects of collective discrimination. Physical (racial) or cultural (ethnic) differences can serve as the basis of the unequal treatment.

Surprisingly, the term *minority group* does not necessarily refer to a *numerical* minority. For example, before India's independence in 1947, a handful of British colonial rulers discriminated against millions of Indians. Similarly, when

✱ **Explore** the reading "Race Matters" by Cornel West on MySocLab.

This photo, taken in Ashkelon, Israel, illustrates the difficulty that assumptions about race and ethnicity posed for Israel. The Ethiopian Jews look so different from other Jews that it took several years for Israeli authorities to acknowledge their "true Jewishness" and allow them to immigrate.

South Africa practised apartheid, a small group of Dutch discriminated against the black majority. All over the world, women are a minority group. Accordingly, sociologists refer to those who do the discriminating not as the *majority*, but rather as the **dominant group**, since they have greater power, privileges, and social status.

The dominant group almost always attributes its privileged position to its own innate superiority. Possessing political power and unified by shared physical and cultural traits, a dominant group uses its position to discriminate against those with different—and supposedly inferior—characteristics.

EMERGENCE OF MINORITY GROUPS A group becomes a minority in one of two ways. The first is through the expansion of political boundaries. This often occurs as the result of a decisive military victory. When a group expands its political boundaries, it produces minority groups if it incorporates people with different customs, languages, values, and physical characteristics into one political entity. For example, after defeating the French on the Plains of Abraham, the British seized control of New France. Consequently, the French who remained, who had previously been the

dominant group, then became a minority group, a status that significantly influenced their lives (see the section "The Two Charter Groups" on page 181).

The second way a group becomes a minority is through migration. Migration can be voluntary, as with the millions of people who chose to move to Canada, or involuntary, as with Native Canadians, many of whom were forcibly transported to remote regions of the North (see the Down-to-Earth Sociology box called "The Inuit Expulsion" on page 182). Japanese Canadians were labelled "enemy aliens" during World War II, then stripped of their businesses and livelihoods, forcibly relocated from the West Coast, and put to work in concentration camps throughout Canada. Interestingly, the same fate did not befall the many German and Italian Canadians. Instead, cities and towns with identifiable German names were simply renamed.

SHARED CHARACTERISTICS Anthropologists Charles Wagley and Marvin Harris (1958) identified five characteristics shared by minorities worldwide:

1. Membership in a minority group is an ascribed status; that is, it is not voluntary, but comes through birth.

2. The physical or cultural traits that distinguish minorities are held in low esteem by the dominant group.
3. Minorities are unequally treated by the dominant group.
4. Minorities tend to marry within their own group.
5. Minorities tend to feel strong group solidarity (a sense of "we-ness" and of belonging somewhere).

These conditions—especially when combined with collective discrimination—often create a shared sense of identity among minorities, and, in many instances, even a sense of common destiny (Chandra, 1993a).

Prejudice and Discrimination

Prejudice and discrimination are common throughout the world. In Mexico, Hispanic Mexicans discriminate against Native-American Mexicans; in Israel, Ashkenazic Jews, primarily of European descent, discriminate against Sephardic Jews from the Muslim world; and in Japan, the Japanese discriminate against just about anyone who is not Japanese, especially immigrant Koreans and the descendants of the Eta caste. A stigma is still attached to the Eta, now called the Burakumin, who used to perform Japan's dirty work—working with dead animals (stripping hides and tanning leather) and serving as the country's executioners and prison guards (Mander, 1992). All around the world, women are discriminated against by men.

Discrimination is an *action*—unfair treatment directed against someone. When the basis of discrimination is race, it is known as **racism**, but discrimination can be based on many other characteristics—including age, sex, sexual orientation, weight, disease (e.g., AIDS), and disability. Discrimination is often the result of an *attitude* called **prejudice**—prejudgment, usually in a negative sense. Positive prejudice exaggerates the virtues of a group, such as thinking that one group (usually one's own) is more capable than others. Most prejudice, however, is negative, prejudging a group as inferior.

LEARNING FROM ASSOCIATION As with other learned attitudes, we are not born with prejudice; we glean it from the people around us. Kathleen Blee (2005) interviewed women who were members of the KKK and Aryan Nations. Some members were recruited by someone who already belonged to the group, while others learned to be racists after they joined. They were attracted to the community not because it matched their racist beliefs, but because someone they liked already belonged. Blee observed that racism was often not the cause of their joining, but rather the result of their membership.

Focus Question
What is the difference between prejudice and discrimination?

Individual and Institutional Discrimination
Sociologists stress that we need to move beyond thinking in terms of **individual discrimination**, the negative treatment of one person by another. With a focus on the broader picture, sociologists encourage us to examine **institutional discrimination**—that is, how discrimination is woven into the fabric of society to such an extent that it becomes routine, sometimes even a matter of social policy. The system once known as apartheid in South Africa, the forced resettlement and expropriation of property of Japanese Canadians as "enemy aliens" during World War II, or the present-day system of reserves for Native Canadians are all examples of institutional discrimination.

Theories of Prejudice

Why are people prejudiced? The common-sense explanation is that they or someone they know has been harmed by some member of a particular group, and they apply their negative perception to all members of that group. Eugene Hartley (1946) showed that much more is involved when he asked people how they felt about various racial and ethnic groups. Besides blacks and Jews, his list included the Wallonians, Pireneans, and Danireans—names he had made up. Most people who expressed dislike for Jews and blacks also expressed dislike for the three fictitious groups. The significance of Hartley's study is twofold. First, people who are prejudiced against one racial or ethnic group tend to also be prejudiced against others. Second, prejudice does not depend on negative experiences with others. People can be—and are—prejudiced against people they have never met—and even against groups that do not exist!

Social scientists have developed several theories to explain prejudice. We will begin by examining psychological theories, and then explore sociological views.

Psychological Perspectives

FRUSTRATION AND SCAPEGOATS Psychologist John Dollard suggested that prejudice is the result of frustration. People who are unable to strike out at the real source of their frustration (such as low wages) find someone else to blame.

This **scapegoat**, generally a racial, ethnic, or religious minority they unfairly blame for their troubles, becomes a convenient—and safe—target on which to vent their frustrations. Gender and age also provide common bases for scapegoating.

THE AUTHORITARIAN PERSONALITY With the horrors he had observed under the Nazis fresh in his mind, Theodor Adorno wondered whether there is a certain type of individual who is more likely to fall for the racist utterances and policies of people like Hitler or Mussolini, or groups like the Ku Klux Klan.

◉ **Watch** the video "Racial Stereotypes and Discrimination" on **MySocLab.**

✳ **Explore** the reading "Racism Without Racists" on **MySocLab.**

To test the idea, Adorno et al., (1950) developed three scales: a series of statements that measured ethnocentrism, anti-Semitism, and support for strong authoritarian leaders. Testing nearly 2000 people, ranging from university professors to prison inmates, Adorno found that people who scored high on one scale also scored high on the other two. For example, people who agreed with anti-Semitic statements also agreed that it was good for a government to be highly authoritarian and that foreign ways of life posed a threat to the nation.

Adorno concluded that highly prejudiced people have several things in common. They are insecure, are highly conformist, have deep respect for authority, and are highly submissive to superiors. He termed this the **authoritarian personality**. Individuals who possess an authoritarian personality believe that things are either right or wrong. When they confront norms and values that differ from their own, especially in matters of religion or sexual orientation, they become anxious and aggressive.

Sociological Theories

Sociologists find psychological explanations inadequate. They stress that the key to understanding prejudice is not the *internal* state of individuals, but factors *outside* the individual. Thus, sociological theories focus on how some environments foster prejudice, while others reduce it. Let's compare functionalist, conflict, symbolic interactionist, feminist, postmodern, postcolonial, and critical race theories of racism, discrimination, and prejudice.

FUNCTIONALISM In a telling scene from a television documentary, journalist Bill Moyers interviewed Fritz Hippler, a Nazi intellectual who, at age 29, was put in charge of the entire German film industry. Hippler said that when Hitler came to power, the Germans were no more anti-Semitic than the French—probably less so. He was told to create anti-Semitism, which he did by producing movies that contained vivid scenes comparing Jews to rats—their breeding threatening to infest the population.

Why was Hippler told to create hatred? The Jews provided a convenient target because they had businesses, bank accounts, and other property to confiscate. They held key positions (university professors, reporters, judges, and so on), which the Nazis could replace with their own flunkies. Hatred also showed its dysfunctional side, as the Nazi officials who were sentenced to death at Nuremberg discovered.

Harnessing the state machinery—schools, police, courts, mass media, and almost all aspects of the government—to promote hatred as the Nazis did is not as uncommon as we would hope. There have been several recent examples of genocide, such as in Rwanda, where extremists from the Hutu majority launched plans in 1994 to destroy the entire Tutsi civilian population of the country. Over approximately 100 days, from April 6 to mid-July, more than 800 000 men, women, and children were killed—in other words, approximately three-quarters of the Tutsi population. The term *genocide* did not exist before 1944; it was declared an international crime by the 1948 United Nations Convention on the Prevention and Punishment of the Crime of Genocide. **Genocide** is defined as violent acts committed with the intent to destroy, in whole or in part, a national, ethnic, racial, or religious group.

That prejudice is functional and shaped by social environment was dramatically demonstrated by Muzafer and Carolyn Sherif (1953) in a simple but ingenious experiment. At a boys' summer camp, they assigned friends to different cabins and made cabins the basic units of competition. Each cabin competed against the others in sports and for status. In only a few days, strong in-groups had formed, and even former lifelong friends were calling one another "crybaby" and "sissy" and showing intense dislike for one another.

The Sherifs' study illustrates four major points. First, the social environment can be deliberately arranged to generate either positive or negative feelings about people. Second, prejudice can be a product of pitting group against group in an "I win, you lose" situation. Third, prejudice is functional in that it creates in-group solidarity. Fourth, prejudice is dysfunctional in that it destroys wider community social relationships.

CONFLICT THEORY Conflict theorists stress that the capitalist class systematically pits group against group. If workers are united, they will demand higher wages and better working conditions. To reduce workers' solidarity, then, is to weaken their bargaining power, drive down costs, and increase profits. Thus, the capitalist class exploits racial and ethnic strife to produce a **dual labour market** (also called a split labour market)—workers divided along racial, ethnic, and gender lines (Du Bois, 1935/1992; Reich, 1972; Lind, 1995). Usually, one ethnic group holds down the good jobs while other identifiable ethnic or racial groups work in low-paying, ordinarily non-unionized jobs.

Unemployment is a useful weapon to help maintain a split labour market. Keeping some people unemployed, however, provides a **reserve labour force** from which owners can draw when they need to expand production. Minority workers, including women, are especially useful as members of the reserve army of labour because their presence poses a potential threat to the dominant group of workers—usually, but not always, white males (see "Feminism: Multiracial Feminism and Inequality" below).

The consequences are devastating, say conflict theorists. Just like the boys in the Sherif experiments, black Canadians, Native Canadians, Quebecois, anglophones, and others see themselves as able to make gains only at one another's expense. Thus, their frustration, anger, and hostility are deflected away from capitalists and directed toward others whom they see as standing in their way.

✳ **Explore** the reading "Race-Specific Policies and the Truly Disadvantaged" on **MySocLab.**

Pitted against one another, racial and ethnic groups learn to fear and distrust each another instead of recognizing their common class interests and working for their mutual welfare (Blackwelder, 1993).

SYMBOLIC INTERACTIONISM Symbolic interactionists stress that no one is born prejudiced. Instead, at birth, each of us becomes a member of some particular family and racial or ethnic group, where we learn our beliefs and values. There we learn to like—or dislike—members of other groups and to perceive them positively or negatively. If discrimination is common practice, we learn to observe it routinely. Just as we learn other attitudes and customs, we learn prejudice and discrimination.

Words are not simply meaningless labels. Rather, *the labels we learn colour the way we see the world*. Symbolic interactionists stress that labels are an essential ingredient of prejudice. Labels cause **selective perception**; that is, they lead people to see certain things and blind them to others. Through labels, people look at the members of racial and ethnic groups as though they are all alike. The terms *honky*, *spic*, *mick*, *kike*, *limey*, *kraut*, *dago*, or any of the other scornful words people use to belittle ethnic groups are not simply nicknames—they are emotionally laden stereotypes. Such words overpower us with emotions, blocking out rational thought about the people they refer to (Allport, 1954).

STEREOTYPES AND DISCRIMINATION: THE SELF-FULFILLING PROPHECY The stereotypes we learn can even produce the behaviour they depict. Let's consider Group X. Negative stereotypes, which characterize Group X as lazy, seem to justify withholding opportunities from this group (because they are lazy and undependable) and place its members in inferior economic positions. The result is a *self-fulfilling prophecy*. Denied jobs that require high dedication and energy, Group X members are confined to "dirty work," seen as more fitting for "that kind" of people. Since much dirty work is irregular, members of Group X are also liable to be readily visible—standing around on street corners. The sight of their idleness then reinforces the original stereotype of laziness, while the discrimination that created the "laziness" in the first place passes unnoticed.

FEMINISM: MULTIRACIAL FEMINISM AND INEQUALITY Multiracial feminism (otherwise known as multicultural or multiethnic feminism) has emerged from the challenges put forward by women of colour. Simply put, they argue that white men *and women* oppress lower-class women and men of disadvantaged races and ethnicities. However, the inclusion of race and ethnicity in social class inequality complicates the picture. While sex is a dichotomy (generally speaking, you are either a man or a woman), race, ethnicity, and social class are continuums of privileges and disadvantages. Multiracial feminists contend that it is not enough to simply dissect inequality from a woman's point of view.

Analysis must include the experiences of women and men of different racial and ethnic groups and their class differences. Therefore, multiracial feminism discusses the outlooks and behaviours of men and women of different ethnic and racial backgrounds, such as black working-class men and women, wealthy white men and women, poor Chinese men and women, and so on.

Eating disorders provide a useful example. Among young, white, middle-class women who desire a thin, sexually attractive body, anorexia nervosa and bulimia can be the negative consequences of a culture of thinness in Western society. Much has been written about this social problem and a great deal of television time has been devoted to it. Eating disorders are now defined as a significant social problem for this group. Among many African-American and Hispanic women, binge eating and purging are ways of coping with the traumas of their social lives, such as poverty, racism, and sexual abuse. Their eating disorders have not received the same level of attention because of their lower social-class position; in other words, lack of access to the levers of power make their social problems "invisible."

The important point made by multiracial feminists is that a member of a disadvantaged ethnic or racial group (man or woman) is not oppressed because of her or his gender, race, ethnicity, or social class position alone; it is a multiple system of domination that requires a multifaceted remedy. In contrast to liberal feminists, who have focused their energies on the oppression of women by men and on raising the status of women through legal changes, and to Marxist and other radical feminists, who have argued that women's oppression is linked to working-class political struggles, multiracial feminists point to complexities in the struggle for equality. "Men" are not the enemy, nor is the "ruling class"; the system of oppression experienced by men and women of colour demonstrates the complexity of inequality and how difficult it is to resolve (Lorber, 1998:134–147).

POSTMODERNISM AND THE ETHNIC/RACIAL EXPERIENCE The postmodernist position on understanding racism and discrimination is reasonably clear-cut: only those who directly experience racism and discrimination can understand what it means to be "black," "brown," and so on. It is only through their "voices" that we all can come to understand what it means to be a member of a disaffected minority group. According to postmodernists, no middle-class white female or male academic could possibly put her- or himself in the place of a visible minority, let alone write about the social and cultural fabric of these communities.

POSTCOLONIALISM, ETHNICITY, AND CULTURAL IDENTITY **Postcolonialism**, also known as postcolonial theory or post-oriental theory, refers to regions of the world that have regained political independence from European domination and are therefore technically no longer colonial. Examples include postcolonial India and postcolonial Algeria.

However, long periods of imperialism and forced dependency have profoundly affected the cultural fabric of these societies. As a result, postcolonial theory seeks to understand how the colonial legacy of racism persists in so-called postcolonial societies and how it interacts with their refusal to accept white European notions of race, ethnicity, and cultural identity (individual and collective). Therefore, most postcolonial theorists are concerned with understanding the cultural products (print and visual media, literature, the arts, and language) of these societies. To what degree are they influenced (even dominated) by their one-time colonial masters?

Franz Fanon, in his 1962 book, *The Wretched of the Earth*, laid the theoretical foundation for much postcolonial writing today. A French-speaking native of Martinique, Fanon knew that language played a vital role in shaping the consciousness of colonized people. As we discussed in Chapter 3, a vibrant culture nurtures and is nurtured by an evolving language. The flip side of this equation is that a colonizer's language must denigrate the local indigenous culture if it is to successfully replace it. After decades, even centuries, of English or French as the master language, for example, indigenous languages and cultures fade into the background. Some locals learn the dominant language and are rewarded. Others may keep their language and culture but pay the price of poverty. Such differences in the response of colonized peoples to the institutions of the colonizer make understanding and theorizing the postcolonial experience a complex and ongoing undertaking.

In the zeal to overthrow cultural imperialism, however, many advocates of postcolonial theory seem willing to toss the baby out with the bath water. A case in point is the issue of homosexuality. For many postcolonials and postcolonial theorists in Africa (Fanon was among the earliest homophobes), the Middle East, and Asia, homosexuality is considered a white European "disease," and any cultural contributions and all experiences of gays and lesbians in the former colonies are prohibited, censored, or ignored. This ignorant and judgmental position is a waste of energy and has become a self-defeating invective in the face of the global AIDS epidemic. In an otherwise progressive movement to affirm the diversity of racial, ethnic, and cultural identities worldwide, throwbacks such as misogyny and homophobia must be rigorously challenged and eradicated.

CRITICAL RACE THEORY Critical race theory accepts that racism is an "endemic facet of life in our society and that neutrality, objectivity, colorblindness, and meritocracy are all questionable constructs" (Pizarro, 1998:62). This perspective sees racial inequalities in housing, the legal system, employment, and the educational system persisting over time. Research by critical race theorists acknowledges an interactive relationship between researchers and participants (Guba & Lincoln, 1994), and between participants and their stories. Within this world view, people's stories of their experiences are counted as empirical evidence, as fact. This paradigm negates the assumption that narratives from the disenfranchised are biased and subjective. Stories, experiences, and voices are the mediums through which critical race theorists uncover the "hidden past" of racial minorities (Pizarro, 1998:62).

Focus Question
How do sociologists differ from psychologists in their explanations of prejudice?

Global Patterns of Intergroup Relations

In any society, basic patterns develop between the dominant group and minorities. Let's look at each of the patterns shown in Figure 8.1.

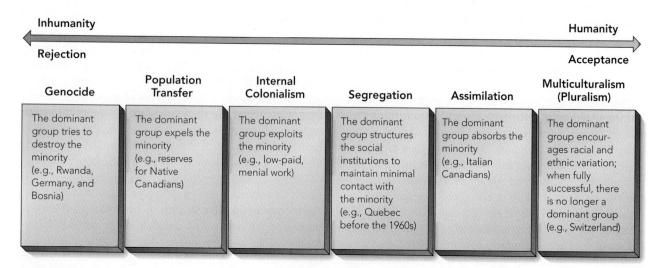

FIGURE 8.1 Patterns of Intergroup Relations: A Continuum

Amid fears that Japanese Canadians were "enemy aliens" who would sabotage industrial and military installations along the Canadian and American west coast, the property of Japanese Canadians in British Columbia in the early days of World War II was confiscated and the people were transferred to "relocation camps" in other provinces, including small towns in Quebec such as Farnham.

Genocide

The twentieth century's most notorious examples of genocide are Hitler's attempt to destroy all Jews and, as mentioned earlier, the Hutus' attempt to destroy all Tutsis in Rwanda in 1994. One of the most horrifying aspects of these slaughters is that those who participated were ordinary citizens—whose participation was facilitated by labels that singled out the victims as enemies worthy of death.

Labels are powerful forces in human life. Labels that dehumanize others help people to **compartmentalize**—to separate their acts from feelings that would threaten their self-concept and make it difficult for them to participate in killing (Bernard, Ottenberg, & Redl, 1971; Markusen, 1995). Thus, *genocide is facilitated by labelling the targeted group as less than fully human.*

Population Transfer

Population transfer can be indirect and direct. *Indirect* population transfer is achieved by making life so unbearable for members of a minority group that they leave "voluntarily." Under bitter conditions in czarist Russia, for example, millions of Jews made this "choice." *Direct* transfer takes place when a minority is expelled. Examples include the relocation of Native Canadians to reserves and the transfer of Canadians of Japanese descent to relocation camps during World War II.

Internal Colonialism

The term *colonialism* refers to the exploitation of the world's least-industrialized nations by the most-industrialized nations. Conflict theorists use the term **internal colonialism** to refer to a dominant group's exploitation of minority groups. The "routine" form is to use existing social institutions to deny minorities access to the full benefits of a society. The system of reserves for Canada's Native peoples is an example of internal colonialism.

Segregation

Segregation—the formal separation of racial or ethnic groups—accompanies internal colonialism. Segregation allows a dominant group to exploit the labour of the minority (butlers, chauffeurs, housekeepers, nannies, street cleaners) while maintaining social distance (Collins, 1986). In the southern United States until the 1960s, by law African-Americans and whites had to use separate public facilities such as hotels, schools, swimming pools, bathrooms, and even drinking fountains. In 38 states, laws prohibited interracial marriage. Violators could be sentenced to one to five years in prison (Mahoney & Kooistra, 1995). The legal structure also upheld residential segregation (Massey & Denton, 1993).

Assimilation

Assimilation is the process by which a minority is absorbed into the mainstream culture. There are two types. In *forced assimilation*, the dominant group refuses to allow the minority to practise its religion, speak its language, or follow its customs. In Armenia prior to the fall of the Soviet Union, for example, the dominant group, the Russians, required that Armenian schoolchildren be taught in Russian and that Armenians honour Russian rather than Armenian holidays. *Permissible assimilation*, in contrast, permits the minority to adopt the dominant group's patterns in its own way and at its own speed. In Brazil, for example, an ideology favouring the eventual blending of diverse racial types into a "Brazilian stock" encourages its racial and ethnic groups to intermarry.

Multiculturalism (Pluralism)

A policy of **multiculturalism**, also called **pluralism**, permits and even encourages racial and ethnic variation. Switzerland provides an outstanding example of multiculturalism. The Swiss are made up of four separate groups—French, Italian, German, and Romansh—who have kept their own languages and live peacefully in political and economic unity. Multiculturalism has been so successful that none of these

 Watch Professor Woody Doane discuss why certain groups become assimilated into the dominant group, and others do not, on **MySocLab.**

TABLE 8.1 Language and Culture in Canada: Some Important Dates

Federal Initiatives on Language and Culture	Date
Canadian Bill of Rights	1960
Royal Commission on Bilingualism and Biculturalism	1963
The Canadian Radio-television and Telecommunications Commission (CRTC)	1968
Official Languages Act	1969
Promotion of multiculturalism as a national policy (Canada becomes the first country in the world to promote multiculturalism)	1971
James Bay and Northern Quebec Agreement (first major agreement between the Crown and First Nations Cree and Inuit)	1975
Canadian Human Rights Act	1977
Canadian Charter of Rights and Freedoms	1982
Multiculturalism Act	1988
Department of Canadian Heritage includes a Secretary of States for Multiculturalism and the Status of Women portfolio	1993
Establishment of the Canadian Race Relations Foundation	1996
Department of Citizenship and Immigration takes over responsibility for multiculturalism	2008

groups can properly be called a minority. Table 8.1 details Canada's initiatives to promote multiculturalism.

Focus Question
What is the difference between multiculturalism and assimilation?

The Major Classifications in Canada

Canadians can be classified into three categories: Native peoples, including status Indians, non-status Indians, Métis, and Inuit; the two "charter groups," the French and English white settlers whose historical relations span over 400 years; and other immigrants from all over the world who entered and settled in Canada over the course of the past 100 years or so.

Native Peoples
Native peoples comprise a small but extremely disparate constituency. Roughly 4 percent of Canada's population, or 1 319 980 people, reported in the 2001 census that they had Aboriginal ancestry. Native Canadians encompass a rich diversity of customs, languages, and cultural differences that stretch back to pre-European contact (Frideres & Gadacz, 2001). However, not many of them share or have shared in Canada's development. There are wide differences in access to social, health, and education programs and in levels of development for Native Canadians both on and off the reserve system.

For this and other reasons, Native Canadians did not consent to the patriation of the Canadian constitution (the *British North America Act*) and even sent a delegation to London, England to lobby British parliament not to pass the *Canada Act*.

The federal government has made efforts to gain Native Canadians' support for the *Charter of Rights and Freedoms* by making provision for their self-government. On April 1, 1999, the territory of Nunavut was created. It is the largest land claim settlement in Canadian history. Nunavut means "Our Land" in the Inuktitut language, and the territory is nearly one-fifth the size of Canada.

Status or registered Indians have the highest profile in Canada. According to the 2001 census, there are 558 180 registered Indians. To be considered a member of this category, a person must (1) be admitted to a general registry in Ottawa; (2) be affiliated with one of the 622 bands; (3) be granted the entitlement to reside on band reserve lands; and (4) come under the legal jurisdiction of the *Indian Act* passed in 1876 (see Chapter 3, Table 3.3, page 58).

Approximately half of status or registered Indians (49 percent in 2001) live on reserves created by one of the 61 treaties signed with the British Crown. The federal government allocates approximately $5 billion a year to this group. However, only a small percentage of this sum, roughly 5 percent, is directed to the economic development of Native reserves. The bulk of the money is monopolized by administrative costs to run Indian and Northern Affairs Canada (or INAC for short) and by social spending.

Today, the interests of status Indians are represented by 633 chiefs, who make up the Assembly of First Nations; however, not all bands are members, nor are the Métis.

Part 2 of the *Constitution Act, 1982* recognizes Native Indians, Inuit, and Métis. Inuit are Native people whose ancestral home is the Arctic, while Métis are the children

Multiculturalism (or pluralism) permits, and even encourages, racial and ethnic variation—in Canada, this allows minority groups to maintain their separate identities but also participate in the country's social institutions.

of Native and non-Native parents. The Charter entrenches "existing aboriginal and treaty rights" (see Ponting, 1986:302). Nevertheless, the use of the term "existing" remains unsatisfactory to Native groups, because many of their land claims are not recognized by provincial governments. For example, only recently (since 2001) did the government of British Columbia enter into agreements with its First Nations peoples through an initiative called New Era.

Despite much-publicized conflicts with Natives, such as those related to the James Bay project and the "Oka Crisis" (1990), Quebec has a better record, in some respects, than the rest of Canada when it comes to its dealings with Native peoples. Evidence can be found in the favourable rate of Native language retention, the levels of prosperity of Native peoples resident in Quebec compared to other provinces, and lower rates of imprisonment.

The Two Charter Groups

In John Porter's *The Vertical Mosaic* (1965), the term *charter groups* was used to characterize the two linguistic and culturally distinct white settler groups in Canada, the French and the British. This term gained ready use among academics and policymakers. The history of the two charter groups began with the French colonization of North America in 1534, when Jacques Cartier led the first of three voyages of exploration into the St. Lawrence River region. By the beginning of the eighteenth century, the French colony stretched from Hudson Bay to New Orleans. The 13 British Atlantic colonies, later to become the United States of America, were encircled by the French. However, the nucleus of the French Empire in North America was centred along the St. Lawrence and stretched from Montreal to Quebec City, with Louisburg as the military beachhead on Cape Breton.

The population of "New France" never exceeded 65 000. The colony depended on trade in fur, a luxury item used in the making of fashionable clothing for the aristocracy of Europe. Neither agriculture nor industry of any significant kind was developed in New France. Therefore, resources—both material and human—were stretched extremely thin to maintain the presence of the French Empire in North America. War with the British Atlantic colonies was inevitable given the need to expand westward to support a growing and prospering colony. The British succeeded militarily in expelling the French colonial government from North America in 1763 with the Peace of Paris.

North America was now under British control. American colonists had been known to grumble for more autonomy from their British overlords before 1763, but they had to worry about the French knocking at their door. Now that the French colonial government was gone, renewed interest in political sovereignty quickly gained momentum. The British government, realizing it might lose everything if it lost a war with its American colonists, passed the *Quebec Act of 1774*. This Act extended extraordinary rights to the newly conquered French Catholic colonists to keep them on side in any conflict with their American counterparts. Among these non-assimilationist rights were the rights to keep the French civil law and to practise Catholicism. The strategy worked: the Americans tried but were unsuccessful in gaining support from the French colonists along the St. Lawrence. The Americans won their war of independence from the British, however. Unlike the French government, the British were able to keep the northern tier in their hands.

The nineteenth century was a period of rapid growth in British immigration to its North American colony and the natural expansion of Catholic Quebec. The hundred

The Inuit Expulsion

The harm that befalls some communities does not necessarily stem from sinister conspiracies. Even the best intentions can lead to suffering and death. The coerced relocation of Native Canadians from one community to another provides an example of how "helping" can sometimes dissolve into "hurting." It also gives us the opportunity to reconsider who is the guilty party in the so-called "Indian problem."

Native Canadians have been afflicted by about 100 forced removals since Confederation. Consider the case of the Inuit. In 1953, southern Canadian bureaucrats dispatched 10 ill-equipped Inuit families, mostly from Quebec, to a life of northern hardship in a bleak and inhospitable environment. The 85 Inuit were identified by dog tags, kept in cargo holds like livestock throughout the 2000-kilometre trip, separated from their families, abandoned to confront harsh Arctic conditions, left in near-starvation conditions for many years, and discouraged from returning home. The fact that these Inuit had little say in what was happening reflected a callous and arrogant indifference at odds with Canada's increasingly vaunted reputation on the global stage.

The rationale given by the federal government included political expediency, cost-cutting, and human compassion—all justified within the framework of "national interests." Within the federal bureaucracy, the resettlement was viewed as an "experiment" to determine whether the Inuit had gone "soft" or could survive when reunited with a wilderness environment. The government saw Inuit settlements as a bulwark in defence of a de facto sovereignty over the northernmost limits of Canada—not an inconsequential challenge given U.S. strategic interests in the northern Arctic when only 140 permanently settled Canadians provided evidence of Canada's sovereignty in the region.

The relocation was also viewed as a way of paring government costs. The solution lay in providing an environment where the Inuit could once again become self-sufficient through resumption of traditional living patterns. However, relief costs were largely underwritten by the Inuit families themselves. Tragically, these Inuit were forced to subsidize their own victimization; they were charged exorbitant prices for necessities but offered reduced payments for the fur pelts they brought to government supply stores. Old colonial practices of exploitation are hard to break.

The injustice of the relocation is rarely disputed. The Inuit were little more than pawns in a Canadian society-building experiment. The lack of cultural sensitivity to a people who were deeply attached to their homeland contributed to the sorry outcome. They were powerless to resist—a powerlessness that continues to plague many Native communities. While Prime Minister Stephen Harper apologized to Canada's Native peoples in June 2008 for residential schools, the government's refusal to issue an apology or a measure of redress commensurate with the gravity of the "white collar" crime of relocation is unjust.

Source: Adapted from Fleras & Elliott (1996:218–219).

years leading up to Confederation and beyond witnessed the development of the two charter groups. Each controlled its own institutional elites—the British presided over commerce and the French Catholics controlled the professions (lawyers, doctors, and clergy) and farming. This unequal distribution of economic power between the two charter groups was meant to be balanced by political accommodation, especially at the federal level.

As Hubert Guindon (1964, 1967, 1978, 1988, 2001) observed, this accommodation "worked" as long as there was room for the French Catholics of Quebec to grow. The late nineteenth and early twentieth centuries saw an exploding population in rural Quebec. The province had the highest birth rate in the country. When arable land became scarce in Quebec by the late nineteenth century, and when the vacant Prairie provinces were closed off to emigration, discontent incubated (see the Down-to-Earth Sociology box "The Legacy of Louis Riel"). The solution to the social and political problem of "too many people and not enough arable land" was the industrialization of rural Quebec (see also Hughes, 1943).

The Legacy of Louis Riel

The French Canadians who supported Confederation expected to establish many new communities on the Prairies. This was a realistic vision: the first European explorers on the great plains had been French, and their numbers increased with the fur trade. French Canadians and Cree Natives intermarried, and their offspring were called Métis, who formed a distinctive community with their own language, Michef. French-Canadian missionaries converted the region's Native population to Catholicism.

French Canadians and Métis comprised the majority of the population when the Prairies entered Confederation through the purchase of the territory from the Hudson's Bay Company.

The first major crisis after Confederation came when the French-Canadian Catholics of the plains protested that they had not been properly consulted regarding the Hudson's Bay Company purchase. The resulting conflict was the Red River Rebellion, the insistence by the residents of Red River on negotiating their entry into Confederation. They were successful. A new province was created by the *Manitoba Act* (1870), and the French-Canadian majority was guaranteed the right to their own school system.

There was a major difference, however, between the liberal spirit of the *Manitoba Act* and the administration of the new province during its first years. Canadian militia in the province terrorized the French-Canadian leaders, prompting many of them to leave before their land claims could be resolved. However, between 1876 and 1881, over 40 000 immigrants, mainly Ontario British, moved to Manitoba, lured by the prospect of profitable wheat farming. Some leaders, notably Louis Riel, moved to the United States. Most Métis left for present-day Saskatchewan. There, the Second Red River Rebellion, or "Riel Rebellion," broke out in 1885 over a concern about the lack of legal protection for French lands and schools. The rebellion was crushed by 5000 militia. Though Riel was a hero in French Canada, he was vilified in Ontario and executed, despite an appeal for clemency by Queen Victoria. Because the French Canadians were clearly upset about their treatment in the West, their migration to the Prairies slowed to a trickle. Instead, they moved north, to "New Quebec," a region inhabited largely by Native peoples.

When Keewatin, part of the Northwest Territories, was transferred to Manitoba in the latter part of the nineteenth century, no protections were extended for its French-Canadian residents. Public opinion about the matter in Quebec was outrage. By way of appeasement, Ungava, a large territory that today comprises the northern section of the province—and the site of the massive James Bay Hydro-Electric Project—was transferred to Quebec.

Métis leader Louis Riel, led the Second Red River Rebellion in 1885 over a concern about the protection of French lands and schools on the Prairies.

Source: Adapted from Spencer (1996:379)

Industrialization was welcomed by the people and clergy of Quebec. Most residents were employed and Quebec's Catholic clergy had parishioners. However, all was not well, especially after World War II. Quebec's government had not kept up with the changing times, and a small group of rogue intellectuals—Pierre Elliott Trudeau, Jean Marchand, and Gerald Pelletier—took on the Quebec government of Maurice Duplessis in a journal called *Cité Libre* ("free city"). Duplessis was accused of corruption and anti-democratic politics. The Catholic Church was also singled out for its authoritarian character and support of the Nazis. Quebec, it was argued, had been shackled by the old elites; it was time to modernize her and bring her into the twentieth century as a free, democratic, and secular province.

The death of Maurice Duplessis and his replacement by Paul Sauvé (not Jean Lesage, as Guindon rightly notes) began what became known as the Quiet Revolution in Quebec. It was not and has not been quiet, nor was it much of a revolution. Its goal was the secularization of Quebec society. Where the Catholic Church had once controlled and staffed social welfare, education, and hospitals, the provincial government took over. The provincial government had access to the resources to affect massive changes in these three areas, and did so by creating jobs in the public sector of the economy. Taking over the hydroelectric power plants in the province by the mid-1960s was tantamount to catching up to Ontario, which had nationalized its hydroelectric power facilities half a century earlier.

Focus Question
Can you describe Canada's two charter groups?

At the beginning of the twentieth century, industrialization in rural Quebec had eased the demographic pressure brought on large family farms by keeping sons and daughters in the province. The post-Duplessis era set the agenda for the secularization of Quebec (the Quiet Revolution) by providing good jobs in the public sector. What was the fate of the private sector? That preserve was to be left largely to the English-speaking population of the province, who had enjoyed its privileges for over a hundred years. Some Quebecois thought otherwise, and the not-so-quiet politics of language in Quebec has been the result.

The chosen few from the English charter group, according to John Porter (1965), kept their status as the pre-eminent economic leaders of the country for several generations. Just as often, though, other members from the English charter group could be found in the country's political and media elites, the upper echelons of the Protestant clergy, and even in the trade union elites. Canada was, in Porter's phrase, a "vertical mosaic"—a pyramid in which the apex was composed of one dominant charter group: the English. A select few from the French charter group constituted a subordinate political elite located mostly, but not exclusively, in the province of Quebec. Even as late as the mid-1960s, immigrant minorities had barely touched any significant levers of power or authority in Canada.

However, Porter believed that once Canada expanded and opened its postsecondary educational institutions to all who qualified, more opportunities would become available to a greater number of Canadians. Moreover, he felt that education would help break down the secrecy and exclusivity of Canada's elites and bring about a more democratic society. The economic benefits of modernization and development could be shared among all Canadians: Natives, both charter group members, and new immigrants.

Unfortunately, according to Wallace Clement (1975, 1977), a student of Porter who updated his mentor's work, the economic elite has grown more insular and exclusive. While the Canadian economy has expanded since Porter's day, Clement, and now others, see a greater integration of Canada's economic elite with powerful economic interests south of the border. And while many Canadians have benefited from the expanding economy and many others have access to postsecondary education, not all Canadians share in these benefits (an exception is our publicly funded health care system, in which we all share equally).

The Other Ethnic Groups in Canada
Canada's ethnic or multicultural minorities occupy a uniquely different status than either the Native peoples or the two charter groups. Their situation in Canada is based on their standing as immigrants or descendants of immigrants. Their interests, therefore, centre on equality instead of the more political demands made by the other groups.

That said, Canada embraces a rich diversity of immigrants and refugees from different parts of the world. At Confederation, barely 8 percent of Canada's population was not British or French. Today, the majority of Canadians have neither British nor French ancestry.

Table 8.2 is based on the 2001 census and provides a breakdown of selected characteristics of eight principal ethnic groups in Canada. All groups are compared with the

The position of Canada's ethnic or multicultural minorities is based on their standing as immigrants or descendants of immigrants. Their interests, therefore, centre more on equality than on political demands.

TABLE 8.2 Ethnic Composition of Canada with Selected Ethnic Groups and Characteristics, 2001

Selected Characteristics	Canadian	English	French	Italian	East Indian	Jewish	American	Jamaican	Native/Aboriginal
Average full-time income	$44 286	$47 698	$42 220	$46 314	$40 622	$73 928	$72 243	$35 505	$30 527
Less than high school diploma	33.4%*	27.3%	29.7%	35.2%	28.4%	18.1%	22.3%	28.8%	55.2%
University degree	11.9%*	16.7%	14.9%	14.6%	26%	39.4%	23.9%	9.9%	3.1%
Trades certificate	11.2%	10.9%	11.1%	9.8%	6.6%	5.1%	9.6%	11.4%	11.3%
Income $60 000 and over	8.8%	12.4%	9.5%	11.3%	8.5%	22%	13.4%	6.5%	4.6%
Unemployment rate	7.7%	6.5%	7.8%	5.4%	8.6%	6%	6.4%	8.6%	24.6%

*Percentages derived from Canadians 15 years and older.

Canadian average. With the exception of Canada's Native peoples and Jamaicans, all groups reported higher levels of university qualifications than the national average, with Jews reporting the highest at almost 40 percent compared with the national average of 12 percent. Americans and Jews stand out as having the highest average full-time incomes, while Native Canadians and Jamaicans report the lowest incomes. Interestingly, of those respondents who had less than a high school education, Jamaicans reported lower incomes than the national average, but of those with trade certificates, Jamaicans reported higher incomes than the

national average. This discrepancy between educational qualifications and income could be due to the more recent immigration of Jamaicans to Canada. Notwithstanding the incredible statistics for Americans and Jews (both groups are small in number compared to the English), the English remain a privileged category in Canada, with higher-than-average incomes (over $60 000 on average per year), university degrees, and lower-than-average unemployment rates.

Table 8.3 draws data from the 2006 census and makes a projection of what Canada's visible minority population will look like in 2031. In 2006, Canada had more than 5 million

TABLE 8.3 Visible Minority Groups in Canada: Projections for 2031

Visible Minority Groups	2006		2031	
	32 522	100	42 078	100
Total visible minority	5285	16.3	12 855	30.6
Chinese	1269	3.9	2714	6.4
South Asian	1320	4.1	3640	8.7
Black	815	2.5	1809	4.3
Filipino	427	1.3	1020	2.4
Latin American	317	1.0	733	1.7
Southeast Asian	250	0.8	449	1.1
Arab	276	0.8	930	2.2
West Asian	164	0.5	523	1.2
Korean	148	0.5	407	1.0
Japanese	85	0.3	142	0.3
Other visible minorities	213	0.7	489	1.2
Rest of population	27 237	83.7	29 222	69.4

Source: Statistics Canada, 2010, Projections of the Diversity of Canadian Population, 2006-2031, Catalogue no. 91-551-X,

TABLE 8.4 Top Ethnic Origins Reported for Montreal, Toronto, and Vancouver

Ethnic Origin	Montreal	Toronto	Vancouver
Canadian	1 670 655	651 635	278 360
English	148 095	804 100	464 340
French	936 990	241 395	137 270
Irish	216 410	531 865	251 695
Scottish	119 365	561 050	337 225
Chinese	82 665	537 060	402 000
Italian	85 785	466 155	76 345
Quebecois*	72 445		
German	**	259 015	203 720
Jewish	68 485	141 685	**
East Indian	39 305	484 655	181 895
North American Indian	74 565	**	43 190
TOTAL	3 588 520	5 072 075	2 097 965

* Reported for Montreal only.
** Not among the top 25 reported.

Source: Statistics Canada, 2007c, Ethnic origins. 2006 counts for census metropolitan areas and census agglomerations—20 percent sample data. Ethnocultural portrait of Canada Highlight 2006 Census, cat no. 97-562-XWE2006002, Ottawa, accessed April 28, 2008.

persons belonging to visible minority groups. At that time, visible minorities accounted for 16 percent of the overall population, compared to only 5 percent in 1981. The projection in Table 8.3 indicates that by 2031, Canada's visible minority population could rise to almost 13 million. In other words, about three Canadians in ten could belong to a visible minority group in 2031. Interestingly, between 4 million and 5 million (or one third of) persons belonging to a visible minority group in 2031 will be Canadian-born, either as the children of immigrants (second generation) or members of families settled in Canada for three generations or more.

Table 8.4 shows data from the 2006 census of reported ethnic origins for the three major metropolitan areas in Canada: Montreal, Toronto, and Vancouver. Not surprising, Montreal reported the largest number of respondents stating "Canadian" and "Quebecois"—evidence that language and politics remain salient. Vancouver and Toronto are important cities for those reporting Chinese and East Indian origins, while Montreal and Vancouver report relatively large Native populations. All three major cities report significant numbers who state English, Scottish, and Irish origins, while Montreal is the only city with a large French origin population. While there is evidence for the increasing ethnic diversity of Canada's three major cities, the two charter groups remain numerically significant.

According to Metta Spencer (1996), the actual economic experience of moving to and living in Canada has fallen far short of the expectations of many immigrants. The hope of a better life took longer than expected for most or failed to materialize at all. Faced with unemployment and discrimination, up to 20 percent of some groups, says Spencer, have returned to their native countries. She contends that while British and American immigrants do well in Canada, others are apt to be less successful.

Canada needs immigration to continue benefiting from our renewed prosperity. It is no secret that our population is aging and our fertility rate is too low to keep the population at its present level. Any remaining barriers to jobs based on racial or ethnic discrimination must be eradicated. The past is rife with examples of discrimination against immigrants. At first, the Irish and French were likely taking jobs away from "Canadians," then it was the Italians or Jews, and now it is Asians or Africans or Caribbeans—all myths with terrible consequences for those who have to bear the brunt of such prejudices. Far from taking employment away from Canadians, immigrants create more jobs than they fill (Dirks, 1995). While it is no easy task, it is time that

✺ **Explore** the statistics in "Immigration" and look at the important changes in origins of people coming to Canada on **MySocLab.**

Over Half a Century of Citizenship

Most Canadians do not realize that our citizenship is a relatively new achievement. As late as 1946, Canadians were considered British subjects residing in Canada, not Canadian citizens.

It was not until 1947, with the passage of the first *Citizenship Act*, that the idea of a distinctly Canadian citizenship was introduced. The year 1997 saw the fiftieth anniversary of this step toward true nationhood for Canada.

The *Citizenship Act* came into being largely due to the efforts of Paul Martin, Sr., father of the former prime minister of Canada. It has been said that while visiting a military cemetery in France just after World War II, Paul Martin, Sr. was visibly shaken by the rows and rows of wooden crosses marking the graves of Canadians who had given their lives in the service of their country and for the peace and freedom that everyone now enjoys.

Martin was impressed by the various ethnic and religious backgrounds of the names on the graves. Despite their differences, these soldiers had come together in a struggle against the Nazi dictatorship and fascism and had died for what they believed in. When Martin returned to Canada, he set wheels in motion that led to the establishment of the *Citizenship Act* as a tribute to their memory. On January 1, 1947, Canada took a bold step toward independence when the Act came into being, and in so doing established a separate Canadian identity, new rights for Canadian women, and our own Canadian passport.

Source: Adapted from Citizenship and Immigration Canada website.

we recognize that we are all "immigrants" in one way or another, and the sooner we get over our hang-ups about our fellow Canadian residents, the better our society and ourselves will be for it.

Looking Toward the Future

Canadians will face two major issues as we progress through the twenty-first century. The first is a persistent demand for the increased political autonomy, if not outright independence, of Quebec from Canada. Second, we will encounter new challenges of racial and ethnic diversity due to the immigration of people, including refugees, from less-developed nations. Clearly, there will be increased racial and ethnic diversity and tension, especially in the three major cities of Toronto, Montreal, and Vancouver. And for all intents and purposes, it is already here. Neither issue will be easy to resolve.

What we do about these issues depends on our vision of and for Canadian society. If we seek a tolerant, progressive, and pluralistic society, we can achieve one where Native peoples, the two charter groups, and a racially and ethnically diverse population coexist in harmony. We will be the envy of the world and a model for others to follow.

SUMMARY AND REVIEW

LAYING THE SOCIOLOGICAL FOUNDATION

How do race and ethnicity differ?

In the sense that different groups inherit distinctive physical characteristics, race is a reality. In the sense of one race being superior to another and the idea that there are "pure races," however, race is a myth. The *idea* of race is powerful, shaping basic relationships among people. pp. 172–173.

Race refers to supposed biological characteristics; ethnicity, to cultural ones. Ethnic groups identify with one another on the basis of common ancestry and cultural heritage. p. 173.

What are minority and dominant groups?

Minority groups are people singled out for unequal treatment by members of the dominant group, the group with more power, privilege, and social status. Minorities originate with the expansion of political boundaries or migration. pp. 173–175.

Are prejudice and discrimination the same thing?

Prejudice is an attitude; discrimination is an act. Some people who are prejudiced do not discriminate, while others who are not prejudiced do. p. 175.

How do individual and institutional discrimination differ?

Individual discrimination is the negative treatment of one person by another, while institutional discrimination is discrimination built into a society's social institutions. Institutional discrimination often occurs without the awareness of either the perpetrator or the object of the discrimination. p. 175.

Sociological theories focus on how different social environments increase or decrease prejudice. Functionalists stress the benefits and costs that come from discrimination. Conflict theorists look at how groups in power exploit racial and ethnic divisions to hold down wages and otherwise maintain power. Symbolic interactionists stress that labels create selective perception and self-fulfilling prophecies. Multiracial feminists argue that white men and women oppress lower-class women and men of disadvantaged races and ethnicities. Postmodernists argue that only those who directly experience racism and discrimination can understand it. Postcolonial theorists seek to understand the ways in which the colonial legacy of racism persists in so-called postcolonial societies.

Critical race theorists hold that racial inequalities in housing, the legal system, employment, and the educational system in developed nations persist over time. pp. 177–178.

THE MAJOR CLASSIFICATIONS IN CANADA

What are the major ethnic groups in Canada?

The major classifications of ethnic groups in Canada are Native peoples, the two charter groups, and other ethnic groups. p. 180.

Why don't all Native peoples in Canada support the Charter of Rights and Freedoms?

The use of the term "existing Aboriginal and treaty rights" remains unsatisfactory to many Natives because many land claims are not recognized by some provincial governments. pp. 180–182.

What was the Quiet Revolution in Quebec?

The Quiet Revolution refers to rural industrialization and secularization of religious institutions in Quebec around health, education, and welfare. pp. 183–184.

TALKING ABOUT THEORY

Theoretical Paradigms

	CLASSICAL PARADIGMS			RECENT PARADIGMS			
	Structural-Functional Paradigm	Social-Conflict Paradigm	Symbolic-Interaction Paradigm	Feminist Paradigm	Postmodernist Paradigm	Postcolonial Paradigm	Critical Race Paradigm
What is the level of analysis?	Macro level	Macro level	Micro level	Macro level	Micro level	Macro level	Micro level
What is the social significance of the inequalities of race & ethnicity?	Prejudice creates in-group solidarity (inclusive = functional); it also destroys wider community social relationships (exclusive = dysfunctional).	Reduces worker solidarity by exploiting racial and ethnic rivalry; for example, the dual or split labour market.	Labels create selective perception; for example, the self-fulfilling prophecy.	White men and women oppress lower-class women and men of disadvantaged races and ethnicities.	Hear only the "voices" of those who have experienced racism and discrimination.	The persistence of the colonial legacy of racism in postcolonial societies; homosexuality viewed as a white European "disease;" patriarchy and misogyny are indigenous characteristics.	Racism is a fact of life; meritocracy, colour-blindness, objectivity, and neutrality are questionable.
Have the inequalities of race and ethnicity changed over time? How?	No/Yes. Without changing social environments, it is difficult to affect prejudice toward minority groups.	No. Capitalist societies need a reserve army of labour.	Yes. Education and changing social environments.	No/Yes. The complexities of understanding the nature of the oppression of men and women of colour.	N/A	Yes. Confronting the nature of the colonizer's culture, especially language and rules of property and governance.	No/Yes. Racism exists but there is a struggle to make legal changes to discrimination in housing, employment, and so on.

assimilation   179
authoritarian
   personality   176
compartmentalize   179
discrimination   175
dominant group   174
dual labour market   176

ethnic (and ethnicity)   173
ethnic work   173
genocide   176
individual
   discrimination   175
institutional
   discrimination   175

internal colonialism   179
minority group   173
multiculturalism (also called
   pluralism)   179
population transfer   179
postcolonialism   177
prejudice   175

race   172
racism   175
reserve labour force   176
scapegoat   175
segregation   179
selective perception   177

WEBLINKS

All URLs listed are current as of the printing of this text.

University of Toronto: Ethnic, Immigration, and Pluralism Studies
www.utoronto.ca/ethnicstudies
The University of Toronto's Robert F. Harney Professorship and Program in Ethnic, Immigration, and Pluralism Studies is a seat of research, training, and the dissemination of knowledge in the area of ethnic studies. The links page provides access to useful Canadian and non-Canadian web references.

Centre for Refugee Studies
www.yorku.ca/crs
The Centre for Refugee Studies is engaged in research on refugee issues. It informs public discussion; participates in policy development and practical innovation by international, governmental, advocacy, and service organizations; and supports teaching in refugee and migration studies.

Hate on the Net
www.sociology.org/content/vol003.002/kallen.html
This 1998 paper by Evelyn Kallen of York University shows that messages promoted on the internet by organized political and religious groups incite hatred and promote harmful action against racial, ethnocultural, religious, and same-sex-oriented minorities. High-tech hate-mongering violates minority members' fundamental right to freedom from group defamation and harassment.

CRITICAL THINKING QUESTIONS

1. Is ethnic or cultural assimilation of immigrants to the dominant culture the only workable public policy for a national society such as in the United States, France, or Canada?

2. Many sociologists assume that a society is held together by the common values and beliefs of its members. What beliefs and values hold Canadian society together today?

3. After you have given some thought to what holds Canada together as a society, consider the ethnic or national forces pulling Canada apart. What solutions might you offer to help minimize cultural and national divisions?

4. Does Aboriginal self-government contribute to nation-building in Canada, or do race-based politics serve to undermine the Canadian state?
   Access Research Navigator through MySocLab and use keywords such as "assimilation," "emigration and immigration," "ethnic," "multiculturalism," and "public policy" to locate relevant and recent scholarly and popular press publications to help you answer these questions.

MySocLab

Explore the topics covered in this chapter on MySocLab. Interactive resources include a study plan, cumulative exams, a multimedia library, MySocLab eReadings, and access to the MySocLab Video Series.

9

INEQUALITIES OF AGE

LEARNING OUTCOMES

After you have studied this chapter, you will be able to answer the following questions:

1. Is aging a global crisis?
2. What does the term "greying of Canada" mean?
3. What factors influence perceptions of aging?
4. How does aging affect men and women differently?
5. Is there conflict among different age groups?
6. What are some of the problems faced by the elderly today?

I AM 64 years old and just a few months shy of the age at which my mother died of cancer. Last year, I was diagnosed with early stage breast cancer, received treatment, and am now back to my "normal" life. But this is a new normal. Suddenly, or so it seems, I need to address the issues attached to aging. Will I retire? After all, I mostly enjoy my work and my work friends, and more than 30 years of my life have been constructed around it. Can I afford to retire? After the 2008 recession, my pension looks a tad weathered and fragile. What will I do if I retire? I am a feminist and I know that it's important to continue to combat the violence (emotional, psychological, economic, and social) that is routinely inflicted on women around the world. More generally, I support social justice advocacy, so I want to make a difference beyond having fun. But I also want to have fun. As other feminists of my generation have said, "I don't want a revolution that I can't dance to."

I certainly can no longer ignore the fact that my life is finite and that, however distant or close, the end of my life is approaching. Close friends and relatives have already died, and aging family members are struggling with a litany of health issues ranging from dementia to diabetes. Ironically, in this context, the framework of my early twenties has resurfaced. I am again living with the contradiction between the sometimes daunting freedom to look on my life as a "beginning" and the awesome pressure to decide what that life will look like. Just as in my twenties, I am again constrained by stereotypes; no longer too young and inexperienced, I am now often treated, very subtly, as too old and out of date. Even youthful economic concerns of not having enough money and being forced to the social margins are again present. At its most intense, when I look directly at my life, it is in equal measures exhilarating and daunting.

These comments from a 64-year-old woman speak to some of the complexities and contradictions of aging. Loss, fear, and fatalism interweave with feelings of freedom, possibility, and accomplishment. For the first time in history, hundreds of millions of people around the globe are living well into their seventies and eighties. Their experience with the process of aging and their struggles with its contradictions are likely to have a profound impact on Canadian society in the coming decades.

The "Age-Quake"

Until the 1970s, aging and the elderly received relatively little attention from Canadian social researchers. Other forms of social inequality—racism, sexism, and classism—were all seen as much more consequential. However, as the post-war baby boomers (Canadians born between 1946 and 1965) now surge toward the final chapters of their lives, efforts to examine the social construction of aging in Canada have gained momentum (Statistics Canada, 2012). In 1999, the International Year of Older Persons, the federal government instituted the National Advisory Council on Aging to advise the federal minister of health, scholars established the Canadian Association on Gerontology, and almost every university in Canada created a gerontology or aging studies program. These and various other efforts are providing increased insight into the personal and societal dimensions of aging.

For most of us, aging and old age will become an issue in the course of our personal lives. We will experience important shifts in our fundamental sense of self. Not only will this be necessitated by biological changes—declining physical fitness and increasing disabilities—but also by profound alterations in our social roles. Important elements that were carefully socialized into our identities when we were children and young adults will eventually be pruned away. Our grandparents and parents will die, and we will no longer be grandchildren or sons and daughters. With divorce or widowhood, the maturation of children, and changes or losses in employment identities because of retirement, we will learn to think of ourselves in terms of a dramatically different constellation of relationships and abilities.

For young people reading this text, the intellectual understanding of these changes may seem perfectly clear, but it is difficult to actually enter into the lived experiences of the elderly. In his classic study of racism, *Black Like Me* (1961), John Griffin, a white social researcher, dyed his skin brown and travelled throughout the southern United States in the late 1950s. He sought to truly know the experience of being black and living in a racist society. It would be wonderfully instructive if, for a few hours, young people could similarly immerse themselves in the lives of seniors.

Walking down a street, the senior is often socially invisible. Unlike "attractive" young men and women, the senior fades into the social setting and often passes unnoticed. As reinforced in popular culture, and particularly in the mass media, our culture is not about the elderly, and their images are rarely reflected in movies, television, or magazines. If they do appear, they are often caricatures—the snoopy old woman, the cranky old man. There are, of course, a few notable exceptions—particularly older white men, such as Christopher Plummer, Leonard Cohen, and Farley Mowat, who remain important cultural figures well past age 65. However, in most instances, cultural images are about the relatively young. Indeed, celebrity women are typically only able to hang on to their status if they maintain a youthful appearance. In the films nominated for Academy Awards in recent years, for example, seniors were almost completely absent from the storylines. An alien visitor might legitimately assume that the elderly are extremely uncommon (and unimportant) in the social landscape or that they have little of significance to communicate about the human condition. In a recent study of animated Disney films, researchers found that although the majority of older characters were portrayed positively, a significant number were depicted in such a way that children might develop negative feelings toward them (Robinson, Callister, Magoffin & Moore, 2007). Older characters, for example, might appear as toothless, feeble, and hunched over, with cracking voices. Older men might be depicted as sinister, conniving villains, while older women often play witches (or witch-like characters) with sagging breasts, unshapely bodies, and unattractive features. A similar portrayal is presented on television, where seniors are either absent as characters, are contestants on games shows, or (particularly for women) are obsessed with their wrinkles (Clarke, 2001; Katz, 2005).

A variety of popular ageist values underlie this tendency to ignore or gloss over seniors. Often, the unstated assumption when interacting with seniors is that they are not intellectually sharp, not up to date, incapable of learning new skills, unambitious and unfocused, and simply not worthy of attention. In a society in which attention is dispensed based on social power and position, the lack of attention shown to seniors speaks volumes.

Examining the way we, as a society, socially construct aging is not only important for one's own future life course and for a full understanding of social inequalities in Canada, it is key to any formulations about our future evolution. Throughout the world's industrialized nations, the population bubble that appeared after World War II has matured into senior citizenry. The result is a historically unparalleled transformation in the age structure of post-industrial and industrialized societies. The possible outcomes are raising concerns among many analysts.

With industrialization, urbanization, and modernization came a dramatic increase in lifespan and a remarkable swell in the numbers of seniors in the population.

⊙ **Watch** the video "The Longevity Revolution" on **MySocLab.**

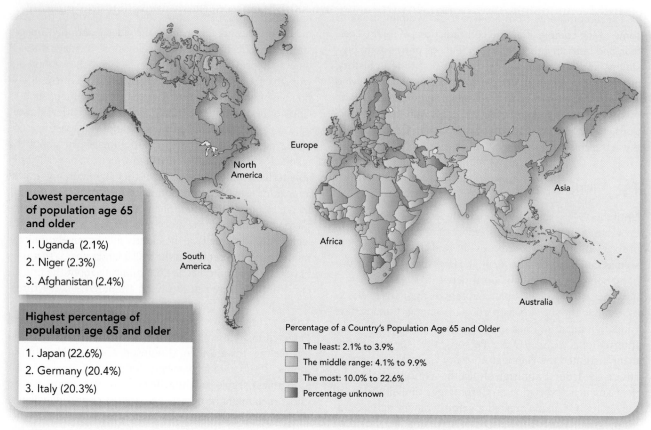

Lowest percentage of population age 65 and older

1. Uganda (2.1%)
2. Niger (2.3%)
3. Afghanistan (2.4%)

Highest percentage of population age 65 and older

1. Japan (22.6%)
2. Germany (20.4%)
3. Italy (20.3%)

Percentage of a Country's Population Age 65 and Older

The least: 2.1% to 3.9%
The middle range: 4.1% to 9.9%
The most: 10.0% to 22.6%
Percentage unknown

FIGURE 9.1 The Greying of the Globe

Source: By the authors. Based on *Statistical Abstract of the United States, 2011:* Table 1333.

The combination of improved sanitation, nutrition, and medical care ensures that Canadians—and the citizens of industrialized countries around the world—have an excellent likelihood of living into their seventies, eighties, or nineties (see Figures 9.1 and 9.2). The demographic effects of industrialization were magnified by World War II. From 1939 to 1945, birthrates dropped as military conflict and the large deployment of soldiers overseas interrupted family patterns. At the end of the war, men and women made up for lost time by marrying and forming families. A period of economic prosperity encouraged couples to have relatively large numbers of children. The net result was the "baby boom"—a dramatic increase in the population generated between 1946 and 1965. Today, the baby boomers range in age from 47 to 66 and, according to data recently released from the 2011 census, they number 9.6 million persons and comprise nearly a third (29 percent) of the total Canadian population (Statistics Canada, 2012b:2). Today, 15 percent of Canadians are age 65 or over, a figure that is anticipated to increase to 23 percent by 2031 (Statistics Canada 2012b:3). Figure 9.3 illustrates the steady increase in the number of seniors in Canada over the 55-year period from 1956 to 2011. The post–World War II shift in the age profile of developed countries

was so momentous that it is sometimes referred to as an "age-quake."

From 1965 to 2007, there was a decline in the number of children born into a typical family from a high of 3.7 during the baby boom to 1.7 currently (Statistics Canada, 2012b:2). Improved access to reliable birth control, the advent of the women's movement, the decline in family income, and an increased need for mothers to enter paid employment all contributed to a "baby bust" from 1966 to 1971—a segment of the population sometimes referred to as Generation X. There was a brief relief from the yearly decline in births when the baby boomers reached the age of marriage and began to have children between 1972 and 1992. These children of the baby boomers now comprise 27 percent of the Canadian population.

The growth spurt was short-lived, however, and in the years following, there was a fairly steady decline in the number of births per year in Canada until very recently. The population born between 1993 and 2011 are often termed Generation Z, or the Internet Generation, and comprise 22 percent of the total population (Statistics Canada, 2012b:6). Interestingly, according to the latest census (2011), there was a marked increase in the population of children aged four and under between 2006 and 2011.

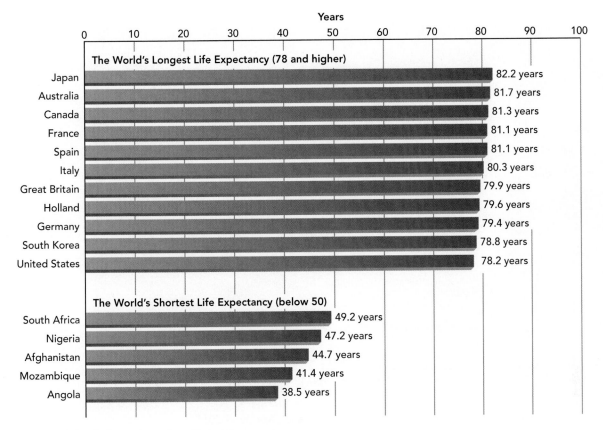

FIGURE 9.2 Life Expectancy in a Global Perspective

Source: By the authors. Based on *Statistical Abstract of the United States, 2011:* Table 1338.

The 11 percent increase was the highest growth rate for this age group since the 1956 to 1961 period of the baby boom (Statistics Canada, 2012n:6) Despite these ups and downs, it is readily apparent that without the steady influx of immigrants (approximately 225 000 per year), Canada's total population would be in decline.

The net result is that the age pyramid that characterizes most traditional societies—many children, fewer adults, and very few elders—has disappeared in Canada and most other industrialized nations, and older Canadians increasingly predominate the population. This is reflected in the median age of Canadians—that is, the point at which exactly half of the population is older and the other half is younger. In 1901, the median age in Canada was 22.7; in 1966, it was marginally higher at 25.4 years. According to census results, the median in 2006 was 39.5, a number that is expected to increase to 44 by 2031 (Statistics Canada, 2007a).

The shift in Canada toward an older society poses significant issues. Will older citizens who continue to occupy positions in the labour force block the entry and advancement of younger Canadians? With the elimination of mandatory retirement, will today's university and college students find it increasingly difficult to gain a foothold in the economy? Or will older workers increasingly become the victims of ageist discrimination in the workplace; for example, facing higher rates of unemployment as well as longer job searches (Bernard, 2012)? Will older workers continue to be pushed out of the productive arena, expected to take up "volunteer" unpaid work, while pension provisions become increasingly insecure and insufficient?

Will seniors who are disabled or ill become an overwhelming burden for young citizens who are directly or indirectly (through taxation) involved in the provision of care for the elderly? As a nation's elderly population increases, so too does the bill footed by its younger citizens to provide for their needs. In the world's most industrialized countries, this bill has been increasingly portrayed as a major social issue. Even though Canada has remained one of the "demographically youngest of the developed countries" (compared, for example, to Japan, where 23 percent of the population is 65 or over, or Italy, where 20 percent are), many analysts express concern about these shifts in population patterns. Of course, these developments are dwarfed by the dramatic increases in aging in China and India. Both of these countries have experienced an historic decrease in their birth rate and today are home to close to one in three seniors (Statistics Canada, 2012m:6–8; McDaniel & Rozanova, 2011:512).

As the senior population continues to grow, and particularly the number of aged seniors (80 years and older), it is

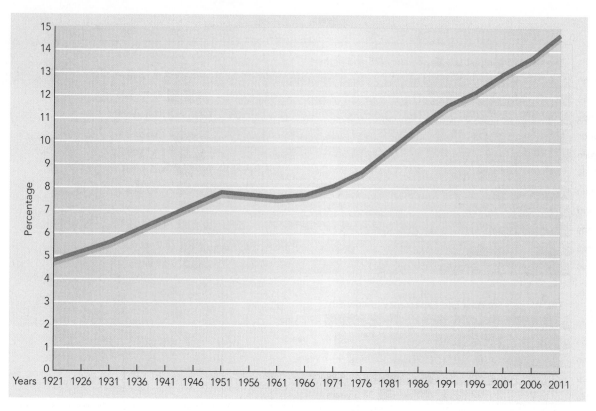

FIGURE 9.3 Proportion of the Canadian Population Aged 65 Years and Over, 1956–2011

Source: Statistics Canada, 2007a. 2006 Census: Portrait of the Canadian Population, By Age and Sex: National Portrait. July 16, 2007. www12.statcan.ca/english/census06/analysis/agesex/charts/chart2.htm, from Statistics Canada, Censuses of Population, 1956 to 2006. Derived from Statistics Canada, 2002c. *Profile of the Canadian Population by Age and Sex: Canada Ages.* Catalogue No. 96F0030XIE2001002, Statistics Canada, 2012c:4.

likely that debates over other public expenditures, such as health care, will greatly intensify. Over the past five years, the proportion of seniors aged 65 and over increased (by 1.4 percent) in every province and territory in Canada, whereas the number of youth aged 14 and under decreased by 0.5 percent (Statistics Canada, 2012c:3). As of this writing, there were 5825 centenarians in Canada, a number that has increased by 25.7 percent since 2006 (Statistics Canada, 2012c:3). Barring any dramatic changes in health practices and employment patterns, this change in the demography of Canada will likely have significant implications. Notably, in 2011, for the first time there were more people aged 55 to 64, presumably moving toward leaving the labour force, than there were Canadians aged 15 to 24, presumably about to enter the labour force (Statistics Canada, 2012c:3).

Such changes raise the question of how scarce resources will be allocated when the interests of seniors conflict with those of the young. For example, should limited research funding be directed toward the diseases of the elderly, such as arthritis and heart disease, or health concerns of the young, such as reproductive technologies? Is a 65-year-old man a less worthy candidate for surgery than a baby born prematurely? Will we be able to provide for the consumption needs of increasing numbers of elderly, many of whom

will presumably join the ranks of the retired? As reflected in the recent heated debate over euthanasia in British Columbia, an aging population, along with increased numbers of persons with dementia and terminal illness, will necessarily intensify the debate over whether Canadians can be afforded the choice to opt for death, for example, through doctor-assisted suicide (CARP, 2012).

These complex societal issues swirl around the shifting age profile in Canada. Certainly, some commentators predict increased tension and conflict between the young and aged if appropriate action is not taken, and others argue that there is a growing malaise and frustration among the young, who see themselves increasingly burdened by their aging societies. There have been a variety of important developments on age-related matters. As explored later in the chapter, academics, especially gerontologists, are theorizing and documenting the senior experience; seniors' organizations are lobbying governments against age discrimination in employment and for changes in retirement practices and options; individuals are taking claims of age discrimination to court (see Selvin & Goldman, 2007:D16; Pigg, 2012); and governments in many industrialized countries are actively exploring ways to maintain old age social security benefits as the first wave of baby boomers reaches retirement age. In a number of societies, seniors and their caregivers are mobilizing in support of a re-examination of the relationship between the state and assisted suicide and demanding the legalization of euthanasia. Most promising, as discussed below, a number of analysts are investigating the possibility of using the broad issue of ageism to rethink the structure and meaning of our lives. Pursued from this perspective, the study of ageism may join racism, sexism, and heterosexism as a core element in social justice campaigns and as a source of fundamental positive social change.

The Greying of Canada

Figure 9.3 documents the dramatic increase in the numbers of seniors (65 and above) in the Canadian population over the past 55 years. In large measure, this is the result of marked improvements in Canadian **life expectancy**. A hundred years ago, the majority of Canadians would not live to see age 65; by 2051, wholly a quarter of all Canadians will be over that age, according to projections (Statistics Canada, 2012b:1). In fact, analysts project that the population of Canadian centenarians will triple by 2031 to 17 600 and reach a staggering 78 300 by 2061 (Statistics Canada, 2012b:1). This suggests a stark contrast to Canadian society in 1901, when the average Canadian woman could expect to live to age 50, and the average man to age 47. While these figures reflect high mortality rates among infants and children in the early twentieth century, there is no question that elderly Canadians were relatively uncommon and centenarians almost unheard of.

As shown in Table 9.1, a Canadian woman born in 2008 can expect to live to age 83, and a man to age 79. Despite illness, accidents, and other factors that may cut life short, the overwhelming majority of Canadians live at least to retirement age. More than 80 percent of men and almost 90 percent of women can expect to live to at least age 65 (Gorrie, 2001; Martel & Belanger, 2000). Further, life expectancy continues to increase, so that every five years Canadians can add about another year to their life expectancy. It is clear that more and more Canadians are living longer lives. What is not clear and has momentous implications is whether the growing population of seniors will be able to participate as productive members of society or whether many—aged seniors, in particular—will continue

to experience high rates of disability, frailty, and dependency (Aaron & Harris, 2003). Not surprisingly, research suggests that the longer seniors survive, the higher the likelihood that they will experience the transition from independent living to intergenerational and institutional living arrangements (Sarma, Hawley, & Basu, 2009).

The term **greying of Canada** has been coined to refer to the increasing proportion of older people in the Canadian population. According to the 2011 census, there are over 4.9 million Canadian seniors (Statistics Canada, 2012b:1). Canadian society has become so "grey" that by 2011 seniors made up almost as much of the population (14.1 percent) as children aged 14 and younger, who made up 16.7 percent (down 0.5 percent). And the greying is far from complete: the number of Canadians aged 60 to 64 nearing retirement is the fastest growing segment of the population, increasing to 4.4 million in 2011 (Statistics Canada, 2012b:11). Although Canada's life expectancy ranks among the highest in the world (see Table 9.1), other countries, such as Japan, Germany, and Italy, have surpassed us in terms of the proportion of seniors in their populations. As Canada follows suit in the coming years, seniors will take an increasingly prominent place in our society.

The impact of this aging population has not been felt uniformly across the country. As with almost every aspect of Canadian social life, important regional differences exist. Atlantic Canada, followed by Quebec and British Columbia, reported the highest proportions of seniors over 65 in 2011, hovering around one-sixth of the population, while Nunavut reported the lowest (3.3 percent) (Statistics Canada, 2012c:11). As a result of low fertility and outmigration, populations in Atlantic Canada and Quebec are expected to continue to age more rapidly than the rest of the country over the next decade. Higher-than-average fertility rates in the Prairie provinces means those regions have relatively younger populations. Alberta's booming economy has attracted so many young workers and families that in 2011 it recorded the lowest provincial population aged 65 and over (11 percent) (Statistics Canada, 2012c:12,13). These differences are important to recognize, since aging issues are likely to resonate very differently in various regions of Canada.

Further, populations of urban areas are generally younger than those of rural areas, since most young rural adults leave their communities for school or work. In 2011, seniors 65 and older made up only 14 percent of Canadians living in census metropolitan areas (CMAs are areas with populations of 100 000 or more), while regions remote from CMAs had higher proportions of seniors (Statistics Canada, 2012b:15,16). However, certain cities, such as Peterborough, Trois-Rivieres, and St. Catharines-Niagara, had particularly

TABLE 9.1 Life Expectancy in a Global Context*

	Women	Men
Canada (2008)	83.1	78.5
United States (2007)	80.8	76.6
Japan (2009)	86.4	79.6
Russia	74.0	68.0

*Derived from Statistics Canada (2012e).

❋ **Explore** the MySocLab eReading "Chinese Community Pushes for 500 New Nursing Home Beds" on **MySocLab**.

CARP (Canada's Association for the Fifty-Plus), in collaboration with the Ontario Human Rights Commission, developed a campaign to combat age discrimination.

high rates of seniors (19 percent). Further, certain smaller cities (termed census agglomerations, with populations of at least 10 000), such as Parksville, British Columbia (39 percent seniors), Elliot Lake, Ontario (35 percent seniors), and Thetford Mines, Quebec (25 percent seniors), have exceptionally high concentrations of older residents and are often considered "retirement communities" (Statistics Canada, 2012c:19). These important demographic differences across Canada mean that the impact of the aging population—such as a dearth of younger workers or increased pressures on the health care system—will be experienced disproportionately throughout the country.

Seniors Organize

As seniors have become a more prominent demographic and economic element in Canadian society, they have predictably established their own support groups and organizations. Some of these efforts are intended to provide assistance and support to seniors in terms of specific issues and concerns, while others provide a more general sense of community and solidarity and advance their interests and perspectives. While interest and involvement in current events varies by level of education, overall the majority of seniors (89 percent) report keeping up with news and current affairs on a daily basis, outnumbering their younger counterparts at all educational levels (Turcotte & Schellenberg, 2007:171–172).

The first significant organizational step in advancing the interests of seniors was taken in the 1960s when Margaret Kuhn helped establish the Gray Panthers in the United States. This organization played a foundational role in advocating seniors' issues and providing a focus for mobilizing older people around a variety of social concerns. Since that time, a growing number of organizations have flourished in Canada and the United States. In 1973, the Fédération de l'Âge d'Or du Québec was created, which lobbies the government on seniors' issues, publishes a newspaper, and writes briefs regarding senior concerns. Similarly, Albertans established the Alberta Council of Aging in the 1970s to identify seniors' needs and mobilize senior leaders to act (Novak, 1993).

In the ensuing years, a variety of other groups emerged. Grandparents Raising Grandchildren provides support and advocacy for grandparents who become primary caregivers for their grandchildren. Across the country, there are organizations that target elder abuse—the Ontario Network for the Prevention of Elder Abuse, for example—and seek to educate the public and provide support for victims (Community Information Centre of Metropolitan Toronto, 1997).

Not surprisingly, as the number of seniors in Canada has increased, more organizations, services, and products have been mobilized in the interests of this demographic. Following the lead of the American Association of Retired Persons (AARP), one of the largest non-profit seniors' advocacy organizations in the United States, Canadians created the Canadian Association of Retired Persons (CARP). For

((• Listen to "NORCs" to see how NORCs differ from nursing homes on **MySocLab.**

a number of years, its magazine was entitled *50Plus* and provided information and advocacy on behalf of Canada's older citizens. In recent years, the organization has become increasingly high profile under the leadership of Susan Eng, and the magazine has been transformed by Toronto businessman Moses Znaimer into *Zoomer Magazine*, Canada's boomer lifestyle magazine).

Through these and other organizations and forums, such as the Canadian Snowbirds Association, seniors have been able to mobilize effectively and rapidly across the country in response to important issues. Most notably, the 1985 federal government plan for pension de-indexation was effectively quashed by massive protests and national petitions mobilized by seniors groups. Since this time, seniors have simply become even better organized. CARP, with local chapters across Canada, launched a vigorous nationwide campaign against age discrimination. Working with the Ontario Human Rights Commission, the group helped create a province-wide campaign to increase public awareness of ageism and its impact. Its publications communicate that discrimination against older workers is detrimental to business, since older workers are highly productive, have on-the-job experience, and have lower absenteeism and turnover rates than younger workers (Pasternak, 2002). Other initiatives, such as demanding improvements in the health care system and challenging efforts to increase long-term institutional care costs, reflect the dynamism of this and other seniors' organizations. In short, it is clear that Canadian seniors, as well as seniors in other industrialized countries, have forged organizations through which they hope to ensure that their voices are heard and their interests advanced, particularly when new social policies are crafted (Beard & Williamson, 2011).

Not all seniors' organizations are formal or mainstream. The Raging Grannies, founded in 1987 in Victoria, British Columbia, is made up of groups of older women in communities across Canada, the United States, Australia, and the United Kingdom who have lent support to a variety of social justice movements. Dressed as stereotypical "old ladies"— with bargain bin big hats and frilly dresses—the Raging Grannies sing satirical songs poking fun at governments, prime ministers, and presidents. They were, for example, denied admission to the B.C. legislature to "present their briefs" when they showed up carrying a clothesline filled with undies. In recent years, they have been a visible presence at protests against militarism, the G20, and pipeline expansions (www.vcn.bc.ca/ragigran; Acker & Brightwell, 2004).

Aging: Differences by Gender, Social Class, and Ethnicity

Not everyone in society has an equal chance of becoming old. Prior to 1951, men were more likely than women to reach old age since many women died in childbirth. Once medical care for mothers improved, the average Canadian woman could reasonably expect to live longer than the average male. However, since the late 1970s, men have been catching up in terms of life expectancy as differences in gender mortality narrow. Accordingly, in 1921 women made up 49 percent of all seniors, and in 1991 they peaked

At age 116, Besse Cooper is the world's oldest living person. Cooper was born in 1896 in Sullivan County, Tennessee. The world's record for age that has been documented by a birth certificate is held by Jeanne Calment of France, who died in 1997 at the age of 122.

at 58 percent of seniors. By 2011, they had dropped to 56 percent, and it is projected that by 2026, they will hover around 53 percent of seniors (Milan & Vezina, 2011:6). The gender gap has not been completely eliminated, a phenomenon evident among the growing numbers of Canadian seniors: of the over 1.3 million Canadians aged 80 or over in 2010, about two-thirds (63 percent) were women (Milan & Vezina, 2011:7).

Women's life expectancy is about four years longer than men's. Not surprisingly, as a result, women tend to predominate in the ranks of the oldest Canadians, and extreme aging is a strongly female phenomenon throughout G8 countries. Currently, women comprise 84 percent of Canadians 100 years of age and older (Statistics Canada, 2012e:2). This greater percentage of women, especially among aged seniors, is one of the reasons aging often draws the attention of feminist researchers (discussed in more detail below).

In old age, as in other stages of life, having money improves your prospects for health and personal satisfaction. Not surprisingly, research indicates that socioeconomic factors such as income and education are directly related to health. Healthy Canadians over the age of 50 with higher incomes and levels of education are less likely to see their health deteriorate over a two-year period than are those with lower education and income levels (Statistics Canada, 2004e). In this context, it is not surprising that more well-to-do seniors are less likely to be institutionalized while seniors with restricted personal resources will face more limited opportunities for social engagement. However, gender intersects with these patterns, since a greater proportion of impoverished seniors are women, and women's social lives are routinely constricted by the gendered expectation that they will provide caregiving for family members and even friends (Rozanova, Keating, & Eales, 2012; Sarma, Hawley, & Basu, 2009). Social class—in complex association with gender and other elements—colours the aging experience.

Predictably, being poor and old is a problematic status. Toward the end of the 1970s, Canada's population of poor seniors was a social embarrassment. Almost one third (31 percent) of Canadian seniors were living below the Statistics Canada low income cut-off in 1976 and many were deeply impoverished. By the end of the twentieth century (thanks in large measure to improved government income support for seniors through Old Age Security, the guaranteed income supplement, and the Canada/Quebec pension plans), those figures had been dramatically reduced. Although improvements have levelled off in recent years, only about one in eight Canadians over age 65 was poor and living below the low income cut-off in 2008 (Williams, 2010:31; Milan & Vezina, 2011:24; Turcotte & Schellenberg, 2007:68).

However, the statistics reveal that many older people continue to live in poverty or near the poverty line, and the economic well-being of certain groups of seniors is particularly precarious. Predictably, women are at particular risk. In 2008, almost 16 percent of women over 65 lived below the low income lines (after tax), in contrast to about 8 percent of senior men (Williams, 2010:31). Gender maintains its negative effect when seniors live alone. In 2008, 17 percent of women, and only 12 percent of men, who lived alone lived in low income (after tax) (Milan & Vezina, 2011:24). In short, gender, social class, and age intersect to put women at an increased risk of impoverishment as they age, even while senior poverty rates overall improve. Not surprisingly, additional factors such as advanced age, visible minority status, and recent immigration intensify the likelihood that older women will be poor.

Research suggests that ethnic and cultural differences also intersect with social class and gender to affect the structure and experience of aging. For example, people living in remote and northern areas of Canada, the majority of whom are Aboriginal, experience markedly lower life expectancies

The socially accepted definition of old age, along with social expectations of seniors' activities, varies around the world. This photo by James Henslin of a 65-year-old bonded labourer in Chennai, India, reveals how culturally relative our views may be. This "senior" woman makes her living carrying heavy rocks all day in the burning, tropical sun. She works alongside her 18-year-old son, who breaks the rocks into a size his mother can carry.

than the average Canadian. For example, residents of Region de Nunavik in Quebec have the lowest life expectancy in Canada, at 66.7 years for both males and females. This means that their life course is more in line with individuals living in the Dominican Republic or Egypt than with Canadians living in large urban centres. In recent years, Aboriginal life expectancies have improved, but they remain below the national average. The argument here is not that some groups are inherently less healthy. Rather, some ethnic populations (for example, Aboriginals in Canada and African-Americans in the United States) are more likely to be affected by socioeconomic and historical circumstances (inadequate housing, high rates of impoverishment, and social marginalization, for example) that ultimately lead to dramatically reduced life expectancy (Wilson, Rosenberg, & Abonyi, 2011; Statistics Canada, 2005b; National Council of Welfare, 2006a).

Focus Question

Why did industrialization have such an impact on the greying of Canada?

In short, ethnicity appears to affect the number of years you will spend as a senior and, in a complex manner, your quality of life. Given Canada's yearly immigration figures, along with the rapid increases in visible minorities, ethnic diversity is a pivotal consideration when approaching our aging population. For example, seniors who do not speak English or French may be more subject to isolation, have fewer opportunities for paid employment, and be more reliant on their immediate family and ethnic community. Seniors who are sponsored as family-class immigrants to Canada (in which case their family sponsor must support and house them for up to 10 years) may be also more isolated and dependent. However, the very vitality of large immigrant communities in Vancouver, Montreal, and Toronto may provide a sense of social support that nourishes seniors' well-being. Similarly, culturally appropriate nursing homes where workers are fluent in the immigrant language and familiar with customs may transform institutional care into an agreeable experience (Keung, 2012).

As the ethnic profile of Canada continues to change, experiences of aging will be impacted (Statistics Canada, 2004h). Importantly, researchers have identified the increasing ethnic and racial diversity among older Canadians, along with the experiences of social exclusion and "othering" of seniors who are visible minorities or immigrants, as an area in need of research (McDaniel & Rozanova, 2011:519).

IN SUM

As a result of industrialization and its accompanying improvements in sanitation, disease prevention, nutrition, and so on, more humans around the globe are growing old. The shift in the age pyramid of industrialized countries poses a variety of important issues, such as the distribution of national resources and the role of citizens in and out of the paid labour force. As with other social categories such as gender and ethnicity, we should refrain from "essentializing" seniors; that is, viewing them as an undifferentiated group. Seniors comprise a diverse population and the experience of aging is importantly enmeshed with various social dimensions, including gender, social class, ethnicity, and immigrant status.

Symbolic Interactionist Perspectives on Aging

To study how aging is socially constructed, symbolic interactionists examine how the symbols associated with age affect our perceptions. Let's look, then, at how culture underlies our ideas of when a person becomes "old" and how negative stereotypes and the mass media may affect the self-perceptions of older Canadians.

Before examining the processes by which age is socially, rather than biologically, constructed, it might be helpful to first consider a woman who gave birth to a daughter at age 16, who in turn had a child at age 18. In this scenario, the first woman became a biological grandmother at 34. Would you consider her old? Most likely, the woman will not play any stereotypical role—spending her days in a rocking chair, for example—but knowing she is a grandmother likely has an impact on her self-concept as well as her relationships with others. At a minimum, she must deny that she is old. With this scenario in mind, consider how we socially define aging and seniors.

Labelling and the Onset of Old Age

You can probably remember when you thought a 12-year-old was "old"—and anyone older than that was beyond reckoning, just "up there" someplace. You were probably five or six at the time. Similarly, to a 12-year-old, someone who is 21 seems "old." At 21, 30 may mark that line, and 40 may seem "very old." And so our patterns of perception persist, with "old" gradually receding from the self. To people who turn 40, 50 seems old; at 50, the late-60s look old (not the early-60s). The passing of years seems to accelerate as we age, and at 50, the 60s don't seem far from the horizon (Thorpe, 2002).

At some point, an individual must apply the label "old" to him- or herself. Often, cultural definitions of age force this label on people sooner than they are ready to accept it. In the typical case, the individual has become used to what he or she sees in the mirror. Changes have taken place very gradually, and each change, if not exactly taken in stride, has been accommodated. Consequently, it comes as a shock when meeting a friend one has not seen in years to see how much that person has changed. At class reunions, no one can believe how much older *the others* appear!

If there is no single point at which people automatically cross a magical line and become "old," what, then, puts someone in this category? We can point to several factors that spur people to apply the label to themselves. The first factor is *biology*, which seems to establish very broad parameters for aging. Within these biological boundaries, one person may experience "signs" of aging—wrinkles, balding, aches, difficulty in doing some things he or she used to take for granted—much earlier than another. Consequently, one person might feel "old" at an earlier or later age than others, and only at that time *adopt the role of an "old person"*—that is, begin to act in ways that old people in their society are thought to act. In short, our experience with and perception of biological changes affect our sense of "self." Laura Hurd Clarke (2001) looked at how women's aging bodies—including the deterioration of health and functional abilities—affected women's sense of identity. For some, the body becomes a mask and a prison that traps their "real" self.

As evident in this cover photograph from the October 2003 edition of *50Plus* magazine, media images of seniors can play an important role in creating a more positive public perception of the "old." Given the growing numbers of Canadian seniors and their high degree of organization, media campaigns are likely to continue to promote a more vital and healthy view of aging Canadians.

Personal history or biography also influences the point at which people "discover" that they are old. The death of close friends is likely to mark an important signpost in the process of aging. Indeed, the loss of close relationships may come to be seen as a normative indicator. In the words of one woman, "I just noticed that I'm at the stage in my life where in one page of obituaries, among the decedents, one half are below my age and one half are above. Up to now they were always older than me" (quoted in De Vries & Johnson, 2002:315). Not surprisingly, many Canadian seniors find that the death of their spouse is particularly momentous and becomes the triggering mechanism that results in their loss of independent living arrangements and the move to institutionalization or co-residence with others (Strohschein, 2011).

A third factor in determining when people label themselves as "old" is societal **timetables**, the signals societies use to inform their members of their aged status. As noted throughout this text, societal forces play a crucial role in establishing our self-definition and expectations about aging. Further, our expectations are interwoven with gender, sexual orientation, ethnicity, (dis)ability, and social class. With this complex array of factors at work, there is no predefined age at which people become "old." The definition varies around the world and throughout history and is communicated through a variety of means (Gilleard, 2002). Government and workplace regulations around retirement and pension eligibility, media images of "seniors," advertising campaigns for cosmetics, and day-to-day comments from friends and family combine in complex ways with our biology and personal history to create our sense of ourselves as "old" or "not old." Consider, for example, seniors' discounts—in one setting they are tagged to 50-year-olds, and in another to 65-year-olds.

Some of this diversity follows cultural lines. One cultural group may choose a particular birthday, such as the sixtieth or sixty-fifth, or a particular physical event, such as menopause, to signal the onset of old age. Of course, our biology is also influenced by social forces (as evidenced by increasing longevity in industrialized societies), so it is not surprising that our social timetables are regularly amended. Most contemporary Canadian seniors who reach older ages tend to "live in a relatively healthy state for a long time" (McDaniel & Rozanova, 2011). Today, many analysts refer to a "third age" (a period of good health, free of many work and family obligations) followed by a "fourth age" (a period when health deteriorates and activity is limited). Further, as discussed in "The Dependency Crisis" section of this chapter (pages 209–210), it appears that the dependence-free "third age" is expanding as more Canadians adopt healthy lifestyles (Martel & Belanger, 2000).

Canadian Society: Changing Social Constructions of Aging

Physician Robert Butler coined the term **ageism** in 1969 to refer to prejudice, discrimination, and hostility directed against people because of their age (Blytheway & Johnson,

2005). Research into ageism in Canada suggests that the elderly were neither uniformly venerated nor detested in the past (Markson, 2003:93). In traditional Canadian Inuit culture, for example, elders were always considered valued members of the group as long as they contributed to its survival. In contemporary Aboriginal society, seniors may be feted as an invaluable resource in terms of the transmission of accumulated cultural knowledge and traditional languages. More generally, the stereotypes of seniors as, for example, cranky and out-of-step have typically been somewhat balanced by more positive images of seniors as caring and kind.

It seems likely that there was never a "golden era" in human history when the elderly were uniformly respected and valued. An elderly individual's experience of well-being and social status has always been rooted in his or her health and physical abilities and relative social ranking as determined by the interplay between age and other personal characteristics such as gender, social rank, and ethnicity. Recognizing that the history of aging is complex and contradictory, it can be argued that the Industrial Revolution corresponded not only with an increase in the number of seniors, but also with a significant downturn in the social position of the great majority of seniors—those who were working-class, female, immigrants, and/or disabled. The new industrial order experienced by workers was decidedly a young man's—and, to a lesser degree, a young woman's—world. Any respect that older individuals might have accrued from their skills in domestic work or crafts or through the apprenticeship system was rapidly eroded as skilled craftsmen and household workers were displaced by machinery and mass-marketed products. At the centre of the new order was the industrial factory, which made unrelenting demands on even the most fit men and women. As economic opportunities for many seniors were undermined, so too were social institutions—notably the patriarchal family and traditional religious structures—that tended to support an age-based system of respect and deference.

Modern Canadian society has inherited long-held contradictory perspectives on aging and the elderly along with the economic marginalization of many seniors, as reflected in the popular acceptance of a range of stereotypes about the elderly. Certainly, old age is not seen as necessarily synonymous with disability, frailty, incompetence, or dependence—and positive notions of older citizens do exist. However, research suggests that since seniors are often denied important productive social roles, they tend to be stereotyped in negative terms. Interestingly, U.S. researchers reported that 95 percent of research respondents held negative views about older people—a higher proportion than held such views along either racial or gendered dimensions (as cited in Bennett and Gaines, 2010:436).

Support for this negative understanding of seniors is not difficult to unearth. For example, recent research from the University of Ottawa found that student research participants embraced negative stereotypes of "typical older drivers" as overly cautious, uncomfortable behind the wheel, and unsafe and dangerous. While younger drivers were believed to engage in reckless and speedy on-road behaviours, the stereotypes of older drivers were predominantly negative. Indeed, 75 percent of comments made by participants fell into negative categories. Also, importantly, the results revealed a tendency to respond to older drivers as a homogeneous group, in effect essentializing them. These results are provocative given that research indicates that healthy, older drivers who drive regularly are "the safest cohort of drivers" and, when compared to their younger counterparts, are more experienced, respectful of the rules of the road, and less likely to drive under the influence of alcohol (Joanisse, Gagnon, & Voloaca, 2012).

These and other negative stereotypes of older individuals are embedded in socialization practices. Research suggests that children as young as age three express negative stereotypes toward older adults, and certainly by late childhood and adolescence, such prejudices are well established. One important source of these patterns is the mass media. For example, a recent content analysis of the representation of seniors in the 60 most popular teen movies from the 1980s, 1990s, and 2000s revealed an anti-age bias. When seniors are not being ignored in these films, they are portrayed in stereotypic and negative ways. Indeed, one-fifth of older characters were portrayed only in negative terms. Given these messages, it is not surprising that many young people grow up viewing seniors as some combination of "ineffective, dependent, lonely, poor, angry, overly wrinkled, ugly, dirty, disabled, and less physically active and healthy than younger adults" (Robinson, Callister, Magoffin, & Moore, 2009).

Admittedly, the media—for example, advertisers—employ scenarios in which healthy seniors plan cruises, are sexually active, and learn new skills. Consider, for example, the recent television enthusiasm for sexy "older" women who are described as "cougars." However, such positive representations exist alongside persistent negative stereotypes. In a revealing study, Tiina Vares (2009) asked males and females aged 49 to 82 to view a copy of the film *The Mother* (2003) at their leisure and then come together in male- and female-only focus groups to discuss it. The film contains sexually explicit scenes between a female character in her late sixties (played by Anne Reid) and Darren, a man in his mid-thirties played by Daniel Craig. Interestingly, while the male focus groups felt that the film gave them permission to think about femininity, aging, and sexuality in new ways, many of the female participants, while critical of the invisibility of older women, had great difficulty extricating themselves from the notions that the older female body is somehow disgusting and shameful.

As suggested by Vares's research, such negative stereotypes of seniors are particularly powerful when they become integral to *implicit ageism*; that is, they are reflected in our

The Social Construction of Age as a Contemporary Social Problem

In his book, *Forever Young* (2003), University of Toronto social analyst Marcel Danesi argues that contemporary Western culture has embraced the view that age is bad and youth is good. Consider, for example, the images of adults in 1950s sitcoms such as *Father Knows Best* and *The Adventures of Ozzie and Harriet*. Whatever their foibles, the parents were mature and in charge and were capable of skillfully guiding their children. In contrast, in the late 1960s and early 1970s, the father on the popular television program *All in the Family* was portrayed as an uneducated, uninformed bigot and the mother as a simpleton. By the 1990s, the dumbing down of adults was complete with the rise in popularity of *The Simpsons* (1987) and *Family Guy* (1999), programs that imply that many adults are rude and stupid. Danesi suggests that the message here and elsewhere in popular culture is clear: only the young are "cool," and aging is a deterioration to be fought on every front. The net result, he suggests, is a culture in which adults vainly attempt to mimic the young while failing to cultivate the skills, experience, and wisdom that should be the companions of age. In his provocative book, Danesi proposes that Western cultures would dramatically benefit from a rethinking of their current social constructions of aging and adolescence. Who would want to grow older when it is translated into a deteriorating body, a loss of sexual identity and attractiveness, and social and economic marginalization? As the proportion of seniors in the population increases, it is not surprising that there are growing calls for an end to ageism and gerontophobia along with demands for a more positive social construction of what it means to grow old (Chapman, 2005)

thoughts, feelings, and behaviours toward elderly people without our conscious awareness or control. As elements in the very fabric of our social relationships, such views do not exist "out there," but rather are incorporated into older and younger people's self-perceptions and their experiences of their own bodies.

Predictably, the internalization of negative perceptions of aging, combined with the unrelenting media preoccupation with youthfulness, have been found to produce internal conflicts for aging women. A recent study of 16 rural Australian women aged 60 and over concluded that continually viewing sexualized images of women premised on a distorted youthful ideal of beauty had a negative impact on their mental health. In particular, women experienced sadness, anger, concern, envy, marginalization, and discomfort with their own appearance. While specific strategies reduced these negative outcomes—holding a strong sense of self apart from appearance and feeling valued by family and community—these results underscore the societal roots of aging women's struggles (Hine, 2011). Very similar internalized struggles were discovered by a Canadian researcher who interviewed women aged 60 to 69 about their body image. The researcher found that older women struggled to find balance between a desire for change and longing for contentment: "'Yes, I worry about my weight . . . but for the most part I'm content with my body'" (Liechty, 2012).

As discussed earlier, a basic principle of symbolic interactionism is that people perceive both themselves and others according to the symbols of their culture. In terms of aging, we are being assailed by, at best, mixed messages not only about seniors' wisdom and experience, but also the undesirability of being viewed as old. Predictably, young and old Canadians are struggling to sort out the personal and societal meanings attached to aging.

In a provocative study, Canadian researchers Julie Ann McMullin and John Cairney (2004) explored the relationships between self-esteem, age, class, and gender. Using data (from Statistics Canada's National Population Health Survey) on 19 600 Canadian households, they found that self-reported self-esteem levels tended to decline as men and women aged, that women of all ages reported lower levels than men, and that higher social class characteristics are related to higher self-esteem results. Examining the interrelationships between these characteristics, they reported that after about age 62, men and women in the high social class enjoy higher self-esteem than their lower-class counterparts. Men, more than women, were particularly advantaged by social class as they aged.

These results lend credence to the view that aging is socially constructed as a negative experience in contemporary Canada and that certain groups, notably women and the less well-off, are particularly vulnerable to the negative conceptions of age in our culture. However, the stigma attached to aging and the elderly reflects an ongoing struggle over the symbolic meanings of these constructs in Canada.

The Clueless Generation? Seniors and the New Technology

One of the more popular stereotypes of seniors is that they are at a loss when it comes to understanding and utilizing new technologies. As with many stereotypes, there is some truth in this idea, since many seniors grew up in a profoundly different technological era. As a result, they may indeed struggle to embrace technological innovations in their homes, personal lives, and workplaces. A recent Canadian survey of internet use, for example, reported that, among Canadians, seniors used the internet the least. However, seniors are also the fastest growing group of users. Indeed, seniors' internet use increased fourfold between 2000 and 2007. Predictably, seniors undertake a smaller variety of online activities—using email, particularly to connect with family, but making significantly less use of blogging, instant messaging, and online media. Nonetheless, particularly given that 80 percent of boomers (45 to 64 years of age) are current internet users, the technological divide is likely to continue to narrow (Veenhof & Timusk, 2009).

This increased use of information technologies is particularly likely to occur in certain segments of the senior population. Not surprisingly, seniors who are immigrants report that the internet is a crucial ingredient in their lives. Older immigrants in Israel, for example, report that the internet is key to successful aging since it provides a mechanism for managing their health, nurturing professional interests, maintaining and extending social networks, appreciating the past, and enjoying their leisure (Khvorostianov, Elias, Nimrod, & 2011). Similarly, seniors struggling with chronic health concerns, living in rural communities, or living away from their extended families will benefit from advances in technological communication. Significantly, more and more support services are using the internet to direct assistance to seniors.

On May 31, 2012, Seniors In Need, a national website sponsored by not-for profit agencies across Canada was launched. The site—www.seniorsinneed.ca—allows agencies to post a synopsis of a senior's location, needs, and circumstances. A donor or volunteer can then respond to the agency on the website with offers of time, money, or equipment (Teotonio, 2012). As technology advances and more resources are mobilized online, seniors will likely become more computer savvy.

Age stereotypes are a frequent source of humour in our society, whereas racist, sexist, and heterosexist stereotypes are usually viewed as out of bounds.

IN SUM

Symbolic interactionists have drawn our attention to a number of important aspects of aging. First, whether someone is labelled old or labels him- or herself as such depends on a variety of factors, not simply biological age. Physical signs of aging, such as wrinkles, may contribute to the labelling process, but personal history (having grandchildren at a young age) and gender (men "mature" while women "age") may also have an impact on how we see ourselves getting older. Some societies set certain timetables, such as retirement at age 65, that tend to be seen as key signals of aging.

Given that aging responds to a variety of social factors, it is not surprising that attitudes toward the elderly vary considerably from one society to another. Further, these attitudes may shift over time. For example, industrialization and related changes in Canadian society served to diminish the social position of many seniors as traditional age-structured institutions, such as the patriarchal family and the craft guild, were replaced. In recent times, the consumer market economy has played a central role in promoting negative societal perceptions of aging and the elderly. At the same time, improved health and nutrition allow increasing numbers of older Canadians to lead healthy, longer lives and prolong their positions as powerful members of society.

The media, including social media, play a particularly important role in promoting both negative and positive images of the aging process. On one hand, seniors are often ignored, pitied, or marginalized by the mass media and advances in technology. On the other, media, and particularly social media, may be mobilized by seniors' interest groups to increasingly promote a more positive and inclusive perspective on aging and the elderly.

Focus Question

How do the most popular television programs, such as *Mad Men* and *Canada's Got Talent*, reflect our attitudes toward aging and the elderly?

Feminist Perspectives

As women who were active in the modern women's movement moved into "middle age" in the 1980s and 1990s, aging was increasingly viewed as a feminist issue (Macdonald & Rich, 1991). Many of the most well-known spokeswomen of the movement—including Betty Friedan (1993), Germaine Greer (1991), and Gloria Steinem (1992)—examined their own personal experiences of growing older and exposed the inequities faced by older women. In more recent years, as feminists sought to embrace the diversities and complexities of women's experiences, they incorporated various intersecting patterns of privilege, domination, and oppression (such as sexual orientation, ethnicity, and disability) into the feminist paradigm (Reinharz, 1997; Shaw & Lee, 2001; Abu-Laban & McDaniel, 2005). Today, although ageism is still not as central a concern in society as it is within feminist scholarship (Colasanti, Slevin, & King, 2006), an increasing number of feminists are playing key roles in challenging mainstream gerontology and articulating a critical approach to the study of aging (Clarke, 2001).

Feminist analysts have pointed out that aging exacerbates the problems of power and inequality for women (Copper, 2001). As women age, they are likely to find themselves increasingly marginalized and dismissed. This is apparent in patterns of marriage, for example. Around the globe, compared to women, most men are able to marry much younger spouses. Indeed, the popular media often poke fun at older men with much younger "trophy" wives. In part, this pattern reflects the belief that men retain their attractiveness and sexuality longer than women. On men, greying hair and even a few wrinkles may be seen as signs of "maturing," while on women those same features are likely to be interpreted as signs of being "old." As Canadian sociologists Sharon McIrvin Abu-Laban and Susan McDaniel (2005) state, "Women are said to be older sooner than men. While aging is seen as empowering for many men,

it is not seen to be so for women. His facial lines are seen as signs of character; her lines are signs of decrepitude and decreasing sexual attractiveness" (p. 101). This difference in the social evaluation of "old women" and "mature men" is also revealed when older male news anchors are likely to be retained, while female anchors of the same age are likely to be transferred to less visible positions. Reflecting a similar preoccupation with women's physical aging, Hillary Clinton's appearance and clothing were considered by the media to be relevant in her role as Secretary of State. In movies, older men are much more likely than older women to play leads—often opposite much younger female stars (50-year-old Tom Cruise, for example, is routinely paired with much younger women). Canadian actress Kim Cattrall (Samantha Jones in *Sex and the City*), who is over 50, said of the ageist-sexist Hollywood ideal, "'You can't ever talk about the big 5-0 . . . You turn 35 in Hollywood and your auditions get cut in half. They're just not interested'" (Goodman, 2008:Go19).

The relative "attractiveness" or "beauty" of women is related in a complex way to their social and economic positions in society. Access to the best cosmetics, health clubs and spas, and cosmetic surgeons requires considerable time and economic resources. Only elite women (Oprah Winfrey is a high-profile example) can afford the personal chefs, personal trainers, and other assistants who make the beauty ideal attainable. The overwhelming majority of women must accept that as they age they will fall further and further short of this artificial, socially prescribed goal (Clarke and Korotchenko, 2011).

Women's lack of economic resources is, in turn, related to their traditional role in the economy. Numerous women who are now approaching senior status have devoted themselves to home and family, and while they may have had paid employment, they often interrupted their careers or worked part-time. As a result, as discussed in Chapter 7, the overwhelming majority of corporate chiefs, leaders in professions such as medicine and law, and social-political power elite are male (Williams, 2010). Indeed, many women will find that contributions to the family do not result in economic security in old age. It is likely that such patterns of economic marginalization and insecurity contribute to images of older women as "unattractive."

Needless to say, older women struggling with additional societal prejudices are likely to have even more difficulties. As Abu-Laban and McDaniel (2005) observe, "The prospects for women of colour, Aboriginal women, women with disabilities, or lesbian women are even worse. Aged women with out-of-date eyewear, bad teeth, unfashionably sized bodies, limited education, and whose only (or main) work

✳ **Explore** the reading "Men and Women: Together and Apart in the Later Years" on **MySocLab.**

experience is raising children on social assistance" are even more likely to end up economically and socially peripheralized in old age (p. 109). As a result of heterosexist patterns, lesbians (and gays) may experience aging without the support of all or part of their extended families and without children. Further, concern at the prospects of institutionalization or co-residence with others may be intensified by fears of being surrounded by homophobic or transphobic residents and staff (Taylor & Ristock, 2011).

There are exceptions to the gendered patterns. Some women marry much younger men, and we have seen increasing numbers of female celebrities (Goldie Hawn, Susan Sarandon, and Jane Fonda, for example) employed in their sixties and seventies. However, such exceptions, simply because they are noteworthy, are evidence of the powerful social norms surrounding women and aging. For example, the "mature" women celebrities are outstanding in large measure because of their youthful appearance rather than their age. Fonda, who attributes her appearance to health and fitness while acknowledging a years-long battle with bulimia, is presented in magazines as an enviable (if unattainable) role model for aging women. In short, even powerful, respected women find themselves constrained by corrosive cultural standards of femininity.

The Mass Media: Invisible Older Women

Much contemporary postmodern feminism has explored cultural representations of gender and age in mediums such as art, literature, and the mass media. Contemporary efforts to deconstruct embedded messages have exposed the complex and nuanced meanings that society attaches to gender and age. However, no deconstruction is needed to reveal the messages about gender and aging that are incorporated into contemporary media.

Laura Hurd Clarke (2011) undertook a content analysis of anti-aging print advertisements in women's magazines (*Harper's Bazaar*, *Ladies' Home Journal*, *More*, *O: The Oprah Winfrey Magazine,* and *Vogue*). She reports that the majority of these ads promoted products that specifically targeted the face and the treatment of facial wrinkles. The clear message to the female consumer is that signs of aging (deep wrinkles; expression lines; dull, tired skin; and so on) were abhorrent and "worthy of ridicule." Women were being exhorted to "resist aging" and "turn back the clock." Implicitly, failure to do so reflected not only on their ugliness but their lack of discipline and good consumption patterns. While women interviewed by Clarke were critical of the airbrushed and staged images accompanying these advertisements, they were also conflicted. Many felt so bombarded and overwhelmed by these messages that they felt a limited ability to resist. When they looked in the mirror, they were dragged in by the ageist and sexist ideologies and their sense of identity and well-being were eroded.

Conflict Perspectives: The Political Economy of Aging

Various conflict perspectives suggest that the guiding principles of social life are competition, disequilibrium, and change. Conflict analysts draw attention to the potential for discord among society's age groups. Recent comments from Canada's Association for the Fifty-Plus (CARP) speak to this concern: "Predictions that seniors will break the health care and pension banks are myths. But, if we don't prepare for the aging population now, these myths could become realities" (Gleberzon & Cutler, 2005:5). As the baby boomer generation retires, analysts project that in 2031 there will be two workers for every retired person in Canada, which represents a dramatic fall from five workers per retiree in the 1980s (CBC News, 2008b). Drawing a more global perspective, journalist Ted Fishman argues that the current aging of the world's population will pit young against old, child against parent, and nation against nation (Pigg, 2011a). The ongoing tensions over retirement issues provide a revealing example of the complexities and contradictions in these age-based struggles.

The Pension Crisis, Employment, and Generational Conflict

Until recently, almost all Canadians were required by law to retire at age 65. As documented in Table 9.2, retirement rules have changed profoundly across Canada. This traditional age of 65 reflected a standard established in 1889 by Count Otto von Bismarck, Germany's first chancellor. To counter the growing popularity of Marxism and earn the loyalty of workers, von Bismark created public pensions. The idea caught on in England, France, and the United States in the early twentieth century. In 1927, Canada produced its first old-age pension—$20 a month for those older than 70 and destitute (Barmak, 2011). At that point in history, most surviving citizens in industrialized economies were in physical decline by age 65 and increasingly incapable of work. Further, few survived many years postretirement.

We now live in a very different world. Improvements in medical care, nutrition, physical fitness, and technology have meant that many workers are capable of continuing their paid employment well beyond the traditional age of retirement. At the same time, dramatic increases in the numbers of retiring seniors have raised concerns about the long-term viability of publicly funded pension schemes. Nowhere is this more of an issue than in the financially troubled Eurozone. In 2009, state pension fund obligations in 19 EU nations were five times higher than their combined gross debt. The net result is a pension bomb. In Germany, for example, in 2011 there were 4.1 active workers for every pensioner; by 2050 that is predicted to drop to 1.6 (*Toronto Star*, 2012:B4). In Europe and North America, the fear is that the number of people who collect government pensions

TABLE 9.2 Retirement Rules across Canada

Province or Territory	Retirement Rules
Nunavut	No mandatory retirement age
Northwest Territories	No mandatory retirement age
Yukon	No mandatory retirement age
British Columbia	Law to eliminate mandatory retirement took effect January 1, 2008
Alberta	No mandatory retirement age
Saskatchewan	Law to eliminate mandatory retirement took effect in November 2007
Manitoba	No mandatory retirement age
Ontario	Law to eliminate mandatory retirement took effect December 12, 2006
Quebec	No mandatory retirement age
New Brunswick	No mandatory retirement, but companies are allowed to enforce it under the terms and conditions of any retirement or pension plan
Nova Scotia	Mandatory retirement at age 65, if required by the employer. Law to eliminate this took effect July 1, 2009
Prince Edward Island	No mandatory retirement age
Newfoundland and Labrador	Law to eliminate mandatory retirement took effect May 26, 2007

CBC News, 2008b. Available at www.cbc.ca/news/background/retirement/mandatory_retirement.html.

will grow, while the proportion of working people—those who pay for these benefits out of their wages—will shrink. Currently, there are four working taxpayers for every non-working pensioner in Canada. But when this ratio drops to two to one, as analysts predict, will the public pension plans be sustainable?

This shift in the **dependency ratio**—the number of workers compared with the number of QPP/CPP recipients—certainly raises questions about future pension funding. These concerns are compounded by the growing trend among both public and private employers to off-load retirement funding onto employees. In the past, good public and private sector employment typically came with a defined-benefit plan. In this arrangement, the employee and employer both paid into the pension fund and, once retired, the retiree was guaranteed a specific income that was calculated based on the retiree's average salary and years of work. In addition, these pension incomes, especially in the public sector, were often indexed to increases in inflation. As the cost of living increased, so, too, did the pension. Such pensions are becoming the dodo bird of retirement: in a recent survey, the majority of private sector employers were moving to eliminate their defined benefit plans (Vuket, 2011; McFarland, 2011). Needless to say, the process of eliminating or reducing pension benefits for employees has triggered heated confrontations between organized labour and public and private employees. For

example, Air Canada, the Canadian Autoworkers Union, the Province of Ontario, and the Ontario Public School Teachers' Federation recently were at loggerheads over pension issues (Lu, 2011).

Increasingly, employers are pushing for an arrangement that dramatically reduces their future pension liabilities. From the employers' perspective, the ideal arrangement is one in which the employee assumes full responsibility for his or her retirement through contributions to RRSPs and other voluntary pension plans. A common middle ground is the increasingly popular "defined contribution" plan, in which the employer and employee agree to each contribute a specified amount to the employee's pension fund. Once retired, the employee is guaranteed the proceeds from this fund, but any market downturns and economic upheavals that affect the income generated are entirely the employee's problem. In addition, there are a variety of plans that provide some combination of defined benefit and defined contribution plans.

Importantly, the overarching trend is away from employer responsibility for pensions. By 2011, 39 percent of Canadian pension plan sponsors had closed their defined benefit plans to new entrants, and in Britain and the United States, the figure was closer to 80 percent. This is being achieved not only through new pension plan arrangements but also through the proliferation of contract, part-time, and other precarious forms of employment. At present, about

60 percent of Canadians have no formal pension plan, 75 percent of Canadians eligible for RRSPs do not have one, and the average Canadian is putting aside only $60 000 in RRSP savings (Crocker, 2011; Vukets, 2011). Necessarily, this new pension landscape raises serious questions about the quality of life to be enjoyed by Canadian retirees.

According to John Crocker, president and CEO of the Healthcare of Ontario Pension Plan, reduced pension coverage and increased reliance on the Canada Pension Plan may produce widespread senior poverty (Crocker, 2011). In 2010, the average Canadian received $6058 per year from CPP, or $504.83 per month. For those of us who have not contributed the maximum amount to CPP, this monthly sum is reduced. This retiree also qualifies for Old Age Security benefits of $6318 a year ($526.50 per month) and the guaranteed income supplement provides another $665 a month. The net result (including income from $60 000 in RRSPs) is a retirement income of more than $23 000 per year, slightly above the Statistics Canada low-income line for people living in large cities and less than half the average wage in Canada in 2011. At present, 1.6 million Canadian seniors are living on less than $15 000 in government support (Vukets, 2011).

Governments in Canada and elsewhere are concerned that they will not be able to afford to continue these pension plans. In Spain and Greece, pensioners have been confronted by a dramatic reduction in pension benefits. In Canada, in 2012, the government passed legislation that postpones receipt of government-funded pensions until age 67. While the change came with substantial notice for future retirees, it underlines once again the apparent conflicting needs of young and old Canadians.

From the perspective of young Canadians, not only is retirement a receding reality, its affordability is in question. Difficulties funding retirement, particularly in terms of purchasing RRSPs, are likely to persist, even intensify, as more young Canadians devote more years and funds to "higher education." For example, more university graduates are entering community colleges in search of job-related skills. The net result is not only more years either outside the labour force or marginally employed, but also mounting student debt. Given other financial pressures, including high housing costs in many major urban centres, young Canadians are often hard-pressed to locate RRSPs in their budgets.

Until the Quebec student protests of 2012, the concerns of younger Canadians tended not to be vigorously represented by particular lobby groups, but their views—in particular, concerns about escalating education costs and difficulties entering and advancing in the labour market—have been increasingly voiced by college and university student organizations and in the media. In this context, some analysts suggest that many young Canadians face high rates of unemployment and are forced to settle for "McJobs" with low pay and little challenge in the retail or service industries

because they are being denied the opportunities enjoyed by their parents and grandparents. This conflict perspective suggests that the "good" jobs and the opportunities for a prosperous life are being obstructed by a "boomer bottleneck" in which older Canadians continue to hang on to their positions for privilege, power, and wealth. The resulting resentment is compounded by concerns that the younger generation will face either higher taxes or reduced services in order to provide pensions and health care for the boomer generation.

However, this notion of generational conflict is being challenged by numerous researchers. In a recent comparative of Canada's aging population in 1986 and 2009, noted Canadian researchers Susan A. McDaniel and Julia Rozanova concluded that the fears about generational strife in Canada are unlikely (2011:513). Similarly, the prestigious MacArthur Foundation Research Network on an Aging Society rejects the notion of a young–old conflict as a myth and suggests that there is no evidence of generational disagreements about entitlements such as Social Security and Medicaid (2009:19).

These conclusions are drawn from the ways in which many aging workers have responded to the pension and retirement crisis by redefining and realigning their approach to retirement (McDonald and Donahue 2011). In particular, seniors are facing down debt and inadequate pension income by continuing to work past 60 and, indeed, well into their seventies. Between 2009 and 2012, seniors (60 and older) accounted for about one-third of net new job gains while comprising only 8 percent of the total labour force (Lu, 2012). Not only are seniors continuing to work, some are taking on new careers and others are shifting to non-standard (for example, part-time), low-intensity jobs as a way to ease into retirement (Goar, 2012; Pigg, 2011b).

The question of generational conflict is far from closed. Youth are currently facing an unemployment rate of 14.5 percent, well above the rate for other sectors of the labour force (Lu, 2012). Leading analysts acknowledge that changes in the broader social and economic environment might set the stage for conflict. For example, in the United States, grievances might coalesce around youth, ethnic identity, and immigrant status. Will young minority workers happily support the needs of aging whites? In Canada, as long as the economy continues to struggle, it is not clear how older workers can be retained while allowing for job prospects and mobility for younger workers (MacArthur Foundation, 2010; McDaniel & Rozanova, 2011).

Evidence does not suggest that gender inequities in aging are resolved. However, shifts in pensions have tended to close one of the gender gaps. As male-dominated jobs in the manufacturing sector, along with their good pension plans, disappeared, so, too, did gender differences in pension protection. In 2005, employed men with pension plans outnumbered women by 265 000. By 2011, this gap had almost completely closed and employed women and men were equally likely to enjoy pension plans (McFarland, 2011).

Older women continue to be twice as likely as older men to live on low income. Traditional gender arrangements in the home and in the paid workforce mean that many women will continue to have "very limited prospects for retirement and old age" (McDaniel & Rozanova, 2011:513). It is important to point out that these financial limitations may be significantly offset by the stronger informal support networks enjoyed by many older women (Ryser & Halseth, 2011; Yew, 2011).

Critical Social Gerontology and Life Course Analysis

The advancing age of the baby boomer generation and the global dimensions of age concerns have helped to stimulate an upsurge of academic interest in aging and the elderly. In recent years, analysts have increasingly challenged traditional gerontological approaches to the study of seniors. In particular, the tendency to approach age in biomedical terms, almost as an ailment that can be "cured" by medical intervention, has been extensively criticized as homogenizing seniors rather than acknowledging the important differences among them (Auger & Tedford-Litle, 2002). Today, pressure continues to mount for more societal and psychological investigation into the aging process and an improved awareness of the diversity (ethnicity, immigrant/non-immigrant status, gender, rural/urban residence, and so on) of the aging population (Chappell et al., 2003). This has resulted in many more studies of the actual experiences of seniors, as well as increasing interest in global research and cross-cultural comparisons (Zhou, 2012; Bosworth & Keys, 2004; de Jong Gierveld, & Havens, 2004; van Dijk, 2004).

Other analysts are mounting a strong argument against the separation of elderly studies as a separate and distinct discipline. They contend that aging must be located in terms of the overall life course and that seniors should be considered within a complex web of relationships. Canadian sociologist Susan McDaniel (2002) made a particularly important contribution to these developments with her concept of *intergenerational interlinkages* (IGILs). In contrast to earlier formulations that tend to locate seniors in terms of relationships (caregiving relationships between adult children and their parents, for example) and transfer from one generation to another (such as provision of public health care), she suggests an approach that moves beyond one-dimensionality and narrowness to explore intergenerational linkages in a variety of directions, contexts, and forms. In a three-generation typology—parents, children, and grandchildren—each generation is both receiving and giving, and transfers between generations are monetary, public, and global (including intangibles such as attention and joy). In short, McDaniel's approach challenges our assumptions about seniors and family life and opens a wide array of research possibilities, in particular regarding "whether or how generation works with or against other dimensions of societal cleavage such as class, gender, ethnicity, and/or immigration recency" (p. 59).

A useful example of this new approach is its perspective on the popular notion of the "sandwich generation." For decades, this term has been employed to refer to the burden experienced by mid-life women and men who must satisfy the simultaneous demand of their teenage children and elderly parents. According to a 2004 Statistics Canada study, 30 percent of Canadians aged 45 to 64 with unmarried children living at home were also caring for an aging relative (Johne, 2008:E5). Women in this group spent, on average, 29 hours a month caring for seniors, while their male counterparts spent 13 hours. Eighty percent of these individuals also had paid employment (Stobert & Cranswick, 2004). Not surprisingly, a significant number of family caregivers (40 percent) faced financial costs as a result of their "labours of love," including the costs of renting medical equipment, reducing work hours, and forfeiting extra income (Johne, 2008:E5).

Over the past 30 years, the rate of institutionalization of seniors declined and then stabilized with the vast majority (93 percent) currently living in private households (Turcotte & Schellenberg, 2007:138). About one in three seniors aged 75 and over lives alone, and nearly one in six lives with children or grandchildren (Turcotte & Schellenberg, 2007:191). Whether seniors are living alone or with family members, care and social support arrangements are complexly interwoven into the schedules of adult children, who may share the responsibilities with their siblings. Analysts question what the future will hold for the baby boomers, who, on average, have had fewer children than their parents and may therefore have a smaller circle of family members involved in their support in their later years.

As theorists have pushed toward more sophisticated and complex understandings of aging and the elderly, **life course analysis** has gained in popularity. The life course approach takes into consideration the complex and fluid nature of our lives. Further, our experiences occur on varied levels—individual, familial/community, and societal. After all, aging is a lifelong process and our understanding of the elderly and ourselves as seniors begins in childhood. Necessarily, our life course is moulded around historical and cultural locations. Further, our experiences of aging are linked with those of others who share our social contexts. Aging as one of the boomers is likely very different from aging at the beginning of the 1900s. A life course perspective also incorporates notions of human agency. Seniors are not only constructed by personal, community, and societal forces, they act as agents on those realities. These actions may be individual or collective and may have profound or minimal impact. The advantage of the life course perspective is that it allows for a nuanced and complex understanding of the aging process and for linkages to other theoretical approaches such as critical theory and symbolic interactionism (Hemphill, 2011).

IN SUM

Conflict theorists contend that all members of a society do not share common interests, and the interests of the young may be in direct opposition to those of seniors. For example, as a society, we must decide on the allocation of resources. With finite resources, difficult decisions must be made. One source of potential conflict is the role of seniors in the paid labour force. At present, there is much discussion in the media about the prospects for generational conflict as seniors and younger workers contest the question of retirement. However, closer examination suggests that the issue is much more nuanced than a generational dispute.

Focus Question

In what ways does the "pension crisis" reflect a significant shift in the lives of Canadians, young and old?

The Dependency Crisis

As seniors age, many will become increasingly vulnerable to physical and mental disability. Those who live long lives can reasonably expect to enter the so-called fourth stage of frailty and vulnerability. It is not surprising, therefore, that most Canadian seniors (81 percent) living at home have at least one chronic health problem and that one in four are living with chronic pain (Lindsay, 1999; Crompton, 2000). Between one-fifth and one-quarter of Canadians in their seventies and more than one-third of men and women in their eighties identify as having an "activity" limitation; that is, they have a long-term health problem or chronic condition that prevents them from participating in necessary or leisure activities (Crompton, 2011). Currently, about 450 000 Canadian seniors suffer from Alzheimer's or a related disease, and it is estimated that by 2031 this number will double, with a cost of $872 billion to Canadian society (Alzheimer's Society of Toronto, n.d.). These figures must prompt the question of who will care for dependent seniors.

Significantly, because of a variety of factors, support for very old, frail elders is a particularly central issue for Canada. The rapid growth in lone-person households, along with the decrease in family size, means there are often fewer family members to provide support, for example, to aging parents. Further, our geographic size and the dispersal of our population across the country may make caregiving particularly difficult. In 2007, 359 700 Canadians were providing help to a parent despite living more than an hour away (Vezina & Turcotte, 2010:5). In contrast to our European counterparts, we have relatively high numbers of frail elders who need support, and our increased longevity means that this need will last for a longer period of time. This is a challenge that

is yet to be adequately addressed (McDaniel & Rozanova, 2011:520).

The eldercare scene in Canada is characterized by an uneven mix of home care, hospital care, and institutional care. About 5 percent of seniors over age 65, and 18 percent of those 80 and over, are cared for in an institution. Seniors living at home are typically cared for by elderly spouses (usually wives), adult daughters, and, to a lesser degree, adult sons. In addition, there is an evolving network of community care centres intended to provide support for ailing seniors who do not need hospitalization but are unable to access outpatient care.

Analysts question whether this patchwork of solutions will adequately address the masses of seniors flooding the system. As the baby boom generation ages, and as disease and disability take their toll, the pressure on caregivers, both paid and unpaid, will dramatically intensify. A recent U.S. survey estimated that between 9 and 13 percent of U.S. households are made up of adults aged 30 or over who work and who provide care to both aging parents and children (Hammer & Neal, 2008). This "sandwich generation" presents a significant social pattern, and concern is being raised about the emotional and physical pressures on adult daughters and sons, most with their own family and paid-work responsibilities, who provide informal care for a seriously disabled senior family member (Ho et al., 2003). Research with family caregivers suggests a litany of problems, including "difficulty balancing work and family, lack of free time, wishing that someone else would take over and anger with the person they were looking after," and being forced to take time off work (Frederick & Fast, 1999; Keating et al., 1999; Vezina & Turcotte, 2010). Further, the expectation that wives and daughters will shoulder the lion's share of this burden is seen by many to perpetuate traditional patterns of gender inequity.

Paid community providers and institutional caregivers are not necessarily the solution, however. Analysts complain that many such public facilities and services are underfunded, resulting in long waiting lists, poorly trained workers, and inadequate supervision of patient treatment (Martin-Matthews, 2005). Recent media coverage of the abuse and neglect of seniors in seniors' residences underscores these concerns. In addition, private facilities and services may be so prohibitively expensive that they are only available to the wealthiest seniors.

Some commentators argue that the composite of isolation, disability, illness, and dependency accounts for many of the social problems with which aged seniors are identified. For example, this constellation is seen as the root cause

✳ **Explore** the reading "Is Frailty Inevitable? Some Experts Say No" on **MySocLab.**

◉ **Watch** the video on a new form of elder care—combining seniors and daycare—on **MySocLab.**

DOWN-TO-EARTH SOCIOLOGY

Connecting Isolation, Dependency, Dementia, and Abuse

It is important to realize that the issues of dependency, disability, and isolation may intersect with other social concerns, such as elder neglect and abuse. The New Brunswick case of 82-year-old Kenneth Leadlay, who pleaded guilty to killing his 81-year-old wife, speaks to these interconnections.

Alice Leadlay suffered from severe dementia and, as a result, often roamed the house and sometimes screamed for hours on end. In September 2004, Kenneth, desperate after days without sleep, tied his wife up and gagged her. She apparently suffocated as a result. The judge ruled that the husband had been negligent and was clearly responsible for his wife's death. He was sentenced to two years to be served in the community.

In his defence, Kenneth affirmed his love for his wife, whom he had met when she was 12 years old, and who had been not only his sweetheart but also his best friend. Other witnesses testified to the happy, loving relationship between the couple, and the judge noted that there were no prior indications of abuse.

Although Kenneth Leadlay was punished for his "bad judgment," it seems likely that other societal factors entered into the tragic end to their relationship. While the husband may be at fault for refusing to admit that his wife was "too big a burden to him," the local community and society at large should consider its failure to be aware of the situation and to provide adequate support and alternatives.

Source: CBC News. (2005, April 7). "Elderly man sentenced in wife's gagging death." Available at www.cbc.ca/story/canada/national/2005/04/06/nb-elder-050406.html.

---

of the relatively high rates of suicide among aged seniors and the tendency for suicide among older adults to increase in recent decades. In 2007, 221 Canadians aged 75 to 89 committed suicide, up from 172 in 2002 (Rakobowchuk, 2011). It is also seen as an important factor in the increasing numbers of murder-suicides in the United States in which older males killed their wives and then themselves. Predictably, causes are seen as linked to undiagnosed depression, failing health, caregiver stress, and loss of independence (Vann, 2002).

As critical social gerontologists would be quick to emphasize, the interplay between dependency, caregiving, illness, and state funding are not restricted to the plight of Canadian seniors. All individuals, regardless of age, who are so ill or disabled that they are incapable of participating productively in the economic order risk societal marginalization. For example, all women with activity limitations, regardless of age, face an income deficit of about 25 percent when compared with other Canadian women (Compton, 2011). While numbers of affected seniors are higher, the social attitudes toward their plight, the underfunding of support services, and the downloading of responsibilities onto family members are by no means peculiar to this group. The mentally and physically disabled, regardless of age or cause, have typically been invisible in modern society. Seriously addressing their plight and that of their caregivers necessarily raises fundamental questions about the social value placed on life, the meaning of "quality of life," and the responsibility of the state and community in maintaining minimal standards.

Dependency and Elder Abuse

By the 1980s, activists working on family violence issues—child abuse, wife abuse, and so on—increasingly recognized that seniors were also subject to violence, both within families and outside. The first national survey of elder abuse was undertaken in 1992, and today we have a growing body of research on the topic. Canadians now generally understand that seniors are vulnerable to a variety of forms of victimization, including physical, sexual, financial, mental, and emotional abuse. The abuse may be perpetrated by a spouse, son or daughter or other relative, neighbour, paid caregiver or caregiver in an institutional setting, or by the senior him- or herself. The physical and mental deterioration that often accompanies aging renders them both dependent upon others and vulnerable to victimization. The precise form of abuse varies considerably—from a physically abusive spouse or family member to financial con artists to attendants in seniors' residences who neglect their patients. Within these broad parameters, there are disputed estimates about the numbers of seniors subject to some form of physical, psychological, and/or financial abuse. We do not have a grasp on the actual numbers of abuse incidents or whether these are increasing (McDonald, 2011).

Very few of these incidents are included in police reports, and those that are tend to involve non-family members. With this stipulation in mind, it may be noted that

⊚ **Watch** the video "Physical Challenges of Living Longer" on MySocLab.

in 2010, nearly 2800 seniors were victims of family violence, according to police-reported data. Of the elder abuse within families, women were more frequently the victims. For example, in incidents of senior spousal violence, women were twice as likely as men to be the victims and were also slightly more likely than men to be victimized by their children. Further, two-thirds of these family-based instances of elder abuse involved physical assaults (Sinha, 2012:2–3). Older Canadians are also vulnerable to victimization outside the home. Although we know very little about abuse in institutional settings, surveys of nurses and nursing assistants suggest that many have witnessed rough handling (hitting or shoving patients, inappropriate use of restraints, overmedicating) and emotional abuse (yelling, swearing, and humiliation of patients) (Momirov & Duffy, 2011:137–138).

Why are elderly Canadians victimized? Increasingly, analysts point to the complex and intersecting ways in which ageism, sexism, ableism, racism, heterosexism, classism, and other patterns of power and oppression may be implicated in generating elder abuse (Walsh et al., 2011). Reflecting this approach, some Canadian researchers report that a feminist perspective (focusing on gender inequalities and the subordination of women), along with a situational model, is helpful in identifying elderly individuals that are more likely to be victims of physical abuse (Smith & Hightower, 2004). The feminist perspective on the issue does not, of course, discount that other factors—such as ethnicity, recent immigrant status, and rural residence—may further compound the vulnerability of older women and men.

IN SUM

Aging, especially for older seniors, almost always involves becoming somewhat dependent. Although both men and women confront the issue, women in particular are likely to end up on their own. Isolation may become a serious issue when coupled with disability, particularly dementia. Chronic illness requires intense support from families and/or health care institutions. As the number of seniors grows, senior dependency is likely to become an increasingly important social issue. The health care system is already experiencing severe pressures, and the burden of family support often falls disproportionately on adult women. In this context, it is troubling to note that elder abuse and neglect may be taking place. Isolated and disabled seniors may be particularly vulnerable to abuse from both professional and family caregivers.

Focus Question

Is it reasonable to rely on family members to provide care and support for aging seniors, or should other social support mechanisms be put in place?

SUMMARY AND REVIEW

THE "AGE-QUAKE"

Is aging a global crisis?
The so-called developed countries are experiencing a dramatic increase in the proportion of seniors in their populations. Differences between developed and developing countries are reflected in differing life expectancy rates, dependency ratios, and age profiles. Globally, the trend is for more people to live longer, and this may have momentous implications for emerging economies such as China and India. However, right now, this concern primarily involves developed countries. pp. 191–196.

What does the term "greying of Canada" mean?
The phrase **greying of Canada** refers to the growing proportion of Canadians reaching old age. Not only are more Canadians reaching age 65—the traditional cut-off for being a senior—many are entering their eighties and nineties, and there are a surprising number of centenarians. The cost of health care for the elderly has become a social issue, and sentiment about the elderly may be shifting. pp. 196–199.

SYMBOLIC INTERACTIONIST PERSPECTIVES ON AGING

What factors influence perceptions of aging?
Symbolic interactionists stress that, by itself, reaching a particular age has no meaning. They identify three factors that influence when people label themselves as "old": biological changes, biographical events, and cultural timetables. Cross-cultural as well as historical comparisons demonstrate the role of culture in determining how individuals experience aging. **Ageism**, or negative reaction to the elderly, is based on stereotypes, which are influenced by the mass media. pp. 199–204.

FEMINIST PERSPECTIVES

How does aging affect men and women differently?
Extensive feminist analysis has shown that the aging process affects men and women differently. Aging women are more likely to be socially marginalized and dismissed, as evidenced by the popular belief that men are more attractive and sexual at an older age than

women. Women are also likely to find themselves economically disadvantaged, particularly if they have taken "time out" to devote themselves to their home and family. Older women who are also members of minority groups—Aboriginal women, lesbians, disabled women—are likely to experience additional societal prejudices. pp. 206–209.

CONFLICT PERSPECTIVES: THE POLITICAL ECONOMY OF AGING

Is there conflict among different age groups?

Government legislation is an example of one generation disputing the demands made by another generation for limited resources. As the **dependency ratio**—the number of workers who support one retired person—decreases, workers may become resentful. It seems, in particular, that the right to retire from paid employment is an increasingly contested issue between younger and older citizens in industrialized countries. pp. 206–209.

THE DEPENDENCY CRISIS

What are some of the problems faced by the elderly today?

Care for isolated and frail aged citizens is an issue that Canadians have yet to successfully address. Due to differences in mortality and their gendered work histories, older women are particularly likely to end up living alone, in poor health, and on restricted incomes. pp. 209–211.

TALKING ABOUT THEORY

Theoretical Paradigms

| | CLASSICAL PARADIGMS | | | RECENT PARADIGMS | |
	Structural-Functional Paradigm	Social-Conflict Paradigm	Symbolic-Interaction Paradigm	Feminist Paradigm	Postmodernist Paradigm
What is the level of analysis?	Macro level	Macro level	Micro level	Micro and macro levels	Micro and macro levels
How is age discrimination explained?	Older people are not discriminated against, but are regarded as being in a separate and distinct stage of life. They contribute to the maintenance of tradition within families and communities.	Older people generally stand outside of productive activity, as they are no longer in the labour force, and they have fewer resources within society.	Older people are labelled in such ways that they appear to be less capable and require more help with everyday tasks than younger people.	Aging exacerbates problems of power and inequality for women. Older women are even more marginalized than their younger counterparts.	Older people—particularly older women—are invisible in cultural representations such as art, literature, and mass media. Images are often negative or absent—giving the impression that the elderly do not count.

KEY TERMS

All URLs listed are current as of the printing of this text.

Elder Web
www.elderweb.org
An online community of older adult computer users.

Aging and Seniors
www.phac-aspc.gc.ca/seniors-aines/index_pages/whatsnew_e.htm
Health Canada's division of Aging & Seniors provides federal leadership in areas pertaining to aging and seniors, and serves as a focal point for information and a centre of expertise.

Canadian Association on Gerontology
www.cagacg.ca
The Canadian Association on Gerontology (CAG-ACG) is a national, multidisciplinary association established to provide leadership in matters relating to the aging population in Canada. CAG fosters research, education, and policy aimed at improving the quality of life of the elderly in Canada.

Canadian Institutes of Health Research—Institute of Aging
www.cihr-irsc.gc.ca
The CIHR established the Institute of Aging to support research, promote healthy aging, and address a wide range of conditions associated with aging. The goal is to improve the quality of life and health of older Canadians. Its website provides publications, resources, and news relevant to this mission.

The Canadian Network for the Prevention of Elder Abuse
www.cnpea.ca
The CNPEA website provides information and raises awareness about abuse and neglect in later life. This information includes Canadian laws on abuse and neglect and strategies for preventing abuse.

Alzheimer Society of Canada
www.alzheimer.ca
Alzheimer Society of Canada is dedicated to preventing and treating the cognitive decline of Alzheimer's disease and to providing practical, up-to-the-minute information that empowers caregivers to manage the disease more confidently, effectively, and economically.

Canada's Association for the Fifty-Plus (CARP)
www.carp.ca
CARP provides information of interest to Canadian seniors 50 and over and seeks to lobby on their behalf with federal, provincial, and local governments.

1. When you envision your own life course, how do you imagine your life after 65, and how does that vision relate to your attitudes toward the elderly in Canada today?
2. In what ways are gender differences in aging intensified or reduced by other factors such as being a recent immigrant, belonging to a specific ethnic group, or being well-off?
3. What kinds of research projects on aging would critical social gerontologists want to pursue?
4. Thinking about the last half-dozen movies you watched, do you think that media images of older men or women are becoming more positive?
5. If the social construction of adolescence and old age are going to be revised in the next generation, what kinds of changes in our values and social institutions would have to take place?
6. Do you think it is likely that seniors and young Canadians will face conflict over access to resources such as health care and employment? Access the Research Navigator through MySocLab and use keywords such as "ageism," "seniors," and "retirement" to locate relevant and recent scholarly and popular press publications to help you answer this question.

MySocLab

Explore the topics covered in this chapter on MySocLab. Interactive resources include a study plan, cumulative exams, a multimedia library, MySocLab eReadings, and access to the MySocLab Video Series.

10

BUREAUCRACY AND THE CORPORATION

LEARNING OUTCOMES

After you have studied this chapter, you will be able to answer the following questions:

1. How did the rationalization of society come about?
2. What are formal organizations?
3. What dysfunctions are often associated with bureaucracies?
4. What are the functions of voluntary associations?
5. What is the "iron law of oligarchy"?
6. How does the corporate culture affect workers?
7. What does "humanizing the workplace" mean?
8. What is lean production?

ELSIE believed in maintaining her independence and dug her heels in firmly whenever anyone suggested that she consider moving closer to her family. At 80, she was a spry and active senior who remained involved in her community. She had lived in her home for more than 40 years and couldn't bear the thought of leaving the warmth of her kitchen, her well-maintained garden, and, most of all, her memories. Her family—two sons, two daughters-in-law, and grandchildren—lived an hour's drive away. Although it would have been much more convenient to have them all close at hand, she knew that moving to the "big city" would be costly. She was afraid she'd have to give up her independence and move into a seniors' residence.

Admittedly, it was becoming increasingly difficult for Elsie to manage her personal care and a number of her household chores on her own. On the advice of her children, she agreed to apply for some help through the Community Elderly Assistance Program—a program designed to lend a hand to seniors who wished to remain independent. From the government's point of view, with the rapidly aging population, community-based programs to assist seniors in their homes were cost efficient alternatives to institutionalized care. After a lengthy process that involved completing a number of forms, having home visits by care workers and their supervisors, agreeing to rules and regulations, and obtaining medical reports indicating her need for assistance, Elsie was provided with a caregiver who would visit her home for 10 hours a week to help with personal care and household chores.

The arrangement was wonderful—a blessing, according to Elsie. She had the support she needed to stay where she wanted.

A few months after Elsie's home care plan was approved, her son invited her to spend the summer with him and his family at the lake. Elsie hadn't been to the old family cottage for a decade or more. She was overjoyed with the idea of spending a summer by the lake.

Without delay, she began to plan for her adventure. First on her agenda was to inform her caregiver and the Elderly Assistance Program that she would be away for two months. She excitedly explained to the program's administrator that she wanted to temporarily suspend her caregiver's visits since she would be away for the summer. But she was quickly informed that there was no such thing as a "temporary" suspension of services. Her choice was to maintain in active status with the program or to resign permanently. The rules did not allow for time away. "It's a matter of efficiency," explained the administrator.

What a dilemma. Not wanting to risk her future independence by losing the caregiver, possibly forever, Elsie's dream of a summer at the lake quickly vanished. Later that evening, Elsie reluctantly called her son to turn down his generous offer, saying, "A summer by the lake does not fit the agency's agenda. Life's choices are often difficult ones. In this case, the agency's goal of efficiency trumps fun."

The Rationalization of Society

We can all understand Elsie's dismay. The assistance program allowed seniors to maintain their independence, but only as defined by the program's rules and regulations. This concept could have been made a lot clearer to Elsie during the application process. But the program administrators had to fit together a giant puzzle—seniors requiring care, allotted home care hours, and caregiver availability. Disruptions of any kind would throw the planning process off course. As a result, program administration involved strict adherence to hundreds of regulations, usually with little room for exceptional circumstances. As Elsie discovered, tightly planned schedules and rigid rules do not easily accommodate life's preferences.

In this chapter, we will examine how society is organized to "get jobs done." As you read, you may be able to trace the source of some of your frustrations to this form of social organization, as well as see how your welfare depends on it.

Over the course of history, societies have undergone transformations so extensive that whole new types of societies emerged. In addition to these transformations, a major development has been **rationality**—the idea that rules, efficiency, and practical results should guide human affairs. We assume that rationality, and an emphasis on efficiency and results, should be the basis for much of our social interactions, including how schools, hospitals, and businesses operate. An emphasis on rationality underlies even the relatively recent shift to a globalized information society. We have come to accept interacting with computers when banking, scheduling appointments, accessing technical support services, and so on as normal, and we are oftentimes surprised when we are greeted by real human voice. Let's examine how this approach to life—which we often take for granted today—came about.

The Contribution of Max Weber

Max Weber (1864–1920), a sociologist whose studies incorporated an amazingly broad sweep of world history, concluded that until recently, the world's groups and nations were immersed in a **traditional orientation** to life—that is, the idea that the past is the best guide for the present. In this view, deep, lifelong obligations and responsibilities and personal relationships characterize society. What exists is good because it has passed the test of time. Customs—and relationships based on them—have served people well and should not be lightly abandoned. A central orientation of traditional society is to protect the status quo. Change is viewed with suspicion and comes slowly, if at all.

The traditional orientation stands in the way of industrialization, which requires willingness—even eagerness—to change. If a society is to industrialize, a deep-seated shift must occur in people's thinking—from wanting to keep things as they are to seeking the most efficient means of accomplishing tasks. Under capitalism, the primary concern is with results, not with who might be affected by decisions taken. This change requires an entirely different way of looking at life and is in opposition to the basic orientation of all human societies prior to industrialization. Weber referred to this change as the **rationalization of society**. This new *rationality* meant that things were to be judged according to the "bottom line" instead of by personal relationships and considerations. Rationality has become so deeply embedded in our ways of life that it is difficult to grasp how fundamentally different society and human relationships were prior to industrialization. How, then, did the rationalization of society come about? How did people break through their profound resistance to change?

To Weber, this problem was like an unsolved murder is to a detective. Weber's primary clue was that capitalism thrived only in certain parts of Europe. If he could determine why this was so, he was convinced he could discover the root of this fundamental change in human society. As Weber pursued the matter, he concluded that religion held the key, given that capitalism flourished in Protestant countries while Roman Catholics held on to tradition and were relatively untouched by the ideology.

Why did Roman Catholics resist change while Protestants embraced the new emphasis on practical results? Weber's answer to this puzzle has been the source of controversy since it was first proposed in his highly influential book, *The Protestant Ethic and the Spirit of Capitalism* (1904–05/1958). He concluded that essential differences between the two religions held the answer. Roman Catholic doctrine emphasized the acceptance of present arrangements, not change: "God wants you where you are . . . Accept your

✳ **Explore** the reading "Asceticism and the Spirit of Capitalism" by Max Weber on **MySocLab**.

lot in life and remain rooted." But Protestant theology, especially Calvinism, was quite different, Weber argued. Calvinists (followers of the teachings of John Calvin, 1509–1564) believed that before birth, people are destined to go either to heaven or to hell—and they would not know their destiny until after death. Weber believed that this idea filled Calvinists with an anxiety that pervaded their entire lives. Salvation became their chief concern in life—they wanted to know now where they were going after death.

To resolve their spiritual dilemma, Calvinists came up with an ingenious solution: God did not want those chosen for heaven to be ignorant of their destiny. Consequently, he would bestow signs of approval on them. But what signs? The answer, they claimed, was to be found not in mystical, spiritual experiences, but in tangible achievements that people could see and measure. The sign of God's approval became success: those whom God had predestined for heaven would be blessed with visible success in life.

This idea transformed Calvinists' lives, serving as an extraordinary source of motivation to work hard. Because Calvinists also believed that thrift is a virtue, their dedication to work led to an accumulation of money. Calvinists could not spend the excess on themselves, however, for to purchase items beyond the basic necessities was considered sinful. **Capitalism**, the investment of capital in the hope of producing profits, became an outlet for excess money, while the success of such investments became a further sign of God's approval. As such, worldly success was transformed into a spiritual virtue, and other branches of Protestantism, although less extreme, adopted the creed of thrift and hard work. Consequently, said Weber, Protestant countries embraced capitalism.

What does this have to do with rationalization? Simply put, capitalism demands *rationalization*, the careful calculation of practical results. If profits are your goal, you must compute income and expenses. You must calculate inventories and wages, the cost of producing goods, and how much they bring in. You must find ways to lower your costs, which often means decreasing labour costs. For example, you might require that workers produce more units per hour or that work be intensified in such a way that fewer workers are needed to do the job. You must determine "the bottom line." Under this arrangement, efficiency, not tradition, becomes the drum to which you march. Traditional ways of doing things, if inefficient, must be replaced, for what counts are the results.

Marx on Rationalization

Another sociologist, Karl Marx (1818–1883), the originator of conflict theory, also observed that tradition had given way to rationality. When he analyzed the problem, however, Marx came up with an entirely different explanation. Marx dismissed Weber's notion that commitment to particular religious beliefs accounted for the rise of capitalism. He did not think religion had anything to do with breaking the bonds of tradition. Rather, Marx concluded that the switch to rationality was the result of capitalism itself. When people saw that capitalism was more efficient, that it produced things they wanted in much greater abundance, and that it amassed profit and wealth, they embraced rationality, giving up their traditional thinking. Thus, Marx reversed the equation: the transition to capitalism, he said, changed the way people thought about life, not the other way around.

Marx criticized capitalism's rationality and emphasis on efficiency. He argued that capitalism produces inequalities within societies, separating people on the basis of wealth, social class, ideologies, and power. He argued that the values and practices of capitalism contributed to feelings of **alienation**. The needs of workers became secondary to the interests of capital and the capitalists' persistent pursuit of profit—often at any cost.

When society began to rationalize, production of goods was broken up into its various components, with individuals assigned only specific tasks. Shown in this wood engraving is the production of glass in Great Britain in the early 1800s.

Which theory—Weber's or Marx's—provides the best explanation for rationality? Weber's, with its conclusion that Protestantism produced rationality, which then paved the way for capitalism? Or Marx's, which concluded that capitalism produced rationality? No analyst has yet reconciled the two opposing answers to the satisfaction of sociologists.

Focus Question
How did Marx and Weber differ in their views on rationality and how it came to permeate society?

Feminist and Critical Approaches to the Study of Organizations

For many years, textbooks and studies of organizations have presented facts about organizational structures, but have overlooked the characteristics and roles of the people who make up organizations. Feminists and other critical thinkers contend that this omission presents a problem for women and minorities, whose voices and perspectives are not taken into account in "generic" descriptions of the organization. These critics argue that the "generic" presentations are not "faceless," but rather are representations of a dominant (male) perspective (Mills, Simmons, & Helms Mills, 2005).

Feminist analyses of organizations take into account the ways in which women are affected by organizational arrangements. They question the distribution of power and authority and seek to understand why and how women are discriminated against within organizational structures. They ask, for example, why women are rarely found in corporate boardrooms as decision-makers, despite their high numbers in the lower levels of organizational hierarchies and in clerical or other female-dominated fields. Radical feminists take such questions further, seeking change to organizational structures that allow men to dominate.

Following this critical tradition of questioning the ways in which organizations are gendered are more recent approaches that include the experiences of diverse groups and how their concerns and rights as workers, consumers, and clients may be excluded, ignored, or cast aside within organizations. Along with concerns raised by feminists, the newer critical approaches to organizations are inclusive, accounting for the experiences of racialized minorities, Aboriginal peoples, people with visible and invisible disabilities, and sexually diverse groups—gay, lesbian, bisexual, queer, and transgendered people.

Formal Organizations and Bureaucracy

Rationality transformed the way society is organized and permeated societal institutions. As a result, **formal organizations**—secondary groups designed to achieve explicit objectives—have become a central feature of contemporary society. We engage in multiple and complex sets of interactions with formal organizations—in schools, workplaces, hospitals and other care-providing institutions, governments, religious organizations, businesses, and so on. In our daily routines—attending classes, shopping, visiting a nursing home resident, paying a parking ticket, playing organized sports, or picking up dinner from a fast-food chain—we interact with dozens of formal organizations, most of which share similar central characteristics.

Formal Organizations

Prior to industrialization, only a few formal organizations existed. The guilds of Western Europe during the twelfth century are an example. People who performed similar work organized to control their craft in a local area. They set prices and standards of workmanship (Bridgwater, 1953; "Guilds," 2005). Much like modern unions, guilds also prevented outsiders (those who were not members) from working at a particular craft. Another example of an early formal organization is the army, with its structure of senior officers, junior officers, and ranks. Formal armies date back to early history.

With industrialization, secondary groups became common. Today we take their existence for granted and, beginning with grade school, spend a good deal of time participating in them. Formal organizations tend to develop into bureaucracies and, in general, the larger the formal organization, the more likely it is to be bureaucratic.

The Essential Characteristics of Bureaucracies

Although a police department, a post office, a university, and General Motors may not seem to have much in common, they are all bureaucracies. As Weber (1913/1947) analyzed them, the essential characteristics of a **bureaucracy** are as follows:

1. *A hierarchy with assignments flowing downward and accountability flowing upward.* The organization is divided into clear-cut levels. Each level assigns responsibilities to the level beneath it, while each lower level is accountable to the level above for fulfilling those assignments. The bureaucratic structure of a typical university is shown in Figure 10.1.

2. *A division of labour.* Every member of a bureaucracy has a specific task to fulfill, and all tasks are then coordinated to accomplish the purpose of the organization. In a university, for example, a professor does not run the heating system, the president does not teach, and a secretary does not evaluate textbooks. These tasks are distributed among people who have been trained to do them.

3. *Written rules.* In their attempt to become efficient, bureaucracies stress written procedures. In general, the longer a bureaucracy exists and the larger it grows, the more written rules it has. The rules of bureaucracies may cover just about every imaginable situation. Often an

✱ **Explore** the reading "Characteristics of Bureaucracy" by Max Weber on **MySocLab**.

The McDonaldization of Society

There are more than 33 000 McDonald's restaurants worldwide, located in 118 countries (with more than 18 500 in the United States and over 1400 in Canada) (http://en.wikipedia.org/wiki/List_of_countries_with_McDonald%27s_restaurants).

Sociologist George Ritzer (1993; 2011) believes that the McDonald's restaurants that dot the North American landscape—and increasingly, the world—have much greater significance than the convenience of fast food. He coined the term "the **McDonaldization** of society" to refer to the increasing rationalization of the routine tasks of everyday life. Ritzer argues that the modern fast-food restaurant presents a better paradigm for rationalization than Weber's conceptualization of bureaucracy (Ritzer, 1998).

He points out that Ray Kroc, the founder of McDonald's, applied principles developed by Henry Ford to the preparation and serving of food. A 1958 operations manual spelled out exact procedures:

> It told operators exactly how to draw milk shakes, grill hamburgers, and fry potatoes. It specified precise cooking times for all products and temperature settings for all

McDonald's in Beijing, China

equipment. It fixed standard portions on every food item, down to the quarter ounce of onions placed on each hamburger patty and the thirty-two slices per pound of cheese. It specified that french fries be cut at nine thirty-seconds of an inch thick ... Those working the grill were instructed to put hamburgers down on the grill moving from left to right, creating six rows of six patties each. And because the first two rows were farthest from the heating element, they were instructed (and still are) to flip the third row first, then the fourth, fifth, and sixth before flipping the first two.

Efficiency may bring reduced prices and dependability, but at a cost—the loss of something difficult to define, a quality of life washed away by rationalization—as predictability replaces spontaneity. If you travel and take packaged tours, for example, you may never have enjoyable, eye-opening experiences that could add to your appreciation of human diversity.

For good or bad, most of us are experiencing McDonaldized lives, complete with the predictability of pre-packaged offerings determining our social destiny. When education becomes rationalized—which is now in process—our children will no longer have to put up with the idiosyncrasies of real professors, people who think ideas must be discussed endlessly and who never come to decisive answers. We seem to want instant, preformed solutions to social issues, like those we find in mathematics and engineering. Our children will be instructed in computerized courses, in which everyone learns the same answers—approved, "politically correct," precise, and proper ways to think about social issues. This will certainly be efficient—and proof that the "iron cage" of bureaucracy has entrapped us, as Weber predicted.

---

free to raise its prices. According to Walmart Watch, an organization of citizens affected by Walmart's policies, three jobs are lost for every two that are created when Walmart moves into a community (Ribeiro, 2005; Fishman, 2003).

Walmart is aggressively anti-union, has intimidated unionists (Pier, 2007; Marotte, 2005), and has closed stores (as in Jonquière, Quebec) or threatened closure (as in Saint-Hyacinthe, Quebec) at the mention of unionization (Peritz, 2005; Greenhouse, 2009). Moreover, it uses sophisticated technologies and tracking devices to monitor consumer choices and customers' buying patterns in different geographic areas, not only through cash register and bar coding systems, but through the implantation of microchips that allow information to be relayed through wireless

technologies long after products have left manufacturers and warehouses in China. For many, Walmart is synonymous with power and control.

"Ideal" versus "Real" Bureaucracy

Just as people's actions often stray from the norm, so do those of bureaucracies. The characteristics of bureaucracies

👁 **Watch** the video of George Ritzer talking about the development of his theory on the McDonaldization of Society on **MySocLab**.

✱ **Explore** the reading "The McDonaldization of Society" by George Ritzer on **MySocLab**.

This is the way that some people view bureaucracies: stilted, slow-moving, and destructive to the individual. Bureaucracies can be like this, but not all bureaucracies are alike. Some are innovative and unleash creative energy.

identified by Weber are ideal types; that is, they are a composite of characteristics based on many specific examples. Think of a judge at a dog show. He or she has a mental image of what a certain breed of dog should look like and judges each dog according to that mental image. No one dog will have all the characteristics, but all dogs of that breed put together have them. Thus, a particular organization may be ranked high or low on some characteristic and still qualify as a bureaucracy. Instead of labelling a particular organization as a "bureaucracy" or "not a bureaucracy," it might make more sense to think in terms of the extent to which an organization is bureaucratized (Udy, 1959; Hall, 1963).

As such, a bureaucracy often differs from its ideal image. The actual lines of authority in an organization ("going through channels"), for example, may be quite different from those portrayed on organizational charts such as that shown in Figure 10.1. Suppose that, before being promoted, a university president taught in the history department. As a result, friends from that department may have direct access to him or her. In giving their "input" (ranging from opinions about how to solve problems to personal grievances or even gossip), these individuals may skip their chairperson or even the dean of their faculty altogether.

Dysfunctions of Bureaucracies

Although Weber recognized that no other form of social organization has been found to be more efficient in the long run, his model accounts for only some of the characteristics of bureaucracies. They do not always operate smoothly and efficiently. We will now discuss some of bureaucracy's dysfunctions—red tape, lack of communication, alienation, goal displacement, and incompetence. The Thinking Critically about Social Controversy box below presents a teenager's dilemma as she is caught between bureaucracies and their policies.

RED TAPE: A RULE IS A RULE As Elsie from the opening vignette discovered, bureaucracies can be filled with so much red tape that they impede the purpose of the organization.

For a single parent trying to escape poverty and make life a little more comfortable for her children, for example, rules regarding eligibility for benefits are too inflexible. After working only a few extra hours at her part-time job as a bank teller, provincial social services declared a single mother ineligible for a daycare subsidy because she earned a few dollars more than the maximum allowed (Daly, 2006). Her choices were to quit her job and apply for welfare or keep the job and

THINKING CRITICALLY ABOUT SOCIAL CONTROVERSY

Cornered by Bureaucracies

One bureaucracy's rules may clash with another's, creating a situation in which it is impossible for people to have their needs met fairly. Bureaucratic dysfunction may inadvertently result in tremendous disadvantage to people who question or challenge rules, policies, or procedures, or even jeopardize their opportunities or threaten their well-being.

Consider the case of Jackie B., a high school student and athlete. After graduating with honours from her local public middle school, Jackie left her friends behind to attend a separate secondary school in her area. Her reason was simple, or so she thought: Jackie was a highly competitive soccer player and wanted to take up the sport of rowing. The separate school supported not only a rowing team, but also the most highly successful and well-regarded girls' soccer program in the province.

Jackie's Grade 9 school year began with the usual awkwardness experienced by most students beginning high school. But soon after the year began, Jackie found herself a victim of bullying and harassment. At first she ignored it and fully expected that it would end as she continued to prove herself on the field and as an outstanding newcomer to the rowing crew. As the year went on, she became increasingly despondent. She found herself alone and depressed and her marks began to drop. She feared reporting the bullies. The situation was brought to the attention of the school's senior administration, and, when pressed, Jackie divulged the name of one of the leading bullies. However, the situation was poorly handled, and Jackie's sense of security both within the school and in public places, such as movie theatres, was threatened. For many, the solution would be simple: transfer to the public high school. For an athlete, however, this simple solution can be very costly.

To prevent coaches from "shopping" for star athletes and luring students from one school to another, either inside or outside home boundaries, all provincial athletic associations have a rule regarding transfers. If a student transfers schools, she or he will not be allowed to participate in any sport (falling under the association's umbrella) in which she or he was involved during the previous school year. Jackie was devastated by her situation. Transferring schools would possibly mean sitting out of sports for a year, and staying put would be increasingly difficult to deal with. However, exceptions are sometimes made to this rule, and Jackie had an opportunity to appeal her case. Her chances of winning were slim, but would be considerably improved if she could obtain a statement by an official from the separate school confirming that she had been a victim of bullying and harassment and transferred as a result.

Jackie's coaches and teachers at the new school were highly accommodating and helped her and her parents with the appeal. Nevertheless, they ran into a major roadblock: no one from Jackie's previous school would help. Her parents' phone calls were not returned and the situation was swept under the carpet. Even several teachers who had been well aware of the problems Jackie had experienced refused to help her. It seems that they were under strict orders from the principal not to get involved. Worried that perhaps their careers might suffer, they turned a blind eye to Jackie's plight, despite their knowledge of the situation and their willingness to agree that bullying and harassment are serious problems in schools and that steps should be taken to eliminate them.

Without supporting documents from the separate school, Jackie lost her appeal. She paid the price for being on the receiving end of the bullies' actions. It would have cost her, whether or not she had chosen to transfer. If she had remained at the separate school, she would have continued to be victimized at the expense of her marks and well-being. Her decision to transfer to the public high school was supported by family and friends as the only reasonable choice, but the price she paid for this decision was clearly outrageous.

For Your Consideration
How was Jackie limited by bureaucratic decision-making? What does her situation tell us about bureaucratic alienation, careerism, communication within or between bureaucracies, and lines of authority? What message would this incident have given to the bullies?

pay the full cost of day care. Neither option is very appealing. Unable to afford day care without a subsidy and unable to live on the income from her part-time job, this mother found herself between the proverbial "rock and a hard place."

LACK OF COMMUNICATION BETWEEN UNITS Each unit within a bureaucracy performs specialized tasks, which are designed to contribute to the organization's overall goals. At times, units fail to communicate with one another and end up working at cross-purposes. When an elderly woman required help after falling in the lobby of a Niagara area hospital after visiting her husband, a staff member advised her to call an ambulance, warning the woman that no one would be able to help her unless she made the call.

There she lay on the floor of the hospital's lobby for half an hour, with the emergency department only 50 metres away, waiting for the paramedics to arrive (Stone and Boyle, 2011:A1,A17). Fortunately, the woman eventually received adequate treatment, but a number of other similar cases resulted in tragedy. With the bureaucracy's various units out of sync with one another, the costs—including human lives—were devastating.

BUREAUCRATIC ALIENATION Many workers find it disturbing to deal with others in terms of roles, rules, and functions rather than as individuals. Similarly, they may dislike sending messages instead of talking to people face to face. It is not surprising, then, that workers in large organizations sometimes feel more like objects than people, or, as Weber (1922/1978) described, " . . . only a small cog in a ceaselessly moving mechanism which prescribes to [them] an endlessly fixed routine . . . " Because workers must deal with one another formally, and because they constantly perform routine tasks, some come to feel that no one cares about them and that they are misfits in their surroundings.

Marx termed these reactions *alienation* and attributed them to the fact that workers are cut off from the finished product of their labour. Although assigning workers to repetitive tasks makes for efficient production, Marx argued that it also reduces their satisfaction by limiting their creativity and sense of contribution to the finished product. Underlying alienation is the workers' loss of control over their work, because they no longer own their own tools or make decisions. Before industrialization, individual workers used their own tools to produce an entire product, such as a chair or table. Now, capitalists own the machinery and tools and assign each worker only a single step or two in the entire production process. Relegated to repetitive tasks that seem remote from the finished product, workers lose a sense of identity with what they produce. Ultimately, they come to feel estranged not only from their products, but from the work environment as a whole.

RESISTING ALIENATION Alienation is not a pleasant experience. Because workers want to feel valued and have a sense of control over their work, they resist alienation. As a major form of resistance, workers band together in informal settings—at lunch, around desks, for a drink after work—to give one another approval for jobs well done and express sympathy for the shared need to put up with cantankerous bosses, meaningless routines, and endless rules. They relate to one another not only as workers, but as people of value. They laugh and tell jokes, and talk about their families, problems, goals, and even their love lives.

Consider the common sight of work areas in an office decorated with family and vacation photos. The sociological implication is that of workers striving to overcome alienation by putting their own stamp on their workspaces. Staking a claim to individuality and adding multidimensionality to work relationships restores workers' sense of being individuals rather than mere cogs in an endlessly moving machine.

When they decide to take collective action about workplace struggles, workers form a union. A union provides strength in numbers, a source of action and support, and a legal avenue through which workers' rights are sanctioned and their concerns addressed.

THE ALIENATED BUREAUCRAT Not all workers succeed in resisting alienation, however, and some become extremely alienated. They remain in an organization because they see no viable alternative or because they have "only so many years until retirement." They hate every minute of it, and it shows—in their attitudes toward clients, fellow workers, and especially toward authority in the organization. The alienated bureaucrat does not take initiative, will not do anything for the organization beyond what he or she is absolutely required to do, and uses rules to justify doing as little as possible. Recently, there has been an increase in the incidence of "work rage," in which workers who are stressed and facing growing workloads or are disrespected by co-workers or managers vent their frustrations at work by hurling things across a room, yelling at or threatening others, or swearing. A British survey of over 1200 workers found that almost four out of five admitted to losing their tempers and lashing out at the office (Immen, 2008). The growth in technology has resulted in new expectations that workers be available to respond instantaneously to clients' and managers' requests, and this has contributed to skyrocketing levels of stress and anxiety. Almost 30 percent of Canadians aged 35 to 44 (including a whopping 43 percent of Torontonians in this age group) describe most days as stressful, and researchers attribute much of this stress to smart phones, apps, and devices designed to save labour, ease lives, and increase productivity—an irony of the modern world (Globe and Mail, 2012; Meece, 2011). Because of these devices, workers feel pressured to respond immediately and, as a result, have less "free" time away from their jobs, making it next to impossible to balance work and family life (Galt, 2011).

Such circumstances are detrimental to all workers. Managers might find ways to ease workers' frustrations by limiting the use of smart phones, encouraging workers to turn them off periodically and involving them in decisions regarding their jobs, workloads, and unreasonable demands on their time. As a matter of policy, two German corporations, Henkel and Volkswagen, have responded to workers' complaints about having to respond to email on their own time by stopping email flows after the end of a shift and during holidays ("No More Emails," 2011: A18).

Some managers deal with such situations poorly by shunting off alienated workers into small bureaucratic

✳ **Explore** the reading "Hanging Tongues: A Social Encounter with the Assembly Line" by William E. Thompson on **MySocLab.**

result, an elite inner group, insulated from the masses below, maintains power by passing the leading positions from one clique member to another.

What many find depressing about the iron law of oligarchy is that it applies even to organizations strongly committed to democratic principles. Even Canadian political parties, for example, supposedly the backbone of the nation's representative government, have fallen prey to it. Run by an inner group that may or may not represent the community, political parties often pass their leadership positions from one elite member to another.

The iron law of oligarchy is not without limitations. Do members of an organization simply adopt a passive stance, thereby allowing a small group to continue to lead, or are the voices of the majority silenced or simply not heard by an elite that is far removed from the day-to-day operations? To maintain democracy, members of the inner group must remain attuned to the opinions of the others, regardless of their personal feelings. If the oligarchy gets too far out of line, the majority may rebel and throw the elite group out of office. Good leadership remains responsive to the needs and interests of the group.

Focus Question

How is the power structure within most formal organizations described?

Working within Bureaucracies

Most of you will spend the majority of your working years working within a bureaucracy. Even if you are self-employed, you will spend a great amount of time interfacing with corporations of various sizes as well as with governments and agencies within the public sector. Although entrepreneurs often talk about setting up their own businesses in order to escape the drudgery of the inflexible hours and rules associated with working in a bureaucratic organization, it is almost impossible to avoid conducting business or settling one's affairs without interaction with bureaucrats.

The Corporate Culture: Consequences of Hidden Values

Who gets ahead in a large corporation? Although we might like to think that success is the consequence of intelligence and hard work, many factors other than merit underlie salary increases and promotions. Historically in Canada, family ties have secured many individuals to the power structure, or what author Peter C. Newman refers to as the "Canadian Establishment." Although a number of historically dominant family dynasties, such as the Eatons, have recently tumbled, others, such as the Irvings, Sobeys, Ganongs, Molsons, and McCains, maintain control over their corporate empires (Newman, 1999). A few among the group of Canada's most wealthy and powerful may trace their roots back to more humble origins. Paul Desmarais, Sr., former CEO of Power Corporation, launched his career by revitalizing a small one-route bus line in Sudbury, Ontario; Jean Coutu and Murray Koffler, retail pharmacy magnates, each started with one corner drugstore; and diving for salvage was the first job of Newfoundland's premier businessman, Craig Dobbin, a lumberjack's son (Newman, 1999). While hard work and a cunning business sense certainly helped a number of Canada's most prominent corporate executives,

Volunteer work has become an intricate part of the social fabric of Canadian communities. With cutbacks in funding to hospitals, social service agencies, long-term care facilities, and other public sector organizations, Canadians relying on these agencies have come to depend on this army of unpaid workers.

the largest group succeeded with the help of familial and social interrelations. Some have even enjoyed continued prosperity despite incompetence. Senior executives with companies such as Bell Canada, ArcelorMittal Dofasco Inc., Scotiabank, Confederation Life, and others have, at one time or another, misjudged business prospects; yet, despite their poor decision-making, they were actually promoted and given raises with bonuses (Newman, 1999). As sociologist Rosabeth Moss Kanter (1977, 1983) stresses, the **corporate culture**—the orientation that characterizes a corporate work setting—is crucial in determining people's corporate fate. She explains how a corporation's "hidden values"—those not officially part of the organization, but that nevertheless powerfully influence its members—operate as self-fulfilling stereotypes. The elite hold ideas about who are the best workers and colleagues, and those who fit this mould get better access to information and networking and are put in "fast-track" positions. Not surprisingly, these people perform better and become more committed to the organization, thus confirming initial expectations. In contrast, those judged to be outsiders find opportunities few and far between. They tend to work at a level beneath their capacity, come to think poorly of themselves, and become less committed to the organization.(www.powercorporation.com/en/governance/senior-management/#profile_intro).

The 2010 blockbuster film, *The Social Network,* tells the story of the founding of Facebook and examines the early trials of a corporation led by a highly energetic and shrewd yet inexperienced entrepreneur, Mark Zuckerberg. The film captures the birth and development of Facebook, from its beginning in 2003 in a Harvard dorm room to its early struggles over ownership and rights. Zuckerberg started with a relatively simple idea designed to help lonely college students make connections on campus and quickly became a megacorporation that has revolutionized social communication. Now, less than a decade after the first blogs spread with lightning speed across Harvard and to campuses around the globe, Facebook is more valuable than McDonald's (Rusli, Perlroth, & Bilton, 2012).

The hidden values that create the self-fulfilling prophecy remain invisible to most. What are visible are the promotions of people with superior performances and greater commitment to the company.

The Down-to-Earth Sociology box below explores how hidden values contribute to the iron law of oligarchy, for the corporate elite—the tight inner group that heads a corporation—sets in motion a self-fulfilling prophecy that tends to reproduce itself with people who "look" like its members—generally white males. Although women and minorities who don't match the stereotype are often "showcased"—placed in highly visible positions with little power—in order to demonstrate to the public that the company engages in diversity practices, looking beyond these few reveals that workers are often placed, promoted, and

rewarded according to gendered and racialized assumptions and stereotypes (Jackson, 2010).

While a number of sociologists have discussed the ways in which women are overlooked in their pursuit of upward social mobility and how organizations may become more open to promoting women, Kathy Ferguson, in her 1984 book, *The Feminist Case Against Bureaucracy*, identifies the power structures within bureaucratic capitalist society as a primary source of oppression for both women and men. She advocates elimination, rather than amelioration, of these structures (Ferguson, 1984). Moreover, it is important to develop a critical approach to organizations that focuses on inequalities of power and opportunity within hierarchical structures and to examine how women, minorities, Aboriginal people, and the working class are disadvantaged within organizations (Mills & Simmons, 1999, 2005).

Kanter found that the level people reach in an organization shapes their behaviour and even their attitudes toward

Some members of the "Canadian Establishment," such as Paul Desmarais, Sr., CEO of Power Corporation, trace their roots to humble origins and owe their powerful positions to their own entrepreneurial efforts. Others secured their positions within the Canadian power structure through family ties. Desmarais's sons, Paul, Jr. and André, are now co-CEOs of Power Corporation.

bureaucracies that makes them *inherently* insensitive to people's needs or that prevents them from humanizing corporate culture. However, under capitalism, the pursuit of efficiency and profit relegates social relationships and people's needs or interests to the "back court."

Moreover, to humanize corporate culture does not necessarily require huge expense; nor does it mean loss rather than profit. Kanter (1983) compared 47 companies that were rigidly bureaucratic with more flexible competitors of the same size. The more flexible companies were also more profitable—probably because their greater flexibility encouraged greater company loyalty, creativity, and productivity. Claims of efficiency and profits are a matter of degrees. The garment industry, for example, is noted for its "sweatshop" conditions. Historically, the term **sweating** has been used in reference to working conditions in the garment industry, with its detailed division of labour separating the craft process (design, cutting, and marketing) from the labour-intensive tasks of sewing and finishing. Under this form of organization, even today, garment workers—who are primarily women—are among the most exploited workers worldwide, receiving very low rates of pay despite their extraordinary sewing skills. Sweatshops are located around the world, and giant retailers import their stock or have their own private labels made in countries where there are no, or very few, policies protecting workers (Ross, 1999). Small clothing manufacturing operations with "no sweat" and "fair trade" practices may be profitable and efficiently run, but they present little competition to corporate giants in the industry.

Quality Circles

In light of such findings, many corporations have taken steps to humanize their work settings, motivated not by any altruistic urge to make life better for their workers but by self-interest—the desire to make their organization more competitive. Some have developed **quality circles**, which consist of perhaps a dozen workers and a manager or two who meet regularly to try to improve the quality of both the work setting and the company's products.

However, many companies report that quality circles yield few benefits. Disappointed with the results, companies such as Whirlpool and GE have abandoned the idea. (Part of the reason may be that they set up quality circles for reasons of publicity, not intending to take employee suggestions seriously.) Regardless of whether they formally implement such measures, companies often solicit ideas from their employees, who have a wealth of knowledge about how things might work best. In some cases, workers are not credited for their ideas, but in others, companies might use town hall-type meetings to allow employees to air their ideas publicly and/or may reward workers with cash and stock options.

Employee Stock Ownership

Many companies offer an opportunity for their employees to purchase stock at a discount or as part of their salary,

and numerous Canadian companies, including Canadian Tire Corporation, are now partially owned by employees. Because each employee typically owns only a tiny amount of stock, such "ownership" is practically meaningless. In a small percentage of companies, however, employees own the majority of the stock. On average, companies with at least 10 percent of stock owned by employees are more profitable than other firms, probably because the workers are more committed and the managers take a longer-term view (White, 1991).

One might think that employee ownership of a company's stock would eliminate problems between workers and management. Profitability, however, not ownership, appears to be the key to reducing these problems. Unprofitable firms put more pressure on their employee-owners, creating tension between workers and managers, while profitable companies resolve problems more quickly.

Work Teams

Small work groups or self-managed teams were pioneered in the computer industry to increase productivity and cut down on absenteeism. Work teams stimulate creative ideas

Co-operatives provide workers with an alternative work arrangement. As owners, organization members collectively make decisions, determine goals and policies, and set salaries and work tasks. Decision-making, even on routine matters, is often very time-consuming, since all members participate. Co-operatives strive to provide members with a high level of satisfaction for work performed.

and imaginative solutions to problems, and some argue that employees who work in them feel a greater sense of loyalty to the company, work harder, and reduce their absenteeism. The small work group establishes primary relationships among its members, and workers' identities become tied up with their group. This reduces alienation; rather than being lost in a bureaucratic maze, workers' individuality is appreciated and their contributions more readily recognized. The group's successes become the individual's successes—as do its failures—reflecting positively or negatively on the individual. As a consequence of their expanded personal ties, workers make more of an effort. The downside for these workers is that their increased efficiency may encourage employers to reduce the group's size by laying off members, thereby increasing the workload of those remaining.

Work–Life Balance

Canadians report that they are seriously time-crunched—stressed by demanding jobs, caring for children, tending to elderly parents, and maintaining their homes. All of these demands are leaving Canadians with little time to "smell the flowers" and enjoy a leisurely stroll. Our busy lifestyles are taking the toll on our well-being, and that in turn affects children, families, relationships, health, and work performance.

There are a number of workplace practices that may help to establish a more favourable work–life balance and ease the stress of working Canadians. Family-friendly practices may include workplace daycare facilities, options for more flexible working hours, more realistic workloads, and supportive and understanding management teams (Higgins & Duxbury, 2009; Galloway & Wingrove, 2010).

Developing an Alternative: The Co-operative

While measures such as those described above generally make the workplace more hospitable to workers, these management strategies are ultimately aimed at increasing profit and productivity. In the 1970s, many workers across North America, especially those opposed to capitalism and what they considered to be the deadening effects of bureaucracy, began to seek an alternative organizational form. They began to establish co-operatives—organizations owned by members who collectively make decisions, determine goals, evaluate resources, set salaries, and assign work tasks. Tasks are carried out without a hierarchy of authority, and all members can participate in the decisions of the organization. In Canada there are approximately 345 worker-managed companies, most of which are located in Quebec. All together, these companies have over 12 876 members (Rural and Co-Operatives Secretariat, 2010). As sociologists Joyce Rothschild and Allen Whitt (1986) state, co-operatives are not new. Farmers' co-operatives, once popular in western Canada, have a long and rich history. Co-operatives attempt to achieve some specific social good (such as lowering food prices and improving food quality) and provide a high level of

personal satisfaction for their members as they work toward that goal. Most self-managed enterprises are small companies in which workers are ultimately concerned with controlling their own labour. Some companies were bought out by workers in order to save their jobs. Northern Breweries in Sault Ste. Marie, Ontario, was the first employee-owned brewing company in North America, although it closed its doors in late-2006 (Rinehart, 2006).

Because all members can participate in decision-making, co-operatives spend huge amounts of time deciding even routine matters. The economic results of co-operatives are mixed. Many are less profitable than private organizations, others more so. A few have been so successful that they have been bought by major corporations.

The Conflict Perspective

Conflict theorists suggest that the basic relationship between workers and owners is confrontational regardless of how a work organization is structured (Edwards, 1979; Rinehart, 2006). Each walks a different path, with one exploiting workers to extract a greater profit, and the other trying to resist that exploitation. Since their basic interests are fundamentally opposed, conflict theorists argue, employers' attempts to humanize the work setting (or to manage diversity) are mere window dressing—efforts to conceal their fundamental goal of exploiting workers. If these efforts are not camouflage, they are worse—attempts to manipulate workers into active co-operation in their own exploitation. This analysis does not apply to co-operatives, however, since they are owned by the workers.

Technology and the Control of Workers

The microchip has rapidly changed our lives. Many people continue to rejoice over the computer's capacity to improve their quality of life. Through mobile apps, patients may even connect with their physicians from across the globe, have electrocardiograms and other tests performed, and have prescriptions delivered, saving millions in health care dollars and, most importantly, saving lives (Priest, 2012). But computers also hold the potential for severe abuse. They may allow governments to operate a police state, monitoring our every move. The Big Brother in George Orwell's classic novel *1984* may turn out to be a computer. Technology has, in many ways, transformed work into Aldous Huxley's vision of a "Brave New World," according to writer and activist Heather Menzies. In the new workplace, individuals play a secondary role to advanced technologies that are not only capable of levels of production and efficiency beyond human capability, but also can simultaneously connect to and manage facilities and labour forces across the globe (Menzies, 1996). The technologically advanced workplace has the capacity to eliminate and de-skill workers, resulting in high levels of unemployment and a deep sense of insecurity experienced by workers in various settings (Noble, 1995; Huws, 2003). With computers and instant messaging, there is still room for error, however. A misdirected email meant for one worker at a giant British insurance company accidentally fired 1300 employees around the globe, asking them to pack their belongings and leave the premises (Yew, 2012). While the company quickly apologized, the incident reminded workers of their vulnerability.

Perhaps the most concerning issue regarding technology at work is the degree of control over workers computers provide. Many analysts contend that computers allow managers to increase surveillance without face-to-face supervision (Silverman, 2008; Mosco & McKercher, 2008; Mosco, 2009). Computers let managers know the number of strokes a word processor makes every minute or hour, or inform supervisors how long each teleworker takes per call. Call centre workers who are "underperforming" are singled out for discipline. It does not matter that the slower operators may be more polite or more helpful, only that the computer reports slower performance (Pupo & Noack, 2010).

With technologies capable of monitoring workers' every movement, are we moving toward "maximum-security" workplaces? Consider this: when workers at a leading hotel punch in, a device scans their eyes, comparing their retinas with computerized data on file. This prevents employees from punching in one another's time cards. Facial recognition technology is even capable of alerting sales clerks to the type of customer walking into the store or to project electronic ads appropriate for the individuals within reach (Tossell, 2011).

Although companies employ monitoring techniques to increase productivity, researchers have found that excessive surveillance may have the opposite effect on workers. In a British study, researchers discovered that workers whose activities, including keyboard strokes and emails, were highly monitored reported feeling exhausted and anxious compared to workers who were not monitored (Silverman, 2008). A truck driver at Safeway used to enjoy his job. He says, "No one was looking over your shoulder, and you felt like a human being." Now, the driver says he feels "pushed around." A small computer in the dashboard of his truck (called, appropriately, a Tripmaster) keeps track of his speed, shifting, and excessive idling, and even reports when and how long he stops for lunch or a coffee break. The driver says he will retire early.

The computer's awesome capacities in the workplace may be just one part of a "maximum-security society" (Marx, 1995).

Focus Question

From the worker's perspective, what are some of the advantages and disadvantages of the various techniques or strategies employed by management to "humanize" the corporate culture?

Virtual Organizations

Virtual organizations are companies "without walls," often transcending time, space, and culture. The image of the virtual organization is that of an edgeless, permeable entity, capable of rapid results and characterized by temporary, depersonalized relationships. Some companies engage in what has come to be known as **hotelling**, whereby they provide employees with laptops, but only assign desks to employees on a temporary basis, much like one rents a room in a hotel—only when needed. Some companies seek to bring like-minded groups and people together in a shared location. But the emphasis is on flexibility and temporariness, addressing workers' trepidation or inability to commit to a conventional "multi-year lease" (Immen, 2011).

While this arrangement may certainly dissuade the development of a work "community" or identification with a workplace, proponents of hotelling see underused office space as dollars lost in profits. Such dollar amounts are especially significant in major cities like Toronto, Montreal, and Vancouver, where land costs are at a premium.

A twist on the idea of hotelling is the newer craze of co-working, with sites popping up around the globe from "Argentina to Australia and many places in between" (Fost, 2008). In co-working, a company or lone entrepreneur sets up an office and rents out the desks to people who have different jobs but who desire a community of others with whom they might share ideas. One such organization, In Good Company Workplaces, is dedicated to providing women entrepreneurs with a positive and professional space to work alongside other female entrepreneurs (Alboher, 2008). Rather than seeing modern offices as disparate working environments in a networked world, networking is re-imagined as physical—being near other similarly focused individuals and groups. For some, this arrangement combines the idea of a traditional office with the contemporary notion that workers' physical location is of minor importance.

Most of us have had experiences interacting through telemediated business processes—perhaps having had an evening meal interrupted by a telemarketer attempting to sell us insurance, vacation packages, financial services, or any other number of goods or services. The telemarketer may be calling from a location thousands of miles away from your Canadian home—even from as far away as India! He or she will have been trained to develop a Canadian "accent" and will rely on a script to deliver his or her sales pitch. Similarly, when you call for hotel reservations, the reservations clerk may be half a world away from the hotel of your choosing and therefore may not be able to answer your questions about the weather at the hotel location or the distance from the hotel to a particular landmark.

Professor Ursula Huws has studied the revolution in microtechnology and the ways in which it has transformed work. Huws (2003) notes that in industrialized countries, information technology (IT) has affected skills and the division of labour, and has also sometimes removed work from a central location to remote areas, including workers' homes—a process known as telework. Huws has studied

To meet the goal of production efficiency, under lean production most workers are replaced by machinery. Even in very large production facilities, there are few workers on the shop floor.

Postindustr
of the Infor

In 1973, sociol
type of society v
society. He ide
(1) a service se

offshoring or outsourcing and argues that IT has enabled information processing work to be relocated across the globe, thereby creating an "internationalization of the division of labour in white collar work." Even fast-food restaurants may engage in outsourcing. In an effort to reduce waiting times at their drive-throughs, McDonald's has been testing the use of remote call centres in the United States to process orders. Your order from a drive-through off the Interstate in Missouri may be taken by a call centre worker in Colorado Springs, more than 1450 kilometres from your car. With lightning speed, your order will be sent by high-efficiency data lines to the McDonald's outlet where you are making your purchase (Fitzgerald, 2004). Centralizing order taking in this manner is expected to keep the individual outlet's workers focused on the already Taylorized, subdivided, and scripted work process within the restaurant. Moreover, this is another step toward complete standardization of the service and product, allowing for minimal variation from one location to the next.

Lean Production and Corporate Efficiency

How were the Japanese able to arise from the defeat of World War II, including the nuclear destruction of two of their main cities, to become a giant in today's global economy? Some analysts trace part of the answer to the way their major corporations are organized. One of the Japanese production techniques contributing to organizational efficiency is **lean production**. Unlike Fordist production, which relies on enormous inventories of parts and massive warehouse spaces, lean production employs a **just-in-time (JIT)**

strategy. Under this system, parts inventories are limited to the amount needed at the time, reducing the demand for huge parts warehouses and large work stations. Work is flexible. Workers easily rotate through various jobs and share job classifications. Overall, there are fewer problems with faulty assemblies and poor-quality production (Rinehart, 2006).

Central to the process of lean production is work standardization. The Japanese model incorporates the practice of **kaizen**, which means continuous improvement. Under kaizen, production techniques are constantly evaluated in search of more efficient and improved methods. While workers are involved in discussions around these improvements, ultimately the goal of *kaizen* and lean production is to reduce the labour force, minimizing inefficiency. Lean production is particularly pertinent in the auto industry, and the success of Toyota has attracted the attention of the North American automakers. In Canada, the CAMI plant in Ingersoll, Ontario, a General Motors facility, is organized according to lean production techniques. Despite the reputation of lean production strategies for minimizing labour disputes, workers at the CAMI plant have engaged in strikes and protests after realizing that work rotation and continuous improvement in practice eliminated jobs and intensified their work (Rinehart, 2006).

Although there are many facets to the Japanese organizational model in addition to lean production and *kaizen*, another interesting aspect is the commitment to lifetime security. Once hired, employees can expect to work for the same firm for the rest of their lives. Similarly, the firm expects them to be loyal to the company, to stick with it through good times and bad. On one hand, employees will not be laid off or fired; on the other, they do not go job

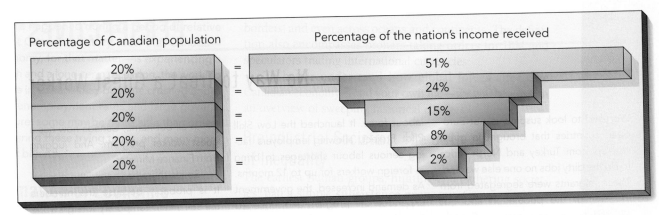

Percentage of Canadian population

20%	=
20%	=
20%	=
20%	=
20%	=

Percentage of the nation's income received

| 51% |
| 24% |
| 15% |
| 8% |
| 2% |

FIGURE 11.1 The Inverted Income Pyramid: The Proportion of Income Received by the Top 20 Percent, the Middle 60 Percent, and the Bottom 20 Percent (1976–2007)

Source: HRSDC calculations based on Statistics Canada. Adjusted and unadjusted market, total, and after-tax income by economic family type and adjusted after-tax income quintiles, 2007 constant dollars, annual (CANSIM TABLE 202-0706). Ottawa: Statistics Canada, 2009.

The consequences of this explosion are unevenly distributed. Most of us will become as comfortable with the new society as our predecessors were with theirs, but not everyone will find a comfortable niche in the global village.

Focus Question
What are the differences between preindustrial, industrial, and postindustrial societies?

Where are the Careers in a Postindustrial Society?

Two main locations for jobs in a postindustrial society are the public sector—which, in Canada, includes the three levels of government: federal, provincial, and municipal—and the private sector, consisting of businesses run for private profit. The latter group includes companies with only one entrepreneur as well as those employing thousands of workers that have a global reach. A third location also deserves mention; it has been identified as a growing segment of the economy (Evers, 2004; Bell, 1976). This not-for-profit, voluntary sector includes organizations such as the March of Dimes and credit unions.

Social Inequality in Canada

In preceding chapters, we examined inequalities—from inequalities generated by globalization to inequalities of social class, gender, race, and age in Canada. There is little to add to that extensive presentation, but an overall snapshot of how income is distributed in Canada may be useful.

Consider the inverted pyramid shown in Figure 11.1. The proportion of the nation's income going to the wealthiest fifth of the Canadian population is at the top; the middle 60 percent is followed by the proportion going to the poorest fifth, at the bottom. Over the 30-year span covered by the three figures, you can see that a small increase in the

middle and bottom quintile occurred from 1976 to 1981, which came at the expense of the top 20 percent. However, in recent years, the squeeze has been put to the middle and bottom 20 percent in order for the top 20 percent's share to increase.

Recent data (presented in Table 11.1) convey an even more dramatic story. Between 1970 and 2007, the top 1 percent of Canada's income earners reported a dramatic increase in their share of total income, from 8.1 percent in 1980 to 13.3 percent in 2007. Rather than ushering in equality, the postindustrial society has perpetuated the income inequalities of the industrial society.

While the percentage of income going to each segment of the population in Canada resembles the skewed distribution in the United States, the inequalities between the richest and poorest Canadians are due to two main factors: a widening disparity in labour earnings between high and low paid workers and less redistribution; that is "taxes and benefits reduce inequality LESS in Canada than in most OECD countries" (OECD, 2011a).

YOUNG CANADIANS ARE POORER In an article in *MoneySense* magazine entitled "Poorer than Ever," author Sarah Efron (2010), referring to Roger Sauvé's research of Statistics Canada data, writes that the incomes of Canadians aged 25 to 34 have not increased for over three decades! In fact, the incomes for this cohort have actually dropped by 2 percent. She contends that when young men and women finally have enough education to get a job, those jobs aren't

✶ Explore "Types of Societies in Today's World" on MySocLab.

◉ Watch "Diminishing Opportunity" to view how job opportunities changed in different types of societies on MySocLab.

argum
prospe
and th
serious
and th
the wei
ment d
to hold
will slip

The T
Syste

The typ
opening
stagnant
the mid
box "Ca
on page
Toda
distribut
radically
The term
touch yo
from loca
somethin
definition
imperson
which we
services,
exchange
City, and
the mover

TABLE 11.1 Top 1 Percent: Share of Total Income

	1970	1980	1990	2000	2007
Canada	9.2	9%	8.1	12.4	13.3%
United States	7.8	8.2	13%	16.4%	18.3%
United Kingdom	7.1	—	9.8	12.7	14.3 (2005)
Japan	8.2%	7.2	8.1	8.2	9.2 (2005)
France	8.2	8.8%	7.8	8.3	8.9 (2006)

Dan Glenday. Derived from Table 9.1 Share of top 1 percent in selected years, OECD: Divided We Stand, 2011a:349 (www.keepeek.com/Digital-Asset-Management/oecd/social-issues-migration-health/the-causes-of-growing-inequalities-in-oecd-countries_9789264119536-en).

easy to come by. Canada's youth unemployment rate is 14.9 percent, much higher than the overall rate of 8 percent. Often the jobs that are available to recent graduates are contract or temporary positions, a situation that can persist even as people move into their thirties and beyond.

World Economic Systems

Now that we have outlined the main economic changes in history, let's compare capitalism and socialism.

Capitalism

If we distill the businesses of Canada into their basic components, we can see that **capitalism** has three essential features: (1) **private ownership of the means of production** (individuals own the capital, land, machines, and factories and decide what shall be produced); (2) the pursuit of profit (selling something for more than it costs); and (3) **market competition** (an exchange of items between willing buyers and sellers).

WELFARE (OR STATE) CAPITALISM VERSUS LAISSEZ-FAIRE CAPITALISM Pure capitalism, known as **laissez-faire capitalism** (loosely, "leave alone"), means that **market forces** operate without interference from the government. Such is not the case in Canada or the United States, where many restraints to the laissez-faire model are in force. The current form of Canadian capitalism is **welfare or state capitalism** and is made-up of three sectors: the public, private, and voluntary or not-for profit organizations.

Consider a few Canadian examples. Crown corporations are companies owned by the provincial or federal government but managed at "arm's length" (see Table 11.2). Crown corporations have a long standing existence in Canada and have been instrumental in the formation of the federal state. They are involved in everything from the distribution, use, and price of certain goods and services to energy development, resource extraction, public transportation, cultural promotion, and property management. The largest federal Crown corporation is Canada Post, which

reported a profit every year for the past 13 years and in 2006 earned $119 million, with over 72 000 full- and part-time employees.

Before the provincial government passed legislation that split it into separate entities, the largest provincial Crown corporation in Canada was Ontario Hydro, with 1998 profits of almost $2 billion and 26 000 persons on the payroll. The largest provincial Crown corporation today is Hydro-Québec, with a 2006 profit of more than $2.8 billion and a full-time workforce numbering over 19 500.

Why does the development of capitalism require continuous government intervention? Suppose you have discovered what you think is a miracle tonic: it will grow hair, erase wrinkles, and dissolve excess fat. If your product works, you will become an overnight sensation—not only a millionaire, but also the toast of television talk shows.

TABLE 11.2 Federal and Provincial Crown Corporations

Crown Corporation	Net Income (2010)	Employment (2010)
BC Hydro and Power Authority	$477 million	5842
LCBO	$2.3 billion	3500 (full-time) 3900 (part time)
Hydro Quebec	$2.52 billion	23 092
Canada Post	$439 million	57 000 (full-time and part-time) 12 000 (full time and part-time Canada Post subsidiaries)

Source: Canada Post, 2010. Annual Report; BC Hydro Annual Report, 2011; LCBO www.lcbo.com/aboutlcbo/media_centre/faq.shtml; Hydro Québec, Financial Profile, 2010–2011.

✳ **Explore** the reading "The End of Welfare as We Know It" on **MySocLab.**

Canada's state capitalism at work: pictured here is one of the "convenience store" postal outlets of Canada Post. Canada Post is the largest Canadian federal Crown corporation, with reported earnings of $119 million in 2006 and a staff of over 72 000 full- and part-time employees.

Before you count your money, you must reckon with **market restraints**, the laws and regulations of welfare capitalism that limit your capacity to sell what you produce. First, you must comply with municipal, provincial, and federal rules. You are required to register your company's name with a provincial registry—or, better yet, obtain a charter of incorporation from the province, a business license from your municipality if you are operating a retail store or outlet, and a GST number from the federal government that allows you to make untaxed purchases.

Second, you cannot simply take your item to local stores and ask them to sell it; you must first seek approval from federal agencies that monitor compliance with the *Food and Drug Act* (FDA). In addition, the *Hazardous Products Act* forbids the advertising, sale, or import of unsafe products that might be an ingredient in your "miracle" cure or the cure itself. This means you must prove that your product will not cause harm to the public. Moreover, you must be able to substantiate your claims—or face being shut down by provincial and federal agencies that monitor the market for fraud.

Suppose you succeed in overcoming these obstacles, your business starts to prosper, and you begin hiring. Other provincial and federal agencies will monitor your compliance with regulations concerning employment. For example, if your employees are not unionized, you must comply with the provincial *Employment Standards Act*. If they become unionized, relations with your employees will fall under the *Labour Relations Act* of your province. Provincial and federal human rights statutes cover discrimination in the workplace on the basis of sex, race, ethnicity, and—at the federal level and in almost every province—sexual orientation. Income tax, employment insurance, and CPP contributions are handled by the federal government, and on occasion the

Supreme Court of Canada has adjudicated issues dealing with unionized workplaces (see Glenday, 1997).

Focus Question
What makes Canada a welfare capitalist society?

IN SUM

As currently practised, capitalism is far from the classical laissez-faire model. Canada's economic system encourages the first two components of capitalism: private ownership of the means of production and the pursuit of profit. A vast system of government regulations both protects and restricts the third, market competition.

Socialism/Communism

Socialism also has three essential components: (1) public ownership of the means of production; (2) central planning; and (3) the distribution of goods without a profit motive.

In the few socialist/communist economies that remain in the world (China, North Korea, and Cuba), the governments own the means of production—not only factories, but also land, railroads, oil wells, and gold mines. In a socialist economy, *everyone* in the economic chain works for the government. By narrowing the huge pay gaps that characterize capitalist nations, socialist nations are able to establish considerably greater equality of income.

DEMOCRATIC SOCIALISM Dissatisfied with the greed and exploitation of capitalism and the lack of freedom and individuality of socialism, most European Union nations developed **democratic socialism**, or welfare socialism. The New Democratic Party represents democratic socialism in

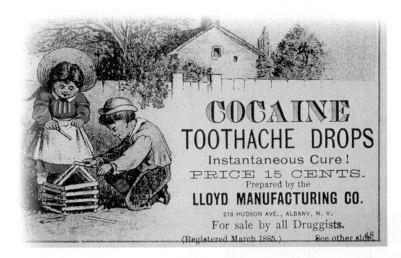

This advertisement from 1885 represents an earlier stage of capitalism. Today, the production and marketing of goods take place under detailed, complicated government regulations.

Canada. In this form of socialism, both the state and individuals engage in production and distribution for profit (see the discussion of Canada's Crown corporations on pages 243–244).

Criticisms of Capitalism and Socialism

The primary criticism levelled against capitalism is that it leads to social inequality. Capitalism, according to critics, produces a tiny top layer comprised of wealthy, powerful people who exploit a vast bottom layer of poorly paid workers, many of whom are underemployed (**underemployment** is having to work at a job beneath one's training and abilities or being able to find only part-time work). Another major criticism is that the tiny top layer wields vast political power. To further their own wealth, the few who own the means of production and reap huge profits are able to get legislation passed that goes against the public good.

The primary criticism levelled against socialism is that it does not respect individual rights (Berger, 1991). In the case of China, the government even controls how many children families may have (Mosher, 1983). Critics also argue that central planning is grossly inefficient (Kennedy, 1993) and that socialism is not capable of producing sufficient quantities of consumer goods.

Changes in Capitalism and Socialism

CHANGES IN CAPITALISM Over the years, Canada has adopted several public policy practices, such as universal health care and accessible, free education, into which the federal and provincial governments redistribute tax dollars to pay for benefits given to all Canadians, no matter where they live in the country. Besides health care and education, Canadians have access to Employment Insurance (formerly Unemployment Insurance, established in 1940), welfare, the Canada Pension Plan (1966), and Old Age Security (1952).

CHANGES IN SOCIALISM In 1989, the Soviet Union, which headed a bloc of Eastern European nations (East Germany,

Czechoslovakia, and Hungary, among others), concluded that its system of central planning had failed. Suffering from shoddy goods and plagued by shortages, the former Soviet Union began to reinstate market forces.

China, the second major socialist power, watched in dismay as its one-time ally abandoned the basic principles of socialism (Szelenyi, 1987). In 1989, at the cost of many lives and despite world opposition, Chinese authorities put down a hunger strike by students and workers in Tiananmen Square who were demanding greater freedom and economic reforms. Despite its repressive measure, however, China began to endorse capitalism. Its leaders solicited Western investment and encouraged farmers to cultivate their own plots on communal farms. They allowed the use of credit cards, approved a stock market, and even permitted pieces of the Great Wall to be sold as souvenirs for profit (McGregor, 1992). While still officially proclaiming Marxist-Leninist-Maoist principles, China's admission into the World Trade Organization in 2001 is an example of its integration into the world economy. Since its adoption of the "Four Modernizations" a generation ago (agriculture, industry, science and technology, and defence), China's share of world economic output grew from 3.4 percent to almost 12 percent in 2000. China's economic transformation has helped to create a large middle class in the main urban areas of Shanghai (12.8 million people) and Beijing. However, more than 60 percent of the population still works in agriculture; the country's "economic miracle" has yet to make an appearance in much of the country (CBC, 2006).

Neoliberalism and Social Conservatism

As a capitalist business and political ideology, neoliberalism is not the same as classical market liberalism, even though they share a belief in the centrality of private property, inheritance, and the pursuit of profit. Market liberalism or classical liberalism has origins in the Enlightenment ideas of human rights or individual rights to life, liberty, and the pursuit of property. According to classical liberalism, the state should protect these rights.

Cultural Diversity around the World: The New Capitalism, Cars, and Social Status in China

Cars are status symbols in every country in the world, whether it is a plutocrat's Rolls Royce or a government leader's armoured Mercedes. No more so than in China, where the famed Flying Pigeon bicycle once ruled roads now crowded with plebeian Toyotas and high-status Audis, Buicks, and Hummers.

The Chinese, especially residents of Beijing, are very aware of the automotive pecking order and that's why Canadian Ambassador David Mulroney's post on the Chinese-language microblog site Weibo caused such a stir. Mulroney posted photos of his official car, a Toyota Camry Hybrid. Canadian officials have only modest budgets for transportation, he explained. Even federal cabinet ministers can spend only $32 400 for an official car.

The Globe and Mail reported Mulroney's post got more than 1100 responses and sparked a debate over the rides of the China's governing elite. "A vice-minister in Beijing drives the Audi A6, which costs over 500 000 yuan (about $80 000), and they also have a full-time driver," one person posted, according to the Globe. "A local township official might drive a Benz." "Ambassador Ma," wrote another

Weibo user, addressing Mulroney by his Chinese name, Ma Dawei, "A Chinese mid-level cadre wouldn't lay an eye on your car!"

Man and son ride a bicycle past an Audi car in Shanghai. Photo by James D. Schwartz, The Urban Country (www.theurbancountry.com/2011/09/bicycle-as-status-symbol.html).

Globe Beijing correspondent Mark MacKinnon said a local cab driver he uses regularly helped him figure out who drives what. Toyotas are favoured by ordinary (fairly prosperous) people, while black Mercedes SUVs are invariably carrying laoban—"bosses" from China's burgeoning private sector. Audi A6 sedans are recognized as rides for senior officials, while Hummers and other high-end luxury vehicles are driven by the privileged offspring of the rich and powerful, MacKinnon's cabbie advised.

Chinese have seized on Mulroney's post as a hook to discuss the whole issue of their leaders' vehicular perks. In an interview with the English-language Global Times, which the Globe says is affiliated with the ruling Communist Party, Mulroney explained that in Canada, only ministers or deputy-minister-level bureaucrats get government vehicles. "Many web users (responding to Mulroney's Weibo post) approved of the Canadian government's rules on official car use, saying it is better than China, where a village official can use an Audi or a Bentley," the Times observed. The Times reported there were 62 026 government vehicles in Beijing in 2010 but noted a program on the state-run CCTV network put the figure at closer to 700 000.

"Government vehicle issue in China is a mess, and our government is the most unwilling in the world to talk about it," Ye Qing, a National People's Congress deputy who's studied the issue, told the Times. "I really appreciate the ambassador's attitude and their government's transparency."

Source: Steve Mertl. Daily Brew, January 31, 2012 (http://ca.news.yahoo.com/blogs/dailybrew/canada-beijing-ambassador-posts-modest-official-toyota-sparking-215253135.html.

Neoliberalism refers to expansion of the free market in time and space: nothing less than a 24-hour global economy will satisfy neoliberals. This type of economy is made possible by the rapid growth of global information and telecommunications technologies.

SOCIAL CONSERVATISM In the developed world, including Canada and the United States, social conservatism, a set of beliefs often linked to the economic changes associated with neoliberalism, has been on the rise for the past thirty years or so. **Social conservatism** is a value system

characterized by the belief in conventional morality and social mores and a desire to preserve them, often aggressively, through civil law and regulation. For Protestants or Roman Catholics, for example, social conservativism means politically supporting the legal definition of marriage as a union only between a man and woman. Another example is abortion, as social conservatives believe it is their right to use the government to enact laws that make abortion illegal. In contrast, more traditional conservatives in Canada, the United States, and elsewhere, who embrace similar beliefs about family, church, and public morality, are suspicious, even intolerant, of government intervention in the private lives of a nation's citizens. More discussion of neoliberalism and social conservativism can be found in Chapter 6.

IN SUM

At this point in history, we must note that there is no pure capitalism (and likely never was). Today, capitalism speaks in a variety of accents, some softer than others, with versions in China, the former Soviet Union, Great Britain, Japan, Germany, Sweden, Canada, and the United States each differing from the others.

Applying Sociological Theories

The Symbolic Interactionist Perspective

PROFESSION OR JOB? WORK AS A STATUS SYMBOL We know that selling hamburgers from a drive-through window is not a profession, but why isn't selling shoes? Sociologists who adopt a symbolic interactionist perspective on work identify five characteristics of **professions** (Parsons, 1954; W.J. Goode, 1960; Greenwood, 1962; Etzioni, 1969).

1. *Rigorous education.* Today, the professions require not only a university degree but also completion of graduate school, followed by an examination that determines whether you will be allowed to practise in the field.
2. *Theory.* Education is theoretical, not just "hands-on." For example, in medicine, microbes, viruses, and genetics are used to explain disease, while in sociology, social structure and social interaction are used to explain human behaviour.
3. *Self-regulation.* Members of a profession claim that only they possess sufficient knowledge to determine the profession's standards and to certify those qualified to be admitted. A group's members also determine who shall be decertified as a result of incompetence or moral problems.
4. *Authority over clients.* Members of a profession claim authority over clients on the basis of their specialized education and theoretical understanding. Unlike carpentry, in which any of us can see that a nail is bent, members of a profession claim that related matters are complex and therefore entreat the client to follow their exclusive instructions.
5. *Professional culture.* Public good, or service to society, not self-interest, lies at the heart of a professional culture. The professions claim that they exist "to provide service to whomever requests it, irrespective of the requesting client's age, income, kinship, politics, race, religion, sex, [sexual orientation,] and social status" (Greenwood, 1962; Hall, 1994).

Today, we expect the basic motivation of a physician to be not unlike that of a businessperson or automobile

TABLE 11.3 The Education–Job Market Connection

Level of Education (25–65 years old)	Change in Number of People Employed, 1990–2001
Grade 8 or less	285 000
Some high school	560 000
High school graduate	198 000
Some postsecondary	32 800
Postsecondary certificate	+834 000
University degree (bachelor's)	+1 110 300
Above bachelor's degree	+172 600
Total	+1 041 100

Source: Statistics Canada, March 2002b, Labour Force Historical Review 2001 (revised edition). Catalogue no. 71F0004XCB.

mechanic—that is, making money. However, educational credentials, membership in professional associations, and the professional culture of physicians distinguish their work from that of automobile mechanics and businessmen.

As shown in Table 11.3, there has been a significant gain in employment among the better educated, and a net loss of jobs among the less educated in Canada in the past decade. This trend is indicative of the increase in status of the many new professional careers created as a result of the information explosion, something we have discussed and that will continue to be a point of interest later in this chapter and in subsequent chapters.

The Functionalist Perspective

Work is functional for society. It is because people work that we have electricity, hospitals, schools, automobiles, and homes. Beyond this obvious point, however, lies a basic sociological principle: *work binds us together.* Let's review Durkheim's principles of mechanical and organic solidarity.

MECHANICAL SOLIDARITY In preindustrial societies, people do similar work, directly share most aspects of life, and look at the world in similar ways. Durkheim used the term **mechanical solidarity** to refer to the sense of unity that arises from performing similar activities.

ORGANIC SOLIDARITY As societies industrialize, a division of labour develops, and people work in different occupations. Functioning as an organism, each is part of the same economic system, and the welfare of each depends on the others. Durkheim called this economic interdependence **organic solidarity**.

THE GLOBAL DIVISION OF WORK Organic solidarity has expanded far beyond anything Durkheim envisioned.

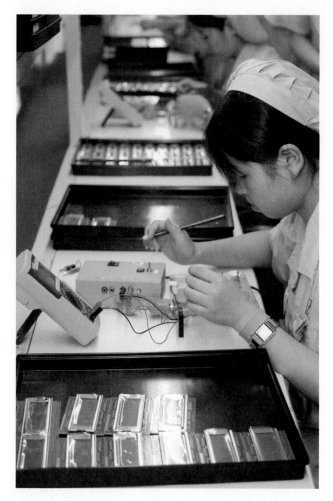

In their march toward globalization, multinational companies locate their corporate headquarters in one country, manufacture components in another, assemble them in still another, and sell the finished product throughout the world. This factory in Guangzhou, China, fills orders from North American corporations.

People who live in Vancouver or Calgary—or even St. John's, Newfoundland—depend on workers in Tokyo to produce cars. Tokyo workers, in turn, depend on Saudi Arabian workers for oil, South American workers to operate ships, and South African workers for palladium for their catalytic converters. Although we do not feel unity with one another—in fact, we sometimes feel threatened and hostile—interdependence links us all in the same economic web.

Driving this interdependence is the dominance of capitalism. As capitalism globalizes, the world's nations are being divided into three primary trading blocs: North and South America, dominated by the United States; Europe, dominated by Germany; and Asia, dominated by Japan. Multinational corporate giants, benefiting from the new world structure, promote free trade. If free trade is put into practice worldwide, its functions will include greater competition over scarce resources on a global scale. Another

dysfunctional consequence—already felt by millions of U.S., U.K., French, and German workers—is the vast loss of production jobs in the most industrialized nations.

The Conflict Perspective

Central to conflict theory is an emphasis on the benefit of the wealthy at the expense of workers. Conflict theorists also focus on the impact of technology and the economic and political power of capitalism's inner circle.

TECHNOLOGY: WHO BENEFITS? Conflict theorists suggest that the jobs destroyed by new technologies are not located at the top levels of the multinationals, nor are they held by the wealthy individuals who own large blocks of stock. For the power elite, by lowering production costs, new technologies increase profits and fatten their dividend cheques. The people who bear the brunt of the change are low-level workers, who suffer the ravages of uncertainty, the devastation of job loss, and, often, the wrenching adjustments that come with being forced into lower-paying jobs.

THE INNER CIRCLE OF POWER Multinational corporations are headed by a group that Michael Useem (1984) calls the *inner circle*. Members of the inner circle consult with high-level politicians, promote legislation favourable to big business, and serve as trustees for foundations and universities. They also endorse political candidates who stand firmly for the private ownership of property. On a global level, they fiercely promote the ideology of capitalism and move capital from one nation—or region—to another in their relentless search for greater and more immediate profits.

As stressed in previous chapters, conflict theorists focus on power. Although multinational corporations enshroud much of their activities in secrecy, on occasion their subterranean abuse of power comes to light. One of the most notable examples occurred in 1973, when a U.S. multinational, the International Telephone & Telegraph Company (ITT), joined the CIA in a plot to unseat Chile's elected government. They first attempted to bring about the economic collapse of Chile. When this failed, they plotted a coup d'état, which resulted in the assassination of the Chilean president, Salvador Allende (Coleman, 1995).

Feminist Perspectives

As discussed in Chapter 1, there are a range of feminist theories that tackle the various issues facing women in the world today. In some respects, these theories correspond to the distinctive stages or "waves" of feminism. "First-wave" feminists were primarily concerned with the political right to vote and were known as "suffragists." In Canada and the United States, women were granted the vote after World War I. In France, Charles de Gaulle enfranchised women after World War II for their courage and determination in

👁 **Watch** the video "Money and Power" on **MySocLab.**

the underground fight against the Nazis and the collaborationist Vichy government. In some Muslim countries, women still cannot vote, leave the house without their husband's permission, drive cars, or appear in public unveiled.

Rights concerned with property ownership, earning a living, and achieving higher education—many of which were granted at the end of the nineteenth century—contributed to increasing women's economic independence in twentieth-century Canada and the United States.

Second-wave feminism is believed to have begun with the publication of Simone de Beauvoir's *The Second Sex* in France in 1949. She argued that men were the first sex because they dominated the economic realm and set the standards and values women were to follow. De Beauvoir insisted that this inequality was not the result of biological differences but was a *social creation*. It wasn't until the 1960s, however, that second-wave feminism took hold and the struggle for equality in the workplace gained momentum. Equal pay for equal work and employment equity (in Canada) or Affirmative Action (in the United States) became the rallying cry of women for several decades. While many have made advances in the world of work and entrepreneurship, job ghettoes and glass ceilings remain in force. **Job ghettoes** (also called **pink ghettoes**) are those employment areas where women dominate, such as nursing, elementary school teaching, child care, and so on. **Glass ceiling** refers to the barriers to social advancement that many women face in the work world.

Third-wave feminism concentrates on sex, sexuality, and gender and offers very little to our understanding of inequality in the workplace. Today, the feminist view of what makes women and men unequal is less unified than it was with first-wave feminism, in large part because of a new focus on the complexity of gender inequality.

Focus Question

What are the differences between the symbolic interactionist, functionalist, conflict, and feminist perspectives on work?

Work In Canadian Society

We will now turn our focus to work in Canadian society. To understand the present situation, we must review the large-scale changes that have taken place in what are called economic sectors.

Three Economic Sectors

Sociologists divide economic life into three sectors: primary, secondary, and tertiary. In the **primary sector**, workers extract natural resources from the environment. Canadians who fish for a living or mine copper and gold in northern Ontario and Quebec work in the primary sector. So do hunters, cattle raisers, farmers, and lumberjacks. In the **secondary sector**, workers turn raw materials into manufactured goods. They package fish, process copper into electrical

wire, and turn trees into lumber and paper. The secondary sector dominates industrial economies.

The main focus of the **tertiary sector** is providing services. Some workers, such as computer technicians and automobile mechanics, install or service products. Others, such as private detectives and cab drivers, provide personal services. Although most of the labour force in postindustrial societies works in the tertiary sector, all three sectors exist side by side. Consider the common lead pencil. People who extract lead and cut timber work in the primary sector; those who turn wood and lead into pencils are employed in the secondary sector; and those who advertise and sell pencils work in the tertiary sector.

Farming provides a remarkable example of the change in sector employment in Canada (Drucker, 1987, 1994). Table 11.4 shows the dramatic decline in employment in farming (the primary sector) since World War II in Canada, from a high of almost 20 percent in 1951 to its present low of 0.8 percent. There has been a similar trend in the other primary sectors (forestry, mining, oil, and natural gas) of the Canadian economy. Manufacturing (the secondary sector) also shows a decline in employment from two in seven workers in 1951 to only one in seven today. In both cases, the declines arose because technological changes in the way food is grown and goods are produced dramatically increased crop yields and manufacturing output. For example, while the production of steel in Canada increased threefold to almost 14.5 million tonnes a year since 1960, the number of people employed fell from 36 500 to 27 200 in 2002 (*Maclean's*, January 23, 2003: 32).

Although a postindustrial society requires fewer people to produce food or basic materials and fewer people to process them, the information explosion demands that large numbers of people work in the tertiary sector. Consequently, we have experienced a surge in "knowledge and information work"—managing information and designing, servicing, and marketing products—that requires higher levels of education, as illustrated in Table 11.4. However, as we become more reliant on the export of our natural resources such as oil and gas, some of the highest paying jobs in the Canadian economy are among those found in these and related industries. This development can be referred to as the Double Bubble effect: a group of careers in the knowledge-based segment of the economy and a second group in the natural resource, utilities, and construction sectors. Each group requires a different skill set and contains high and low paying portions. Examples in the knowledge-based industries include executive coaching, medical researchers and specialists, university professors, personal support workers, and administrative assistants, while the second group

✱ Explore the reading "When Work Disappears" to see how certain jobs disappeared from inner-city neighbourhoods in the United States on **MySocLab**.

✱ Explore the World's Labour Force by Sector and World Bank Stratum on **MySocLab**.

TABLE 11.4 Employment by Industry, 1951–2011 (percentage of total employed), and Average Weekly Full-Time Earnings, August 2008–2010

Industry**	1951	1981	2011	Avg. weekly wage Aug 2010	Avg. weekly wage Aug 2008
Agriculture	18.4%	4.3%	< 1%		
Manufacturing	26.5%	19.5%	10%		
Construction	6.8%	6.3%	7.3%		
Forestry, mining, oil and gas	4.4%	3.0%	2%		
Services	56–57%		78.1%		
Average salaries in Canada*					
Forestry, logging				$971	$812
Mining and quarrying, and oil and gas extraction				$1801	$1524
Utilities				$1,516	$1,422
Construction				$1,071	$1,023
Manufacturing				$977	$943
Wholesale Trade				$1,024	$960
Retail Trade				$501	$486
Transportation & warehousing				$900	$873
Information & Cultural industries				$1,100	$992
Finance & Insurance				$1,050	$1,014
Real estate & rental & leasing				$784	$783
Professional, scientific & technical services				$1,170	$1,065
Management of companies & enterprises				$1,105	1,038
Administrative and support				$727	$677
Educational services				$946	$865
Health care and social assistance				$792	$752
Accommodation & food services				$354 ***	$331***

Sources: *www.livingin-canada.com/work-salaries-wages-canada.html; **Statistics Canada, CANSIM, table 282-0008. Last Modified: 2012-01-06; ***Statistics Canada, CANSIM, table 281-0027 and Catalogue no. 72-002-X. Last modified: 2011-03-31.

includes oil riggers, surface diamond drillers, carpenters, pilots, servers, bartenders, and chambermaids.

Table 11.4 shows that between 1951 and 2011, a major transition occurred in Canada. Employment in the services sector grew rapidly and remains the major engine of job growth in the Canadian economy today.

The Double Bubble is one way of looking at the changes in the occupational structure brought about by technological change and globalization. Another way is by spreading out the high and low paying jobs. Examination of Table 11.4 reveals that in addition to high-paying careers, there are significant numbers of low-paying service jobs. For example, the reported

average weekly earnings between 2008 and 2010 of people employed in mining and petroleum, construction, and utilities businesses are considerably higher than the average weekly earnings of those in booming tourist and food services enterprises. This difference is due in large part to two major factors: the increased productivity of technological changes and the highly unionized nature of the higher-paying workforce.

Focus Question

What are the three highest-paying jobs in Canada (by average full-time weekly earnings)?

Women and Work

One of the chief characteristics of the Canadian workforce has been the steady increase in the number of women in paid employment outside the home. In the early 1900s, only one in six women worked in the paid labour force, while today the proportion has narrowed to one in two. As Figure 11.2a illustrates, the ratio of men to women in the labour force by province is roughly similar with but some regional variation. Newfoundland and New Brunswick have the lowest percentage while Alberta, PEI, Saskatchewan, and Manitoba record the highest. Women continue to fall below men in every province; however, the differences are not substantial.

The likelihood of a woman working in the paid labour force depends on several factors. One is marital status. In a recent study by Statistics Canada, families in which the wife reported employment income had higher household incomes than in other family structures. In 1995, less than 5 percent of two-income families had a total income of less than $20 000, while 14 percent had an income of over $100 000. These findings stand in contrast to one-income families, where 21 percent had incomes of less than $20 000 and less than 5 percent reported incomes of at least $100 000 (Statistics Canada, 1998: 12–17).

Researchers have found some major distinctions between women and men in the world of work. For one, women tend to be more concerned than men with maintaining a balance between their work and family lives (Statham, Miller, & Mauksch, 1988; Duffy, Mandell, & Pupo, 1989). For another, men and women generally follow different models for success: men tend to emphasize individualism,

power, and competition, while women are much more likely to stress collaboration, persuasion, and helping (Miller-Loessi, 1992). A primary concern of many women is the extent to which they must adopt the male model of leadership in order to be successful in their careers. Note that these findings reflect tendencies only and many people can and do diverge from them.

THE QUIET REVOLUTION Because the changes it has brought about have been both gradual and profound, sociologists in the United States use the term **quiet revolution** to refer to the growing proportion of women in the labour force. This trend has transformed consumer patterns, relations at work, self-concepts for both men and women, and relationships with husbands and children. One of the most significant aspects of the quiet revolution is the increased proportion of women with preschool children working for wages. In 1981, 47 percent of married women in Canada were employed; by 1997 that proportion had increased to 57 percent. As previously discussed, dual-income families tend to be better off than single-income families, and are increasingly becoming the norm in the Canadian labour force.

Figure 11.2b describes the impact of unemployment by gender by province for 2012. The unemployment rate is roughly similar for both genders in the Prairie provinces. The Atlantic provinces and British Columbia, on the other hand, report men with significantly larger percentages of unemployment than women. The implications of these and other related changes to Canada's families are discussed in Chapter 13.

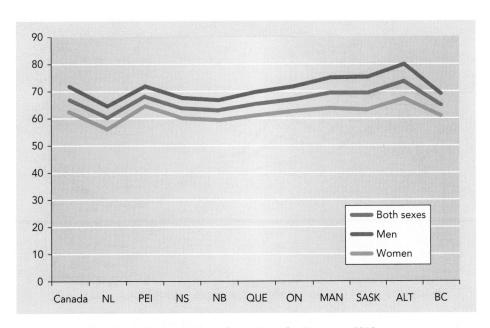

FIGURE 11.2A Percentage of Men and Women in the Labour Force by Province, 2012

Source: Dan Glenday. Statistics Canada, CANSIM, table (for fee) 282-0002.Last modified: 2012-01-06.

Women in Business: Manoeuvring the Male Culture

This box was written by an insurance executive in one of your authors' introductory sociology class. Concerned about retaliation at work, she has chosen to remain anonymous.

I work for a large insurance company. Of its 2500 employees, about 75 percent are women. Only 5 percent of the upper management positions, however, are held by women.

I am one of the more fortunate women, for I hold a position in middle management. I am also a member of the 12-member junior board of directors, of whom nine are men and three are women.

Recently one of the female members of the board suggested that the company become involved in Horizons for Tomorrow, a program designed to provide internships for disadvantaged youth. Two other women and I spent many days developing a proposal for our participation.

The problem was how to sell the proposal to the company president.

From past experiences, we knew that if he saw it as a "woman's project" it would be shelved into the second tier of "maybes." He hates what he calls "aggressive bitches."

We three decided, reluctantly, that the proposal had a chance only if it were presented by a man. We decided that Bill was the logical choice. We also knew that we had to "stroke" Bill if we were going to get his co-operation.

We first asked Bill if he would "show us how to present our proposal." (It is ridiculous to have to play the role of the "less capable female," but, unfortunately, the corporate culture sometimes dictates this strategy.) To clinch matters, we puffed up Bill even more by saying, "You're the logical choice for the next chairmanship of the board."

Bill, of course, came to our next planning session, where we "prepped" him on what to say.

At our meeting with the president, we had Bill give the basic presentation.

We then backed him up, providing the background and rationale for why the president should endorse the project. As we answered the president's questions, we carefully deferred to Bill.

The president's response? "An excellent proposal," he concluded, "an appropriate project for our company."

To be successful, we had to maneuver through the treacherous waters of the "hidden culture" (actually not so "hidden" to women who have been in the company for a while). The proposal was not sufficient on its merits, for the "who" behind a proposal is at least as significant as the proposal itself.

"We shouldn't have to play these games," Laura said, summarizing our feelings.

But we all know that we have no choice. To become labelled "pushy" is to commit "corporate suicide"—and we're no fools.

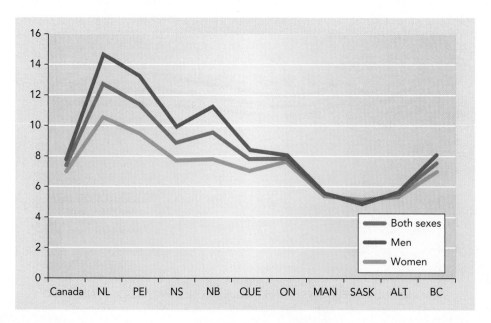

FIGURE 11.2B Percentage of Unemployed Men and Women by Province, 2012

Source: Dan Glenday. Statistics Canada, CANSIM, table (for fee) 282-0002.Last modified: 2012-01-06.

Statistics Canada says the paying out of unreported income is most prevalent in the construction industry.

The Underground Economy

It has a sinister ring—suggestive of dope deals struck in alleys and wads of dollar bills hastily exchanged. The underground economy is this, but is also a lot more. If you pay the plumber with "cash," if you purchase a pair of sunglasses from a street vendor or a kitchen gadget at a yard sale, if you so much as hand a neighbour's kid a $20 bill (or accept one) to mow the lawn or baby sit, you are participating in the underground economy (Pennar & Farrell, 1993).

These day-to-day transactions, which make up the **underground economy**, are difficult to measure, but Statistics Canada estimated their size to be worth nearly $36 billion in 2008, almost double the size in 1992.

Where is the underground economy in Canada? Two-thirds derive from household expenditures. These include private payments to contractors, undisclosed rental income, or tips. Statistics Canada believes that the underground economy is shrinking, in part because of the move to electronic payments and away from cash transactions.

Shrinking Paycheques

The record profits reported by Canada's banks and other corporations give weight to the assumption that the pay of Canadian employees is increasing. According to Statistics Canada, however, both average income and average family income decreased from 1990 until after 1995, when both started to increase again. These averages do not appear to have been affected by the recent global recession. Statistically, the fact that Canadian incomes have increased over the past 10 years gives the impression that all is well with Canadian families. This is far from the truth. The experiences of the two-income middle-class family of four described in the chapter's opening vignette tell a different story of struggle and sacrifice. As shown in Table 11. 4, the average weekly earnings of workers in 2010 appeared high in the Double Bubble sectors of the Canadian economy—that is, knowledge-based companies and the utilities, mining, oil, and natural gas industries. However, even with the sharp rise in the number of working mothers, and the pressure to consume has put a pinch on the average Canadian. Consumers have responded by going increasingly into debt. A 2011 Vanier Institute of the Family report stated that the debt-to-income ratio for Canadian families has steadily increased over the past 20 years, reaching a record high of 150 percent in 2010. For every $1000 of after-tax income, Canadian families owe $1500. This is not a recipe for a financially secure future.

Some workers aren't able to bring home even shrinking paycheques. Imagine making payments on rent, a car, food, and, if you had anything left over, entertainment on the approximately $354 a week provided to employees in the accommodation and food service industries (see Table 11.4). Many young people are forced to work two or more jobs and "bunk up" with others their age or return home to live with their parents. The Perspectives box looks at the declining middle class in Canada's cities as a serious problem faced by many Canadians in today's job market.

Patterns of Work and Leisure

TRENDS IN LEISURE **Leisure** is time not taken up by work or required activities such as eating and sleeping. Consider driving a car. If you do it for pleasure, it is leisure, but if you are an on-duty police officer or commuting to the office, it is work. If done for enjoyment, horseback riding and reading a book are leisure—but these activities are work for jockeys and students.

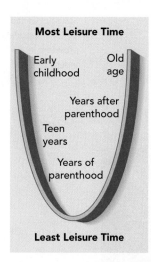

Most Leisure Time

Early childhood — Old age

Years after parenthood

Teen years

Years of parenthood

Least Leisure Time

FIGURE 11.3 Leisure and the Life Course: The "U" Curve of Leisure

TABLE 11.5 Paid Time Off With 10 Years' Tenure

Country	Minimum Paid Vacation Days	Paid Public Holidays	Total
Israel	24	16 (avg.)	40
France**	30	10	40
Greece**	25	12	37
Japan	20	15	35
Germany**	24	10	34
Canada	10	10 (avg.)	20
USA	15* (9)***	10* (6)***	25* (15)***

* These numbers reflect typical practice among *large* U.S. firms. There is no U.S. federal law requiring employers to give a minimum number of vacation days and holidays off, paid or unpaid.

** All members of the European Union must provide workers with a minimum of 20 paid vacation days a year (four weeks), plus public holidays.

*** "No-Vacation Nation," Rebecca Ray & John Schmitt, May 2007, Center for Economic and Policy Research (CEPR) included companies of all sizes.

From: Dan Glenday. Mercer Human Resources Consulting: 2007 reported by Jeanne Sahadi, CNN Money.com senior writer (http://money.cnn.com/2007/06/12/pf/vacation_days_worldwide.

Patterns of leisure change with the life course, as illustrated by the U-curve shown in Figure 11.3. Ideally, young children enjoy the most leisure. However, teenagers are under increasing pressure to get a part-time job that is meant to either boost confidence, encourage saving or, most likely, to be able to buy the latest clothes and electronic gadgets. Parents with small children have the least leisure, but after their children leave home, the possibility for leisure picks up again. After the age of 60 or so, the amount of leisure enjoyed by adults is supposed to peak.

WORK IN THE POSTINDUSTRIAL SOCIETY While some workers today enjoy plenty of leisure time, increasing numbers of Canadian workers are feeling the stress of working more but enjoying life less. Table 11.5 compares the amount of paid vacation in seven countries for employees who have worked for a large organization for 10 years. Canada is at the bottom of the list, with two weeks paid vacation (five plus five working days) and 10 paid public holidays. Israel, the European Union, and Japan provide four to six weeks paid vacations, while Japan and Israel provide 15 and 16 paid public holidays, respectively, to their employees. The United States is the only country that does not mandate federal paid holidays. According to a recent report entitled "No-Vacation Nation," the vacation picture is even more dismal in the United States when companies of all sizes are included in the statistical measure (see figures marked with ***).

For several decades after the Second World War, unionization helped many Canadians increase the amount of time they could spend in leisure activities. Today, the assault on trade unions by businesses and governments makes increasing vacation time for their members a luxury when faced with more pressing issues such as job security.

Shortening the workweek is one way to increase leisure time. In Germany, for example, Volkswagen was the world's first global corporation to adopt a 30-hour workweek (Rifkin, 1995). In addition, German workers work on average 1419 hours per year and take home over six weeks of paid vacation each year (see Table 11.5). Unlike Western Europe, however, the trend in Canada and the United States is the opposite: Canadian workers now average 1702 hours of work a year, with U.S. workers averaging 1778 hours. For Japanese workers, the norm is 1733 hours (statistics on average annual hours of work derived from OECD; StatExtracts, 2012).

The Future: Facing the Consequences of Global Capitalism

A little over a decade and a half ago, a small number of sociologists in Great Britain and France were celebrating the coming "Leisure Revolution" (Sherman, 1985; Jenkins & Sherman, 1981; Gorz, 1982, 1985). We were told then that within our lifetime, the application of new microelectronics-based technology by businesses and governments would steer us into a future where the nature of work and the work ethic would be defined by what we did in our leisure time, be it simple relaxation or starting our own business. True, we would still have to work at something that was not of our own choosing; however, there would be limitations on the length of time we would be exposed to this kind of work.

◉ **Watch** the video "Global Financial Crisis" on **MySocLab.**

Canada Income Inequality: Toronto's Cabbagetown

In 2003, $350 000 bought Toronto resident Steven de Blois and his wife a house in Toronto's colourful Cabbagetown neighbourhood. Eight years and two children later, the couple was looking to buy again. They settled on purchasing another home in the same neighbourhood—this time for just under $1 million.

"I don't enjoy taking on more debt," 36-year-old de Blois says. "You never know what tomorrow holds, but today my money is on Cabbagetown."

For de Blois, a product manager for online and mobile channels married to a real estate agent, those million-dollar figures may not be too daunting when it comes to buying a stately Victorian home. But the numbers reflect a new

reality in Toronto, as well as elsewhere throughout the Western world: the disappearance of the middle class.

Cabbagetown, once an eclectic mix of rich, poor, and everything in between, is losing its middle class, and an ever-larger proportion of its population hails from either the top of the income ladder or the bottom. It's a phenomenon that is repeating across the city of Toronto and around the Western world—the seemingly inevitable result of a growing income gap.

Cabbagetown is one of the clearest examples of shrinking middle-class neighbourhoods in the city. In 2005, median household income in Toronto was $52 833. The median income by private household was $54 654 in Cabbagetown-South St. James Town—nearly the same as the city as a whole.

However, of the 6050 households in the neighbourhood, the largest group of—1325 or 22 percent—had incomes above $100 000. The second-

largest group—830 or 17 percent—had incomes of $10 000 to $19 999. Of these households, slightly more than half made less than the city's median income. These numbers—showing plenty of high-income earners, even more low-income earners, and little in between—suggest that Cabbagetown's middle-class past is far behind it.

"Would I want to live in a more homogeneous area? No, I don't think so," says de Blois. "I'm sure I'd be happy in other parts of the city but this is what is home now." De Blois and others like him have the good fortune of being able to pick and choose where in the city they would like to live. But as Cabbagetown shows, that freedom is becoming a luxury fewer and fewer can afford.

Source: Adapted from Daniela Costa, January 22, 2012. The Huffington Post Canada.

As one of the "Paths to [this] Paradise," André Gorz (1985) spoke of a lifetime work schedule of 20 000 hours. Can you imagine working for only 20 years at a rate of only six hours a day, four days a week, for 42 weeks a year? Imagine starting employment after university with a four-day workweek, two-and-a-half months' paid vacation, and retirement before your forty-fifth birthday!

Clearly, this is not our present-day reality, nor is it likely to become reality in the immediate future. What happened to the transformation of work? Is the idea of a shortened workweek and meaningful jobs an impossible utopia?

The new realities of work deal with the nature of jobs and skills-based change. The transformation of work has witnessed the rise of a knowledge/information/service economy

based on the universal application of microelectronics technology that has created new occupational categories—a rush of change that has left in its wake thousands of lost jobs, leaving most of the remaining positions "retooled."

What does this mean for the future of occupational choice for young Canadians? When governments are divesting themselves of people and assets and large companies are shedding "excess" human resources, what are the prospects for the future? Will there be enough good service jobs created by the private sector in this country? What would it take to rescue the dream of the "Leisure Revolution"?

The Thinking Critically about Social Controversy box that follows focuses on the far-reaching implications of the global transformation of our economy.

THINKING CRITICALLY ABOUT SOCIAL CONTROVERSY

New Technology and the Restructuring of Work: What Type of New Society?

How do you envision the future of work? Maybe you think the future will be a lot like the present, with a few more gadgets, a little more globalization, a smidgen more flexibility, and a bit less job security. Perhaps you imagine that most employees will be skilled, telecommuting, well-paid free agents who work for the highest bidder in a super-flexible, highly connected global network of employers. Or maybe you visualize a more pessimistic world dominated by a winner-take-all toxic capitalism in which a group of super-rich Haves lord it over a majority of Have-Nots who work longer and longer hours for less pay. Possibly, you foresee the day when employment-based work will be replaced by government provided living wages, worker-owned enterprises, and volunteer associations.

These are just a few examples of what may come to pass, and none can be written off as impossible. The future may contain aspects of each (or none) of these visions, or each one may arise in different regions of the world or at different times. Even the best strategists can not be certain.

For Your Consideration
Given the discussion in this chapter about (1) the effects of new technologies on work and (2) the direction of capitalism, which of these futures appears more likely?

Source: Adapted from Canadian Management Centre, Special Report. "The Future of Work 2015." Published September 2005.

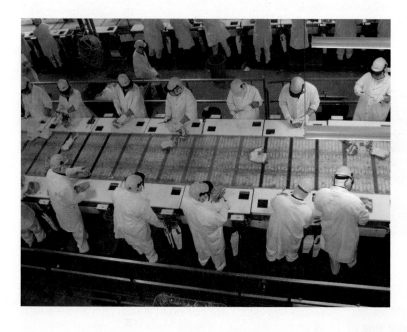

Some 1500 migrant workers are employed by Maple Leaf Consumer Foods in Brandon, Manitoba. They toil on the "disassembly" line, dismembering animals, but as one worker says, it "pays well and has good benefits."

SUMMARY AND REVIEW

APPLYING SOCIOLOGICAL THEORIES

How do four of the major sociological perspectives apply to paid work?
Symbolic interactionists analyze meanings and self-perceptions, asking why work is a job or a profession, what gives work status, and what makes work satisfying. From the *functionalist perspective*, work is a basis of social solidarity. Preindustrial societies foster **mechanical solidarity**, identifying with others who perform similar tasks. With industrialization comes **organic solidarity**, economic interdependence brought about by the division of labour.

Conflict theorists, who focus on worker exploitation and alienation, note how the new technology and global capitalism affect workers and owners. Workers lose jobs to automation, while the inner circle maintains its political power and profits from these changes. *Feminist theories* concentrate on gender inequality and how men dominate the more important good jobs while women can be found in **pink ghettoes**. Those that do enter the mostly male occupations tend to experience **glass ceilings**. p. 247–249.

WORK IN CANADIAN SOCIETY

What are the three economic sectors of the labour force?

In the **primary sector**, workers extract raw materials from the environment. In the **secondary sector**, workers turn raw products into manufactured goods. In the **tertiary sector**, workers produce services. Most Canadians now work in the tertiary, or service, sector. p. 249.

Where are the careers in canada's postindustrial society?

The "Double Bubble" pertains to a group of careers in the knowledge-based segment of the economy and a second group in the natural resource, utilities, and construction sectors. Each group requires a different skill set and contains high and low pay levels. Examples in the knowledge-based industries include executive coaching, medical researchers and specialists, university professors, personal support workers, and administrative assistants;, examples in the second group include oil riggers, surface diamond drillers, carpenters, pilots, servers, bartenders, and chambermaids.pp. 249–250.

What is the underground economy?

The **underground economy** consists of any economic activity not reported to the government, from babysitting to prostitution. The size of the underground economy is likely 15 to 20 percent of the regular economy. p. 253.

How have patterns of work and leisure changed?

Industrialization initially brought a dramatic decrease in **leisure**, but workers have gained some back. Among the industrialized nations, currently only the Japanese work more hours per year than Canadian workers. pp. 253–254.

THE FUTURE: FACING THE CONSEQUENCES OF GLOBAL CAPITALISM

Expanding global trade, new technologies, and downsizing will continue to force a restructuring of work. Choices made now can lead to either a shortened workweek and more leisure time or to high unemployment with increasing numbers of workers needing to be "retooled.". pp. 254–255.

TALKING ABOUT THEORY

Theoretical Paradigms

	CLASSICAL PARADIGMS		RECENT PARADIGMS	
	Structural-Functional Paradigm	Social-Conflict Paradigm	Symbolic-Interaction Paradigm	Feminist Paradigm
What is the level of analysis?	Macro level	Macro level	Micro level	Micro and macro levels
What is the social significance of the economy?	Work binds us together as a society and increasingly as members of a global economy (inclusive = functional).	The economic system maintains the status quo. New technology benefits the few at the expense of the many.	The distinction between working at a job and having a career as a professional.	"Pink ghettoes" and the "glass ceiling" point to the social mechanisms of discrimination in the workplace.
Has the economy changed over time? How?	Yes. Globalization divides the world into three trading blocks.	No. As changing technology provides new opportunities for capital and profit, the wealthy benefit economically.	Yes. New information and communications technologies have created new professions.	Yes/No. Changes in legal prohibitions against sexual harassment and workplace discrimination are significant positive changes. Patriarchy remains.

capitalism 243

conspicuous
    consumption 241

debit card 241

democratic socialism 244

economy 240

glass ceiling 249

job ghettoes 249

laissez-faire capitalism 243

leisure 253

market 240

market competition 243

market forces 243

market restraints 244

mechanical solidarity 247

neoliberalism 246

organic solidarity 247

pink ghettoes 249

primary sector 249

private ownership of the
    means of production 243

professions 247

quiet revolution 252

secondary sector 249

social conservatism 246

socialism 244

subsistence economy 240

tertiary sector 249

underemployment 245

underground economy 253

welfare (state) capitalism 243

All URLs listed are current as of the printing of this text.

Centre for Research on Work and Society (CRWS)
www.yorku.ca/crws
The Centre for Research on Work and Society at York University brings together academic researchers with labour movement partners to engage in research and education on work and labour matters. One of the centre's most recent projects is an electronic journal entitled *Just Labour*. You can reach the *Just Labour* website through the CRWS home page.

Canadian Business
www.canadianbusiness.com
The homepage for Canada's premier business periodical. Each year, it carries the most complete and authoritative list of that year's most successful Canadian companies and business personalities.

World Economic Forum
www.weforum.org
The World Economic Forum is an independent, non-partisan international organization committed to improving the state of the world by engaging leaders in partnerships to shape global, regional, and industry agendas. The World Economic Forum was incorporated as a foundation in 1971 and is based in Geneva, Switzerland.

1. Some sociologists and most public officials believe that microelectronics-based computer technologies hold the promise of a better future for most Canadians. Do you believe this is an accurate assessment?

2. Most students today work while going to university. Describe the ways you would make your workplace a better place to work. Why can't you implement your ideas? Do you think having a trade union in your workplace would matter?

3. Some sociologists believe work is important because it provides all of us with status and meaning. It is not uncommon to hear someone say, "I am a sociologist" or "I am a university student" or "I am a teacher." If work is important for our well-being, why do so many people hate their jobs and look forward to retirement?

4. Access the Research Navigator through MySocLab and use keywords such as "new technology," "work," and "future" to locate relevant and recent scholarly and popular press publications to help you answer these questions.

MySocLab

Explore the topics covered in this chapter on MySocLab. Interactive resources include a study plan, cumulative exams, a multimedia library, MySocLab eReadings, and access to the MySocLab Video Series.

For centuries, widows in the Mediterranean were expected to dress in black. Their long dresses were matched by black stockings, black shoes, and black head coverings. Widows conformed to this socially defined expression of ongoing sorrow not because of law, but because of custom. Today, however, as industrialization erodes traditional authority, few widows follow this practice.

Gandhi is an example of a charismatic leader who led a peaceful revolution.

specific individuals become chief, king, or queen. Queen Elizabeth II is Canada's titular head of government. She wasn't elected queen, she was crowned because of her royal lineage or kinship.

Gender relations in most human groups are a good example of traditional authority, since they are based on custom. In the villages of Spain and Portugal, for example, widows are expected to wear only black until they remarry—which generally means they wear black for the rest of their lives, or risk being ostracized by the community.

Traditional authority is undermined by industrialization, because people are exposed to new experiences. This opens up new perspectives on life and traditional authority no longer goes unchallenged. Thus, in Spain and Portugal, you can still see old women dressed in black from head to toe—and you immediately know their marital status.

Younger widows, however, are likely to be indistinguishable from other women.

Even in postindustrial societies, parental authority provides an excellent example of traditional authority (M. Schwartz, 1990). From generations past, we inherit the idea that parents are responsible for providing their children with food and shelter and also have the right to discipline them, choose their doctors and schools, and teach them religion and morality.

Rational-Legal Authority

Rational-legal authority, the second type of authority identified by Weber, is based on written rules. "Rational" means reasonable, and "legal" means part of law. Matters agreed to may be as broad as a constitution that specifies the rights of all members of a nation or as narrow as a contract between two individuals. Because bureaucracies are based on written rules, rational-legal authority is also called *bureaucratic authority*.

Rational-legal authority comes from the position an individual holds, not from the person who holds the position. In a democracy, for example, the prime minister's authority comes from the office, as specified in a written constitution, not from custom or the individual's personal characteristics. Her/his pronouncements are subject to the law, rather than the law being subject to her/his personal fads and foibles.

Pierre Elliott Trudeau at the 1968 Liberal leadership convention. Trudeau is a good example of someone who combined rational-legal and charismatic authority.

Charismatic Authority

A charismatic individual is someone to whom people are drawn because they believe that person has been touched by God or has been endowed by nature with exceptional qualities (Lipset, 1993). Joan of Arc is an example of someone with **charismatic authority**, the third type of authority identified by Weber. (*Charisma* is a Greek word that describes a gift freely and graciously given [Arndt & Gingrich, 1957].) People followed her because they were drawn to her outstanding traits. They saw her as a messenger of God, fighting on the side of justice, and accepted her leadership as a result of these appealing qualities.

THE THREAT POSED BY CHARISMATIC LEADERS Queen Elizabeth II owes allegiance to tradition, while Prime Minister Harper is bound to written laws. To what do charismatic leaders owe allegiance? Their authority resides in their ability to attract followers, which is often based on their sense of special mission or calling. Not tied to tradition or the rule of law, charismatic leaders pose a threat to the established political system. Accordingly, they can inspire followers to disregard—or even overthrow—traditional and rational-legal authorities.

Authority as Ideal Type

Weber's classifications—traditional, rational-legal, and charismatic—represent ideal types of authority. Any given leader may show a combination of characteristics.

Consider Pierre Elliott Trudeau, who combined rational-legal and charismatic authority. As the elected head of the Canadian government, Trudeau represented rational-legal authority. Yet his mass appeal, especially in English-speaking Canada, was so great that his public speeches could arouse feelings of patriotism and national identity.

On the other hand, for nationalists in Quebec, Trudeau's authority was far from legitimate. Trudeau's policy of bilingualism and biculturalism (later changed to multiculturalism) was portrayed as an exercise in the assimilation of the French majority in Quebec because it did not challenge the entrenched privileges of the anglophone minority in the province. In addition, Quebec francophones' hostility toward Trudeau's actions during both the October Crisis (see page 270) and the air traffic controllers' and airline pilots' strike of 1976 had a significant role in the subsequent election of the nationalistic Parti Québécois (PQ) to power in 1976 (Guindon, 1988, 2001). Trudeau may have had mass appeal in English Canada, but he was far from a hero in his home province of Quebec. Such are the "dangers" of a charismatic leader. Not everyone supports his or her cause, and there are many who will openly oppose it.

Charismatic and traditional authority can also overlap. Mother Teresa, the 1979 winner of the Nobel Peace Prize, is widely recognized as someone who combined both charismatic and traditional authority. Her Society of Missionaries, for example, undertakes relief work for those affected by natural disasters such as floods, famines, and epidemics, and also provides assistance to the very poor in several countries in Asia, Africa, and Latin America. There are also houses in her name that take care of shut-ins, alcoholics, homeless, and AIDS patients in North America, Europe, and Australia (Nobelprize.org, 2012).

The Transfer of Authority

The orderly transfer of authority from one leader to another is critical for social stability. Under traditional authority, people generally know who is next in line. Under rational-legal authority, people may not know who the next leader will be, but they do know how that person will be selected. South Africa provides a remarkable example of the orderly transfer of authority under a rational-legal organization. In spite of being ripped apart by decades of racial strife accompanied by deep suspicions, hatreds, and many murders, South Africa was able to peacefully transfer power from the white minority group led by President de Klerk to the black

Over the years, rights have been extended, and citizenship and its privileges now apply to all Canadians. Property, sex, and ethnicity no longer determine the civil rights of citizens.

Focus Question

Why is the parliamentary system in Canada a form of democracy?

Dictatorships and Oligarchies: The Seizure of Power

A government run by a single person who has seized power is known as a **dictatorship**. If a small group seizes power, the government is called an **oligarchy**. Although one individual may be named president, often a group of high-ranking military officers, working behind the scenes, makes the decisions. If their designated president becomes unco-operative, they remove him from office and designate another.

Monarchies, dictatorships, and oligarchies vary in the amount of control they exert over their people. **Totalitarianism** is almost total control of a people by a government. In Nazi Germany, for example, Hitler kept the populace in tight control through the Gestapo, a ruthless secret police force that looked for any sign of dissent. Control was so thorough that spies even watched moviegoers' reactions to newsreels, reporting those who did not respond "appropriately" (Hippler, 1987). A more recent example is the armed squads in Taliban-ruled Afghanistan that patrolled the streets looking for anyone who transgressed the religious rules of the regime. Women were often the prime targets of these vigilante-style operations. Another incidence of totalitarianism is the deterioration of women's rights in Ayatollah Khomeini's Iran, as described in Azar Nafisi's *Reading Lolita in Tehran* (2004).

The ideas of citizenship and representative democracy are appealing to people around the world. Those who have no say in their government's decisions or who face prison for expressing dissent find hope for a brighter future in these ideas. With today's electronic communications, people no longer remain ignorant of whether they are more or less privileged politically than others. This knowledge produces pressure for greater citizen participation in government. With continued development in communications, this pressure will continue to mount.

The Canadian Political System

The Canadian system of government can be described as a *parliamentary democracy*. Parliament is, constitutionally, the supreme national lawmaking authority for all matters that fall within its jurisdiction. Canada has a federal system of government. This means that some areas of legal jurisdiction or real powers of enforcement are reserved for the federal parliament and other residual powers are distributed

TABLE 12.2 Voter Turnout at Federal Elections

Date of Election	Voter Turnout (%)
May 2, 2011	61.1
October 14, 2008	58.8
January 23, 2006	64.7
June 28, 2004	60.9
November 27, 2000	61.2
June 2, 1997	67
October 23, 1993	69.6
November 21, 1988	75.3%

Source: www.elections.ca/content.aspx?section=ele&dir=turn&document=index&lang=e.

among provincial and municipal governments. Examples of Parliament's powers include interprovincial and international trade, communications, banking and finance, and some criminal matters. However, in Canada, the provinces have evolved a number of separate and significant powers of their own, such as control over natural resources, most labour legislation (approximately 90 percent of trade union members come under provincial jurisdiction), and most criminal matters.

Canada is a democracy, as the people elect their politicians in periodic elections. Since World War II, between 70 and 80 percent of Canadians have participated in the electoral process (see Table 12.2). This contrasts with only 50 to 55 percent of Americans who voted for their president and less than a majority of eligible voters who cast ballots for their representatives to Congress. Since the 1990s, however, a downward trend in voter turnout in Canada may be evidence of a growing cynicism among the electorate toward our political system. Interestingly, we are approaching the U.S. average voter turnout for presidential elections. Can you think of ways to get more Canadians excited about their political system? Recent studies have tackled the thorny issue of low electoral participation by young Canadians (O'Neill, 2003; Gidengil et al., 2005; Milner, 2007). Some point to their limited political knowledge about Canada's political system; others to the lack of trust in whether voting in elections actually influences the political decision-making process. Some propose lowering the voting age from 18 to 16; others suggest using new communications technologies to reach out to young voters. Still other Canadians believe proportional representation, an option that will be discussed in more detail later in the chapter, is a solution.

Canada's form of federal government is unlike a **unitary state**, in which all power resides with the central government. Neither does Canada's parliamentary democracy resemble a **confederal union**, in which provinces have most of the powers and the central government has little authority to enforce national decisions on the "sovereign" provinces.

Canada has evolved a system of government that is somewhere in between the two extremes. Nevertheless, to most Canadians, the year 1867 is commonly known as that of "Confederation." As Garth Stevenson notes, the use of that term to denote our system of government is inaccurate. The Fathers of Confederation desired a unity state. Many citizens in Quebec, New Brunswick, Nova Scotia, and Prince Edward Island, however, were interested in preserving their distinctive cultural and social qualities and meeting the particular economic needs of their provinces. This could only be accomplished if they could retain control over matters that would allow them to preserve their local character and institutions. Therefore, a unitary national state of any kind was out of the question, and a confederal union was appealing to Quebec and the Maritime provinces. Stevenson goes so far as to say that the use of the word "Confederation" to denote our federal system of government was purposely encouraged to "confuse those [such as the people of the Maritimes and Quebec] who might find such a project [a unitary state] alarming" (1987: 9).

What Is the Parliamentary System in Canada?

Constitutionally, there are three major levels of national government in Canada: the Queen, the Senate, and Parliament. However, the Queen has no powers to make laws in Canada, and the Senate, an appointed body, is a minor player in the lawmaking process. Therefore, only Parliament has the ultimate power to make law in Canada.

While Parliament makes the laws, there are limits to what it can do. It cannot make laws in areas reserved exclusively for the provinces. And, since 1982, Parliament's formal powers have been limited by the *Charter of Rights and Freedoms*.

Most Canadians realize that the lion's share of the federal government's policymaking authority comes from the prime minister's office (PMO) and the Cabinet. The power to spend money and introduce tax legislation is limited to the Cabinet, while the prime minister has the exclusive power to open, postpone, and dissolve Parliament. Ultimately, the prime minister wields the real power in Canada's federal government. He or she appoints the Cabinet, whose members become the heads of various federal government departments such as Finance, Human Resources, Transportation, and so on.

In a majority government like the one at the federal level, the role of the opposition parties at the federal and provincial levels is basically informational and adversarial. The opposition parties have no real power to change government policy. During Question Period, they debate the government's policies, suggest alternatives, and try to keep the public informed about issues relating to how the government spends its money. However, in a minority government, the governing party must rely on enough support from the opposition parties to give it a majority number of seats; otherwise, a vote of non-confidence will trigger a new election.

Canadians elected a Liberal minority government in 2004 under Paul Martin. Two short years later, Canadians voted twice for a Conservative minority government under Stephen Harper, on January 23, 2006 and October 14, 2008—a first in Canadian history. On May 2, 2011, Stephen Harper achieved his first majority government. The final number of seats in the House of Commons included 166 Conservatives, 103 NDP, 34 Liberals, 4 Bloc Québécois, and 1 Green Party member.

Table 12.3 provides a chronology of the prime ministers in Canada since Confederation, their political party affiliations, the dates they held office, and the lengths of their tenures as prime minister. (The only woman prime minister in Canada's history has been Kim Campbell, whose short-lived status as the head of government came after Brian Mulroney left the post late in his second term of office.) The fourth column provides a number of significant contributions to Canadian political culture and institutions.

The Evolution of the Political Party System in Canada: From the Two-Party to the Multiple-Party System

John A. Macdonald was Canada's first prime minister (1867–1873). He headed a coalition Conservative government comprised of Ontario Tories and Quebec Liberals, or *Bleus*, as they were called. His first term in office as head of the coalition ended in scandal (the "Pacific Scandal") when it was revealed that he and a number of his colleagues had accepted large sums of money as kickbacks from the promoters of the Canadian Pacific Railway. By 1878, there were two political parties in Canada—the Conservatives and the Liberals.

Canada, in 1867, counted only five provinces. Manitoba was added in 1870, and British Columbia in 1871. Alberta and Saskatchewan did not enter Confederation until 1905. As Canada was still in the process of nation-state building, the two-party system of the Liberals and the Conservatives dominated Canadian politics until well into the twentieth century.

The end of World War I (1914–1918) saw the emergence of a coalition of farmers' organizations based in Alberta and extending to Ontario that became known as the Progressive Movement. It was populist in ideology (i.e., grassroots democracy with regional agricultural-based policies) and had a short life nationally. However, the party continued to dominate western provincial governments until World War II. The end of the Progressive era in Canadian politics came when Manitoba premier John Bracken moved to the federal Conservative party in 1942 on the condition that its name be changed to the Progressive Conservative Party.

The demise of the Progressive movement in the West led to the dramatic election in the 1935 Alberta legislature of another grassroots, populist protest party known as Social Credit. Unlike the Progressive Movement, the Social Credit Party was able to achieve a beachhead in Quebec with its sister party, known as the *Ralliement des Créditistes*, under

TABLE 12.3 Prime Ministers of Canada from Confederation to the Present

Prime Minister	Dates in Office (Tenure)	Remarks
John A. Macdonald (Conservative)	1867–1973, 1878–1891 18 years, 359 days	Served until 1873 when the Pacific Scandal—the soliciting of bribes by the Macdonald government in the order of $360 000 from the promoter Hugh Allen for the 1872 General Election—led to Macdonald's resignation. He was elected once again in 1878 and served until he died in office in 1891.
Alexander Mackenzie (Liberal)	1873–1878 4 years, 356 days	Became prime minister as a result of the Pacific Scandal.
John Abbott (Conservative)	1891–1892 1 year, 161 days	He was one of four prime ministers to serve out the end of John A. Macdonald's last term after his death. He could not finish his term because of his own health problems.
John Thompson (Conservative)	1892–1894 2 years, 7 days	Second prime minster to serve out the end of John A. Macdonald's last term. He died in office.
Mackenzie Bowell (Conservative)	1894–1896 1 year, 128 days	Third prime minister to serve out the end of John A. Macdonald's last term. He lost the confidence of his cabinet and resigned before the end of the term.
Charles Tupper (Conservative)	1896 68 days	Fourth prime minster. He was prime minister during the 1896 election campaign.
Wilfrid Laurier (Liberal)	1896–1911 15 years, 86 days	Four full terms in majority governments.
Robert Borden (Conservative)	1911–1920 8 years, 274 days	During his tenure, women were awarded the right to vote in 1918. He resigned in 1920.
Arthur Meighen (Conservative)	1920–1921 1926 1 year, 260 days	Served out the end of Robert Borden's term. He briefly took over from William L.M.King's term after the King-Byng Affair.
William Lyon Mackenzie King (Liberal)	1921–1926, 1926–1930, 1935–1948 21 years, 154 days	The King-Bing Affair was a constitutional crisis over the power of the Governor General (Lord Byng) to refuse Mackenzie King's request in 1926 to call a general election. Eventually, the Statute of Westminster (1931) granted greater national autonomy in all self-governing dominions of the British Empire.
R.B. Bennett (Conservative)	1930–1935 5 years, 77 days	One-term majority government.
Louis St. Laurent (Liberal)	1948–1957 8 years, 218 days	After Mackenzie King retired, he served as prime minister. He won the next election with a majority.
John Diefenbaker (Progressive Conservative)	1957–1963 5 years, 305 days	Oversaw the cancellation of Canada's Avro Arrow jet fighter, the most advanced of its kind in the world.
Lester Pearson (Liberal)	1963–1968 4 years, 364 days	Two minority governments. He helped establish NATO. He inaugurated Canada's national flag in 1965; won the Nobel Peace Prize in 1957.
Pierre E. Trudeau (Liberal)	1968–1979, 1980–1984 15 years, 86 days	Eventful period in Canadian politics, including the October Crisis 1970, Québec Referendum 1980, and the Constitution Act of 1982 with the entrenched Charter of Rights & Freedoms.
John Turner (Liberal)	1984 79 days	Served out Pierre Trudeau's term after he retired.

Brian Mulroney (Progressive Conservative)	1984–1993 8 years, 281 days	Canada-U.S. Free Trade in 1988 and NAFTA in 1994. GST in 1991, Meech Lake Accord in 1987, and Charlottetown Accord in 1992.
Kim Campbell* (Progressive Conservative)	1993 132 days	Served out Brian Mulroney's term after he retired.
Jean Chrétien (Liberal)	1993–2003 10 years, 38 days	Elimination of the deficit and budget surplus for five consecutive years.
Paul Martin (Liberal)	2003–2006 2 years, 56 days	Served out Jean Chretien's term for six months; led a short-term minority government.
Stephen Harper (Conservative)	2006–present	After two minority governments, won a majority in the 2011 election with a scripted campaign based on fear of a Liberal-NDP coalition government.

* Canada's first woman prime minister. She was not elected to the position.

the leadership of Réal Caouette, a Rouyn-Noranda, Quebec, radio commentator. Except for the one-time electoral success of the *Ralliement des Créditistes* in the 1962 federal election (26 seats from rural Quebec), Social Credit remained a provincial party contender in Manitoba, Alberta, and British Columbia until the early 1970s, when it disappeared for good from Canada's political landscape.

The Cooperative Commonwealth Federation (CCF), later the New Democratic Party (NDP), was founded by representatives from the co-operative movement, labour leaders, and academics in Regina, Saskatchewan, in 1933. The founding principles of the party are contained in the Regina Manifesto. The party remains Canada's national social democratic party. Its provincial strongholds are Saskatchewan, Manitoba, and British Columbia. While never achieving a majority in the House of Commons, the NDP formed a coalition government with the Liberals for two years from 1972 to 1974.

The Conservative Party of Canada is the latest addition to the federal political landscape. On December 8, 2003, the Canadian Alliance Party (formerly the Reform Party) merged with the Progressive Conservative Party to become the Conservative Party. Before the merger, the Progressive Conservatives held 15 seats in the House of Commons and the Canadian Alliance held 63 seats. Stephen Harper and Peter MacKay acted as principal spokespersons for the Canadian Alliance and Progressive Conservative caucuses respectively. Once the two parties merged, Harper ran for the leadership of the newly formed party in January 2004, along with Belinda Stronach and Tony Clement. Harper won the leadership contest in March 2004, and MacKay became deputy leader.

Like its predecessor, the Canadian Alliance Party, the Conservative Party does not have provincial parties as the Liberals and the NDP do. Instead, the Conservative Party maintains relationships with provincial Progressive Conservative parties at the provincial level.

The Conservative Party occupies the "right" of the political spectrum in Canada. The party endorses the major tenets of social conservatism, such as upholding and valuing traditional, intolerant views about the nation (e.g., anti-multiculturalism, anti–Aboriginal rights, anti-immigration, and pro-military), family, and religion, as well as promoting a strong work ethic and stricter law enforcement. These values came to the party via the western Canada–based Canadian Alliance Party. However, unlike the U.S. Republican Party, neither gay marriage nor abortion are political hot potatoes for many federal Conservative members of Parliament.

The lack of a coherent political right in Canada is probably due to at least two factors not shared with the United States. First, although there are pockets of right-wing Christian fundamentalism in Canada, especially in western Canada and parts of Ontario, this votership is dramatically less than south of the border. Indeed, as will be discussed in Chapter 14, one of the largest growing segments of the population is those who profess to have no religion. Second, unlike the United States, Canada is not a superpower with a large military to support. Therefore, while there will be continued support for the Conservative Party of Canada, its association with social conservatism will keep many Canadians (and certainly most Quebecois) from voting for the party.

First elected in 1990, the Bloc Québécois is the newest social democratic political party on the national scene in Canada. Its roots are exclusively in the province of Quebec. Unlike the NDP, the Bloc Québécois was formed from a coalition of dissident Quebec MPs who had left the Liberal and Progressive Conservative parties. It upholds a social democratic platform of policies and is committed to increased sovereignty for Quebec. During the last federal election (May 2011), Quebec voters ran from the Bloc Québécois and, not surprisingly embraced the NDP. With the untimely death of Jack Layton and the leadership reins now in the hands of Thomas Mulcair, the NDP remains a significant presence in Quebec.

The Structure of the Canadian Bureaucracy

Today, employees of the federal government who work for one of the ministries are called *public servants*. Under the 1967 *Public Service Employment Act*, public servants are allowed the right to bargain collectively with their employer. However, *public sector employees* in Canada are a much larger group, which includes both federal and provincial public servants and employees of Crown corporations, the military, and other nondepartmental agencies of the government. Taken together, all categories of public sector employees at all levels of government make up over 40 percent of the total labour force.

The *federal bureaucracy* is comprised of employees in the armed forces, the RCMP, various government agencies, and the public service. At the federal level, the main categories of the bureaucracy are government departments, departmental corporations, Crown corporations, the Canadian Armed Forces (115 000 employees), and the RCMP (22 500 employees).

Quebec: The Social Basis for the Quiet Revolution and the Rise of the Sovereignty Movement

Politically, the Quiet Revolution in Quebec began in 1959 with the death of Maurice Duplessis and his replacement by Paul Sauvé, his right-hand man in the Union Nationale Party. Premier Sauvé died after only a hundred days in office but had begun the process of modernization in Quebec. The election of the provincial Liberal Party under the leadership of Jean Lesage in 1960 carried forward the initiatives begun by Sauvé: the creation of professionally qualified jobs in the modernizing sectors of the health, education, and welfare bureaucracies of the provincial government and the eventual nationalization of the hydroelectric power companies under Hydro-Québec.

The social basis for the rapid expansion of the public sector in Quebec during the 1960s began with the industrialization of rural Quebec in the first half of the twentieth century. During this time, rural Quebec came under the pressure of a "demographic contradiction"; that is, there were too many people and not enough arable lands to settle. Where was the surplus population to go? Some went to northern Quebec and northern Ontario to work in the mines; others went in search of work to Montreal and towns springing up in the Eastern Townships, such as Drummondville; still others went to the New England states of Vermont, New York, and New Hampshire. The only employment open to the children of rural farmers was labouring jobs in the factories owned by foreign or English Canadian capital.

Everett Hughes, in his classic study of the industrialization of rural Quebec entitled *French Canada in Transition* (1943), paints a graphic picture of what he calls an "ethnic division of labour," in which the bosses in the factories were all English-speaking and Protestant while the workers were all French-speaking and Catholic. Contrary to what one might expect, Hughes argued that it was not the rural working-class Quebecois that had difficulty adapting to their new situation; it was members of the traditional Quebec middle class of lawyers and doctors. According to Hughes, so long as Quebec remained rural and agricultural, members of the small middle class could survive by passing on to their sons (and some daughters) their education and class privileges. Industrialization changed this system, however, because the workers' sons and daughters would soon acquire better educations and would be able to compete for the small number of middle-class jobs once held

Bill 101, otherwise known as the Charter of the French Language, was passed in 1977. Its purpose was "to make French the language of Government and the Law, as well as the normal and everyday language of work, instruction, communication, commerce and business". Above is an example of an advertisement in French for a chicken dinner at a well-known BBQ franchise in Québec.

by their class "betters." The only remedy for the situation was to expand the number of middle-class jobs available. Modernizing and professionalizing the Quebec government bureaucracy was a viable solution. Moreover, and equally important, jobs in the public sector would ensure the continuation of the French language and culture (but not religion) in the decades subsequent to the Quiet Revolution. This was not an easy task, however, and it had to wait until the death of Maurice Duplessis and the election of Jean Lesage and the provincial Liberal Party in order to be successful.

The Quiet Revolution gave hope to many Quebecois seeking to modernize their province through the expansion of the health, education, and welfare bureaucracies while taking on other more daring projects such as nationalizing the province's hydroelectric power companies. It unleashed a tidal wave of energy in the province that included the rise of the terrorist group known as the Front de Libération du Québec (FLQ) and the creation of the Parti Québécois.

In 1970, the bubble burst with the October Crisis: the FLQ kidnappings of James Cross, the British trade commissioner, on October 5, and Pierre Laporte, the Quebec minister of labour in the ruling provincial Liberal Party, on October 10. Prime Minister Trudeau invoked the *War Measures Act* on October 16, 1970, marking the first time these extraordinary powers were used in peacetime. On October 17, Pierre Laporte was found dead in the trunk of a parked car at the airport in St. Hubert, Quebec.

This was an unsettling period for many Canadians both inside and outside Quebec. The fact that the kidnappers had been found by conventional police methods strongly indicated to many that the invocation of the *War Measures Act* was at best an overreaction on the part of Pierre Trudeau and the federal Liberals, and at worst a disguised attempt to undermine the credibility of the Parti Québécois and the sovereignty movement in the province. In any event, the tide shifted back toward the sovereignty movement when, in 1976, the Parti Québécois was elected for the first time. One of the first pieces of legislation passed by the newly formed PQ government was Bill 101—"the language law."

As is the case in other provinces where English signs speak to the majority population, in Quebec, French signs predominate. The sign in this photo tells onlookers that from Sunday to Wednesday, they can get two, full-course chicken meals for $25.

Language in the workplace had become a major political issue in Quebec before 1976. Starting with the Report of the Royal Commission on Bilingualism and Biculturalism in 1968, the stage was set for a lingering feud over language in the province that continues to this day. The passage of Bill 22, the *Official Languages Act*, by the Liberal Party of Quebec in 1972 and Bill 101 by the dissatisfied Parti Québécois in response should have been wake-up calls to the rest of Canada—reminders that language and culture are significant social issues that go beyond petty party politics.

What is the social basis for the politics of language in Quebec? For those of us in the rest of Canada to begin to understand, we need to set aside the complex political wrangling over the repatriation of the Constitution in 1982 and the "failures" of the Meech Lake Accord (1987) and the Charlottetown Accord (1992). Instead, we must see the preservation of language and culture in Quebec as tied to "jobs." A language does not flourish by being taught at school. Languages are nurtured or languish in the workplace. Speaking a language at work is the primary vehicle for sustaining its survival and culture. We constantly exercise our language at work, a place where cultural experiences are shared and nurtured. Therefore, making French the language of work for everyone in Quebec makes sense to the majority of French speakers in the province. The English-speaking minority recognizes the significance of work for language preservation and struggles against the majority's language bills.

This is the essence of the political strife in Quebec. The struggles over language in that province are just as much struggles over who gets which jobs. In other words, the social basis of language and culture is a necessary starting point for all of us if we hope to achieve an understanding of the growing complexity of politics of Quebec, either in or out of Canada. To bury our heads in the sand or to fall back on old and tired clichés will not resolve our difficulties as a maturing nation. As Canadians, we must begin an intelligent and reasonable discussion of the issues if we are to participate in their resolution.

Focus Question

Why are language and culture so important for many Quebecois?

Democratic Systems in Europe

We tend to take our political system for granted and assume that any other democracy looks like ours. This is not the case. To achieve a comparative understanding, let's look at the European system.

Most European countries base their elections on a system of **proportional representation**; that is, the seats in the national legislature are divided according to the proportion of votes received by each political party. If one party wins 51 percent of the vote, for example, that party is awarded 51 percent of the seats; a party with 49 percent of the votes receives 49 percent of the seats, and so on.

Proportional representation encourages minority parties. The proportional representation followed in most European countries means that if a party gets 10 percent of the voters to support its candidate, it will get 10 percent of the seats. This system encourages the formation of **noncentrist parties**, those that propose less popular ideas.

Three main results follow from being able to win even a few seats in the national legislature. First, if a minority party has officeholders, it gains access to the media throughout the year, receiving publicity that helps keep its issues alive. Second, because many parties compete in elections, no single party is likely to gain a majority of the seats in the national legislature. To muster the required votes to make national decisions, the party with the most seats must align itself with one or more of the smaller parties and form a **coalition government**. A party with only 10 or 15 percent of the seats, then, may be able to trade its vote on some issues for the larger party's support on others. Third, because coalitions break down, the governments tend to be less stable. Italy, for example, has had more than 50 different governments since World War II, in contrast to the 13 prime ministers of Canada (see Table 12.3).

In April 2001, Fair Vote Canada (FVC) was launched in Ottawa. Its goal is to bring some form of proportional representation to Canada's political system by a national referendum. Voters during the recent Ontario election rejected the mixed member proportional (MMP) system advocated by the FVC. The group remains active and is committed to electoral reform in Canada (see www.fairvotecanada.org).

Sociological Theories and Canadian Politics

The Functionalist Perspective: Pluralism
Functionalists view the state as having arisen out of the basic needs of a social group.

Functionalists say that **pluralism**, a diffusion of power among many interest groups, prevents any one group from gaining control of a government and using it to oppress the people. In other words, the Canadian government functions like a healthy human body (Polsby, 1959; Huber & Form, 1973; Dahl, 1961, 1982).

From the functionalist perspective, ethnic groups, women, men, farmers, the unemployed, and the retired are all parts of our pluralist society. As special-interest groups such as women or the disabled negotiate with one another and reach compromises, conflict is minimized, and the resulting policies gain wide support.

The Conflict Perspective: Power Elite/Ruling Class
Conflict theorists propose a different answer. The important question is who holds the power that determines the overarching policies for Canada. For example, who determines how many Canadians will be out of work by raising or lowering interest rates? Who sets policies that transfer jobs from Canada to the United States or countries with low-cost labour? And the ultimate question of power: Who is behind decisions to go or not to go to war?

C. Wright Mills (1956) took the position that the decisions that have the greatest impact on the lives of Americans—and of Canadians and people across the globe—are made by a coalition of individuals whose interests coincide and who have access to the centre of political power in the United States. Mills called them the **power elite**. As depicted in Figure 12.1, the power elite

⊙ **Watch** "Democracy: Those Who Don't Participate" on **MySocLab.**

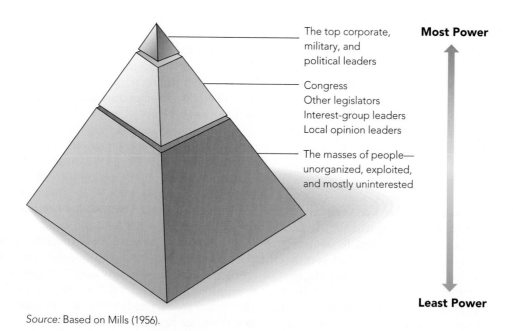

The top corporate, military, and political leaders

Congress
Other legislators
Interest-group leaders
Local opinion leaders

The masses of people—unorganized, exploited, and mostly uninterested

Most Power

Least Power

Source: Based on Mills (1956).

FIGURE 12.1 Power in the United States: The Model Proposed by C. Wright Mills

Source: Based on Mills (1956).

consists of the top leaders of the largest corporations, the most powerful generals and admirals of the armed forces, and certain elite politicians. They wield the most power and make the decisions that direct the country—and shake the world (Hellinger & Judd, 1991; Ferguson, 1995).

Conflict theorists contend that we should not think that the behaviour of the ruling class stems from some grand conspiracy to control the country. Rather, it is grounded in mutual interests in solving problems faced by large businesses (Useem, 1984). The ruling class consists of people whose backgrounds and orientations to life are so similar—they attend prestigious private schools, belong to exclusive private clubs, and are millionaires many times over—that they automatically share the same values and goals.

As mentioned in other chapters, in *The Vertical Mosaic* (1965), John Porter identified several elites in Canadian society, not just the industrial-military complex identified by C. Wright Mills for the United States. In addition to the economic elite, he identified elites in the media, religion, organized labour, and the political sector of Canadian society.

The common characteristics of an elite presented by Porter were similar to those put forth by C. Wright Mills. The Canadian economic elite, for example, attended similar if not the same private schools as members of the U.S. elite and completed their education at the "right" universities. British Protestants (primarily Anglican) still dominate the Canadian group, with very few French-Canadians, Jews, or Catholics. The members of the economic elite attend the same social (private) clubs and recruit one another to serve on various boards of directors.

Wallace Clement's (1975, 1977, 1983) studies classified three components of Canada's corporate elite: a Canadian component based mainly in banking, insurance, and other related financial institutions; a foreign (mainly U.S.) component that dominates the manufacturing and natural resource sectors of the economy; and a component Clement calls a comprador elite—native-born directors and senior managers of foreign-controlled corporations operating in Canada.

Dennis Olsen (1980), a graduate student of John Porter, studied the Canadian state elite. While Olsen discovered that members of the federal bureaucratic elite (judges, politicians, and senior federal and provincial bureaucrats such as deputy ministers) were more open to recruitment and were a much larger group than the economic elite, most came from middle-class backgrounds and were channelled to executive positions through "acceptable" bureaucratic means. They were able to stay in regular contact through what Olsen calls "executive federalism."

Unfortunately, very little recent research has been carried out to investigate the changing social characteristics of Canada's political elites.

Feminist Perspectives: Gender Reform, Resistance, and Rebellion

Current feminist theorizing about the nature of gender inequality is linked to whether theorists seek to reform the present system or struggle to achieve some fundamental change. That is, the main reasons given for women having a lesser social status and fewer advantages than men of similar education, class background, race/ethnicity, and religion lead to proposed solutions or remedies, including political ones. Proponents of liberal feminism, for example, hold the current system of democratic government as legitimate. They have been instrumental in making visible the pervasiveness of overt discrimination. The solutions they have proposed, such as pay and employment equity in Canada and Affirmative Action in the United States, have sparked debate and discussion.

EMPLOYMENT EQUITY Since the 1970s, the Canadian government has attempted to change the manner by which employees are recruited into the federal bureaucracy. The major policy initiative has been employment equity, or recruitment targeting the designated groups of women, Aboriginal people, visible minorities, and the physically disabled. Table 12.4 provides a portrait of the "success" of this policy at the "executive category" level.

Clearly, women have made important strides since the early 1990s, though they remain underrepresented at the "executive level." Aboriginal numbers remain low, at just under 3 percent, and visible minorities have made only minor advances, holding just 4.2 percent of executive-level positions in 2003.

In addition, the number of jobs at this level over the six-year period from 1993 until 1999 decreased from a high of 4155 in 1993 to a low of 3421 in 1999, a drop of nearly 20 percent. The number rose somewhat between 1999 and 2001, although it was still 15 percent lower than in 1993. By 2003, however, the numbers advanced to 4213—a marginal increase of 1 percent over the 1993 figure. It has taken 10 years to reach levels comparable to those in 1993.

Gender resistance feminisms, such as radical and lesbian feminisms, claim that the gender order cannot be made gender-neutral by seeking legislative changes. Instead, these feminists propose a woman-centred society and seek to create a women-oriented culture, ethics, and even religion. Gender rebellion feminisms, such as multiracial, postmodern, and queer theories, attack the gender order directly by undermining the boundaries that separate men from women, male from female, and homosexual from heterosexual. Using the language of postmodernism, these feminists

✳ **Explore** the reading "The Power Elite" by C. Wright Mills on **MySocLab**.

◉ **Watch** the video "Lobbying and Special Interest Groups" on **MySocLab**.

TABLE 12.4 Employment Equity at the "Executive Category" Level in the Federal Civil Service

	1993 Number	%	1999 Number	%	2001 Number	%	2003 Number	%	2006 Number	%
Women	731	17.6	919	26.9	1057	30.0	1424	33.8	1749	38.8
Aboriginal people	44	1.1	64	1.9	70	2.0	114	2.7	153	3.4
People with disabilities	81	1.9	101	3.0	125	3.5	193	4.6	248	5.5
Visible minorities	N/A	N/A	103	3.0	118	3.4	177	4.2	247	5.5
Total executive category	4155		3421		3522		4213		4505	

Source: Adapted from Treasury Board of Canada, Employment Equity in the Federal Public Service—Annual Report, Ottawa, Communications and Coordination Directorate, 1994–present.

deconstruct the categories of sex, sexuality, and gender and thereby undermine the legitimacy of favouring one group over another.

War and Terrorism: A Means to Implement Political Objectives

As previously noted, an essential characteristic of the state is that it claims a monopoly on violence. **War**—armed conflict between nations or politically distinct groups—is often part of national policy.

Is War Universal?

War is one option that groups may choose for dealing with disagreements, but not all societies choose this option. The Mission Indians of North America, the Arunta of Australia, the Andaman Islanders of the South Pacific, and the Inuit of the Arctic, for example, follow procedures to handle

aggression and quarrels, but do not have organized battles that pit one tribe or group against another. These groups do not even have a word for war (Lesser, 1968).

Focus Question

What are some examples of recent wars that would fit one or more of Timasheff's objectives?

Sowing the Seeds of Future Wars

With incredible hypocrisy, the most industrialized nations of the world lament regional conflicts that can escalate into larger wars while zealously pursuing profits by selling advanced war technology to the least industrialized nations. When one least industrialized nation buys high-tech weapons, its neighbours get nervous, sparking an arms race among them (Cole & Lubman, 1994; Ricks, 1994).

Table 12.5 illustrates that the United States is the chief merchant of death, even though the Cold War is over and

TABLE 12.5 The Business of Death

The Top 10 Arms Sellers	The Top 10 Arms Buyers
1. United States $58 billion	1. Saudi Arabia $32 billion
2. Russia $36 billion	2. China $14 billion
3. Great Britain $21 billion	3. India $14 billion
4. France $12 billion	4. Egypt $12 billion
5. China $11 billion	5. Israel $10 billion
6. Germany $6 billion	6. U.A.E. $9 billion
7. Israel $3 billion	7. Taiwan $8 billion
8. Sweden $2 billion	8. South Korea $7 billion
9. Ukraine $2 billion	9. Pakistan $6 billion
10. Italy $1 billion	10. Singapore $4 billion

Note: For years 2002–2009. U.A.E. is United Arab Emirates.

it can no longer claim the "communist threat" as a reason for arming the free world. The seeds of future wars are also sown by nuclear proliferation, and several least industrialized nations, such as India, Pakistan, and China, now have nuclear weapons. Always a threat to the world's safety, in the hands of a dictator these weapons can mean blackmail or an attack to settle personal or nationalistic grudges.

Terrorism

With hatred fanned across generations, terrorism directed against a civilian population is a continuing threat. Groups nurture bitterness by endlessly chronicling the atrocities committed by their arch-enemy. One of the few options open to a weaker group looking to retaliate against a powerful country for its suppression is "suicide terrorism"—which usually involves bombs capable of blowing up only a few people at a time. However, as we witnessed on September 11, 2001, suicide terrorism can also strike on a grander scale, killing thousands.

War and Dehumanization

Proud of his techniques, the U.S. trainer was demonstrating to the South American soldiers how to torture a prisoner. As the victim screamed in anguish, the trainer was interrupted by a phone call from his wife. His students could hear him say, "A dinner and a movie sound nice. I'll see you right after work." Hanging up the phone, he then continued the lesson. (Stockwell, 1989)

Exposure to brutality and killing often causes **dehumanization**, the process of reducing people to objects that do not deserve to be treated as humans. Consider the four characterizations of dehumanization (Bernard, Ottenberg, & Redl, 1971):

1. *Increased emotional distance from others.* People are seen as subhuman—as "the enemy."
2. *An emphasis on following procedures.* People are likely to say, "We all have to die some day. What difference does it make if these people die now?"
3. *Inability to resist pressures.* Fears of losing one's job, losing the respect of one's peers, or having one's integrity and loyalty questioned take precedence over individual moral decisions.
4. *A diminished sense of personal responsibility.* People do not see themselves as responsible for what they do because they are simply following orders.

A Vietnam vet who read this section remarked, "You missed the major one we used. We killed kids. Our dehumanizing technique was a saying, 'The little ones are the soldiers of tomorrow.'"

Dehumanization does not always insulate the self from guilt, however, and its failure to do so can bring severe personal consequences. During a war, soldiers are surrounded by army buddies who agree that the enemy is less than

human and deserves inhuman treatment. After a solider returns home, the concept of dehumanizing is more likely to break down. Many soldiers find themselves seriously disturbed by what they did during a war.

POST-TRAUMATIC STRESS DISORDER (PTSD) While trauma-stress reactions date back to descriptions in Classical Greek literature, it was not until 1980 that the *American Psychiatric Association Diagnostic and Statistical Manual* recognized post-traumatic stress disorder. PTSD is a severe psychological disorder. For returning Canadian soldiers, the number who have received disability pensions related to mental injuries including PTSD jumped five times, from 2137 in 2002 to 11 888 in 2009—what it was when troops first arrived in Afghanistan (CBC News, 2009c).

A New World Order?

The globalization of capitalism, accompanied by the worldwide flow of information, capital, and goods discussed in Chapter 11, is little affected by national boundaries. The United States, Canada, and Mexico formed the North American Free Trade Association, to which all of South America will eventually belong. European countries have formed an economic and political unit known as the European Union, which supersedes their national boundaries. The euro is now the single cross-national currency, with only one exception—the United Kingdom. Similarly, the United Nations, transcending national borders and moderating disputes between countries, can authorize the use of international force against individual nations—as it did against North Korea in 1950, Iraq in 1990, and, on a smaller scale, Somalia in 1993 and Bosnia in 1994 and 1997.

Will this process continue until a single state or empire envelops the earth? This is a possibility. Set against it is the demand for self-determination and self-government from nations within the bosom of states in the developed part of the world. Examples include Scottish and Quebec independence, the Palestinians, Aboriginals, and so on. As borders shift, as occurred with the breakup of the Soviet Union, previously unincorporated nations such as Lithuania and Azerbaijan demand their independence and the right to full statehood. The Perspectives box explores the anxieties and tensions many Canadians experience when trying to seek accommodation with ethnic and religious minorities.

If global political and economic unity does come about, it is fascinating to speculate on what type of government will result. If Hitler had had his way, his conquests would have resulted in world domination—by a world dictator and a world totalitarian regime based on racial identification. If a progressive world order emerges from current trends—that's a big "if"—the potential for human welfare is tremendous.

Marriage, Divorce, and Inheritance: Saying "No" to Sharia Law in Canada

In 1991, Ontario was looking for ways to ease the burdens of a backlogged court system. As such, the province changed its Arbitration Act to allow "faith-based arbitration"—a system where Muslims, Jews, Catholics, and members of other faiths could use the guiding principles of their religions to settle family disputes such as divorce, custody, and inheritances outside the court system.

It was voluntary—both parties (a husband and wife) had to agree to go through the process. But once they did, the decisions rendered by the tribunal were binding. The Ontario government, in its review of the Arbitration Act, released a report on December 20, 2004, conducted by former attorney general Marion Boyd. Among her 46 recommendations was that:

> The Arbitration Act should continue to allow disputes to be arbitrated using religious law, if the safeguards currently prescribed and recommended by this review are observed.

In her report, Monica Boyd noted that some "participants in the Review fear that the use of arbitration is the beginning of a process whose end goal is a separate political identity for Muslims in Canada, that has not been the experience of other groups who use arbitration." Boyd stressed that any faith-based system would have to conform to the Charter of Rights and Freedoms. Earlier in the year, the Islamic Institute of Civil Justice said it wanted to set up its own faith-based arbitration panels under the Arbitration Act, based on Sharia law.

The Boyd proposal ran into opposition from women's groups, legal organizations, and the Muslim Canadian Congress, which all warned that the 1400-year-old Sharia law does not view women as equal to men. The National Association of Women and the Law, the Canadian Council of Muslim Women, and the National Organization of Immigrant and Visible Minority Women of Canada argued that men

and women are not treated equally under Sharia law, and that women fare far worse in divorce, child custody, and inheritance matters. For instance, men have the right of unilateral divorce under classical Sharia; a woman can only inherit half as much as a man can. If a divorced woman remarries, custody of the children from her previous marriage may revert to the children's father.

Attempts to set up Sharia courts in Canada in 2005 were abandoned after protests. The Jewish and Catholic communities did not want Muslims introducing Sharia into Canada, so they accepted the decision to ban all religious arbitration in Ontario, including their own respective tribunals. In May 2005, the Quebec National Assembly unanimously supported a motion to block the use of Sharia law in Quebec courts.

Source: Adapted from CBC News, "Sharia law: FAQs." May 26, 2005 (www.cbc.ca/news/background/islam/shariah-law.html); www.canadianlawsite.ca/sharia-law-canada.htm.

SUMMARY AND REVIEW

POWER, AUTHORITY, AND VIOLENCE

How are authority and coercion related to power?

Authority is power that people view as legitimately exercised over them, while **coercion** is power they consider unjust. The **state** is a political entity that claims a monopoly on violence over a particular territory. If enough people consider a state's power illegitimate, **revolution** is possible. p. 261.

THE CANADIAN POLITICAL SYSTEM

What are the main characteristics of the Canadian political system?

Canada is a federal state with a parliamentary democracy. Sometimes, though rarely, Canada's parliamentary system can have

a **coalition government**, unlike the "winner take all" system of the United States. Most European democracies have **proportional representation** with legislative seats divided among political parties according to the percentage of votes each receives. If no single party wins a majority of votes, proportional representation creates the need for a coalition government. pp. 266–267.

What political parties are there at present in the House of Commons?

The Liberal Party, the Conservative Party, the Bloc Québécois, the Green Party, and the New Democratic Party. pp. 267–270.

What is at the root of the political strife in Quebec politics?

The preservation of language and culture in Quebec is tied to jobs. Speaking at work is the primary vehicle for sustaining a language and culture. We constantly exercise our language at work, a place where cultural experiences are shared and nurtured. This is the essence of the political strife in Quebec. pp. 270–271.

WAR AND TERRORISM: A MEANS TO IMPLEMENT POLITICAL OBJECTIVES

How are war and terrorism related to politics, and what are their costs?

War, common in human history, is a means of attempting to reach political objectives. The least industrialized nations, which can least afford it, spend huge amounts of money on technologically advanced weapons. Another cost is **dehumanization**, whereby people no longer see others as worthy of human treatment. pp. 274–275.

A NEW WORLD ORDER?

Is humanity headed toward a one-world political order?

The global expansion of communications, transportation, and trade; the widespread adoption of capitalism and the retreat of socialism; and the trend toward larger political unions may indicate that a world political system is developing. The oppositional trend is a world totalitarian regime based on racial or religious identification. If a new world order develops, the possible consequences for human welfare range from excellent to calamitous. p. 275.

TALKING ABOUT THEORY

Theoretical Paradigms

	CLASSICAL PARADIGMS		RECENT PARADIGMS
	Structural-Functional Paradigm	Social-Conflict Paradigm	Feminist Paradigm
What is the level of analysis?	Macro level	Macro level	Micro and macro levels
What is the social significance of politics?	Various interest groups compete (inclusive = functional)	A power elite or ruling class dominates politics. The members usually come from upper-class backgrounds.	Male domination at the societal level (patriarchy) explains the continued inequality of women in politics.
Have politics changed over time? How?	Yes. Different interest groups, such as women, ethnic groups, and gays/lesbians, can effect changes in legislation.	No.	Yes/No. Changes in the legal prohibitions against women voting and pay and employment equity are significant positive changes. Patriarchy remains.

KEY TERMS

All URLs listed are current as of the printing of this text.

Mother Jones Online
www.mojones.com
Mother Jones is a magazine of investigation and ideas for independent thinkers. Provocative and unexpected articles inform readers and inspire action toward positive social change.

Canadian Political Parties
www.synapse.net/radio/can-pol.htm
A comprehensive array of links to parties and to other indexes. Highly recommended.

Fair Vote Canada
www.fairvotecanada.org
Fair Vote Canada is committed to electoral reform and has the goal of bringing some form of proportional representation to Canada's political system.

CRITICAL THINKING QUESTIONS

1. According to Max Weber, the state is an organization with a monopoly on the legitimate use of violence. In a democracy, what other forms of power are there for citizens to express their point of view?
2. Some sociologists contend that democracy as a form of government and capitalism as an economic system are two sides of the same coin. Is it true that democracy and capitalism are directly related?
3. The democratic institutions we have inherited in Canada are apparently unable to resolve some of the political demands being made by Quebec nationalists. Is Quebec sovereignty inevitable? Can you think of any public policy alternatives to the present dilemma, or do we need to completely change the way we practise politics in Canada?

   Access the Research Navigator through MySocLab and use keywords such as "Quebec," "independence," and "sovereignty" to locate relevant and recent scholarly and popular press publications to help you answer the previous question.

MySocLab

Explore the topics covered in this chapter on MySocLab. Interactive resources include a study plan, cumulative exams, a multimedia library, MySocLab eReadings, and access to the MySocLab Video Series.

13

THE FAMILY: DOORWAY TO SOCIETY

LEARNING OUTCOMES

After you have studied this chapter, you will be able to answer the following questions:

1. Why do contemporary sociologists refer to "families" and reject the notion of "the family"?
2. What are the differences between the functionalist, conflict, and symbolic interactionist theoretical approaches to family life?
3. What are the key patterns that persist within the rich diversity of family life experiences?
4. What are some of the major changes that have occurred in Canadian families over the past 20 years?
5. How have economic and legislative changes resulted in profound changes in family living?
6. What are some of the social causes of family violence and abuse?

SAMRA took a long, deep breath. This was the third job interview this month and she was starting to anticipate rejection. Having sent out over 200 résumés since her university graduation nine months earlier, she knew she was lucky to even get an interview. So far all of her efforts had not produced a "real" job offer in her field. At one point, getting top marks and getting into teachers' college had seemed like the big hurdle. Now, she realized that the credentials were no guarantee of employment. This afternoon she would be back at the mall, working her retail shift until 9:30 p.m., and on the weekend she had two shifts at the Cineplex. Thirty hours a week at minimum wage were barely keeping her and her husband, Das, afloat. And her evening and weekend schedule meant they had very little time to spend together.

Samra's parents had been so delighted when she and Das had married last spring in a traditional ceremony in India. The opulent festivities and days of celebration now seemed a lifetime ago. After returning to Canada, they had moved into the basement apartment at Das's parents' house. This was to be a temporary arrangement until they both found jobs, and it had seemed like a great way to save money. But it had quickly become a tense and unpleasant situation. Samra's mother-in-law had become increasingly vocal in her criticism of Samra's housekeeping and cooking skills and constantly made comments about the dowry she felt was owed to Das and his parents. When they married, even though it was arranged by her parents, Samra felt she and Das had left those old-fashioned ways of thinking behind, but here they were, dominating their everyday lives. Samra grimaced at the thought of going home to more nasty remarks, but her parents had made it clear—she had to be a good daughter-in-law and make a "go" of this marriage. There was no going back.

But was there any going forward? Das had finally landed a six-month, unpaid internship at a major newspaper, although there was no guarantee that it would turn into a permanent position. Samra was thinking about taking some community college courses to improve her employment prospects, but she and Das already had $40 000 in student debt. How were they ever going to get to the point where they had a nice home, secure jobs, and children? She had dreamed about driving her kids to soccer matches and enjoying lazy afternoons in the backyard pool. The family life she had imagined for herself seemed to be evaporating before her eyes.

Adult children living at home, immigrant families dealing with generational conflicts, women juggling the combined pressures of paid work and family responsibilities, gay marriages, middle-aged couples juggling their "sandwich generation" roles as parents and as sons and daughters—all reflect profound transformations in Canadian family lives.

Despite the fact that the media often refer to some abstract notion of "the family," it is not clear what it means to live in a family. Everyone has heard the phrase "nothing is more important than family," but what does this signify and whom does it include? As we will see, family lives are complex, nuanced, and sometimes conflicted experiences and many Canadian families are in the midst of dramatic transformations. To navigate through these changes and come to terms with the new realities of many families, we need to appreciate the established patterns, significant diversities, and emerging trends that characterize contemporary lives.

Marriages and Families In a Global Perspective

To better understand Canadian patterns of marriage and family, let's first sketch a cross-cultural portrait of family lives.

Defining Families

From the 1950s to the turn of the century, the "ideal" family arrangement was often described in terms of the so-called traditional family: a married man who brought home the bacon and his wife, who cooked it, and their two children, hopefully a boy and a girl. Such a view is today anachronistic. Gay couples with kids, single-parents, common-law relationships, and a myriad other changes have transformed family experience. Even the preferred number of children has changed. Where only children were once pitied and assumed to be lonely and even spoiled, they have become increasingly popular. In 2006 (the latest available census data), 44 percent of Canadian families were single-child families, and throughout Europe (46 percent of families in England are single-child; 30 percent of families in Spain and Portugal are single-child) the trend suggests that one child may be the new norm in families as parents confront economic and time pressures (Kopun, 2011).

According to the 2006 census, most Canadians (84 percent) live in some kind of census family (married, common-law, or lone parent) rather than alone or with non-relatives, but the nature of those families is shifting dramatically. Only about one in 10 families now follows the so-called traditional form where one parent works full-time and the other stays home. The family type characterized by different-sex, legally married couples with children is the only family structure that is declining in Canada (Flavelle, 2011; Harder, 2011). A scant one in three (34.6 percent) of all census families in 2006 were made up of married couples with children aged 24 and under. This was markedly down from the one in two reported in the 1986 census. Meanwhile, the percentage of common-law couples (with and without children), lone-parent families (with and without children), and married couples without children grew significantly in the decade before 2006 (Harder, 2011; Milan, Vezina, & Wells, 2007). We live in a time of transition in terms of both our beliefs about family life and our lived experiences (Meadow & Stacey, 2006: 55).

This diversity in family experiences is consistent with what social scientists, especially anthropologists, have been documenting for generations. Around the globe, there is no single clear standard for *the* family. In some cultures, men are expected to have more than one wife (**polygyny**) and in others women have more than one husband (**polyandry**). Consider, for example, the Banaro of New Guinea. Among this group a young woman must give birth before she can marry, and she cannot marry the father of her child (Murdock, 1949). And so it goes. For just about every element you might consider essential to marriage or family, some group has a different custom. Even the sex of a bride and groom may not be what you expect.

Focus Question
What beliefs and values might the following families have in common: a refugee family recently arrived from Afghanistan living in downtown Toronto; a single-parent Native family living in northern Alberta; and a childless gay couple living in a Victoria retirement community?

Watch "Defining Families" to learn how definitions of the family have changed throughout history on **MySocLab**.

Explore the reading, "The Way We Weren't: The Myth and Reality of the 'Traditional' Family" on **MySocLab**.

Listen to Julie McCarthy's report "Defending and Attacking Polygamy in Saudi Arabia" on **MySocLab**.

Finding Facts about Canadian Families

We have heard startling generalizations about Canadian families: "Today, most marriages end in divorce" or "There are now as many single dads as single moms." Neither of these statements are true of Canadian families; nevertheless, when we hear such pronouncements, it is difficult to know if they are accurate. Some media comments, for example, reflect realities in the United States that do not apply in Canada. Other statements may be derived from inaccurate and flawed research.

Statistics Canada remains an excellent source for good data on Canadian families. Every five years, the General Social Survey (GSS) provides detailed information on Canadian families including numbers of marriages, common-law unions, children, and fertility intentions. Most recently, in 2011, the GSS conducted a telephone survey, using random digit dialling, in a sample of all non-institutionalized Canadians 15 years and older living in the 10 provinces. The data from the more than 22 000 contacts was available

in fall 2012. The "gold standard" for Canadian statistics is the Canadian Census. Also conducted every five years, it seeks to obtain information directly from every Canadian, including those living in the Yukon, the Northwest Territories, and Nunavut. While census data is far from perfect (it has recently been subject to considerable criticism after the elimination of the mandatory long form), it does provide exceptionally accurate data on a variety of Canadian dimensions, including families.

Common Cultural Themes

Within tremendous diversity, several common themes run through many marriages and families. Table 13.1 illustrates the ways in which traditional and industrial/postindustrial societies typically pattern mate selection, descent, inheritance, and family authority.

These patterns, however, are the product of history, which means they are changing. Fifty years ago, for example, childbirth routinely occurred in hospitals and was attended only by medical staff. Family and friends were exiled to the waiting room. Today, many Canadian women opt for home births or birthing centres and the presence of an increasing

TABLE 13.1 Common Cultural Themes: Marriage in Traditional and Industrial Societies

Perspective	Traditional Societies	Industrial (and Postindustrial) Societies
What is the structure of marriage?	Extended (marriage embeds spouses in a large kinship network of explicit obligations)	Nuclear (marriage brings fewer obligations toward the spouse's kin)
What are the functions of marriage?	Economic production, socialization, care of the sick and aged, recreation, sexual control, and reproduction	More limited (many traditional social functions are fulfilled by other institutions)
Who holds authority?	Highly patriarchal (authority is held by males)	Although some patriarchal features remain, authority is more evenly divided
How many spouses at one time?	Most have one spouse (monogamy), while some have several (polygamy)	One spouse
Who selects the spouse?	The parents, usually the father	Individuals choose their own spouse
Where does the couple live?	Most commonly with the groom's family (patrilocal residence); less commonly with the bride's family (matrilocal residence)	In a new home (neolocal residence)
How is descent figured?	Most commonly from male ancestors (patrilineal kinship); less commonly from female ancestors (matrilineal kinship)	From male and female ancestors equally (bilateral kinship)
How is inheritance figured?	Rigid system of rules; usually patrilineal, but may be matrilineal	Highly individualistic; usually bilateral

diversity of family relations and friends. Not only the baby's father, but also the couple's children, their mothers and fathers, and various friends are sometimes invited to witness the birth (Sokoloff, 2008: L1).

NORMS OF MATE SELECTION Every human group establishes formal or informal norms to govern who forms a formal or informal marital bond with whom. Norms of **endogamy** specify that people should marry within their own group. Groups may prohibit interracial marriages, for example. In contrast, norms of **exogamy** specify that people must marry outside their group. The best example is the incest taboo, which prohibits sex and marriage between designated relatives. Even when informal, these norms are powerful. For example, in Canada people tend to "couple up" with individuals from similar educational backgrounds. This educational "homogamy" is reflected in the fact that in 2006, 67 percent of men with a university degree were married to women with the same level of education (up from 38 percent in 1981) (Martin & Hou, 2010).

RECKONING PATTERNS OF DESCENT Family generally involves some sense of belonging to a particular group. This sense is typically formalized in a society's **system of descent**, the way people trace kinship over generations. To us, a **bilateral** system seems logical—and natural—for we think of ourselves as related to both our mother's and our father's side of the family. Interestingly, this is only one logical way to reckon descent. In a **patrilineal** system, descent is traced only on the father's side, and children are not considered to be related to their mother's relatives. In a **matrilineal** system, descent is figured only on the mother's side, and children are not considered to be related to their father's relatives. The most direct evidence of these patterns is found in naming ceremonies. When a woman assumes her husband's name upon marriage and when children automatically are identified by their father's surname, a patrilineal system of descent is maintained. In Canada and the United States, there is considerable diversity in these practices, although patrilineal naming remains prevalent (Nugent, 2010). The primary exception is the province of Quebec, where wives (both common-law and legal) routinely retain their maiden names and children adopt a hyphenated combination of their parents' surnames (Noack & Wiik, 2008).

RIGHTS OF INHERITANCE Historically, one of the most important functions of the family was to regulate the passage of property and wealth from one generation to the next. In bilateral systems, property is passed to both males and females; in a patrilineal arrangement only to males; and in the matrilineal system (the rarest form) only to females. Each system matches a people's ideas of justice and logic.

PATTERNS OF AUTHORITY Some form of **patriarchy**, a social system in which men dominate women, has formed a

Non-traditional families take many forms. Families from across Canada have moved to Alberta to take advantage of the high paying jobs provided by the oil industry. In many instances, husbands are away at remote work locations for weeks or months at a time.

thread running through the histories of most societies. Many of our marriage and family customs developed within a framework of patriarchy. Today, in Canada, Europe, and elsewhere around the globe, many individuals are adopting more **egalitarian** attitudes toward, for example, family decision-making, household work, and childcare. In many instances, shifting economic realities demand new patterns of authority. Single mothers and the growing numbers of women who are the primary or only breadwinner in the family are unlikely to accept a patriarchal authority structure. Similarly, oil-patch "widows" whose male partners have moved to Alberta to take advantage of high-paying jobs in the oil industry must take over all the responsibilities of parenting, household maintenance, and, in many instances, paid employment for months at a time (Agrell, 2008). Put simply, the old "father knows best" scenario no longer applies.

Focus Question

How are issues of authority, descent, mate selection, and inheritance managed in your family?

Definitions of "the Family": The Problem of Monolithic Bias

Until the 1970s and 1980s, North American sociologists tended to downplay the amazing diversity of family life and adopted a structural-functional perspective focused on common cultural themes and functions. As a result, they broadly defined the **family** as two or more people who consider themselves related by blood, marriage, or adoption. A **household** may or may not be a family, since it is defined as consisting of all people who share the same housing unit. Within the broad category of **family**, some sociologists classify families as **nuclear** (husband, wife, and children) and **extended** (including people such as grandparents, aunts, uncles, and cousins in addition to the nuclear unit). Sociologists also refer to the **family of orientation** (the family in which an individual grows up) and the **family of procreation** (the family formed when a couple have their first child). Regardless of its form, **marriage** is a group's approved mating arrangement—usually marked out by a ritual of some sort (e.g., a wedding) to indicate a couple's new public status.

While it is important to understand these sociological terms, it is also crucial to realize that many Canadian (and American) sociologists have explicitly rejected this approach to "the family" as a **monolithic structure** (Renzetti, Curran, & Maier, 2012). Noted Canadian sociologist Margrit Eichler developed an extensive critique of this traditional approach to family studies (1988a, 1997). As she suggests, the popular definition of the nuclear family appears to support a very limited view of family life. If we assume that all or most families include a mother and father who are married to one another, who live together, and who have biological children who reside with them, we are ignoring the hundreds of thousands of Canadians who are same-sex couples, who live in single-parent families, who do not live together (commuting couples), who do not have children, who do not have children living at home, who have stepchildren, who have adopted children, or who are working so that their children can join them as immigrants to Canada (Harder, 2011; Mandell & Duffy, 2011; Powell et al., 2010). Indeed, the list of exceptions seems to become longer and longer as we scrutinize the complex realities of family life.

This **monolithic bias** in traditional sociology not only lends itself to a very incomplete approach, but also tends to support a **conservative bias**. It implies that the "normal" and "natural" family is the one composed of two heterosexual adults who reside with and raise their biological (or adopted) children. Other families are "deviant." The mass media frequently draw on this monolithic "ideal" family to fuel "scary" news stories about the decline of the family (Scott, 2010; Luxton, 2010). Such an approach ignores the fact that Canadian families have always been diverse in their response to changing historical and economic

realities, and that the "nuclear" family is far from a perfect solution to family relationships. The so-called "normal" nuclear family was a short-lived product of the prosperous post-war era, and, despite the *Happy Days* image, these families were often plagued with problems such as child abuse, woman abuse, senior abuse, and incest. Not surprisingly, the monolithic perspective on families and its implied conservative bias has been marginalized in sociological thought.

Focus Question
Why does Canadian sociologist Margrit Eichler reject the monolithic approach to the family?

IN SUM

The basic question of what constitutes a family is much more complex than we might first think. There is tremendous variation in family life around the globe and within North American families. Providing a narrow definition of the "normal" family is both misleading and inaccurate. If the "real" or "normal" family is restricted to heterosexual couples with male primary breadwinners, female secondary breadwinners, biological children living at home, and so on, then the majority of Canadians are not living in a family. When these narrow definitions are used to restrict the numbers of families who qualify for legal recognition and therefore for social benefits, such as child-tax credits or social welfare support, the political agenda behind the definitions is clear (Harder, 2011).

Marriage and Family In Theoretical Perspective

The Functionalist Perspective: Functions and Dysfunctions

As noted in Chapter 1, functionalists stress that to survive, a society must meet certain basic needs or functions. When functionalists look at families, they examine how families are related to other parts of society, especially how they contribute to its overall well-being.

IS THE FAMILY UNIVERSAL?   Functionalists argue that although the form of families may vary from one human group to another, they are universal in that they fulfill six needs basic to every society's well-being. As described in Table 13.1, these needs, or functions, are economic production, socialization of children, care of the sick and aged, recreation, sexual control, and reproduction.

As Eichler (1997) and other sociologists have pointed out, many groups that consider themselves "families" do not fulfill all or even most of these basic needs. Childless couples and couples whose children are fully grown do not actively socialize children, yet still consider themselves

Breastfeeding and Motherhood Anxieties

On May 21, 2012, *Time* magazine published a cover story that rattled collective insecurities about families, mothering, and sexuality. On the cover, a sexy blond woman was shown breastfeeding her almost four-year-old son. Mother and son are looking directly into the camera. Beside the photograph is the caption, "Are You Mom Enough?" Not surprisingly, the image generated a torrent of public debate that spoke, among other things, to the responsibilities of mothers. The article discussed the movement for "attachment parenting," which includes in its program support for the notion that women should breastfeed their children well into their toddler years. This practise, it is suggested, not only provides the child with a healthy start to life in terms of nutrition but also helps to ensure psychological well-being. The

furor surrounding the image speaks profoundly to many social issues, but most significantly to our unsettled and hotly contested standards for "good mothering."

Contrary to any disclaimer that each woman should decide for herself how she will mother, in reality, women are subject to enormous pressures about every aspect of their role. Breastfeeding is no exception. From Dr. Spock's 1960s primer on childcare to contemporary breastfeeding advocates, many analysts point to the importance of women breastfeeding each child for at least six months. Interestingly, a strong backlash against the breastfeeding lobby has emerged in public discourse. Advocates argue that the pressure to breastfeed is more fear than fact-based, and that breastfeeding

campaigns leave many women feeling unnecessarily inadequate (Wolf, 2011; Wolf, 2012). They suggest that rather than pointing an accusatory finger at women who "fail" to breastfeed, proponents should tackle the social, cultural, workplace, and health care obstacles that make breastfeeding difficult, particularly for specific populations of mothers (Artis, 2009).

As the debate rages, mothers are left wondering what their primary responsibilities are. How much time and energy should be devoted to accomplishing breastfeeding? How pivotal is it to their success as a parent? As with natural childbirth and home birthing, conflicting social messages promise to leave many women feeling guilty and confused about their first steps as a new mother.

members of a family. In some families, the socialization of children is entirely the responsibility of others—consider, for example, children placed in homes for young offenders or sent to boot camps, or those attending private residential schools or raised by nannies. Similarly, families do not necessarily provide a medium for legitimate sexual activity. Some engage in illegal or socially stigmatized sexual behavior, such as marital rape, child sexual abuse, or "swinging." In other families, the "couple" has no sexual relations or has them only with partners outside the family relationship. The examples are endless. The bottom line is that any enumeration of universal needs fulfilled by families should be understood only as a useful analytic tool, not as an accurate or complete description of familial realities and not as a foundation for social policies.

CONNECTION TO OTHER PARTS OF SOCIETY Functionalists make the important point that "the family" is not an isolated unit, but is vitally connected to other parts of society. They note, for example, that industrialization and urbanization have made many families more fragile. Modernization ushered in formal organizations, some of which replaced the family's traditional functions. Medical treatment began to be provided by hospitals, recreation by businesses, and

sex education by schools. To weaken family functions is to weaken the "ties that bind," reducing the motivation or necessity to struggle together against hardships. One consequence is higher divorce rates. From the functionalist perspective, increased incidence of divorce does not represent "incompatible personalities" or personal conflicts but the increased viability of alternative personal living arrangements, including living alone.

ISOLATION AND EMOTIONAL OVERLOAD Functionalists also analyze the dysfunctions that arise from the relative isolation of today's nuclear family (another consequence of industrialization and urbanization). Unlike extended families in traditional societies, which are more likely to be enmeshed in complex kinship networks, members of nuclear families can count on fewer people for material and emotional support. This makes nuclear families vulnerable to "emotional overload." That is, the stress that comes with crises such as the loss of a job—or even the routine stress of a harried life—is spread around among fewer people. This puts a greater strain on each family member. In addition, the relative isolation of the nuclear family makes it vulnerable to a "dark side"—which we will examine later in the chapter.

The Conflict Perspective: Gender, Conflict, and Power

As we have discussed, central to conflict theory is the struggle over scarce resources. The recurring struggle over who does housework is an example of such a struggle over time, energy, and the leisure to pursue interesting activities. Feminist sociologists (working from a variety of perspectives, including feminist political economy and poststructrualism) continue to draw attention to the social issues surrounding unpaid work conducted in the household.

THE POWER STRUGGLE OVER HOUSEWORK When the second wave of feminism swept the globe in the 1960s, social researchers realized that family structures that dictated who washed the dishes and who diapered the baby were a reflection of significant social forces. Canadian sociologists working from a conflict perspective quickly picked up on the issue and developed a wealth of material on the experience of Canadian women. Among the most notable work was that of Meg Luxton, an anthropologist

As India rapidly modernizes and more women assume roles in the paid labour force, the traditional roles of husbands and wives will necessarily be challenged.

who lived for several years in Flin Flon, Manitoba, and chronicled the day-to-day lives of women in that community (1980). From this and other research, it became clear that in Canada, as elsewhere, women were doing the lion's share of housework and childcare. The implicit agreement in many Canadian families, especially in the 1950s and 1960s, was that the husband would "bring home the bacon" and the wife would "cook it," while also taking care of the home and children.

Unfortunately, as the research record increasingly documented, this arrangement contained significant drawbacks for women. Like many forms of low-paid, semiskilled work, housework was often tedious, time-consuming, repetitious, boring, and socially marginalized. Women with young children reported shouldering onerous amounts of work, while receiving little support within their families or communities (Mandell, Wilson, & Duffy, 2011; Duffy, Mandell, & Pupo, 1989). Indeed, for many women, housework and childcare was a socially isolating experience in which they felt cut off from adult realities. These problems were intensified for women who were poor or were recent immigrants or disabled. Most important, unlike other work, housework and childcare was unpaid and socially ignored. This reality could have devastating implications in women's lives. In particular, women whose marriages failed or who became widows (as most eventually would) often found that years of cooking, cleaning, and care translated into economic insecurities, even poverty, when they were on their own.

While in the booming 1950s and 1960s, many families could afford to have a mother working as a full-time homemaker, growing financial pressure on family resources now means that very few families can afford a full-time parent in the home (Vanier Institute of the Family, 2011a). In particular, the sharp decline in well-paid, secure industrial employment, along with dramatic increases in housing and education costs, make it extremely difficult to support the average family on one income. Instead, more mothers have moved into the paid labour force. In 1971 Canadian mothers living in couples with children younger than age 18 worked for pay an average of 8.2 hours per week; by 2006, this number had jumped to 26.1 hours of paid work. As shown in Table 13.2, there has been a dramatic shift in how even the mothers of very young children spend their days.

Interestingly, despite the movement of mothers into paid employment, equality in the division of domestic labour has not been achieved. Although most Canadians agree that both parents should take equal responsibility for

> **Watch** the video "Motherhood Manifesto" on **MySocLab**.

> **Watch** the videos "Women in the Workplace" and "Working Women and Childcare" on **MySocLab**.

TABLE 13.2 Employment Rate of Women with Children, by Age of Youngest Child, 1976 and 2009]

	2009	1976
Youngest child less than 3	64.4 %	27.6%
Youngest child aged 3 to 5	69.7%	36.8%
Youngest child less than 6	66.5%	31.4%
Youngest child 6 to 15	78.5%	46.4%
Youngest child less than 16	72.9%	39.1%
Women under 55 with no children at home	80.4%	60.9%

Source: Ferrao (2010: 9).

raising children and carrying out household duties (Bibby, 2004–5: 9) and there have been noteworthy changes, women continue to shoulder the bulk of domestic work. A generational examination of patterns of unpaid work reveals this continued inequity. Married women born between 1981 and 1990 with children spend on average two-and-a-half hours on housework per day, down from three hours per day performed by such women born between 1957 and 1966. Married men born between 1981 and 1990 with children spend an hour and a half on housework per day, up from one hour per day for those born between 1957 and 1966. So mothers are doing a bit less and fathers are doing a bit more household work. Despite the improvement in men's involvement, women who combine marriage, paid employment, and mothering continue to devote almost a full day (seven hours) per week more to household work than their male counterparts (Marshall, 2011).

In sum, women continue to do more of the childcare as well as other household work even when they also hold full-time or part-time paid employment. Predictably, the hours devoted to these activities are especially heavy when there are very young children in the home. Although women's participation in paid employment appears to have been related to reductions in domestic inequality, it has not been eliminated (Milan, Keown, & Urquijo, 2011).

Not surprisingly, this dramatic shift into increased paid employment for both parents puts pressures on family members. In particular, many young families report they are "squeezed for time" but cannot afford any reductions in family income (Gordon, 2011). As a result of this inequity, many women are experiencing considerable stress (Crompton, 2011; MacDonald, Phipps, & Lethbridge, 2005). Two-thirds of workers who report that they are highly stressed by family concerns are women. Understandably, children in the home, low income, less than postsecondary education, and

immigrant status are factors that are complexly related for these workers (Crompton, 2011).

Some analysts (see Hochschild, 1989) have suggested that the stressful, burdened lives of young mothers around the globe are a direct result of male resistance. Fathers avoid assuming equal responsibility for the home and children and conceptualize themselves as "babysitting" their kids or "helping out" their wives (Gregory & Milner, 2011). Feigning incompetence or prolonging simple tasks, for example, are strategies that have been identified as evidence of male reluctance to domestic equality. However, men in many countries of the world, including Canada, are slowly increasing their household and familial contributions. In 1986, when 56 percent of couples with dependent children were dual-earner families, only 54 percent of men participated daily in housework; by 2006, when 78 percent of families were dual earners, three-quarters of men were doing daily housework (Marshall, 2006).

There is also evidence that conceptions of men's roles as fathers are shifting. Certainly, there is extensive media coverage of the "new fathers" who are prioritizing their parenting role over paid work obligations (Douglas, 2012). Evidence of this shift is suggested by the fact that men's participation rate in primary childcare (reading to children, helping with homework, driving them to activities, and so on) in dual-earner families increased from 57 percent in 1986 to 73 percent in 2005 (Marshall, 2006). Research also suggests that our socialization practices now include increased representations of "involved" fathers in children's picture books (Adams, Walker, & O'Connell, 2011; Gerson, 2010).

Unfortunately, these changes have not produced equality in the division of unpaid work, and negotiating the time crunch remains a significant problem for many families—especially those with young children in the home and those caring for both children and aging parents—the so-called "sandwich generation." The combined facts that men are increasing their contributions to household work and childcare and that family members, especially mothers, still experience a severe time crunch suggest that the problem is not due simply to resistant husbands. Many professional careers—held by men and women—allow little time for attending to family responsibilities, and average Canadians are now spending more time in paid employment than they did a decade ago. Both husbands and wives, particularly at certain points in their family lives, are simply "running as fast as they can" (Turcotte, 2007). Noted Canadian researchers Roderic Beaujot and Robert Andersen conclude from their research that solving the time crunch in Canadian families requires a reduction in hours of paid work for men and women (2007: p. 311). We are simply spending too many hours at work.

This examination of the time crunch experienced by dual-parent, dual-income families ignores the struggles of other forms of families, as well as important differences among dual-parent families. In particular, numerous single-parent families struggle to manage time and income demands. Significantly, the time crunch experienced by lone mothers has been found to exceed that of married mothers and to have increased notably between 1992 and 2005. Similarly, low-income parents are significantly more time stressed than their better-off counterparts (Burton & Phipps, 2011). It appears that in terms of managing paid and domestic work, we are dividing into a population of haves and have-nots.

Focus Question
Why do employed mothers still assume most of the responsibility for household work?

The Symbolic Interactionist Perspective: Gender and Its Meanings in Marriage

As noted in Chapter 1, symbolic interactionists focus on the meanings people give to the roles they play in society.

HOUSEWORK, PAYCHEQUES, AND MASCULINITY The first pattern of findings is probably what you'd expect—the more a woman earns from her paid employment, the more housework men tend to take on (Marshall, 2006: 11). (However, when women are the primary wage earners, husbands do not typically equal or surpass their wives' household work time.) More than a quarter of wives (29 percent) in dual-earner couples earned more than their husbands in 2008. This is a remarkable increase from 11 percent in 1967 (Williams, 2010: 19; Marshall, 2006: 10). Rather than the husbands in these families taking over household responsibilities while the wives occupy the traditional breadwinner role, these couples are more likely to purchase home services such as cleaning or childcare. And, further, when women earn much more than their husbands, couples may engage in complicated "systems of shifting money" to maintain the appearance that the man is the major provider (Marshall, 2006: 11).

Researchers suggest that the key is gender role. Not only are boys socialized to perform certain tasks in the home, but they also associate their self-esteem with a particular notion of masculinity. If a wife earns more than her husband, it may threaten his masculinity if he endorses traditional gender roles. To do housework—"women's work"—threatens it even further. By avoiding housework, he "reclaims" his masculinity (Pitt & Borland, 2008; Hochschild, 1989; Brines, 1994).

TWO MARRIAGES IN ONE Another interesting finding of symbolic interactionists is how husbands and wives perceive their marriages. When asked how much housework each does, they give different answers. They even disagree about whether they fight over doing housework (Sanchez,

1994). Groundbreaking sociologist Jessie Bernard studied this marital gulf and noted in a classic work (1972) that when researchers

> ask husbands and wives identical questions about the union they often get quite different replies. There is usually agreement on verifiable items (duration of marriage), although not, for example, on length of premarital acquaintance, on age at marriage and interval between marriage and birth of first child.

Bernard suggests that men and women often experience quite different marital realities. Given gender socialization differences, this proposal makes sense. For example, women are much more likely to be immersed in and buy into "intimacy discourse." As a result of female socialization (consider all the romance movies and novels that target women), women embrace the ideology of romance from an early age and typically assume responsibility for maintaining the romance in the marital relationship. This may range from reminding husbands about anniversaries to wearing sexy lingerie. Here, women's experience of and involvement in the marriage relationship often differs significantly from that of men (Langan & Davidson, 2011).

Symbolic interactionists conclude that because husbands and wives hold such different viewpoints, they perceive marriage differently. Their experiences contrast so sharply that *every marriage contains two separate marriages—his and hers*. Viewed from this perspective, it is not surprising that marital interaction and communication have been long experienced as problematic, and efforts to improve marriages through marriage counselling have flourished throughout modern history (Davis, 2010).

IN SUM

Working from very different and sometimes opposing theoretical orientations, sociologists of the family have focused on a number of important features of family life. Functionalists tend to emphasize the interconnections between families and other social institutions such as the economy. The conflict perspective, and feminist sociologists in particular, explores conflicts, including those over scarce resources (such as time) that often emerge in family life. Nowhere is this strain more apparent than in the struggle over household work, particularly in a dual-earner family. Symbolic interactionists focus on the "meaning" family members construct in family roles and the divergent realities of "his" marriage and "her" marriage.

Focus Question
What contributions would structural functionalists, conflict theorists, and symbolic interactionists make to explaining family struggles over who should assume responsibility for housework?

THINKING CRITICALLY ABOUT SOCIAL CONTROVERSY

Is it Greed or Need? Why Canadian Mothers Work for Pay

From the 1970s to the end of the 1990s, the Canadian family mobilized increasing numbers of income earners. Wives, mothers, and teenage family members moved into the paid labour force. Not only are more family members employed, but they are working more continuously. Indeed, as noted Canadian sociologist Amber Gaszo has pointed out, the moral codes in Canada surrounding motherhood have increasingly embraced the notion that being a "good mother" means combining paid work with unpaid work in the home.

Much has been made of the reasons why family members, particularly mothers, have become so deeply involved with paid work, particularly when it often results in considerable time stress for not only mothers but all family members. There has been an ongoing debate in the media between those who are advocates for mothers who "opt out" of high-pressure professional. careers and those who urge stay-at-home moms to get to work in order to find financial and personal freedom in paid employment.

The issue was front and centre in the mass media when Anne-Marie Slaughter, a senior member of the U.S. State Department, quit her job and penned an article for *The Atlantic* explaining that despite a helpful husband, her life as a "working" mother was "freaking impossible" (Mallick, 2012). In an article triggered by this essay, Cherie Blair, wife of former British Prime Minister Tony Blair and an accomplished barrister,

commented that today young women are asking why they should bother struggling and sacrificing so that they can have both a career and a family. Once again, in the absence of real changes in the structures of employment, it appears that many women are concluding that they "can't have it all."

However, most women do not have the luxury of leaving a prestigious professional career, and most stay-at-home mothers will find the path to economic freedom bumpy at best. Rather than "choosing" whether to have a paid job, most women and their families face harsh economic pressures that typically demand several incomes.

Controlling for inflation, incomes in Canada have grown only minimally for almost two decades. Average hourly wages are actually lower now than they were 15 years ago, and overall, salaries and wages are up only $0.25 since 1991. Importantly, despite significantly increased hours of paid labour for both parents, middle-income families saw their incomes stagnate between 1971 and 2006 (Burton & Phipps, 2011). Given that real income gains for all households grew by a mere 5 percent from 1990 to 2006, while household spending increased by over 18 percent, it is not surprising that the average household saving rate dropped to the same as the average rate during the Great Depression of the 1930s—and household debt has skyrocketed.

In order to make ends meet in a period of increasing employment

insecurity for almost all workers and amid dramatic increases in the costs of education, housing, energy, medical care, health services, and so on, families are cashing in their RRSPs and going deeper into debt. Household indebtedness (the sum of mortgage and consumer debt) in Canada increased from $147 billion in 1982 to a staggering $1454 billion by 2010 (Chawla, 2011). Put simply, many Canadian families, particularly young families (19 to 34 years of age) and lone-parent and immigrant families, owe more than they own (Hurst, 2011; Sauve, 2011). In this economic context, it is not surprising to see many families, middle-income and poor, mobilizing every available wage-earner.

For these reasons, women play an increasingly crucial role in family economics. Employed wives are contributing, on average, about 30 percent of dual-earner family income, and couples with only one income earner have a poverty rate five times larger than dual-earner families (Sauve, 2007). While many Canadian families could "survive" without women's income, and some women work for reasons other than economic survival, it is important to realize the pivotal role played by economic pressures on women's paid employment.

For Your Consideration

Identify the sources of economic pressure for the contemporary Canadian family, and explore why it is so difficult for many families to extricate themselves from debt.

The Family Life Cycle

We have seen that forms of marriage and family vary widely, and we have examined marriage and family from different sociological perspectives. Now let's discuss love, courtship, and the family life cycle.

Love and Courtship in Global Perspective

Until recently, social scientists thought romantic love originated in Western Europe during the medieval period

(Mount, 1992). When anthropologists William Jankowiak and Edward Fischer (1992) surveyed the data available on 166 societies around the world, they found that this was not so. **Romantic love**—people being sexually attracted to and idealizing one another—showed up in 88 percent (147) of

⊙ **Watch** the video "The Welfare of Children" on **MySocLab.**

⊙ **Watch** the video "Women Entering the Workforce" on **MySocLab.**

Finding a "Significant e-Other": Looking for Romance in All the New Places

Just as marriage rates have changed, so, too, have the mechanisms for locating a "significant other." Canadians are increasingly turning to the internet to find friends, dates, and potential mates.

On some websites, there is a fascinating array of photographs of people searching for a relationship. Some seem to be lovely, attractive, and vivacious, and one wonders why they are posting their photos and personal information online. Internet dating sites appear to be frequented by people of every description—the needy, the pitiful, the desperate, and, of course, regular, ordinary people. In an increasingly time-stressed culture, it is not surprising that many people embrace these efficient, cost-effective mechanisms for meeting suitable potential mates. Predictably, internet postings and online services are losing their stigma and more singles are finding mates via electronic matchmaking or Facebook connections.

these groups. The role of love, however, differs sharply from one society to another. For example, people in India don't expect love to occur until *after* marriage—if at all.

Focus Question
Using a functional perspective, explain why notions of romantic love vary from one culture to another.

Marriage

Despite sharp declines in the rates of Canadian marriages, marriage itself remains popular. According to the latest census data, almost 60 percent of Canadians are in a "conjugal union," and 80 percent of those individuals are married. The structure of these relationships may have changed, but the relationships themselves persist. Between 1961 and 2006, the traditional married couple with children pattern declined from 55 percent of census families to 39 percent, but common-law couples with children increased from 2 percent to 8 percent of families; such couples without children grew from 4 to 9 percent (White, Martin, & Bartolic, 2013: 117–8). Clearly, marriage is still envisioned as a path to adult fulfilment.

THE SOCIAL CHANNELS OF LOVE AND MARRIAGE When Canadians marry, we generally think we have freely chosen our spouse. With few exceptions, however, our choices follow highly predictable social channels, especially age, education, social class, race, and religion. A young woman with a university degree whose parents are both physicians is likely to fall in love with and marry a young man slightly older than her who has graduated from university. Similarly, a female high-school dropout whose parents are on welfare is likely to fall in love with and marry a male who comes from a similar background. Race and ethnicity are particularly significantly social factors. Even though Canadian attitudes toward interracial unions have significantly liberalized, in 2006 only 3.9 of married or cohabiting couples were racially mixed (Ambert, 2012).

Sociologists use the term **homogamy** to refer to the tendency of people with similar characteristics to marry one another. Homogamy occurs largely as a result of *propinquity*, or spatial nearness. That is, we tend to fall in love with and marry people who live near us or whom we meet at school, church, or work. The people with whom we associate are far from a random sample of the population, for social filters produce neighbourhoods, schools, and churches that follow racial-ethnic and social class lines.

In a multicultural country such as Canada, many persons enter into "mixed unions." As Canada relies ever more heavily on immigration to expand its population, and the student bodies in high schools, colleges and universities reflect this growing racial, ethnic, and religious diversity, more "mixed unions" are expected. By forming unions across cultural status lines, such individuals may be seen as an important "engine of social change" (Milan & Hamm, 2004). Movement in this direction is certainly suggested by the significantly higher rates of mixed unions among young Canadians aged 25 to 34. In this age group, 6.8 percent of unions are "mixed," up from the 5.4 percent reported a mere five years earlier (Vanier Institute of the Family, 2012a). "Mixed" unions may not only challenge racial categories but also provide a mechanism for social integration and social mobility.

In a very contentious survey involving mixed marriages in Toronto, Spanish social scientist Rodriguez-Garcia found that visible minorities were more likely to marry whites even if whites were less educated and earned a lower income. The author suggested that members of minority groups tend to compensate for their relative status by bringing more educational or economic resources to the marriage market when they marry someone from an ethnic group with higher social standing. Needless to say, these suggestions were considered offensive by some readers, but the logic of Rodriguez-Garcia's analysis underscores the point that mate

education program, full-day kindergarten, and after-school day care were introduced for all families regardless of income (Albanese, 2012).

While non-familial childcare has become increasingly normalized, there remains concern that this new social reality jeopardizes parents' roles in child rearing or has negative implications for the children themselves. Research consistently indicates that childcare does not necessarily undermine child rearing. The children of employed parents feel loved and valued, provided they know they are their parents' priority (Galinsky, 1999). Indeed, the Canadian National Longitudinal Survey of Children and Youth suggests that although childcare has drawbacks, such as fewer positive mother–child interactions and less reading with parents between the ages of two to four, children in non-parental care exhibit lower hyperactivity, more pro-social behaviour, and less anxiety at age four. In short, depending on the type and quality of childcare and the mothers' parenting, childcare may benefit children (Nomaguchi, 2006).

Another major shift in child-rearing experiences has been the growth in divorce rates. Today, many children are being parented in the context of family separation and divorce. Estimates suggest that about one in five children born in 1984 experienced their parents' divorce by age 18 (Ambert, 2012: 350). As a result, many Canadian children grow up in lone-parent families (typically living with their mothers, even in joint custody arrangements) or, if their parent(s) remarried, in new, blended families. Research reveals that marital dissolution has a particularly negative impact on the role of the father in child rearing. In Canada, 15 percent of non-custodial fathers never visit their children, and an additional 25 percent do so irregularly. Not surprisingly, research also indicates that children of divorce do better (have fewer behavioural, mood, and academic problems) when their non-residential fathers are more fully involved in their lives as parents (Ambert, 2012: 352–3).

The Family in Later Life

The later stages of family life bring their own pleasures to be savoured and problems to be solved. Let's look at common-law unions among older Canadians, "boomerang" kids, and living alone.

COMMON-LAW UNIONS AMONG OLDER CANADIANS It is difficult to believe that in the not-too-distant past, entering a common-law relationship (at one time termed "shacking up") was considered somewhat daring and even socially deviant. In recent years, common-law relationships have increasingly become accepted, something that is reflected in the emergent patterns among older Canadians. Between 2001 and 2006, the growth rate in common-law relationships for Canadians aged 50 to 54 was 43.5 percent; 63.9 percent for those aged 55 to 59, and 77.1 percent for seniors aged 60 to 64. In contrast, the rate of increase in

common-law-couple families among the general population was only 18.9 percent.

This dramatic increase among older Canadians likely reflects a variety of factors. The size of the boomer generation means that as they age, boomers will impact on all marriage forms, but it is also likely that adults who have been living their lives in common-law families for a long time are now entering the ranks of older Canadians—the Woodstock generation is growing old.

It seems that new normative patterns have emerged. After the dissolution of an earlier marriage, many individuals choose a common-law form for their subsequent relationships. Reflecting general trends, older Canadians are increasingly likely to find themselves divorced (Milan, Vezina, & Wells, 2007: 21–22). The proportion of divorced persons among seniors tripled from 1981 to 2001, and by 2001, 11 percent of women aged 55 to 64 had been divorced (Turcotte & Schellenberg, 2007: 139). In addition, it seems that after age 50, people who have been widowed also often opt for common-law arrangements. In general, while older men may welcome maintaining a relationship with a partner (since men typically benefit highly from living in a relationship), older women may relish their independence and opt for cohabitation rather than more formal marital arrangements (Ambert, 2012: 196). Together, these factors underscore the fact that throughout the life cycle, marriage is becoming less frequently defined as a legal contract or religious ceremony.

Focus Question

Considering the changes that are impacting the Canadian family, what kinds of issues might be faced by a man and woman living in a common-law relationship as they mature from 50 to 70 years of age?

BOOMERANG KIDS A generation ago, analysts were discussing the impact of "empty nest" syndrome on older parents. Having devoted much of their adult lives to the care and well-being of their children, fathers and, in particular, mothers, it was suggested, were troubled by their abrupt lack of purpose in life. While the empty nest theory has always been questioned, it has become outdated as a result of recent trends. Today, many mothers have long been employed full-time in the paid labour force, so the exit of adult children and the transition to reduced familial responsibilities may create more of a sense of relief and opportunity rather than a personal vacuum (Green, 2010).

However, adult children are not all moving out, and many of those who have moved out are returning home. As a result of various factors, including a very problematic job market for Canadian young people, more extended periods of education, growing educational costs, an increasing cultural preoccupation with consumerism, and dramatic rises in the costs of housing in metropolitan centres, many mothers and fathers are finding that their adult children are living at home.

In the past, reflecting patterns of earlier marriage and child-bearing, young adults tended to leave the parental home to form their own households. In 1986, slightly less than a third of young adults (aged 20 to 29) were still living with their parents. In contrast, in 2006, almost half (43.5 percent) had either stayed in their parental homes or had moved back. While the figures are particularly high for those in the first half of their twenties (60.3 percent), even among young adults aged 25 to 59, more than one in four (26 percent) were living "at home" in 2006 (Milan, Vezina, & Wells, 2007).

Further, adult children living with their parents is an increasingly globalized pattern. In Italy, 55 percent of young people (up to age 34) are single and have never cohabited, and most still live at home (Ambert, 2012: 301). According to recent news accounts, the 50 percent youth unemployment rate in Spain has meant that many young people have been forced to live with and off their parents and grandparents. Even those who are married and have children of their own may find that they have no choice. Interestingly, by moving grandchildren in with grandparents, parents may gain access to the pension income stream while being spared the expense of sending grandparents to nursing homes. Regardless of the family constellation, it is clear that economic pressures have pushed many adult children back into their childhood homes (Blitzer, 2012).

Whether this trend will be long-lived depends on a variety of social factors. There is no doubt that, at present, there is a new reality in many families. As reflected in popular humour on the topic ("for my kids, when they're 24, it's out the door!), the presence or even the possibility of "boomerang" kids may be unsettling. The daily presence of adult children may result in frustrations for parents who must continue to share their living space and who may lose their privacy. However, Canadian research suggests that, typically, this inconvenience is balanced by a sense of personal satisfaction in continuing to provide for children. While parents report arguments over adult children's contributions to chores or their drain on family resources, as well as reduced opportunities for couple intimacy, the evidence does not suggest that significant family turmoil is common (Mandell, Wilson, & Duffy, 2008: 96–97).

LIVING ALONE In the final stages of the family life cycle, as they enter their senior years, men and women may find that they are increasingly "on their own." This has long been more the case for women than men. The cultural pattern of women marrying older men, and the higher longevity rates for women, increase the likelihood that even when marriages endure for decades, a woman is more likely than her male partner to be widowed and living alone. This is reflected, for example, in the fact that only 46 percent of women aged 65 and older live as part of a couple, while 76 percent of men

in this age category are coupled (Milan & Vezina, 2011: 10). Cultural patterns surrounding ageism, beauty, and economic wealth also mean that in the event of widowhood or divorce, women are less likely to remarry than their male counterparts, although 20 years post divorce, 69 percent of divorced women and 82 percent of divorced men have entered into a committed relationship at least a second time (White, Martin, & Bartolic, 2013: 251). The net effect of these various patterns is that although seniors in general are likely to end up alone, it is particularly the case for senior women.

In 2006, 37 percent of women aged 65 and over lived alone, in contrast to only 17 percent of comparable men. With increasing age, the gender discrepancy grows. More than half (54 percent) of women 80 and older lived alone, compared to only 24 percent of men (Milan & Vezina, 2011: 11). In sum, a variety of biological, social, and cultural factors conspire to dramatically increase the likelihood that many women will spend some portion of their senior years on their own.

Only recently have social researchers begun to critically examine the quality of life and experiences of post-family older women. The picture is not necessarily bleak, particularly for women with sufficient economic resources and good health. Many maintain extensive social networks with friends and family and live busy, fulfilled lives (de Vries, 2010). However, as discussed in Chapter 6, many older women on their own struggle with economic marginalization and its implications. As the tidal wave of baby boomers moves into old age, it is likely that the economic plight of older women living alone will be increasingly seen as a social problem (Mandell, Wilson, & Duffy, 2008).

> **IN SUM**
>
> Following the family through the life course—from romance and courtship to widowhood and death—provides an appreciation for the complexities of family life. Certainly, not every family follows the same path, and an examination of other cultures and other historical periods reveals profoundly different experiences of love, childbirth, and child rearing.

Diversity In Canadian Families

There are many varieties of family life throughout Canada.

Ethnic Diversities

For several generations, families have not produced sufficient numbers of children to maintain the size of the population, let alone to allow for growth. As a result, immigration has been key to Canadian growth. In 2006, the proportion of foreign-born people in Canada reached its highest level in 75 years. There are now members of more than 200 different ethnic groups living in Canada, and immigrants make up almost 20 percent of our population

(Chui, 2011; *The Daily*, 2007a; Momirov & Kilbride, 2005:88). Decades of immigration have literally changed the complexion of Canada. In total, 16.2 percent of Canadians are visible minorities (usually Chinese, South Asian, or black)—a 27.2 percent increase between 2001 and 2006 alone—and in certain areas, the numbers are much higher. For example, about half of Torontonians are members of a visible minority group (Chui & Maheux, 2011; Chui, 2011; *The Daily*, 2008).

These statistics underscore the continuing importance of recognizing the diversity of cultures that influence Canadian families. Some differences, as in national costume or dates of religious events, may seem trivial, but many, such as differences in cultural beliefs and values and familial roles, may have a profound impact on almost every aspect of family life. For example, Lee and Pacini-Ketchabaw's (2011) research in Victoria, British Columbia, points to the often overlooked role played by immigrant girls in serving as caregivers to their younger siblings. In cash-strapped immigrant families, older daughters may be expected to pitch in as childcare providers for younger family members. There is also evidence that Chinese-Canadian immigrant mothers are indeed more likely to embrace so-called "tiger mothering"—no sleepovers, no grades less than an A, and so on (Chua, 2011). Among Chinese-Canadian immigrant mothers, researchers have found a tendency to embrace authoritarian parenting, although this pattern complexly intersects with levels of stress and the amount of support in the immediate social environment (Su & Hynie, 2011). In short, it is not surprising that differing cultural backgrounds, along with immigrant status, may produce quite different views on the rights and responsibilities of family members (Leavell et al., 2012).

Cultural diversity similarly affects the nature and significance of families in Canada's First Nations. In the 2006 census, 1 678 200 people (5.4 percent of the Canadian population) reported Aboriginal ancestry. There is considerable diversity within this population, since these individuals are divided among 48 First Nations, ranging from the 120 000-member Cree to the 85-member Potawatomi, and some are living in large metropolitan areas while others are on remote reserves. However, family life for members of the First Nations is still conditioned by long-standing patterns that have tended to marginalize Native Canadians economically and socially (Castellano, 2002). While individual lives vary, simply by reason of being a Native Canadian, Aboriginals are more likely to be in a low-income category, more likely to commit suicide, more likely to have a variety of serious illnesses, and less likely to have high levels of formal education (O'Donnell & Wallace, 2011). Aboriginal analysts point to the importance of families—extended family networks in rural communities and reserves, nuclear families and two-generation families in urban and rural communities, and "intentional families" of the heart (voluntary communities)—in supporting efforts to create a vibrant new Aboriginal presence in Canada (Castellano, 2002).

It is important to keep in mind that the family lives of members of various racial and ethnic groups are also affected by the explicit responses of the dominant culture. Members of visible minorities, including immigrants and Native peoples, have frequently been subjected to direct and indirect manifestations of discrimination and cultural domination that have affected the quality, and even the possibility, of family life among minority communities. Historically, immigration policies have intentionally blocked family formation among working-class Chinese, South Asian, and Japanese men and women, and more recently black Caribbean women. Missionary-led residential schools and, later, non-Native child-welfare agencies similarly jeopardized family life among Canadian Native peoples by removing children from their communities, undermining familial relationships, while exposing children to abuse—and terminating Native cultures, languages, religions, education, and economies (Henry & Tator, 2010).

One-Parent Families

From television talk shows to government officials, the growing numbers of one-parent families have long been a matter of public concern. The increase is no myth, but it is not a new phenomenon. After all, in the early 1930s, more than one family in 10 was a single-parent family. However, the overwhelming majority of those families were created by the death of a parent. As the adult death rate lessened due to improvements in medicine and nutrition, so, too, did the proportion of single-parent families. By 1961, there were only 347 400 single-parent families in Canada. The country then began to witness an enormous increase. In 2006, there were 1 414 060 such families in Canada and 16 percent (a staggering one in six) of all census families were lone-parent families—the highest recorded census figure in the past 75 years. The majority (80 percent) of single-parent families are headed by women; however, the numbers of father-headed lone-parent families grew by 14.6 percent between 2001 and 2006, while mother-headed lone-parent families grew by only 6.3 percent (Flavelle, 2011).

This shift in family configuration has triggered a heated debate on the implications of divorce and single-parent families for children (White, Martin, & Bartolic, 2013: 247–255).

To understand many one-parent families, we need to view them through the lens of poverty, which is often the primary source of strain. When a household becomes

Explore "Trends for Marital Status in Canada" on **MySocLab.**

Listen to "Fathers Taking a More Active Role in Raising Children" on **MySocLab.**

Explore the reading "Life Without Father: What Happens to the Children?" on **MySocLab.**

essentially reliant on the income of one income-earner or when a household's income must be divided to support two separate units, there are frequently not enough financial resources to go around. As a result, the average total income for two-parent families with children in Canada in 2008 was $100 200, but for female lone-parent families it was $42 300 and for male lone-parent families $60 400. Predictably, one in five female lone parents and fewer than one in ten (7 percent) of male lone parents were categorized as low-income (Williams, 2010: 9, 21).

The results are serious. Children from poor families are penalized with respect to physical, mental, and social health. Level of income is clearly related to a sense of identity and purpose, social contacts, and opportunities for personal growth. For example, children from low-income families are likely to achieve lower levels of education, which, in turn, is likely to translate into higher levels of unemployment (Cumming & Duffy, 2012). Although poverty does not inevitably repeat generation after generation, children of poor families are certainly not set up to succeed.

Childless or Child-free Families?

Why do some couples not have children? With increasing economic and employment pressures, it is not surprising to find that many couples do not "choose" childlessness so much as they delay child-bearing and find that as they age, fertility issues make the decision for them. Other couples, however, consciously opt for childless marriages (Ambert, 2012: 233). Sociologist Kathleen Gerson (1985) found that some women see their marriage as too fragile to withstand the strains a child would bring. Other women believe they would be stuck at home—bored and lonely with diminishing career opportunities. Many couples see a child as too expensive or feel that having a child would limit their options in life. Not surprisingly, couples who opt for childless relationships find that they have more time for their marital relationship and enjoy greater equality in their gender roles. Women, in particular, benefit in terms of economic advances relative to women who elect to become mothers (Ambert, 2012: 233).

In 2006, 43 percent of census families (married and common-law couples) had no children living in the home (Milan, Keown, & Urquillo, 2011) (see Table 13.3). This was the first time that there were more census families living without than with children in Canada. Many of these families were empty-nesters whose children had gone off to establish families of their own (Berry et al., 1999: 72), and others were young couples who had not yet had children. However, over the past 20 years, as the population aged, the proportion of married couples with children declined from almost half (49.4 percent) to slightly more than a third (34.6 percent) (Milan, Vezina, & Wells, 2007).

Some analysts suggest that one factor at work is a shift toward the acceptance of childlessness as a family alternative. Current research indicates that about 10 percent of

TABLE 13.3 Percentage of Canadian Families by Living Arrangement, 2006

Married couples with children	34.6
Married couples with no children	34.0
Common-law couples with children	6.8
Common-law couples with no children	8.7
Lone-parent mother-headed families	12.7
Lone-parent father-headed families	3.2

Source: Derived from Milan, Vezina, & Wells (2007).

Canadian women never give birth (Nelson & Robinson, 2002). In part, this reflects the intentions of some men and women not to have children—7 percent of Canadian women and 8 percent of Canadian men aged 20 to 34 do not intend to have children (Stobert & Kemeny, 2003). Recent U.S. surveys suggest that there has been a shift toward more positive attitudes among students about childlessness as a life choice and an acceptance that parenthood will be delayed (Koropeckyj-Cox, Romano, & Moras, 2007). In particular, it seems that women are increasingly accepting childlessness as "one possible life path" (Koropeckyj-Cox & Pendell, 2007).

On occasion, the popular media, notably online media, have paid positive attention to voluntary childlessness as a life option (as embodied, for example, in the lives of Oprah Winfrey and Condoleza Rice) and challenged the pro-natalist view that all women want to become mothers. Several social groups have also emerged that are devoted to extolling the virtues of adults-only communities, vacation spots, and so forth. For example, the non-profit social club "No Kidding" provides support for couples who do not have or never want children. Created in 1984, the organization now has 70 chapters throughout North America, with 7000 members and a very active website (McNeely, 2002).

Focus Question

In what ways have major changes in Canadian institutions increased the likelihood of both single-parent and childless-by-choice families?

Focus Question

What kinds of societal issues are raised by the use of high-tech reproduction assistance by infertile couples?

Blended Families

An increasingly significant type of family formation found in Canada is the **blended family**, resulting from the remarriage of adults who are parenting one or more children from prior relationships and possibly one or more children they have had together. Since divorce in Canada now approaches

High-Tech Reproduction and the Formation of Families

One of the unintended consequences of delayed marriage and child-bearing has been an upsurge in infertility among married couples. While infertility impacts about 7 percent of females aged 18 to 24, by ages 40 to 44, the rate more than doubles to 14.3 percent (Vanier Institute of the Family, 2012b). In response, a variety of technological solutions—such as in vitro fertilization (IVF) and the use of donor insemination and donor eggs—has garnered public attention. The first successful IVF took place in 1978, when a woman in England gave birth to Louise, the world's first "test-tube" baby. Well over 250 000 children worldwide have been born as a result of the procedure since then (T. Harper, 2000: L1, L3). Not surprisingly, as more young women experience later marriages and child-bearing, technologies, such as freezing eggs and using surrogate mothers, have become increasingly significant, especially among well-to-do parents (Gootman, 2012). In 2010 the government of Quebec became the first to shoulder the costs of reproductive technologies for couples experiencing infertility issues.

Ongoing technological advances in the field have generated heated public debate over the ethical and social implications. Should 65-year-old women be allowed to use this technology to become mothers? Who should "own" the frozen embryos of deceased couples? Should donors and surrogates be allowed to "sell" their services? Which fertility services (egg retrieval and freezing costs between $8000 and $18 000) should be covered by the government-funded health insurance program? Each year, an estimated 330 000 Canadian couples

Although large families are essentially a thing of the past, unintended consequences of fertility treatments may be the unexpected creation of multiple babies and very large families.

seek fertility assistance, so this important social issue is likely to stay with us.

---

40 percent of marriages and most divorced people repartner and/or remarry, this is an increasingly common family experience (Sev'er, 2011). In 2006, 5.3 percent of all census families were stepfamilies; that is, families in which at least one of the children was from a previous relationship of one of the parents, and 2.4 percent of Canadian families were blended stepfamilies where children of both spouses from one or more unions along with one or more children from the current union were members (Bechard, 2007). With divorce common, many children spend some of their childhood in stepfamilies or blended families. In addition, even if they grow up in a single-parent home, they may have biological parents living elsewhere with new partners and new half-siblings.

Same-sex Families

In 1989, Denmark became the first country to legalize marriage between people of the same sex. Since then, the

Netherlands (2001), Belgium (2003), Spain (2005), South Africa (2006), Norway, and Sweden have made same-sex marriage legal. In 2001, the Netherlands provided same-sex couples with the right to marriage, adoption, and divorce, placing them at the vanguard of gay rights internationally (Deutsch, 2000). The issue remains contentious and largely unresolved in the United States.

In Canada, there has been steady progress toward acceptance of same-sex marriage. In 1996, the government amended the Canadian Human Rights Code, adding sexual orientation as a prohibited ground of discrimination. Health care benefits were extended to same-sex partners, and the term "common-law spouse" in collective agreements was interpreted to include same-sex couples. In 1998, British Columbia became the first jurisdiction in North America to

✳ **Explore** the reading "Ideas and Trends: Legal License; Race, Sex and Forbidden Unions" on **MySocLab.**

give same-sex couples the same privileges and obligations as opposite-sex couples (including custody, access, and child support) (O'Brien & Goldberg, 2000). On July 12, 2002, the Ontario Superior Court ruled that the current legal definition of marriage is discriminatory and ordered it changed to include recognition of same-sex marriages. And in June 2005, the Canadian federal government fully recognized and legalized same-sex unions (Larocque, 2006).

These changes reflect greater social acceptance of the 45 300 same-sex couples living in Canada in 2006. The 2006 census, for the first time, recorded the number of married same-sex couples; 7500, or 16.5 percent of same-sex couples, are legally married (Statistics Canada, 2010k:7). In Canada, as in other countries such as New Zealand, Australia, Ireland, and the United States, it appears that slightly less than 1 percent of all households are same-sex households. In most of these countries, including Canada but excluding New Zealand, male same-sex couples tend to predominate.

Over half of same-sex married couples (53.7 percent) in Canada were male in 2006 and 46.3 percent were female. Children were present in slightly less than one in ten (9 percent) of same-sex-couple homes. Women in same-sex couples were more likely (16.3 percent) than comparable men (2.9 percent) to have children in the home, and same-sex married couples were more likely to have children in the home. As a result of these combined factors, almost a quarter (24.5 percent) of women in same-sex married couples have children. Possibly reflecting the recent changes in social attitudes, men and women in same-sex couples tend to be younger than opposite-sex couples. A quarter of same-sex couples were aged 34 or younger in 2006, and only 3.8 percent were aged 65 or older (Statistics Canada, 2012k:8; Milan, Vezina, & Wells, 2007).

These national statistics suggest that there is greater social acceptance of gay and lesbian families. A recent survey reported that almost half of Canadians approve of same-sex marriages and of adoption by homosexual men and women, and the majority (61 percent) of respondents indicated that they feel same-sex couples "can do a good job of raising children" (Bibby, 2004–5: 9). Further, there is now a growing body of research scholarship on LBGTQ families (Taylor & Ristock, 2011).

However, despite this progress, it is important to recognize that many gay and lesbian relationships in Canada and elsewhere continue to be directly affected by a sometimes hostile, even violent, social context. In 2009 there were 188 hate crimes perpetrated against individuals on the basis of sexual orientation, up 18 percent from the previous year (Statistics Canada, 2010b). There has been a long tradition of legal discrimination against gays and lesbians, and growing up gay, lesbian, transgendered, or two-spirited continues to be a difficult and stressful process as negative stereotypes and discriminatory practices abound. In this context, families and communities may take on even greater significance.

Intentional Families

The segmented relationships of contemporary society may make many of us feel emotionally aloof or disconnected from others. Many would like to find a solution to this problem—to enjoy long-term relationships and feel closer to others. To overcome problems of loneliness, some people have started **intentional families**. The members, though not related by blood or marriage, declare themselves a family. They often live separately, but near one another. They meet regularly and share experiences, which adds satisfaction to their lives. The first intentional family, formed in Providence, Rhode Island, has been together for 25 years (Graham, 1996). Analysts suggest that a similar phenomenon exists among contemporary "urban tribes." With growing numbers of 30-something singles living in urban centres (consider the close-knit groups featured on television shows such as *Friends* and *Sex and the City*), young adults may be creating their own family-like support structures to foster a sense of community and belonging (Watters, 2003).

Focus Question

Why would be it be very important for a Grade 1 school teacher to be aware of the possible diversity of family forms?

IN SUM

It is important to keep in mind not only the patterning of family life, but also the diversity of experiences within these patterns. We have considered racial and ethnic diversities, one-parent families, families without children, families formed through reproductive technology, blended families, same-sex families, and intentional families. Many families combine these diversities, and there are other diversities not included here.

Trends In Canadian Families

Marriage and family life patterns in Canada are in the midst of profound change (Statistics Canada, 2012k). The "traditional" or nuclear Canadian family, comprised of a married heterosexual couple with children, is in the minority and continues to decline. In 2006, only about 39 percent of Canadian census families were heterosexual married couples with children (Milan, Vezina, & Wells, 2007; Harder, 2011). The remainder consisted of married couples (same-sex and opposite sex) without children, same-sex married couples with children, common-law couples with and without children at home, single-mother-headed families, and single-father-headed families.

Alongside the decline in "traditional" families, there has been a dramatic increase in non-traditional arrangements. The incidence of common-law-couple families continues to increase and is growing faster than married-couple families.

Between 2001 and 2006, the number of common-law-couple families grew by 18.9 percent, while married-couple families increased by only 3.5 percent. For example, the share of women aged 25 to 29 years of age living in common-law relationships increased from 7.1 percent in 1981 to 23 percent in 2006 (Milan, Keown, & Urquijo, 2011: 8). The 2006 census recorded for the first time that unmarried Canadians (aged 15 and older) outnumbered married Canadians. Over half of the population aged 15 and older had never been married, divorced, separated, or widowed, and only 48.5 percent were legally married in 2006. Twenty years ago, only 38.6 percent of this population was unmarried.

In large part as a result of increased rates of divorce, numbers of lone-parent families also grew faster than married-couple families. Reflecting a trend toward more joint-custody arrangements, lone-father families grew dramatically. The number of households made up of individuals living alone also increased (Milan, Keown, & Urquijo, 2011). When linked with other profound changes in the experiences of family life—the dramatically aging population, the shift toward employed mothers, the dramatic growth in the immigrant population, the general urbanization of Canadians, delays in relationship formation and child-bearing, the application of fertility technologies, and so on—it is not far-fetched to suggest that many Canadian families are in the midst of foundation-shaking turmoil.

Postponing Marriage and Parenting

The age at which couples enter into marriage has changed dramatically in the past hundred years. In 1925, the average bride was 25 and her groom was almost 30. A drop in age meant that by 1975, brides averaged 22 years of age and grooms only 24. Today, the average bride and groom are older than at any other time in the twentieth century (see Table 13.4).

TABLE 13.4 Changes in the Average Age of Marriage, Canada, 1925–2008

Year	Average Age of Marriage Brides	Grooms
1925	25.3	29.8
1940	24.4	27.7
1950	25.3	28.5
1960	24.7	27.7
1970	24.9	27.3
1980	22.8	25.0
1990	25.5	27.4
2008	29.1	31.1

Sources: Statistics Canada e-Book, (2005c), "Marriage," The People. Available at http://142.206.72.67/02/02d/02d_001a_e.htm; *The Daily*, January 17, 2007; Vanier Institute of the Family (2011b).

This increased age reflects the fact that both marriage and child-bearing are increasingly being postponed or put off all together. Growing pressures to spend longer periods in education and employment prior to getting married and having children mean that many women and men are starting families at an older age. In the mid-1960s, the average age of women at first birth was 23.5 years old; by 2008 the average age for first-time mothers was 28.1 years. Half of the women giving birth in 2008 were 30 or older (double the rate in 1981) (Milan, Keown, & Urquijo, 2011: 14).

When women have children later in life, they have fewer children. In 1961, about one in six Canadian families was made up of six or more persons, and the average family size was 3.9 people. Today, large families make up a scant 2.6 percent of families (Statistics Canada e-Book, 2005b). It is now estimated the average woman will have 1.68 children in her lifetime, up only slightly from the record-low fertility rate for Canada set in 2000 (Milan, Keown, & Urquijo, 2011: 13). Postponed marriages and fewer children appear related to fewer marriages overall and increased numbers of single-person households.

Focus Question
Do the postponement of marriage and child rearing and increases in divorce signal disillusionment with family life?

Going It Alone: Opting out of Marriage and Famiy

For a variety of reasons, more Canadians are living on their own, and the social implications of this popular arrangement are hotly debated. Is this a reflection of the demise of our communities and families? Are Canadians living isolated and lonely lives? Since Robert Putnam's popular book *Bowling Alone* was published in 2000, many analysts have expressed concern about this emerging global reality. Indeed, a recent survey of Vancouver community leaders reported that a "growing sense of isolation" was considered the most important issue facing the city. The fact that Vancouverites were found to be more addicted to social media than other Canadians and that those living on the West coast self-reported as the loneliest in Canada seems to affirm the idea that increasing numbers of us are trapped living alone (Mason, 2011).

However, another side to this debate is becoming increasingly prominent in the mass media (Bielski, 2012). Commentators suggest that many of us enjoy the luxury of living alone. From this perspective, when people can afford to live alone, they choose to do so. American sociologist Eric Klineberg recently laid out this argument in his *Going Solo: The Extraordinary Rise and Surprising Appeal of Living Alone* (2012). The dramatic expansion in the service sector of the economy, along with technological advances such as

● **Watch** the video "Common-Law Marriage" on MySocLab.

Global Delays in Marriage and Child-Bearing

The global economic upheavals of recent years have had particularly negative consequences for youth around the world. With youth unemployment rates approaching 50 percent in some countries, many youth are reporting that they have no options but to continue to reside at home and rely economically on their parents. While Canadians have not been as hard hit, and in 2011 youth (under age 30) unemployment was only 11.8 percent, concern persists that a significant portion of youth will become detached from schooling and employment (Marshall 2012). Research suggests that the consequences may be long term, with young people who graduate into a "poor" economy plagued by higher debt loads, higher levels of economic insecurity, and longer transitions into paid employment (Vanier Institute, 2011c). Such economically and socially marginalized youth are clearly at a disadvantage in terms of marriage and child-bearing patterns.

Postponement of marriage and child-rearing is not simply the result of absent employment options. In the growing middle class in India, China, Vietnam, Thailand, and the Philippines, more young women are postponing marriage as they pursue education and careers. As with Canadians, these delays may ultimately result in late or foregone marriage and fewer or no children. Echoing complaints heard in North America during the first wave of the women's movement in the 1920s, there is much talk in the popular press of a "flight" from marriage and the family. Not surprisingly, educated women are being criticized for "imperiling the country's future (i.e., the next generation)" by putting personal interests and careers ahead of traditional responsibilities as wives and mothers (Williams & Guest, 2005).

the internet and Facebook, means that it is possible to have a perfectly comfortable, even luxurious, life and to connect socially with many people while still living alone. Recent research suggests that people living alone have more frequent contact with friends than do couples (Vezina, 2011). These positive outcomes explain, according to Klineberg, the explosion of single-person households not only in urban centres such as Paris and Stockholm, where they comprise more than half of all households, but also in the booming economies of India, China, and Brazil.

The dialogue on the benefits and drawbacks of living an independent, solitary life hark back to feminist criticisms of marriage and the family from the 1960s and 1970s. Early advocates for "women's liberation" argued that traditional forms of marriage and the' family tended to both imprison and subordinate women, and they urged a revolution in how we respond to our emotional, sexual, and reproductive needs. As evidenced by subsequent shifts in family lives, there has, indeed, been revolutionary change in terms of patterns of divorce, maternal employment, the division of domestic labour, and alternative family formations. At the same time, many of our prejudices about "singletons" being neurotic, self-centred, or immoral have dissipated (Coontz, 2006).

Any rethinking of marriage and the family is far from complete, however, and marriage and children remain the dominant social pattern. For example, the great efforts to secure the legalization of same-sex marriages and the dramatic growth in reproductive technology both certainly attest to our ongoing investments in marriage and children.

Similarly, we still draw on pro-family ideology when we want a positive description of social groups. Army buddies and sports teams are "bands of brothers" and women's close personal friendships are a "sisterhood." It seems that even when we do not have the family idealized in the mass media, we long for it. It remains to be seen whether future social developments will include an "unhitching" of the presumed connections between love, marriage, and family (Stacey, 2011).

Common-law Marriage

Fifty years ago, most Canadians would have been scandalized by the notion of two people living together without a formal married union. Since the 1981 census—the first time the number of common-law families was counted—the numbers have increased by 200 percent (Statistics Canada e-Book, 2005a). Today, although the overwhelming majority of couples are formally married, common-law unions make up 18 percent of all couples and the numbers are rapidly increasing. Between 2001 and 2006, the number of married couples increased by 3.5 percent, while common-law unions grew by 19 percent. Common-law arrangements are particularly popular in Quebec, where, in 2006, 35 percent of couples were common-law (Milan, Keown, & Urquijo, 2011: 7–8). This sharply contrasts not only with the rest of Canada, but with other countries such as Sweden (25.4 percent), Finland (23.9 percent), New Zealand (23.7 percent), and Denmark (22.2 percent) (Milan, Vezina, & Wells, 2007).

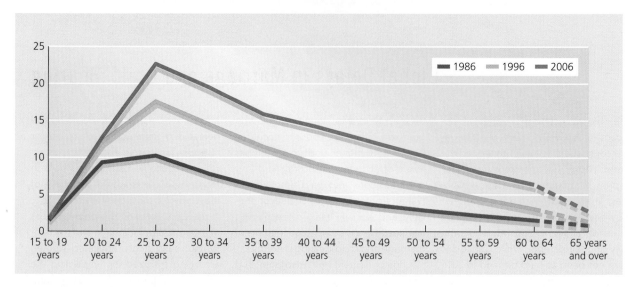

FIGURE 13.2 Persons in Common-law Couples Increasing for All Age Groups

It seems that for many common-law couples, the relationship may be a trial run. In 2006, 23 percent of women living common-law were aged 25 to 29 (up from 7.1 percent in 1981) (Milan, Keown, & Urquijo, 2011: 8). They live together as long as the relationship works, and if it sours, they can move out. In line with this pattern, first common-law relationships are twice as likely as first marriages to end in separation. Given the generalized social acceptance of common-law unions, other individuals may opt for a common-law arrangement in the wake of a divorce or widowhood. This may explain the dramatic increases, revealed in Figure 13.2, between 2001 and 2006 in the number of women and men aged 55 and over living in common-law unions (Milan, Keown, & Urquijo, 2011: 7). Common-law arrangements may offer older Canadians a less formal and legalistic union while allowing them to be part of a couple.

Divorce and Remarriage

A generation ago, divorce was a key theme in any treatment of Canadian families, and analysts expressed alarm at the dramatic increases in family breakups. Today, divorce has become part of the landscape and rates have stabilized. While the minority (19 percent of divorces end marriages that last four years or less, the overwhelming majority involve marriages of some duration. In 2008, 41 percent of all marriages that had endured 30 years or less ended in divorce. While this is below the American divorce rate, which involves approximately 50 percent of all marriages, it does indicate that divorce is far from rare (Milan, Keown, & Urquijo, 2011: 16). In both Canada and the United States, the overwhelming majority of divorced men and women subsequently remarry or form common-law unions.

In the wake of divorce, men are more likely to remarry and to remarry more quickly than women. This may reflect not only the smaller pool of potential partners for women, but also men's greater motivation to remarry. Research has consistently indicated that men derive greater benefit from marriage—in terms of increased life expectancy, for example—than women. Presumably, men derive considerable benefit from the familial gender roles in which women are expected to bring to the marriage companionship skills and housekeeping abilities.

Today, everyone knows personally or through friends that many marriages end in separation, and divorce has lost much of its public shame. Nonetheless, divorce may be a difficult event for a family, with possible long-term negative consequences for all members. Children may be particularly vulnerable to divorce-related distress. Sixty-eight percent of Canadians who were children in divorced or separated families indicate that "life was harder for us" because of their parents' divorce or separation (Bibby, 2004–5: 10). Similarly, the Canadian National Longitudinal Survey of Children and Youth, which tracked children over time, found that children whose parents later divorced exhibited higher levels of anxiety, depression, and antisocial behaviour than children whose parents remained married (Strohschein, 2005).

One of the most important outcomes of divorce and one that is interwoven with other post-divorce problems is economic. There have long been very significant economic consequences to family breakdown. In particular, women

Explore "Perceived Reasons for Divorce, by Gender" on **MySocLab.**

Explore "Physical Child-Custody Arrangements in Divorce" on **MySocLab.**

Explore the MySocLab eReading "Kids of Divorce Face Challenges at School" on **MySocLab.**

THINKING CRITICALLY ABOUT SOCIAL CONTROVERSY

Social Policy and Changes in the Family

Divorce rates provide an excellent example of the interplay between social policy and social patterns. For years, restrictive divorce laws were maintained in Canada to ensure against the "liberal excesses" of the United States. Once legislators capitulated to the need for change, we witnessed a shift in divorce rates, which then fed further changes in attitudes toward divorce, which were in turn reflected in further liberalization of divorce laws. This underscores the importance of the role of social policy in changing the possibilities in family life. For precisely these reasons, some jurisdictions, such as Turkey and Egypt, have resisted liberalization of their divorce laws. There is a fear that any such changes in the law would constitute a slippery slope that would inevitably result in societal changes unacceptable to the powers that be.

Similarly, policies surrounding parental leave, child tax credits, and childcare profoundly impact decisions about the timing and number of children as well as the likelihood and nature of fathers' early involvement in their children's lives and mothers' paid labour force engagement. For example, with the introduction of Quebec's low-cost daycare service in 1997, the labour force participation rate of mothers with pre-school children went from the lowest in Canada to the highest in a mere five years (Gaudet, Cooke, & Jacob, 2011: 176). Legislative differences mean that some nations and regions offer much more support in these areas than others. For example, Italian legislation allows for five months of maternity leave at 80 percent of wages as well as 10 months of parental leave at 30 percent of wages. In contrast, the United States provides 12 weeks of unpaid parental leave. While private employers may offer much better support, government legislation establishes the "bottom line" for all families.

who become single parents (children typically reside with their mothers post-divorce) experience very high rates of low income and economic insecurity. In a society premised on dual-earner families, single parents are likely to struggle financially, and, given our persistent patterns of gender inequality, women are particularly likely to face labour–market inequities (Ferrao, 2010). The global economic upheavals triggered by the 2008 recession have pushed many single parents and their children around the world into particularly harsh circumstances, including homelessness (Povoledo, 2012).

In the past, divorce was a distinctly uncommon event in part because of legal obstacles. Until 1968, adultery was the only legal grounds for divorce in most of Canada. Formal divorces were uncommon, but informal separations and family desertions provided a way out for many. In 1968, in response to social pressure, the *Divorce Act* was changed, the grounds for divorce were expanded, and a number of "no-fault, no-blame grounds" were added. In particular, if a couple could demonstrate that they had lived separately for three or more years, they could petition for divorce.

This change in the law opened the floodgates to a backlog of divorce actions. Couples that had been informally divorced made their status official. In 1985, the *Divorce Act* was amended again: a couple living separately for a period of not less than one year, and adultery or mental or physical cruelty, were viewed as indicative of marriage breakdown and legitimate grounds for divorce (Ambert, 2009). The changes in the law were again reflected in dramatic increases in the number of Canadians obtaining divorces (see Table 13.5).

Focus Question

What sociological factors would be particularly important in explaining the negative impact of divorce and remarriage on children?

TABLE 13.5 Rates of Divorce in Canada, 1921–2008 per 100 000 population

1921	6.4
1941	21.4
1968**	54.8
1969	124.2
1981	271.8
1985+	253.6
1987++	362.3
1997	224.8
2008	211

* Reform of divorce laws
+ *Divorce Act* (no fault)
++ Peak Year

Source: Ambert (2005: 5); Milan, Keown, & Urquijo (2011: 16).

While contemporary families are under tremendous pressures from society, they remain for their members an important source of joy, fulfillment, and social connection.

IN SUM

Not only is it vital to appreciate the variety of family forms in Canada, but we must recognize that familial structures are fluid. At present, increasing numbers of Canadians are postponing marriage and parenting. They are also much more likely to enter into common-law relationships. Although divorce statistics appear to have hit a plateau, divorce is a common ingredient of family life for Canadians.

Focus Question

What social factors would be useful in explaining the different rates of divorce across Canada and elsewhere around the world?

The Dark Side of Family Life

Aspects of family life may bring with them enormous personal benefits and satisfactions; conversely, it may incorporate the worst aspects of human existence. Let's acknowledge family troubles and their implications for Canadian society.

Child Abuse, Battering, and Incest

CHILD ABUSE Most of us are appalled by child abuse—helpless children victimized by their own parents, the adults who are supposed to love, protect, and nurture them. The most gruesome of these cases make the evening news—a four-year-old girl beaten and raped by her mother's boyfriend or six-to-ten-year-old children videotaped in sex acts by their stepfather. But few of the less-sensational child abuse cases come to our attention: children who live in filth, those who are neglected, those who are left alone for hours or days at a time, and those who are "disciplined" with extension cords. In 2008, an estimated 235 842 investigations into "child maltreatment" were conducted in Canada and 85 440

were substantiated. The most common forms of child abuse were neglect and exposure to intimate partner violence—both accounting for 34 percent of all cases. Physical abuse made up 20 percent of cases; 9 percent involved emotional abuse and 3 percent sexual abuse (Vanier Institute of the Family, 2011d).

Although since 1998 (through the Canadian Incidence Study of Reported Child Abuse and Neglect) we have national statistics on child mistreatment in Canadian families, the survey methodology changed so much in 2003 and 2008 that it is not possible to draw any conclusions about changes in rates of abuse. Reflecting dramatic and ongoing shifts in our understanding of child abuse, the term has been expanded over the past decade and remains open to debate. For example, the line between abuse and corporal punishment continues to be hotly contested. While some jurisdictions, such as Sweden (1979), have banned all forms of physical force in disciplining children, Canada has resisted this step. In 2004, the Supreme Court of Canada ruled that parents and teachers have the right to spank a child between the ages of two to 12 as long as they use "reasonable corrective force" (Jackson, 2011). While spanking is a contentious issue in Canada, the debate itself speaks to the complexity of our ideas about child abuse. Currently there are calls to include pre-natal violence (typically, intimate partner violence against pregnant women) under the rubric (Momirov, with Duffy, 2011)

Not surprisingly, girls are much more likely (three times) to be victims of sexual assault by family members than boys. Reflecting the intersecting patterns of sexuality, gender, and age, boys are more likely to be sexually assaulted when they are between the ages of three and five, while girls' rates are highest between 12 and 15 years of age. Suggesting that physical violence may be rooted in power struggles among family members, overall rates of family-related physical assaults tend to increase with the age of the victim. Physical assaults peak at age 17 for girls and at age 12 for boys (Momirov, with Duffy, 2011).

Family violence against children and youth is not insignificant. Between 2000 and 2010 the family homicide rate was highest for infants under one, and 90 to 98 percent of infant and toddler homicides were committed by parents. In 2010, children and youth were almost as likely to be physically injured by a family member as by a non-family member (Sinha, 2012: 6).

While physical and sexual abuse and murder capture the headlines, numerous Canadian children are routinely abused by being neglected or exposed to growing up in a violent home. Recent research suggests that when children witness physical fights between adults or teenagers in their home, they are more likely to be physically aggressive or to be the victims of physical violence and to display emotional disorders (Morton, 2011). In addition, recent research indicates that between 2004 and 2009, more children were exposed to spousal violence (Sinha, 2012: 6).

Globally, in many countries, social practices result in the routine abuse of children, especially female children. The routine acceptance of physical punishment (including spanking) continues to contribute to child maltreatment and child deaths (Gracia & Herrero, 2008). In some countries, it has been socially accepted to deliberately allow certain children to die of exposure or to smother or drown unwanted children. Age-old patterns of infanticide and neglect (along with sex-selective abortion) are reported to have resulted in the elimination of 60 million girls from Asian populations. Honour killings (or rapes) of young girls suspected of dishonouring their families by losing their virginity or acting in an "unchaste" manner are a socially sanctioned form of child murder. Female genital mutilation, which has been performed on at least 130 million girls and often results in persistent gynecological problems, may be viewed as a socially accepted expression of child sexual abuse. Child labour, particularly in the form of child prostitution, is a culturally embedded practice that destroys childhoods around the world. It is estimated that 2 million girls between the ages of five and 15 are introduced, often by family members, to the commercial sex market each year, some ending up on the streets of Toronto and Vancouver (United Nations Population Fund, 2000; Seager, 2003). Child abuse, when viewed from this perspective, is a complex, growing, and global reality.

BATTERING   Violence against intimate partners primarily consists of violence against females. In general, Canadian females have more than double the risk of males of being the victims of family violence (407 female victims per 100 000 population versus 180 male victims). Most of these women are victims of spousal violence (Sinha, 2012: 6).

Thanks in large measure to Statistics Canada's landmark 1993 *Canadian Violence Against Women Survey* and the now yearly family violence statistical profiles, we have excellent national statistics concerning intimate partner abuse. In the 1993 survey, almost one woman in three (29 percent) who had ever married or lived in a common-law relationship revealed at least one episode of violence by a husband or live-in partner (H. Johnson, 1996). Although spousal violence reported to police has declined in recent years, it remains an important social issue. In 2010, there were 102 500 victims of police-reported intimate partner violence (including spousal and dating violence). An alarming 51 percent of victims of intimate partner violence reported to police suffered injuries and resulted in criminal charges being laid (Sinha, 2012: 5).

The global picture is alarmingly similar. A quick review of the literature indicates that violence against women in intimate relationships remains commonplace. In South Africa, 13 to 29 percent of women say they have experienced physical abuse by a male intimate; in India, 26 to 40 percent, and in Norway, 18 percent (Seager, 2003: 26–27; Amnesty International, 2004). In the United States between 2000 and 2006, more than 8000 women were killed by the intimate males in their lives (Vallee, 2008). In some countries, abuse is amplified by a cultural tolerance for violence against women—a view shared by both sexes. In rural Egypt, for example, 80 percent of women surveyed said that beatings were common and justified, especially if the woman refused her partner sex. In some countries (such as the case of dowry murder in India), prevailing laws and practices mean that male attackers are seldom punished and women have little access to alternative shelter (Sandhu, 2012; United Nations Population Fund, 2000; Rudd, 2001).

Focus Question
How is violence in the family connected to age and gender inequalities in society?

OTHER FORMS OF FAMILY VIOLENCE   This brief discussion leaves aside other significant aspects of family violence. A quick survey of your friends will reveal that sibling violence is very common and not always innocuous (Momirov, with Duffy, 2011). In addition, although it is assumed to be relatively uncommon, analysts are paying more attention to violence against men in intimate relationships. Growing research is also documenting the extent to which aging parents may be the victims of violence at the hands of their adult children. In 2010, 2800 seniors were victims of police-reported family violence (Sinha, 2012: 5-6).

IN SUM

Social researchers are increasingly aware that numerous families, of all kinds, are often troubled and even violent. Abuse is particularly troublesome when the victims are children or seniors, since they are often trapped by the power of their "caregivers." Women are also common victims of family violence. Our growing knowledge of the nature and extent of violence within families will hopefully set the stage for proactive measures that not only assist victims but reduce the likelihood of future familial abuse.

The Future of Marriage and Family
What can we expect of marriage and family in the future?

It seems very likely that the Canadian and global economies will continue to play a significant role in marriages and families in the near future. High rates of unemployment, postponement of retirement, and rising household debt, to name a few economic factors, have direct implications for not only the timing of marriage and childbirth but also

▶ **Watch** the video "Violence in Lesbian Relationships" on **MySocLab.**

▶ **Watch** the video "Domestic Violence" on **MySocLab.**

for the stresses of familial interactions (Chawla & Uppal, 2012; Duffy, 2011). There may, for example, be increased pressures on families to provide direct economic support to the households of both younger and older family members (Chung, 2011).

Other trends are also firmly in place in Canada as well as globally (Trask, 2010). Family events—home-leaving, first marriage, first child—will continue to be delayed. There will be increasing individualization in terms of both the timing of family changes and the nature of family forms. For example, cohabitation, mother-headed families, and blended families will signify a diversity of family types. Married women will continue to join the workforce, and, as a consequence, will gain marital power. There is likely to be a continued shift toward greater equality in family life as men spend more of their youth living independently (in college dorms, for example) and learning the skills needed to share the responsibilities of housework (Pitt & Borland, 2008). Importantly, the number of elderly will dramatically increase, and more couples will find themselves "sandwiched" between caring for their parents and their own children.

At the same time, our culture will be haunted by distorted family ideologies—ranging from the family as an abusive prison to the family as a blissful haven. Sociological research can help correct these distortions and allow us to see how our own family experiences are complexly rooted in shifting social realities. Sociological research can also help to answer the big questions of how to formulate social policy that will support and enhance the quality of family and personal life as we move ever further into "uncharted territory" (Bianchi, Robinson, & Milkie, 2006).

Focus Question

Given the major changes affecting Canadian society, what will Canadian families look like in 20 years?

SUMMARY AND REVIEW

MARRIAGE AND FAMILIES IN A GLOBAL PERSPECTIVE

Why do contemporary sociologists refer to "families" and reject the notion of "the family"?

The notion of "the family" implies that there is one standard type of family. Certainly for a short period of time in the past, the expected family form was a mother and father, legally joined in marriage, living with their biological children in a common residence. Today, a minority of families share these characteristics. One-parent, blended, same-sex, and many other forms of families have proliferated. As a result, using the term "the family" harkens back to this "traditional" model of families and is not only inaccurate but may hide a conservative agenda; that is, that families ought to have these characteristics. pp. 280–283.

MARRIAGE AND FAMILIES IN A THEORETICAL PERSPECTIVE

What are the differences between the functionalist, conflict, and symbolic interactionist theoretical approaches to family life?

Functionalists tend to examine families in terms of the services they provide for the larger society and for other institutions in that society. They are inclined to argue, for example, that all societies have families because they must have a mechanism of socializing children, caring for the sick and aged, and providing for the production of the next generation. Conflict theorists tend to focus on the power struggles and inequalities within and between families. For example, feminists have focused on the struggle over the division of household work and the pressures on women to contribute to household incomes as important elements in family satisfaction and changes in familial roles. Symbolic interactionists are particularly interested in the construction and perpetuation of meanings in family lives. Being a father is complexly interwoven with the meanings attached to masculinity in a particular society. pp. 238–288.

THE FAMILY LIFE CYCLE

What are the key patterns that persist within the rich diversity of family life experiences?

From a life cycle perspective, families typically go through a series of stages. First, there is some form of mate selection and relationship formation. In many western societies, couples date, fall in love, and become engaged (often reflected in a decision to live common-law). Whether or not they formalize their relationship with a legal or religious ceremony, most couples will confront the possibility of child-rearing. The majority of couples will bear children or adopt and will spend several decades raising these children. In later life, contemporary couples may find that their adult children remain in the home. As a result of divorce or widowhood, most parents (especially mothers) will find themselves on their own in their later years. However, within these patterns, there is considerable diversity. Contemporary Canadian families include married couples with and without children, common-law couples with and without children, and lone-parent families headed by either mothers or fathers. These families include same-sex families, step-, and blended families. pp. 288–293.

TRENDS IN CANADIAN FAMILIES

How have economic and legislative changes resulted in profound changes in family living?

There are trends toward decreased numbers of traditional families and increased numbers of common-law families, blended and stepfamilies, and father-headed lone-parent families. There are increased numbers of households made up of individuals living alone. Marriage and child-bearing are being delayed longer. Mothers continue to move into the paid labour force, and more fathers are taking time off work to partake of parental leave when their children are born. There are more Canadian families without children. Many of these changes can be traced back directly to new laws concerning marriage dissolution, parental leave, the provision of childcare, and the legalization of birth control. pp. 297–302.

TWO SIDES OF FAMILY LIFE

What are some of the social causes of family violence and abuse?

Long-standing patterns of gender inequality contribute to abuse of children and wives. The patriarchal tradition in many societies has tended to legitimate violence against girls and women. This tradition is echoed in some familial relationships; for example, husbands may feel that they own their children or wives and may treat them as property. The long-standing acceptance of punishment of children (and, previously, wives) also serves to provide a rationale for contemporary "disciplining" of children. Many other forms of child abuse—notably, neglect—are the direct results of poverty and patterned economic inequality. pp. 302–304.

TALKING ABOUT THEORY

Theoretical Paradigms

	CLASSICAL PARADIGMS		RECENT PARADIGMS
	Structural-Functional Paradigm	Symbolic-Interaction Paradigm	Feminist Paradigm
What is the level of analysis?	Macro level	Micro level	Macro level
What is the importance of families for society?	Society depends on families for reproduction, socialization of children, support for educational processes, and economic activities.	Family roles are crucial to our sense of meaning and identity. Being a father or a mother, for example, is a key ingredient in the social construction of masculinity or femininity.	Struggles over division of household labour within the home reflect larger social patterns of inequality surrounding gender. The expectation that women will do the "lion's share" in the home reflects and reinforces the generalized subordination of women in society.
Have families changed over time? How?	Yes, many of the traditional functions of the family have been taken over by other agents—including the school system, daycare centres, and even Molly Maid.	Yes, the meanings people attach to family roles have shifted. Being a mother, for example, is now generally accepted as compatible with paid employment.	Yes and no. The division of domestic labour has moved toward greater equality, but there still remains a tendency for women to take the majority of responsibilities for children and chores.

KEY TERMS

All URLs listed are current as of the printing of this text.

National Clearinghouse on Family Violence
www.phac-aspc.gc.ca/nc-cn
The National Clearinghouse on Family Violence is a national resource centre for all Canadians seeking information about violence inside the family and looking for new resources being used to address it. The Clearinghouse seeks to help Canadian communities work toward the eventual elimination of all forms of family violence.

The Vanier Institute of the Family
www.vifamily.ca
The Vanier Institute of the Family was established in 1965 under the patronage of their Excellencies Governor General Georges P. Vanier and Madame Pauline Vanier. It is a national voluntary organization dedicated to promoting the

well-being of Canada's families through research, publications, public education, and advocacy. The website is a very useful resource for examining trends in Canadian families.

The Childless by Choice Project
www.childlessbychoiceproject.com
This site provides an interesting example of the ways in which the social media seek to explore and legitimate certain familial configurations. This advocacy site provides information that supports the decision to remain childless.

Children's Defense Fund
www.childrensdefense.org
The mission of the Children's Defense Fund is to "ensure every child a Healthy Start, a Head Start, a Fair Start, a Safe Start, and a Moral Start in life and successful passage to adulthood with the help of caring families and communities."

1. Why is it so uncommon for intimate partners to work out the division of domestic labour before they move in together?
2. How are the interconnections between Canadian families and the education system likely to change in the near future?
3. Given that the Canadian family is going through a number of important changes, what particular family issues confront children and adolescents today?
4. Have the dramatic changes in family life in Western countries benefited women? Access the Research Navigator through MySocLab and use keywords such as "divorce," "single-parents," "full-day kindergarten," and "housework" to locate relevant and recent scholarly and popular press publications to help you answer this question.

MySocLab

Explore the topics covered in this chapter on MySocLab. Interactive resources include a study plan, cumulative exams, a multimedia library, MySocLab eReadings, and access to the MySocLab Video Series.

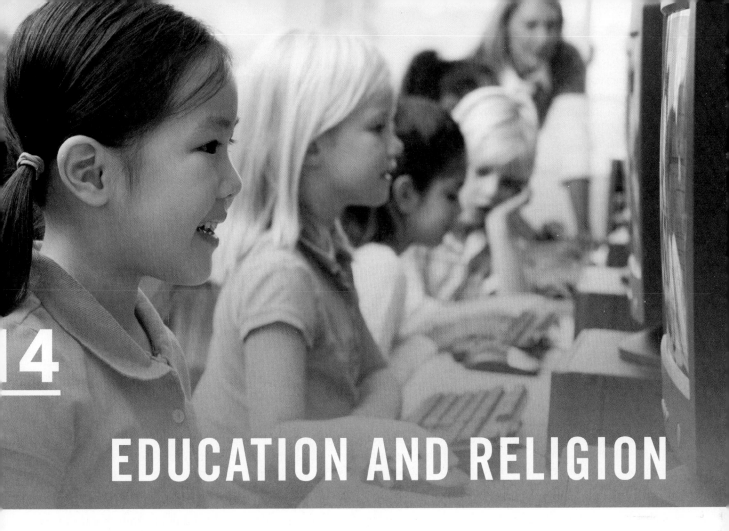

14

EDUCATION AND RELIGION

NEHA still feels resentment when she recalls the memo that greeted her that Monday morning:

> With growing concern about international competition for our products, the management is upgrading several positions. The attached listing of jobs states the new qualifications that must be met.

Neha quickly scanned the list. The rumours had been right, after all. The new position the company was opening up—the job she had been slated to get—was listed.

After regaining her composure somewhat, but still angry, Neha marched into her supervisor's office. "I've been doing my job for three years," she said. "You always gave me good evaluations, and you said I'd get that new position."

"I know, Neha. You'd be good at it. Believe me, I gave you a high recommendation. But what can I do? You know what the higher-ups are like. If they decide they want someone with a university degree, that's just what they'll get."

"But I can't go back to university now, not with all my responsibilities. It's been five years since I was in university, and I still have a year to go. I promise to finish my degree by taking courses online, but with five full courses to complete, it will be at least a year before I will graduate."

The supervisor was sympathetic, but she insisted that her hands were tied and that upper management was insisting on hiring someone whose degree is in hand. Neha would have to continue working at the lower job classification—and stay at the lower pay.

It was Neha's responsibility to break in Melissa, the newcomer with the freshly minted university degree. Those were the toughest two weeks Neha ever spent at work—especially since she knew that Melissa was already being paid more than she was.

EDUCATION: TRANSFERRING KNOWLEDGE AND SKILLS

Today's Credential Society

Sociologist Randall Collins (1979) observed that industrialized nations have become **credential societies**, that employers use diplomas and degrees to determine who is eligible for a job. In many cases, the diploma or degree is irrelevant for the work that must be performed. The new job that Neha wanted, for example, did not suddenly change into a task requiring a university degree. Her immediate supervisor knew Neha's abilities well and was sure she could handle the responsibility just fine—but the new company policy required a credential that Neha didn't have. Similarly, a high school diploma is not necessary to pump gas or to sell shoes, yet employers routinely require such credentials.

In fact, it is often on the job, not at school, that employees learn the specific knowledge or skills a job requires. A high school diploma teaches no one how to sell tacos or be polite to customers. Neha had to teach Melissa the ropes. Why do employers insist on diplomas and degrees? Why don't they simply use on-the-job training?

A major reason credentials are required is the large size, urbanization, and consequent anonymity of industrial societies. Diplomas and degrees serve as automatic sorting devices. Because employers don't know potential workers personally or even by reputation, they depend on schools to weed out the capable from the incapable. By hiring graduates, the employer assumes that they are hiring responsible people; for evidently they have shown up on time for numerous classes, have turned in scores of assignments, have obeyed—or at least have not detoured too far from—the many rules of universities, and have demonstrated basic writing and thinking skills. The specific job skills that a position requires can then be grafted onto this base certified by the academic institution.

In other cases, specific job skills must be mastered before an individual is allowed to perform certain work. As a result of changes in technology and knowledge, simple on-the-job training will not suffice for physicians, engineers, and airline pilots, which is precisely why doctors prominently display their credentials. Their framed degrees declare that they have been certified by an institution of higher learning, that they are qualified to work on our bodies.

A high school diploma is regarded as the minimum qualification for young Canadians entering the labour market. Between 2008 and 2010, there were 280 000 new jobs requiring a university degree created in Canada, while 260 000 for those without degrees were eliminated (Bradshaw, 2011), In fact, for many Canadians, a bachelor's degree isn't enough to get them the job they really want; it is simply a "stepping stone" to their ultimate career goal. Between 1999 and 2009, while full-time undergraduate enrollment increased by 40 percent, graduate enrollment rose by 70 percent, with rates of master's students skyrocketing (ibid.). The explosion in graduate education has left many Canadians questioning the value of their undergraduate degrees.

In general, unemployment rates are lower among the more highly educated. In Canada in 2011, the unemployment rate among university graduates aged 25 to 54 was 4.7 percent. In contrast, within the same age group, 11.2 percent of those who did not finish high school were unemployed (Statistics Canada, 2012b).

Without the right credentials, you will not get hired. It doesn't matter that you can do the job better than someone else. You will never have the opportunity to prove what you can do, if, like Neha, you lack the credentials to even be considered for the job.

The Development of Modern Education

Credentials are only one indicator of how central the educational institution is in our lives. Before exploring the role of education in contemporary society, let us first look at education in earlier societies, and trace the development of universal education.

Education in Earlier Societies

In earlier societies, there was no separate social institution called education. There were no special buildings called schools, and no people who earned their livings as teachers. Rather, as an integral part of growing up, children learned what was necessary to get along in life. If hunting or cooking were essential skills, then people who already possessed those skills taught them. *Education was synonymous with* **acculturation**, the transmission of culture from one generation to the next—as it still is in today's tribal groups.

Education can be a dangerous thing. Socrates, who taught in Greece about 400 years before the birth of Christ, was forced to take poison because his views challenged those of the establishment. Usually, however, educators reinforce the perspectives of the elite, teaching students to take their place within the social structure.

In some societies, when a sufficient surplus accumulated—as in China, North Africa, and classical Greece—a separate institution developed. Some people then devoted themselves to teaching, while those who had leisure time—the children of the wealthy—became their students. In ancient China, for example, Confucius taught a few select pupils, while in Greece, Aristotle, Plato, and Socrates taught science and philosophy to upper-class boys. **Education** came to be something quite distinct from informal acculturation; education is a group's *formal* system of teaching knowledge, values, and skills. Such instruction stood in marked contrast to the learning of traditional skills such as farming or hunting, for it was clearly intended to develop the mind.

Education flourished during the period roughly marked by the birth of Christ, then slowly died out. During the Dark Ages in Europe (the thirteenth and fourteenth centuries), the candle of enlightenment was kept burning by monks, who, except for a handful of the wealthy and nobility, were the only people who could read and write. Although they delved into philosophy, the intellectual activities of the monks centred on learning Greek, Latin, and Hebrew so that they could read early texts of the Bible and writings of the church fathers. Similarly, Jews kept formal learning alive as they studied the Torah. Baghdad was the educational hub for the Arab world; here the focus was on the Quran, poetry, philosophy, linguistics, and astronomy.

Formal education, however, remained limited to those who had the leisure to pursue it. (In fact, school comes from a Greek word meaning "leisure.") Industrialization transformed this approach to learning, as new machinery and new types of jobs brought a general need to be able to read, write, and work accurately with figures—the classic "three Rs" of the nineteenth century ("Reading, 'Riting, and 'Rithmetic").

Industrialization and Universal Education

The development of universal education is linked to industrialization. Let's see how free universal education developed in Canada.

Prior to Confederation, mainly religious groups were most involved in education. The primary goal, particularly among Christian groups, was to "civilize" First Nations Canadians, along with other children, by teaching them a curriculum based on the "three Rs." The church's influence on education, however, was significant, and lessons usually included guidance in morality and obedience. Both Catholic and Protestant (or public) school systems were created even before Confederation. The *School Act* of 1851 provided Roman Catholics with public funds for their schools, a topic of ongoing controversy even today. The development of higher education was also linked to religious bodies. North America's oldest institution of higher learning, Laval University in Quebec City, was founded by Jesuit priests in 1636. The founders of both the University of Toronto and McGill University were linked to the Church of England.

By the time of Confederation, the makings of a free and universal education system had been firmly entrenched. A number of school acts were passed throughout Upper and Lower Canada providing for schools within bounded areas, and school attendance gradually began to increase as the value of education was recognized across communities. Commitment to education was regarded not only as a personal benefit, but also as a civic responsibility, since schooling the masses was considered to be the means to social improvement. Education was a matter of **political** socialization, the way young people would be inculcated with beliefs, ideas, and values and would embrace the civil order, all of which was necessary for the developing capitalist and industrial order. A universal system of schooling based on standardized texts instilled patriotism and taught the principles of democratic government.

In Ontario, Reverend Egerton Ryerson, who was the province's superintendent of schools from 1844 to 1876, was instrumental in establishing the system of free, publicly supported schools. His work in Ontario was eventually followed by educational activists throughout Canada. Prior to Ryerson's work, formal education was optional for working-class children. Most children learned from their parents in and around the home or in small workshops that dotted the Canadian landscape. Upper-class children attended costly private schools or were taught in their homes by tutors. In 1871, schooling was made compulsory and the relationship between the school and the state tightened. The common school became "a public institution in the modern sense of the term, an institution not only paid for out of public funds, but with publicly defined goals" (Prentice, 1977: 17). It is no coincidence that universal education and industrialization occurred simultaneously. Seeing that the economy was undergoing fundamental change, political and civic leaders recognized the need for an educated workforce. They also feared the influx of foreign values and looked on public education as a way to socialize immigrants into the Canadian way of life.

Over time, the amount of education considered necessary continued to expand. By 1920, most provinces had compulsory education laws requiring children to attend school, usually until they had completed Grade 8 or turned 16, whichever came first. In the early 1900s, graduation from Grade 8 was considered to be a full education for most people. "Dropouts" were students who did not complete grade school. High school, as its name implies, was viewed as a form of "higher" education.

As industrialization progressed and as fewer people made their living from agriculture, formal education came to be thought of as essential to the well-being of society. Industrialized nations then developed some form of the credential society described earlier. Graduation with a post-secondary certificate or university degree is increasingly common in Canada. Between 1980 and 2005, the income gap between less educated young workers and those who were well-educated widened significantly. There are a number of reasons why this difference in income levels exists. Some argue that technological change requiring a more highly skilled labour force accounts for the difference, while others point to losses in manufacturing and other highly unionized jobs together with growth in economic sectors, such as retail, where wages are typically low (Chung, 2006: 5). With the loss of many assembly jobs as industries move to China, India, or other lower-wage countries, there have been fewer opportunities available to Canadian workers who do not graduate from high school (ibid.).

Predominant among those who have not completed high school are older workers over the age of 55. Between 1980 and 2005, the percentage of Canadians in the labour force without a high school diploma decreased from 29 percent of those aged 25 to 34 in 1980 to 9 percent in 2005. Among Canadians aged 35 to 54, 47 percent had some high school or less in 1980 but only 13 percent had less than a high school diploma in 2005 (Chung, 2006: 5). Between 1999 and 2009, the proportion of Canadians aged 25 to 64 holding college or university certificates or degrees increased from 39 to 50 percent (Statistics Canada, 2011f: 15).

Today, the majority of university graduates (60 percent) are women (Statistics Canada, 2011f). Women with college diplomas outnumber college-educated men, while the majority of those holding trade certificates or licenses are men (Statistics Canada, 2011f). Despite women's achievement in education, the average annual incomes of women with higher educational degrees are 61 percent of that of men; in 2008, women's earnings were still only 63 percent of men's incomes. This does not mean that women should abandon their educational aspirations. Although men's incomes are higher than women's at every level of educational attainment, the gap narrows as women ascend the educational ladder, indicating that the financial payoff from additional education is greater for women than it is for men (Statistics Canada, 2011f: 62).

Canadians who don't make it through high school are condemned to a difficult economic life. Analysts have estimated that university graduates may earn up to $1 million more over their lifetimes than high school graduates (Brown, 2006: A4). On average, the unemployment rate among high school leavers is higher, their wages are lower, and they are less likely to work full-time, full-year compared to high school graduates (Statistics Canada, 2011e). Moreover, the International Adult Literacy Survey concluded that, as compared to their counterparts in other countries, poorly educated Canadians with less than a high school education tend to perform poorly in simple daily literacy tasks (Statistics Canada, 2011e).

The rates of high school graduation are not evenly distributed across the provinces. Relatively higher numbers in Newfoundland, the Northwest Territories, Prince Edward Island, and Saskatchewan leave school before completing high school. To some degree, the rates of school leaving correlate with the distribution of poverty within the provinces, with the relatively poorer provinces having a higher number of school leavers and the relatively well-off having greater numbers of university graduates.

Canada ranks fourth among developed countries for the percentage of its labour force holding a university degree (20 percent). Further, among those with a university degree, one-quarter of Canadians aged 25 to 64 compared to just over one-fifth in OECD countries on average had attained this level of education in 2009 (Statistics Canada, 2012b).

Canada is behind Norway (26 percent) and the Netherlands (21 percent), and ahead of the United Kingdom

(18 percent), Sweden (17 percent), Korea (17 percent), and Australia (19 percent). However, Canada ranks second (21 percent), trailing only Iceland (22 percent), in the percentage of the labour force holding college diplomas (OECD, 2002). If we consider only younger adults aged 25 to 34, Canadians have shown considerable improvements in post-secondary attainment as compared to other OECD countries (OECD, 2011b). In 2009, Canada, Japan, and Korea stood well ahead of other OECD countries, with over 50 percent of those aged 25 to 34 having obtained higher educational credentials (OECD, 2011b:40). However, Canada's commitment to education may be questioned. Canada ranked fifteenth among 39 OECD countries in 2005 on the proportion of the GDP it spent on research and development, a number that had not changed since 2001. And on another measure, Canada ranked twentieth out of 291 OECD countries in the number of science and engineering degrees as a percentage of all new degrees granted in 2004 and 2006 (Canadian Council on Learning, 2009: 96).

Focus Question
What is political socialization and how does it take place through education?

The Functionalist Perspective: Providing Social Benefits

As stressed in previous chapters, a central position of functionalism is that when the parts of society are working properly, each contributes to the well-being or stability of the society as a whole. The intended consequences of people's actions are known as **manifest functions**, while those that are not intended are called **latent functions**. As we examine the functions of education, its manifest and latent functions will become evident.

Teaching Knowledge and Skills

Education's most obvious manifest function is to teach knowledge and skills, whether they are the traditional three Rs or more contemporary competencies such as computer literacy and internet skills. Every society must train the next generation to fulfill its significant positions. From a functionalist perspective, the reason schools are founded, supported by parents, and financed by taxes is to meet the needs of the labour market. But why are employers requiring workers to obtain diplomas or degrees for jobs that appear to have little or no relation to the subject matter studied in school and that did not require higher educational credentials a generation ago?

Cultural Transmission of Values

At least as significant as teaching knowledge and skills is a function of education called **cultural transmission**, a process by which schools pass on a society's core values from one generation to the next. In addition to responding to the demands of the economy, the need to produce an informed electorate, and the desire to "Canadianize" immigrants, in what other ways does the educational system reflect—and transmit—cultural values?

Schools are such an essential part of Canadian culture that it is difficult to know where to begin. Outside Quebec, instruction takes place primarily in English, reflecting the dominant British influence on Canadian institutions and culture. The perspective conveyed in the classroom is predominantly Western. The Western perspective, essentially the point of view of the dominant group, neglects to tell the stories of minority groups, often those that have suffered at the hands of these dominant groups. Aboriginal or First Nations groups are sometimes portrayed in negative ways or might be absent from school texts and discussions. Slavery and other acts of discrimination, such as the treatment of Japanese-Canadians during World War II, are introduced as unfortunate, inexcusable, and isolated events that should not have happened, but are now in the past. There is little in the curriculum on working-class or union history, politics, arts, and culture. Similarly, the architecture of school buildings themselves reflects Western culture, and their often distinctive appearance—typically low-rise, boxy buildings with adjacent playing fields or running tracks—identify them as schools on sight.

If we think of political teaching and cultural training within schools as running on a continuum from a very conservative approach to one incorporating more liberal viewpoints, then situated on the extreme right would be fundamentalist groups from the Christian right. The Oscar-nominated and award winning documentary *Jesus Camp* (2006) follows the lives of a group of young children as they are trained to assume leadership roles within a particular sect of evangelical Christianity. This training includes homeschooling, thereby isolating the children from a wider range of viewpoints and ideas. Many question the extreme training practices in which the children are repeatedly reduced to tears to atone for their sins. Coupled with homeschooling, where the children are taught that creationism has all the answers and that science is evil, these practices are considered by many to be intense forms of indoctrination.

With just under 5.1 million students attending elementary and high schools in 2008–09 (Statistics Canada, 2010c), and over 1 million enrolled in universities in 2005–06 (Statistics Canada, 2008i), Canadian education is big business. In 2008–09, the total expenditure on public education was $55 billion; in other words, the cost to Canadian taxpayers was $11 614 per student (Statistics Canada, 2010c).

Education institutions at all levels are major employers, providing relatively well-paid work for thousands of professionals. In addition to classroom teachers and university professors, thousands more work providing classroom support as aides, administrators, bus drivers, janitors, and secretaries. Others earn their living in industries that service schools—from building schools to manufacturing pencils, paper, computers, and desks to providing insurance, cleaning supplies, and food. In 2004, 43 percent of Canadian households each spent an average of $2500 on educational expenses for books, supplies, and tuition (Statistics Canada, 2008). Canada spent about 6 percent of the gross domestic product (GDP) on education in 2007—similar on average to what was spent by the OECD countries. But Canada outspent other OECD countries on college and university programs, with an outlay of 42 percent of the education share of the GDP on higher education (Statistics Canada, December 20, 2010). To better understand the connection between education and values, let's look at how the educational system transmits individualism, competition, and patriotism.

INDIVIDUALISM   Individualism forms a thread integrally woven into the Canadian educational system. Unlike their Japanese counterparts, Canadian teachers and students seldom focus on teamwork. Where Japanese schools stress that the individual is only one part of a larger, integrated whole, Canadian students learn that the individual exists on his or her own. Pervasive but often subtle, such instruction begins in the early grades, when teachers point out the success of particular students, sometimes awarding them with small tokens or minor privileges. Some might say, for example, "Everyone should be like Joey," or "Why can't you be like María, who got all the answers right?" In such seemingly innocuous statements, the teacher thrusts one child ahead of the rest, holding the individual up for praise. Schools continue to select class valedictorians, reward high achievers, sponsor athlete-of-the-year banquets, and participate in science fairs, math competitions, and spelling bees. In each

of these events, in the end, usually only one student takes home the coveted prize.

COMPETITION   Competitive games in the classroom and the schoolyard provide an apt illustration of how schools transmit this core value. In the classroom, a teacher may divide the class into competitive groups for a math challenge, while on the playground children are encouraged to play hard-driving competitive games and sports. A school's formal sports programs—baseball, football, basketball, soccer, hockey, volleyball, and so on—pit students against one another as they try out for spots on the teams and then pit team against team in head-to-head confrontations, driving home the lesson that the competitive spirit is highly valued. Although organized sports stress teamwork, the individual is held up for praise. The custom of nominating an "outstanding player" (emphasizing which of these persons is the best) reinforces the related lesson of individualism.

PATRIOTISM   As in schools around the world, schools in North America teach patriotism. Canadian students are taught that Canada is the best country in the world; Americans learn that no country is better than the United States; and French, German, British, Spanish, Japanese, Chinese, Afghani, and Egyptian students all learn the same about their respective countries. To instill patriotism, elementary school teachers in every country extol the virtues of their society's founders, their struggle for freedom from oppression, and the goodness of the country's basic social institutions.

Sociologist Randle Nelsen (2002) argues that, in today's schools, education has become infused with popular culture in such a way that education has evolved into

Corporations can sometimes play a significant role in the education system. Over the years, some schools have negotiated agreements with specific corporations in return for funding. However, while students may benefit from the extra money their school has managed to acquire in this way, the students' ideas, values, and overall school experiences are often influenced by that company's corporate agenda.

"edu-tainment" and the corporate presence at schools and on college and university campuses represents the encroachment of the corporate agenda into curriculums and therefore into the heart of education. In the United States, the amount of company sponsorship at the elementary and high school levels has rapidly increased, with global and local companies footing bills for sports programs and football stadiums. It is becoming commonplace to see advertisements around schoolyards, on uniforms, on walls, and even sculpted into the landscape (Pennington, 2004).

In step with practices in the United States, highbrow fundraisers are becoming commonplace in Canada. A national study by the Canadian Teachers' Federation found that public schools on average raised almost $16 000 per year, with some schools netting close to $50 000 (Alphonso, 2005: A6). In Toronto there are stark differences in the amounts schools can fundraise. Between 2007 and 2010, 20 primary schools in the most affluent neighborhoods raised 36 times the amounts raised by the 20 least affluent schools. In dollar terms, the difference was $249 362.51 per school compared to $6922.98 per school (Social Planning Toronto, 2011: 2). The same pattern was repeated in the secondary schools, with the wealthiest 20 schools raising 920 times more funds than the poorest 20 schools, or a difference of $33 653 compared to $36.56 per school (ibid.).

Corporate sponsorships buy basics, including textbooks, library materials, and classroom technology, and pay for special events, such as school trips and athletic programs and clubs. Many parents and educators worry about the long-term outcomes of what might seem like innocuous activities. In particular, concerns have been raised that fundraising and corporate sponsorships recreate inequality and widen the gap in opportunities and resources between wealthier and poorer neighbourhoods. There is a growing dependency on raising funds and the differences across communities are contributing to the gap. Recognizing the growing inequality, many schools are questioning the responsibility of the state in providing equal opportunities to children and youth through education.

As elaborated below in the Thinking Critically about Social Controversy box on page 314, not only have schools, and particularly university and college campuses, taken on a "shopping mall" appearance, but the transformation in the appearance of the "ivy walls" represents long-term contracts and agreements that institutions have struck with big business—and such relationships that have affected dominant values, ideas, and experiences of the school system.

Focus Question

How does the educational system transmit values of individualism and competition?

Social Integration

Schools also perform the function of social integration, helping to mould students into a more or less cohesive unit.

Schools socialize students politically by incorporating, however subtly, dominant values, ideas, and experiences. Most school lessons are taught primarily from a white, middle-class, male, non-Native perspective.

Indeed, forging a national identity by integrating immigrants into a common cultural heritage was one of the manifest functions of establishing a publicly funded system of education in Canada. When children enter school, they come from many different backgrounds. Their particular family and social class may have taught them speech patterns, dress, and other behaviours or attitudes that differ from those generally recognized as desirable or acceptable. In the classroom and on the playground, those backgrounds take new shape. The end result is that schools help socialize students into the mainstream culture.

Peer culture is especially significant, since most students are eager to fit in. From their peers, they learn ideas and norms that go beyond their family and their little corner of the world. Guided by the powerful world of mass media, many succumb to peer pressure, particularly during early and middle adolescence (Ambert, 2001; 2006). While peer pressure may result in students in all parts of the country sporting the same brands and styles of jeans, shirts, shoes, and jackets and using similar speech patterns, sharing ideas, and interacting with the opposite sex in similar ways, there are aggressive, nasty, harmful, and even violent sides to peer pressure (Corsaro, 2004).

Peer culture may also turn awry, with those not seen as fitting in becoming targets for insults, pranks, or more serious and violent words and actions, as evident in the increased incidence of bullying in Canadian schools. Bullying, often a topic for community forums, professional development days, and public discussion, is a growing problem within schools. It has also been the theme of a number of recent films, including the highly acclaimed *Bully*, a 2011 film that documented the lives of five students in the United States who endure bullying on a daily basis. Although bullying is sometimes the subject of light humour, it is a serious concern. In many episodes of the popular TV series *The*

THINKING CRITICALLY ABOUT SOCIAL CONTROVERSY

Education and Corporatization

For decades, critics have exposed the intricate ways that the corporate agenda has directed and shaped the structural forms and intellectual pathways of educational institutions, starting with the seemingly linear links realized through individuals who play pivotal roles in connecting the two. The encroachment of the corporate agenda into the sphere of education is no longer debated as it was throughout the last century, when those defending the form and structure of educational institutions argued that non-partisan educational decision-makers should be drawn from among those men (and sometimes women) who held esteemed positions within the economy and broader society. With insights drawn from their professional experience largely within the corporate world and as members of academic governing boards, these prominent players were expected to protect the academy's autonomy and ensure that its researchers and educators maintained their course in the pursuit of knowledge, while drawing interest, respect, and material support from corporate and political networks.

In the past, corporate connections to education were less obvious, and were traced by critics primarily through members of boards of governors, the majority of whom had résumés that included an impressive list of directorships in both top-ranking and local business concerns. Schools maintained their autonomy, at least in appearance. Today, corporate presence is striking, and academic administrators covet long-term contracts and reciprocal agreements with big business. Ontario university campuses, for example, have become the site of Pepsi–Coke cola wars. A number of schools have signed deals with either company, stipulating that the competitor's products will not be sold anywhere on campus.

The agreements give Pepsi or Coke full rights at the exclusion of the other (as well as the less popular brands), thereby guaranteeing a market of primarily young consumers whose preferences (for Pepsi or Coke) may be formulated or confirmed during their years at school. Similar binding agreements are signed with fast-food chains, many of which are located within the same corporate empire, such as the well-known Pepsi–Pizza Hut relation. And these agreements are not only signed at colleges and universities, where it is generally easier for students and staff to access alternative businesses within their local communities, but an increasing number of high schools have committed to such arrangements in exchange for sponsorship of events (basketball tournaments, band exchanges, ski trips) and the provision of resources and equipment (sports scoreboards, computers).

For the institutions, a successful corporate campaign has been key to economic survival. Those spearheading corporate fundraising campaigns argue that such initiatives are necessary to support an increasingly expensive academic infrastructure, particularly in light of the state's dismantling of the welfare state, including its former commitments to higher education and its adoption of a monetarist economic program. Within the context of globalization, one of the primary goals for the state is to reduce the costs of production and reproduction. This is accomplished in part through cutbacks in health care, social programs, and education. For some, the invitation to establish corporate agreements is a reasonable course in heading off the inevitable tide of privatization. However, as Nelsen (2002) poignantly observes, "education becomes edu-tainment" and a student culture, marked by political dissent, is replaced by popular culture. The campus, once a site of protest and resistance, becomes even more firmly ensconced within the throes of corporatism.

As schooling is transformed into edutainment, the educator steps into the role of performer. Those professors who have taught large undergraduate classes with any degree of success will readily describe the experience as physically exhausting, largely because of demands for a flawless performance that is somewhat entertaining and well-paced to maintain interest and allow for salient points to be noted. Within mass culture, scholarship and intellect may be confused with Trivial Pursuit. The "game show" format to some degree conditions our understanding of intellect and provides rewards for straightforward facts. As schools become further corporatized, it is within similarly narrow parameters that their curricula and institutional form will be shaped as corporatization demands compartmentalization. We may not wish to reconstruct the traditional academy of past decades and we certainly do not want to reproduce the exclusivity of the past. However, we might struggle to revive the intellectual culture that is today lost within the edu-business framework.

Source: Adapted from Pupo (2002).

Big Bang Theory, the main characters, who are all science nerds and academics, quip about the number of times they were humiliated, "pantsed," razzed, beaten up, ribbed, and ridiculed during their adolescent years. While the characters are portrayed to be socially inadequate, presumably due to their somewhat sheltered and socially isolated pasts as teens, they are all successful in their fields. However, as

 Explore the reading "How Corporations Are Buying Their Way into America's Classrooms" on **MySocLab.**

well-publicized cases in both Canada and the United States indicate, bullying in its extreme form has pushed many to suicide and others to violent actions, including murder. The case of Reena Virk, who was swarmed, beaten, and drowned by seven girls and a boy, aged 14 to 17, under a bridge in Saanich on Vancouver Island in 1997, stands as testimony to the strong pressures teens face to fit in and the price they may pay in doing so.

A Canadian study reports that among children aged 12 to 19, 6 percent admit they bully others on a weekly basis, 8 percent are victimized weekly, and a further 1 percent are both bullied and bully others weekly (cited in Public Safety Canada, 2011). Boys are more likely to be both victims and aggressors and are more likely to demonstrate behaviours that are physical, including punching, hitting, and beating others. Girls more often resort to more passive forms of bullying, including socially isolating victims, ridiculing, spreading rumours, and slandering (ibid.). Some argue that social media—Facebook, forum postings, and so on—along with cellphones, often used as vehicles of harassment, have worsened the situation for many victims. Researchers suggest that schools need well-developed policies, and that teachers require training to recognize and deal with bullying in order to provide safe and comfortable learning environments for all children (Mishna, Scarcello, Pepler, & Wiener, 2005).

Social Integration and Political Socialization

The classroom itself helps to produce social integration. As students learn about Confederation and the Canadian *Charter of Rights and Freedoms*, take Civics class in high school, or sing "O Canada," they become aware of the "greater government," and their sense of national identity grows. One indicator of how education promotes political integration is the millions of immigrants who have attended Canadian schools, learned mainstream ideas, and given up their earlier national and cultural identities as they became Canadians. Schools also socialize students politically by incorporating and emphasizing, however subtly, dominant values, ideas, and experiences. Teaching is primarily done from a white, middle-class, male, non-Native perspective. Many critics have exposed the ways that structural barriers, such as racism, classism, and sexism, operate within the Canadian school system to limit the level of participation and success of minority students (C. James, 2003).

How significant is this integrative function of education? It goes far beyond similarities of appearance or speech. To forge a national identity is to stabilize the political system. If people identify with a society's social institutions and perceive them as the basis of their welfare, they have no reason to question or rebel. This function is especially significant when it comes to the working classes, in which the greatest desire for and the strongest pursuit of social and political change ordinarily develops. The wealthy already have a vested interest in maintaining the status quo, but to get the working classes to identify with the Canadian social system as it is goes a long way toward its preservation.

Gatekeeping

Gatekeeping, or determining which people will enter what occupations, is another major function of education. Credentialing, the subject of the opening vignette, is an example of gatekeeping. Because Neha did not have the required credentials, but Melissa did, education closed the door to one person and opened it to the other. Yet, as sociologist David Livingstone (1999) argues, many workers are vastly underemployed, and this may be so because we usually focus on the question of how schools should prepare students for work, rather than how work might make use of people's education, continuing learning capacities, and knowledge. As feminists argue, knowledge and skills acquired through cultural teachings and practices, or through experience in managing households or engaging in caring and other family and community-related work, for example, are disregarded. Exclusively emphasizing school learning as preparation for jobs disadvantages those who are unable to acquire the specified credentials.

Essential to the gatekeeping function is **tracking**, or sorting students into different educational programs on the basis of real or perceived abilities. Tests are used to determine which students should be directed into "university-bound" programs, while others are put on a vocational track. The impact is lifelong. As we saw with Neha and Melissa, throughout adulthood, opportunities for jobs, raises, and promotions open or close on the basis of education.

Tracking begins in elementary school, where, on the basis of test results, most students take regular courses, but some are placed in programs for the "gifted" or in advanced sections of English and mathematics. In high school, tracking becomes more elaborate. In many schools, students are funnelled into university-bound, non-university-bound, or vocational programs. Others are placed in classes for students with "special needs." All students who complete their sequence of courses receive high school diplomas, but not all graduates are eligible to go on to higher education. Those in vocational or non-academic streams are most likely to enter the workforce after high school or perhaps take a vocational or trade course; those in the academic streams enter university; and those in between may attend a community college to obtain a diploma or certificate in one of a number of semiprofessional, technological, or vocational fields.

Recent studies have confirmed results consistent with a number of previous studies that indicate that in general, the likelihood of attending university increases as family incomes increase (Drolet, 2005; Canadian Council on Learning, 2009) (see Table 14.1). As indicated in Table 14.2, along with income, parents' education is also strongly related to participation in higher education. In 2006, only 23 percent of youth whose parents had a high school education or less attended university, compared to 57.6 percent with at

TABLE 14.1 Postsecondary Participation by Household Income in Canada, 2006

Before-Tax Parental Income Range	University Participation Rate	College Participation Rate	Total Participation Rate
Less than $25 000	27.5%	40%	58.5%
$25 001–$50 000	21.7%	45.5%	60.8%
$50 001–$75 000	30.6%	45.2%	64.9%
$75 001–$100 000	40.9%	44%	73.1%
More than $100 000	48.6%	44%	80.9%

Source: Statistics Canada. Survey of Labour Income and Dynamics (SLID), 2006. Cited in Canadian Council on Learning, 2009: 44.

least one university-educated parent (Canadian Council on Learning, 2009: 43). Tables 14.1 and 14.2 provide data on postsecondary participation by household income and by parental education.

In an earlier study of Ontario schools, researchers concluded that children whose parents are in unskilled jobs are 10 times more likely than children whose parents are professionals to be directed toward non-college-or-university-bound high school programs. Also, working-class children are far less likely than others from higher social class backgrounds to go to university, a result of the way the school system sorts students. Not only is this a shameful waste of human potential, but it discriminates against working-class and poor children (Curtis, Livingstone, & Smaller, 1992).

Besides academic achievement, which many suggest is related to social class, students are provided with opportunities on the basis of other characteristics, such as gender. Today, the educational attainment of females in Canada is surpassing that of males. In 2006, 58 percent of students in bachelor degree programs in Canadian universities were women (Canadian Council on Learning, 2009: 52). This represents an enormous increase in female participation rates since the 1970s, when only one in three students in full-time programs was female. In addition, today women account for about half of the master's degrees awarded and 43 percent of PhDs earned in Canada (Canadian Council on Learning, 2009: 54). Not only are women outnumbering males in classrooms and lecture halls, but the graduation

rates for women have been consistently increasing since the 1970s, whereas the rates for males have been declining (ibid.). In 2008, 45.8 percent of university graduates were women, while men accounted for 28.3 percent (Statistics Canada, 2011b:44). However, some fields, such as engineering, are still male-dominated. Males earn over 75 percent of engineering degrees, and at the undergraduate level, women are underrepresented in mathematics and the physical sciences. At the same time, men are underrepresented in nursing, rehabilitation medicine, social work, languages, education, and a number of the social sciences, including psychology and sociology (Statistics Canada, 2010h). Considering these patterns, we might conclude that males and females are sent down separate, gender-specific career paths and that these paths are to some degree mapped out by their school-related experiences, including advice from guidance counsellors, encouragement from teachers and parents, and reception from other students.

The first hurdle that young Canadians must jump is getting access to schooling and, as the discussion above indicates, social class—wealth and income—matter a great deal. For those who complete a higher educational program, there may still be a number of bumps along the way to finding success in the labour market, as evidenced in the Down-to-Earth Sociology box below.

Gatekeeping sorts people on the basis of merit, according to functionalists. Sociologists Talcott Parsons (1940) and Kingsley Davis and Wilbert Moore (1945), who pioneered this

TABLE 14.2 Postsecondary Participation by Parental Education in Canada, 2006

Highest Level of Parental Education	University Participation Rate	College Participation Rate	Total Participation Rate
University	57.6%	47.4%	88.4%
Postsecondary certificate/diploma	35.2%	54.1%	76.5%
High school or less	23%		47.6%

Source: Statistics Canada, Survey of Labour and Income Dynamics (SLID), 2006. Special data run for Canadian Council on Learning, cited in Canadian Council on Learning, 2009, p. 43. Note: The sum of the values in the first two columns exceeds the value of the third column because some students participate in more than one kind of postsecondary education. Accessed at: www.ccl-cca.ca/pdfs/PSE/2009/PSE2008_English.pdf.

The Higher Education–Jobs Conundrum

All the signs indicate that staying in school is the best option for labour market success. Not only are graduates generally more employable, but eventually they will earn higher incomes compared to members of their cohort who packed away their books and headed for the labour market after Grade 12. But the path from the ivy walls to the labour market is not as direct and smooth as it once was. Many students will hit a few bumps along the way.

Today most students work during the school terms. This means having to juggle school and work schedules—even to the point of choosing courses that fit with employers' demands, rather than those that hold the greatest interest or most promise for future labour market or postgraduate plans. Not only is balancing school and work stressful, but college and university students who work are more likely to drop out—with those who work 20 hours or more twice as likely not to finish their programs and graduate (Brown, 2010: A19).

The effects are obvious in the classrooms and lecture halls. Instructors often find students dozing off in class, especially after working late-night shifts, or cutting class a few minutes early in order to make it to work on time. This scenario is not only stressful for the individual in terms of managing time, but it robs students of the joys of the classroom experience and it distracts classmates, sometimes to the point of quelling discussion. Even after all the effort of balancing school and work, students are frequently faced with enormous debts after graduation, and as a result are forced to take any job offered or keep working at the part-time jobs they held as students until something else comes along. Some sectors within the service industry—notably, food service and bartending—are chockfull of graduates with newly minted degrees. Being waited on by a university graduate may in fact be the "new normal" within the food-service industry.

While graduation is a joyful occasion, for many the celebration is bittersweet. Many graduates—even those who continued to work throughout their undergraduate years—face substantial debt. Upon graduation, on average, student debt is about $19 000 (Statistics Canada, 2010d).

And with many having to start paying off their loans before landing a permanent job within their career track, decision-making about buying a home, having children, and other life events is very difficult. Many resort to moving back to their parents' home or delaying their decision to strike out on their own—a phenomenon sometimes referred to as "rebounding." Such scenarios may be challenging for parents and adult children alike—often pressuring aging parents to delay their retirements and young adults to postpone aspirations of independence.

In order to insulate themselves from the exigencies of the labour market, some prefer to go on to graduate school to earn a master's degree or PhD. But many who graduate with advanced degrees are finding themselves underemployed or unemployed. According to an OECD study of 12 countries, for example, Canada's rate of unemployment for PhD graduates in engineering and medical sciences was the highest (Lu, 2011: A8). For some students, then, even the highest degree does not necessarily guarantee a smooth ride to labour market security.

---

view, also known as **social placement**, argued that a major task of society is to fill its positions with capable people. Some positions, such as that of a physician, require a high intellect and many years of arduous education. Consequently, to motivate capable people to postpone immediate gratification and submit to many years of rigorous education, high income and prestige are held out as rewards. Other jobs require far fewer skills and can be performed by people with fewer educational qualifications. Thus, functionalists look on education as a system that, to the benefit of society, sorts people according to their abilities. Clearly education plays a role in promoting personal change; broadens people's outlooks, networks, and perspectives; and often contributes to social change.

Mainstreaming

A new function of education is **mainstreaming**, incorporating people with disabilities into regular social activities. As a matter of routine policy, students with disabilities used to be placed in special schools. Educators concluded that in these settings, such students learned to adjust only to a world of the disabled, leaving them ill-prepared to cope with the dominant world. The educational philosophy then changed to having students with disabilities attend regular schools.

Mainstreaming is easiest for students whose disabilities are minor, since they fit more easily into regular schools. For people who cannot walk, schools (and other public facilities) have been required to build wheelchair ramps; for those who cannot hear, "signers" (interpreters who use their hands) may attend classes with them. Most blind students still attend special schools, as do people with severe learning disabilities. There is wide variation across Canada with regard to the integration of students with disabilities into regular classes. For example, in 2001, among 5- to 14-year-olds with a disability, 73 percent (highest) in Prince Edward Island and 48 percent (lowest) in Quebec were taught in regular classrooms. The national average stood at 59 percent (Statistics Canada, 2008). Access to regular classrooms is only one concern of many parents of children with disabilities. Some question the quality of education provided and worry about literacy, test scores, and other scholastic measures.

Replacing Family Functions

Canadian schools have begun to rival some family functions. Childcare is an example. Elementary schools do double duty as babysitting services for working parents. Childcare always has been a *latent* function of formal education, as it was an unintended consequence of schooling. Now, however, since most families have two wage earners, childcare has become a manifest function. Some schools even offer childcare both before and after formal classes. Another example is providing sex education and birth control advice, which has stirred controversy. Some families resent this function being taken from them. Many parents object to schools usurping their role, and to their children being taught values that violate their own. Many would condemn a graphic presentation of how to put on a condom. Disagreement with school curricula, to some degree, has prompted some parents to opt for home schooling.

The Conflict Perspective: Reproducing the Social Class Structure

Unlike functionalists, who see education as a social institution that performs functions for the benefit of society, conflict theorists see the educational system as a tool used by those in dominant positions in society to maintain their power and keep people in line.

The Hidden Curriculum

The term **hidden curriculum** refers to the unwritten rules of behaviour and attitudes, such as obedience to authority and conformity to cultural norms, that are taught in schools in addition to the formal curriculum (Gillborn, 1992). Conflict theorists contend that this hidden curriculum perpetuates social inequalities.

To better understand this central point, consider the values and work habits that students are taught in school: obedience to the teacher, punctuality, and turning in neat work on time. These traits are highly desired by employers, who want dependable, docile, subordinate workers. Or just consider the emphasis on "proper" English. Members of the elite need people to run their business empires, and they are more comfortable if their managers possess the "refined" language and manners that they themselves are used to. Consequently, middle-class schools, whose teachers know where their pupils are headed, stress "proper" English and "good" manners. In contrast, because fewer children from working-class or minority backgrounds will occupy

According to conflict theorists, the primary functions of bureaucratically organized schools are to teach acceptance of hierarchal control, obedience to authority, and acceptance of rules regardless of their logic or purpose.

managerial positions, their teachers will be more lenient in allowing street language in the classroom and are less concerned with students' grammatical skills.

Each type of school helps reproduce the social class structure, then, by preparing students to work in positions similar to those of their parents. They are "taught" to internalize negative perceptions of the working class that reproduce their status and, therefore, reinforce such perceptions, creating and perpetuating the cycle (Willis, 1981). Some children, socially destined for higher positions, learn "refined" speech and manners. Others are simply taught to obey rules so they can take their place in the closely supervised, low-status positions for which they are socially destined (Bowles & Gintis, 1976; Olneck & Bills, 1980). From the conflict perspective, even kindergarten has a hidden curriculum, as illustrated in the Down-to-Earth Sociology box.

Tilting the Tests: Discrimination by IQ

Even intelligence tests play a part in keeping the social class system intact. For example, how would you answer the following question?

A symphony is to a composer as a book is to a(n)

paper _____
sculptor _____
musician _____
author _____
man _____

You probably had no difficulty coming up with "author" as your choice. Wouldn't any intelligent person have done the same?

In point of fact, this question raises a central issue regarding biases in intelligence and standardized testing. Not all intelligent, capable, or skilled people would know the answer, because the question contains *cultural biases*. In other words, children from some backgrounds are more familiar with the concepts of symphonies, composers, sculptors, and musicians than other children. Consequently, the test is tilted in their favour (Turner, 1972; Ashe, 1992).

Perhaps asking a different question will make the bias clearer. How would you answer the following question?

If you throw dice and "seven" is showing on top, what is facing down?

seven _____
snake eyes _____
box cars _____
little Joes _____
eleven _____

This question, suggested by Adrian Dove (n.d.), a social worker in Watts, California, is slanted toward a working-class experience. It surely is obvious that this *particular* cultural bias tilts the test so that children from some social backgrounds will perform better than others.

Speaking a language students understand is key to reaching them. Working with youth in detention centres, Ras Mo Moses, an anti-violence educator, draws on rap to get through to young offenders. Recognizing that youth listened to and identified with rap, he turned to dub poetry, a Jamaican art form popularized in the 1970s. By writing new lyrics and maintaining the rhythm of rap, Moses captured students' attention because his approach was, in his words, "culturally appropriate, something they could relate to" (Borcea, 2007: A3).

It is no different with IQ (intelligence quotient) tests that use such words as *composer* and *symphony*. A working-class child may have heard about rap, rock, hip hop, or jazz, but not about symphonies. In other words, IQ tests measure not only intelligence but also culturally acquired knowledge. Everything else aside, the cultural bias built into the IQ tests used in schools is clearly not tilted in favour of the working classes.

A second inadequacy of IQ tests is that they focus on mathematical, spatial, symbolic, and linguistic abilities. Intelligence, however, consists of more than these components. The ability to compose music, to be empathetic to the feelings of others, or to be humorous or persuasive are also components of intelligence. Questions regarding who composes test questions, what the tests are trying to achieve, and who they are geared toward should be raised. In addition, many parents and educators are aware that standardized testing neglects learning disabilities and different ways of learning and expression.

The significance of these factors, according to conflict theorists, is that culturally biased IQ tests favour the middle classes and discriminate against students from lower-class backgrounds. An important consequence is that children from poor families or who are recent immigrants and whose first language may not be English may score lower than average on standardized tests, and on this basis may be assigned to less demanding courses or streams thought to appropriately match their test scores. This affects their education, and ultimately, their work futures. Conflict theorists view standardized tests as maintaining the social class structure across generations.

Stacking the Deck: Unequal Funding

Conflict theorists stress the central role that funding for education plays in perpetuating social inequalities. Funding is a scarce resource unequally distributed among rich and poor students. The vast regional inequality in Canada affects access to education, and the unequal distribution of resources pushes education out of the reach of students in poorer areas. A greater percentage of the population over age 25 in the relatively richer provinces have university degrees, while at the other end, the relatively poorer provinces have the highest proportion of adults with less than a Grade 9 education (Davies & Guppy, 2006). Moreover, a greater percentage of Aboriginal students compared to non-Aboriginal students drop out of school, although among those living off reserves, there are fewer dropping out today as compared to the number of dropouts in earlier decades (Canadian Council on Learning, 2009:45). Aboriginal and Inuit youth living on reserves are dropping out in greater numbers (ibid.) Although there has been a significant increase in the participation of Native groups in higher education, particularly over the past 20 years, attendance and participation rates of Aboriginal people lag far behind the rates for all Canadians. First Nations peoples living on reserves have identified a number of barriers preventing them from attending university or college. These barriers include inadequate funding, poor academic preparation, having to support their families, and feeling unwelcome on campuses (Canadian Council on Learning, 2007: 76).

The low rate of school completion in the Northwest Territories in part reflects the abysmal way schooling has been provided for Aboriginal Canadians. Under the residential school system, formally operated by the Canadian government through the *Indian Act* of 1876, between 1892 and 1969, Native children were separated from their families, often by force, and taken to boarding schools, where they

Boot Camp or Critical Learning?

After conducting participant observation in a kindergarten, sociologist Harry Gracey (2007) concluded that kindergarten is a sort of boot camp for the entire educational system. Here, tender students from diverse backgrounds are drilled in the behaviours and attitudes deemed appropriate for the "student role" and made to follow classroom routines. The goal of kindergarten is to mould many individuals from diverse backgrounds into a compliant group that will, on command, unthinkingly follow classroom routines.

Kindergarten's famous "show and tell," for example, is not merely a tool for encouraging children to be expressive. It also teaches them to talk only when they are asked to speak ("It's your turn, Jarmay"). The practice also instructs children to request permission to talk ("Who knows what Letitia has?") by raising a hand and being acknowledged. Show and tell also teaches children to acknowledge the teacher's ideas as superior. She is the one who has the capacity to evaluate students' activities and ideas.

Gracey found a similar hidden curriculum in the other activities he observed. Whether drawing pictures, listening to records, or participating in snack time or rest time, teachers would quiet talkative students, even scolding them at times, while giving approval for conforming behaviours. In short, the message is that the teacher—and, by inference, the entire school system—is the authority.

Gracey concluded that this is not merely a side issue—it is the purpose of kindergarten. The kindergarten teacher's job is to teach children to "follow orders with unquestioning obedience." To accomplish this, kindergarten teachers "create and enforce a rigid social structure in the classroom through which they effectively control the behaviour of most of the children for most of the school day."

These early lessons extend well beyond the classroom. As Gracey notes, school serves as a boot camp, preparing students for the routines of the work world, whether on the assembly line or at the office. Mastering the student role prepares them to become docile workers and to follow unquestioningly the routines imposed by "the company."

Within a different learning environment—that is, by putting aside the strict hierarchical structure and "standard" value-laden curriculum of the typical classroom—"show and tell," along with other common classroom exercises, may take on a critical standpoint. Students might be asked to consider how they use and understand everyday objects. Robert Foster, for example, argues that objects might be discussed in terms of the historical and complex relationships underlying them (2008). According to Foster, a bottle of Coke may be central to lessons on globalization, the environmental impact of groundwater depletion, the health consequences of polyethylene terephthalate bottles, the working conditions around the globe in bottling and distribution plants, and so on (ibid.).

Moving the classroom away from a "boot camp" regime to embrace principles of critical pedagogy challenges teachers, parents, and principals to rewrite "standard" lessons, to recognize and engage with children's curiosity about their world, and to take some risks in their lesson planning.

---

were stripped of their Indianness. They were not allowed to speak in their Native languages, nor were they provided with opportunities to learn from within and about their own cultures. Many students suffered sexual, physical, and emotional abuse in these schools, which were eventually abolished (Frideres, 2011:168–169). Overall, about 130 000 Native children were taken into the country's 130 residential schools. After 1969, some of the schools remained in operation, but were run by churches and eventually by band councils. Akaitcho Hall in Yellowknife, the last residential school to remain open, was finally closed in 1994 (Mironowicz, 2002).

Since then, overall education levels on reserves have increased, but there are still wide gaps between levels of school completion for Native populations and those for Canada as a whole. In 2006, 37.8 percent of Aboriginals aged 20 to 24 living off reserves had not completed secondary school. While this represented a drop from previous years, it compares poorly with the general rate for all Canadians in that age group. By 2006, only 12.5 percent of the general population aged 20 to 24 had not completed secondary school (Canadian Council on Learning, 2009:45).

The dropout rate among Canadian youth is relatively low. Calculations indicate that it steadily declined from 19.2 percent to 11.1 percent for males and from 14 percent to 7.3 percent for females between 1990–91 and 2006–07 (Canadian Council on Learning, 2009: 48). In general, school leavers face a number of labour market challenges. Not only are they less likely to find work, but the jobs they do find typically have lower wages, higher rates of unemployment, and less security than those of high school or postsecondary graduates (Raymond, 2008; Canadian Council on Learning, 2009). Across Canada, the rate of dropping out varies, and currently the highest rate is in Quebec (Gilmore, 2010).

School leavers tend to be from lower socioeconomic backgrounds, often from single- and no-parent families, and usually experience pressures to enter the labour market.

On the plus side, an increasing number of dropouts return to school. Three out of ten re-entered in 2005–06, and this upward trend may be the result of increasing labour market pressures and rising job requirements, as well as new programs designed to give those who dropped out a second chance. Almost one in four dropouts were unemployed during the recent 2008 recession; this rate was almost double that of high school completers (ibid.). In 2009–10, high school dropouts earned, on average, $70 less per week as compared to their peers who graduated from high school (ibid.)

Men and women drop out of school for different reasons. For girls, it is most often for personal reasons—29 percent of female dropouts in 2006 were mothers with one or more children (Faulkner, 2008: A4). Boys' reasons tend to relate to jobs—labour market conditions and wages—or to their performance—grades and disinterest (ibid.). Among those who dropped out of high school in 2004, 21 percent of girls, compared to 14 percent of boys, went on to postsecondary education (Shaienks, Eisl-Culkin, & Brussiere, 2006: 32).

The disparities across Canada in educational attainment may be explained by a variety of additional factors, including distance from a postsecondary institution (Statistics Canada, 2004a) and parents' educational attainment. Education is a provincial matter, and there are vast economic differences between provinces in the tax bases from which funding is drawn. Decisions made by local school boards may also account for variations between and within provinces. Some provinces have larger urban areas, and generally rural areas are relatively poorer. In urban areas, the demand for higher educational credentials is higher and relates to the types of industries and work available. Provinces such as Ontario, for example, house high-profile law and medical schools that attract students from across Canada. The existence of a degree-granting institution within a community is a drawing card for a highly educated workforce. The Northwest Territories does not have a university. Many young residents who leave never return, eventually settling in the community where they graduated (Humphreys, 1998).

Conflict theorists go beyond these observations, however. They stress that in each province and community, the deck is stacked against the poor. Because public schools are largely supported by local property taxes, the richer communities (where property values are higher) have more to spend on their children, while the poorer communities end up with much less. Consequently, the richer communities are able to offer higher salaries (and take their pick of the most highly qualified and motivated teachers); afford the latest textbooks and computers, teach additional courses in languages, music, and arts; and provide better opportunities for young athletes interested in sports programs. Because schools so closely reflect the Canadian social class system, the children of the privileged emerge from elementary and middle schools best equipped for success in high school. Wealthier families are often more able to afford opportunities such as private schooling or tutoring in addition to being more likely to afford university or a prestigious postsecondary institution. In turn, they come out of high school best equipped for success in university. Their greater likelihood of success in university, and in high-status professional programs such as medicine and law, in turn, serves to maintain their dominance.

The Correspondence Principle

Conflict sociologists Samuel Bowles and Herbert Gintis (1976) used the term **correspondence principle** to refer to the ways schools reflect the social structure of society. This term means that what is taught in a nation's schools corresponds to the characteristics of that society. Thus education helps to perpetuate a society's social inequalities. The following list provides some examples.

CHARACTERISTICS OF SOCIETY

1. Capitalism
2. Social inequality
3. Racial-ethnic prejudice
4. Bureaucratic structure of the corporation
5. Need for submissive workers
6. Need for dependable workers
7. Need to maintain armed forces and agents of control

CHARACTERISTICS OF SCHOOLS

1. Promote competition
2. Unequal funding of schools, track the poor to job training
3. Make minorities feel inferior, track minorities to job training
4. Provide a model of authority in the classroom
5. Make students submissive, as in the kindergarten boot camp
6. Enforce punctuality in attendance and homework
7. Promote nationalism (to fight for capitalism)

Thus, conclude conflict theorists, the Canadian educational system is designed to produce dependable workers that will not question their bosses, and produce some individuals who will go on to be innovators in thought and action but can still be counted on to be loyal to the social system as it exists (Olneck & Bills, 1980).

The Bottom Line: Family Background and the Educational System

The end result of unequal funding, standardized tests, and so on is that family background proves more important than test scores in predicting who attends university. In 1977, Bowles compared the college attendance of the brightest

⊙ **Watch** the video "Education and Financial Success" on MySocLab.

25 percent of high school students in the United States with the intellectually weakest 25 percent. Of the brightest 25 percent, 90 percent of those from affluent homes went to college, while only half of those from low-income homes did. Of the weakest students, 26 percent from affluent homes went to college, while only 6 percent from poorer homes did.

Canadian sociologists also found that in Canada, students from a higher class background were far more likely to go to university than poorer students within the same cohort (Porter, Porter, & Blishen, 1979; Davies & Guppy, 2006). The same general relationship still holds today. If you rank families from the poorest to the richest, as the income increases, the likelihood that the children will attend institutions of higher learning also increases (Manski, 1992–1993; Curtis, Livingstone, & Smaller, 1992; Davies & Guppy, 2006).

Conflict theorists point out that the educational system reproduces the wealth–poverty divide within the Canadian social class structure. Like Neha in the opening vignette, those without degrees have less access to jobs with better pay and potential for advancement. Then, too, there is the program and the type of institution attended. Wealthy Canadians are more likely than others to attend private schools and prestigious and internationally renowned universities.

The purpose of the educational system, according to conflict theorists, is to reproduce inequality, to help keep the social class structure intact from one generation to the next. Consequently, most children from less privileged families are funnelled into job training programs, while children of the middle classes attend universities and community colleges. The offspring of the elite, in contrast, attend exclusive private schools, such as Upper Canada College, where their learning environment includes small classes and well-paid teachers (Persell et al., 1992). Here they inherit a cozy social network between the school's advisors and the admissions officers of the nation's and the world's most elite institutions. Some of these networks are so efficient that a majority of these private schools' graduating classes are admitted to McGill, University of Toronto Law School, or Schulich School of Business at York University, or to Harvard, Yale, or Princeton in the United States.

Focus Question

What are some of the ways the education system reproduces inequality?

The Feminist Perspective

Feminist approaches to the sociology of education raise questions regarding women's place in schools at all levels, in knowledge production and distribution, and in the construction of research questions and programs about education. A primary concern of feminism is to promote social justice, and in developing their analysis of education and schools, feminist approaches are interconnected with analyses of inequalities, including race, class, disabilities, sexual orientation, and ageism.

Liberal feminists are most concerned with basic equality issues within schools and educational institutions. They want to see women have equal opportunities, and catch up to men with regard to educational attainment, access to educational programs, and respect and consideration in academic circles. Radical feminists are more interested in giving women a "voice" within classrooms, within the sphere of knowledge production, and within all levels of education. Their concern is less in accessing the avenues that will allow them to achieve equity with men, but more in developing a woman-centred approach to education that denies men systematic power and dominance over women. In this scenario, women's experiences and understandings of social processes are foremost. Socialist feminists are concerned with the intersections of race, class, and gender, and argue that patriarchal relations, including those intertwined in the fabric of schools and educational programs and processes, must be dismantled in order to establish a truly just society.

The Symbolic Interactionist Perspective: Teacher Expectations and the Self-Fulfilling Prophecy

Whereas functionalists look at how education functions to benefit society and conflict theorists examine how education perpetuates social inequality, symbolic interactionists study face-to-face interactions in the classroom. They have found that the expectations of teachers have profound consequences for their students.

The Rist Research

Symbolic interactionists have uncovered some of the dynamics of educational tracking. In what has become a classic study, sociologist Ray Rist conducted participant observation in an African-American grade school with an African-American faculty. Rist (1970) found that after only eight days in the classroom, the kindergarten teacher felt that she knew the children's abilities well enough to assign them to three separate worktables: one for "fast learners," the second for "slow learners," and a third for "average" students.

This pattern seemed strange to Rist. He knew that the children had not been tested for ability, yet the teacher was certain that she could differentiate between bright and slow children. Investigating further, Rist found that social class was the underlying basis for assigning the children to the different tables. Middle-class students were separated out for Table 1, children from poorer homes to Tables 2 and 3.

👁 **Watch** the video "Inequities in Education" on **MySocLab.**

✴ **Explore** the reading "Detours on the Road to Equality: Women, Work, and Higher Education" on **MySocLab.**

The teacher paid the most attention to the fast learners, and as the year went on, those labelled "fast learners" perceived that they were treated better and came to see themselves as smarter. They became the leaders in class activities and even ridiculed children at the other worktables, calling them "dumb." Eventually, the children at the other tables, particularly children at the "average" table, whom the teacher paid least attention to, disengaged themselves from many classroom activities. Not surprisingly, at the end of the year only the children at Table 1 had completed the lessons that prepared them for reading.

This early tracking stuck. When these students entered Grade 1, their new teacher looked at the work they had accomplished and placed students from Table 1 at her Table 1. She treated her tables much as the kindergarten teacher had, and the children at Table 1 again led the class.

The children's reputations continued to follow them. The Grade 2 teacher followed the pattern and distributed readers once again according to the previously determined ability groups. Rist concluded that the child's journey through school was determined at the eighth day of kindergarten! What had occurred was a **self-fulfilling prophecy**, a term coined by sociologist Robert Merton (1949/1968) to refer to an originally false assumption of what is going to happen that comes true simply because it was predicted. Labels are powerful. They can set people on courses of action that affect the rest of their lives. That, of course, is the significance of Rist's observations of these grade school children.

How Do Teacher Expectations Work?

How do teacher expectations work? Observations of classroom interaction have given us some idea (Leacock, 1969; Rist, 1970; Buckley, 1991; Farkas, 1996; Farkas, Sheehan, & Grobe, 1990; Farkas, Grobe, Sheehan, & Shuan, 1990). To some degree teachers are not adequately prepared to deal with the diversity of interests, experiences, and backgrounds of their students, and as a result, unknowingly replicate patterns of racism and inequality within the wider society (Mujawamariya, 2007). A teacher's own middle-class background comes into play, for teachers are pleased when middle-class students ask probing questions. They take these as a sign of intelligence. When working-class students ask similar questions, however, teachers are more likely to interpret their questions as "smart aleck." In addition, working-class children are more likely to reflect a subculture that "puts down" or doesn't value intellectual achievements, causing teachers to react negatively. As with social class, there are also questions regarding the intersection of race and education. While most educators do not see racism as present in the school system, many teachers and students have preconceived notions pertaining to members of racial minorities. As a result, unfair expectations or unrealistic demands are placed on some students based on their backgrounds and minority group status (Gillborn, 2008).

We do not yet have enough information on how teachers form their expectations, how they communicate them to students, or exactly how these expectations influence teacher–student interaction. Nor do we know very much about how students "signal" messages to teachers, nor how marginalized students might negotiate structures of opportunity within the educational system to find or create positive spaces for themselves (James, 2007).

Rethinking Schools: Problems and Solutions

To conclude this section on education, let's list some of the major problems facing Canadian education today—and consider potential solutions.

The Rising Tide of Mediocrity

While more and more Canadians are staying in school longer, a significant number of Canadians experience illiteracy. At the same time, dropout rates have declined significantly across the country. Teachers' groups may claim that teachers are doing a better job. They are getting more students to stay in high school and to go on to university. Is it possible that higher retention rates today mean that fewer students are failing due to poorer standards and a deflation in expectations?

In the United States, sociologist Robert Benford (2007) obtained a copy of a 20-question final examination given to basketball players taking a credit course on coaching at the University of Georgia. Some of the questions were:

1. How many goals are on a basketball court? a. 1 b. 2 c. 3 d. 4
2. How many players are allowed to play at one time on any one team in a regular game? a. 2 b. 3 c.4 d. 5
3. How many halves are in a college basketball game? a. 1 b. 2 c. 3 d. 4
4. How many points does a three-point field goal count for in a basketball game? a. 1 b. 2 c. 3 d. 4

Some point their fingers at low standards: "frill" courses, less homework, fewer term papers, grade inflation, and burned-out teachers who often find themselves working under dismal classroom conditions due to recent cutbacks and restructuring in many areas of the school system. Professors in Canadian universities often find students in their classes who experience great difficulties in summarizing researchers' findings in social science courses, who read too slowly or without adequate comprehensive skills to keep up with weekly reading assignments, or who are unable to write well. As discussed below in the textbox "Electronic Classrooms: A High-Tech Pedagogical Nightmare?" technology is producing new forms of interaction and learning, some of which may not intersect well with critical thinking objectives.

Watch the video "Storytelling" to see how storytelling in the classroom can bridge the divide between races and social classes on **MySocLab.**

Electronic Classrooms: A High-Tech Pedagogical Nightmare?

For 12 years, my teaching load at the university was reduced as I took on a number of administrative posts—graduate program director, departmental chair, research unit director. During this time, I taught only small classes for graduate or fourth-year undergraduate students. There was no need for PowerPoint, course websites, or new forms of electronic communication. There were few, if any, laptops perched in front of the students around the seminar tables. But I have always enjoyed teaching and looked forward to the day I would complete my administrative commitments and return to a full-time teaching load.

Finally, my chance came. I completed my term as research director, declined an offer to chair the department again, and turned toward spending more time in classrooms and lecture halls. Admittedly, I anticipated my "new" role in teaching with trepidation. I knew things had changed and I had a lot of catching up to do—familiarizing myself with electronic course systems, writing lectures and preparing accompanying PowerPoint presentations, and delivering lectures to students who grew up in the electronic age—whose high schools and even elementary schools had been digitized.

After a couple of lectures to my mid-size classes of 50 and 75 students, I fell completely back into my element—lecturing, inviting comments and discussion, posing questions, and challenging those who were most absorbed in the material. However, at times I yearned for the pre-electronic classroom. Without a remote control, my first challenge was to teach myself how to "stay put" at the lectern so that I could smoothly change the PowerPoint slides. While this lesson came easily— I quickly learned "my place" at the front of the class, fingers poised over the keyboard—others required more adjustment.

The electronic classroom challenges the professor to share the spotlight with onscreen messages—outlines of lectures, definitions of terms, statistical relationships, lists of points, short texts, quotes, and so on—in such a way that whatever bits of information are presented on the screen *become* the lecture, the focal point of the class. The problem with this is that teaching and learning in a discipline like sociology requires more than producing lists of information on PowerPoint slides. As you read in previous chapters, sociology employs theoretical perspectives

and analysis to make sense of the social world. Sociologists build an argument about aspects of our social world and examine or present data that supports their argument. With the new electronic format, however, students tend to focus on the material presented on the slides—the "bits" or "bytes"—rather than on the analysis—the whole picture—or the social meanings behind the information. To use an old metaphor, it is akin to seeing the trees, rather than the forest. In actual fact, we are asking students to examine the whole forest rather than the individual trees.

Each time a new slide is posted, a physical change comes over the classroom—the sounds of laptop keyboards tapping or pens scratching down notes fill the room. The space again falls silent as the professor moves from the definitions and points onscreen to provide the key aspects of the lecture—analyses of social processes and social relationships. Unfortunately, for many students, the critical essence of what sociology is becomes lost as they drum their fingers on their desks or check their Facebook profiles, waiting for the professor to move along to the next slide. Source: Norene Pupo (2012).

Cheating and Essay-Writing Mills

Almost every year, stories of essay-writing services are uncovered in major urban centres. These services offer recycled or hastily prepared essays for sale. With enough cash, students may purchase a made-to-order term paper that conforms closely to the particular requirements of their course. These illegal operations boom at peak periods during the academic year, and the arrogance of their proprietors is demonstrated by their bold advertisements littering Canadian campuses.

In addition to buying these services, some students engage in other forms of academic dishonesty, including plagiarism, cheating, and misrepresentation at examinations.

The extent of such problems is unknown, possibly due to difficulties in detection, but surveys in the United States indicate that the majority of undergraduates admit to cheating on assignments and exams. This has, in turn, prompted many professors to rely on detection services, such as the popular Turnitin (Gabriel, 2010).

Grade Inflation, Social Promotion, and Functional Illiteracy

At the same time that learning may be declining, grades are going up. In the 1960s, high school teachers gave out about twice as many Cs as As, but now the As exceed the Cs. Grade inflation in the face of declining standards has

Internet University: No Walls, No Ivy, No Keg Parties

Distance learning—courses taught to students who are not physically present with their instructor—is not new. Correspondence courses have been around for decades.

Today, however, telecommunications—satellites, computers, television, iPads, and video cameras—are changing the face of education by making cybercolleges part of mainstream learning. With computer linkups, students may watch a professor on their laptop. Clicking an icon, they can "raise their hands" to ask a question. Programs let the instructor know who is emailing others and who is not participating. Such software is also capable of scrutinizing the instructor by storing information that may be retrieved by department chairs or deans on how long it takes him or her to answer students' questions by email.

Until recently, most distance learning has been either slow (a correspondence course) or one-way (students passively receiving instruction, usually providing feedback only through tests). New technologies, such as teleconferencing, however, permit students and teachers to see one another, talk with one another, and share documents worldwide.

The potential is staggering. Why should our learning be limited to walled classrooms? When studying human culture, for example, wouldn't it be intriguing to be able to compare notes on eating, dating, or burial customs with fellow students in Thailand, Iceland, South Africa, Germany, Egypt, China, and Australia?

Some educators suggest that new technologies—such as podcasts—allow students to self-direct and "attend" lectures at their own convenience. As a bonus, this flexible learning system provides a solution to the "space crunch" in university lecture halls and to the "time crunch" experienced by most students (Faulkner, 2006: A7).

While the virtual classroom has been part of the educational system for many years, new technologies are reshaping administrative structures within academic circles. With the development of telephone and internet registration options, long line-ups of students waiting to enroll in classes, pay tuition, or access administrative

This student is taking a credit course in economic crime investigation from home.

services within universities and colleges have disappeared. The application and recruitment processes have also been recently reorganized, with potential students being lured by podcasts or online advertising.

Will we eventually go from kindergarten to graduate school, proceeding at our own pace, with classmates from around the world? While it may sound intriguing, no walls also means no flirting after class, no joking in the hallway or dorm, and no keg parties.

---

been accompanied by social promotion, the practice of passing students from one grade to the next even though they have not mastered basic materials. One unfortunate result is functional illiteracy, difficulty with reading and writing even though one has graduated from high school. Some high school graduates cannot fill out job applications; others can't figure out if they are being given the right change at the grocery store.

Violence in Schools

The shooting spree at Columbine High School in the spring of 1999, a jolting incident and the subject of Michael Moore's documentary film *Bowling for Columbine*,

and what has been called the worst mass shooting in U.S. history on the Virginia Tech campus in April 2007 in many ways represent the intensity of the violence many young people live with on a daily basis. Many U.S. schools have deteriorated to the point that basic safety is an issue, putting students' lives at risk, a condition that decades earlier would have been unimaginable. In some schools, uniformed guards have become a fixture, while in others students can gain entrance only after passing through metal detectors. While Canadian schools are much safer, the growing number of incidents of violence, including the possession and use of weapons, beatings, drug trafficking, and other serious offences, have prompted school boards

A secure learning environment is basic to a good education. The growing number of violent incidents in Canadian schools has prompted school boards to confront the problem with strict, no-nonsense policies such as "zero tolerance."

to adopt "zero tolerance" policies, which expel or suspend students at their first offence for even minor infractions. Without programs in place to prevent students from committing "offensive" behaviour in the first place, critics say that such policies are too punitive and may backfire, turning students away from school altogether (Canadian Press, 2002: A3). However, a report on the Toronto District School Board, the country's largest school system, found it to be rife with violence, including robberies and sexual assaults—most of which were not reported by school officials or staff, who felt that exposing the violence would be akin to criticizing the Board, something they thought would have career implications for them (Alphonso & El Akkad, 2008: A1, A10). It was not until the unfortunate shooting death of Jordon Manners, a 15-year-old victim of violence on school property, that the depth of the problem began to come to light.

Solutions: Retention, Safety, Standards, and Other Reforms

It is one thing to identify problems, but quite another to find solutions for them.

A SECURE LEARNING ENVIRONMENT The first criterion for a good education is security, a guarantee of students' physical safety and freedom from fear. Fortunately, most Canadian schools are relatively trouble-free, and those that are not can be changed. School administrators and teachers can reclaim the schools by expelling all students who threaten the welfare of others and by refusing to tolerate threats, violence, drugs, and weapons. However, the extent of problems such as bullying and harassment—problems that may be even less obvious and that are difficult to address—are beginning to surface. Unfortunately, many school administrators seem to "bury their heads in the sand" when it comes to confronting these problems head-on.

HIGHER STANDARDS Within a secure learning environment, steps can be taken to improve the quality of education.

Students perform better when they are expected to achieve. Somehow, this basic principle seems to be lost on many teachers, who end up teaching at a low level—and on school administrators, who accept low student performance. The reason is probably not their lack of awareness of such basics, but rather the organizational constraints in which they find themselves, the bureaucracies in which ritual often replaces performance. Ultimately, we must not only expect more from students, but also from teachers and administrators.

Reform in anything needs a guiding principle. The problem lies not with the ability of students, but rather with the educational system itself. That this is true becomes apparent when we consider the results reported in the Thinking Critically about Social Controversy box on page 327.

THINKING CRITICALLY ABOUT SOCIAL CONTROVERSY

Breaking through the Barriers: The Jaime Escalante Approach to Restructuring the Classroom

Called "the best teacher in America," Jaime Escalante taught in an East Los Angeles inner-city school plagued with poverty, crime, drugs, gangs, and miserably low student scores. In this self-defeating environment, he taught calculus. His students scored so highly on national tests that test officials, suspecting cheating, asked his students to retake the tests. They did. Again they passed—this time with even higher scores.

How did Escalante overcome such odds? His success was not due to a recruitment of the brightest students. Students' poor academic performance did not stand in the way of being admitted to the math program. The only requirement was an interest in math. What did Escalante do right, and what can we learn from his approach?

"Success starts with attitude" could be Escalante's motto. Few Latino students were taking math. Most were tracked into craft classes and made

jewellery and birdhouses. "Our kids are just as talented as anyone else. They just need the opportunity to show it. And for that, they must be motivated," he said. "They just don't think about becoming scientists or engineers."

Here are the keys to what Escalante accomplished. First, teaching and learning can't take place unless there is discipline. For that, the teachers, not gangs, must control the classroom. Second, students must believe in themselves. The teacher must inspire students with the idea that they can learn (remember teacher expectations). Third, students must be motivated to perform, in this case to see learning as a way out of the barrio, as a path to good jobs.

Escalante uses a team approach. He has his students think of themselves as a team, of him as the coach, and the national exams as a sort of Olympics for which they are preparing. To stimulate team identity, the students

wear team jackets, caps, and T-shirts with logos that identify them as part of the team. Before class, his students do "warm-ups" (hand-clapping and foot-stomping to a rock song).

His team has practice schedules as rigorous as a championship football team. Students must sign a contract that binds them to participate in the summer program he has developed, to complete the daily homework, and to attend Saturday morning and after-school study sessions. To get into his class, even the students' parents have to sign the contract. To show his students that the principle that self-discipline pays off, Escalante covers his room with posters of sports figures in action—Michael Jordan, Jerry West, Babe Ruth, and Tiger Woods.

The sociological point is that the problem was not the ability of the students. Their failure to do well in school was not the result of something within them. The problem was the system, the

To say that today's schoolchildren can't learn as well as previous schoolchildren would be to blame the victim. Jaime Escalante, shown here, demonstrated that teachers can motivate even highly deprived students to study hard and excel in learning. His experience challenges us to rethink our approach to education.

way classroom instruction was arranged. When Escalante changed the system of instruction, both attitudes and performance changed. Escalante makes this very point—that student performance does not depend on the charismatic personality of a single person, but on how we structure the learning setting. The movie *Stand and Deliver* (1988) is based on Jaime Escalante's work.

Using a similar approach to reach out to his students, educator and author Rafe Esquith teaches fifth graders who are poor, first-generation immigrants and for whom English is a second language. Their classroom, Room 56 at Hobart Boulevard Elementary School, is located in a Los Angeles neighbourhood where guns, gangs, and drugs are the order of the day. Commended by Oprah Winfrey and the Dalai Lama, in Esquith's latest book, *Teach Like Your Hair's is on Fire* (2007), he warns that there are "no shortcuts." His students experience education—performing Shakespeare; playing classical and rock and roll on guitar, keyboards, and drums; doing algebra; travelling the country studying history; discussing the Constitution; and learning to handle money responsibly. Some also score in the top 1 percent on standardized tests and many go on to attend Ivy League universities and colleges (Garrison, 2007: A8).

For Your Consideration

What principles discussed in this or earlier chapters are applied by Escalante and Esquith? What changes do you think we can make in education to bring about similar results all over the country?

Sources: Barry (1989); Meek (1989); Escalante & Dirmann (1990); Hilliard (1991).

RELIGION: ESTABLISHING MEANING

With a call from his mother, Tom's world began to crumble. Amid sobs, she had told him that she had left his father. After 22 years, their marriage was over. Why? It just didn't make sense. Tom knew that his mother and father had problems, that they argued quite a bit. But they always had. And didn't every married couple? Where was he going to go for the summer? His parents had put the house up for sale, and each had moved to a small apartment. There was no home anymore.

Life seemed a little brighter when Tom met Amy in English class. She was the only one he could talk to about his feelings—Amy's parents had divorced three years before, and she understood. When Amy was invited to a meeting of the Unification Church (the church of the "Moonies," followers of Reverend Sun Myung Moon), Tom agreed to go with her.

The meeting was a surprise. Everyone was friendly, and everything was low-key. And everyone seemed so sure. They all believed that Judgment Day was just around the corner.

Amy and Tom found the teachings rather strange, but, since the people had been so friendly, they came back. After Tom and Amy had attended meetings for about a month, they became good friends with Marcia and Ryan. Later they moved into an apartment house where Marcia, Ryan, and other Moonies lived. After a while, they dropped out of university and immersed themselves in a new life as Moonies.

What Is Religion?

Sociologists who research religion analyze the relationship between society and religion and study the role religion plays in people's lives. They do not seek to make value judgments about religious beliefs. Nor is their goal to verify or to disprove anyone's faith. Religion is a matter of faith; sociologists deal with empirical matters, things they can observe or measure. Thus sociologists can measure the extent to which people are religious and can study the effects of religious beliefs and practices on people's lives. They can analyze how religion is organized and how systems of belief are related to culture, stratification systems, and other social institutions.

In 1912, Émile Durkheim published an influential book, *The Elementary Forms of the Religious Life*, in which he tried to identify the elements common to all religions. He found that all religions, regardless of their name or teaching, separate the sacred from the profane. By **profane**, he meant aspects of life that are not concerned with religion or religious purposes but, instead, are part of everyday life. By **sacred**, Durkheim referred to aspects of life having to do with the supernatural that inspire awe, reverence, deep respect, and even fear. Durkheim also found that all religions develop a community around their practices and beliefs. He summarized his findings as follows: a religion is a unified system of beliefs and practices relative to sacred things; that is to say, things set apart and forbidden—beliefs and practices that unite into one single moral community.

Thus, Durkheim argued, a **religion** is defined by three elements:

1. Beliefs that some things are sacred (forbidden, set off from the profane);
2. Practices (rituals) centring around the things considered sacred;
3. A moral community resulting from a group's beliefs and practices. (1912/1965)

Durkheim used the term moral community not to imply morality in the sense familiar to most of us. A **moral community** is simply a group of people united by their religious practices—which includes Aztec priests or Jehovah's Witnesses.

From his review of world religions, Durkheim concluded that all religions have beliefs, practices, and a moral community. Shown here are the colourful and expressive statutes on the roof of a Hindu temple in Chattisgargh, India. The figures represent some of the numerous gods worshipped by Hindus.

To better understand the sociological approach to religion, let's see what pictures emerge when we apply the major theoretical perspectives.

The Functionalist Perspective

Functions of Religion

Around the world, religions provide answers to perplexing questions—such as the purpose of life, why people suffer, and the existence of an afterlife.

Similarly, religious rituals that enshroud critical events such as illness and death provide emotional comfort at times of crisis. The individual knows others care and can find consolation in following familiar rituals.

Religious teachings and practices unite believers into a community that shares values and perspectives ("we Jews," "we Christians," "we Muslims"). The religious rituals that surround marriage, for example, link a bride and groom with a broader community. So do other religious rituals, such as those that celebrate birth and mourn death.

Religion not only provides guidelines for everyday life, but also controls people's behaviours. An example is religious teachings that are incorporated into criminal law. In Ontario, for example, laws once prohibited the sale of alcohol before noon on Sunday. Thankfully, that law no longer exists!

Religion can help people adapt to new environments. By keeping their native languages alive and preserving familiar rituals and teachings, religion provides continuity with immigrants' cultural pasts.

Most religions provide support for the government. An obvious example is the Canadian flag prominently displayed in many Anglican and other churches. Another example is the Queen (or King) of England's coronation as head of state (for Great Britain and Canada), which means she (or he) is also the head of the Church of England. The reading of the Lord's Prayer remains a hallmark of the Ontario legislature, although MPPs voted in June 2008 to add a moment of silence and a rotation of prayers from other beliefs as well.

Although religion is often so bound up with the prevailing order that it resists social change, occasionally it spearheads progressive social and political change. In Canada, a notable example is J.S. Woodsworth's religious movement that began in Saskatchewan and eventually led to the founding of the Cooperative Commonwealth Federation (the CCF), now known as the New Democratic Party (NDP).

Dysfunctions of Religion

Functionalists also examine ways in which religion can be dysfunctional; that is, how it can bring about harm. Two main dysfunctions are war and religious persecution. However, a recent study by Gregory Paul (2005) found that highly secular democracies, such as in France, Japan, and

Tommy Douglas, pictured here, combined his personal experiences with the compelling message of the Social Gospel teachings he received while studying theology at Brandon University, which emphasized the church's responsibility to reform society. He is credited with helping to establish two important institutions in Canada: Medicare and Crown corporations.

Scandinavia, consistently enjoy low rates of societal dysfunction, while pro-religious and anti-evolution America performs poorly. Among the measures of dysfunction he used were homicide, teen pregnancy, STD infection rates, and abortion.

WAR AND TERRORISM History is filled with wars based on religion. Between the eleventh and fourteenth centuries, Christian monarchs conducted nine bloody Crusades in an attempt to wrest control of the Holy Land from the Muslims. Unfortunately, such wars are not a relic of the past. Even in recent years, we have seen Protestants and Catholics kill one another in Northern Ireland, and Jews and Muslims in Israel and Christians and Muslims in Bosnia follow suit. Terrorist acts also are sometimes committed in the name of a god. In the United States, Paul Hill, a minister, was executed in Florida for killing a doctor who had carried out abortions. Another example is Dr. Baruch Goldstein, who was convinced that God (Yahweh) wanted him to go to the Tomb of the Patriarchs and shoot into a crowd of praying Palestinian men and boys (Juergensmeyer, 2000). The all-too-familiar 9/11 acts of terror in New York and Washington were done in the name of religious jihad. It should be noted, however, that religious terrorism often carries a political agenda.

PERSECUTION Beginning in the 1200s and continuing into the 1800s, in what has become known as the Inquisition, special commissions of the Roman Catholic Church tortured women to elicit confessions that they were witches and burned them at the stake. In 1692, Protestant leaders in Salem, Massachusetts, drowned women who were accused of being witches. (The last execution for witchcraft was in Scotland in 1722 [Bridgwater, 1953]). In short, religion has been used to justify oppression and a number of brutal acts.

The Symbolic Interactionist Perspective

Symbolic interactionists focus on the meanings people give their experiences, especially how they use symbols. Let's apply this perspective to religious symbols, rituals, and beliefs to see how they help to forge a community of like-minded people.

Religious Symbols

All religions use symbols to provide identity and social solidarity for their members. A symbol is a condensed way of communicating. In other words, for Muslims, the primary symbol is the crescent moon and star, for Jews the Star of David, and for Christians the cross. For members, these are not ordinary symbols, but sacred symbols that evoke feelings of awe and reverence.

Rituals

Rituals—ceremonies or repetitive practices—are also symbols that help unite people in a moral community. Some rituals, such as the bar mitzvah for Jewish boys and Holy Communion for Christians, are designed to create in the devout a feeling of closeness and unity with one another. Rituals include kneeling and praying at set times, bowing, crossing oneself, singing, lighting candles and incense, a liturgy, scripture readings, processions, baptisms, weddings, and funerals. Boys and, later, men are normally accorded special status or privileges when compared to girls and women. Later, you will read how women in some of the major religions, such as Christianity, Judaism, and Islam, are struggling for equality.

Beliefs

Symbols, including rituals, develop from beliefs. A belief may be vague ("God is") or highly specific ("God wants us to prostrate ourselves and face Mecca five times each day").

One of the functions of religion is to create community—a sense of being connected with one another and, in this case, a sense of being connected with God. To help accomplish this, religions often use rituals. Shown here are Javanese Muslim women in Aramaribo as they celebrate Id al-Fitr at the end of Ramadan.

Religious beliefs include not only **values** (what is considered good and desirable in life—how we ought to live) but also a **cosmology**, a unified picture of the world. For example, the Jewish, Christian, and Muslim belief that there is only one God—who created the universe, is concerned about the actions of humans, and will hold us accountable for what we do—is a cosmology. It presents a unifying picture of the universe.

Community

Finally, the shared meanings that come through symbols, rituals, and beliefs unite people into a moral community. People in a moral community feel a bond with one another: their beliefs and rituals bind them together while separating them from those that do not share their unique symbolic world. Mormons, for example, feel a "kindred spirit" (as it is often known) with other Mormons. So do Baptists, Jews, Jehovah's Witnesses, and Muslims with members of their respective faiths. Removal from a community is a serious matter for people whose identity is bound up in their religious community. Sociologists John Hostetler (1980) and William Kephart and William Zellner (1994) describe the Amish practice of shunning—ignoring an offender in all situations. Persons who are shunned are treated as though they do not exist. Shunning is so thorough that even family members, who themselves remain in good standing in the congregation, are not allowed to talk to the person being shunned.

The Conflict Perspective

The conflict perspective provides an entirely different focus. Conflict theorists examine how religion supports the status quo and helps to maintain social inequalities.

Opium of the People

In general, conflict theorists are highly critical of religion. Karl Marx set the tone for conflict theorists with his most famous statement on this subject: "Religion is the sigh of the oppressed creature, the sentiment of a heartless world. . . . It is the opium of the people" (Marx, 1844/1964). By this statement, Marx meant that oppressed workers, sighing for release from their suffering, escape into religion. For them, religion is like a drug that helps them forget their misery. By diverting their eyes to future happiness in a coming world, religion takes them from their suffering in this one, thereby greatly reducing the possibility that they will rebel against their oppressors.

A Reflection of Social Inequalities

Conflict theorists stress that religious teachings and practices are a mirror of a society's inequalities. Gender inequality illustrates this point. In the mid-nineteenth century, when Canada was evolving into a nation, the Church (like Parliament and other institutions of society that were dominated by men) ordained only men, limiting women to such activities as teaching children's Sunday school or preparing meals for congregational get-togethers, which were considered appropriate "feminine" activities. As women's roles in the broader society changed, however, religion reflected those changes. First, many religious groups allowed women to vote. Then, as women attained prominent positions in the business world and professions, some Protestant and Jewish groups allowed women to be ordained. Similarly, just as women still face barriers in secular society, some congregations still refuse to ordain women. In some religious communities the barriers remain so high that women are still not allowed to vote.

A Legitimation of Social Inequalities

Conflict theorists say that religion legitimates the social inequalities of the larger society. By this, they mean that religion teaches that the existing social arrangements of a society represent what God desires.

In what is perhaps the supreme technique of legitimating the social order, the religion of ancient Egypt held that the Pharaoh was a god. The Emperor of Japan was similarly declared divine. Today, in matters of faith and morals, all Catholics must believe in the infallibility of the Pope.

Conflict theorists point to many other examples of how religion legitimates the social order. One of the more remarkable took place in the decades before the U.S. Civil War. Southern ministers used scripture to defend slavery, saying it was God's will—while northern ministers legitimated their region's social structure and used scripture to denounce slavery as evil (Ernst, 1988; Nauta, 1993; White, 1995). In India, Hinduism supports the caste system by teaching that an individual who tries to change caste will come back in the next life as a member of a lower caste—or even as an animal.

The Feminist Perspective

Female Spirituality

According to Johanna Stuckey (1998), there are a number of reasons to study female spirituality from a feminist perspective. First, the feminist commitment to diversity leads to an acceptance of exploring the positive spiritual experiences of women. Second, feminist endorsement of the personal should recognize that the spiritual is deeply personal. Third, spirituality and its manifestations in religion help to reveal how the male-dominated system controls both women and men. Fourth, the separation of mind and body or rationality and spirituality is a fabrication of Western male epistemologies (i.e., theories of knowledge), which feminists must avoid. And fifth, half the human population—that is, women—have been neglected in religious studies. It is time to include women's religious roles, women's understanding of spirituality, and women-centred religious symbols.

Stuckey (1998) outlines four main categories of the feminist study of spirituality. **Revisionists** are those who believe that the basic message of the major religions is liberating. The major changes to the teachings revisionists would defend include replacing sexist prose with sex-neutral language. **Reformists** advocate revealing the "liberating core" of religious teachings with female imagery and exposing and refusing to accept rituals that are clearly sexist. **Revolutionaries** seek to change the established orthodoxy by importing language, images, and rituals from other traditions. **Rejectionists** are feminists who judge the traditional teachings to be hopelessly sexist and have abandoned them in order to establish a new spiritual tradition. Most practise "Feminist Goddess Worship," which is understood to be completely different from any other religious expression of spirituality.

Themes in Christian Feminism

Several themes have been expressed by feminists interested in female spirituality within the Christian tradition. First is overcoming sexism by taking account of women's experiences in the church. Second, and a very productive area of Christian feminism, is the recovery of Christian women's histories. Rescued names and lives of women from the past include the twelfth-century prophet Hildegard of Bingen, Shaker Ann Lee, and Roman Catholic social activist Dorothy Day. Third is exploring the meaning of Jesus, a debate that has produced heated encounters. One telling example is the statue "Crucified Woman" that stands in a courtyard at Emmanuel College at the University of Toronto (Dyke, 1991). Fourth, the issue of Christian feminist ethics has produced a burgeoning literature tackling issues such as abortion, homophobia, power and sexuality, and suffering and evil.

Themes in Judaism and Feminism

Jewish feminists, like their Christian counterparts, have been questioning the male dominance of their religion and the masculinity of God. For the most part, Jewish feminists are revisionists in that they believe in the core meanings of Judaism and seek to change Judaism from the inside by challenging blatantly sexist rituals and teachings. They have fought to take part in public rituals and to fill leadership roles. Within non-Orthodox Judaism, for example, there are a number of female rabbis. In Conservative, Reform, and Reconstructionist Judaism, women read the Torah in public and can take part in the minyan, the formerly "10 males" prayer ceremony (Elwell, 1996).

Themes in Feminism and Islam

The theoretical core of Islamic feminism is grounded in an interpretation of the teachings of the Quran. The central focus remains the clarification of gender equality in Islam. The first international conference on Islamic feminism, held in Barcelona in 2005, drew participants from old and new Muslim societies. One important Canadian Muslim woman is Irshad Manji, a Canadian journalist and author

of *The Trouble with Islam Today: A Muslim's Call for Reform in Her Faith* (2005), who has been published in almost 30 countries. Another example of bringing Islamic issues including feminist themes to a wider Canadian audience was the CBC television program *Little Mosque on the Prairie*.

Feminist spirituality is a recent development within second-wave feminism. However, the thrust of feminist spirituality resides in the Christian and Jewish traditions and is only now beginning to have an impact on Islam and other world religions. For the most part, feminists interested in spirituality have not given up on their religious upbringing. Very few profess rejectionist sentiments. Most are working for change from within an established religious tradition.

Postmodernism and Religion

Unlike modernism, which celebrated the virtues of individualism, science, reason, and progress, postmodernism extols the intrinsic worth of socially contextualized individual experience, spirituality, and cultural diversity. According to postmodernism, all of our thinking is contextual. There is no place for objective truth derived from science or organized religion. Instead, we find "local narratives" or stories that work for particular communities but are not considered valid outside these communities. Indeed, there is no room for any absolute, universal truths within postmodernism. All religions that profess to know the truth are classed as "metanarratives" (comprehensive world views) and abandoned. However, there is space for individuals to seek out their spirituality. In some ways, postmodernism is the spiritual "'re-enchantment' of the world that modernity tried so hard to disenchant" (Bauman, 1994: x). However, there are a great many forms this "re-enchantment" can take, which is probably why postmodernism has contributed to the rise of New Age religions and all things "spiritual."

Focus Question

What explanations are provided by the functionalist, symbolic interactionist, conflict, feminist, and postmodernist perspectives for the existence of religion in society?

Religion and the Spirit of Capitalism

Weber was intrigued with the question of why some societies embraced capitalism while others clung to their traditional ways. As he explored the problem, he concluded that religion held the key to **modernization**—the transformation of traditional societies to industrial societies.

To explain his conclusions, Weber wrote *The Protestant Ethic and the Spirit of Capitalism* (1904–1905/1958). His explanation is briefly summarized here.

1. Capitalism represents a fundamentally different way of thinking about work and money. To accumulate money (capital) as an end in itself and to consider it a duty to

invest money in order to make profits Weber called the **spirit of capitalism**.

2. Why did the spirit of capitalism develop in Europe, and not, for example, in China or India, where the people had similar intelligence, material resources, education, and so on? According to Weber, religion was the key.

3. What was different about Protestantism, especially Calvinism? Calvinists concluded that church members had a duty to prove that they were one of God's elect and to live as though they were predestined to heaven. This conclusion motivated Calvinists to lead highly moral lives and to work hard, to not waste time, and to be frugal—for idleness and needless spending were signs of worldliness. Weber called this hard-working, self-denying approach to life 'inner-worldly asceticism" or the **Protestant ethic**.

4. As people worked hard and spent money only on necessities, they accumulated wealth, because spending made people pompous and greedy. Therefore, a Calvinist could never be certain, but believed that a frugal way of life, or inner worldly asceticism, was close to what God wanted from "His" followers on earth. Accumulated capital, since it couldn't be spent, was invested—which led to a surge in production.

5. Thus, a change in religion to Protestantism, especially Calvinism, led to a fundamental change in thought and behaviour (the Protestant ethic). The result was the spirit of capitalism. Hence capitalism originated in Europe, and not in places where religion did not encourage capitalism's essential elements: the accumulation of capital through frugality and hard work, and its investment and reinvestment.

Today, the Protestant ethic and the spirit of capitalism are not confined to any specific religion or part of the world. Rather, they have become cultural traits that have spread to societies around the globe (Greeley, 1964; Yinger, 1970). Canadian Catholics have about the same approach to life as Canadian Protestants. In addition, Hong Kong, Japan, Malaysia, Singapore, South Korea, Taiwan, andChina—not exactly Protestant countries—have embraced capitalism (M.J. Levy, 1992).

The World's Major Religions

Of the thousands of religions in the world, most people practise Judaism, Christianity, Islam, Hinduism, Buddhism, or Confucianism (see Figure 14.1). Let us briefly review each.

Judaism

Judaism is one of the first recorded religions based on **monotheism**, the belief that there is only one God.

Contemporary Judaism comprises three main branches: Orthodox, Reform, and Conservative. Orthodox Jews adhere to the laws espoused by Moses. They eat only foods prepared in a designated manner (kosher), observe the Sabbath in a traditional way, and segregate males and females in their religious services. During the 1800s, a group that wanted

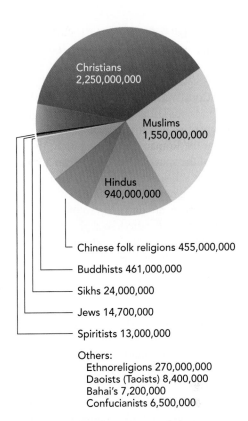

FIGURE 14.1 The World's Largest Religions

Note: With the various classifications of religions, it is sometimes difficult to tell what groups are included in what categories. Ethnoreligions, for example, is a catch-all category that refers to folk religions that are limited to specific ethnic groups.

Source: Turner (2011).

to make its practices more compatible with the secular (nonreligious) culture broke from this tradition. This liberal group, known as Reform Judaism, mostly uses the vernacular (a country's language) in its religious ceremonies and has reduced much of the ritual. The third branch, Conservative Judaism, falls somewhere between the other two.

The history of Judaism is marked by conflict and persecution. For most of Jewish history, they faced prejudice, discrimination, and persecution (called **anti-Semitism**) by many peoples and rulers. The most horrendous example is Hitler's attempt to eliminate the Jews as a people in the Nazi Holocaust of World War II. Under the Nazi occupation of Europe and North Africa, about 6 million Jews were slaughtered, perhaps half dying in gas ovens constructed specifically for this purpose.

Christianity

Christianity, which developed out of Judaism, is also monotheistic. Christians believe that Jesus Christ is the Messiah. At about the age of 30, he began a preaching and healing ministry and was as a result punished by the ruling Romans with death.

The 12 main followers of Jesus, called the apostles, believed that Jesus rose from the dead. The new religion spread rapidly, and in A.D. 317, Christianity became the Roman empire's official religion.

During the first 1000 years of Christianity, there was only one church organization: the Roman Catholic Church. In the eleventh century, after disagreement over doctrine and politics, Greek Orthodoxy was established. It was headquartered in Constantinople (now Istanbul, Turkey).

Although Martin Luther's (1483–1546) original goal of advancing what has become known as the 96 Resolutions was to reform the Roman Catholic Church, the Protestant Reformation of the sixteenth century began a splintering of Christianity. The schism coincided with the breakup of feudalism and the beginning of capitalism.

Today, Christians are divided into hundreds of groups, some with doctrinal differences so slight that only members can appreciate the extremely fine distinctions that significantly separate them from others.

Islam

Islam, whose followers are known as Muslims and number 1 billion people, began in the same part of the world as Judaism and Christianity. Islam is the world's third monotheistic religion. It was founded by Muhammad, who was born in Mecca (now Saudi Arabia) about A.D. 570. His teachings were written in a book called the Quran. When he found out that there was a plot to murder him, Muhammad fled to Medina, where he found a more receptive audience. There he established a theocracy (a government based on the principle that God is the ruler, his laws the statutes of the land, and priests his earthly administrators), and founded the Muslim empire. In A.D. 630 he returned to Mecca, this time as a conqueror (Bridgwater, 1953).

After Muhammad's death, a struggle for control over the empire split Islam into two branches that remain today, the Sunni and the Shi'ite. Shi'ites are generally more conservative and inclined to **fundamentalism**, the belief that modernism threatens religion and that the faith as it was originally practised should be restored. Sunni, who do not share this belief, are generally more liberal.

Like Jews, Muslims trace their ancestry to Abraham. For Muslims, also, Jerusalem is a holy city. It is the duty of each Muslim to make a pilgrimage to Mecca during his or her lifetime.

Hinduism

Unlike the other religions described, Hinduism has no specific founder. For about 4000 years, Hinduism has been the chief religion of India. The term *Hinduism*, however, is Western, and in India the closest word is *dharma* (law). Unlike Judaism, Christianity, and Islam, Hinduism has no texts thought to be inspired by a God. Instead, several books, including the *Brahmanas*, *Bhagavad-Gita*, and *Upanishads*, expound on moral qualities that people should strive after.

Hindus are *polytheists*; that is, they believe there are many gods. They believe one of these gods, Brahma, created the universe. Brahma, along with Shiva (the Destroyer) and Vishnu (the Preserver), form a triad at the centre of modern Hinduism.

A central belief is *karma*, or spiritual progress. There is no final judgment, but, instead, **reincarnation**, a cycle of life, death, and rebirth. Death involves only the body, and every person's soul comes back in a form that matches the individual's moral progress in the previous life (which centres on proper conduct in following the rules of one's caste). If an individual reaches spiritual perfection, he or she has attained nirvana. This marks the end of the cycle of death and rebirth, when the soul is reunited with the universal soul. When this occurs, maya, the illusion of time and space, has been conquered.

Buddhism

About 600 B.C., Siddhartha Gautama founded Buddhism. (Buddha means "enlightened one," a term Gautama was given by his disciples.) Gautama was the son of an upper-caste Hindu ruler in an area north of Benares, India. At the age of 29, he renounced his life of luxury and became an ascetic.

Through meditation, he discovered the following "four noble truths," all of which emphasize self-denial and compassion:

Depictions of Buddha are found throughout the world. Many Buddhists keep small statues in their homes and businesses, to which they make daily offerings of food. This golden Buddha statue is in Bangkok, Thailand.

1. Existence is suffering.
2. The origin of suffering is desire.
3. Suffering ceases when desire ceases.
4. The way to end desire is to follow the "noble eightfold path."

The noble eightfold path consists of

1. right belief
2. right resolve (to renounce carnal pleasure and to harm no living creature)
3. right speech
4. right conduct
5. right occupation or living
6. right effort
7. right-mindedness (or contemplation)
8. right ecstasy

The central symbol of Buddhism is the eight-spoked wheel. Each spoke represents one aspect of the path. Buddhists teach that all things are temporary, even the self. Because all things are destined to pass away, there is no soul. By the fifth century A.D., Buddhism reached the height of its popularity in India, after which it died out. However, Buddhism had been adopted in Sri Lanka, Myanmar, Tibet, Laos, Cambodia, Thailand, China, Korea, and Japan, where it flourishes today.

Confucianism

About the time that Gautama lived, K'ung Fu-tsu (551–479 B.C.) was born in China. Confucius (his name strung together in English), a public official, was distressed by the corruption that he saw in government. He urged social reform and developed a system of morality based on peace, justice, and universal order. His teachings were incorporated into writings called the Analects.

Confucianism was originally atheistic, simply a set of moral teachings without reference to the supernatural. As the centuries passed, however, local gods were added to the teachings and Confucius himself was declared a god. Confucius's teachings became the basis for the government of China.

The basic moral principle of Confucianism is to maintain *jen*, sympathy or concern for other humans. The key to *jen* is maintaining right relationships—being loyal and placing morality above self-interest. In what is called the "Confucian Golden Rule," Confucius stated a basic principle for *jen*: to treat those who are subordinate to you as you would like to be treated by people superior to yourself. Confucius taught that right relationships within the family (loyalty, respect) should be the model for society. He also taught the "middle way," an avoidance of extremes.

Types of Religious Groups

Sociologists have identified four types of religious groups: cults, sects, churches, and ecclesias. Why are some of these groups met with hostility, while others are accepted? For an explanation, consider Figure 14.2.

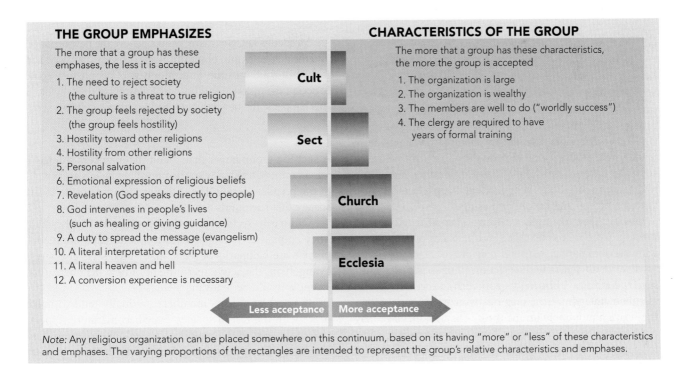

THE GROUP EMPHASIZES

The more that a group has these emphases, the less it is accepted

1. The need to reject society (the culture is a threat to true religion)
2. The group feels rejected by society (the group feels hostility)
3. Hostility toward other religions
4. Hostility from other religions
5. Personal salvation
6. Emotional expression of religious beliefs
7. Revelation (God speaks directly to people)
8. God intervenes in people's lives (such as healing or giving guidance)
9. A duty to spread the message (evangelism)
10. A literal interpretation of scripture
11. A literal heaven and hell
12. A conversion experience is necessary

CHARACTERISTICS OF THE GROUP

The more that a group has these characteristics, the more the group is accepted

1. The organization is large
2. The organization is wealthy
3. The members are well to do ("worldly success")
4. The clergy are required to have years of formal training

Cult

Sect

Church

Ecclesia

Less acceptance ← | → More acceptance

Note: Any religious organization can be placed somewhere on this continuum, based on its having "more" or "less" of these characteristics and emphases. The varying proportions of the rectangles are intended to represent the group's relative characteristics and emphases.

FIGURE 14.2 Religious Groups: From Hostility to Acceptance

Source: By the author. Adapted from Troeltsch (1931); Pope (1942); Johnson (1963).

Heaven's Gate and Other Cults

The news made instant headlines around the world in late March 1997: 39 bodies had been found in an exclusive San Diego neighbourhood draped in purple, diamond-shaped shrouds. Some of the men had been castrated. There was no sign of a struggle.

Reports followed on the beliefs of those who had died—members of the Heaven's Gate cult. A spaceship was hiding behind the Hale-Bopp comet, ready to transport them to a new life. To be beamed aboard, they had to leave their "containers" behind. That meant suicide. For their space travels, each cult member put on new Nike sneakers. Each also packed a bag with clothing, $5 bills, and quarters—and a passport.

Then there is the garbage-eating Brotherhood led by an ex-Marine who claims he is Jesus. His long-haired followers rummage through dumpsters, carefully removing any mould before dining on rotting scraps of the material world they so disdain. They blame their stomach aches on Satan (O'Neill, 1997).

Other Messiahs have been just as influential. In the 1970s, hundreds followed Jim Jones to Guyana. More than 900 committed suicide—or were murdered. In the 1990s, 74 members of the Solar Temple in Switzerland, France, and Canada arranged themselves in the shape of a cross and set themselves afire. They believed they would be transported to the star Sirius (Lacayo, 1997).

Why would anyone fall for such "obvious" deception? Finding meaning in life lies at the centre of religion. Always, people seek to satisfy their spiritual longings. And with today's rapid social change, our traditional meanings are constantly challenged and sometimes uprooted. Newcomers are isolated, cut off from family and friends who would provide a balancing perspective on reality. As a group's views are regularly confirmed by people one has come to like and respect, the bizarreness of these beliefs gradually wears off. Instead, cult members come to be viewed as "insiders" privy to secret messages beyond the grasp of ordinary people.

Heaven's Gate, and its many counterparts throughout the world, matches the public's image of cults—bizarre people with strange teachings whose followers act in repugnant ways. As has been stressed, however, the sociological meaning of "cult" is different. All new religions begin as cults. Some grow and become sects. Others even develop into churches and ecclesias.

Cults

Cults sometimes make instant headlines around the world, as did the ones described in the next Down-to-Earth Sociology box (on page 335). Cults, however, are not necessarily weird, and few practise "brainwashing" or bizarre rituals. In fact, all religions began as cults (R. Stark, 1989).

Cults often begin with the appearance of a **charismatic leader**, an individual who inspires people because he or she seems to have extraordinary qualities. Finding something highly appealing about the individual, people feel drawn to both the person and his or her message.

A **cult**, then, is simply a new or different religion, with few followers, whose teaching and practices put it at odds with the dominant culture and religion.

Every cult meets with rejection from society. Its message is considered bizarre, its approach to life, strange. Its members antagonize the majority, who are convinced that they have a monopoly on the truth. The new message may claim revelation, visions, visits from God and angels, some form of enlightenment, or seeing the true way to God. The cult demands intense commitment, and its followers, confronting a hostile world, pull into a tight circle, separating themselves from nonbelievers.

Most cults fail. Not many people believe the new message, and the cult fades into obscurity. Some, however, succeed and make history. Over time, large numbers of people may come to accept the message and become followers of the religion. If this happens, the new religion changes from a cult to a sect.

Sects

A **sect** is a group larger than a cult. Its members still feel a fair amount of tension with the prevailing beliefs and values of the broader society. The sect may even be hostile to the society that surrounds it.

Ordinarily, sects are loosely organized and fairly small. They emphasize personal salvation, and extemporaneous prayers are hallmarks of sects. Like cults, sects also stress **evangelism**, the active recruitment of new members. One example would be Jehovah's Witnesses.

If a sect grows, its members gradually tend to make peace with the rest of society. They become more respectable in the eyes of the majority and feel much less hostility and little, if any, isolation. To appeal to the new, broader base, the sect shifts some of its doctrines, redefining matters to remove some of the rough edges that created tension between it and the rest of society. If a sect follows this course and becomes larger and more integrated into society, it changes into an institutionalized religion, such as the Roman Catholic Church or Confucianism.

Institutionalized Religions

When a sect becomes an **institutionalized religion**, it becomes highly bureaucratized—probably with national and international headquarters that give directions to local congregations, enforce rules about who can be ordained, and control finances. Rather than being recruited from the outside by fervent, personal evangelism, most new members come from within, from children born to existing members. At some designated age, children may be asked to affirm the group's beliefs in a confirmation or bar mitzvah ceremony.

Ecclesias

Some groups become so well integrated into a culture and so strongly allied with their government that it is difficult to tell where one leaves off and the other takes over. In these state religions, also called **ecclesias**, the government and religion work together to try to shape society. How extensively religion and government intertwine in an ecclesia is illustrated by Sweden, where in the 1800s all citizens had to memorize Luther's Small Catechism and be tested on it yearly (P. Anderson, 1995). Today, Lutheranism is still the state religion, but most Swedes come to church only for baptisms, marriages, and funerals.

Variations in Patterns

Not all religious groups go through all of these stages—from cult to sect to institutionalized religion to ecclesia.

While attendance at religious services in Canada has declined over the past five decades, the vast majority of Canadians still retain a belief in God.

Some die out because they fail to attract enough members. Others, such as the Amish, remain sects. And very few religions ever become ecclesias, with notable exceptions such as Iran.

Although all religions began as cults, not all varieties of a given religion may have done so. For example, some **denominations**—"brand names" within a major religion, such as Methodism or Reform Judaism—may begin as splinter groups. A large group within an institutionalized religion may disagree with some aspects of the religion's teachings (not its major message) and break away to form its own organization.

When Religion and Culture Conflict

Cults and sects represent a break with the past. Consequently, they challenge the social order. Three major patterns of adaptation occur when religion and the culture in which it is embedded find themselves in conflict.

First, the members of a religion may reject the dominant culture and have as little as possible to do with nonmembers of their religion. The practice of polygamy by a breakaway Mormon sect in Bountiful, British Columbia, is a recent example. Withdrawn into a closed community, it is unlikely that the BC government can or will prosecute, even though polygamy is illegal in Canada.

In the second pattern, a cult or sect rejects only specific elements of the prevailing culture. Most elements of the main culture, however, are accepted. Although specific activities are forbidden, members of the religion are able to participate in most aspects of the broader society. They resolve this mild tension either by adhering to the religion or by "sneaking," conducting the forbidden acts on the sly. An example might be Jehovah's Witnesses.

In the third pattern, the society rejects the religious group and may even try to destroy it. The early Christians are an example. The Roman emperor declared them enemies of Rome and ordered all Christians hunted down and destroyed.

Characteristics of Religion in Canada

How can we generalize about religion in Canada, with its hundreds of denominations and sects? What do these many religious groups have in common? It certainly isn't doctrine, but doctrine is not the focus of sociology. Sociologists are interested in the relationship between society and religion, and the role religion plays in people's lives. To better understand religion in Canadian society, we shall focus first on characteristics of members of religious groups, then on the groups themselves.

The picture of religion in Canada is a changing one—but one that recognizes diversity and a degree of continuity with the past.

Historically, Canada has been predominantly Christian, with Roman Catholicism as the majority religion, in contrast to the United States, which remains majority Protestant. Most of the population in Canada is divided between Protestants, living mostly outside the province of Quebec, and Roman Catholics, of whom the majority live in Quebec. Between 1986 and 2001, Roman Catholics numbered over 43 percent of the adult population in Canada, while the proportion of established Protestants, such as Anglican, United, and so on, made up over 29 percent of the adult population in the country.

The only religious groups in Canada that grew to any significant degree over this time period were the Eastern, non-Christian religions of Islam, Hinduism, Sikhism, and Buddhism. Between 1991 and 2001, Muslims were the fastest growing population with an increase of over 128 percent (253 265 to 579 640), followed by Hindus, Sikhs, and Buddhists, with over 85 percent While the proportion is small—between 4 and 5 percent of the adult Canadian population—the percentage of individuals self-identifying as members of these four religions was higher in Canada than in the United States (see Table 14.3).

What is changing in Canada in terms of religion and religious identity? When compared to Americans, Canadians show a dramatic difference when it comes to non-religious residents. Since the 1961 census, the incidence of those reporting "no religion" increased dramatically, from a low of less than 1 percent in 1961 to over 16.5 percent today. Compared to the United States, more than four times the percentage of Canadians profess not to be part of any religious tradition, a trend that does not appear to be slowing down.

TABLE 14.3 Religion in Canada and the United States

Religion	Canada	United States
Roman Catholic	43.6	23.9
Protestant	29.2	51.3
Mormon	—	1.7
Other Christian	4.3	1.6
Muslim	2	.6
Jewish	1.1	1.7
Buddhist	1	.7
Hindu	1	nil
Sikh	.9	nil
Other or unaffiliated	1.3	14.6
None	16.5	4

Sources: www.state.gov/r/pa/ei/bgn/2089.htm; www.cia.gov/library/publications/the-world-factbook/geos/us.html.

TABLE 14.4 Canadians Reporting "No Religion" by Age Group

Age Group	No Religion (%)	Total Population (%)
0–14 years	23.1	19.4
15–24 years	16.2	13.5
25–44	45	30.5
45–54	13.2	14.9
55–64	6.3	9.6
65 years and over	6.2	12.2

Source: Statistics Canada, Cat. # 96F0030XIE2001015—Religions in Canada.

Table 14.4 illustrates that younger Canadians, or those under age 25, are more likely to say they have no religion. In 1996, Queen's University conducted the only recent North American survey, titled "God and Society in North America." In the survey, those expressing no religious affiliation were separated into the following categories: "Agnostic," "Atheist," "Nothing," and "Don't Know." In each category, Canadians scored higher (in percentage terms) than Americans.

Another significant change has been the proportion of Canadians who regularly attend religious services. Since the post–World War II period, Canadians have been attending services on a less frequent basis. Over two-thirds of Canadians in 1951 stated that they had attended religious services during the previous week. The General Social Survey in 2005 reported that fewer than 21 percent of adult Canadians attend religious services every week—down from 30 percent in 1985 (Lindsay, 2008).

While this is true for all age groups in Canada, older Canadians are considerably more likely than their younger counterparts to attend religious services on a regular basis. In 2005, for example, 37 percent of Canadians aged 65 and over attended a religious service at least once a week, whereas only 16 percent of boththose between the ages of 15 and 24, and 25 and 44, did so. In other words, the percentage of seniors attending regularly in 2005 was over twice that reported for 15- to 24- and 25- to 44-year-olds.

Focus Question

What are the religious differences between Canada and the United States?

👁 **Watch** the video "The Persistence of America in Religion" on **MySocLab.**

((• **Listen** to "New Religion in America: Alternative Movements Gain Ground with Flexibility, Modernity" on **MySocLab.**

👁 **Watch** the video "History of Religion in America" on **MySocLab.**

EDUCATION: TRANSFERRING KNOWLEDGE AND SKILLS

TODAY'S CREDENTIAL SOCIETY

What is a credential society, and how does it develop?

A **credential society** is one in which employers use diplomas and degrees to determine who is eligible for a job. One reason that credentialling developed is that large, anonymous societies lack the personal knowledge common to smaller groups; educational certification provides evidence of a person's ability. p. 308.

THE FUNCTIONALIST PERSPECTIVE: PROVIDING SOCIAL BENEFITS

What is the functionalist perspective on education and how does the conflict perspective on education differ from it?

Among the functions of education are the teaching of knowledge and skills, **cultural transmission** of values, social integration, **gatekeeping**, promoting personal and social change, and **mainstreaming**. Functionalists also note that education has replaced some traditional family functions. The basic view of conflict theorists is that education reproduces the social class structure; that is, through such mechanisms as unequal funding and operating different schools for the elite and for the masses, education reinforces a society's basic social inequalities. pp. 311–318.

THE SYMBOLIC INTERACTIONIST PERSPECTIVE: TEACHER EXPECTATIONS AND THE SELF-FULFILLING PROPHECY

What is the symbolic interactionist perspective on education?

Symbolic interactionists focus on face-to-face interaction. In examining what occurs in the classroom, they have found a **self-fulfilling prophecy**: that student performance tends to conform to teacher expectations, whether they are high or low. pp. 322–323.

RETHINKING SCHOOLS: PROBLEMS AND SOLUTIONS

What are the chief problems that face canadian education and what are the primary solutions to these problems?

The major problems are low achievement, grade inflation, social promotion, functional illiteracy, and violence. The primary solution is to restore high educational standards, which can be done only after providing basic security for students. Any solution for improving quality must be based on raising standards and expecting more of both students and teachers. pp. 323–328.

RELIGION: ESTABLISHING MEANING

WHAT IS RELIGION?

What is religion?

Durkheim identified three essential characteristics of **religion**: beliefs that set the **sacred** apart from the **profane**, **rituals**, and a **moral community**. pp. 328–329.

THE FUNCTIONALIST PERSPECTIVE

What are the functions and dysfunctions of religion?

Among the functions of religion are answering questions about ultimate meaning, providing emotional comfort, social solidarity, guidelines for everyday life, social control, adaptation, support for the government, and fostering social change. Groups or activities that provide these same functions are called functional equivalents of religion. Among the dysfunctions of religion are war and religious persecution. pp. 329–330.

THE SYMBOLIC INTERACTIONIST PERSPECTIVE

What aspects of religion do symbolic interactionists, conflict theorists, feminists, and postmodernists study?

Symbolic interactionists focus on the meanings of religion for its followers. They examine religious symbols, rituals, beliefs, experiences, and the sense of community provided by religion. pp. 330–331. Conflict theorists examine the relationship of religion to social inequalities, especially how religion is a conservative force that reinforces a society's social stratification. p. 331. Feminists focus on female spirituality. There are four main categories of the feminist study of spirituality: revisionists, reformists, revolutionaries, and rejectionists. All attempt to eliminate sexist ritual and teachings. pp. 331–332. Postmodernism extols the intrinsic worth of socially contextualized individual experience, spirituality, and cultural diversity. According to postmodernism, all of our thinking is contextual. There is no place for objective truth derived from science or organized religion. Instead, we find "local narratives" or stories that work for particular communities but are not considered valid outside these communities. There is no room for any absolute, universal truths within postmodernism. All religions that profess to know the truth are classed as "metanarratives" (comprehensive world views) and abandoned. However, there is space for individuals to seek out spirituality. p. 332.

RELIGION AND THE SPIRIT OF CAPITALISM

What does the spirit of capitalism have to do with religion?

Max Weber disagreed with Marx's conclusion that religion impedes social change. In contrast, Weber saw religion as a primary source of social change. He analyzed how Protestantism gave rise to the **Protestant ethic**, which stimulated what he called the **spirit of capitalism**. The result was capitalism, which transformed society. pp. 332–333.

THE WORLD'S MAJOR RELIGIONS

What are the world's major religions?

Judaism, Christianity, and Islam, all **monotheistic** religions, can be traced to the same Old Testament roots. Hinduism, the chief religion of India, has no specific founder, unlike Judaism (Abraham), Christianity (Jesus), Islam (Muhammad), Buddhism (Gautama), and Confucianism (K'ung Fu-tsu). Specific teachings and history of these six religions are given in the text. pp. 333–335. Sociologists divide religious groups into cults, sects, churches, and ecclesias. All religions began as **cults**. Those that survive tend to develop into **sects** and eventually into **institutionalized religions**. Sects, often led by **charismatic leaders**, are unstable. Some are perceived as a threat and persecuted by the state. **Ecclesias**, or state religions, are rare. pp. 335–337.

CHARACTERISTICS OF RELIGION IN CANADA

What is one of the principal differences between canada and the united states with regard to religion?

When compared to Americans, Canadians show a dramatic difference when it comes to the non-religious affiliation category. Over 16 (16.4) percent of Canadians reported no religious affiliation in a recent study, while only one in 4 percent of Americans expressed the same sentiment. pp. 337–338.

TALKING ABOUT THEORY

Theoretical Paradigms

	CLASSICAL PARADIGMS			RECENT PARADIGMS	
	Structural-Functional Paradigm	Social-Conflict Paradigm	Symbolic-Interaction Paradigm	Feminist Paradigm	Postmodernist Paradigm
What is the level of analysis?	Macro level	Macro level	Micro level	Macro level	Micro and macro levels
What is the social significance of religion?	Religion provides answers to troubling questions about human purpose, choice, and emotional comfort (inclusive = functional). Religion divides us into believers and non-believers, resulting in conflict between different religious groups (exclusive = dysfunctional).	Religion reinforces social inequality by acting much like a drug, facilitating escape from personal misery.	Religion creates a feeling of belonging to a larger community through symbols, rituals, and cosmology.	Concentrates on how the world's religions have avoided or, more often, suppressed female spirituality.	Emphasizes local narratives as expressions of human spirituality. For example, the rise of New Age religions.
Has religion changed over time? How?	Yes/No. When linked to outstanding political objectives, religious messages change. For example, Christian fundamentalism and social conservatism.	No All religions, regardless of cosmetic changes, remain false consciousness.	Yes/No. Changing social environments can lead to changes in rituals but not fundamental symbols and cosmology. For example, Catholic mass no longer in Latin.	Yes. Recovering the role of women and female spirituality from the three major world religions.	N/A

All URLs listed are current as of the printing of this text.

Canadian Montessori Academy
www.policyalternatives.ca/sites/default/files/uploads/
publications/ourselves/docs/OSOS_Summer10_
Preview.pdf
This site provides a short collection of articles on alternative public education.

Infidel Guy
www.infidels.org
This website, called the Secular Web, is dedicated to promoting and defending a naturalistic world view on the internet.

Becoming a Pagan
www.spiralgoddess.com/Pagan101.html
This website provides information and links about paganism.

1. With technology providing greater out-of-classroom educational opportunities (courses through the internet, for example), will education's role in reproducing inequality be diminished?
2. How might education become a liberator for the poor and other minority groups?
3. What are some of the pressures high school students experience in today's economy and how might these pressures contribute to growing violence within schools?
4. What are some of the ways the education system reproduces inequality? Access the Research Navigator through MySocLab and use keywords such as "hidden curriculum," "political socialization," "gender inequalities," and "racial inequalities" to locate relevant and recent scholarly and popular press publications to help you answer this question.
5. Compared to Americans, a much larger percentage of Canadians report that they have no religious affiliation. What do you think accounts for this difference? Do Weber's ideas of secularization have any merit?
6. Generally speaking, why do you think people from different classes in Canada also differ in their religious preferences? Compare the religious affiliation of small businessmen with the rich and with the more underprivileged members of Canadian society.

MySocLab

Explore the topics covered in this chapter on MySocLab. Interactive resources include a study plan, cumulative exams, a multimedia library, MySocLab eReadings, and access to the MySocLab Video Series.

15

MEDICINE: HEALTH AND ILLNESS IN CANADA

LEARNING OUTCOMES

After you have studied this chapter, you will be able to answer the following questions:

1. What is the role of sociology in the study of medicine?
2. What are the gender differences in causes of death?
3. Which level of government in Canada is responsible for health care?
4. What are the five provisions of the *Canada Health Act* (1984)?
5. Is extra billing a good idea for cutting costs to the health care system in Canada?
6. What is one of the major findings of the sociology of health research in Canada?
7. Why is medically assisted suicide an issue now?
8. Are there alternatives to our current health care system?

Think all chicken McNuggets are made the same?

Think again.

A new study has found the amount of salt in fast food varies significantly between countries, with some foods sold to Canadians among the saltiest. In Canada, for example, a 100-gram serving of McDonald's chicken McNuggets contains two-and-a-half times more sodium than a 100-gram serving in the United Kingdom. And french fries, salads and sandwiches are saltier in Canada than in five other countries, including the United States.

The international team of researchers compared salt levels in breakfast items, burgers, chicken products, french fries, pizza, salads, and sandwiches. The fast food chains scrutinized in the research were Burger King, Domino's Pizza, KFC, McDonald's, Pizza Hut, and Subway.

The international team of researchers compared salt levels in breakfast items, burgers, chicken products, french fries, pizza, salads, and sandwiches. The fast food chains scrutinized in the research were Burger King, Domino's Pizza, KFC, McDonald's, Pizza Hut, and Subway.

"What we found is a large variation in the amount of salt in the different categories," said study co-author Dr. Norm Campbell, a professor at the University of Calgary's faculty of medicine. "Some were very low, most were

Source: Megan Ogilvie, "Some fast foods sold to Canadians among the saltiest." *Toronto Star*, April 16, 2012. Edited by Dan Glenday.

very high, and some were extremely high. What that shows is within each food category you can produce foods that are low in salt."

"What that means is there are really no viable technological challenges the fast food industry faces in reducing the amount of salt in their products," Campbell said. "It can be done."

Food companies often say food processing issues make it hard for them to substantially lower salt content in foods. Campbell and his co-authors suggest that large food companies, such as the six included in the study, do have the ability to reformulate their foods since, for example, a chicken product produced by the same company is saltier in one country than in another.

Campbell wants to know why Canadian fast food companies are serving foods so high in salt. "I think some people feel helpless about this," he said.

Research has shown consuming too much dietary salt leads to high blood pressure, a risk factor for heart disease and stroke. The study's authors conclude their report by suggesting that reducing salt in fast foods is technically feasible and "is likely to produce important gains in population health."

Focus Question
Why do sociologists study health and illness?

Sociology and the Study of Medicine

Increasingly, Canadians are becoming aware of the old adage: "You are what you eat." It is also true that Canadians are eating at more fast-food restaurants than ever before. Becoming knowledgeable about what and how much we eat, including the amount of salt we ingest and its consequences to the human body, is one of the issues Canadians are beginning to take seriously.

As we look at such issues, the role of sociology in the study of **medicine**—society's standard ways of dealing with illness and injury—will become apparent. Medicine is a profession, a bureaucracy, and a publicly funded institution in Canada. In the midst of our publicly funded, universally accessible Medicare system stands what is called the Health-Industrial Complex. The Health-Industrial Complex comprises the pharmaceutical industries, private health insurance companies such as Blue Cross and Green Shield that provide extra medical coverage for Canadians, privately operated home-care industries, and many other for-profit industries that extend across the health and medicine sector of our economy.

Sociologists study how this important and extensive sector is influenced by ideas of self-regulation, the bureaucratic structure, and public policy in Canada. Sociologists also study how illness and health are much more than biological matters—how they are intimately related to cultural beliefs, lifestyle, and social class. Because of such emphases, the sociology of medicine is one of the applied fields of sociology.

The Symbolic Interactionist Perspective

The Role of Culture in Defining Health and Illness

There are biological components of health—a nutritious diet, exercise, the use of antibiotics, and so on. However, there is also an important cultural dimension to physical well-being that is the focus of health and medical sociology.

Consider mental "illness" and mental "health." If a Canadian talks aloud to spirits that no one else can see, and takes direction from them, he or she is likely to be defined as mentally ill. In some tribal societies, someone who talks to invisible spirits might be honoured for being in close contact with the spiritual world—and, for everyone's good, declared a **shaman** (or healer) who will diagnose and treat medical problems.

Around the world, every culture provides guidelines its people use to determine whether they are "healthy" or "sick." This is another example of the vital role the social construction of reality plays in our lives.

What is Health?

In 1941, international health experts identified three components of **health**: physical, mental, and social (World Health Organization, 1946). (See Figure 15.1. In light of recent feminist and postmodern interest in the "spiritual" side of well-being, we have added a spiritual component to the diagram.)

As symbolic interactionists stress, an important concern of sociologists is not to define what "true" health or "true" illness is. Instead, it is to analyze the effects of people's ideas of health and illness on their lives.

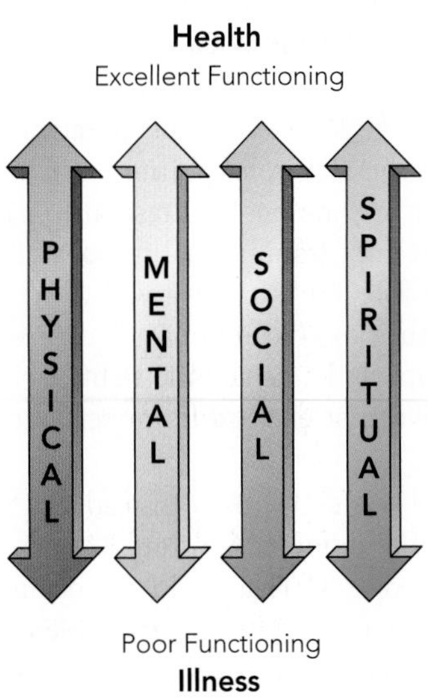

Health
Excellent Functioning

Poor Functioning
Illness

FIGURE 15.1 A Continuum of Health and Illness

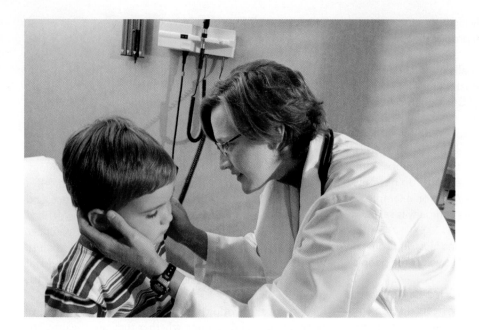

How do you think this doctor's assumptions of the cause and proper treatment of illness might contrast with those of the immigrant parents of her patient?

The Functionalist Perspective

If society is to function well, its people need to be healthy enough to perform their normal roles. One way to control sickness is through a system of medical care societies. Another is to make rules that keep too many people from "being sick."

The Sick Role

Do you remember when you were young and your throat began to hurt and mom or dad took your temperature? The thermometer may have registered 39°C (37°C is normal), and your parents perhaps took you to the doctor. Despite your protests that the next day was (your birthday or the first day of vacation), you had to spend the next three days in bed taking medicines. You were forced to play what sociologists call the **sick role**. What is meant by this term?

ELEMENTS OF THE SICK ROLE Talcott Parsons (1953), who first analyzed the sick role, pointed out that it has four elements—that you are not held responsible for being sick, that you are exempt from normal responsibilities, that you don't like the role, and that you will get competent help so you can return to your routines. People who don't seek competent help can be denied the right to claim sympathy from others and to be excused from their normal routines.

AMBIGUITY IN THE SICK ROLE Instead of a fever of 39°C, suppose the thermometer registers 37.4°C. Do you then "become" sick, or not? That is, do you decide to claim the sick role? Decisions to claim the sick role often are based more on social considerations than physical conditions. Let's also suppose you are facing a midterm for which you are drastically underprepared, and you are allowed to make

it up. The more you think about the test, the worse you are likely to feel—legitimating to yourself the need to claim the sick role. Now assume that you have no test, but your friends are coming over to take you out to celebrate your nineteenth birthday. You are much less likely to play the sick role. Note that in the two cases your physical condition is the same.

GATEKEEPERS TO THE SICK ROLE Parents and physicians are the primary gatekeepers to the sick role. That is, they mediate between our feelings of illness and our claim to being sick. Before parents call the school to excuse a child's absence, they decide whether the child is faking or has genuine symptoms serious enough to allow him or her to remain home. For adults, physicians are the main gatekeepers of the sick role. A "doctor's excuse"—actually official permission to play the sick role—removes the need for employers and teachers to pass judgment on an individual's claim.

The Conflict Perspective

As stressed in earlier chapters, the primary focus of conflict theorists is how people struggle over scarce resources. Since medical treatment is one of those resources, let's examine this competition in a global perspective.

Effects of Global Stratification on Health Care

Our review in Chapter 5 of how globalization stratified the world economy stressed that the nations that industrialized obtained the economic and military power that allowed

 Explore Talcott Parsons' "The Sick Role and the Role of the Physician Reconsidered" on **MySocLab.**

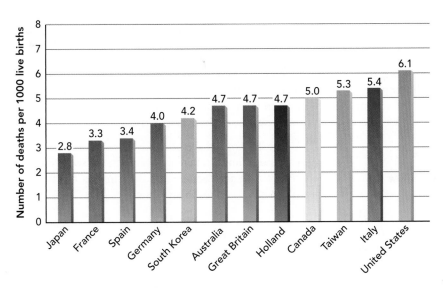

FIGURE 15.2

Note: Infant mortality is the number of babies that die before their first birthday, per 1000 live births. Not all countries with infant mortalities lower than the United States are included.

Source: By the author. Based on *Statistical Abstract of the United States* (2011), Table 1338.

them to become rich and dominate the globe. One consequence is the globalization of medical care.

Life expectancy also illustrates globalization. Whereas most people in the industrialized world can expect to live to about 75, *most* people in Afghanistan, Angola, Cambodia, Haiti, and Rwanda die before they reach 50. The infant mortality rates shown in Figure 15.2 also tell the story. This figure lists some of the world's countries where fewer than 7 out of every 1000 babies die before they are a year old. All of them are industrialized nations.

In contrast to these totals, the infant mortality rates of some countries, such as Angola, are 60 times higher than Japan's rate (*Statistical Abstract* 2011: Table 1338).

Globalization, then, is a matter of life and death. Suppose you were born in one of the least industrialized nation located in the tropics. During your much shorter life, you would face illness and death from four major sources: malaria (from mosquitoes), internal parasites (from contaminated water), diarrhea (from food and soil contaminated with human feces), and malnutrition. A longer life expectancy in the developed industrial nations depends on diseases you are not likely to contract that could kill you early in life. Or, if you do contract malaria or diarrhea, there are "cures" available to you.

Focus Question

What are the differences between the functionalist and the conflict perspectives on health?

The Feminist Perspective

As discussed throughout the text, the primary focus of feminist theorists is how sexism pervades our social institutions and social life. Since medical treatment is an important

institution in our society, let's examine how sexism works in medicine and health.

Sexism in Medicine

Although usually quite subtle, often even below people's awareness, sexism in medicine can carry serious consequences. As we saw in the Down-to-Earth Sociology box entitled "Making the Invisible Visible: Gender Impacts Health" in Chapter 7 (page 156), physicians don't take women's health complaints as seriously as men's. As a result, women with heart disease are operated on at a later stage, making it more likely they will die from their surgery.

Bias against women's reproductive organs has also been reported. Sue Fisher (1986) conducted participant observation in a hospital. When she heard doctors recommend a total hysterectomy (removal of both the uterus and the ovaries) although no cancer was present, she asked why. The doctors explained that the uterus and ovaries are "potentially disease-producing" organs. Also, they added, they are unnecessary after the child-bearing years, so why not remove them?

To "convince" the woman to have this surgery, the doctor told her that, unfortunately, the examination uncovered fibroids in her uterus—and that they *might* turn into cancer. This statement is often sufficient, since it frightens women, who visualize themselves ready to be buried. What the surgeon did not say was that the fibroids would probably not turn into cancer and that many nonsurgical alternatives were available.

Underlying this sexism is the male dominance of medicine in Canada. This is not a worldwide phenomenon. In the former Soviet Union, for example, three out of four physicians are women (Knaus, 1981). Following changes in gender relations, the percentage of Canadian medical degrees earned by women rose from only 24.3 percent in 1975 to 58.4 percent in 2010, in contrast to 48 percent in the United States (Canadian Medical Association, 2010). This changing sex ratio should not only help reduce sexism in medical practice but also contribute to several new changes in health care delivery (see the Down-to-Earth Sociology textbox "Women as Physicians").

The Gendered Experience of Health and Illness: Some Explanations

There are gender differences in causes of death (discussed in the next section) and, although the gap is narrowing, in life expectancy (see Chapter 9). Moreover, we know that men and women experience health and illness differently. For example, having social support is a more important predictor of good health for women than for men.

What could account for these and other gendered differences? Leaving aside any biological answers, there are five sociological explanations for gender differences in the experience of health and illness.

1. First, there is role *accumulation*. This theory suggests that the more roles a person has, the better their health. However, this simple explanation fails to take into account the kinds of roles a woman performs. For example, the benefits of being married and having a job, such as increased income and social support, may be offset by the added burdens of the parental role. Therefore, modifications to this explanation have centred on the kinds of roles women and men perform.
2. A second explanation put forward for the gendered differences in health and illness concentrates on the negative effects of women's roles on their health and well-being. The demands of the *double day* (i.e., family and employment responsibilities) lead to increased stress and excessive demands on women's time and energy.
3. *Social acceptability*, the third explanation, suggests that due to the socialization of women into traditional roles, women are more willing than men to admit to being sick and accept help in dealing with their health problems. On the other hand, men are socialized to control their experiences of pain or illness and are reluctant to adopt the sick role, and, as a result, are reluctant talk about their health. Therefore, women are more likely to share information about the types of symptoms they are experiencing. While men rely on their spouses for social support, women tend to turn to their friends and their children for help.
4. The fact that women experience more illness than men is explained by the *nurturing* tendencies of women. In their role as primary caregiver for their spouses, children, and aging parents, women experience considerable stress with little, if any, time left for themselves. As a result, they may neglect their own health.
5. Finally, there is the suggestion that men are socialized to take more risks than women while women are socialized to be cautious. This *competitive* view of gender role differences sees men engaging in more risky behaviours, such as smoking, drinking alcohol, and accidents, while women take on more preventive and protective behaviours, such as seeking help early.

All these theories have been advanced in order to make sense of the complex differences between the social characteristics of men and women and their impact on the gendered experience of health and illness.

Focus Question

Is there a gendered experience of health and illness?

Historical Patterns of Health

How have patterns of health and illness in Canada changed? The answer to this question takes us into the field of **epidemiology**, the study of how medical disorders are distributed throughout a population.

Physical Health

Table 15.1 provides recent data for the leading causes of death among Canadians. The top two causes of death—cancer and heart disease—affected 51 percent of men and women in Canada who died in 2008 (Statistics Canada, 2008h). Gender differences do exist, however; men dominated in the top 10 of causes of death in 2008. For young adults aged 15 to 24, the top three causes of death, in order, were accidents, suicide, and homicide (ibid.)

Between the provinces, Quebec reported the highest mortality rates for lung and colon cancer, while Alberta reported the lowest rates of lung cancer and British Columbia the lowest rates of colon cancers. Deaths due to suicide have declined in all provinces except Saskatchewan, Alberta, and Quebec. Quebec's rate not only remained the highest but exceeded the margin set the year before for all the provinces and territories in Canada. The reason or reasons for this cause of death is a matter of serious research and public policy remedies in Quebec. Having said this, the highest rates of suicide in Canada are among our Aboriginal populations, especially those located in the Yukon and the Northwest Territories. This must become a high priority for Indian and Northern Affairs Canada (INAC).

WERE CANADIANS HEALTHIER IN THE PAST? Mortality rates can help us answer this question. Because most people today live longer than their ancestors, we can conclude that contemporary Canadians are healthier.

 Explore the reading "Health Care Reform—A Woman's Issue" on **MySocLab.**

DOWN-TO-EARTH SOCIOLOGY

Women as Physicians

More and more women are practising medicine in Canada, but a new Canadian Institute for Health Information (CIHI) report says male physicians still far outnumber women doctors.

The study contains the latest data on the composition of the country's physician workforce, including how many doctors are practising in Canada, where they are, and their demographic characteristics. One of the most noteworthy statistics is the growth rate of female physicians over a five-year period.

Between 2002 and 2006, the number of women doctors in Canada grew by about 13 percent, while the rate for their male counterparts was just under 1 percent. Women are gaining ground in what was once a male-dominated profession and, by 2006, made up more than a third of the physician workforce (33.3 percent), CIHI reported.

Overall, men still far outnumber women doctors in Canada. Family physicians and specialists combined, there was a total of 41 379 men in 2006 compared to 20 646 women. But when the numbers were broken down by age, they show that a sizable number of young women are now in the field. In 2006, women represented almost half (48.6 percent) of the doctors under 40 years old.

And younger doctors in Canada are different from their older counterparts, CIHI said, in terms of how they practice. "Research suggests that younger doctors joining the workforce tend to practice differently than their older counterparts," said Geoff Ballinger, CIHI manager of health human resources, in a release. "They tend to put more emphasis on work-life balance, and may see fewer patients on average than older physicians as a result. It's important for health planners to understand these difference in practice patterns, particularly as a greater number of doctors approach their retirement years" (CanWest News Service, 2007).

For Your Conisderation

In Chapter 7, we learned an interesting principle of gender: Activities associated with women are usually given lower prestige than the activities associated with men. Larger numbers of women entering the medical profession in Canada is an example. As women begin to move ahead of men in the profession, do you think the prestige of practicing medicine will decline? What about the income of physicians?

TABLE 15.1 Selected Leading Causes of Death, by Sex, 2004–2008

Leading Causes of Death*	2004			2008		
	Total Both Sexes	Females	Males	Total Both Sexes	Females	Males
HIV	1.2	0.4	1.9	1.1	0.5	1.6
Cancer	174	147	212	164	140	197
Diabetes	19.6	15.8	24.8	16.7	13.4	20.9
Alzheimer's	12.7	13.7	10.5	12.8	13.8	10.8
Heart Disease	127	94.6	168	108	79.7	143
Cerebrovascular	34.9	32.4	37.9	28.8	27	30.8
Flu and Pneumonia	13.4	11.3	17	11	9.3	13.7
Kidney & Liver	30.8	10.4	20	30.2	10.4	19.3
Accidents	24.7	16	33.8	25.4	16.6	34.8
Suicide	10.8	5.1	16.6	10.4	5.1	15.8
Assault	1.7	0.9	2.4	1.8	0.8	2.8

* Not all diseases were reported.
Note: Age-standardized mortality rates are calculated using the 1991 population of Canada as standard population.
Source: By Dan Glenday. Statistics Canada, CANSIM, table 102-0552 and Catalogue no. 84F0209X.

TABLE 15.2 Canada Health Act, 1984

Criterion	Description
Comprehensive	A province must cover all services provided by physicians (general practitioners and specialists).
Universal	A province must provide insured services to all insured residents and must not impose a residential or waiting period longer than three months.
Public Administration	A provincial plan must be administered and operated on a nonprofit basis by a public authority
Portability	The benefits must be available to insured persons temporarily absent from the province (e.g., on vacation) and to those who move to another province until such time as they qualify for medicare benefits in that province.
Accessibility	A province's health care services must be reasonably accessible to all insured persons.

Mental Health

When it comes to mental health, we have no rational basis for making comparisons. All groups have had their share of mental problems—and common-sense beliefs that mental illness is worse today represent perceptions, not measured reality. Since we don't know how extensive mental illness is now (M.W. Miller, 1993), we certainly can't judge how much there was in the past.

Issues in Health Care

Health Care in Canada

While the provision of health care in Canada is a provincial responsibility, the federal government has played a major role in the past in financing the health care services available to all Canadians.

The primary purpose of national health insurance in Canada is the elimination of financial barriers to health care. Universal, government-funded medical, hospital, and other related health insurance has been available only since 1971, even though there was a federal hospital insurance program in the 1950s and a federal medical insurance program covering physicians and related services in the mid 1960s.

Under Canada's Medicare system, hospitals are financed on the basis of annually negotiated, planned-for budgets. Physicians are reimbursed on a fee-for-service basis (as is the case in the United States). However, these fees are determined by province-wide, negotiated, uniform fee schedules. Private insurance companies offer coverage only for various forms of additional services, such as private-room accommodation in hospitals, eyeglasses (up to a certain dollar limit), and pharmaceutical drugs. (Note that as of 2004, Ontario no longer covers eye examinations under Medicare.)

In 1984, the *Canada Health Act* came into force to ensure that necessary health services would be available to all Canadians regardless of their financial circumstances. The Act sets out a national standard for the provision of Canada's health care with which the provinces are obligated to comply under penalty of withholding transfer payments.

Table 15.2 outlines the five basic criteria: comprehensive scope, universal coverage, public administration, portability, and accessibility.

Federal funding for health care took a severe slashing during Paul Martin's later years as finance minister (1997 and following), when he was tackling the federal deficit and, as a result, slashed health care contributions to the provinces (see Table 15.3). Beginning in 1996–1997, the older Established Programs Financing (EPF) was replaced by the Canada Health and Social Transfer program (CHST). Unlike the EPF, which was divided into separate categories of health insurance, extended health care, and postsecondary education, the CHST is a block transfer payment to the provinces. This makes determining the federal share of health costs extremely difficult. However, we know that the federal government's share of health care funding has been dramatically cut. Even recently, the federal contribution has barely reached pre-1997 funding levels although expenditures have skyrocketed. Despite several years of record budget surpluses, there is little evidence that the federal government has reversed its course voluntarily. Even after Roy Romanow's report (from the Commission on the Future of Health Care in Canada), *Building on Values: The Future of Health Care in Canada*, was tabled in Parliament in November 2002, there was little sustained momentum for advancing the benefits of publicly funded health care.

The recent (2003–2005) transfer of health care monies to the provinces may begin the process of re-establishing the federal government's commitments to publicly funded health care in Canada. However, a June 2005 ruling in Quebec protecting a patient's right to access private services may become more important for the future health of Medicare.

Data for the 2000–2001 fiscal year reveal a total transfer to the provinces and territories under the CHST of almost $33 billion. What amounts go directly to medical health

TABLE 15.3 Federal and Provincial Expenditures on Health, 1989–2008

	Millions of $	% of Total	Millions of $	% of Total
1989	7723	18.7	33 449	81.3
1993	9803	17.6	45 859	82.4
1996	9024	15.9	47 641	84.1
1997	1177	2.4	47 951	97.6
1998	1327	2.6	49 553	97.4
2003	3498	4.7	70 893	95.3
2004	6044	7.3	76 758	92.7
2005	23 774	22.6	81 615	77.4
2007	22 901	19.7	93 289	80.3
2008	25 805	20.4	100 454	79.6

Source: Dan Glenday and Kevin Manual. Data from Statistics Canada, 2005, CANSIM II database, Table 358-0002.

care and what goes to social spending is determined mainly by individual provinces and territories.

One issue that occasionally surfaces is the use of *extra billing*, or charging patients "a little extra" as a means of cutting down on "unnecessary" visits by patients to general practitioners. As early as 1968–1972, Saskatchewan instituted a regime of modest extra billing. This measure was devastating to the poor and the elderly, and little evidence could be found to support the contention that extra billing cut down on unnecessary visits to doctors. On the contrary, R.G. Evans, a health care economist, concluded from his study of the province's "experiment" in extra billing that it involved "perverse wealth transfers from the ill to the healthy and from low-to-high income classes" (Barer, Evans, & Stoddart, 1979: 111).

For the most part, provincial, and territorial health care insurance plans meet the criteria and conditions set out in the *Canada Health Act*. However, on the basis of reports to Health Canada by their respective provincial health ministries, deductions were taken from the March 2011 payments to British Columbia, in respect of extra-billing and patients charges at surgical clinics in the amount of $75 136, and Newfoundland and Labrador, in respect of extra-billing in the amount of $3577, levied during fiscal year 2008–2009 (*Canada Health Act*, Annual Report, 2010–2011).

International Comparisons

In 2008, the latest year for which data is available, per capita spending on health care remained highest in the United States (US$7538), when comparing 26 countries with similar accounting systems in the Organisation for Economic Co-operation and Development (OECD). The United States was followed by Norway (US$5003), Switzerland (US$4627), and Luxembourg (US$4210). At around US$4079 per capita, Canada was in the top five, with spending similar to that of several other OECD countries, including the Netherlands (US$4063), Austria (US$3970), Germany (US$3737), and France (US$3696). The United States is the only country listed above where health care for its citizens is dependent on a privately funded health care system (OECD. 2010).

Focus Question

Describe the publicly funded health care system in Canada.

SARS (Severe Acute Respiratory Syndrome)

Severe Acute Respiratory Syndrome (SARS) became a health issue in Canada about 10 years ago. According to the World Health Organization (WHO), a total of 8098 people worldwide became sick with SARS during the 2003 outbreak. With only sporadic cases reported since the original outbreak, SARS has receded from the public's attention.

It is widely recognized that SARS had a dramatic impact on the tourism industry in Canada. Not until 2005 was there any sign of relief that the industry may be on the rebound. Table 15.4 provides a brief annotated history of the outbreak of the disease.

Watch the video "Cuba's Health Care System" on MySocLab.

Watch the video "Health Care Outside the United States" on MySocLab.

Watch the video "Market Principles in Health Care in the United States" on MySocLab.

TABLE 15.4 A Brief Chronology of SARS

Date	Event
Feb. 15, 2003	China reports 305 cases of atypical pneumonia (later classified as SARS).
March 5, 2003	Sui-chu Kwan, a 78-year-old woman who had travelled to Hong Kong in February, dies of SARS in Toronto.
March 12, 2003	The World Health Organization (WHO) issues a global SARS alert.
March 17, 2003	Health Canada announces 11 suspected cases of SARS in Canada: 9 in Ontario, 1 in B.C., and 1 in Alberta.
March 21, 2003	Canadian scientists say they have isolated the virus that causes SARS. The virus comes from the same family that gives people mumps or measles.
March 26, 2003	Ontario declares a public health emergency and orders thousands of people to quarantine themselves in their homes. There are 27 probable cases of SARS in the province. Toronto hospitals begin barring visitors.
April 1, 2003	WHO advises travellers to stay away from Hong Kong and China.
April 23, 2003	WHO warns against all unnecessary travel to Toronto, Beijing, and China's Shanxi province because of the SARS outbreak. The three locations join Hong Kong and China's Guangdong province on the WHO list.
April 24, 2003	Health Canada sends a formal letter of protest to the WHO, demanding that the UN health agency take back its Toronto travel advisory. Health Canada says the WHO based its warning on outdated information. The U.S. Centers for Disease Control and Prevention says it doesn't believe a travel advisory is warranted for Toronto since public health officials understand the patterns of transmission in the city. British medical officers, meanwhile, support the advisory.
April 29, 2003	The WHO announces it will lift its travel advisory against Toronto, effective April 30, 2003.
May 30, 2003	Thirty SARS-related deaths in Canada are reported—all of them in the Toronto area.
July 2, 2003	WHO removes Toronto from its list of SARS-affected cities.
September 29, 2003	Ontario's SARS inquiry opens the first of three days of public hearings in Toronto.

Source: Dan Glenday. Data from CBC News Timeline, December 15, 2003, www.cbc.ca/news/background/sars/timeline.html.

The Development of the Sociology of Health in Canada

The sociology of health in Canada has passed through at least two major stages. During the 1970s, or stage one, it focused on matters related to the complexity of the health care system, such as the changing relationships between health care professionals, the challenges posed by nurses and chiropractors to the dominance of the traditional model of medicine, and the dynamics of the sick role and patient illness behaviour. During the 1980s, the second stage brought the inclusion of other themes, such as the impact of population aging on health and health care delivery.

The principal focus of research in the field of health care has been the use of large surveys to gauge the health status of Canadians. The most recent is the ongoing longitudinal *National Population Health Survey* (NPHS), conducted by Health Canada and Statistics Canada. This large survey, begun in 1994 and continuing every second year thereafter, is an important source of information about the health and health behaviours of Canadians. The NPHS, which relies on respondents' self-reported health information, surveys the same group of respondents every two years for up to 20 years. In the studies that have been conducted recently, the most significant finding centres on the *causal* links between social status and health status. That is, social factors such as socioeconomic status (e.g., income and education) and gender, age, and ethnicity play a vital part in determining how healthy Canadians are.

The recent Health Behaviour in School-Aged Children study (2008) examined the health, well-being, and health behaviours of young people (aged 11 to 15 years) and their social settings and conditions, especially the school environment. The survey is a continuing, cross-national research project conducted in collaboration with the WHO Regional Office for Europe. The findings are numerous, but a few pertinent results include: between 1981 and 2007/09, obesity rates roughly doubled among both males and females in most age groups in the adult and youth categories, almost two fifths of students reported being victims of bullying, daily smoking is down from 2002, and condom use during respondents' last sexual intercourse is reported by four-fifths

THINKING CRITICALLY ABOUT SOCIAL CONTROVERSY

Euthanasia in Canada

Lawyers representing a 63-year-old B.C. woman with a fatal neurodegenerative disease wants the B.C. Supreme Court to grant her the right to a doctor-assisted suicide. Gloria Taylor, a West Kelowna woman with amyotrophic lateral sclerosis, also known as ALS and Lou Gehrig's disease, says she wants her doctor to be able to help her end her life before she becomes incapacitated.

Taylor is one of five plaintiffs in the case, which was fast-tracked in August because of her illness. She was not in court on Monday morning in Vancouver for the start of the hearing, but her case is being presented by Joseph Arvay of the B.C. Civil Liberties Association.

The other plaintiffs include a couple who helped their aging mother fly to Switzerland for an assisted suicide, a Victoria doctor seeking the right to help his grievously and irremediably ill patients have assisted suicides, and the B.C. Civil Liberties Association. Arvay read an affidavit from another man,

Peter Fenker, who was 71 years old and a strong active man until he was diagnosed with ALS. Later, he could not physically take any action to end his life—besides refusing food and water. He said he wished for physician-assisted suicide, and was angry that was not a possibility. "The government should not be able to control my body," he wrote.

He has since died from the disease, wrote his wife Grace, in a separate affidavit read in court. She wrote that he suffered incredibly, gasping for breath over days as though he was drowning in water. She wrote that her husband often said to her, "Humans show animals that are suffering more compassion."

The challenge is being opposed by the federal and provincial governments and the Euthanasia Prevention Coalition, which has intervener status in the case. Donnaree Nygard, the lawyer for the attorney general of Canada, said their argument will be that the good of alleviating suffering is outweighed

by the probability of wrongful death. She said those particularly vulnerable are the elderly, disabled, and people who may worry about being a "burden to society." In Canada, it is illegal to counsel, aid, or abet a person to commit suicide, and the offence carries a maximum punishment of 14 years in prison. However, three U.S. states and four European countries do allow it. The Supreme Court of Canada last ruled on the right-to-die debate in 1993, when Victoria resident Sue Rodriguez, who also had ALS, took her case to court. It ruled against her request for a doctor-assisted suicide, but Rodriguez did find an anonymous doctor who helped her carry out her dying wish.

For Your Consideration
What do you think?

Source: "Assisted suicide challenge begins in B.C. court." CBC News, November 14, 2011. Edited by Dan Glenday.

---

of sexually active boys in Grades 9 and 10. A 2005 study by Morris et al. provides data on an opposite phenomenon—the "drift hypothesis," or how a deterioration in a person's health can lead to a reduction in her or his income. In addition to these studies, others have confirmed that the organization of work and family life are important predictors of the health status of Canadians.

Focus Question
What is the sociology of health in Canada?

Depersonalization

One of the main criticisms levelled against the medical profession is its **depersonalization**, the practice of dealing with people as though they are cases and diseases, not individuals. Many patients get the impression they are being treated by a physician who, while talking to them, is impatiently counting minutes.

Participant observation of medical students at McMaster University by sociologists Jack Haas and William Shaffir

(1978/1993) provides insight into how physicians learn to depersonalize patients. Haas and Shaffir found that students begin medical school wanting to "treat the whole person." As vast amounts of material are thrown at them, their feelings for patients are overpowered by the need to be efficient. These students' statements pick up on the change:

> Somebody will say, "Listen to Mrs. Jones' heart." It's just a little thing flubbing on the table. And *you forget about the rest of her . . .* The advantage is that *you can go in a short time and see a patient, get the important things out of the patient, and leave* [italics added].

> Someone comes in who has croaked (died) [and you say], "Well, come on. Here is a chance to practise your intubation" [inserting a tube in the throat].

Medicalization of Society

As we have seen, women's reproductive organs have become defined as medical matters. Sociologists use the term **medicalization** to refer to the process of turning something that was not previously considered medical into a medical matter. Examples include balding, weight, wrinkles, acne, anxiety, depression, a sagging chin or buttocks, small breasts, and even the inability to achieve orgasm. There is nothing inherently medical in such human conditions, yet we have become so used to medicalization that we tend to consider them somehow naturally medical concerns. As Susan Sontag (1994) says, even many criminal behaviours have become matters to be medically understood and treated.

Bioethics

Medicine and ethics are by no means strangers—on the contrary, medicine started out as an aspect of early philosophy. Bioethics began with the Oath of Hippocrates, some of whose tenets included: treat the sick to the best of one's ability, preserve patient privacy, and teach the secrets of medicine to the next generation. Today, the advent of new reproductive and genetic technologies has opened the door to a number of new ethical concerns never contemplated by Hippocrates. Human cloning, stem cell research, abortion, euthanasia, and the selling of organs are a few of the issues we are confronted with today. Let's look at euthanasia.

Medically Assisted Suicide

Jack Kevorkian, a retired pathologist, helped over 100 people commit suicide (Denzin, 1992). Some defend Kevorkian as a courageous trailblazer, while others decry his acts as perverted. A how-to book on suicide, *Final Exit*, has sold over half a million copies. The Hemlock Society is a group advocating voluntary **euthanasia**—mercy killing—for terminally ill people. The case of "Nancy B." (a pseudonym), a terminally ill patient at Hôtel Dieu hospital in Quebec City, although considered by some to be an instance of euthanasia, is more properly an example of the right to refuse medical treatment. For two and a half years, Nancy suffered from a neurological disease called Guillain-Barré syndrome, for which there is no cure. She was totally helpless and physically dependent on the health care staff at the hospital. Nancy wanted to have her life-sustaining equipment disconnected, and when she went to court in 1992 to plead for this right, Justice Jacques Dufour ruled in favour of the patient's right to self-determination. Some argue that the Nancy B. case is an example of "passive euthanasia," a situation in which the person is rational (according to legal definitions) but requires assistance to stop artificial treatment of an incurable illness.

At the opposite end of the euthanasia spectrum is the situation depicted in the Oscar-winning film *Les Invasions Barbares* (*The Barbarian Invasions*) by acclaimed Quebec director Denys Arcand. The film tells the moving story of Rémy, a history professor in his fifties who is dying of cancer. Rémy opts to die while he is still in control of his faculties. Assisted by his son, Sébastien, his family, and close friends, Rémy is administered an overdose of morphine and dies quietly in the countryside, surrounded by those who love him.

With new technology that can keep the body alive even after the heart, lungs, and other vital organs no longer function on their own, a burning question, yet undecided, is "Who has the right to pull the plug?" Should someone's body be kept alive for years even though their mind can no longer work? To resolve this issue, some people sign a **living will**—a declaration they make while in good health of what they want medical personnel to do in case they become dependent on artificial life support systems.

Our technology and the acts of Dr. Kevorkian have brought us face to face with matters of death that are both disturbing and unresolved. Should "medically assisted suicide" be legal? Few find this medical-ethical issue easy to resolve. The Thinking Critically about Social Controversy box on the previous page explores these issues.

Threats to Health

In this section we will examine the following threats to health: AIDS, the globalization of disease, drugs, and disabling environments.

AIDS

Perhaps one of the most pressing health issues today in Canada—and globally—is Acquired Immune Deficiency Syndrome (AIDS). Let's look at some of its major characteristics.

ORIGIN The origin of AIDS is unknown. The most prevalent theory is that the virus was first present in monkeys in Africa and then transmitted to humans. If so, how the transmission to humans took place remains a matter of conjecture. It may have occurred during the 1920s and 1950s, when, in a peculiar experiment for malaria, people were inoculated with blood from monkeys and chimpanzees. The blood may have been infected with viral ancestors of HIV (Rathus & Nevid, 1993). Since monkeys are considered food in several parts of Africa, another possibility is that the virus was transmitted through inadequately cooked meat. Some suggest an opposite theory, that the disease originated in Europe or the United States and was somehow transmitted to Africa (Rushing, 1995).

THE TRANSMISSION OF AIDS AIDS is known to be transmitted through the exchange of blood and semen, and, in rare cases, through mother's milk to newborns. Since the virus can be present in all bodily fluids, including sweat, tears, spittle, and urine, some people think AIDS can also be transmitted in these forms. The U.S. Centers for Disease

👁 **Watch** the video "Medical Ethics and Morality" on MySocLab.

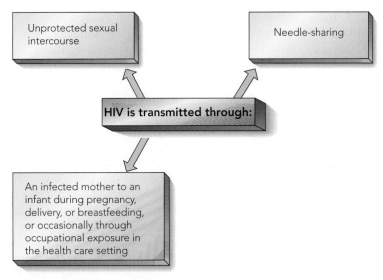

FIGURE 15.3 How Do I Get HIV/AIDS?

Control and Prevention, however, says that AIDS cannot be transmitted by casual contact in which traces of these fluids would be exchanged. The correct use of condoms is the best preventative measure against AIDS and other STDs (see Figure 15.3).

THE STIGMA OF AIDS One of the most significant sociological aspects of AIDS is its stigma, another example of how social factors are essential to health and illness. From the outset, the notion of AIDS as a "gay disease" was spread rapidly by television evangelists and other Christian conservatives in Canada and the United States. Even today, in many parts of the world, including our own, some remain convinced that AIDS is a "divine" message from God. Some people even refuse to be tested because they fear the stigma they would have to bear if they tested positive. One unfortunate consequence is the further spread of AIDS by people who "don't want to know." The stigma is so great in Africa and some Asian countries that government officials refuse to acknowledge how widespread the disease is. Burying their heads in the sand, however, makes them unable to sponsor preventive measures, so the epidemic grows (Shenon, 1995). If this disease is to be brought under control, its stigma must be overcome: AIDS must be thought of as being, like other lethal diseases, simply the work of a destructive biological organism.

AIDS is devastating huge areas of Africa. In some countries, a third or more of the population has AIDS. Millions of children have been orphaned. Governments that first ignored the problem are now trying to battle the disease. This anti-AIDS billboard is posted in Blantyre, Malawi.

THE GLOBALIZATION OF AIDS Today's global travel has facilitated the globalization of this disease. Africa has been hit hardest (Haub, 1997). In some countries ravaged by AIDS, life expectancy may be cut in half (Olshansky, Carnes, Rogers, & Smith, 1997). Botswana, Uganda, and Zimbabwe are likely to lose a quarter of their populations (Stout, 1992). In Kampala and Kigali, a third of all pregnant women have AIDS (Scommegna, 1996). The bubonic plague is considered to have killed about 30 million people in medieval Europe. The U.S. Census Bureau projects that by 2010, as a result of AIDS deaths and the loss of future population from the deaths of women of child-bearing age, sub-Saharan Africa will have 71 million fewer people than it would otherwise (Christensen, 2000). In the former Soviet Union, AIDS is multiplying, primarily due to the rise in prostitution and drug use since the fall of communism (Kaminski & Palchikoff, 1997). AIDS is also flourishing in Asia, partly because of its huge sex industry.

IS THERE A CURE FOR AIDS? The number of deaths due to AIDS in Canada began to decline in 1996. Does this mean we have found a cure? With thousands of scientists searching, the media have heralded every new breakthrough in research as a possible cure, but this has yet to appear.

The most promising treatment to date, the one that lies behind the reduction in deaths, was spearheaded by David Ho, a virologist (virus researcher). If patients in the very early stages of the disease take a "cocktail" of drugs (a combination of protease inhibitors, AZT, and 3TC), the "visible" signs of the virus can be erased from their bodies. Their immune systems then rebound (C. Gorman, 1997b). No one is yet calling this a cure, however; apparently the virus lingers undetected, ready to flourish if the drugs are withdrawn.

While most praise this new treatment, some researchers have issued a warning (Rotello, 1996). They suggest that the cocktail may become this decade's penicillin. When penicillin was introduced, everyone was ecstatic with its results. But over the years, the microbes it targets mutated, producing "super bugs" against which we have no protection. If this is the case with AIDS, then a new, "super AIDS" virus may hit the world with even more fury than the first devastating wave.

Weight: How Much Is Just Enough?

You read earlier about the ongoing Canadian sociological research on the substantial increase in obesity among children and young adults. Obesity has been described as a global epidemic. It has been linked to diabetes, hypertension, cardiovascular disease, and some forms of cancer. Comparing Canada to the United States, between 2007 and 2009, almost a quarter of Canadians (24.1 percent) were obese, over 10 percentage points lower than in the United States (34.4 percent) (Statistics Canada, 2011a). However, we should not be complacent. Obesity is on the rise in this country. The consumption of high calorie foods, especially junk food, and decreases in activity levels are helping to fuel

this increase. While it is viewed as a medical condition to treat, a variety of other options to combat obesity include taxing junk food, regulating salt (sodium) consumption, and limiting access to junk food in schools and universities.

Drugs: Alcohol and Nicotine

Let's examine some of the health consequences of alcohol and nicotine, the most frequently used drugs in Canada.

ALCOHOL Alcohol is the standard recreational drug of Canadians. Is it bad for your health? This beverage cuts both ways. About two drinks a day for men and one drink for women reduce the risk of heart attacks and blood vessel diseases. (Women weigh less on average and produce fewer enzymes that metabolize alcohol.) Beyond these amounts, however, alcohol increases the risk of a variety of diseases, from cancer to stroke. It also increases the likelihood of birth defects.

NICOTINE Of all drugs, nicotine is the most harmful to human health. Smokers in their thirties are six times more likely to have heart attacks than nonsmokers of the same age (Winslow, 1995). Smoking doubles the risk of blindness in old age (Lagnado, 1996). It also causes progressive emphysema and several types of cancer that kill an increasing number of Canadians every year. Between 1991 and

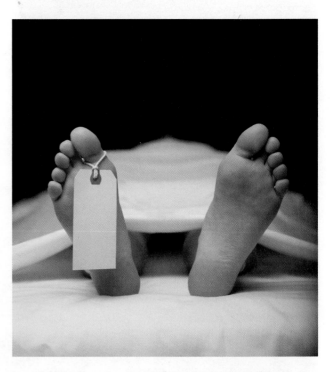

In a mind-boggling attempt to justify cigarette smoking, Philip Morris reported that the Czech government saves $1227 in pensions and health care every time a smoker dies. Following this reasoning, to reduce government deficits we might want to require smoking classes in kindergarten—for the sooner people begin to smoke, the sooner they get sick and die, and the more the government saves.

2001, deaths due to smoking increased from over 41 000 to almost 47 000, or over 20 percent of *all* deaths in Canada. By far, nicotine is the most lethal of all recreational drugs.

Stressing the health hazards of smoking and of second-hand smoke, an anti-tobacco campaign is being waged successfully in Europe and North America. It helped end smoking on Canadian airlines and led to nonsmoking regulations in bars, restaurants, and offices across the country.

Why do people still smoke? There are two main reasons. First, nicotine is addictive, maybe even as addictive as heroin (Tolchin, 1998). The second reason is advertising. Although the tobacco companies deny it, they target youth, often by associating cigarette smoking with success, high fashion, and independence. The tobacco industry is relentless in its pursuit of adolescent smokers, and in 2004 introduced cigarettes spiked with candy flavours in the United States (O'Connell, 2004).

Disabling Environments

A **disabling environment** is one that is harmful to health. The health risk of some occupations is evident: mining and the construction industry are obvious examples. In many occupations, however, people become aware of the risk only years after they worked at jobs they thought were safe. For example, several million people worked with asbestos during and after World War II. Now the government estimates that a quarter of them will die of cancer from having breathed asbestos dust. It is likely that many other substances we have not yet identified also cause slowly developing cancers (Meier, 1987).

Although industrialization has increased the world's standard of living, it also threatens to disable the basic environment of the human race, posing what may be the greatest health hazard of all time. The burning of vast amounts of carbon fuels is leading to the *greenhouse effect*, a warming of the earth that is changing the globe's climate. Use of fluorocarbon gases in such items as aerosol cans, refrigerators, and air conditioners has threatened the ozone shield, the protective layer of the earth's upper stratosphere that screens out a high proportion of the sun's ultraviolet rays. High-intensity ultraviolet radiation is harmful to most forms of life. Additional risks to life on our planet come from the pollution of land, air, and water, especially by nuclear waste, pesticides, herbicides, and other chemicals.

To identify environmental threats to world health is only the first step. The next is to introduce short- and long-term policies to reduce such problems. The sociology of the environment is discussed in Chapter 17.

The Globalization of Disease

In the movie *Outbreak*, when a new disease threatened the world, government epidemiologists were transformed into Indiana Jones–style heroes in order to save it. But despite its overdramatization, the movie's depiction of the rapid spread of disease is not far from reality. As noted in Chapter 5, the

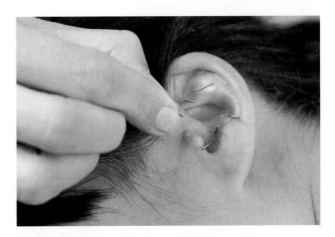
In auriculotherapy, reflex points of the ear are stimulated to relieve chronic pain and alleviate substance abuse.

globalization of modern travel has wiped out the frontiers that used to contain diseases. In fact, many political scientists and demographers already refer to the twenty-first century as the "century of migration" (Leaning, 2002).

Migrant populations are among the most vulnerable to emerging and reemerging infectious diseases such as multidrug-resistant tuberculosis (Knobler, Mahmoud, Lemon, & Pray, 2006: 21). When SARS appeared in 2003 (discussed earlier in the chapter), the fear was that it would encircle the globe, killing millions of people in a short time. Each person with SARS was isolated and cities and regions were declared off limits to visitors. The same thing happened with outbreaks of Asian bird flu (avian influenza) and the Marburg virus in Angola (LaFraniere, 2005).

However, initiatives such as the U.S. Global Health Initiative, which is investing $63 billion over six years (2011–2017) to tackle AIDS, malaria, and tuberculosis, and the continuing involvement of the Canadian Society for International Health in reducing health inequities and strengthening health systems globally are confronting the challenges of the globalization of disease.

The Search for Alternatives

What alternatives are there to the way medicine is usually practised? The suggestion we explore here is to shift the emphasis away from the treatment of disease to the prevention of it.

Treatment or Prevention?

EFFECTS OF VALUES AND LIFESTYLES Prevention implies both an individual and a group responsibility. At the individual level, exercising regularly, eating nutritious food, having protected sex, and avoiding smoking and alcohol abuse go a long way to preventing disease. Following these guidelines can add years to our lives.

At the group level, one alternative is preventive medicine. Instead of the treatment of disease, medicine could

THINKING CRITICALLY ABOUT SOCIAL CONTROVERSY

Sociology, Stress, and the Canadian Workplace

In June 2011, the federal government announced that it would provide funding to the Canadian Mental Health Commission to help develop new voluntary standards to safeguard psychological health and safety in the workplace. The action is part of an ongoing response to the prevalence of depression and anxiety reported by Canadian workers.

Numerous studies link chronic stress to anxiety, depression, insomnia, fatigue, and substance abuse (Godin et al., 2005) Others point to the relationship between long-term stress with the development and progression of many chronic physical diseases, such as heart disease, arthritis, ulcers, asthma, and migraines (Kudielka & Wust, 2010).

Work-related stress has been the focus of much of the public discussion about chronic stress and mental health. Numerous studies have identified some of its key causes—including having little control over the terms and conditions of the work one is doing, occupying a job that does not match one's skills and abilities (either too demanding or not demanding enough), and having insufficient support from supervisors and/or colleagues (Shields, 2006; Shigemi et al., 2002).

For Your Consideration

Have you experienced high levels of stress either at university or during work? Have you experienced any of the key causes identified above? Can you provide any other causes of undue levels of stess?

---

have "wellness" as its goal. What would it require to implement a national policy of "prevention, not intervention"? This would necessitate a program of education in schools and the media showing how some practices of nutrition, exercise, sex, and judicious prescription drug use pay off with healthier lives. For example, diet is a significant factor in many types of cancer, and an educational program to replace fatty, low-fibre foods with a diet rich in fruits, vegetables, and green tea would go a long way in saving lives. Unfortunately, rather than making such basic changes, most Canadians still seem to prefer that their doctors prescribe drugs.

On yet a broader scale is comprehensive prevention—eliminating disabling environments and the use of harmful drugs. Some businesses continue to spew industrial waste into the air and use rivers and oceans as industrial sewers, while others use advertising to seduce youths to use harmful drugs. These acts are unconscionable. Since we now live in a global village, the creation and maintenance of a health-producing environment requires international controls and co-operation.

SUMMARY AND REVIEW

SOCIOLOGY AND THE STUDY OF MEDICINE

What is the role of sociology in the study of medicine?

Sociologists study **medicine** as a social institution. As practised in Canada, three of its primary characteristics are professionalization, bureaucracy, and public policy. p. 343.

HISTORICAL PATTERNS OF HEALTH

What are the gender differences in causes of death?

The two leading causes of death—cancer and heart disease—are experienced more by men than women in Canada. Women are more likely than men to die from mental and behavioural disorders such as Alzheimer's. However, among the top 10 causes of death, including infectious diseases such as HIV/AIDS and other causes such as accidents, assaults, and suicides, men fare far worse than women. p. 346.

ISSUES IN HEALTH CARE

Which level of government in Canada is responsible for health care?

While the provision of health care in Canada is a provincial responsibility, the federal government has played a major role in financing the health care services available to all Canadians. p. 348.

What are the five provisions of the Canada Health Act (1984)?

The five provisions of the Canada Health Act (1984) are comprehensive scope, universal coverage, public administration, portability, and accessibility. p. 348.

Is extra billing a good idea for cutting costs to the health care system in Canada?

Research has shown that although extra billing has meant that the poor and the elderly were dissuaded from going to their general practitioner, there was no support for the contention that extra billing cut down on unnecessary visits to doctors. p. 348.

What is one of the major findings of the sociology of health research in Canada?

The most significant finding centres on the causal links between social status and health status of Canadians. pp. 350–351.

BIOETHICS

Why is medically assisted suicide an issue now?

As a result of advanced technology, people can be kept technically alive even when they have no brain waves. However, physicians who openly assist in suicides can face up to 14 years in prison in Canada. Yet, from the Sue Rodriquez case in 1993 to Gloria Taylor's most recent challenge before the B.C. Supreme Court, **euthanasia** continues to be an important issue facing Canadians. pp. 351–352.

THE SEARCH FOR ALTERNATIVES

Are there alternatives to our current health care system?

The primary alternative discussed in this chapter is a change from treatment to the prevention of disease. pp. 355–356.

TALKING ABOUT THEORY

Theoretical Paradigms

	CLASSICAL PARADIGMS			RECENT PARADIGMS
Theoretical Paradigms	Structural-Functional Paradigm	Social-Conflict Paradigm	Symbolic-Interaction Paradigm	Feminist Paradigm
What is the level of analysis?	Macro level	Macro level	Micro level	Micro and macro levels
What is the social significance of medicine?	The sick role and sick role behaviours allow individuals to be exempt from normal responsibilities. The sick role is a temporary, medically sanctioned form of deviant behaviour.	The globalization of health care increases the risks of illness and death in less developed nations.	Different cultures provide guidelines for who is "healthy" and who isn't.	Gendered differences in the diagnosis and treatment of illness.
Has the sociological study of medicine changed over time?	No.	Yes/No. As changing technology provides new opportunities for curing illness, those with the fewest resources in either rich or less developed countries will be denied access.	Yes. As social attitudes change toward what constitutes health and the role of medicine.	Yes/No. Changes in legal prohibitions against women in medicine are significantly positive. Patriarchy remains.

KEY TERMS

depersonalization 351
disabling environment 355
epidemiology 346
euthanasia 352
health 343
living will 352
medicalization 351
medicine 343
shaman 343
sick role 344

All URLs listed are current as of the printing of this text.

World Health Organization (WHO)
www.who.int
WHO's objective is the attainment by all peoples of the highest possible level of health—defined in the WHO constitution as a state of complete physical, mental, and social well-being and not merely the absence of disease or infirmity.

Centers for Disease Control and Prevention
www.cdc.gov
An agency of the U.S. Department of Health and Human Services, located in Atlanta, Georgia. Its mission is to "promote health and quality of life by preventing and controlling disease, injury, and disability."

AIDS Treatment News Archive Online
www.aids.org
The mission of AIDS.org is to help prevent HIV infections and to improve the lives of those affected by HIV and AIDS

by providing education and facilitating the free and open exchange of knowledge at an easy-to-find, centralized website.

Canadian Alliance on Mental Illness and Mental Health
www.camimh.ca
Established in 1998, the Canadian Alliance on Mental Illness and Mental Health (CAMIMH) is an alliance of mental health organizations comprised of health care providers and the mentally ill and their families.

Public Health Agency of Canada (PHAC)
www.phac-aspc.gc.ca
The PHAC deals with the public health of Canadians through disease surveillance, disease and injury prevention, health protection, health emergency preparedness and response, health promotion, and relevant research undertakings.

1. Canadians are not all equally likely to become sick or to suffer an injury. Some are more likely to develop particular diseases or disabilities. Why do you think there are differences in the health and illness of Canadians based on sex and class?

2. Virtually everyone recognizes the life-saving value of medicine and the advances being made in medical research on such diseases as cancer and AIDS. However, are there any social factors that negatively contribute to our physical, mental, and spiritual well-being?

3. Is the medicalization of society a good thing? Apply the functionalist and conflict perspectives to help answer this question.

4. How do lifestyles and values affect our health? What does this have to do with sociology? Access the Research Navigator through MySocLab and use keywords such as "lifestyles," "health," and "values" to locate relevant and recent scholarly and popular press publications to help you answer this question.

MySocLab

Explore the topics covered in this chapter on MySocLab. Interactive resources include a study plan, cumulative exams, a multimedia library, MySocLab eReadings, and access to the MySocLab Video Series.

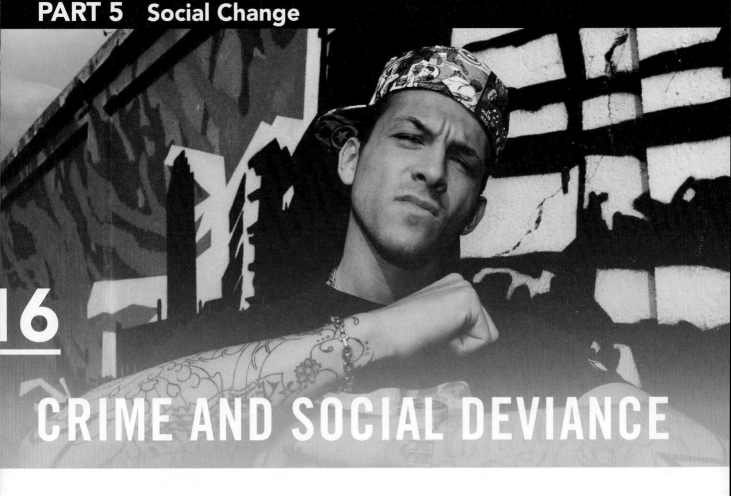

16

CRIME AND SOCIAL DEVIANCE

LEARNING OUTCOMES

After you have studied this chapter, you will be able to answer the following questions:

1. How do psychological, biological, and sociological explanations of social deviance differ?
2. How do symbolic interactionists, functionalists, conflict theorists, feminists, and postmodern theories explain social deviance?
3. What is the medicalization of social deviance?
4. Why do men commit acts of violence against women?
5. What can be done about male violence against women?
6. What are the main components of the Canadian criminal justice system?

ON January 1, 2011, Pittsburgh Penguins star centre Sidney Crosby dropped heavily to the ice after he took a blindsided hit to the head by then–Washington Capital's centre David Steckel. Four days later, Crosby was driven into the boards headfirst by Tampa Bay Lightning's Victor Hedman. On January 7, Crosby announced that he was suffering from a concussion. After 11 months of therapy, Crosby returned to the ice on November 21, but was once again sidelined on December 12.

Crosby is not the only NHL player to suffer a concussion. During the 2011 season, Chris Pronger, Claude Giroux, Shea Weber, and Jeff Skinner also experienced concussions. Reporting on the seven seasons between 1997 and 2004, the largest and most detailed study of concussions in the NHL found 559 concussions—or 5.8 concussions for every 100 players (Benson et al., 2011). In many instances, players suffered two or more concussions.

Concussions are serious brain injuries that require specialized medical supervision and can end athletic careers. This kind of violence is not necessary to the game of hockey, a concept that appears to receive only token recognition from the leaders of the NHL. Many commentators have witnessed the rise in often senseless violence in professional hockey and have made suggestions on how the NHL might clamp down on the kind of brutality that sidelines stars and gives hockey a bad name. From the comfort of their living rooms, Don Cherry–types may covet this kind of rock 'em, sock 'em stuff on skates. But if such violence ever happened in a bar where a hockey game was being

Source: Dan Glenday (2012); *Toronto Star* editorial (1992), Cnews (March 28, 2008).

broadcast, or when hockey fans took to the streets after a big loss, there would be criminal charges.

Violence on the ice filters down to junior and minor league hockey teams across Canada. The recent (2008) incident involving Patrick Roy's son, Jonathan Roy, who charged at and repeatedly pounded the opposing goaltender during a Quebec Remparts versus Chicoutimi Sagueneens game, caught national attention and was broadcast across the country. Jonathan was suspended for seven games and fined $500, while his father, the coach of the Remparts, was suspended for five games and fined $4000. After the Quebec Minister of Public Safety investigated the incident, Jonathan was charged with assault and faced up to five years in prison. In October 2009, after pleading guilty, he was granted an absolute discharge on the condition that he donate $5000 to five local charities.

It is doubtful that such a fate will act as a deterrent to curb violence in hockey, whether it be players on the ice or parents in the stands. Neither will the lure of high salaries, the heightened expectation of sports bravado, and the need for attention-getting headlines in print and electronic media.

Violence on the ice can and does spill out into the streets. When the Vancouver Canucks lost the seventh game in the Stanley Cup final series in 2011 to the Boston Bruins, fans took to the streets to vent their frustration. However, unlike the hockey players, whose brutality on the ice carries few, if any, criminal consequences, when fans get aggressive outside the arena, they are subject to criminal action by the police and the courts. Do you believe there is a double standard: relaxed punishment for the players and a more punitive one for the fans?

Gaining a Sociological Perspective on Crime and Social Deviance

In Canadian society, violence has become culturally acceptable in sports, particularly in hockey. We frequently hear that a game was good because of a "good brawl" (or brawls). But when does "acceptable" violence in a sport step over the line and become criminal? As we saw with the case of Jonathan Roy, even when criminally charged, his absolute discharge with no criminal record communicates what appears to be a separate set of consequences for hockey players who are criminally charged. Another example of this line-crossing occurred in a 1988 hockey game, when Minnesota North Star Dino Ciccarelli pleaded guilty to assault charges in Toronto for slashing Maple Leaf Luke Richardson in the head. He was jailed for only one day.

Whether the NHL should police its own players or whether the responsibility should fall to the state is a complex issue. The nature of, and reaction to, violence in sports depends on a society's culture. Whether the subject is violence in the bull-fight or violence in soccer, much can be learned about a society as a whole by studying its sports.

Examples such as the Sidney Crosby, Jonathan Roy, and Dino Ciccarelli cases demonstrate that cultural norms, values, and mores shape the social acceptance or non-acceptance of certain behaviours. Canadians continually debate what is acceptable and unacceptable behaviour, whether related to sports, morality, or the criminal justice system. What Canadians view as criminal behaviour or social deviance, then, depends on whose behaviour it is, who is affected by it, and in what context it occurs.

Violence has always been part of NHL hockey. In recent years, however, the level and intensity of violence has dramatically increased. Instead of throwing down the gloves, the elbow to the head and the hockey stick have become the weapons of choice for some players. A culture of violence has emerged—encouraged, in part, by the demand for bigger and stronger players, by the competition for huge salaries, and by some in the media.

How Norms Make Social Life Possible

Norms make social life possible by making behaviour predictable. Only because we can count on most people most of the time meeting the expectations of others can social life as we know it exist. However, the social context of the encounter with others determines how we should behave.

You can depend on grocery clerks to sell you milk. You also can depend on paying the same price as everyone else and not being told to attend a party in the store before paying for your groceries. Why is this so? Because we are socialized to follow norms, to play the basic roles society assigns to us so long as they conform to the social situation we find ourselves.

Norms lay out the basic guidelines for how we play our roles and how we interact with others. In short, norms allow for **social order**, a group's usual and customary social arrangements. Our lives are based on these arrangements, which is why social deviance and criminal behaviour in particular are often seen as threatening, for they undermine predictability, the foundation of social life. Consequently, human groups develop a system of **social control**, formal (legal) and informal means of enforcing norms.

Comparing Psychological, Biological, and Sociological Explanations

Since norms are essential for society, why do people violate them? To better understand the reasons, it is useful to know how sociological explanations differ from biological and psychological ones, and to examine how the five sociological perspectives explain crime, social deviance, and social control.

Psychologists and *sociobiologists* explain crime and social deviance by looking for answers *within* individuals. They assume that something in the makeup of people leads them to become criminal or socially deviant.

Some *psychologists* focus on abnormalities *within* the individual, or what are called **personality disorders**. Their supposition is that deviating individuals have deviating personalities (Barnes, 2001; Mayer, 2007). That is, various unconscious urges drive people to criminal activity or social deviance.

Biological explanations, like their psychological counterparts, focus on **genetic predispositions** to such social deviance as juvenile delinquency and crime (Lombroso, 1911; Goozen et al., 2007). When it comes to explaining criminal behaviours, biological explanations include (but are not restricted to) the following three theories: (1) intelligence—low intelligence leads to crime; (2) the "XYY" theory—an extra Y chromosome in males leads to crime; and (3) body type—people with "squarish, muscular" bodies are more likely to commit **street crimes**, acts such as mugging, rape, and burglary.

How do these theories hold up? Some criminals are very intelligent, and most people of low intelligence do not commit crimes. Most criminals have the normal "XY" chromosome combination, and most men with the "XYY" combination do not become criminals; in addition, no women have this combination of genes, so the theory is lacking in explanation

for female criminals. Criminals also run the range of the body types exhibited by humanity, and most people with "squarish, muscular" bodies do not become street criminals. No specific childhood experience is invariably linked with social deviance or criminality. For example, children who had "bad toilet training," "suffocating mothers," or "emotionally aloof fathers" may become good accountants—or embezzling bookkeepers. Just as university students, professors, and police officers represent a variety of good—and bad—childhood experiences, so do social deviants and criminals. Similarly, people with "suppressed anger" can become military heroes or hockey goons—or anything else. In short, these supposed "causes" of criminal behaviours are even more common among the general population of people who do not commit crimes. There is no inevitable outcome of any childhood experience. Therefore, the causes of criminal behaviours and social deviance cannot be answered by biological or psychological explanations that focus solely on personality or genetic "disorders." One sociological explanation, for example, is that some of the expectations of the masculine role in Canadian society—to be braver, tougher, more independent, and less tolerant of insult—increase the likelihood that males will become involved in violence.

In contrast to the biological and psychological perspectives, *sociologists* search for factors *outside* the individual. Since crime and social deviance are relative, why, they ask, should we expect to find anything constant within people to account for a behaviour that is conforming in one society and socially deviant in another? Sociologists also look for social influences that "recruit" some people rather than others to break norms. To account for why people commit crimes, for example, sociologists examine such external influences as socialization, subcultural membership, and social class. Social class, a concept discussed in depth in Chapter 6 and the next two chapters, refers to people's relative standing in terms of education, occupation, and especially income and wealth.

The Relativity of Social Deviance

In just a few moments I was to meet my first Yanomamo. What would it be like? I looked up (from my canoe) and gasped when I saw a dozen burly, naked, men staring at us down the shafts of their drawn arrows. Immense wads of green tobacco were stuck between their lower teeth and lips. We arrived at the village while the men were blowing a hallucinogenic drug up their noses.

The Indians would blow their noses into their hands, flick as much of the mucus off that would separate in a snap of the wrist, wipe the residue into their hair, and then carefully examine my face, arms, legs, hair, and the contents of my pockets. . . . I wondered why I ever decided to switch from civil engineering to anthropology in the first place. (Chagnon, 1977)

Sociologists use the term **social deviance** to refer to any violation of norms—whether the infraction is as minor as jaywalking, as serious as murder, or as humorous as Chagnon's encounter with the Yanomamo. This deceptively simple definition takes us to the heart of the sociological perspective of social deviance, which sociologist Howard S. Becker (1966)

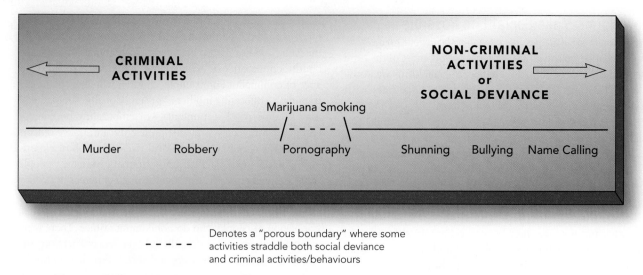

Denotes a "porous boundary" where some
activities straddle both social deviance
and criminal activities/behaviours

FIGURE 16.1 Crime and Social Deviance—A Continuum

identified this way: *it is not the act itself*, but the reactions to the act, that make something socially deviant. In other words, people's behaviours must be viewed from the framework of the culture in which they take place. What was socially deviant to Chagnon was *conforming* to the Yanomamo. From their viewpoint, you *should* check out strangers, as they did—and nakedness is natural, as are hallucinogenic drugs.

Chagnon's abrupt introduction to the Yanomamo allows us to see the *relativity of social deviance*. Thus, acts perfectly acceptable in one culture—or in one group within a society—may be considered socially deviant in another culture, or in another group within the same society.

Unlike the general public, sociologists use the term *social deviance* nonjudgmentally, to refer to any act to which people respond negatively. To sociologists, then, *all of us* are social deviants of one sort or another, for we all violate norms from time to time. Figure 16.1 depicts the violation of norms along a continuum, from non-criminal to criminal activities.

To be considered socially deviant, a person may not even have to *do* anything. Sociologist Erving Goffman (1963) used the term **stigma** to refer to attributes that discredit people. These attributes include violations of norms of ability (blindness, deafness, mental handicaps) and norms of appearance (a facial birthmark, obesity). They also include involuntary membership in groups, such as being the victim of AIDS or a close friend of Paul Bernardo or Karla Homolka. The stigma becomes a person's *master status*, defining him or her as socially deviant. Recall from Chapter 5 that a master status cuts across all other statuses that a person occupies.

Knowing how relative social deviance is, sociologists wonder why anyone would expect to find factors within people to explain social deviance. For example, because **crime** is the violation of norms that have been written into law, what a crime is varies from one human group

to another. Why, then, should we expect to find anything constant within people to account for crime—or any other behaviour that is conforming in one group but socially deviant in another? The media's interpretation of crime often insists on "explaining" criminal behaviours as the result of "abnormal" or nonconforming personality traits.

Who Defines Social Deviance?

If social deviance does not lie in the act, but in definitions of the act, where do those definitions come from? To see how sociologists explain social deviance, especially criminal behaviour, let's contrast the five main sociological perspectives—symbolic interactionism, functionalism, conflict theory, feminism, and postmodernism.

Focus Question

What is social deviance? What is crime?

> **IN SUM**
>
> In sociology, the term *social deviance* refers to all violations of social rules, regardless of their seriousness. In other words, social deviance can be viewed as a continuum, with minor rule- or norm-breaking at one end and serious criminal violations at the other. The term is not a judgment about the behaviour. Social deviance is relative; what is socially deviant in one group may be conforming in another. Consequently, we must consider social deviance from within a group's own framework, for it is the group's meanings that motivate its members' behaviour.

◉ **Watch** the video "Piercings Perceived as Deviance" on **MySocLab.**

◉ **Watch** the video "Sociologists' Approach to Crime and Deviance" on **MySocLab.**

The Symbolic Interactionist Perspective

As we examine symbolic interactionism, it will become more evident why sociologists are not satisfied with explanations of social deviance that are rooted in biology or personality. A basic principle of symbolic interactionism is that each of us acts according to our interpretations of situations, not according to blind predispositions. Let's consider how our membership in social groups influences our views of life, which affect our individual behaviours.

Differential Association Theory of Criminal Behaviours

THE THEORY Contrary to theories of biology and personality, sociologist Edwin Sutherland stressed that people *learn* criminal behaviours. He coined the term **differential association** to indicate that learning to deviate or to conform to society's norms is influenced most by the people with whom we associate (Sutherland, 1924, 1947; Sutherland & Cressey, 1974; Sutherland, Cressey, & Luckenbill, 1992). On the most obvious level, boys and girls who join street gangs learn a way of looking at the world that is more likely to get them into trouble with the law than boys and girls who join the Boy Scouts or Girl Guides.

Sutherland's theory is actually more complicated, but his basic assertion was that social deviance is learned rather than the result of biology or personality.

FRIENDS AND NEIGHBOURHOODS The longer someone has friends who commit criminal acts, the more likely he or she will follow in the friends' footsteps (Warr, 1993). This comes as no surprise to parents, who generally are eager to keep their kids away from "bad" friends or neighbours.

SUBCULTURES All subcultures impart particular attitudes about social deviance and conformity that are learned by their members. For example, the contemporary hipster is a subcultural figure that emerged from the 1990s youth culture known as alternative or indie and was, in the beginning, defined by her or his rejection of consumerism. Among the identifiers of this subculture are Buddy Holly–style glasses, Pabst Blue Ribbon beer, tattoos, undershirts called "wife beaters," and skinny jeans. The fashion magazine *Vice* (launched as the *Voice of Montreal* in 1994) relocated from Montreal to New York in 1999 and has a recent readership of over 900 000 in 22 countries. Some have argued that hipster subculture died in the aftermath of the recent recession, while others suggest it is undergoing a transformation (Greif, 2010).

For members of the Mafia, ideas of manliness are intertwined with criminal behaviour. In that society, *killing is a primary measure of their manhood*. Not all killings are accorded the same respect, however: "The more awesome and potent the victim, the more worthy and meritorious the killer" (Arlacchi, 1980). Some killings are very practical matters. A member of the Mafia who gives information to the police, for example, has violated the omertà (a vow of secrecy taken by all members). Such an offence can never be tolerated, for it threatens the very existence of the group. This example further illustrates how relative even criminal behaviour is. Although the act of killing breaks a legal norm of mainstream society, for the Mafia, *not* killing after certain rules are broken, such as "squealing" to the cops, is the criminal act.

PRISON OR FREEDOM? Symbolic interactionists stress that we are not mere pawns in the hands of others. We are not destined by our group membership to think and behave as our groups dictate. Rather, *we help produce our own orientations to life*. Our choice of membership (differential association), for example, helps to shape the self. One university student may join a feminist group that is trying to change the treatment of women in university; another may associate with a group of women who smoke cigarettes. Their choice of groups points them in two different directions. The one who associates with cigarette smokers may or may not find herself becoming a smoker, while the one who joins the feminist group may develop an even greater interest in producing social change.

Focus Question

According to symbolic interactionists, are we mere pawns in the hands of others when we socialize with either "bad people" or "good people"?

Labelling Theory

Labelling theory focuses on the significance of labels (names, reputations) given to people. Labels tend to become a part of our self-concept. Depending on the kind of pressure coming from others, labels such as whore, slob, genius, or entrepreneur help set people on paths that propel them into or divert them from social deviance and crime.

REJECTING LABELS: HOW PEOPLE NEUTRALIZE SOCIAL DEVIANCE Most people resist the negative labels others try to pin on them. Some are so successful that even though they persist in criminal behaviour, they still consider themselves conformists. For example, some bullies consider themselves to be conforming members of society, even though they beat up people. How do they do it?

Sociologists Gresham Sykes and David Matza (1988) studied boys like this. They found that the boys used these

((• **Listen** to"Deviance"—Susan Stamberg's conversation with professor Felton Earls and the results of his study—on **MySocLab**.

❋ **Explore** the reading "The Code of the Streets" on **MySocLab**.

five **techniques of neutralization** to help deflect society's norms:

1. *Denial of responsibility.* The youths frequently said, "I'm not responsible for what happened because . . . " The act may have been an "accident," or they may see themselves as "victims" of society, with no control over what happened—like billiard balls shot around the pool table of life.

2. *Denial of injury.* Another favourite explanation of the boys was "What I did wasn't wrong because no one got hurt." Vandalism becomes "mischief," gang fighting is seen as a "private quarrel," and stealing cars is simply "borrowing." The boys might acknowledge that they have done something illegal, but claim it was "just having a little fun."

3. *Denial of a victim.* Sometimes the boys thought of themselves as avengers. Vandalizing a teacher's car would be getting revenge for an unfair grade, while shoplifting might even the score with "crooked" store owners. In short, they protected their self-concept by claiming that people "deserved what they got."

4. *Condemnation of the condemners.* Another technique the boys used was to accuse people who pointed their fingers at them of being "a bunch of hypocrites": the police are "on the take," teachers have "pets," and parents cheat on their taxes. In short, they say, "Who are they to accuse me of something?"

5. *Appeal to higher loyalties.* A final technique to justify antisocial activities was to consider loyalty to the gang more important than following the norms of society. They might say, "I had to help my friends. That's why I got in the fight."

IN SUM

The five techniques of neutralization have implications far beyond these boys. It is not only delinquents who try to neutralize the norms of mainstream society. Consider them again: (1) "I couldn't help myself." (2) "Who really got hurt?" (3) "Don't you think she deserved that, after what she did?" (4) "Who are you to talk?" (5) "I had to help my friends—wouldn't you have done the same thing?" Do these statements have a familiar ring? All of us attempt to neutralize some of the labels we are given.

REJECTING LABELS: BECOMING A PROSTITUTE Sociologist Nanette Davis (1978) interviewed young prostitutes to find out how they had entered the profession and discovered that most had made a gradual transition from sexual promiscuity to prostitution. Their first acts of selling sex were casual. As one girl said, "I never thought about it one way or another." At this point, the girls were in a stage of social deviance that sociologist Edwin Lemert (1972) termed **primary social deviance**—fleeting acts that do not become part of the self-concept. The young women did not yet think of themselves as prostitutes.

Girls who are engaged in the "business" for a longer time, however, do come to think of themselves as prostitutes. When this occurs, they have entered **secondary social deviance**.

The movement from primary to secondary social deviance may be gradual. Through *self-labelling*, bit by bit, the social deviance becomes part of the self-concept. Self-jarring labels such as "pervert" and "whore" tend to lock people out of conforming groups and push them into contact with others like themselves.

In **tertiary social deviance**, socially deviant behaviour is normalized by *relabelling* it as nondeviant (Kitsuse, 1980; de Young, 1989). Most people in this stage simply reject the judgment that the behaviour is wrong. For example, prostitutes in Canada have formed an organization called Canadian Organization for the Rights of Prostitutes (CORP). This group takes the position that prostitutes perform a service to society, and it is therefore a reasonable occupational choice and legislation should allow prostitutes to operate without interference from the government. Similar

UFC (Ultimate Fighting Championship, sometimes called cage fighting) has a large following in Canada and the United States among both men and women. Many Canadians label those who watch this form of violence social deviants. What do you think?

Sex worker rights are human rights.

organizations exist in the United States (COYOTE—Call Off Your Old Tired Ethics), Europe (ICPR—International Committee for Prostitutes' Rights), and Australia (PROS—Prostitutes Rights Organization for Sex Workers).

In March 2012, Ontario's Appeal Court struck down the ban on brothels saying prostitutes should be allowed to work safely indoors and pay staff to protect them. However, the ban on street soliciting was upheld. In the preamble to the judgement, the court said prostitution is legal in Canada. The government has one year to rewrite Canada's laws against prostitution.

What do you think? Should Canada's prostitution laws be changed?

INVITING LABELS: THE EMBRACE OF SOCIAL DEVIANCE

Although most of us resist being labelled socially deviant, others revel in a socially deviant identity. Some teenagers, for example, make certain by their choice of clothing, music, and hairstyles that no one misses their intentional rejection of adult norms. Their status among fellow members of a subculture—goths, for example—within which they are almost obsessive conformists, is vastly more important than any status outside it.

One of the best examples of a group that embraces criminal activities is motorcycle gangs. Sociologist Daniel Wolf (1991) conducted participant observation as a graduate student at the University of Toronto with the Canadian outlaw biker gang known as The Rebels. In contrast to the conventional view of outlaw biker gangs as a deviant fringe group, Wolf's analysis begins with The Rebels as a rational social organization that is deviant but not necessarily engaged in criminal behaviours. Wolf outlines a five-part analysis of the gang members' personal search for identity and community. First, the biker sees himself as an anti-hero. Second, he discusses their notion of brotherhood and the lengthy process of socialization from

novice biker to friend of the club, to striker or prospective member and then initiation. Third, limiting female participation to either a sex object or personal property of one member encourages male bonding through misogyny. Fourth, involvement with club activities such as the club "run" (a tour) integrates the individual's life with those of all group members. Finally, each member is viewed as an equal partner in the formulation and enforcement of policy.

THE POWER OF LABELS: THE SAINTS AND THE ROUGHNECKS

We noted in Chapter 6 that social class is a powerful predictor of human behaviour. We can illustrate how powerful social class labelling is by referring to Chambliss's study (1973/2007) of two groups of high school boys known as the "Saints" and the "Roughnecks." Both groups were "constantly occupied with drinking, wild parties, petty theft, and vandalism," yet their teachers looked on the Saints as "headed for success" and the Roughnecks as "headed for trouble." By the time they finished high school, not one Saint had been arrested, while the Roughnecks had been in constant trouble with the police.

Why did the community perceive these groups differently? Chambliss concluded that the double vision was the result of family background, especially *social class*. The Saints came from respectable, middle-class families, while the Roughnecks came from less respectable, working-class families. Because of their respective backgrounds, teachers and other authorities expected good, law-abiding behaviour from the Saints and trouble from the Roughnecks. And, like the rest of us, both the teachers and police saw what they expected to.

Social class allowed the Saints' lawbreaking to be *less visible*. They had automobiles, and they made their drinking and vandalism inconspicuous by spreading it around neighbouring towns. Without cars, the Roughnecks couldn't even make it to the edge of town. Day after day, they hung around the same street corners, where their boisterous behaviour made them conspicuous, confirming the negative ideas that the community held about them.

The boys' social class backgrounds had equipped them with distinct *styles of interaction*. When questioned by police or teachers, the Saints put on apologetic and penitent faces. Their "respect for authority" elicited positive reactions from teachers and the police, allowing them to avoid serious legal problems. People in authority believed them. In contrast, the Roughnecks' attitudes often expressed open hostility to the authorities, and even when they showed respect, their teachers and the police did not believe they were sincere. Consequently, while the police let the Saints off with

✳ **Explore** William Chambliss's "The Saints and the Roughnecks" on **MySocLab.**

warnings, they came down hard on the Roughnecks, interrogating and arresting them when they had the chance.

While a lifetime career is not determined by a label alone, the Saints and the Roughnecks lived up to the labels the community had given them. All but one of the Saints went on to university, after which one earned a doctorate, one became a lawyer, one a doctor, and the others business managers. In contrast, only two Roughnecks went to university, both on athletic scholarships, after which they became coaches. The other Roughnecks did not fare as well. Two of them dropped out of high school, later became involved in separate killings, and received long prison sentences. One became a local bookie, and no one knows the whereabouts of the other.

How do labels work? While the matter is extremely complex, involving self-concept and individual reactions, we can observe that labels open and close the doors of opportunity. In many respects, how others in authority react to what is expected from members of the lower social classes affects how we are labelled. It is not *what* they do so much as who they do it to.

IN SUM

Symbolic interactionists examine how people's definitions of a situation underlie their rejection of or conformity to social norms. They focus on group membership (differential association) and the significance of labels placed on people (labelling theory).

The Functionalist Perspective

When we think of crime and social deviance, its dysfunctions are likely to come to mind. Functionalists, in contrast, are as likely to stress the functions of social deviance rather than dysfunction itself.

How Crime and Social Deviance Are Functional for Society

According to Émile Durkheim (1893/1933, 1895/1964), social deviance, including crime, is functional for society. Its three main functions are as follows:

1. *Crime and social deviance clarify moral boundaries and affirm norms.* A group's ideas about how people should act and think mark its *moral boundaries*. Social deviance, and especially more serious crimes, challenge those boundaries. To say, in effect, "You broke an important rule, and we cannot tolerate that," affirms a group's norms and clarifies the distinction between conforming and deviating behaviour.
2. *Crime and social deviance promote social unity.* To affirm a group's moral boundaries fosters a "we" feeling among the group's members. In saying, "You can't get away with that," the group collectively affirms the rightness of its own ways.

Social control refers to messages that persuade—such as the one above—or to law enforcement and military intervention.

3. *Crime and social deviance promote social change.* Groups do not always agree on what to do with people who push beyond their acceptable ways of doing things. Boundary violations that gain enough support become new, acceptable behaviours. Thus, social deviance may force a group to rethink and redefine its moral boundaries, helping groups, and whole societies, change their customary ways. Same-sex marriage in Canada is a case in point.

FUNCTIONALISM AND SOCIAL CONTROL If some group threatens to upset the equilibrium, efforts are made to restore balance. For example, in a pluralistic society, the central government often plays a mediating role between groups. In Canada, the federal and provincial governments and the Supreme Court mediate the demands of the various groups that make up our society, accommodating diverse communities whose basic ideas deviate from those held by most members of Canadian society (Porter, 1965). This view of mediation and balance among competing groups is broadly representative of what may be called the Canadian Mosaic, or the **pluralistic theory of social control**.

Focus Question

Are crime and social deviance always bad for society?

✻ **Explore** Peter Berger's "The Meaning of Social Control" on MySocLab.

Strain Theory: How Social Values Produce Crime

Functionalists argue that crime is a *natural* part of society, not an aberration or some alien element in our midst. To understand how the acceptance of mainstream values can generate crime, they say, we must consider what sociologists Richard Cloward and Lloyd Ohlin (1960) identified as the crucial problem of the industrialized world: the need to locate and train the most talented people of every generation—whether born in wealth or in poverty—to enable them to take over the key technical jobs of modern society. To get the most talented people to compete with one another, society tries to motivate everyone to strive for success. It does this by arousing discontent—making people feel dissatisfied with what they have so that they will try to "better" themselves.

Most people end up with strong desires to achieve **cultural goals** such as wealth, high status, or "the good life." Not everyone, however, has equal access to society's **institutionalized means**, the legitimate ways of achieving success. Some people, for example, find their path to higher education and good jobs blocked. The more entrepreneurial among these people experience *strain* or frustrations and find it difficult to identify with these norms. They may even feel wronged by the system, and its rules may seem illegitimate.

This perspective, known as **strain theory**, was developed by sociologist Robert Merton (1956, 1968). Merton's classic outline of how people react to cultural goals and institutionalized means is depicted in Table 16.1. The first reaction, which Merton said is the most common, is *conformity*, using socially acceptable means to strive to reach cultural goals. In industrialized societies, most people try to get good jobs, a good education, and so on. If well-paid jobs are unavailable, they take less desirable jobs. Others take night classes and attend vocational schools. In short, most people take the socially acceptable road.

FOUR SOCIALLY DEVIANT PATHS The remaining four responses represent reactions to strain. *Innovators* are people who accept the goals of society but use illegitimate means to try to reach them. Drug dealers, for instance, accept the goal of achieving wealth but reject legitimate avenues for doing so. Other examples are embezzlers, robbers, and con artists.

The second socially deviant path is taken by people who become discouraged and give up on achieving cultural goals, but who still cling to conventional rules of conduct. Merton called this response *ritualism*. Although ritualists have given up on excelling and advancing in position, they survive by following the rules. Teachers who suffer from "burnout" but continue to go through the motions of classroom performance after their idealism is shattered are examples of ritualists.

People who choose the third path, *retreatism*, reject both cultural goals and the institutionalized means of achieving them. Those who drop out of the pursuit of success by way of membership in mystical religious sects are retreatists. So are long-term welfare recipients. Such people do not even try to appear as though they share the goals of their society.

The final type of response is *rebellion*. Rebels, like retreatists, reject both society's goals and its institutionalized means. Unlike retreatists, however, they seek to replace existing goals with new ones. Revolutionaries are the most committed type of rebels. More important are those who seek change in the name of social justice, such as environmentalists, gay and lesbian activists, or feminists.

Strain theory underscores the main sociological point about social deviance—namely, that social deviants are not pathogenic individuals. Simply put, if a society emphasizes the goal of material success, groups deprived of access to this goal will be more involved in property crime. During periods of economic recession, we can expect to find an increase in property crimes simply because there aren't enough good jobs to go around to all who want or need them, especially hard-hit young males (see the following Down-to-Earth Sociology box).

Illegitimate Opportunity Theory: Explaining Social Class and Crime

Social class position is an important predictor of economic success in our society. Just as different classes carry different

TABLE 16.1 How People Match Their Goals to Their Means

Do They Feel the Strain That Leads to Anomie?	Mode of Adaptation	Cultural Goals	Institutionalized Means
No	Conformity	Accept	Accept
Yes	**Deviant Paths:**		
	1. Innovation	Accept	Reject
	2. Ritualism	Reject	Accept
	3. Retreatism	Reject	Reject
	4. Rebellion	Reject/Replace	Reject/Replace

Source: Based on Merton (1968).

Mean Streets and Hard Times: Youth Unemployment and Crime in Canada

Newspaper headlines from Western Canada in 1993 announced that "Tough Times Drive Kids out of Class, into Crime" (*Winnipeg Free Press*, September 5, 1993). A few months earlier, the same newspaper reported that "Young Canadians have the highest unemployment rate, account for a large share of criminal activity and are especially vulnerable to economic downturns" (March 16, 1993: A3). According to the same article, students who work more than 15 hours a week are more likely to drop out of school. Even those who stay in school see grim prospects for good jobs. Corey, a 15-year-old, said, "There are more offers from gangs than offers of jobs."

Among Canadian criminologists, the link between unemployment and property crimes has been ignored in favour of more "sophisticated" theories. "Dysfunctional" family background is often used by more conservative theorists who point out single-parent households or a parent's alcoholism as negatively affecting the children's actions. Others are more prone to differential association theory—that is, a person's prior exposure to socially deviant beliefs—and/or labelling theory—that is, a person's passage through successive stages of negative stigmatization.

Clearly, youth unemployment affects different young people differently. In Great Britain, the increase in suicide rates among young people has been linked with prolonged periods of unemployment (*Calgary Herald*, April 2, 1993). That said, the relationship between youth unemployment and crime is also real. But what types of crime are associated with prolonged periods of unemployment?

It is crimes against property that are most commonly related to unemployment. Prostitution is another course of action, especially for teenage girls and boys who have nothing to eat and nowhere to go. However, for many young adults, poorly paid part-time work and/or seasonal work, a growing sector of the economy and population, can lead many young adults to commit property crimes such as robbery, larceny, auto theft, and burglary. Or, to paraphrase from Gary O'Bireck's (1993) ethnographic study of Toronto youth, "Why work at McDonald's when you can sell drugs or steal stereos?"

What's the answer to prolonged periods of youth and young adult unemployment and property crimes? Better and more secure jobs for young adults, not prison time.

For Your Consideration
What do you think? Which theory or theories do you feel helps explain property crimes among Canada's young offenders?

Source: *From Not a Kid Anymore, Canadian Youth, Crime, and Subcultures*, by G. O'Bireck, PhD. © 1996. Reprinted with the permission of Nelson, a division of Thomson Learning: www.thomsonlearning.com.

---

cultures of dress, speech, and mannerisms, social classes have distinct styles of crime.

THE POOR AND CRIME Functionalists point out that industrialized societies have no trouble socializing the poor into wanting to possess things. Like others, they, too, are bombarded with messages urging them to buy everything from the latest iPod to Xboxes and cellphones. The vivid images in movies and on television of the middle class enjoying luxurious lives reinforce the myth that all Canadians can afford society's many goods and services. The bombardment of messages also unintentionally produces the idea that all Canadians have a *right* to these items.

The school system, however, which constitutes the most common route to success, fails the poor. It is run by the middle class, and when poor children enter it, they are already at an educational disadvantage, confronting a bewildering world for which their background ill prepares them. Their grammar and nonstandard language—liberally punctuated by what the middle class considers obscene and foul words and phrases—their ideas of punctuality and neatness, and their lack of preparation in computer skills are a mismatch with their new environment. Facing these barriers, the poor drop out of school in larger numbers than their more privileged counterparts. Educational failure, in turn, closes the door on many legitimate avenues to financial success (recall from Chapter 14 our discussion of the "hidden curriculum").

Not infrequently, however, a different door opens to them, one that sociologists Richard Cloward and Lloyd Ohlin (1960) called **illegitimate opportunity structures**. Woven into the texture of life in poor urban neighbourhoods are gambling and other remunerative crimes, commonly called "hustles" (Liebow, 1967/1999; E. Anderson, 1978, 1990, 2006; Bourgois, 1994). For many of the poor, the "hustler" is a role model—glamorous, in control, the image of "easy money," and one of the few people in the area who comes close to the cultural goal of success. Those who tell their urban "buds" that they have made lots of

Former Montreal financial adviser Earl Jones was sentenced to 11 years in prison after pleading guilty to two fraud charges related to his $50-million Ponzi scheme.

money from internet casino gambling point out it is an "easy way" to make it for the less educated but talented poor. For some, then, such illegal income-producing activities are functional—they provide income—and they attract disproportionate numbers of the poor.

WHITE-COLLAR AND STREET CRIME The more privileged social classes are not crime free, but they find a different illegitimate opportunity structure beckoning. More privileged people encounter "opportunities" for income tax evasion, bribery of public officials, stock manipulation, embezzlement, false advertising, and so on. Sociologist Edwin

Sutherland (1949) used the term **white-collar crime** to refer to crimes that people of respectable and high social status commit in the course of their occupations.

Although the general public seems to think that the lower classes are more crime prone, numerous studies show the devastating impact of corporate crime (Weisburd, Wheeler, & Waring, 1991; Zey, 1993). This difference in perception is based largely on visibility. While crimes committed by the poor are given much publicity, the crimes of the more privileged classes seldom make the evening news and go largely unnoticed. Yet the dollar cost of "crime in the suites" is considerably higher than "crime in the streets,"

For over five years, Conrad Black, the one-time media mogul and darling to some of the Toronto media and business class found himself on the other side of the cameras. Initially convicted of three counts of fraud and one count of obstruction of justice in 2007, he was sentenced to 6 1/2 years in prison. On appeal, two of the charges were overturned. In 2011, he was re-sentenced to a prison term of 42 months and fined $US 125,000. Conrad Black was released on May 4, 2012.

totalling in the billions of dollars a year. This estimate refers only to dollar costs, however. No one has yet figured out a way to compare, for example, the suffering of a rape victim with the pain experienced by an elderly couple who have lost their life savings to white-collar fraud.

Although white-collar crime is not as dramatic as a street killing or an abduction and rape—and therefore usually considered less newsworthy—it, too, can involve physical harm, and sometimes even death. Unsafe working conditions, for example, many resulting from executive decisions to put profits ahead of workers' safety, killed 2 million workers worldwide in 2002, according to the International Labour Organization (ILO) (ILO, 2002).

In Canada, work-related fatalities kill 1000 Canadians each year. Of five countries surveyed for the ILO, Canada's record for occupational injuries at work was the worst in all three economic sectors surveyed—manufacturing, mining, and construction (Glenday, 1996). Nevertheless, Canadians are becoming more and more worried about street crime, since the media is diligent about reporting any and almost all encounters with violence on the street.

IN SUM

Functionalists conclude that much street crime is the consequence of socializing the lower social classes into equating success with material possessions, while denying them the means to attain that success. People from higher social classes are exposed to opportunities to commit fraud or embezzlement or to do nothing even when they know that intervention could save lives and property.

The Conflict Perspective

Class, Crime, and the Criminal Justice System

Conflict theorists stress that the state's machinery of social control, which includes the **criminal justice system**—the police, courts, and prisons that deal with people who are accused of having committed crimes—represents the interests of the wealthy and powerful.

The Law as an Instrument of Oppression

According to conflict theorists, the idea that the law is a social institution that operates impartially and administers a code shared by all is a cultural myth promoted by the capitalist class. In contrast, they see the law as an instrument of oppression, a tool designed to maintain the powerful in their privileged position (Spitzer, 1975; Reiman, 2004; Chambliss, 2000, 2007). Because the working class holds the potential to rebel and overthrow the current social order, when its members get out of line they are arrested, tried, and imprisoned. Wealthy property holders, on the other hand, are punished much less severely.

CONFLICT THEORY AND SOCIAL CONTROL Conflict theorists stress that every society is dominated by a group of elite, powerful people, and that the basic purpose of social control is to maintain the current power arrangements. For this reason, the criminal justice system does not focus on the owners of corporations and the harm they do through manufacturing unsafe products, creating pollution, and manipulating prices. Instead, it directs its energies against violations by the working and middle classes. The violations of the capitalist class cannot be ignored totally, however, for if they become too outrageous or oppressive, the working class may rise up and revolt. To prevent this, a flagrant violation by a member of the capitalist class is occasionally prosecuted. The publicity given to the case helps to stabilize the social system by providing evidence of the "fairness" of the criminal justice system.

Although political power is not as naked in Canada as it is in dictatorships, conflict theorists note that an elite group of wealthy, largely white, males maintains power, working behind the scenes to control the federal government by making certain that the group's interests are represented in Cabinet (Porter, 1965; Clement & Myles, 1994; Olsen, 1980; McQuaig, 1995). Thus, it is this group's views of capital and property—the basis of its power—that are represented in the laws of society.

The Trouble with Official Statistics

Both the findings of symbolic interactionists concerning authorities' reactions to such groups as the Saints and the Roughnecks and the conclusions of conflict theorists that the criminal justice system exists to serve the ruling elite demonstrate the need for caution in interpreting official crime statistics. Statistics are not objective, tangible objects, like apples in a supermarket, waiting to be picked up. They are a human creation, produced within a specific social and political context for some particular purpose.

According to official statistics, working-class boys clearly emerge as much more delinquent than middle-class boys. Yet, as we have seen, who actually gets arrested for what is directly affected by social class, a point that has far-reaching implications. As symbolic interactionists point out, the police use a symbolic system as they enforce the law. Their ideas of "typical criminals" and "typical good citizens," for example, permeate their work. The more a suspect matches their ideas of the "criminal profile," the more likely that person is to be arrested. *Police discretion*, or the decision whether or not to arrest someone or even to ignore a matter, is a routine part of police work. Consequently, official crime statistics always reflect these and many other biases.

Usually, the powerful bypass the courts altogether, appearing instead before some agency with no power to imprison. Most cases of illegal sales of stocks and bonds,

✻ **Explore** the reading "The Rich Get Richer and the Poor Get Prison" on **MySocLab.**

price-fixing, restraint of trade, collusion, and so on are handled by "gentlemen overseeing gentlemen." Such agencies are directed by people from wealthy backgrounds who sympathize with the intricacies of the corporate world. It is not surprising, then, that the typical sanction is a token fine. In contrast, the property crimes of young offenders from the lower classes are handled by courts that do have the power to imprison. Burglary, armed robbery, and theft by the poor and their children not only threaten the sanctity of private property but, ultimately, the positions of the powerful.

IN SUM

From the perspective of conflict theory, the small penalties imposed for crimes committed by the powerful are typical of a legal system designed to mask injustice, play down workplace health and safety interests of the majority of the country's workers, and, ultimately, stabilize the social order. From this perspective, law enforcement is a cultural device through which the capitalist class carries out self-protective and oppressive policies (Silver, 1977).

The Feminist Perspective

Feminist theories stress the importance of gender inequality in society. Patriarchy implies male power over women, and social deviance from a feminist perspective evokes male violence against women. Let's examine this aspect of social deviance.

Feminist Theories and Male Violence against Women

As has been mentioned in previous chapters, there are several feminist theories—Marxist feminist theories, liberal feminist theories, non-Marxist radical feminist theories, and postmodern feminist theories. However, when it comes to feminist theories of social deviance—more specifically, male violence against women—a number of common principles are shared by all feminist theories, of which the most important is patriarchy.

First and foremost, **patriarchy** is characterized as a "sexual system of power in which the male possesses superior power and economic privilege" (Eisenstein, 1980: 16). Michael Smith (1990) identified two related forms of patriarchy, the "social" and the "familial." The first refers to male domination at the societal level, whereas the latter pertains to male control in domestic arrangements, including dating and nonmarriage or common-law relationships.

When it comes to male violence against women, virtually all feminist theorists agree that men assault their female partners to maintain control over them and, if they happen to live in a relationship, over their "domestic" situation. Control over women has been measured as (1) sexual fidelity, (2) obedience, (3) respect, (4) loyalty, (5) dependency, and (6) sexual access.

Several studies have been conducted that confirm the relationship of a patriarchal ideology of control and male violence against women (D.E. Smith, 1987, 1990). Feminist contributions to our understanding of male violence against women are pioneering. However, this approach is not without its detractors and progressive critics. Conservative critics, for example, are quick to regard theories of patriarchy as political philosophies rather than social scientific theories (Gelles & Cornell, 1985; Levinson, 1989). The empirical work of Smith and others challenges this notion.

More serious criticisms come from those who point out that feminist theories ignore the effects of class and ethnicity/race on violence against women. It is too simple to point to some empirical studies that have shown that violence against women is more prevalent among lower-class males. And, as we have seen in this chapter, official statistics tend to hide as much as they may reveal about criminal activity. These critics entreat feminists to explain how certain class-based cultural characteristics interact with gender relations and how these circumstances put some women more at risk than others.

Ethnicity/race is another significant factor in assessing male violence against marginalized women. For example, Statistics Canada data show that Aboriginal women are murdered at rates between five and ten times higher than those for non-Aboriginal women (Gartner et al., 1998). Recently, Amnesty International (2004) took issue with the Canadian government's failure to protect Aboriginal women from violence. The report noted that Aboriginal women aged 25 to 44 were five times more likely than other Canadian women of the same age to die of violence. Further, despite controversy about its composition (due to alleged underrepresentation of marginalized women), the Canadian Panel on Violence Against Women (1993) reported that lesbians, teenagers, and seniors are also especially vulnerable. In fact, a 1993 Statistics Canada Survey found that just over half (51 percent) of all sexual assaults were on young women between the ages of 16 and 27. Feminist theories and researchers are only now becoming sensitive to the issue of violence in same-sex relationships, whether gay or lesbian. The fact that there is little research on violence in these relationships does not signify its absence. Same-sex relationships may be an accepted social fact among many urban-based gays and lesbians in Canada, but violence in such relationships is probably still in the closet (Kinsman, 2001). A recent National Film Board film entitled *Prisoners of Violence: Same Sex Partner Abuse* (2003) spoke to this growing issue. The video stressed the importance of education and awareness to break down barriers. Domestic violence is violence, regardless of sexual orientation.

Feminist Theories and Issues of Public Policy in Canada

Four strategies for coping with male violence against women are discussed in this section: policing, job creation, social services, and anti-sexist male collectives. The first involves raising the sensitivity of police to the reality of male violence against women. Where once police officers, most of whom are males, would not want to arrest or lay charges against a man, today there has been a change in attitude and training across Canada. This change has been largely the result of feminist research findings and effective lobbying. This is not to say all is well—far from it. For example, while arrests for violence against women have increased, some feminists charge that simply enforcing arrest policies can make a bad situation even worse. They contend that many women do not want to report their husbands, companions, or boyfriends simply because they believe their partner's arrest will destroy the relationship. They suggest that only implementing aggressive charging policies fails to address wider issues of patriarchy, including many women's economic dependence on men.

The second strategy includes all levels of government participating in good job-creation programs. DeKeseredy and Hinch (1991), for example, argue that economic policy reforms such as paid work leaves, flexible hours (flextime), pay equity, and improving the quality of work available to disadvantaged people, to name just a few, can lower the rate of male violence against women.

The need for expanded social services such as short-term emergency shelters and housing assistance is the third strategy for coping with male violence against women. Since 1979, the number of Canadian women's shelters has tripled. Nevertheless, most emergency shelters in this country are usually overcrowded and understaffed. All levels of government, in their cost-cutting frenzy, were quick to cut these essential social services. Instead of returning to their violent partners, women who find themselves with little money and who are unable to buy a house or rent an apartment should be assured of some measure of safety and autonomy by living in state-subsidized housing or co-ops.

Anti-sexist self-help groups for violent men are beneficial so long as the men are attending for the right reasons. If men are attending because they were told to change before returning home, or were caught by the police and ordered by a judge to take counselling, the success of these programs may be jeopardized. Only if there is a genuine willingness to change can the issues have any hope of being resolved. Examples of anti-sexist male self-help groups include AMEND, EMERGE, New Directions, and Vivre sans Violence.

The costs for these initiatives should not come from the limited amount of money available for the victims of violence. Shelters for women and other social services are beneficial and necessary to cope with male violence against women. Instead, governments must adequately fund both initiatives.

Postmodern Theories of Crime and Social Deviance

The postmodern approach emphasizes the need to "deconstruct" or decode the meaning of concepts such as "law and order" and the "criminal justice system." Postmodern feminist analyses of "the law," for example, have uncovered the ingrained bias of the legal system against women because certain aspects of this system are premised on conceptions of the "reasonable man" (Naffine, 1990). Many postmodern analysts try to uncover the "hidden text" of oppression. More often than not, the media are singled out as the major culprit in the creation of a false public perception of "reality." When television or newspapers "expose the truth" about crime in a city by using particular images, text, or film that focus on particular groups, postmodernists seek out the hidden agendas—the biased subtexts—of these stories.

Postmodern theorists also argue that we are living in a "**risk society**." That is, whether sitting at home, driving, or walking on the streets, we are bombarded by information in the media about the risks that we take—from air pollution and environmental hazards on and off the job to everyday choices about what we eat and drink. The postmodern conception of society is characterized by risk and how it should be managed at both the institutional and personal levels. Canadians and Americans are increasingly feeling at risk of being victimized by crime, based on what they read and see in the media. This is what postmodernists call the media-created "risk society" (see, for example, the now classic work by Ulrich Beck, 1992).

Let's look at the representations of youth crime in Canada as one example of a risk society.

YOUTH CRIME AND THE RISK SOCIETY Canadian society, like American society, is focused on the notion that the criminal element has taken over almost all aspects of everyday living. This widespread belief in crime as a pervasive and global phenomenon helps to create a risk society. In the media's discussion of youth crime, for example, today's youth are presented as the source of the perceived risk we all face. In response to this media-created "reality" of the high incidence of youth crime, social policymakers and criminal law legislators impose rules and regulations in an attempt to effectively manage the perceived dangers of the risk society.

In an attempt to uncover the facts about youth crime, sociologists and criminologists study (1) the external forces that create the social conditions leading to youth crime, (2) the incidence of youth crime, and (3) the nature of the crimes themselves, in order to "decode" the messages generated by the media. Public perceptions of the increase in youth crime have, in fact, been disproved by a study conducted by the John Howard Society of Alberta (1999). Covering the period from 2000 to 2010, Table 16.2 shows a recent drop in violent and property crime by young people in Canada. However, with significant exceptions of the Northwest Territories and Nunavut in 2010, Manitoba and Saskatchewan continue to be the Western Canadian provinces with the highest rates of serious assaults and robbery by young people, while Ontario, Manitoba, and Saskatchewan have the highest rates of homicide (Brennan & Dauvergne, 2011: 41. Nunavut reported the highest homicide rate in

TABLE 16.2 Youth[1] Accused of Police Reported Crime in Canada, 2000–2010

Year	Total Crime (Crime Rate*)		Violent Crime (Crime Rate*)		Property Crime (Crime Rate*)		Other Criminal Offences (Crime Rate*)	
	Number	Rate	Number	Rate	Number	Rate	Number	Rate
2000	171 148	6914	48 130	1944	96 760	3909	26 258	1061
2002	175 537	6945	47 960	1898	98 021	3878	29 556	1169
2004	179 670	6959	49 695	1925	99 601	3858	30 374	1176
2006	178 839	6812	51 144	1955	94 835	3612	32 552	1240
2008	169 747	6577	49 130	1903	88 878	3443	31 739	1230
2010	152 700	6147	45 653	1838	78 366	3155	28 681	1155

*Crime Rate = calculated on the basis of 100 000 population.
[1] Youth refers to young adults aged 12 to 17.

Source: Adapted by Dan Glenday from Shannon Brennan and Mia Dauvergne, Police Reported Crime Statistics in Canada, 2010. Ottawa: Statistics Canada, July 21, 2011: 39.

Canada—at twice that of Saskatchewan—while both the Northwest Territories and Nunavut reported the highest incidence of serious assaults.

Popular opinion would tell us that young offenders commit crimes, get a slap on the wrist, and are then released without receiving effective rehabilitation, which results in most young offenders re-offending. This public perception is overwhelmingly generated by media reports (John Howard Society of Alberta, 1999). Public concerns regarding the "deficiencies" of the current criminal justice system and the treatment of young offenders, as presented by the media, led to the replacement of the *Young Offenders Act* by the more stringent (yet still ineffective) *Youth Criminal Justice Act* in April 2003 (Gardner, 2004). Negative public sentiment hinders the implementation of more effective alternative programs such as vocational instruction, alternate custodial arrangements, and so forth. The example in the Perspectives box on page 376 is indicative of how the current treatment of young offenders by the criminal justice system in the United States and Canada is ineffective in preventing further crime.

The Need for Multiple Theories

Feminist theories, differential association, labelling, blocked opportunities, illegitimate opportunities, and the privileged position of the elite all help explain the range of social deviance in society, including crime.

The Canadian Criminal Justice System

The Canadian criminal justice system comprises three principal components: the police, the courts, and the corrections system. Each division is made up of its own subsystems that include both public and private sectors. Some provinces, such as Ontario and Quebec, have their own provincial

police forces, while others, such as New Brunswick and Saskatchewan, rely on the Royal Canadian Mounted Police (RCMP). (The Canadian court system is discussed in detail below.) The corrections system includes such facilities as federal penitentiaries, provincial correctional centres, halfway houses, treatment programs, youth programs, boot camps, and parole.

The Organization of the Court System in Canada

The court system in Canada is composed of four basic levels. At the lowest, most local level, are the provincial courts, which handle the great majority of cases that come into the system: most criminal offences, family law matters (except divorce, which is dealt with at the federal level), young offenders (from the ages of 12 to 17), and traffic violations. At the second level are the provincial and territorial superior courts, which deal with more serious crimes and also take appeals from provincial court judgments. There is also the Federal Court Trial Division. At the third level are the provincial courts of appeal and the Federal Court of Appeal. The Supreme Court of Canada comprises the fourth and highest level (see Figure 16.2).

Federal Authority over Criminal Courts

Unlike the United States, where states' rights prevail in criminal matters, in Canada the federal government has exclusive authority over the procedures in the criminal court. While criminal cases are tried in provincial courts, any appeals go to a superior court, the highest level of court in the provinces. The federal government appoints and pays provincial superior court judges. The highest-level court of appeal in Canada is the Supreme Court, which has nine judges, three of whom must be from Quebec. The Supreme Court also has a second function: to decide important questions

Why Shouldn't Young Offenders Be Treated as Adult Criminals?

The first federal government legislation dealing with youth in Canada was called the *Juvenile Delinquents Act* of 1908. Over several decades, it was criticized for inconsistent and disparate sentencing for the same or similar offenses and failing to recognize the rights of the child. In 1984, the *Young Offenders Act* was passed in order to tighten the legal framework by allowing charges to be laid on specific offences and placing responsibility for the offence on the young person charged.

Once again, the new laws were criticized for being too soft on the offender, for laying inconsistent and unfair sentences, and for not properly addressing serious and violent offences. The *Youth Criminal Justice Act* officially replaced the *Young Offenders Act* on April 1, 2003. It, too, has been criticized, for many of the same reasons as those levelled against the *Young Offenders Act*. In early 2006, the Conservative Harper government lobbied for harsher sentences as a deterrent to would-be young criminals and to cut down on repeat offenders. However, in June 2006, the Supreme Court of Canada stated that there was no basis to mete out harsher sentences to young people than those already in place.

Source: Adapted by Dan Glenday. CBC News Online, "*Youth Criminal Justice Act*: Changing the Law on Young Criminals." June 23, 2006. Retrieved from www.cbc.ca/news/background/crime/ycja.html.

concerning the Constitution and controversial areas of public law.

The criminal justice system in Canada is a complex web of institutions, organizations, professional and voluntary associations (e.g., police associations), and groups with particular vested interests in matters such as abortion or youth justice. It is a system of criminal and law enforcement behaviours and organizations that all the major theories discussed in this chapter—functionalist, conflict, symbolic interactionist, postmodern, and feminist—have something to say about.

Reactions to Social Deviance

Whether cheating on a sociology quiz or drinking under the legal age, any violation of norms invites reaction.

Sanctions

Responding to social deviance is vital to the welfare of groups, since groups must maintain their boundaries if they are to continue to claim a unique identity. Disapproval of social deviance, called **negative sanctions**, ranges from frowns and gossip for breaking folkways to imprisonment

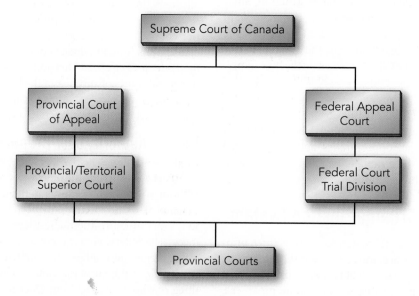

FIGURE 16.2 The Organization of the Court System in Canada

Degradation ceremonies are intended to humiliate norm violators and mark them as "not members" of a group. This photo was taken by the U.S. army in 1945 after U.S. troops liberated Cherbourg, France. Members of the French resistance shaved the heads of these women, who had "collaborated" (had sexual contact) with the occupying Nazis. They then marched the shamed women down the streets of the city, while the public shouted insults and spat on them.

and capital punishment for breaking mores. **Positive sanctions**, in contrast—from smiles to formal awards—are used to reward people for conforming to norms. Getting a raise is a positive sanction; being fired for misconduct is a negative sanction. Getting an A in basic sociology is a positive sanction; getting an F is a negative one.

Degradation Ceremonies

Sociologist Harold Garfinkel (1956) referred to formal attempts to mark an individual with the status of an outsider as **degradation ceremonies**. The individual is called to account before a group, witnesses denounce him or her, the offender is pronounced guilty, and, most importantly in sociological terms, steps are taken to *strip the individual of his or her identity as a group member.* Following a court martial, for example, officers found guilty stand at attention before their peers while the insignia of rank are ripped from their uniforms. A priest may be defrocked before a congregation; a citizen forced to wear a prison uniform. In other words, it is a ritual shaming of an individual. It is an ordered process whereby a person is stripped of their position of responsibility.

Focus Question

What is the more important strategy for reducing crime—punishment or rehabilitation?

Imprisonment

Today, the prison experience follows a degradation ceremony involving a public trial and the public pronouncement that the person is "unfit to live among decent, law-abiding people" for some specified period of time.

IN SUM

Reactions to the spectrum of criminals and social deviants vary from such mild sanctions as frowns and stares to such severe responses as imprisonment and death. Some sanctions are formal—court hearings, for example—although most are informal, as when friends refuse to talk to each other. One sanction is to label someone a social deviant, which can have powerful consequences for the person's life, especially if the label closes off conforming activities and opens up socially deviant ones. The degradation ceremony, in which someone is publicly labelled "not one of us," is a powerful sanction. So is imprisonment. Official statistics must be viewed with caution, for they reflect a strong social class bias.

The Medicalization of Social Deviance: Mental Illness

Another way society deals with social deviance is to *medicalize* it. To medicalize something is to make it a form of illness that properly belongs in the care of physicians.

NEITHER MENTAL NOR ILLNESS? For the past 100 years or so, especially since the time of Sigmund Freud (1856–1939), the Viennese physician who founded psychoanalysis, there has been a growing tendency toward the **medicalization of social deviance.** In this view, social deviance, including crime, is a sign of mental sickness. Rape, murder, theft, cheating, and so on are external symptoms of internal disorders, consequences of a confused or tortured mind.

Thomas Szasz (1986, 1998), a renegade in his profession of psychiatry, argues *that mental illnesses are neither mental nor illnesses. They are simply problem behaviours.* Some

Incarceration: Canada versus the United States

There are substantial differences between the United States and Canada in terms of rates of imprisonment for violent crime and other forms of social deviance. Canada's imprisonment rate of 110 is almost seven times lower than the rate in the United States, which had 738 prisoners for every 100 000 people in 2005–2006. However, the U.S. rate only counts adult prisoners, while the Canadian rate counts all prisoners, including those under the age of 18.

Rates in Western Europe, which also count prisoners of all ages, were closer to the Canadian rates in 2005–2006: Sweden's rate was 82, France's was 85, and in England and Wales the rate was 148.

The average number of youths (aged 12–17) in jail in Canada has fallen 58 percent since 2003, the year the Youth Criminal Justice Act came into effect and began diverting young offenders from the jail system.

These differences in incarceration have been explained in a number of ways. A widely recognized theory was offered by Seymour Martin Lipset (1990), who pointed to our counter-revolutionary history and its traditions of respect for institutional authority. The revolutionary history of the United States, by contrast, boasts of traditions respecting "rugged individualism" and irreverence for authority. What is more, the U.S. constitution guarantees every individual the right to life, liberty, the pursuit of happiness, and to bear arms. This makes for a lethal cultural cocktail. In Canada, the *British North America Act* promises peace, order, and good government, while the Charter of Rights and Freedoms contains provisions for both individual and collective rights.

Canadian economic history has also been used to explain the cultural differences between the two countries. Canada has relied much more on large commercial enterprises, such as the Canadian Pacific Railroad, for nation-building, while major U.S. industries were frequently begun by individuals, often "robber barons" known to bend the rules on their way to fame and fortune. Because of the size of Canadian enterprises, our economic development relied more heavily on government subsidies than that of our U.S. capitalist counterparts. Therefore, the government and the police were active in the settlement of Western Canada, in contrast to the "frontier spirit" of conquest over nature and people that symbolized U.S. westward expansion.

Source: Adapted by Dan Glenday. CBC News Online, "Canada's prison population grew in 2006: StatsCan." November 21, 2007. Retrieved from www.cbc.ca/news/canada/story/2007/11/21/stats-prisons.html.

forms of so-called mental illnesses have organic causes; that is, they are physical illnesses that result in unusual perceptions and behaviour. Some depression, for example, is caused by a chemical imbalance in the brain, which can be treated with drugs. Depression, however, manifests as crying, long-term sadness, and the inability to become interested in anything. When a person becomes socially deviant in ways that disturb others, who cannot find a satisfying explanation for why the person is "like that," they conclude that a "sickness in the head" causes the inappropriate, unacceptable behaviour.

All of us have troubles. Some of us face a constant barrage of problems as we go through life. Most of us continue the struggle, encouraged by relatives and friends, motivated by jobs, family responsibilities, and life goals. Even when the odds seem hopeless, we carry on, not perfectly, but as best we can.

Some people, however, fail to cope well with the challenges of daily life. Overwhelmed, they become depressed, unco-operative, or hostile. Some strike out at others, while some, in Merton's terms, become retreatists and withdraw into their apartments or homes and refuse to come out.

These are *behaviours, not mental illnesses*, stresses Szasz. They may be inappropriate coping devices, but they are coping devices, nevertheless, not mental illnesses. Thus, Szasz concludes that "mental illness" is a myth foisted on a naive public by a medical profession that uses pseudoscientific jargon to expand its area of control and force nonconforming people to accept society's definitions of "normal."

Szasz's extreme claim forces us to look anew at the forms of social deviance called mental illness. To explain behaviour that people find bizarre, he directs our attention not to "things hidden deep within the subconscious," but instead to how people learn such behaviours. To ask, "What is the origin of inappropriate or bizarre behaviour?" then becomes similar to asking, "Why do some women steal?" "Why do some men rape?" "Why do some teenagers cuss their parents and stalk out of the room slamming doors?" *The answers depend on people's particular experiences in life, not some illness in their mind.* In short, some sociologists find Szasz's renegade analysis refreshing because it indicates that *social experiences*, not illness of the mind, underlie bizarre behaviours—as well as social deviance in general.

THE HOMELESS MENTALLY ILL

Jamie was sitting on the low wall surrounding the landscaped area of an exclusive restaurant. She appeared unaware of the stares elicited by her many layers of mismatched clothing, her dirty face, and the ever-present shopping cart overflowing with her meagre possessions.

Every once in a while Jamie would pause, concentrate, and point to the street. I asked her what she was doing.

"I'm directing traffic," she replied. "I control where the cars go. Look, that one turned right there," she said, now withdrawing her finger.

"Really?" I said.

After a while she confided that her cart talked to her.

"Really?" I said again.

"Yes," she replied. "You can hear it, too." At that, she pushed the shopping cart a bit.

"Did you hear that?" she asked.

When I shook my head, she demonstrated again. Then it hit me. She was referring to the squeaking wheels!

I nodded.

When I left Jamie, she was looking toward the sky, her finger upraised, for, as she told me, she also controlled the flight of airplanes.

To most of us, Jamie's behaviour and thinking are bizarre. They simply do not match any reality we know. Jamie might be mentally ill. Some organic problem, such as a chemical imbalance in her brain, might underlie her behaviour. But perhaps not. Could you or I become Jamie?

Suppose for a bitter moment that you are homeless and have to live on the streets. You have no money, no place to sleep, no bathroom, do not know if you are going to eat, much less where, have no friends or anyone you can trust, and live with the constant threat of rape and violence. Do you think this might be enough to drive you "over the edge"?

Consider the problems involved in not having a place to bathe. (Shelters are often so dangerous that the homeless prefer to take their chances sleeping in public settings.) At first, you might try to wash in the toilets of gas stations, bars, the bus station, or a shopping centre. But you are dirty, and people stare when you enter and call the management when they see you wash your feet in the sink. You are thrown out and told in no uncertain terms never to come back. So you get dirtier and dirtier. Eventually you come to think of being dirty as a fact of life. Soon, maybe, you don't even care. No longer do the stares bother you—at least not as much.

No one will talk to you, and you withdraw further into yourself. You begin to build a fantasy life. You talk openly to yourself. People stare, but so what? They stare anyway. Besides, they are no longer important to you.

How long would it take us to engage in bizarre behaviours if we were homeless? What if we were homeless and hopeless for years? The point is that *just being on the streets can cause mental illness*—or whatever we want to label socially inappropriate behaviours that we find difficult to classify (McCarthy, 1983; Belcher, 1988; R.K. Nelson, 1989). *Homelessness and mental illness are reciprocal:* just as "mental illness" can cause homelessness, so the trials of being homeless, of living on cold, hostile streets, can lead to unusual and unacceptable thinking and behaviours.

The Need for a More Humane Approach

As Durkheim (1895/1938: 68–69) pointed out, social deviance is inevitable—even in a group of saints:

> Imagine a society of saints . . . Crimes, properly so called, will there be unknown; but faults which appear [invisible] to the layman will create there the same scandal that the ordinary offense does in ordinary [society].

With social deviants being inevitable, one measure of a society is how it treats them. Social class position remains an important predictor. White-collar criminals continue to get by with a slap on the wrist, while street criminals are severely punished. Taking refuge in shelters and cardboard boxes in city streets is not a humane answer to homelessness. Neither is enforcing arrest policies the answer for violence against women. Although no one has the answer, it does not take much reflection to see that there are more humane approaches than these.

The larger issues of social deviance involve protecting people from socially deviant behaviours that are harmful to themselves or others, tolerating those that are not, and developing systems of fairer treatment for social deviants. In the absence of the fundamental changes that would bring about a truly equitable social system, most efforts are, unfortunately, Band-Aid work. What is needed is a more humane social system, one that would prevent the social inequalities that were the focus of Chapters 6 through 9.

GAINING A SOCIOLOGICAL PERSPECTIVE ON CRIME AND SOCIAL DEVIANCE

How do psychological, biological, and sociological explanations of social deviance differ?

To explain why people deviate, psychologists and biologists look for reasons within the individual, such as **genetic predispositions** or **personality disorders**. Sociologists, in contrast, look for explanations *outside* the individual, in social relations. pp. 360–362.

HOW DO SYMBOLIC INTERACTIONISTS, FUNCTIONALISTS, CONFLICT THEORISTS, FEMINISTS AND POSTMODERNISTS EXPLAIN SOCIAL DEVIANCE?

The symbolic-interactionist perspective

Symbolic interactionists have developed several theories to explain social deviance such as **crime** (the violation of norms written into law). According to **differential association** theory, people learn to deviate from associating with others. **Labelling theory** focuses on how labels (names, reputations) help to propel people into or divert people away from social deviance. Many people commit socially deviant acts and still think of themselves as conformists. They apparently use five **techniques of neutralization**. Studies of prostitutes show three ways in which the self-concept is involved in socially deviant acts. In **primary social deviance**, the acts are fleeting and have little effect on the self-concept. In **secondary social deviance**, people incorporate their socially deviant acts into their self-concept. In **tertiary social deviance**, acts commonly considered socially deviant are relabelled as normal. Although most people resist being labelled socially deviant, some embrace social deviance. pp. 363–366.

The functionalist perspective

Functionalists point out that social deviance, including criminal acts, is functional for society. Functions include affirming norms and promoting social unity and social change. According to **strain theory**, societies socialize their members into desiring **cultural goals**, but many people are unable to achieve these goals in socially acceptable ways—by **institutionalized means**. Social deviants, then, are people who either give up on the goals or use socially deviant means to attain them. Merton identified five types of responses to cultural goals and institutionalized means: conformity, innovation, ritualism, retreatism, and rebellion. Illegitimate opportunity theory stresses that some people have easier access to illegal means of achieving goals. pp. 366–367.

The conflict perspective

Conflict theorists see power and social inequality as the primary characteristics of society. They stress that the state's machinery of social control, which includes the **criminal justice system**—the police, courts, and prisons that deal with the accused—represents the interests of the wealthy and powerful, a group that determines the basic laws essential to preserving its own power. pp. 370–371.

The feminist perspective

When it comes to male violence against women, virtually all feminists agree that men assault their female partners to maintain control over them, and, if they happen to live in a relationship, over their "domestic" situation. Control over women has been measured as (1) sexual fidelity, (2) obedience, (3) respect, (4) loyalty, (5) dependency, and (6) sexual access pp. 371–372.

The postmodern perspective

The postmodern approach emphasizes the need to "deconstruct" or decode the meaning of concepts such as "law and order" and the "criminal justice system." Postmodern theorists also argue that whether we are sitting at home, driving, or walking the streets, we are bombarded by information in the media about the risks we take—from air pollution and environmental hazards on and off the job to everyday choices about what we eat and drink pp. 372–373.

WHAT CAN BE DONE ABOUT MALE VIOLENCE AGAINST WOMEN?

Four strategies for coping with male violence against women are: (1) training the police to identify and charge offenders; (2) good job-creation strategies; (3) social services such as shelters and co-op housing; and (4) anti-sexist male collectives. DeKeseredy and Hinch, for example, argue that economic policy reforms such as paid work leaves, flexible hours (flextime), pay equity, and improving the quality of work available to disadvantaged people, to name just a few, can lower the rate of male violence against women. p. 371.

THE CANADIAN CRIMINAL JUSTICE SYSTEM

What are the main components of the Canadian criminal justice system?

The Canadian criminal justice system comprises three principal components: the police, the courts, and the corrections system. The court system in Canada is composed of four basic levels. The first level is the provincial courts, which handle most criminal offences, family law matters (except divorce, which is dealt with at the federal level), and traffic violations. At the second level are the provincial and territorial superior courts, which deal with more serious crimes and also take appeals from provincial court judgments. There is also the Federal Court Trial Division. At the third level are the provincial courts of appeal and the Federal Court of Appeal. The Supreme Court of Canada comprises the fourth and highest level. pp. 373–374.

THE MEDICALIZATION OF SOCIAL DEVIANCE: MENTAL ILLNESS

What is the medicalization of social deviance?

The medical profession has attempted to medicalize many forms of social deviance, claiming that they represent mental illnesses. Thomas Szasz disagrees, claiming that they are just problem behaviours, not mental illnesses. Research on homeless people illustrates how problems in living can lead to bizarre behaviour and thinking. pp. 375–377.

TALKING ABOUT THEORY

Theoretical Paradigms

	CLASSICAL PARADIGMS			RECENT PARADIGMS	
	Structural-Functional Paradigm	Social-Conflict Paradigm	Symbolic-Interaction Paradigm	Feminist Paradigm	Postmodernist Paradigm
What is the level of analysis?	Macro level	Macro level	Micro level	Micro and macro levels	Micro and macro levels
What is the social significance of crime and social deviance?	Social deviance and crime clarify and affirm normative boundaries for the majority (positive, or functional). The capitalist ethic that says that happiness and the good life come as a result of affluence influences some individuals in minority groups to resort to crime as the quickest means to achieve the good life (negative, or dysfunctional).	The criminal justice system maintains the status quo.	The groups that individuals associate with directly influences their attitudes and behaviours.	Male domination at the societal and familial level (patriarchy) explains violence toward women as a means of control.	The media-created "risk society" generates anxieties over the perpetrators of crime, such as visible minorities and youth.
Have crime and social deviance changed over time? How?	No. Social deviance and crime continue to have the same root causes and explanations. (For example, Merton uses four paths of social deviance and "illegitimate opportunity structures" to explain social class and crime.)	Yes/No. As changing technology provides new opportunities for capital and profit, the laws must change to maintain class privilege and power.	Yes. As social attitudes change toward social deviance, old labels carry less weight.	Yes/No. Changes in legal prohibitions against women's right to vote and discrimination at work are significant positive changes. Patriarchy remains.	N/A

All URLs listed are current as of the printing of this text.

Journal of Prisoners on Prisons
www.jpp.org
A prisoner-written, academically oriented journal with the purpose of bringing "the knowledge and experience of the incarcerated to bear upon more academic arguments and concerns and to inform public discourse about the current state of our carceral institutions."

SocioSite
www.sociosite.net
A site designed to provide access to information and resources relevant to sociologists and other social scientists. Subjects include crime and deviance.

Internet Crime Archives
www.mayhem.net/Crime/archives.html
Information on all manners of illegal deviant behaviour.

The American Society of Criminology
www.asc41.com
An international organization concerned with criminology that embraces scholarly, scientific, and professional knowledge concerning the etiology, prevention, control, and treatment of crime and delinquency.

Art Crimes: The Writing on the Wall
www.graffiti.org
A gallery of graffiti art from cities around the world, providing cultural information and resources that aim to preserve and document constantly disappearing graffiti paintings. "We do not advocate breaking the law, but we think art belongs in public spaces and that more legal walls should be made available for this fascinating art form."

1. According to Robert K. Merton, when people lack the opportunities to legitimately pursue culturally approved goals, they may turn to crime. Two ways of circumventing this are to (1) teach people to be satisfied with less and (2) provide more legitimate opportunities. If you alone had the means to decrease crime in Canadian society, which strategy would you pursue and why?

2. According to one of the authors of this text (Dan Glenday), Canadian criminologists have largely ignored the link between unemployment and property crimes in Canada. Instead, they have focused on more "sophisticated" theories that suggest "dysfunctional family backgrounds" as the cause for property crimes or differential association and labelling theories. Why do you think Canadian criminologists have ignored the link between unemployment and property crimes?

3. Probation officers and social workers usually want to identify "young offenders" as early as possible so that they may be "treated" before their "socially deviant" character is firmly established. Is this the right or wrong approach to take with young offenders?

4. What do you think should be done about the Canadian crime problem? What sociological theories either support or oppose your view? Access the Research Navigator through MySocLab and use keywords such as "crime," "solution," and "Canada" to locate relevant and recent scholarly and popular press publications to help you answer this question.

MySocLab

Explore the topics covered in this chapter on MySocLab. Interactive resources include a study plan, cumulative exams, a multimedia library, MySocLab eReadings, and access to the MySocLab Video Series.

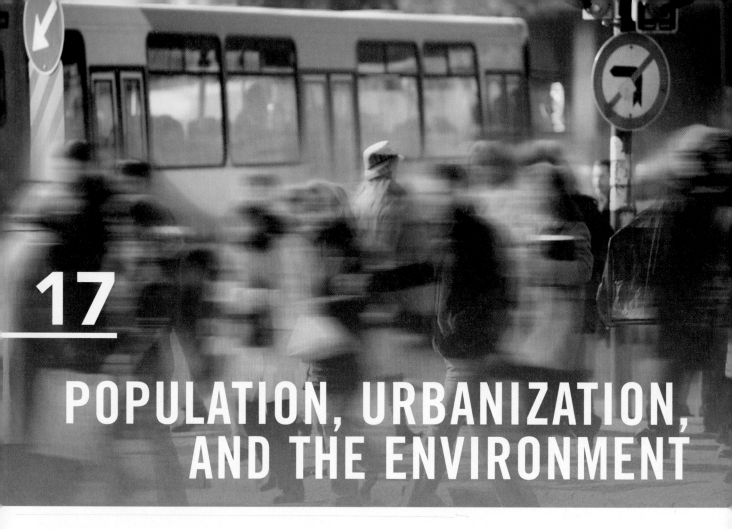

17

POPULATION, URBANIZATION, AND THE ENVIRONMENT

LEARNING OUTCOMES

After you have studied this chapter, you will be able to answer the following questions:

1. What debate did Thomas Malthus initiate?
2. Why are people starving?
3. Why do the poor nations have so many children?
4. What models of urban growth have been proposed?
5. Is the city inherently alienating?
6. What are the environmental problems of the most industrialized nations?
7. What is environmental sociology?
8. What is ecofeminism?

THE federal government recently dispatched Environment Canada media officers to an international polar conference in Montreal to monitor and record what Environment Canada scientists said to reporters. According to the *Vancouver Sun*, the media instructions included the following: "If you are approached by the media, send a message to your media relations contact and they will organize the interview. They will most probably be with you during the interview to assist and record."

Mark Johnson, an Environment Canada spokesman, described the plan as "standard practice" and consistent with the government's overall communication policy.

Others see it differently. "Until now such a crude heavy-handed approach to muzzle Canadian scientists, prior to a significant international Arctic science conference hosted by Canada, would have been unthinkable," a senior scientist who has worked for Environment Canada for decades told Margaret Munroe of the *Vancouver Sun*. He asked not to be identified due to the possibility of repercussions from Ottawa.

Climatologist Andrew Weaver at the University of Victoria views these federal media police who take charge of arranging interviews and sending

Source: Adapted by Dan Glenday. Margaret Munro, "Critics pan instructions to Environment Canada scientists at Montreal conference." *Vancouver Sun*, April 23, 2012. Retreived from www.canada.com/technology/Critics+instructions+Environment+Canada+scientists+ Montreal+conference/6500175/story.html; Krista Fickes, senior communications advisor Environment Canada, email to Environment Canada scientists attending International Polar Year Conference (www.canada.com/news/Email+sent+Environment+Canada+scientists/6500182/story. html#ixzz1t4zlmXD1).

recordings to Ottawa as reminiscent of the way the Soviets used to send KGB agents to conferences with scientists during the Cold War. "It's an affront to democracy," Weaver said.

There is growing concern in many quarters about what is being viewed as the government's excessive information control. In February 2012, the *Ottawa Citizen* reported how a reporter's simple question about a Canada–U.S. study on snow was torpedoed by the media police at the National Research Council. While an American NASA scientist was free to answer questions in a simple 15-minute interview, the NRC declined to let anyone speak with the reporter about the snow study. Instead, 11 people in the Canadian agency eventually produced a list of equipment used in the study—information of little use in the story.

Faced with staffing cuts, 23 000 federal scientists are operating in a culture of fear, said Johanne Fillion, a spokeswoman with the Professional Institute of the Public Service of Canada.

Fillion went on to point out that "Public science is paid for by taxpayers and our scientists want to promote Canadian research that is being recognized internationally . . . These scientists are essential to making the right decision in public policies and the government shouldn't be able to stop them from doing science and talking to the public about what they are doing."

Several organizations say they are concerned with the silencing of Canada's federal scientists. Most recently, PEN Canada, a member of the an international association of writers defending freedom of expression, called on the government to ensure that any restraints on the free flow of scientific information are lifted immediately.

POPULATION IN A GLOBAL PERSPECTIVE

Demography is the study of the size, composition, growth, and distribution of human populations. It brings us face to face with questions of whether our planet will be able to support its growing population. Will chronic famine and mass starvation be the sorry fate that awaits most of us in this millennium? Let's look at how these concerns began, and then at what today's demographers have to say.

A Planet with No Space to Enjoy Life?

Sometimes, the cultural diffusion of a simple item can have far-reaching consequences on nations. An example is the potato, which the Spanish Conquistadors found among the natives of the Andes. When the Spanish brought this food back to Europe, the people there came to gradually accept it. Eventually, the potato became the principal food of the lower classes. With more abundant food, fertility increased and the death rate dropped. As a result, Europe's population soared, almost doubling during the 1700s (McKeown, 1977).

This rapid growth alarmed Thomas Malthus (1766–1834), an English Protestant theologian. He saw it as a sign of coming doom. In 1798, he wrote *An Essay on the Principle of Population*, a book that became world famous. In it, Malthus proposed what became known as the **Malthus theorem**. He argued that while population grows geometrically (from 2 to 4 to 8 to 16, and so forth), the food supply increases only arithmetically (from 1 to 2 to 3 to 4, and so on). This meant, he claimed, that if births go unchecked, the population of a country, or even of the world, will outstrip its food supply. War and famine would be the inevitable result.

The New Malthusians

Was Malthus right? One group, whom we can call the "New Malthusians," is convinced that today's situation is at least as grim, if not grimmer, than what Malthus ever imagined. Figure 17.1 shows how fast the world's population is growing. *In just the time it takes you to read this chapter, another 15 000 to 20 000 babies will be born!*

The New Malthusians point out that the world's population is following an **exponential growth curve**. To illustrate, sociologist William Faunce (1981) told a parable about a man who saved a rich man's life. The rich man was grateful and said he wanted to reward the man for his heroic deed:

> The man replied that he would like his reward to be spread out over a four-week period, with each day's amount being twice what he received on the preceding day. He also said he would be happy to receive only one penny on the first day. At the end of the first week, the rich man owed only $1.27 . . . On the

◉ **Watch** the video "Population Growth and Decline" on **MySocLab.**

✳ **Explore** the reading "Sixteen Impacts of Population Growth" on **MySocLab.**

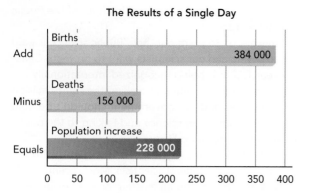

The Results of a Single Day

Add	Births	384 000
Minus	Deaths	156 000
Equals	Population increase	228 000

0 50 100 150 200 250 300 350 400

The Accumulating Increase

Each second 2.63	Each minute 158	Each hour 9 480	Each day 228 000
Each week 1 597 000	Each month 6 940 000	Each year 83 000 000	

FIGURE 17.1 How Fast is the World's Population Growing?

twenty-first day, however the total had grown to $20 971.51. When the twenty-eighth day arrived the rich man was shocked to discover that he owed $1 342 177.28 for that day alone and that the total reward had jumped to $2 684 354.56!

This kind of situation is precisely what alarms the New Malthusians. They contend that it took all of human history for the world's population to reach its first billion around 1800. It then took about 130 years (1930) to add the second billion. Just 30 years later (1960), the world population hit three billion. The time needed to reach the fourth billion was cut in half, to only 15 years (1975). Today, the world population has surpassed 7 billion (www.census.gov/population/popclockworld.html).

The Anti-Malthusians

It seems obvious that no one wants to live in a shoulder-to-shoulder world and fight for scraps. How, then, can anyone argue with the New Malthusians?

A much more optimistic group of demographers, whom we can call the "Anti-Malthusians," claim that such an image of the future is ridiculous. Anti-Malthusians argue that people simply do not blindly reproduce until they run out of room (Simon, 1992, 1996; Mosher, 1994, 1997).

The Anti-Malthusians believe that Europe's **demographic transition** provides a more accurate picture of the future. This transition is diagrammed in Figure 17.2. During most of its history, Europe was in Stage 1. High birth rates offset by high death rates led to a fairly stable population. Stage 2, the "population explosion," was what upset Malthus. Europe's population surged because birth rates remained high, while death rates went down. Finally, Europe made the transition to Stage 3—the population stabilized as people brought their birth rates into line with the lower death rates.

This, contend the Anti-Malthusians, is what will happen in the least industrialized nations. Their current surge in

In earlier generations, large farm families were common. Having many children was functional—there were many hands to help with crops, food production, and food preparation. As the country industrialized and urbanized, this changed—children became expensive and nonproducing. Consequently, the size of families shrank as we entered Stage 3 of the *demographic transition* (as shown in Figure 17.2), and today Canadian families with 10 children are practically non-existent.

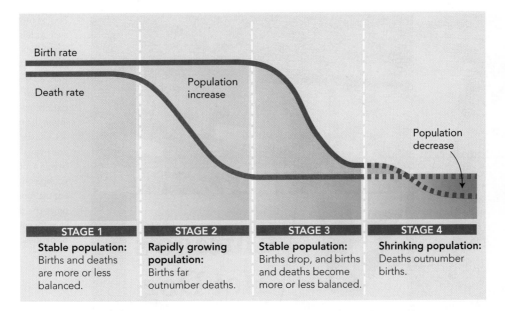

FIGURE 17.2 The Demographic Transition

Note: The standard demographic transition is depicted by Stages 1–3. Stage 4 has recently been suggested by some Anti-Malthusians.

growth simply indicates that they have reached the second stage of the demographic transition. Hybrid seed and modern medicine imported from the most industrialized nations have cut their death rates, but their birth rates remain high. When they move into the third stage, we will wonder what all the fuss was about.

Some Anti-Malthusians go even further (Mosher, 1997). As shown at the far right of Figure 17.2, they foresee a "demographic free fall." They predict that the world's population will peak at about 8 or 9 billion and then begin a long descent. As countries industrialize, women will become more educated, postpone marriage, and reduce the number of children they bear. The result will be **population shrinkage**.

The shrinking population of Europe—Germany and Italy already fill more coffins than cradles—has begun to alarm policymakers. Closer to home, the demographic picture of Quebec society over the past 50 years illustrates the Anti-Malthusian claim. Quebec went from having the highest birth rate in the country to one of the lowest in just two generations. In recent years, the birth rate has inched upward, but still remains at a dismal 1.54 children per woman. The number of births dropped to a 55-year low in 2000. Since then, the number of births has gone up every year except 2002. In 2005, 342 418 babies were born in Canada, a jump of 1.5 percent from the previous year. The two main concerns for Anti-Malthusians are not enough young workers to support a rapidly growing elderly population, and race–ethnic problems that develop as workers from other parts of the world migrate to depopulating countries. Surprising almost everyone, the fourth stage of the demographic transition has also begun to hit Asia: Japan has had

a declining population since the early 1990s. The success of South Korea's population policy to lower its population growth rate during the 1960s and 1970s resulted in the government implementing *Saero-Maji*, or the "New Beginning" plan, from 2006 to 2010 to provide a more favourable environment for childbearing (Statistical Handbook of Japan, 2011: 13; Haub, 2010).

In short, the Anti-Malthusians stress that the world's problem will not be a population explosion, but population shrinkage—too few children in the world rather than too many.

Who Is Correct?

Who is right? Like the proverbial pessimists who see the glass of water half empty, the New Malthusians interpret population growth negatively. And like the optimists who see the same glass half full, the Anti-Malthusians view the figures positively.

However, in addition to the Mathusian debate, we should consider another perspective: feminism and population control.

Feminism and the Population Debate

Feminists reject the "solutions" favoured by the New Malthusians to limit population growth in the industrializing and least industrialized countries. The New Malthusians proposed, for example, forced sterilization of women in the industrializing and least industrialized nations. This idea and others like it were rightly analyzed as patriarchal policies. That is, such heavy-handed decisions, thought up by governments, are mainly rules created by older men to be imposed on younger men, women, and children. Feminists

Photos of starving people, such as this mother and child, haunt Canadians and other citizens of the most industrialized nations. Many of us wonder why, when some people are starving, we should live in the midst of such abundance, often overeating and even casually scrapping excess food. We even have eating contests to see who can eat the most food in the least time. The text discusses reasons for such unconscionable disparities.

object to these policies because they deprive women of the freedom to make decisions for themselves—decisions about their own bodies.

The feminist perspective on the topic of population control begins with the emancipation of women from patriarchal decision-making. Feminists argue that women's rights, especially the right to decide about one's reproductive future, must be recognized as basic human rights. Unlike their Victorian predecessors, who rejected contraception, the contemporary feminist perspective recognizes the importance of birth control.

How should population control be achieved? By providing women with economic opportunities, education about birth control, and rights. Women who work, especially in cities, generally want to limit the number of children they will bear. This is a "policy" that does not have to be imposed; it simply involves making available opportunities for employment. There is strong evidence to support the argument that educating women is another important step. Women who can read are better able to care for their children, leading to lower infant mortality rates and lower fertility rates.

For most feminists, the course of action is clear: Empower women by giving them opportunities to find and keep meaningful employment, provide free public education, and enshrine women's rights in national and international legislation, and they will voluntarily lower their fertility.

Focus Question
What is the feminist viewpoint on the population debate?

Why Are People Starving?

Pictures of starving children haunt us. Why don't children around the world have enough food?

The basic question is this: Does the world produce enough food to feed everyone? On this issue, the Anti-Malthusians make a point that seems irrefutable. As Figure 17.3 shows, *the amount of food produced for each person in the world is now much more than it was in 1950.* Although the world's population has more than doubled during this time, improved seeds and fertilization have made more food available for every person on earth.

Then why do people die of hunger? From Figure 17.3, we can conclude that some countries produce more food than their people can consume; others make less than they need for survival. In short, the cause of starvation is an imbalance between supply and demand. It is important to understand the underlying basis of such human misery, some of which could certainly be alleviated by transferring food from nations that have a surplus.

One of the most notable examples is that at the same time as widespread famine is ravishing West Africa, Canadian farmers are having trouble selling their grain on the global market. The result: the lack of adequate incomes from cash crops has forced many western Canadian family farmers to give up and move to the cities.

Africa has been the site of recent pockets of starvation. Many images presented in the media leave the impression that Africa is overpopulated. Why else would all those people be starving? The truth is far different, however. Africa has 23 percent of the earth's land surface but only 15 percent of the world's population (Haub & Kent, 2008; Haub, 2011). The continent has vast areas of fertile land that have

* **Explore** the reading "Meager Harvests in Africa Leave Millions at the Edge of Starvation" on **MySocLab.**

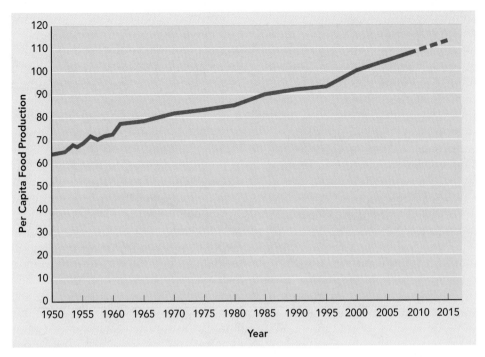

FIGURE 17.3 How Much Food Does the World Produce Per Person?

Source: Dan Glenday, based on Simon (1981). Food and Agriculture Organization of the United Nations, 2006. *Statistical Abstract of the United States* 2010: Table 1335.

yet to be farmed. The reason for famines in Africa, then, cannot be that too many people live on too little land.

Population Growth

Why the Least Industrialized Nations Have So Many Children

To understand why populations increase so much more rapidly in the least industrialized nations, let's consider three scenarios.

First, in the least industrialized nations, the more children a woman bears, the more she is thought to have achieved the purpose for which she was born—motherhood. Similarly, a man proves his manhood by fathering children. The more children he fathers, especially sons, the better—for through them his name lives on.

Second, the community views children as a blessing and encourages a couple to have many children. The barren woman, not the woman with a dozen children, is to be pitied.

Third, poor people in the least industrialized nations consider children economic assets. They have no social insurance or medical and employment insurance. As a result, when parents become sick or too old to work—or when no work is to be found—the more children they have, the more each child can contribute to the family income at a young age.

Figure 17.4 illustrates how children can be net income earners for a least industrialized nation family. For example, consider the following incident, reported by a government worker in India:

Chinese officials have become concerned about the lopsided gender ratio that their "one couple, one child" policy has produced. Recent billboards continue to promote this policy, but by featuring a female child in the poster, the government hopes to reduce female infanticide.

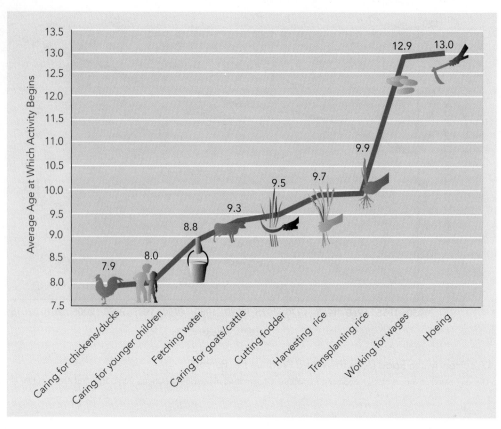

FIGURE 17.4 Why the Poor Need Children

Surviving children are an economic asset in the least industrialized nations. This figure, based on a survey in Indonesia, shows that boys and girls can be net income earners for their families by the age of nine or ten.

Source: U.N. Fund for Population Activities.

Thaman Singh [a very poor man, a water carrier] . . . I have six sons and two daughters and I sit at home in leisure. They are grown up and they bring me money. Now, you see, because of my large family I am a rich man." (Mamdani, 1973, italics added)

Feminists offer a different view of why women in poor nations bear so many children. They stress that in these cultures, men dominate women in all spheres of life, including reproduction. Feminists argue that women have internalized values that support male dominance. For example, in Latin America, *machismo* is common. This emphasis on male virility and dominance includes fathering many children as a means of achieving status in the community. From a feminist perspective, then, another reason poor people have so many children is that men control women's reproductive choices.

Estimating Population Growth: The Three Demographic Variables

How many people will live in Canada 50 years from now? What will the world's population be then? These are important questions. Educators want to know how many schools to build. Manufacturers want to anticipate changes in demand for their products. The government needs to know how many doctors, engineers, and executives to train, as well as how many people will be paying taxes and how many young people will be available to fight a war.

To project population trends, demographers use three **demographic variables**: fertility, mortality, and net migration.

FERTILITY The **fertility rate** is the number of children the average woman bears. A term sometimes confused with fertility is **fecundity**, the number of children that women are *capable* of bearing. The fecundity of women around the world is around 20 children each. Their fertility rate, however (the actual number of children they bear), is much lower. The world's overall fertility rate is 3.0, which means that the average woman in the world bears three children during her lifetime. As we saw earlier in the chapter, at 1.54 (2005), the fertility rate of Canadian women is considerably less than the world average.

To compute the fertility rate of a country, demographers figure the country's **crude birth rate**, the annual number of live births per 1000 population.

TABLE 17.1 Demographic Profile of Canada from the First Census in 1851–2007 (thousands)[1]

Period	Births	Deaths	Immigration	Emigration	Population of Canada at the End of the Period
1861–1871	1370	760	260	410	3689
1871–1881	1480	790	350	404	4325
1901–1911	1925	900	1550	740	7207
1921–1931	2420	1060	1200	970	10 377
1931–1941	2294	1072	149	241	11 507
1941–1951	3186	1214	548	379	13 648
1961–1966	2249	731	539	280	20 0151
1971–1976	1755	824	1053	496	23 550
1981–1986	1872	885	677	384	26 101
1986–1991	1933	946	1189	256	28 031
1996–2001	1660	1114	1137	321	31 081
2006–2007	353	238	260	41	31 240

[1]Includes Newfoundland since 1951.

Note: Figures are approximate.

Source: Statistics Canada, Annual Demographic Statistics, 2001 (corrected), Catalogue no. 91-213-XPB; CANSIM table 051-0004. Last modified 2011-09-28.

MORTALITY The second demographic variable, **crude death rate**, is the number of deaths per 1000 population.

MIGRATION The third major demographic variable is the **net migration rate**, the difference between the number of *immigrants* (people moving in) and *emigrants* (people moving out) per 1000 population. To understand migration, we need to look at both *push* and *pull* factors. Push factors are the things people want to escape—poverty, a lack of religious and political freedoms, even political persecution. Pull factors are the magnets that draw people to a new land, such as a chance for higher wages and better jobs.

Around the world, the flow of migration is from the least industrialized nations to the more industrialized countries (Kalish, 1994). After "migrant paths" are established, immigration often accelerates as networks of kin and friends become further magnets that attract more people from the same nation—and even from the same villages.

Table 17.1 shows the demographic profile of Canada from 1861 up to 2010. Note the rapid increase in births just after World War II, signalling the beginning of the "baby boom" generation. Also take note of the periods on the table from 1986–1991 and 1996–2001. The number of births and deaths decreased significantly over the last period while the numbers of new immigrants increased. The latest data for 2010 reveals a similar pattern, with immigration helping to offset Canada's low birth and death rates. Immigration to Canada is the key to supporting population growth and with it sustaining our standard of living.

The Basic Demographic Equation and Problems in Forecasting Population Growth

The total of the three demographic variables—fertility, mortality, and net migration—gives us a country's **growth rate**, the net change after people have been added to and subtracted from a population. What demographers call the **basic demographic equation** is quite simple:

Growth rate = Births – Deaths + Net migration

With such a simple equation, it might seem that it would be a simple matter to project a country's future population. But social factors—economic booms and busts, wars, plagues, and famines—push rates up or down.

The primary factor that influences a country's growth rate is its rate of industrialization. *In every country that industrializes, the growth rate declines.* Not only does industrialization open up economic opportunities, it also makes children more expensive. Significantly, the basis for conferring status also changes—from having children to attaining education and displaying material wealth. People in industrializing countries then begin to see life differently, and their motivation to have many children drops sharply. Not knowing how rapidly industrialization will progress or how quickly

Canada's Multicultural Cities

What is a multicultural city in Canada? Some look to spatial divisions such as ethnic neighbourhoods to define multiculturalism, while others look to the degree of social inclusion or the juxtaposition of ethnic identifiers such as mosques located close to temples and churches. Other examples include restaurants, boutiques, and cafés located close to one another that cater to varying ethnic tastes.

According to Statistics Canada, between now and 2031, the foreign-born population could reach a high of 12.5 million, up from the over 6.1 million enumerated in the 2006 census. Each major Canadian city hosts its own unique combination of multiculturalism. About 18 percent of 1990s immigrants to Montreal, for example, are from Africa, Haiti, China, Algeria, France, and Lebanon. The city is home to 85 percent of Canada's immigrants from Haiti and 76 percent of immigrants from Morocco, while Toronto is home to 77percent of Jamaicans, 80 percent of

Celebrants along Granville Street in Vancouver after Canada won the gold medal in the Winter Olympics in February 2010.

Guyanse, and 80 percent of Sri Lankans living in Canada. Most immigrants from Taiwan and Fiji live in Vancouver. That city's ethnic makeup also includes Malaysians, South Koreans, South Africans, and Iranians. The demographic trend is similar in Calgary, where about 200 000 residents are foreign-born.

Most Canadian cities celebrate ethnic and cultural diversity by hosting events such as Nuits d'Afrique, the Montreal Jewish Film Festival, Fierté Montréal, and the Festival du Monde

Arabe in Montreal; the International Dragon Boat Race, Corso Italia, Gay Pride, and the Caribbean Carnival in Toronto; Heritage Days in Edmonton; and Folklorama in Winnipeg. Are these events enough? Are they too much?

For Your Consideration:
Many European countries believe multiculturalism is a failed experiment. Germany, the United Kingdom, the Netherlands, and France hold multiculturalism largely responsible for separating peoples, weakening national cohesion, and encouraging Islamic extremism. Do you believe multiculturalism discourages assimilation into Canadian society and begets cultural walls between Canadians?

Sources: Dan Glenday; Statistics Canada "The Daily." March 9, 2010; *Touch Base*, "Today, Canada's multicultural cities set the tone for peaceable communities." March 7, 2010.

---

changes in values and reproductive behaviour will follow adds to the difficulty of making accurate projections.

Because of such complications, demographers play it safe by making several projections of population growth (Haub, 1997). For example, what will the population of Canada be in the year 2020? In Canada, as in the United States, no long-term population decline is projected. Nevertheless, Canada is slowly heading toward zero growth. **Zero population growth** occurs when every 1000 women gives birth to 2100 children. (The extra 100 children make up for those who do not survive.) Will a larger proportion of women go to university? (The more education women have, the fewer children they bear.) How will immigration change during the coming years? Will AIDS be brought under control? Will some other horrible disease appear? What will happen to the global economy?

The Challenge of the Twenty-First Century

Let's look at a different aspect of population: where people live. Since the world is rapidly becoming urban, we will concentrate on urban trends and urban life.

Urbanization

The Development of Cities

Perhaps as early as 7000 to 10 000 years ago, people built small cities with massive defensive walls, such as the biblically famous Jericho (Homblin, 1973).

The key to the origin of cities is the development of efficient agriculture (Lenski & Lenski, 1987). Only when

Early cities were small economic centres surrounded by walls that kept out enemies. These cities had to be fortresses, for they were constantly under threat. The photo is of Avila, Spain, whose walls date from 1090.

farming produces a surplus can some people stop being food producers and gather in cities to spend time in other pursuits. The invention of the plow between 5000 and 6000 years ago created widespread agricultural surpluses, stimulating the development of towns and cities (Curwin & Hart, 1961). A **city** can be defined as a place in which a large number of people are permanently based and do not produce their own food.

Most early cities were tiny in comparison to those of today, merely a collection of a few thousand people in agricultural centres or on major trade routes. The most notable exceptions are two cities that reached populations of 1 million for a brief period before they declined—Changan in China around A.D. 800 and Baghdad in Persia around A.D. 900 (Chandler & Fox, 1974). By 1900, the number of such cities jumped to 16 as a result of the Industrial Revolution, which drew people to cities by providing work. The Industrial Revolution also stimulated rapid transportation and communication, and allowed people, resources, and products to be moved efficiently—all essential factors (called infrastructure) upon which large cities depend. Figure 17.5 illustrates the global growth in the number of cities that are home to a million or more people (Brockerhoff, 2000).

The Process of Urbanization

Although cities are not new to the world scene, urbanization is. **Urbanization** refers to masses of people moving to cities, giving cities a growing influence on society. Urbanization is worldwide. Just 200 years ago, in 1800, only 3 percent of the world's population lived in cities (Hauser & Schnore, 1965). In 2008, for the first time in history, more people lived in cities than in rural areas. Today, about 75 percent of people in the industrialized world, 44 percent in the industrializing countries, and 27 percent in the least industrialized nations live in cities (Haub, 2011).

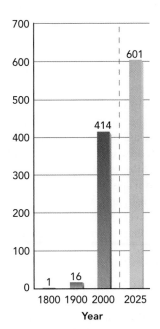

FIGURE 17.5 A Global Boom: Cities with over 1 Million Residents

Sources: Dan Glenday. Based on Chandler & Fox (1974); Brockerhoff (2000); United Nations (2008).

◉ **Watch** the video "New Metropolis" on **MySocLab.**

To understand the city's attraction, we need to consider the "pull" of urban life. Due to its extensive division of labour, the city offers incredible variety—music ranging from rock and rap to country and classic, diets for vegetarians and diabetics, and imported delicacies from around the world. Cities also offer anonymity, which many people find highly refreshing in light of the much tighter social controls of village and small-town life. And the city offers work—of all kinds.

The term **metropolis** refers to a central city surrounded by smaller cities and their suburbs. They are connected economically, sometimes politically through county boards and regional governing bodies, and physically by ties of transportation and communication.

Some metropolises have grown so large and influential that the term **megalopolis** is used to describe them. This term refers to an overlapping area consisting of at least two metropolises and their many suburbs. When a city's population hits 10 million, it is called a *megacity*. In 1950, New York City and Tokyo were the only two megacities in the world. Today, there are 22, including Manila, Shanghai, Lagos, Buenos Aires, and Mexico City. There are no Canadian megacities.

Urban Patterns in Canada

In 1871, only 18 percent of the Canadian population lived in what could be called small cities. Industrialization had not taken off in Canada, so these early cities were geographically small with limited transportation routes connecting the various districts. By 1921, however, in a period of rapid industrialization that saw the influx of thousands of European immigrants, the percentage of Canadians living in cities had jumped to almost half the population. Today, if we rely on Statistics Canada's definition of "urban," over four-fifths of Canadians live in cities. The Statistics Canada definition of urban as 1000 people or more has recently been criticized as overstating the urban character of Canada (MacGregor, 2007).

Not all cities are the same size, however, nor do they grow at the same rate or carry the same commercial or financial weight. There is a hierarchy of urban centres in Canada.

One measure of the importance of cities in Canada is based on population size and its rate of growth over a period of time. In some instances, several towns expand until they run together and form a continuous urban area even though their municipal governments are still separate. Federal statisticians classify a continuous, built-up region of this kind with a population of 100 000 or more as a census metropolitan area (CMA).

Between 1996 and 2001, 6 of the 10 fastest-growing census metropolitan areas were located in Ontario: Oshawa, Toronto, Kitchener, Windsor, Ottawa-Hull, and Hamilton, in that order. The remaining CMAs were Edmonton (third place), Vancouver (fourth place), Abbotsford (Quebec), and Ottawa-Hull (Quebec part). However, between 2006 and 2011, the pattern of growth shifted westward. The four fastest growing cities were Calgary, at 12.6 percent; Edmonton, at 12.1 percent; Saskatoon, at 11.4 percent, and Kelowna, at 10.8 percent. But in sheer numbers, the Greater Toronto Area (GTA) is the country's most populous city, with a growth rate of 5.1 percent and a population (not including Oshawa) of 5.6 million.

Models of Urban Growth

The Concentric Zone Model

To explain how cities expand, using Chicago as his model city, sociologist Ernest Burgess (1925) proposed a *concentric-zone model*. As shown in segment A of Figure 17.6, Burgess noted that a city expands outward from its centre.

Burgess observed, however, that no "city fits perfectly this ideal scheme." Some cities have physical obstacles, such as lakes, rivers, or railroads, which cause their expansion to depart from the model (Palen, 1987; Milbank, 1995a).

The Sector Model

Sociologist Homer Hoyt (1939, 1971) noted that a city's concentric zones do not form a complete circle, and modified Burgess's model of urban growth. As shown in segment B of Figure 17.6, a concentric zone might contain several sectors—one of working-class housing, another of expensive homes, a third of businesses, and so on—all competing for the same land.

What sociologists call an **invasion-succession cycle** is an example of the dynamic competition of urban life. When poor immigrants or migrants enter a city, they settle in the lowest-rent areas. As their numbers swell, they spill over into adjacent areas. Upset at their presence, the middle class moves out, thus expanding the sector of low-cost housing. The invasion-succession cycle is never complete, because later, another group will replace this earlier one, or it may be gentrified by other migrants. **Gentrification** is the movement of middle-class people into rundown areas of a city. They are attracted by low prices for quality housing that can be restored. Montreal's famous St. Urban/St. Lawrence Boulevard corridor has been the home of Jewish, Italian, Portuguese, Spanish, and other ethnic groups for the past 100 years. Vancouver's Victoria-Fraserview neighbourhood and Toronto's Cabbagetown and Spadina Avenue corridors are other examples.

The Multiple-Nuclei Model

Geographers Chauncey Harris and Edward Ullman observed that some cities have several centres or nuclei (Harris & Ullman, 1945; Ullman & Harris, 1970). As shown in segment C of Figure 17.6, each nucleus is the focus of some specialized activity. A familiar example is the clustering of malls and fast-food restaurants in one area

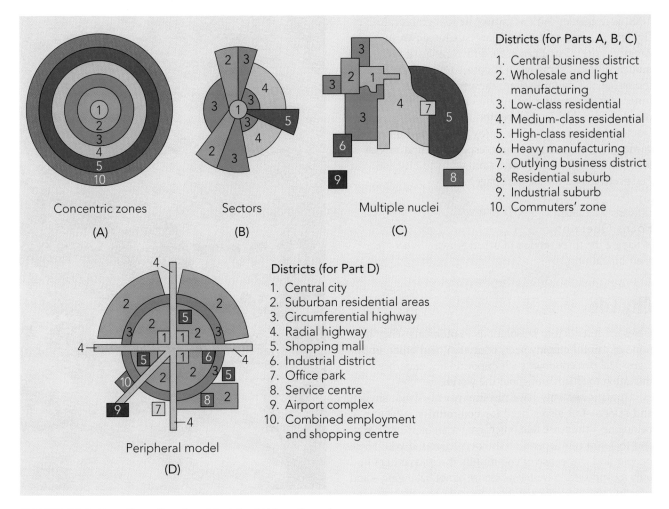

Districts (for Parts A, B, C)

1. Central business district
2. Wholesale and light manufacturing
3. Low-class residential
4. Medium-class residential
5. High-class residential
6. Heavy manufacturing
7. Outlying business district
8. Residential suburb
9. Industrial suburb
10. Commuters' zone

Concentric zones (A)

Sectors (B)

Multiple nuclei (C)

Districts (for Part D)

1. Central city
2. Suburban residential areas
3. Circumferential highway
4. Radial highway
5. Shopping mall
6. Industrial district
7. Office park
8. Service centre
9. Airport complex
10. Combined employment and shopping centre

Peripheral model (D)

FIGURE 17.6 How Cities Develop: Models of Urban Growth

Sources: Cousins & Nagpaul (1970); Harris (1997).

and automobile dealerships in another. Thus, push-pull factors separate areas by activities, and services are not evenly spread throughout an urban area.

The Peripheral Model

Chauncey Harris (1997) developed the peripheral model, shown in segment D of Figure 17.6. This model portrays the impact of radial highways on the movement of people and services away from a city's periphery or outskirts. It also shows the development of industrial and office parks.

Critique of the Models

These models tell only part of the story. For one thing, they are time-bound, for medieval cities didn't follow these patterns. In addition, they do not account for urban planning policies. England, for example, has planning laws that preserve green belts (trees, farmlands) around its cities. This prevents urban sprawl: Walmart cannot buy land outside the city and put up a store, but instead must locate in the downtown core. Norwich, England, has 250 000 people, yet the city suddenly ends, and in its green belt, pheasants skitter across plowed fields while sheep graze in verdant meadows (Milbank, 1995b).

Like Chicago, the three largest cities of Canada—Montreal, Toronto, and Vancouver—grew in relation to a body of water. For Montreal, it was the St. Lawrence River; Toronto, Lake Ontario; and Vancouver, the Strait of Georgia and the Pacific Ocean. Due to a number of factors, including Canada's constitution, innovative urban planning, and coalitions of various interest groups in each city, these cities have reversed the patterns identified above. With its dynamic linguistic and territorial duality, Montreal can claim an old-world character epitomized by Old Montreal and the Vieux Port and the largest gay village in the country. Toronto's Harbourfront, a 28.3-hectare (70 acre) property along Lake Ontario, mixes recreational, cultural, residential, and commercial elements (Church, Greenberg, & McPhedran, 1997). Vancouver boasts the

1000-acre Stanley Park as part of its topographical diversity and is home to the third-largest Chinatown in North America after San Francisco and New York City. The models also fall short when it comes to cities in the least industrialized nations. Here, the wealthy often claim the inner city, where fine restaurants and other services are readily accessible. Tucked behind tall walls and protected from public scrutiny, they enjoy luxurious homes and gardens. In contrast, the poor, especially rural migrants, settle unclaimed fringe areas outside the city (see the Perspectives box on the next page).

Focus Question

What are the three models of urban growth? What are their limitations?

City Life

Cities are intended to be solutions to problems. They hold hope of gainful employment, education, and other advantages. The perception of such opportunities underlies mass migration to cities throughout the world.

Humans not only have physical needs—food, shelter, and safety—but also a need for **community**, a feeling of belonging—the sense that others care what happens to you, and that you can depend on the people around you. Some people find this sense of community in cities; others find only its opposite, *alienation*—a sense of not belonging—and a feeling that no one cares what happens to you. Let's look at these two aspects of city life.

Alienation in the City

Why should cities be alienating? If you live in a large city, you know that impersonality and self-interest are ordinary characteristics. As you navigate city streets, you can expect people to avoid needless interaction with others and to be absorbed in their own affairs. The ubiquitous iPod or similar MP3 device strapped around a head sends a clear signal to everyone on the street—"I am in my own space, thank you. Don't bother me." These are adjustments that people have made to deal with the crowds of strangers with whom they temporarily share the same urban space. Another example of people avoidance is travelling on either the Montreal Metro or Toronto's subway system.

Lacking identification with one another, people often develop an attitude of "It's simply none of my business." In short, the very sense of personal freedom that the city provides may come, for some, at the cost of alienation.

Community

The city is more than a mosaic of strangers who feel disconnected and distrustful of one another. It is also made up of a series of smaller worlds, within which people find

The types of dwellers Gans identified as ethnic villagers find community in cities. Living in tightly knit neighbourhoods, they know many other residents. Some first-generation immigrants have even come from the same village in the "old country."

community, a sense of belonging. Here they live, work, shop, and play. Slums, which to outsiders seem threatening, provide a sense of belonging. In a classic study, sociologist Herbert Gans (1962) noted:

> After a few weeks of living in the West End [of Boston], my observations—and my perceptions of the area—changed drastically. Since much of the area's life took place on the street, faces became familiar very quickly. I met my neighbours on the stairs and in front of my building. And, once a shopping pattern developed, I saw the same storekeepers frequently, as well as the area's "characters" who wandered through the streets on a fairly regular route and schedule.

Living in Boston's West End, Gans gained an insider's perspective. He had located a community, discovering that its residents visited back and forth with relatives and were

✽ **Explore** Ferdinand Tonnies's "Gemeinschaft and Gesellschaft" on **MySocLab**.

Cultural Diversity around the World: Urbanization in the Least Industrialized Nations

Thoughts of the least industrialized nations often conjure images of people tending animals or harvesting crops, enjoying a peaceful life in the lush, green countryside or along babbling brooks. Such images no longer represent the reality faced by most people in the least industrial nations—if they ever did. The rural poor of these countries are flocking to the cities at such a rate that the least industrialized nations now contain most of the world's largest cities. In the most industrialized nations, industrialization generally preceded urbanization, but in the least industrialized nations urbanization is preceding industrialization. These cities cannot support their swelling populations.

Settlement patterns are also different in these cities. When rural migrants and immigrants move to U.S. cities, they usually settle in deteriorating housing near a city's centre. The wealthy reside in suburbs and luxurious city enclaves. Migrants to cities of the least industrialized nations, in contrast, establish illegal squatter settlements outside cities. They build shacks from scrap boards, cardboard, and bits of corrugated metal. Even flattened tin cans are scavenged for building material. Squatters enjoy no city facilities— roads, public transportation, water,

sewers, or garbage pickup. After thousands of squatters have settled an area, the city reluctantly acknowledges their right to live there and adds busservices and minimal water lines. Hundreds of people use a single spigot. About 5 million of Mexico City's residents live in such squalid conditions, with hundreds of thousands more pouring in each year.

At the bottom of a ravine near Mexico City is a dismal bunch of shacks. Some of the parents in the small community have up to 14 children. "We used to live up there," Señora Gonzalez gestured toward the mountain, "in those caves. Our only hope was one day to have a place to live. And now we do." She smiled with pride at the jerry-built shacks. Each one had a collection of flowers planted in tin cans. "One day, we hope to extend the water pipes and drainage—perhaps even pave . . . "

What was the name of this community? Señora Gonzalez beamed. "Esperanza!" (McDowell, 1984: 172). *Esperanza* is the Spanishword for hope. This is what lies behind the rush to cities—the hope of a better life. This is also why the rush won't slow down. In 1930, only one Latin American city had over a million people—now 50 do! The

world's cities are growing by a million people each week (Brockerhoff, 2000).

Why is there a rush to live in cities under such miserable conditions? At its core are the "push" factors that arise from a breakdown of traditional rural life. With a safer water supply and the importation of modern medicine, the death rate in rural areas drops. As a result, rural populations multiply, and there is no longer enough land for parents to divide up among their children. Without land or jobs, there is hunger. People are deeply dissatisfied with the resulting hardscrabble character of rural life. There are also "pull" factors that draw people to cities— jobs, schools, housing, and even a more stimulating life.

Will the least industrialized nations adjust to this vast migration? They have no choice. Authorities in Brazil, Guatemala, Venezuela, and other countries have sent in the police and even the army to evict settlers. It doesn't work. It just leads to violence, and settlers keep streaming in. The adjustments are painful. Infrastructure (roads, water, sewers, electricity, and so on) must be built, but poor countries don't have the resources to build them. As the desperate rural poor flock to the cities, the problems only worsen.

This photo taken in Brazil illustrates the settlement pattern common in the least industrialized and industrializing nations.

involved in extensive networks of friendships and acquaintances. Gans therefore titled his book *The Urban Villagers* (1962).

Types of Urban Dwellers

Whether you find alienation or community in city life largely depends on who you are, for the city offers both. People from different backgrounds experience the city differently. Gans (1962, 1968, 1991) identified the types of people who live in the city. The first three types live in cities by choice and have found a sense of community.

THE COSMOPOLITANS   The cosmopolitans are a city's students, intellectuals, professionals, musicians, artists, and entertainers. They value its conveniences and cultural benefits.

THE SINGLES   Young, unmarried people, who may team up to rent apartments, come to a city seeking jobs and entertainment. Businesses and services such as singles bars, singles apartment complexes, and computer dating services cater to their needs. Their stay in the city often reflects a temporary stage in their life course. After they marry, many move to the suburbs, where housing is usually cheaper than in the city core.

THE ETHNIC VILLAGERS   These people live in tightly knit neighbourhoods that resemble villages and small towns. United by race/ethnicity and social class, their neighbourhoods place an emphasis on family and friends. By doing so, they try to isolate themselves from the dangers and problems of urban life.

THE TRAPPED   This group of people have little choice about where they live. Outcasts of industrial society, they are alienated and always skirting the edge of disaster. They consist of four subtypes: those who could not afford to move when their neighbourhood was "invaded" by another ethnic group; elderly people who are not wanted elsewhere; alcoholics and other drug addicts; and the "downwardly mobile," people who have fallen from a higher social class. The trapped suffer high rates of assault, mugging, robbery, and rape. The homeless are made up of all four types of urban dwellers.

While not complete, Gans's typology provides insight into the variety of ways urban dwellers experience city life. Some find the streets a stimulating source of cultural contrasts. For others, however, the same events pose a constant threat as they try to survive in what for them amounts to an urban jungle.

Focus Question

Why has the world's population tended to move into urban settlements?

Urban Sentiment: Finding a Familiar World

Sociologists note that *the city is divided into little worlds* that people come to know, down to their smallest details. Gregory Stone (1954) and Herbert Gans (1970) observed how city people create a sense of intimacy for themselves by personalizing their shopping. By frequenting the same stores, they become recognized as "regulars," and after a period of time customers and clerks greet each other by name. Particular taverns, restaurants, laundromats, and shops are more than just buildings in which to purchase items and services. They become meeting places where neighbourhood residents build social relationships with one another and share informal news about the community.

Spectator sports also help urban dwellers find a familiar world (Hudson, 1991). When the Hamilton Tiger-Cats won the Grey Cup in 1999, the city of Hamilton celebrated the victory of "their" team with a downtown parade and week-long festivities. And when the underdog Toronto Argonauts won in 2004, the victory parade went from Union Station north up Bay Street and ended in Nathan Phillips Square. The 2007 Grey Cup, the Battle of the Underdogs, ended with the Saskatchewan Roughriders as the victors. The ninety-ninth Grey Cup was won by the B.C. Lions, and last year marked the hundredth anniversary of the event, which was hosted by Toronto. Sociologists David Karp and William Yoels (1990) note that such identification is so intense that long after moving to other parts of the country, many people maintain an emotional allegiance to the sports teams of the city in which they grew up.

As sociologists Richard Wohl and Anselm Strauss (1958) observed, city dwellers even develop strong feelings for particular objects and locations in the city, such as buildings, rivers, lakes, parks, and even trees and street corners. In some cases, objects become a type of logo that represents the city—for example, Kensington Market in Toronto, the Latin Quarter in Montreal, or Granville Island in Vancouver.

Urban dwellers find community not in buildings and space, then, but in their social relationships. Regardless of where they live in the city, people who are not integrated into social networks find alienation, while those who are integrated find community.

Suburbanization

Suburbanization, which refers to people moving from cities to **suburbs**—the communities located just outside a city—is not new. The dream of a place of one's own with green grass, a few trees, and kids playing in the yard was not discovered by this generation (Riesman, 1970). For the past 100 years or so, as transportation became more efficient, especially with the development of automobiles, people have moved to towns next to the cities in which they work.

Deindustrialization and Globalization

The development of a global market has left a heavy imprint on Canadian cities. As sociologist Victor Rodríguez (1994) points out, to compete in the global market, many industries have abandoned local communities and moved their factories to places where labour costs are lower. This process has eliminated millions of manufacturing jobs, locking many poor people out of the postindustrial economy engulfing some cities in Canada. They are forced to move, usually taking lower-paying jobs in call centres and large box stores such as Walmart and Home Depot. Many live in despair as a distant economy charges into the uncharted waters of a brave new world without them.

THE ENVIRONMENT

The Natural Environment

The opening vignette pointed out how the Harper government continues to muzzle Canadian scientists working with Environment Canada on projects of international ecological import from discussing their work with the media. What would bring our federal government to act in such an underhanded way? Why would this government appear to be afraid of what scientists might say?

Environmental Problems of Past Civilizations

Contrary to common assumptions, environmental problems are not new to human existence. Several civilizations destroyed themselves by destroying the environments on which their very existence depended.

The most famous is the fall of Mesopotamia, a civilization that was located in the lush river basin of the Tigris and Euphrates in what is now Iraq. About 3000 years before Christ, this civilization flourished as a result of an extensive irrigation system that provided abundant food. Without proper drainage, the water constantly evaporated, gradually growing saltier. Over centuries, the underground water table rose, and the land became too salty to support crops. The Mesopotamians had unwittingly destroyed the agricultural base on which their civilization depended (Jacobsen & Adams, 1958). What once was beautiful, lush, green land that produced fruits, vegetables, and grains in abundance is now desert.

Environmental Problems in the Most Industrialized Nations

Although environmental degradation is not new, the frontal assault on the natural environment did not begin in earnest until nations industrialized. The more extensive the industrialization, the better it was considered for a nation's welfare, and the slogan for the most industrialized nations has been "Growth at any cost."

Industrial growth progressed, but at a high cost to the natural environment. Today, many formerly pristine streams are polluted sewers. Most major Canadian cities have daily air pollution indexes. Montreal's McGill subway station, for example, posts the changing daily pollution count on an overhead electronic bulletin board for commuters to easily see. During the summer months, nearly all Canadian radio and television news programs report on the sun's ultraviolet radiation by telling listeners and viewers how long it is safe to stay outside without sun protection.

Of all the consequences of pollution we could discuss, we will consider—due to space limitations—only the implications of fossil fuels.

FOSSIL FUELS AND ENVIRONMENTAL DEGRADATION The burning of fossil fuels for factories, motorized vehicles, and power plants has been especially harmful to the environment. Fish can no longer survive in some lakes in Canada and the northeastern United States because of **acid rain**. As illustrated in Figure 17.7, acid rain is created when the burning of fossil fuels releases sulphur dioxide and nitrogen oxide, which react with moisture in the air to become sulphuric and nitric acids (Sawyer, 2001).

An invisible but more serious consequence is the **greenhouse effect**. Like the glass of a greenhouse, the gases emitted from burning fossil fuels allow sunlight to enter the earth's atmosphere freely, but inhibit the release of heat. It is as though the gases have closed the atmospheric window through which our planet breathes. The world's scientists have concluded that the resulting **global warming**, or climate change, will melt the polar icecaps and inundate the world's shorelines, causing the climate boundaries to move several hundred kilometres north and making many animal

✱ Explore "World Energy Consumption" and how it varies in different regions on **MySocLab**.

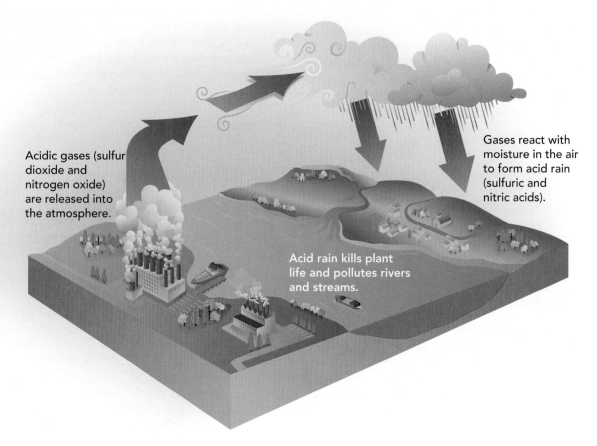

Acidic gases (sulfur dioxide and nitrogen oxide) are released into the atmosphere.

Gases react with moisture in the air to form acid rain (sulfuric and nitric acids).

Acid rain kills plant life and pollutes rivers and streams.

FIGURE 17.7 Acid Rain

and plant species extinct (Kanter & Revkin, 2007; Smith & Tirpak, 1988; P. Thomas, 1988; Weisskopf, 1992).

THE ENERGY SHORTAGE AND MULTINATIONAL CORPORATIONS If you have ever read about an energy shortage, you can be sure the report was false. There is no energy shortage, nor can there ever be. The earth holds the potential of producing unlimited low-cost power, which can help raise the living standards of humans across the globe. The sun, for example, produces more energy than humanity could ever use. Boundless energy is also available from the tides and the winds. In some cases, we need better technology to harness these sources of energy; in others, we need only apply technology we already have.

Since burning fossil fuels in internal combustion engines is the main source of pollution in the most industrialized nations, and vast sources of alternative energy are available, why don't we develop the technology to use these alternative sources? From a conflict perspective, alternative sources of energy threaten multinational corporations' oil monopoly. To maintain their profits, these corporations make certain that internal combustion engines remain dominant. The practical development and

widespread use of alternative sources of power will wait until the multinationals have cornered the market on the technology that will harness them—so they can continue reaping huge profits.

Environmental Injustice

Unequal power has led to **environmental injustice**, with minority groups and the poor suffering the most from the effects of pollution (Mohai & Saha, 2007). Industries locate where land is cheaper, which is not where the wealthy live. Nor will the rich allow factories to spew pollution near their homes (a phenomenon often referred to as NIMBY—not in my backyard). As a result, low-income communities, which are often inhabited by minorities, are more likely to

Watch the video "World Climate Change" on **MySocLab**.

Watch the video "Everything's Cool" on **MySocLab**.

Listen to "Sources of Global Warming" on **MySocLab**.

Explore the reading "Dumping in Dixie: Race, Class, and the Politics of Place" on **MySocLab**.

be exposed to pollution. Sociologists have studied, formed, and joined environmental justice groups that fight to close polluting plants and block the construction of polluting industries.

Environmental Problems in the Industrializing and Least Industrialized Nations

INDUSTRIALIZING NATIONS Negative environmental consequences of industrialization, such as ozone depletion, the greenhouse effect, and global warming, cannot be blamed solely on the most industrialized nations. With their rush to be contenders in global competition, the lack of funds to purchase pollution controls, and few anti-pollution laws, the industrializing nations make their own enormous contributions to this problem. Breathing the polluted air of Mexico City, for example, is the equivalent of smoking two packs of cigarettes a day (Durbin, 1995).

The former Soviet Union is a special case. Until this empire broke up, pollution had been treated as a state secret. Scientists and journalists were forbidden to mention pollution in public. Even peaceful demonstrations to call attention to the problem could net participants two years in prison (Feshbach, 1992). With protest stifled and no environmental protection laws, environmental pollution was everywhere: almost half of Russia's arable land is unsuitable for farming, about a third of Russians live in cities where air pollution is over 10 times greater than levels permitted in Canada, and half of Russia's tap water is unfit to drink. Pollution is so severe that it is likely a contributor to the drop in life expectancy that has occurred in Russia. If so, it is a lesson that should not be lost on the rest of us as we make decisions on how to treat our environment.

LEAST INDUSTRIALIZED NATIONS The great poverty and swelling populations of the least industrialized nations, combined with almost non-existent environmental regulations, destine these countries to become major sources of pollution.

Their lack of environmental protection laws has not gone unnoticed by opportunists in the most industrialized nations, who have seized the opportunity to use these countries as garbage dumps for hazardous wastes and for producing chemicals that their own nations will no longer tolerate (LaDou, 1991; C.S. Smith, 1995). Alarmed at the growing environmental destruction, the World Bank, a monetary arm of the most industrialized nations, has put pressure on the least industrialized nations to reduce pollution and soil erosion (Lachica, 1992). The basic concern of these nations is to produce food and housing first, and to worry about the environment later.

RAIN FORESTS AND EXTINCTION Holding unknown consequences for the future of humanity is the extinction of numerous plant and animal species as tropical rain forests are relentlessly cleared for lumber, farms, and pastures. Although rain forests cover just 7 percent of the earth's land area, they are home to half of its plant species. With these forests disappearing at a rate of nearly 2500 acres (1012 hectares) every hour (McCuen, 1993), it is estimated that 10 000 species become extinct every year—about one per hour (Durning, 1990). As rain forests are destroyed, so are the native communities that live in them.

Canada and the Kyoto Protocol

The Kyoto Protocol is an agreement entered into by a number of countries that is intended to reduce greenhouse gases (climate change) and thereby contribute to sustainable global development. However, not all national leaders support the goals of the protocol and some don't believe global warming is a problem, even though the world's top 2000 climate experts are all on side.

The Kyoto Protocol came into effect on February 16, 2005, prior to which signing nations were required to "ratify" the protocol—commit to achieving the goals set out in it. The Canadian Parliament ratified on December 17, 2002. One hundred and forty-one countries ratified Kyoto, with the most glaring exception being the largest single polluter in the world: the United States. The United States is responsible for about a quarter of the greenhouse gas emissions believed to be causing climate change.

Canada became the first country to withdraw from the Kyoto Protocol when Peter Kent, Minister of the Environment in the Harper government, made the announcement after returning from a UN conference on climate change in Durban, South Africa, in December 2011. This action means Canada has abandoned the world's only legally binding plan to tackle climate change.

The Environmental Movement

Concern about environmental problems has produced a worldwide social movement. In some countries, political parties built around environmental concerns, called *green parties*, campaign in local and national elections. In Europe, especially Germany, green parties have become a political force and have won seats in the national legislatures.

Activists in the environmental movement generally seek solutions in politics, legislation, and education. Seeing that pollution continues, the rain forests are still being cleared, and species are becoming extinct, some activists

((•● Listen to "Amazon Rainforest Update" on **MySocLab.**

✱ **Explore** the MySocLab eReading "Was Rachel Carson Wrong?" on **MySocLab.**

Ecosabotage

Chaining oneself to a giant Douglas fir slated for cutting; pouring sand down the gas tank of a bulldozer; tearing down power lines and ripping up survey stakes; driving spikes into redwood trees; and sinking whaling vessels—are these the acts of dangerous punks, intent on vandalism and with little understanding of the needs of modern society? Or are they the acts of brave men and women willing to put their freedom, and even their lives, on the line on behalf of the planet?

How many 3000-year-old trees remain on Earth? Do fences and picnic tables for backyard barbecues justify cutting them down? Questions like these, as well as the slaughter of seals, the destruction of rain forests, and the drowning of dolphins in mile-long drift nets spawned Earth First! and other organizations devoted to preserving the environment, such as Greenpeace, Sea Shepherds, and the Ruckus Society.

"We feel like there are insane people who are consciously destroying our environment, and we are compelled to fight back," explains a member of one of the militant groups. "No compromise in defence of Mother Earth!" says another. "With famine and death approaching, we're in the early stages of World War III," adds another.

The dedication of some of these activists has brought them close to martyrdom. When Paul Watson, founder of the Sea Shepherds, sprayed seals with green dye, which destroys the value of their pelts but doesn't hurt the animals, hunters hog-tied him, dragged him across the ice, and threatened to toss him into the sea. "It's no big deal," says Watson, "when you consider that 100 million people in this century have died in wars over real estate."

Radical environmentalists represent a broad range of activities and purposes. They are united on neither tactics nor goals. Some want to stop a specific action, such as the killing of whales, or to destroy all nuclear weapons and dismantle nuclear power plants. Others want everyone to become vegetarians. Still others want the earth's population to be reduced to 1 billion, roughly what it was in 1800. Some even want humans to return to hunting and gathering bands. Most espouse a simpler lifestyle that will consume less energy and put less pressure on the earth's resources. These groups are so splintered that the founder of Earth First!, Dave Foreman, quit his own organization when it became too confrontational for his tastes.

Among their successes, the radical groups can count a halt to the killing of dolphins off Japan's Iki Island, a ban on whaling, trash recycling in many communities, and hundreds of thousands of acres of uncut trees.

For Your Consideration

Who are these people? Should we applaud ecosaboteurs or jail them? As symbolic interactionists stress, it depends on your definition. According to conflict theorists, your definition likely depends on your location in the economic structure. That is, if you are the owner of a lumber company, you will likely have a negative image of ecosaboteurs and will not view the actions of your company the way many Native Canadians do—as the destruction of Mother Earth. How does your own view of ecosaboteurs depend on your life situation? What effective alternatives to ecosabotage are there for people convinced we are destroying the life support system of our planet?

Sources: Russell (1987); Borrelli (1988); Guha (1989); Carpenter (1990); Eder (1990); Foote (1990); Martin (1990); Parfit (1990); Reed & Benet (1990); Courtney (1995).

As concern about the environment grows, a social movement to try to change the course of events has developed. Protest groups have rallied around numerous issues, including the seal hunt, whaling, and the destruction of old-growth forests on Canada's west coast.

TABLE 17.2 Comparison of Competing Paradigms, Selected Items

New Environmental Paradigm	Dominant Sociological Paradigm
I. High valuation of nature	*I. Lower valuation of nature*
Environmental protection over economic growth	Human domination over nature
II. Generalized compassion	*II. Compassion only for those near and dear*
Concern for other species, peoples, and generations	Concern for present generation only
III. Careful planning and acting to avoid risk	*III. Acceptance of risk to maximize wealth*
Regulation to protect nature and humans is the government's responsibility	Deregulation by governments—individual responsibility
IV. Limits to growth	*IV. No limits to growth*
Conservation	Production and consumption
V. Completely new society	*V. Present society fine (maintain the status quo)*
Openness and participation	Competition and emphasis on the market
VI. New Politics	*VI. Old Politics*
Emphasis on foresight and planning	Emphasis on market control

Source: Canadian Society: Meeting the Challenges of the Twenty-First Century, 2001, Dan Glenday and Ann Duffy, eds. Toronto: Oxford University Press, copyright © 2001.

are convinced that the planet is doomed unless immediate steps are taken. Choosing a more radical course, they use extreme tactics to try to arouse indignation among the public and thus force governments to act. Convinced that they stand for morality, many are willing to break the law and go to jail for their actions. Such activists are featured in the Thinking Critically about Social Controversy box below.

Environmental Sociology

Environmental sociology, which examines the relationship between human societies and the environment, emerged as a subdiscipline of sociology around 1970 (Dunlap & Catton 1979, 1983; Buttel, 1987; Freudenburg & Gramling, 1989; Laska, 1993). Its main assumptions are:

1. The physical environment is a significant variable of sociological investigation.
2. Human beings are one species among many that are dependent on the natural environment.
3. Because of intricate feedbacks to nature, human actions have many unintended consequences.
4. The world is finite, so there are potential physical limits to economic growth.
5. Economic expansion requires increased extraction of resources from the environment.
6. Increased extraction of resources leads to ecological problems.

7. These ecological problems place restrictions on economic expansion.
8. Governments create environmental problems by trying to establish conditions for the accumulation of capital.

The goal of environmental sociology is not to stop pollution or nuclear power, but rather to study how humans (their cultures, values, and behaviours) affect the physical environment and how the physical environment affects human activities. Environmental sociologists, however, are generally also environmental activists.

Kathleen Riel is an environmental sociologist in Canada who has written extensively on matters affecting our environment. In Table 17.2, she provides contrasting views of society as seen from environmental and traditional sociological perspectives.

Focus Question

What is the relationship between our physical environment and sociological theory?

Ecofeminism and the Environment

Ecofeminists believe human beings are connected to one another and to the nonhuman world—animal, vegetable, or mineral. They point out that we do violence to each other and to nature, congratulating ourselves on providing material abundance for some while militarily protecting our self-interests in the exploitation of the earth's natural resources, such as fossil fuels and other valuable minerals and ores.

They explain the harm done to humanity and the environment by pointing to patriarchy's hierarchical, dualistic, and oppressive ways of thinking. For example, women are "naturalized" when they are described in animal terms such as "foxes, cows, chicks, bird-brains" and so on, while nature is "feminized" when "she" is "raped, conquered, mastered, penetrated, subdued" or "worshipped" as the grandest "mother" of them all. In biblical terms, man is lord over nature and over nature's analogue, woman. These dualistic, hierarchical, and oppressive ways of thinking have brought humanity to the brink of disaster by disrespecting nature and women.

Ecofeminists disagree on the proper "solutions" to this social problem, but most agree that a fundamental and radical change in our thinking must be a necessary start. We can begin individually by respecting ourselves and nature and conserving resources through, for example, recycling and refusing to eat animals that have been grown under cruel conditions, and collectively by supporting environmental causes.

Technology and the Environment: The Goal of Harmony

It is inevitable that humans will continue to develop new technologies. The abuse of our environment by those technologies is not inevitable, however.

If we are to have a world that is worth passing on to coming generations, we must seek harmony between technology and the natural environment. This will not be easy. At one extreme are people who claim that to protect the environment we must eliminate industrialization and return to some sort of preindustrial way of life. At the other extreme are people unable to see the harm being done to the natural environment, and who want the entire world to continue industrializing at full speed. Somewhere, there must be a middle ground, one that recognizes that industrialization is here to stay but that we can control it, for it is our creation. Controlled industrialization can enhance our quality of life. As a parallel to the development of technologies, then, we must develop systems to reduce or eliminate their harm to the environment. This includes mechanisms to globally monitor the production, use, and disposal of technology. The question is whether we have the resolve to take the steps that will preserve the environment for future generations. The stakes—no less than the welfare of the entire planet—are surely high enough to motivate us to make the correct choices.

POPULATION IN GLOBAL PERSPECTIVE

A PLANET WITH NO SPACE TO ENJOY LIFE?

What debate did Thomas Malthus initiate?

In 1798, Thomas Malthus analyzed the surge in Europe's population. His conclusion, called the Malthus theorem, was that because the population grows geometrically but food only arithmetically, the world population will outstrip its food supply. The debate between today's New Malthusians and those who disagree, the Anti-Malthusians, continues, while feminists offer their own analysis and solutions. pp. 383–386.

Why are people starving?

Starvation is not due to a lack of food in the world, for there is now more food for every person on the planet than there was 50 years ago. Starvation is due, rather, to a maldistribution of food. pp. 386–387.

POPULATION GROWTH

Why do the poor nations have so many children?

In the least industrialized nations, children are generally viewed as gifts from God, cost little to rear, and represent parents' social security. Consequently, people are motivated to have large families. pp. 387–388.

What are the three demographic variables?

To compute population growth, demographers use *fertility*, *mortality*, and *migration*. The basic demographic equation is Births – Deaths + Net migration = Growth Rate. pp. 388–389.

Why is forecasting population difficult?

A nation's growth rate is affected by unanticipated variables—from economic conditions, wars, plagues, and famines to government policies and industrialization. pp. 389–390.

URBANIZATION

What is the relationship of cities to farming?

Cities can develop only if there is a large agricultural surplus, which frees people from having to participate in food production. The primary impetus to the development of cities was the invention of the plow about 5000 or 6000 years ago. pp. 390–391.

What are metropolises and megalopolises?

Urbanization is so extensive that some cities have become metropolises, dominating the areas adjacent to them. The areas of influence of some metropolises have merged, forming megalopolises. pp. 391–392.

MODELS OF URBAN GROWTH

What models of urban growth have been proposed?

The primary models are a concentric zone model, a sector model, and a multiple-nuclei model. These models fail to account for medieval cities, as well as many European cities and those in the least industrialized nations. pp. 392–394.

CITY LIFE

Is the city inherently alienating?

Some people experience alienation in the city; others find community. What people find depends largely on their background and urban networks. The types of people who live in cities are cosmopolitans, singles, ethnic villagers, and the trapped. pp. 394–397.

THE ENVIRONMENT

THE NATURAL ENVIRONMENT

What are the environmental problems of the most industrialized nations?

The environmental problems of the most industrialized nations are severe, ranging from city smog and acid rain to the greenhouse effect. Scientists debate whether the greenhouse effect is real; if it is, it may cause global warming that will fundamentally affect social life. The burning of fossil fuels in internal combustion engines lies at the root of many environmental problems, but alternative sources of energy are unlikely to be developed until the multinational corporations can turn them to profitable ventures. pp. 397–399.

What are the environmental problems of the industrializing and least industrialized nations?

Some of the worst environmental problems are found in the former Soviet Union, a legacy of the unrestrained exploitation of resources by the Communist Party. The rush of the least industrialized nations to industrialize is adding to our environmental decay. p. 399.

What is the kyoto protocol?

The Kyoto Protocol is an agreement, entered into by a number of countries, intended to reduce greenhouse gases (climate change) and thereby contribute to sustainable global development. However, Canada abandoned the agreement in a statement made by Peter Kent, Minister of the Environment, on December 12, 2011. p. 399.

What is the environmental movement?

The environmental movement is an attempt to restore a healthy environment for the world's people. This global movement takes many forms, from peacefully influencing the political process to ecosabotage, sabotaging the efforts of people thought to be harming the environment. pp. 399–401.

What is environmental sociology?

Environmental sociology is not an attempt to change the environment, but a study of the relationship between humans and the environment. Environmental sociologists are generally also environmental activists. p. 401.

ECOFEMINISM AND THE ENVIRONMENT

What is ecofeminism?

While there are several variants of ecofeminism, they all agree that the human and nonhuman worlds are interconnected. According to ecofeminists, patriarchy's hierarchical, dualistic, and oppressive ways of thinking explain the environmental predicament facing our planet today. pp. 401–402.

KEY TERMS

All URLs listed are current as of the printing of this text.

Environment Canada
www.ec.gc.ca
Environment Canada's internet resource for weather and environmental information.

WWICS Comparative Urban Studies Project
www.wilsoncenter.org/index.cfm?fuseaction=topics.home&topic_id=1410
This project of the Woodrow Wilson International Center for Scholars brings together scholars and policymakers to discuss problems of urban management from a multidisciplinary, multiregional perspective. Participants organize international conferences and disseminate findings through policy briefs, occasional papers, books, and other publications.

The Office of Population Research at Princeton University
http://opr.princeton.edu
The oldest population research centre in the United States. Many of its graduates occupy important professional positions in developing countries; others are on university faculties worldwide.

EnviroLink: The Online Environmental Community
www.envirolink.org
EnviroLink is a non-profit organization that has been providing access to thousands of online environmental resources since 1991.

1. Should governments try to limit population growth by using such traditional techniques as family planning?
2. All major municipalities in Canada have urban planners. However, their advice for more urban green space, for example, is often ignored because it conflicts with powerful economic interests that benefit from the increases in the price of land that result from building huge skyscrapers, stadiums, or other concrete structures in our cities. How would you try to resolve these conflicts of interest if you were an urban planner promoting the public use of a segment of waterfront or riverfront property in your city?
3. Why is there such a shortage of affordable housing in booming cities like Vancouver, Calgary, and Toronto?
4. Is it true that famine, overpopulation, and disease are destroying the social fabric of our planet? Access the Research Navigator through MySocLab and use keywords such as "famine" and "overpopulation" to locate relevant and recent scholarly and popular press publications to help you answer this question.

MySocLab

Explore the topics covered in this chapter on MySocLab. Interactive resources include a study plan, cumulative exams, a multimedia library, MySocLab eReadings, and access to the MySocLab Video Series.

18

SOCIAL MOVEMENTS AND SOCIAL CHANGE

LEARNING OUTCOMES

After you have studied this chapter, you will be able to answer the following questions:

1. How did early theorists explain the effects of crowds on individuals?
2. What forms of collective behaviour are there?
3. What types of social movements are there?
4. How do social movements select their tactics?
5. How are cellphones and social media related to the spread of social movements today?
6. Why do people join social movements?
7. What types of technology are there, and what effects can a changed technology have on society?
8. What are the contemporary theories of social change?

ON Friday, April 17, 2012, riot police used tear gas and concussion grenades on hundreds of students protesting outside Montreal's Palais des congrès, where Premier Jean Charest was speaking at a symposium on northern development.

The mayhem reached deep inside the convention centre, where Charest's keynote speech was delayed after a group of protesters gained access to the building and confronted police guarding the meetings. Two police officers and at least two protesters were injured in the standoff, and 17 people were arrested.

That day's action was the latest in a string of protests in Quebec's escalating student movement against planned tuition-fee increases. Student groups have organized near-daily demonstrations and declared an unlimited boycott on classes that have lasted nearly two months.

Source: Adapted by Daniel Glenday. "Violent Montreal student protest nets 17 arrests: Premier calls social disruption 'unacceptable,'" CBC News, April 20, 2012.

Why did students in Quebec decide to take to the streets to voice their concerns about a 75 percent increase in their tuition fees over the next five years? What tactics have they used to get the message out? Could some of the recent violence be the result of agent provocateurs? These questions will be addressed in this chapter.

Student protests spurred the Hungarian Uprising in 1956, France's May 1968 General Strike, and the Tiananmen Square massacre in Beijing, China, in 1989, to name just a few. Student demonstrations are an example of **collective behaviour**—a group of people bypassing the usual norms that guide their actions to engage in behaviour that violates social expectations (Turner & Killian, 1987; Lofland, 1993). As such, collective behaviour is group conduct that is considered socially deviant. Before examining its specific forms, we will discuss theories that seek to explain collective behaviour.

Early Explanations: The Transformation of the Individual

When people can't figure something out, they are apt to say, "He must have 'gone nuts,'" or he wouldn't have shot into the crowd." Early explanations of collective behaviour were not far from such assumptions. Let's look at how these ideas developed.

How the Crowd Transforms the Individual

The study of collective behaviour began when British journalist Charles Mackay (1814–1889) observed that "country folks," who ordinarily are reasonable sorts of

About 200 striking students entered the Palais des Congres in Montreal and delayed Premier Jean Charest's speech in April 2012.

people, sometimes "went mad" and did "disgraceful and violent things" in crowd situations. The best explanation Mackay (1852) could come up with was that people had a "herd mentality"—they were like a herd of cows that could suddenly stampede.

About 50 years later, Gustave LeBon (1841–1931) noted that people feel anonymous in crowds, less accountable for what they do. Some even develop feelings of invincibility and come to think that they can do virtually anything. A **collective mind** develops, he said, and people are swept up by almost any suggestion. Contagion, something like mass hypnosis, then takes over, releasing the destructive instincts that society so carefully represses.

The Acting Crowd

Herbert Blumer (1900–1987) synthesized LeBon's ideas with those of another sociologist, Robert Park. As shown in Figure 18.1, Blumer (1939) identified five stages that precede what he called an **acting crowd**, an excited group that moves toward a goal. This model still dominates today's police manuals on crowd behaviour (McPhail, 1989).

1. *Tension or unrest.* At the root of collective behaviour is a background condition of tension or unrest. An example of such a background condition occurred when the PC government of Mike Harris decided in 1997 to place control of Ontario's $14 billion public education system firmly in the hands of the provincial government, and by so doing, eliminate between 7500 and 10 000 jobs and cut billions of dollars from the education budget. As a result, five unions, representing 126 000 teachers, pulled their members out of the classroom and onto the streets of Ontario's cities and towns. This was the first Ontario-wide teachers' strike in more than two decades and the largest strike in Ontario history. It lasted two weeks, from November 3 to 16, 1997, with the leaders of the unions ultimately deciding that little more could be done to effect changes in government policy (Jenish, 1997: 18).

2. *Exciting event.* An exciting event occurs, one so startling that people become preoccupied with it. In the instance described at the beginning of this chapter, that event was students protesting Premier Jean Charest's speech on northern development.

3. *Milling.* Next comes **milling**, people standing or walking around, talking about the exciting event. A circular reaction then sets in. That is, as people pick up cues as to the "right" way of thinking and feeling and reinforce them in one another.

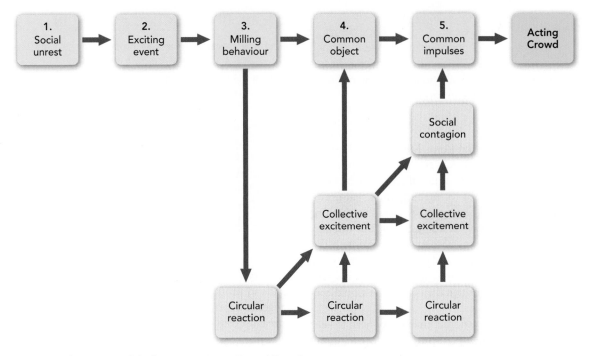

FIGURE 18.1 Blumer's Model of How an Acting Crowd Develops
Source: Based on McPhail (1991: 11).

4. *A common object of attention.* In this stage, people's attention becomes riveted on some aspect of the event. They get caught up in the collective excitement.

5. *Common impulses.* People get the feeling that they are in agreement about what should be done. These common impulses are stimulated by social contagion, a sense of excitement that is passed from one person to another.

Acting crowds aren't always negative or destructive, for they also include spontaneous demonstrations or sit-ins directed against oppression, such as Amnesty International's efforts to free political prisoners in many parts of the globe or the Ontario-wide teachers strike. Nor are they all serious—even "food fights" are acting crowds!

The Contemporary View: The Rationality of the Crowd

If we were to witness a large group of people "taking to the streets"—or a prison riot—most of us probably would agree with LeBon that some sort of "madness" had swept over the crowd. Sociologists today, however, point out that crowds are actually quite rational. By this, they mean that crowds take deliberate steps to reach some desired goal.

The Minimax Strategy

A general principle of capitalist behaviour is that we try to minimize our costs and maximize our rewards. Sociologist Richard Berk (1974) calls this a **minimax strategy**.

Most of the demonstrators at the 1997 APEC conference in Vancouver came from middle-class backgrounds. One of their goals was to increase public awareness of the corporate agenda of this transnational organization.

The fewer costs and the more rewards we anticipate from something, the more likely we are to do it. For example, if we believe that others will approve an act, the likelihood that we will do it increases. Whether in yelling for a referee's blood at a bad call in football, or shouting for the release of a political prisoner, this principle applies.

Emergent Norms

Sociologists Ralph Turner and Lewis Killian (1987) use the term **emergent norms** to express the idea that something new has happened. They suggest that life typically proceeds pretty much as we expect it to, making our usual norms adequate for dealing with everyday events. If something disrupts our customary ways of doing things, our ordinary norms may not cover the new situation. To deal with this situation, new norms may emerge. People may even develop novel definitions of right and wrong, feeling that the new circumstances justify actions that they otherwise would consider wrong.

To understand how new norms emerge, we need to keep in mind that not everyone in a crowd has the same point of view (Snow, Zurcher, & Peters, 1993; Rodríguez, 1994). Turner and Killian (1987) contend that there are five kinds of crowd participants:

1. The *ego-involved* feel a personal stake in the extraordinary event.
2. The *concerned* have a personal interest in the event, but less so than the ego-involved.
3. The *insecure* care little about the particular issue, but they join the crowd because it gives them a sense of power and security.
4. The *curious spectators* also care little about the issue, but they are inquisitive about what is going on.
5. The *exploiters* do not care about the event, but are entrepreneurial and use it for their own purposes, such as hawking food or T-shirts.

Most important for setting a crowd on a particular course of action are the *ego-involved*. Some make suggestions about what should be done; others simply start doing something. As the *concerned* join in, they, too, influence the crowd. If things heat up, the insecure and the *curious spectators* may also participate. Although the *exploiters* are unlikely to get involved, they do lend passive support to the crowd. Once a common mood develops, emergent norms are likely to replace the usual norms of accepted behaviour. Activities "not OK" in everyday life may now seem "OK"—whether throwing bottles at police officers or protesting a provincial government's cuts to public education or health care.

Focus Question
Why don't all sociologists describe collective behaviour in terms of emotions?

Forms of Collective Behaviour

Sociologists treat collective behaviour the same as other forms of behaviour (Turner & Killian, 1987; Lofland, 1993; Turner, 1993). They view it as ordinary people responding to extraordinary situations (Rodríguez, 1994). They ask their usual questions about interaction, such as: How do people influence one another? What is the significance of the members' age, gender, and social class? What role do pre-existing attitudes play? How are people's perceptions translated into action?

Collective behaviour takes many forms, including riots, panics, moral panics, rumours, fads, fashions, and urban legends. Let's look at each.

Riots or Demonstrations

An urban **riot** is violent crowd behaviour aimed against people and property and is usually caused by frustration and anger at deprivation. Frustration at being kept out of mainstream society—limited to a meagre education, denied jobs and justice, and kept out of good neighbourhoods—builds to such a boiling point that it takes only a precipitating event to erupt in collective violence.

Sociologists have found, however, that it is not only the deprived who participate in riots or **demonstrations**. During the June 2010 demonstration against the G20 summit in Toronto, over 400 people were arrested, while many others were bludgeoned and hosed with pepper spray by the police. The G20 is a group of 20 member nations that comprise half the world's economic strength and whose discussions centre on the global financial system and the world economy. Most of the demonstrators were university students, environmentalists, trade unionists, educators, and others from stable, middle-class backgrounds. When violence broke out late into the demonstration, the police reacted vigorously. A spokesman for Prime Minister Stephen Harper and then-Toronto mayor David Miller called the demonstrators "thugs." Why would middle-class people participate in demonstrations? The answer, says sociologist Victor Rodríguez (1994), is the same: frustration and anger. Even though most of the demonstrators had good jobs and were living middle-class lives, they understood the G20's view of globalization as socially and economically damaging to people all around the world. As a result of alleged abuse of police authority and breach of civil liberties, there have been demands from the Council of Canadians and the Canadian Civil Liberties Association, among others, for a public inquiry into the police response during the G20 summit.

* Explore the "Continuum of Collective Behaviour" on **MySocLab**.

* Explore the MySocLab eReading "Forget Freud, Forget Marx. Rioting, Above All, Is Fun" on **MySocLab**.

Panics

On the night before Halloween, a radio program of dance music was interrupted with a report that explosions had been observed on the surface of Mars. The announcer breathlessly added that a cylinder of unknown origin had been discovered embedded in the ground on a farm in New Jersey. The radio station then switched to the farm, where an alarmed reporter gave details of horrible-looking Martians coming out of the cylinder. Their weapons had destructive powers unknown to humans. An interview with an astronomer confirmed that Martians had invaded the Earth.

Nearly 6 million North Americans heard this broadcast by Orson Wells in 1938. In adapting his book *The War of the Worlds* for a radio play, H.G. Wells made an important change: under his direction, the play was written and performed to sound like a news broadcast about an invasion from Mars, a technique that was intended to heighten the dramatic effect. And it did! About a million listeners were frightened, and thousands panicked. Unknown numbers burst into tears, while thousands more grabbed weapons and hid in their basements or ran into the streets.

Of course, there was no invasion. Although the panic reactions to this radio program may appear humorous to us today, to anyone who is in a panic, the situation is anything but humorous. **Panic** occurs when people become so fearful that they cannot function normally, and may even flee.

Why did people panic? Psychologist Hadley Cantril (1941) attributed the result to widespread anxiety about world conditions. The Nazis were marching in Europe. War jitters, he said, created fertile ground for the broadcast to ignite a panic.

Contemporary analysts question whether there even was a panic, however. Sociologist William Bainbridge (1989) acknowledges that some people were frightened, but says most of this famous panic was an invention of the news media. Reporters found a good story and milked it, exaggerating as they went along.

Bainbridge points to a 1973 event in Sweden. To dramatize the dangers of atomic power, Swedish Radio broadcast a play about an accident at a nuclear power plant. Knowing about the 1938 broadcast in the United States, Swedish sociologists were waiting to see what would happen. Might some people fail to realize that it was a dramatization and panic at the threat of ruptured reactors spewing out radioactivity? The sociologists found no panic. A few people became frightened, and some telephoned family members and the police—reasonable responses, considering what they thought had occurred.

But the Swedish media reported a panic. Apparently, a reporter telephoned two police departments and learned that each had received calls from concerned citizens. With a deadline hanging over his head, the reporter decided to gamble. He reported that police and fire stations were jammed with citizens, that people were flocking to shelters, and that others were fleeing south (Bainbridge, 1989).

Panics do occur—which is why nobody has the right to shout "Fire!" in a public building when no such danger exists (if people fear immediate death, they will lunge toward the nearest exit in a frantic effort to escape). Such a panic occurred on January 7, 1995, at a 30-storey apartment building in suburban North York, Ontario. In the early morning hours, around 5 o'clock, residents were awoken by a fire alarm. Most on the lower floors were able to race out of the building, while others screamed from balconies as acrid smoke from a fire that had started on the fifth floor slowly gripped the whole building. In the end, six bodies—two men and four women, one of whom had been six months pregnant, were found dead in the smoke-filled stairwell. One eyewitness, who lived on the eighteenth floor, decided to leave her apartment and descend the stairwell to the ground floor. By the time she reached the eleventh floor, she said,

> The stairwell was full of panicking, half-asleep people carrying their pets, and then the smoke became so thick we couldn't go any further—everybody was choking—I knew we had to turn back, but we had to get everybody turned around because the stairwells were lined. It became even harder to breathe because you're puffing from climbing the stairs. (Canadian Press Newswire, January 5, 1995)

Sociologists have found what other researchers have discovered in analyzing disasters. Not everybody panics. In disturbances, many people continue to act responsibly. Sociologists use the term **role extension** to describe these actions.

Moral Panics

From the witch hunts of the Renaissance to the symbol of outcast and menace posed by "hooded" teenage boys and young adults in the United States and Great Britain, the sociological phenomenon known as **moral panic** occurs when large numbers of people become intensely concerned, even fearful, about some behaviour thought to threaten their accepted values and way of life by the activities of groups defined as socially deviant, and the fear is out of proportion to any supposed danger (Cauthen & Jasper, 1994; Goode & Ben-Yehuda, 1994). The threat is seen as enormous, and hostility builds toward those social deviant individuals thought responsible. Stanley Cohen (1972) labelled these socially deviant individuals as **folk devils**. Cohen and others (see Young, 1971) showed how agents of social control, particularly the police, magnified the pervasiveness of this kind of social deviance. They also demonstrated the media's part in this process and thus started to draw attention to the ideological function of the media in actively constructing meanings, rather than merely reflecting some supposedly shared reality.

Today, moral panics are fuelled by the media. Like other panics, moral panics centre around a sense of danger. Moral panics are further fuelled by **rumour**—information for which there is no discernible source and which is usually unfounded. For example, a rumour, still continuing, is that

Rumours have swirled around the Magic Kingdom's supposed plots to undermine the morality of youth. Could Mickey Mouse be a dark force, and children his victims? As humorous as this may seem, some have taken these rumours seriously.

missing children are sold to Satanists who abuse them sexually and then ritually murder them. This rumour is intensely believed by some, and has been supported by testimony from people who claim to have been involved in such sacrifices. But investigations by the police have uncovered no evidence to substantiate it.

Moral panics thrive on uncertainty and anxiety. Today's changing family serves up a rich source of anxiety. Concerns that children are receiving inadequate care because many mothers have left home to join the workforce become linked with thoughts of dangers to children from sinister sources lurking almost everywhere.

Focus Question

Why aren't all crowds destructive mobs?

Rumours

> In *Aladdin*, the handsome young title character murmurs, "All good children, take off your clothes." In *The Lion King*, Simba, the cuddly lion star, stirs up a cloud of dust that, floating off the screen, spells S-E-X.

A rumour is unverified information that is passed from one person to the next. Thriving in conditions of ambiguity, rumours function to fill in missing information (Turner, 1964; Shibutani, 1966). In response to the rumour that Disney plots to undermine the morality of youth, the filmmaker reports that Aladdin really says, "Scat, good tiger, take off and go." The line is hard to hear clearly, however, leaving enough ambiguity for others to continue to hear what they want, even to insist that it is an invitation to a teenage orgy. Similar ambiguity remains around Simba's dust.

Most rumours arise in a situation of ambiguity, only to dissipate when they are replaced by factual information—or by another rumour. For example, despite a publication ban about the brutal killing of Leslie Mahaffy and Kristin French during the 1993 trial of Karla Homolka and Paul Bernardo, rumours about the details of the crimes were said to be available on the internet for those curious enough to find them.

Why do people believe rumours? Three main factors have been identified. First, rumours deal with a subject that is important to an individual. Second, they replace ambiguity with some form of certainty. Third, they are attributed to a creditable source. An office rumour may be preceded by "Jane has it on good authority that . . . " or "Bill overheard the boss say that. . . ."

Fads and Fashions

A **fad** is a novel form of behaviour that briefly catches people's attention. The new behaviour appears suddenly and spreads by suggestion, imitation, and identification with people already involved in the fad. Publicity by the mass media also helps spread fads (Aguirre, Quarantelli, & Mendoza, 1993).

Sociologist John Lofland (1985) identified four types of fads. First are object fads, such as the Hula Hoop in the 1950s, pet rocks in the 1970s, the Rubik's Cube and Cabbage Patch Dolls in the 1980s, and pogs, beanie babies, and Pokémon in the 1990s. Second are activity fads, such as eating goldfish in the 1920s, bungee jumping in the 1990s, and tattooing and body piercing in the 1990s–2000s. Third are idea fads, such as astrology. Fourth are personality fads, such

((•● Listen to "Rumour Control" on **MySocLab.**

as Elvis Presley, Princess Diana, and Wayne Gretzky. Some fads are extremely short-lived, such as "streaking" (running naked in a public place) or "Tickle Me Elmo" dolls. When a fad lasts, it is called a **fashion**. Some fashions, as with clothing, are the result of a coordinated international marketing system that includes designers, manufacturers, advertisers, and retailers. Billions of dollars worth of clothing are sold by manipulating the tastes of the public. Fashion, however, also refers to hairstyles, home decorating, and even the design and colours of buildings. Lofland pointed out that fashion even applies to language, as demonstrated by these roughly comparable terms: "Neat!" in the 1950s, "Right on!" in the 1960s, "Really!" in the 1970s, "Awesome!" in the 1980s, and "Bad!" in the 1990s, and the resurrection of "cool," "hot," and "buddy" in the early twenty-first century.

Urban Legends

Jerry [or whoever] went to a nightclub last weekend. He met a good-looking woman, and they hit it off. They spent the night in a motel, and when he awoke the next morning, the woman was gone. When he went into the bathroom, he saw a message scrawled on the mirror in lipstick: "Welcome to the wonderful world of AIDS."

Urban legends are stories with an ironic twist that sound realistic but are false. Although untrue, they are usually told by people who believe that they happened.

Another rumour as urban legend recently making the rounds in Canada is that McDonald's is importing beef from South America.

McDonald's claims that there is not enough beef in Canada to support their restaurants. Well, we, Alberta cattle farmers, know that is not so. Our opinion is they are looking to save money at our expense. The sad thing is we are not good enough to provide beef. We Albertan farmers personally are no longer eating at McDonald's, which I am sure does not make a large impact, but if we pass this around maybe there will be an impact felt.

Folklorist Jan Brunvand (1981, 1984, 1986) reported that urban legends are passed on by people who think that the event happened just one or two people down the line of transmission, often to a "friend of a friend." Brunvand views urban legends as "modern morality stories," each teaching a moral lesson about life.

If we apply Brunvand's analysis to these two urban legends, three major points emerge. First, their moral serves as a warning. "The wonderful world of AIDS" warns young people that they should be careful about where they go, with whom they go, and what they do. The world is an unsafe place, and "messing around" without proper protection is risky. McDonald's importing beef from South America contains a different moral: Do you really know the sources of what we eat in fast food restaurants?

Second, each story is related to social change: "The wonderful world of AIDS" to changing sexual morality; McDonald importing South American beef to globalization. Third, each is calculated to instill guilt and fear: guilt—failing to protect your family—and fear, the dangerous unknown—whether unprotected sex, tainted beef, or West Nile virus. Brunvand suggests that most urban legends have a very morally conservative tone to them.

SOCIAL MOVEMENTS

Social movements consist of large numbers of people who organize to promote or resist social change. They have strong ideas about what is wrong with the world—or some part of it—and how to make things right. Examples include the temperance or MADD movement, the women's movement, the animal rights crusade, the Quebec sovereignty movement, and the environmental movement.

At the heart of social movements lie grievances and dissatisfactions. For some people, a current condition of society is intolerable, and their goal is to *promote* social change. Theirs is called a **proactive social movement**. In contrast, others feel threatened because some condition of society is changing, and they organize to resist that change. Theirs is a **reactive social movement**.

To further their goals, people develop **social movement organizations**. Those whose goal is to promote social change develop such organizations as the National Action Committee on the Status of Women (with over 700 member groups), the Council of Canadians, the Canadian Centre for Policy Alternatives, and the National Indian Brotherhood. In contrast, for those who are trying to resist these changes, the National Citizens Coalition, the Western Guard, and REAL Women of Canada serve this purpose. To recruit followers and sympathizers, leaders of social movements use various attention-getting devices, from marches and protest rallies to sit-ins and boycotts. To publicize their grievances, they also may try to stage "media events."

The Quiet Revolution in Quebec, which began in the early 1960s, was a response to the two-decades-long failure of Maurice Duplessis's Union Nationale government to modernize the state institutions of health, education, and welfare in that province. But the Quiet Revolution also unleashed

Watch the video "Defining Social Movements" on MySocLab.

Watch the video "Grievances, Anger, and Hope" on MySocLab.

Watch the video "Organizational Structure of Social Movements" on MySocLab.

Canada and the Occupy Wall Street Movement

The Occupy Wall Street movement spurred grassroots demonstrations against corporate bailouts, income inequality, and high rates of unemployment in cities across the world. Otherwise known as the "99 percent," the movement employed the Arab Spring tactics that were successfully used in Tunisia, Egypt, and, most recently, Libya. The movement flourished online, with groups organizing on social networks such as Twitter and Facebook.

Their tactics involved civil resistance through marches, rallies, and demonstrations, with social media serving to organize, communicate, and raise awareness. The Occupy Wall Street movement became a significant presence in Canadian cities like Vancouver, Montreal, Toronto, and Calgary.

More than 2000 people gathered in front of the Vancouver Art Gallery one afternoon and held a series of marches throughout downtown. In Montreal, hundreds of people descended on Victoria Square. One student, holding a sign that read "You can't eat money," told CBC News, "We place so much importance on money in our society . . . the system is so screwed up [and in the end] money means nothing."

In Toronto, a crowd of about 3000 protestors marched east from their meeting place in the city's financial district to St. James Park at King and Church Streets.

Source: Adapted from CBC News, November 25, 2011. "Map: The Occupy Canada movement." Retrieved from www.cbc.ca/news/interactives/occupy-canada; PremierLife.ca, October 26, 2011. "Occupy Wall Street, Occupy Canada, Occupy London, Occupy the World." Retrieved from www.premierlife.ca/on-campus/occupy-wall-street-occupy-canada-occupy-london-occupy-the-world/.

---

many other social movements, including the indépendence movement and the Front de Libération du Québec (FLQ).

Types and Tactics of Social Movements

Let's see what types of social movements there are and then examine their tactics.

Types of Social Movements

Since social change is always their goal, we can classify social movements according to their target and the amount of change they seek. Figure 18.2 summarizes the classification developed by sociologist David Aberle (1966). If you read across, you will see that the target of the first two types of social movements is *individuals*. **Alterative social movements** seek only to alter some particular behaviour of people. An example of a powerful social movement today is Mothers Against Drunk Driving (MADD), whose goal is to get people to stop driving if they have been drinking any alcohol. Its members are convinced that if they could stop drunk drivers, there would be many fewer deaths on our highways. **Redemptive social movements** also target individuals, but here the aim is for *total* change. An example is a religious social movement that stresses conversion. In fundamentalist Christianity, for example, when someone converts to a particular view of Jesus Christ, the entire person is supposed to change, not just some specific behaviour. The individual becomes a "true believer" of that religious sect or cult.

The target of the next two types of social movements is *society*. **Reformative social movements** seek to *reform* some specific aspect of society. The environmental movement, for

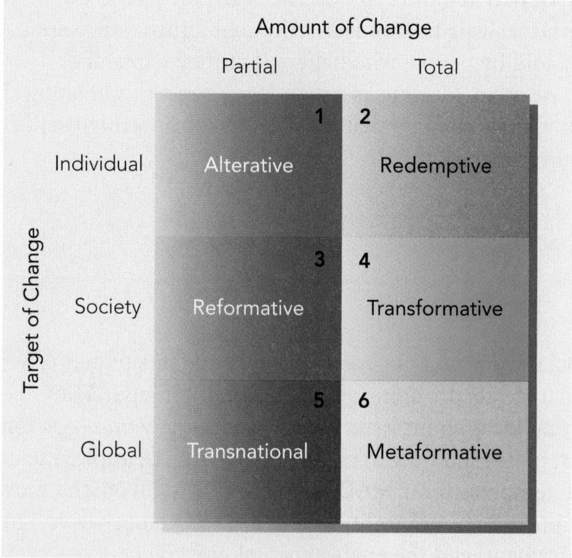

FIGURE 18.2 Types of Social Movements
Source: The first four types are from Aberle (1966); the last two are by the author.

example, seeks to reform the ways society treats the environment, from its disposal of garbage and nuclear wastes to its use of forests and water. **Transformative social movements**, in contrast, seek to *transform* the social order itself and to replace it with a new version of the good society. Revolutions such as those in the American colonies, France, Russia, and Cuba are examples.

((•● Listen to "China's Communists Chart a New Course" on MySocLab.

Nellie McClung and Emmeline Pankhurst in 1916. What kind of tactics did the suffragettes use in their social movement?

Women participating in a Take Back the Night march, which takes place annually in communities across Canada and throughout the world.

A new twist in social movements is global orientation. Rather than focusing on changing a condition within a specific country, the goal of a global social movement is to change this condition throughout the world. As with many aspects of life in our new global economy, numerous issues that concern people transcend national boundaries. Participants in transnational social movements want to change some condition that exists not just in their society but also throughout the world (see Cell 5 of Figure 18.2). These social movements often centre on improving quality of life (Melucci, 1989) The women's, environmental, and animal rights movements are examples. Because of this new focus, some sociologists refer to them as **new social movements** (McAdam, McCarthy, & Zald, 1988).

Cell 6 of Figure 18.2 represents a rare type of social movement. The goal of *metaformative* social movements is to change the social order itself—not just of a specific country, but of an entire civilization, or even the whole world. The objective of metaformative social movements is to change concepts and practices of race/ethnicity, class, gender, family, religion, government, and the globalization of nations. The communist and fascist movements of the first half of the twentieth century are examples. Today, examples include religious fundamentalism, whether Christian, Islamic, or some other variety. In most cases, metaformative social movements are socially and morally regressive; that is, they seek to replace capitalist modernization with their own specific brand of social and moral order.

Tactics of Social Movements

The leaders of a social movement can choose from a variety of tactics. Should they peacefully boycott, march, or hold an all-night candlelight vigil? Or should they bomb a building, blow up an airplane, or assassinate a key figure? To understand why the leaders of social movements choose particular tactics, we need to examine a group's membership, the publics it addresses (or its audience), and its relationship to authorities.

MEMBERSHIP Figure 18.3 shows the composition of social movements. At the centre is the inner core, those people most committed to the movement. The inner core sets the group's goals, timetables, and strategies, and inspires the other members. Those at the second level are also committed to the movement. People at this level, however, can be

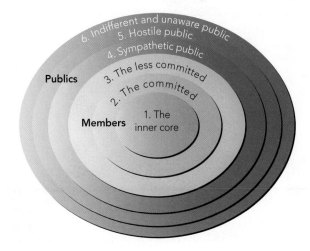

FIGURE 18.3 The Membership and Publics of Social Movements

✳ **Explore** the reading "Overview of U.S. White Supremacist Groups" on **MySocLab.**

counted on to show up for demonstrations and to do grunt work—mailings, passing out petitions and leaflets, making telephone calls. At the third level is a wider circle of people who are less committed and less dependable. Their participation is primarily a matter of convenience. If an activity does not interfere with something else they want to do, they will participate.

The predispositions and backgrounds of the inner core are essential in the choice of tactics. Because of their background, the inner core of some groups is predisposed to use peaceful means while others prefer confrontational means and still others prefer violence. Tactics also depend on the number of committed members. Different tactics are called for if the inner core can count on 700 committed members to show up—as opposed to, say, seven.

THE PUBLICS   Outside the membership of a group is the **public**, a dispersed group of people who usually have an interest in the issue. Just outside the third circle of members, and blending into it, is the sympathetic public. Sympathy

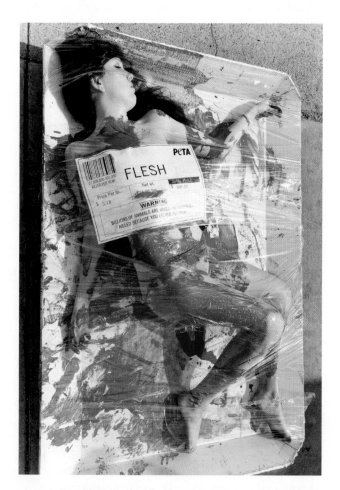

The use of propaganda is popular among those committed to the goals of a social movement. They usually see only one side of the social issue about which they are upset. What attention-getting devices is this demonstrator using? Are they effective? Why is this an example of propaganda?

with the movement's goals makes this public fertile ground for recruiting new members. The second public is hostile; it is keenly aware of the group's goals and dislikes them. This public wants to stop the social movement, for the movement's values go against its own. The third public consists of disinterested people. They are either unaware of the social movement, or if aware, indifferent to it.

RELATIONSHIP TO AUTHORITIES   A movement's relationship to authorities is also significant in determining tactics—especially in choosing peaceful or violent tactics. If a social movement is *institutionalized*—accepted by authorities—violence will not be directed against the authorities, as they are on the same side. This, however, does not rule out violence directed against the opposition. If authorities are hostile to a social movement, aggressive or even violent tactics are more likely.

OTHER FACTORS   Sociologist Ellen Scott (1993), who studied the movement to stop rape, discovered that close friendships, race, and even size of town are important in determining tactics.

Social Movements and the Media

In selecting tactics, the leaders of social movements are keenly aware of their effects on the mass media (Zald, 1992). Their goal is to influence **public opinion**, how people think about some issue. Pictures of bloodied, dead baby seals, for example, go a long way toward getting one group's message across.

A key to understanding social movements, then, is **propaganda**. Although this word often evokes negative images, it is actually neutral. Propaganda is simply the presentation of information in an attempt to influence people. Its original meaning was positive: *propaganda* referred to a committee of cardinals of the Roman Catholic Church whose assignment was the care of foreign missions. (They were to *propagate* the faith.)

Propaganda, then, in the sense of organized attempts to manipulate public opinion, is a regular part of modern life. Advertisements, for example, are a form of propaganda, presenting a one-sided version of reality.

The mass media play a crucial role in social movements. They can become, in effect, the gatekeepers to social movements. If those who control and work in the mass media—from owners to reporters—are sympathetic to some particular "cause," it will receive sympathetic treatment in the media. A case in point is the widely televised "Live 8—The Long Walk To Justice" concerts in 2005, staged in the major cities of the G8 countries and Johannesburg, South Africa, on the eve of the G8 summit in Gleneagles (near Edinburgh), Scotland. This was a showcase of musical talent from around the world, brought together by Sir Bob Geldof. It is estimated that between 2 and 3 billion people worldwide watched the concerts. The aim of these shows was

Live 8 was a series of concerts that took place on July 5, 2005, in the G8 nations and South Africa. More than 1000 musicians performed at the concerts, which were broadcast on 182 television networks and 2000 radio networks. The shows were planned to pressure world leaders to drop the debt of the world's poorest nations, increase and improve aid, and negotiate fairer trade rules in the interest of poorer countries. Pictured here is the crowd outside Park Place in Barrie, Ontario.

to pressure the leaders of the G8 nations (Canada, France, Germany, Italy, Japan, Russia, the United Kingdom, and the United States) to do three things to eliminate poverty in Africa: cancel the debt owed by African nations to rich countries, make trade fairer by changing the rules to allow poor countries to develop and build their own industries, and provide more financial aid in areas such as basic health care and education. If it did nothing else, Live 8—and the media's coverage of it—brought an important social issue to the forefront of young people's consciousness.

If you ever get the impression that the media are trying to manipulate your opinions and attitudes on some particular social movement—or some social issue—you are probably right. Far from conducting unbiased reporting, the media are under the control and influence of people who have an agenda to get across. This doesn't mean, however, that we need to be cynical about the role of the media in our lives. It does mean that we need to be critical at times about what is and isn't reported about particular issues and social movements. We need to be aware of the biases of the media establishment—television, radio, newspapers, magazines, and so on—and of the fact that they select which issues they give publicity to, as well as which ones they ignore, and they

decide whether they will present favourable or unfavourable treatment of issues and movements.

Why People Join Social Movements

As discussed, social movements arise from the conviction that some condition of society is no longer tolerable. Not everyone who feels strongly dissatisfied about an issue joins a social movement, however. Let's look at three explanations for why some people join social movements.

Mass Society Theory

To explain why people are attracted to social movements, sociologist William Kornhauser (1959) proposed **mass society theory**. Kornhauser argued that **mass society**—an impersonal, industrialized, highly bureaucratized society—makes many people feel isolated. Social movements fill a void by offering people a sense of belonging. In geographical areas where social ties are supposedly weaker, such as western Canada, one would expect to find more social movements than in areas where traditional ties are supposedly stronger, such as in Atlantic Canada.

This theory seems to match common-sense observations. Social movements seem to proliferate on the Prairies and the West Coast. But sociologist Doug McAdam and colleagues (1988), who interviewed people who had risked their lives in the civil rights movement, found that these people were firmly rooted in families and communities. It was their strong desire to right wrongs and overcome injustices, not their isolation, that motivated their participation. Ironically, the homeless, among the most isolated, generally do not join anything—except food lines.

Deprivation Theory

A second explanation to account for why people join social movements is *deprivation theory*. According to this theory, people who are deprived of things deemed valuable in society—money, justice, status, or privilege—join social movements in the hope of redressing their grievances. This theory may seem so obvious as to need no evidence. Aren't the Mohawk warriors who occupied their land for 78 days in what became known across Canada as the "Oka Crisis" ample evidence that the theory is true?

Deprivation theory does provide a starting point, but there is more to the matter. We must also pay attention to what Alexis de Tocqueville (1856/1955) noted almost 150 years ago. The peasants of Germany were worse off than the peasants of France, and from deprivation theory we would expect the Germans to have rebelled and overthrown their king. Revolution occurred in France, not Germany, however. The reason, said de Tocqueville, is *relative* deprivation. French peasants had experienced improving living conditions and could imagine even better conditions, while German peasants, having never experienced anything but depressed conditions, had no comparative basis for feeling deprived.

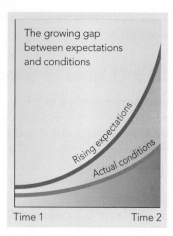

The growing gap between expectations and conditions

Rising expectations

Actual conditions

Time 1   Time 2

FIGURE 18.4 Relative Deprivation and Revolution

According to **relative deprivation theory**, then, it is not people's actual deprivation that matters. The key to participation is relative deprivation—that is, what people *think* they should have *relative* to what others have or relative to their own recent past or even their perceived future. Relative deprivation theory, which has provided insight into revolutions, holds a surprise. Because *improving* conditions fuel human desires for even better conditions, improving conditions can spark revolutions. As illustrated in Figure 18.4, this occurs when people's expectations outstrip the actual change they experience. It is likely that we can also apply this theory to riots.

Moral Issues and Ideological Commitment

Some people join social movements because of *moral shock*—a sense of outrage at finding out what is "really" going on (Jasper & Poulsen, 1995). They feel they must

The "Oka Crisis," during which Mohawk warriors occupied their land for 78 days in Quebec, can be viewed as an example of deprivation theory.

choose sides and do what they can to make a difference. As sociologists put it, they join because of *ideological commitment* to the movement.

Many members on both sides of the Quebec sovereignty issue see their involvement in such terms. Similarly, most activists in the animal rights movement are convinced that there can be no justification for animals to suffer in order to make safer products for humans. For others, matters of the environment are moral issues, and not to act would be an inexcusable betrayal of future generations. The moral component of a social movement, then, is a primary reason for some people's involvement.

A Special Case: The Agent Provocateur

A unique type of social movement participant is the **agent provocateur**, an agent of the government or even of a rival social movement whose job is to spy on the leadership and perhaps sabotage the group's activities. Some are recruited from the membership itself and betray their movement's goals for money, while others are members of the police or a rival group who go underground and join the movement.

Since the social change represented by some social movements is radical, threatening the power elite, the use of agent provocateurs is not surprising. What may be surprising, however, is that some agents get converted to the social movement on which they are spying. Sociologist Gary Marx (1993) explains that, to be credible, agents must share at least some of the class, age, gender, ethnic, racial, or religious characteristics of the group. This makes them more likely to sympathize with the movement's goals and become disenchanted with trying to harm the group. What also may be surprising is how far some agents go. During the 1960s, when a wave of militant social movements rolled across Quebec, the RCMP and other police were busy recruiting agent provocateurs. To sabotage groups, these agents provoked illegal activities that otherwise would not have occurred, setting the leadership up for arrest (Sawatsky, 1980).

Focus Question

Who joins social movements and why?

IN SUM

Perhaps most commonly, people join a social movement because they have friends and acquaintances already in the movement (McCarthy & Wolfson, 1992; Snow, Zurcher, & Ekland-Olson, 1993). Some join because of moral convictions, others to further their own careers, because it is fun, or because they achieve recognition or find a valued identity. As discussed, police officials may join social movements in order to spy on them and sabotage their activities. In no social movement, then, is there a single cause motivating people to join.

THINKING CRITICALLY ABOUT SOCIAL CONTROVERSY

Opposing the MAI: What It Takes to Build a Community-Based Social Movement

On September 25, 1997, Saskatchewan's Broadway Theatre in Saskatoon was the site of the first large-scale rally in Canada against the Multilateral Agreement on Investment (MAI). How is it possible for an apparently invisible issue to become so visible?

This can be attributed to organizing that had occurred previously in the community. Two months earlier, a small group got together to talk about the way the MAI was being secretly negotiated, how to break the code of secrecy, and how to build resistance to it. Organizers decided to concentrate on the negative impacts of the MAI, such as potential job losses, increased regional disparities, and the loss of national sovereignty.

The second stage of organizing grew out of an agreement to work toward a major public event in September. Another organizing meeting was held in August. People from different social justice, antinuclear, development, church, labour, farm, health, and other organizations in Saskatoon attended.

Various people and organizations took on tasks such as distributing posters, developing leaflets, issuing press releases, and getting more groups to support the coming rally. Two Saskatoon organizers wrote articles on the MAI for the local *Saskatoon Star Phoenix*.

Another event helped to spur things forward. A conference of the Asia Pacific Economic Cooperation Forum (APEC) was held in Saskatoon in early September 1997. Because of short notice, only about 30 protestors gathered at the hotel where the conference was being held. As small as it was, the demonstration received positive press coverage; however, as a result of the experience, organizers decided that it was very important to have an active phoning tree.

To keep the momentum growing, the organizing group agreed to meet on a weekly basis leading up to the Broadway Theatre event. Finally, an afternoon workshop on dismantling the corporate agenda was held just prior to the event at the Broadway.

After the rally, participants met at the theatre, where they endorsed a people's charter in opposition to the MAI. Two hundred people signed letters calling for a full and open public debate in the House of Commons and the provincial legislatures. The letters were sent to Prime Minister Jean Chrétien and Premier Roy Romanow.

The key organizing question is how to keep a social movement alive. Participants at the September rally were invited to attend an organizing meeting to be held the next month.

For Your Consideration

Typically, the last stage of a social movement is decline. Does the last stage apply to this social movement? Under what conditions might this movement decline?

Source: Cram & Kossick (1997).

On the Success and Failure of Social Movements

Social movements have brought about extensive social change. The women's movement has led not only to new laws but also to a different way of thinking about relations between women and men. Let's look at the reasons for the success or failure of social movements.

The Life Course of Social Movements

Sociologists have identified five stages in the growth and maturity of social movements (Lang & Lang, 1961; Mauss, 1975; Spector & Kitsuse, 1977; Tilly, 1978; Jasper, 1991).

1. *Initial unrest and agitation.* During this first stage, people are upset about some condition in society and want to change it. Leaders emerge who verbalize people's feelings and crystallize issues. Most social movements fail at this stage. Unable to gain enough support, after a brief flurry of activity they quietly die.

2. *Resource mobilization.* The crucial factor that enables social movements to make it past the first stage is **resource mobilization**. By this term, sociologists mean the mobilization of resources such as time, money, people's skills, technologies such as direct mailing and fax machines, attention by the mass media, and even legitimacy among the public and authorities (Oliver & Marwell, 1992; Buechler, 1993).

3. *Organization.* A division of labour is set up. The leadership makes policy decisions, and the rank and file members carry out the daily tasks necessary to keep the movement going.

✳ **Explore** the reading "The Rise and Fall of Aryan Nations: A Resource Mobilization Perspective" on **MySocLab**.

4. *Institutionalization.* At this stage, a movement has developed a *bureaucracy*, the type of formal hierarchy described in Chapter 10. The collective excitement is gone, and control lies in the hands of career officers, who may care more about their own position in the organization than the movement for which the organization's initial leaders made sacrifices. They may move the group's headquarters to a "good" location, for example, furnish it with expensive furniture and art work, and take pains to be seen with the "right" people in the "right" places.

5. *Organizational decline and possible resurgence.* During this phase, managing the day-to-day affairs of the organization dominates the leadership. Change in public sentiment may even have occurred and there may no longer be a group of committed people who share a common cause. Decline is not inevitable, however, as we shall see.

If most participants desert and those most committed flounder with little support, it does not necessarily mean the end of a movement. After suffragists won the right to vote in Canada in 1919, their movement declined until nothing but a shell remained. During a period researchers call abeyance, only a handful of committed organizers were left, and the best they could do was desperately keep the flame burning. Yet the women's movement was re-energized, and again thrust into national prominence (Taylor, 1997).

The Thinking Critically about Social Controversy box provides an example of the building of a social movement.

Focus Question

Do all social movements have a sociological life (i.e., birth, maturation, and eventual death)?

An Overview of Social Change

Social change is brought about by people organized into social movements. Before we can interpret these changes, decide whether they are progressive, or even whether there is such a thing as progress, it is necessary to make a few introductory comments about the importance of technology in any theory of social change.

How Technology Changes Society

As you may recall from Chapter 3, **technology** carries a double meaning. It refers to both *tools*, items used to accomplish tasks, and the *skills or procedures* to make and use those tools. This broad concept includes in its first meaning tools as simple as a comb and as complicated as computers. Its second meaning refers in this case not only to the skills or procedures used to manufacture combs and computers but also to those required to "produce" an acceptable hairdo or to gain access to the internet. Apart from its particulars, technology always refers to *artificial means of extending human abilities*.

All human groups make and use technology, but the chief characteristic of postindustrial societies (also called **postmodern societies**) is technology that greatly extends our ability to analyze information, communicate, and travel.

These *new information technologies* (ICTs), as they are called, allow us to do what had never been done in history: probe space and other planets; communicate almost instantaneously anywhere on the globe; travel greater distances faster; and store, retrieve, and analyze vast amounts of information.

This level of accomplishment, though impressive, is really very superficial. As we look at how technology spreads, we will stress this sociological aspect of technology—how it affects people's lives.

Modernization

The term given to the sweeping changes ushered in by the Industrial Revolution is **modernization**. Table 18.1 reviews these changes, presenting an *ideal type* in Weber's sense of the term, for no society exemplifies to the maximum degree all the traits listed here. For example, although most Canadians now work in the service sector of the economy, over 2 million are still employed in the natural resource and manufacturing sectors. Thus, all characteristics shown in Table 18.1 should be interpreted as "more" or "less" rather than "either–or."

As technology from the industrialized world is introduced into traditional societies, we are able to witness how far-reaching the changes are. Consider modern medicine. Its introduction into the least industrialized nations helped reduce death rates while birth rates remained high. As a result, the population exploded, bringing hunger and starvation, mass migration to cities, and mass migration to the industrialized nations.

Ogburn's Theory of Social Change

Sociologist William Ogburn (1922, 1961, 1964) proposed a theory of social change that is based largely on technology. As illustrated in Table 18.2, technology changes society by three processes: invention, discovery, and diffusion. Let's consider each.

INVENTION   Ogburn defined **invention** as the combining of existing elements and materials to form new ones. Although we think of inventions as being only material, such as computers, there also are *social* inventions, such as capitalism and the corporation.

DISCOVERY   Ogburn identified **discovery**, a new way of seeing reality, as the second process of change. However, a discovery brings extensive change only when it comes at the right time.

DIFFUSION   The spread of an invention or discovery from one area to another, called **diffusion**, can have far-reaching

TABLE 18.1 Comparing Traditional and Modern Societies

Characteristics	Traditional Societies	Modern Societies
General Characteristics		
Social change	Slow	Rapid
Size of group	Small	Large
Religious orientation	More	Less
Formal education	No	Yes
Place of residence	Rural	Urban
Family size	Larger	Smaller
Infant mortality	High	Low
Life expectancy	Short	Long
Health care	Home	Hospital
Temporal orientation	Part	Future
Material Relations		
Industrialized	No	Yes
Technology	Simple	Complex
Income	Low	High
Material possessions	Few	Many
Social Relationships		
Families	Extended	Nuclear
Respect for elders	More	Less
Gender equality	Less	More
Norms		
View of life and morals	Absolute	Relativistic
Social control	Informal	Formal
Tolerance of differences	Less	More

effects on human relationships. For example, when missionaries introduced steel axes to the Aborigines of Australia, it upset their whole society. Before this, men controlled the making of axes, using a special stone available only in a remote region and passing axe-making skills from one man to another. Women had to request permission to use a stone axe. When steel axes became common, women also possessed them, and men lost both status and power (L. Sharp, 1995).

Diffusion also involves the spread of ideas. The idea of citizenship, for example, changed political structure, for no longer was the monarch an unquestioned source of authority. Today, the concept of gender equality is circling the globe, with the basic idea that it is wrong to withhold rights on the basis of someone's sex. This idea, though now taken for granted in a few parts of the world, is revolutionary. Like citizenship, it is destined to transform basic human relationships and entire societies.

As noted in Chapter 3, Ogburn coined the term **cultural lag** to describe a situation in which some elements of a culture adapt to an invention or discovery more rapidly than others.

Evaluation of Ogburn's Theory

Some find Ogburn's analysis too one-directional, saying it makes technology the cause of almost all social change. They point out that adapting to changing technology is only one part of the story. The other part consists of people

Hamilton Television Station Startles Viewers with Gay Porn

Sometimes when new technologies misfire, the results can be shocking for some, hilarious for others. This happened recently when viewers of Hamilton, Ontario's CHCH-TV program *Morning Live* got some extra programming when the broadcast was interrupted by about a minute of explicit gay pornography.

Spokepersons for CHCH said the morning program was the blameless victim of a mistake by a cable-repair crew, who, while repairing a cut cable, apparently spliced a gay pornographic film into the news station's feed. According to the *Hamilton Spectator*, the mishap quickly went viral, inspiring reports at global websites such as The Hollywood Reporter and several labels on Twitter to aid Seaching—otherwise known as hashtags—including #porngate and #CHPorningLive.

CHCH will not likely face penalties from the Canadian Radio and Television Commission (CRTC) since the problem originated with the cable company and not the broadcaster.

Source: Adapted from www.thespec.com/news/local/article/708898—oops-a-morning-news-broadcast-to-remember.

taking control over technology—developing the technology they need.

Technology and social change, then, actually form a two-way street. Just as technology leads to social change, social change leads to new technology. For example, as the numbers of elderly in our society have grown, their needs have stimulated the development of medical technologies to treat Alzheimer's disease. Changing ideas about the disabled have stimulated the development of new types of wheelchairs that allow people who cannot move their legs to play basketball, participate in the Special Olympics, and enter races.

Transforming Society

As discussed in the Sociology and the New Technology box above, it is easy to inaccurately guess the consequences of a new technology. Let's look at five ways technology can change society.

TRANSFORMATION OF EXISTING TECHNOLOGIES The first impact is felt by the technology that is being displaced. For example, IBM electric typewriters, "state of the art" equipment a few decades ago, have been rendered practically useless by desktop and laptop computers.

CHANGES IN SOCIAL ORGANIZATION Technology also changes social organization. For example, machine technology gave birth to the factory. Then it was discovered that workers could produce more items if each did a specialized task. Henry Ford built on this innovation by developing the assembly line: instead of workers moving to the parts, a machine moved the parts to the workers. In addition, the parts were made interchangeable and easy to attach (Womack, Jones, & Roos, 1991).

CHANGES IN IDEOLOGY Technology also spurs new ideologies. For example, Karl Marx saw the change to the factory

TABLE 18.2 Ogburn's Processes of Social Change

Process of Change	What It Is	Examples	Social Changes
Invention	Combination of existing elements to form new ones	1. Cars 2. Microchip 3. Graphite composites	1. Urban sprawl and long commutes to work 2. Telecommuting and cyber warfare 3. New types of building construction
Discovery	New way of seeing some aspect of the world	1. Columbus—North America 2. Gold in California 3. DNA	1. Realignment of global power 2. Westward expansion of the U.S. 3. Positive identification of criminals
Diffusion	Spread of an invention or discovery	1. Airplanes 2. Money 3. Condom	1. Global tourism 2. Global trade 3. Smaller families

Note: For each example, there are many changes. For some of the changes ushered in by the automobile and microchip, see pages 421–424. You can also see that any particular change, such as global trade, depends not just on one item, but also on several preceding changes.

Source: By the author.

In the photo on the left, Henry Ford proudly displays his 1905 car, the latest in automobile technology. As is apparent, especially from the spokes on the car's wheels, new technology builds on existing technology. At the time this photo was taken, who could have imagined that this vehicle would transform society? The photo on the right is a Renault Twizzy Z.E., a concept car.

system as a source of **alienation**. He noted that workers who did repetitive tasks on a small part of a product no longer felt connected to the finished product. They became alienated from the product of their labour, which bred dissatisfaction and unrest.

TRANSFORMATION OF VALUES Today Canadians and Americans brag about cars, hot tubs, and Jacuzzis—and make certain their jeans have the right labels prominently displayed. In short, the particular emphasis on the social value of materialism often depends on the state of technology.

TRANSFORMATION OF SOCIAL RELATIONSHIPS Technology can also change social relationships. New technological changes flourish in our largest cities. And these cities are growing ever larger. Thriving, vibrant cities provide sufficient social space for individuals living in diverse communities to flourish. Ironically, the bigger the city, the "freer" the individual is to be him- or herself and to pursue his or her interests, often with minimal social pressure. In the age of globalization, new social relationships sparked by living in big cities with people from all walks of life and from all parts of the globe lead to the explosion of new ideas and new inventions.

The Automobile

If we try to pick a single item that has had the greatest impact on social life during the past century, among the many candidates would be the automobile. Consider some of the major effects of this innovation.

DISPLACEMENT OF EXISTING TECHNOLOGY In the beginning, people considered the automobile to be cleaner, safer, more reliable, and more economical than horses. Cars also offered the appealing prospect of lower taxes, for no longer would the public have to pay to clean up the tonnes of horse manure that accumulated on city streets each day.

The automobile also replaced a second technology. Canada had developed a vast system of urban transit, with electric streetcar lines radiating outward from the centres of our cities. As the automobile became affordable and more dependable, Canadians demonstrated a clear preference for the greater convenience of private transportation. Instead of walking to a streetcar and then having to wait for one to arrive, people were able to travel directly from home on their own schedules.

EFFECTS ON CITIES The decline in the use of streetcars actually changed the shape of most North American cities, as it stimulated mass suburbanization.

CHANGES IN ARCHITECTURE The automobile's effects on commercial architecture are clear—from the huge parking lots that decorate malls to the drive-up windows of banks and restaurants. But the automobile also fundamentally altered the architecture of North American homes (Flink, 1990). First, new homes were built with a detached garage, located, like the stable, at the back of the home. As the automobile became a more essential part of the North American family, the garage was incorporated into the home by moving it from the backyard to the side of the house and connecting it by a breezeway. The breezeway was eventually removed and the garage integrated into the home so that people could enter their automobiles without even going outside.

CHANGED COURTSHIP CUSTOMS AND SEXUAL NORMS By the 1920s, the automobile was used extensively in dating.

Most of us take computers for granted, but they are new on the world scene—as are their effects on our lives. This photo captures a significant change in the evolution of computers. The laptop held by the superimposed model has more power than the room-sized ENIAC of 1946.

In 1925, Jewett introduced cars with a foldout bed, as did Nash in 1937. The Nash version became known as "the young man's model" (Flink, 1990). Since the 1970s, mobile love-making has declined, partly because urban sprawl (itself due to the automobile) left fewer safe trysting spots, and partly because changed sexual norms made beds more accessible.

EFFECTS ON WOMEN'S ROLES The automobile may also lie at the heart of the changed role of women in Canadian society. Because automobiles required skill rather than strength, women were able to drive as well as men. This new mobility freed women physically from the narrow confines of the home. As Flink (1990) observed, the automobile changed women "from producers of food and clothing into consumers of national-brand canned goods, prepared foods, and ready-made clothes. The automobile permitted shopping at self-serve supermarkets outside the neighbourhood and in combination with the electric refrigerator made buying food a weekly rather than a daily activity." When women began to do the shopping, they gained greater control over the family budget, and as their horizons extended beyond the confines of the home, they also gained different views of life.

In short, the automobile helped change women's roles at home, including their relationships with their husbands, and facilitated their participation in areas of social life not connected with the home.

IN SUM

With changes this extensive, it would not be inaccurate to say that the automobile shifted basic values and changed the way we look at life. No longer isolated, women and teen-agers began to see the world differently. So did husbands and wives, whose marital relationship had also been altered.

The automobile even transformed views of courtship, sexuality, and gender relations. No one attributes such fundamental changes solely to the automobile, of course, for many historical events, as well as other technological changes, occurred during this same period, each making its own contribution to social change.

The Computer

The second candidate for bringing about the greatest social change is the computer.

None of us is untouched by the computer. Although it has intruded into our daily lives, most of us never think about it. Our grades are computerized, and probably our paycheques, as well. When we buy groceries, a computer scans our purchases and presents a printout of the name, price, and quantity of each item. The computer's novelty has given way to everyday routine; it is simply another tool.

Let's consider how the computer is changing medicine, education, and the workplace, then examine its likely effects on social inequality.

MEDICINE

The patient's symptoms were mystifying. After exercise, one side of his face and part of his body turned deep red, the other chalky white. He looked as though someone had taken a ruler and drawn a line down the middle of his body.

Stumped, the patient's physician consulted a medical librarian who punched a few words into a personal computer to search for clues in the world's medical literature. Soon, the likely answer flashed on the screen: Harlequin's disease. (Winslow, 1994)

The computer was right, and a neurosurgeon was able to correct the patient's nervous system. With computers,

Technology, which drives much social change, is at the forefront of our information revolution. This revolution, based on the computer chip, allows reality to cross with fantasy, a merging that sometimes makes it difficult to tell where one ends and the other begins. A computer projects an image onto the front of a coat in this image, making its wearer "invisible."

physicians can peer within the body's hidden recesses to determine how its parts are functioning or to see if surgery is necessary. Today, a million tiny fragments of genetic DNA can be crammed onto a disposable microchip. Read by a laser scanner, in just a few minutes the chip can reveal such things as whether a patient carries the cystic fibrosis gene or has grown resistant to AIDS drugs (King, 1994).

As the future is ushered in, the microchip is bringing even more technological wonders. In what is called telemedicine, patients have their hearts and lungs checked with a stethoscope—by doctors in another province or country. The data are transmitted by fibre-optic cable (Richards, 1996). Soon a surgeon in Halifax or Vancouver, using a remote-controlled robot and images relayed via satellite to computers, will be able to operate in almost any place or circumstance in the world.

EDUCATION   Almost every grade school in Canada introduces its students to the computer. Successful educational programs use a game-like, challenging format that makes students forget they are "studying." Most classrooms are wired to the internet ("Cyberschool Makes Its Debut," 1996).

The question of social inequality becomes significant in this context. Those schools most able to afford the latest in computer technology are able to better prepare their students for the future, thus helping to perpetuate social inequalities that arise from the chance of birth.

The computer has already transformed the experience of university. Students at Mount Allison University in Sackville, New Brunswick, are provided with laptop computers free of charge (if required for their studies) upon their acceptance at the university. And in every university in Canada, students have direct access to the internet and are provided with free email accounts. Overall, "surfing the net" for research and fun is a mainstay of student life at Canadian universities. If you wish, you can go to MySocLab to give yourself a test—at your chosen level of difficulty—to immediately check your mastery of the material.

THE WORKPLACE   The computer has also transformed the workplace. In some cases it has returned the work location to the home—an arrangement called telework. Already, millions of people perform their jobs at home. As discussed earlier, industrialization caused work to shift from home to factory and office. Since workers can now be "networked" (linked by computers), for many public and private sector workers this historic change is being reversed.

On the negative side are increased surveillance of workers and depersonalization. As a telephone information operator said:

> The computer knows everything. It records the minute I punch in, it knows how long I take for each call . . . I am supposed to average under eighteen seconds per call. . . . Everything I do is reported to my supervisor on his computer, and if I've missed my numbers I get a written warning. I rarely see the guy. . . . It's intense. It's me and the computer all day. I'm telling you, at the end of the day I'm wiped out. Working with computers is the coal mining of the nineties. (Mander, 1992: 57)

Cyberspace and Social Inequalities in the Twenty-First Century

The term *information superhighway*, which evokes the idea of information travelling at high speed between homes and businesses, is most apt to describe what is occurring at present around the world. Just as a highway allows physical travel from one place to another, so homes and businesses are being connected by the rapid flow of information. Already about 300 million people around the world are able to communicate by internet, which allows electronic access to libraries of information. Some programs sift, sort, and transmit scanned images, sound, even video. Email allows people to fire off messages without regard to national boundaries. This is the shape of the future: a world linked by almost instantaneous communication, with information readily accessible around the globe, and with few places being considered remote.

The implications of the information superhighway for national and global stratification are severe. At the national level, we may end up with "information have-nots," thereby perpetuating present inequalities. At the global level, the question is: Who will control the information superhighway? The answer is obvious—the most industrialized nations that are developing the system. This leads to one of the more profound issues of the twenty-first century: Will such control destine the least industrialized nations to endless pauper status?

If the answer is yes, how can we reduce the social inequalities created on a global scale? There are no easy answers.

Contemporary Theories of Social Change

Table 18.3 categorizes the principal contemporary theories about the causes of social change.

1. *Evolutionary theories* presuppose that societies are moving from the same starting point to some similar ending point. Unilinear theories, which assume the same path for every society, have been replaced with multilinear theories, which assume that different paths can lead to the same stage of development.
2. *Marxist conflict theories* are similar to evolutionary theories of progress except that the final stage, communism—otherwise known as "the end of history"—is the ultimate stage of development.
3. *Cyclical theories*, in contrast, view civilizations as going through a process of birth, youth, maturity, decline, and death.
4. *Feminist theories* assume that all societies, with the possible exception of the earliest hunting-and-gathering tribes, are dominated by patriarchy; and only by women achieving equality of condition and taking action on

TABLE 18.3 Contemporary Theories of Social Change

Theories of Social Change	Assumptions	Path(s) of Social Change
Evolutionary Theories of Social Change	All societies progress from simple to more complicated forms of material organization.	From elementary beginnings to more complex stages of development.
1. Unilinear evolution	All societies follow the same path of development.	One road out of a small village that leads to a town, then a city and beyond.
2. Multilinear evolution	Different routes can lead to a similar stage of development.	Multiple roads out of a small village that lead to a town, then a city and beyond.
Marxist Conflict Theories of Social Change	Similar to evolutionary theories of progress, except communism is the last stage of development, otherwise known as "the end of history."	Multiple roads out of a small village that lead to a town, next a city, and end in paradise.
Cyclical Theories of Change	Civilizations, such as those of Greece, Egypt, or the West, not one particular society, are like organisms: they are born, experience decline, and die.	Airborne fireworks display that begins with a trail upward, then a sudden burst, followed by beautiful colours, ends an exuberant youth, matures, and finally begins the long trail downward to the earth.
Feminist Theories of Social Change	Except for possibly the earliest hunting–and-gathering communities, all societies have been dominated by patriarchy.	A "tug of war" in which more and more women are added to one side of the rope until there is an eventual stalemate.
Postmodern Theories of Social Change	There is no progress or purpose or continuity of values, beliefs, and disbeliefs. Identities and localized situations are the basis for change.	A rushing river with multiple currents and fast-moving water, with light sparkling off the top of the water and the surface glimmer being all one sees or wants to see.

global human rights can the privileges and liabilities of patriarchy be overcome.

5. *Postmodern theories* assume the present, so that there is no progress or continuity in values, beliefs, and disbeliefs; belief in scientific progress has been replaced with a belief in appearance or form. To postmodernists, any possibility of social change begins with the acceptance of uncertainty, the acknowledgement of diversity, and the refusal to see concepts such as "justice" or "society" as fixed or as governed by unassailable "truths."

Focus Question

Do all sociologists hold the view that humankind is making progress and will keep getting better?

The Difficult Road to Success

In spite of their significance in contemporary society, social movements as agents of social change seldom solve all of society's social problems. Resource mobilization helps to explain why. To mobilize resources, a movement must appeal to a broad constituency. For example, the fact that workers at one particular plant are upset about their low wages is not adequate to recruit the broad support necessary for a social movement. At best, it will result in local agitation. The low wages and unsafe working conditions of millions of Canadian workers, however, have a chance of becoming the focal point of a social movement.

Many social movements vitally affect society. The Quebec sovereignty movement comes quickly to mind. Some movements, such as trade unions in Canada, become powerful forces for social change. They highlight problems and turn society onto a path that solves those problems. Others become powerful forces in resisting the social change that its members—and the public it is able to mobilize—consider undesirable.

By their very nature, broad social problems are entrenched in society and are not easy to solve. They require more than merely tinkering with some small part. Just as the problem touches many interrelated components of society, so the solutions require changes in those many parts. Social movements and new technology are among the forces that change society.

COLLECTIVE BEHAVIOUR

EARLY EXPLANATIONS: THE TRANSFORMATION OF THE INDIVIDUAL

How did early theorists explain the effects of crowds on individuals?

Early theorists argued that individuals are transformed by crowds. Charles Mackay used the term "herd mentality" to explain why people do wild things in crowd settings. Gustave LeBon said that a collective mind develops, and people are swept away by suggestions. pp. 406–408.

FORMS OF COLLECTIVE BEHAVIOUR

What forms of collective behaviour are there?

Some of the major forms of collective behaviour are **demonstrations**, **riots**, **panics**, **moral panics**, **rumours**, **fads**, **fashions**, and **urban legends**. Conditions of discontent or uncertainty provide fertile ground for collective behaviour, and each form provides a way of dealing with these conditions. pp. 408–412.

SOCIAL MOVEMENTS

TYPES AND TACTICS OF SOCIAL MOVEMENTS

What types of social movements are there?

Social movements consist of large numbers of people that organize to promote or resist social change. Depending on their target (individuals or society) and the amount of social change desired (partial or complete), social movements can be classified as **alternative**, **redemptive**, **reformative**, or **transformative**. pp. 412–414.

How do social movements select their tactics?

Tactics are chosen on the basis of a group's membership, its publics (audience), and its relationship to authorities. The three levels of membership are the *inner core*, *the committed*, and *the less committed*. The predispositions of the inner core are crucial in choosing tactics, but so is the public they wish to address. If relationships with authorities are bad, the chances of aggressive or violent tactics increase. Friendship, size of city, and race of movement participants and their targets may also be significant. pp. 414–415.

How are cellphones and social media related to the spread of social movements today?

Because the mass media are gatekeepers for social movements, and their favourable or unfavourable coverage greatly affects a social movement, tactics are chosen with the media in mind. Social movements also make use of social media, including internet applications such as Facebook, Twitter, and YouTube, and have been identified as key to events as diverse as the rise of student protests in Britain at the end of 2010 and the outbreak of revolution in the Arab world in 2012. p. 415.

WHY PEOPLE JOIN SOCIAL MOVEMENTS

Why do people join social movements?

There is no single, overriding reason why people join social movements. According to **mass society theory**, social movements relieve feelings of isolation created by an impersonal, bureaucratized society. According to **relative deprivation theory**, people join movements in order to address grievances. Morality, values, and ideological commitment also motivate people to join social movements. The **agent provocateur** illustrates that even people who hate a cause can end up participating in it. pp. 415–416.

HOW TECHNOLOGY CHANGES SOCIETY

What types of technology are there, and what effects can a changed technology have on society?

Because technology is an organizing force in social life, when technology changes its effects can be profound. The automobile and the computer were used as extended examples. The automobile changed the development of cities, buying patterns, architecture, and even courtship and women's roles. We looked at how the computer is changing the way we practise medicine, learn, and work. The information superhighway is likely to perpetuate social inequalities at both a national and a global level. pp. 418–423.

CONTEMPORARY THEORIES OF SOCIAL CHANGE

What are the contemporary theories of social change?

Evolutionary theories presuppose that societies are moving from the same starting point to some similar ending point. *Marxist conflict theories* are similar except that communism is the ultimate stage of development. Cyclical theories view civilizations as going through a process of birth, youth, maturity, decline, and death. *Feminist theories* assume that societies are mostly dominated by patriarchy, to be overcome by achieving equality of opportunity for women and securing global human rights. In *postmodern theories*, belief in scientific progress has been replaced with a belief in appearance or form; all change is ephemeral. pp. 424–426.

KEY TERMS

WEBLINKS

All URLs listed are current as of the printing of this text.

Canadian Centre for Policy Alternatives (CCPA)
www.policyalternatives.ca
The CCPA is an independent, non-profit research organization promoting research on economic and social policy issues from a progressive point of view

LGBT Social Movements
http://english.turkcebilgi.com/LGBT+social+movements
This site provides the history of the evolution of LGBT social movements, including in Canada and recent developments globally.

Royal Commission on the Status of Women in Canada
www.swc-cfc.gc.ca/dates/roycom/index-eng.html
The official Status of Women Canada website, announcing the fortieth anniversary of the Royal Commission on the Status of Women in Canada.

1. To understand the pressures of a social group or social movement, imagine yourself at a hockey game. When the Canadian national anthem is sung, instead of standing up with the other members of the audience, you stay seated. How do you feel when you don't join in? Who is behaving rationally in this situation? You or everyone else?

2. How do the media influence the creation or development of social movements?

3. All too often, sociologists describe social movements as examples of social problems and not as solutions to social problems. Do social movements such as trade unions serve any useful functions in Canadian society?

4. While it is true that technology influences the broad nature of social change, human beings also contribute to the direction of a society's transformation. After having read this text, you should know what sociology is and whether it has anything further to offer you. Do you think sociologists should use their skills and knowledge to directly influence Canadian public policy?

5. In what ways does technology change society? Access the Research Navigator through MySocLab and use keywords such as "teenage" and "authority" to locate relevant and recent scholarly and popular press publications to help you answer this question.

MySocLab

Explore the topics covered in this chapter on MySocLab. Interactive resources include a study plan, cumulative exams, a multimedia library, MySocLab eReadings, and access to the MySocLab Video Series.

GLOSSARY

acculturation: the transmission of culture from one generation to the next

acid rain: rain containing sulphuric and nitric acids

acting crowd: Herbert Blumer's term for an excited group that collectively moves toward a goal

ageism: prejudice, discrimination, and hostility directed against people because of their age; can be directed against any age group, including youth

agency: individual or collective actions upon social structures and circumstances

agent provocateur: someone who joins a group in order to spy on it and to sabotage it by provoking its members to commit illegal acts

agents of socialization: people or groups that affect our self-concept, attitudes, or other orientations toward life

alienation: Marx's term for workers' lack of connection to the product of their labour; caused by their being assigned repetitive tasks on a small part of a product

alterative social movement: a social movement that seeks to alter only particular aspects of people

anomie: Durkheim's term for a condition of society in which people become detached or cut loose from the norms that usually guide their behaviour

anticipatory socialization: learning part of a future role because one anticipates it

anti-Semitism: prejudice, discrimination, and persecution directed against Jews

applied sociology: the use of sociology to solve problems—from the micro-level of family relationships to the macro-level of crime and pollution

authoritarian personality: Theodor Adorno's term for people who are prejudiced and rank high on scales of conformity, intolerance, insecurity, respect for authority, and submissiveness to superiors

authority: power that people accept as rightly exercised over them; also called legitimate power

backstage: where people rest from their performances, discuss their presentations, and plan future performances

basic demographic equation: growth rate = births − deaths + net migration

basic sociology: see pure or basic sociology

bilateral (system of descent): a system of reckoning descent that counts both the mother's and the father's sides

biological determinism: the belief that the way we act reflects built-in biological traits such as the need to reproduce, the need to survive, and so on

blended family: a family whose members were once part of other families

boomerang kids: young adults who move out of their parents' homes and then move back in as they go through periods of schooling, employment, and family-building

bourgeoisie: Karl Marx's term for capitalists, those who own the means to produce wealth

bureaucracy: a formal organization with a hierarchy of authority; a clear division of labour; emphasis on written rules, communications, and records; and impersonality of positions

capitalism: an economic system characterized by the private ownership of the means of production, the pursuit of profit, and market competition; the investment of capital with the goal of producing profits

caste system: a form of social stratification in which one's status is determined by birth and is lifelong

charismatic authority: authority based on an individual's outstanding traits, which attracts followers

charismatic leader: an individual who inspires people because he or she seems to have extraordinary qualities

citizenship: the concept that birth (and residence) in a country imparts basic rights

city: a place in which a large number of people are permanently based and do not produce their own food

city-state: an independent city whose power radiates outward, bringing the adjacent area under its rule

clan: an extended network of relatives

clan system: a form of social stratification in which individuals receive their social standing through belonging to an extended network of relatives

class conflict: Marx's term for the struggle between the proletariat and the bourgeoisie

class consciousness: Marx's term for awareness of a common identity based on one's position in the means of production

class system: a form of social stratification based primarily on the possession of money or material possessions

clique: a cluster of people within a larger group who choose to interact with one another; an internal faction

closed-ended questions: questions followed by a list of possible answers to be selected by the respondent

coalition government: a government in which a country's largest party aligns itself with one or more smaller parties

coercion: power that people do not accept as rightly exercised over them; also called illegitimate power

collective behaviour: extraordinary activities carried out by groups of people; includes lynchings, rumours, panics, urban legends, and fads and fashions

collective mind: Gustave LeBon's term for the tendency of people in a crowd to feel, think, and act in extraordinary ways

community: a place people identify with, where they sense that they belong and that others care what happens to them

compartmentalize: to separate acts from feelings or attitudes

confederal union: a system of government in which the provinces have most of the power and the central government has little authority

conflict theory: a theoretical framework in which society is viewed as composed of groups competing for scarce resources

conservative bias: the tendency of analysts to downplay evidence of historical change and to reject evidence of challenges to traditional social patterns

consumer societies: societies in which there has been an explosion in the numbers of goods and services being marketed to meet every possible human need and a dramatic expansion in the time devoted to consumer activities

contradictory class location: Erik Wright's term for a position in the class structure that generates contradictory interests

corporate culture: the orientation that characterizes a corporate work setting

correspondence principle: the sociological principle that schools correspond to (or reflect) the social structure of society

cosmology: teachings or ideas that provide a unified picture of the world

counterculture: a group whose values, beliefs, and related behaviours place its members in opposition to the broader culture

credential society: the use of diplomas and degrees to determine who is eligible for jobs, even though the diploma or degree may be irrelevant to the actual work

crime: the violation of norms that are written into law

criminal justice system: the system of police, courts, and prisons set up to deal with people accused of having committed a crime

critical race theory: linked to the development of African–American legal thought in the post–civil rights era; an interdisciplinary approach that argues that the notions of the social construction of race and race identity, and the reality of discrimination, are ever-present in the writings of known contemporary critical race theorists

crude birth rate: the annual number of births per 1000 population

crude death rate: the annual number of deaths per 1000 population

cult: a new or different religion, with few followers, whose teachings and practices put it at odds with the dominant culture and religion

cultural diffusion: the spread of cultural characteristics from one group to another

cultural goals: the legitimate objectives held out to the members of a society

cultural lag: William Ogburn's term for human behaviour lagging behind technological innovations

cultural levelling: the process by which cultures become similar to one another, and especially by which Western industrial culture is imported and diffused into developing nations

cultural relativism: understanding a people from the framework of its own culture

cultural transmission: in reference to education, the ways schools transmit a society's culture, especially its core values

cultural universal: a value, norm, or other cultural trait that is found in every group

culture: the language, beliefs, values, norms, behaviours, and even material objects passed from one generation to the next

culture of poverty: the assumption that the values and behaviours of the poor make them fundamentally different from other people, that these factors are largely responsible for their poverty, and that parents perpetuate poverty across generations by passing these characteristics on to their children

debit card: a device that allows its owner to charge purchases against his or her bank account

degradation ceremony: a term coined by Harold Garfinkel to describe an attempt to remake the self by stripping away an individual's self-identity and stamping a new one in its place; a ritual designed to strip an individual of his or her identity as a group member—for example, a court martial or the defrocking of a priest

dehumanization: the act or process of reducing people to objects that do not deserve the treatment accorded to humans

democracy: a system of government in which authority derives from the people; derived from two Greek words that translate literally as "power to the people"

democratic socialism: a hybrid economic system in which capitalism is mixed with state ownership

demographic transition: a three-stage historical process of population growth: first, high birth rates and high death rates; second, high birth rates and low death rates; and third, low birth rates and low death rates

demographic variables: the three factors that influence population growth: fertility, mortality, and net migration

demography: the study of the size, composition, growth, and distribution of human populations

demonstration: a public meeting, march, etc. for a political or moral purpose

denomination: a "brand name" within a major religion, for example, Methodist or Baptist

dependency ratio: the number of paid workers required so that dependent individuals, usually seniors and children, can be adequately supported

dependency theory: a sociological theory that stresses how the least industrialized nations became dependent on the most industrialized nations

depersonalization: dealing with people as though they are objects—in the case of medical care, as though patients are merely cases and diseases, not persons

dictatorship: a form of government in which power is seized by an individual

differential association: Edwin Sutherland's term to indicate that associating with some groups results in learning an "excess of definitions" of social deviance and, by extension, a greater likelihood that one will become socially deviant

diffusion: the spread of invention or discovery from one area to another; identified by William Ogburn as the final of three processes of social change

direct democracy: a form of democracy in which eligible voters meet together to discuss issues and make their decisions

disabling environment: an environment harmful to health

discovery: a new way of seeing reality; identified by William Ogburn as the second of three processes of social change

discrimination: an act of unfair treatment directed against an individual or a group

divine right of kings: the idea that the king's authority comes directly from God

documents: in its narrow sense, written sources that provide data; in its extended sense, archival material of any sort, including photographs, movies, etc.

dominant group: the group with the most power, greatest privileges, and highest social status

downward social mobility: movement down the social-class ladder

dramaturgical analysis: an approach, pioneered by Erving Goffman, analyzing social life in terms of drama or the stage

dual labour market: workers split along racial, ethnic, gender, age, or any other lines; this split is exploited by owners to weaken the bargaining power of workers

ecclesia (plural ecclesias): a religious group so integrated into the dominant culture that it is difficult to tell where one begins and the other leaves off; also referred to as state religion

economy: a system of distribution of goods and services

education: a formal system of teaching knowledge, values, and skills

egalitarian: authority more or less equally divided between people or groups; for example, between husband and wife in a family

ego: Freud's term for a balancing force between the id and the demands of society

emergent norms: Ralph Turner's and Lewis Killian's term for the development of new norms to cope with a new situation, especially among crowds

endogamy: the practice of marrying within one's own group

environmental injustice: the result of unequal power relations, where minority groups and the poor suffer the most from the effects of pollution

environmental sociology: a subdiscipline of sociology that examines how human activities affect the physical environment and how the physical environment affects human activities

epidemiology: the study of disease and disability patterns in a population

ethnic (and ethnicity): having distinctive cultural characteristics

ethnic work: the way people construct their ethnicity, either through enhancing and maintaining a group's distinctions or recovering ethnic heritage

ethnocentrism: the use of one's own culture as a yardstick for judging the ways of other individuals or societies, generally leading to a negative evaluation of their values, norms, and behaviours

euthanasia: mercy killing

evangelism: an attempt to win converts

exchange mobility: about the same numbers of people moving up and down the social class ladder, such that, on balance, the social class system shows little change

exogamy: the practice of marrying outside one's group

exponential growth curve: a pattern of growth in which numbers double during approximately equal intervals, thus accelerating in the latter stages

export processing zones: tax-free "factory cities" where young Asian women are often lured by the promise of good jobs manufacturing products for export

extended family: a nuclear family plus other relatives, such as grandparents, uncles, and aunts, who live together

fad: a temporary pattern of behaviour that catches people's attention

false consciousness: Karl Marx's term to refer to workers identifying with the interests of capitalists

family: two or more people who consider themselves related by blood, marriage, or adoption

family of orientation: the family in which a person grows up

family of procreation: the family formed when a couple's first child is born

fashion: a pattern of behaviour that catches people's attention and lasts longer than a fad

fecundity: the number of children women are theoretically *capable* of bearing

feminism: the philosophy that men and women should be politically, economically, and socially equal

feminist theories: all three types of feminist theories—Marxist, liberal, and radical—hold that women are oppressed by gender roles that are products of social, historical, and cultural factors

feminization of poverty: the global tendency for adult women to outnumber men among the impoverished population; this tendency is embedded in women's traditional roles in the family and the economy

fertility rate: the number of children the average woman bears

field interview: see qualitative interview

fieldwork: see participant observation

folkways: norms that are not strictly enforced

formal organization: a secondary group designed to achieve explicit objectives

frontstage: where performances are given

functional analysis: a theoretical framework in which society is viewed as composed of various parts, each with a function that, when fulfilled, contributes to society's equilibrium; also known as functionalism and structural functionalism

fundamentalism: the belief that true religion is threatened by modernism and that the faith as it was originally practised should be restored

gatekeeping: the process by which education opens and closes doors of opportunity; another term for the social placement function of education

gender: the social characteristics that a society considers proper for its males and females; masculinity or femininity

gender inequality: males' and females' unequal access to resources, power, prestige, status, and property on the basis of their sex

gender role: the behaviours and attitudes considered appropriate because one is a female or a male

generalizability: the extent to which the findings from one group (or sample) can be generalized or applied to other groups (or populations)

generalized other: the norms, values, attitudes, and expectations of "people in general"; a child's ability to take the role of the generalized other is a significant step in the development of a self

genetic predispositions: inborn tendencies, in this context, to commit socially deviant acts

genocide: the systematic annihilation or attempted annihilation of a people based on their presumed race or ethnicity

gentrification: the displacement of the poor by the relatively affluent, who renovate the former's homes

gestures: the ways in which people use their bodies to communicate with one another

glass ceiling: barriers to social advancement that many women face in some organizations

global warming: an increase in the earth's temperature due to the greenhouse effect

globalization: the extensive movement of capital and ideas between nations due to the expansion of capitalism

goal displacement: replacement of one goal by another; in this context, the adoption of new goals by an organization; also known as goal replacement

greenhouse effect: the buildup of carbon dioxide in the earth's atmosphere that allows light to enter but inhibits the release of heat; believed to cause global warming

greying of Canada: a term that refers to the rising proportion of older people as a percentage of the Canadian population

growth rate: the net change in a population after adding births, subtracting deaths, and either adding or subtracting net migration

habitus: embracing a set of skills and way of looking at the world that reflects (rather than questions or challenges) hierarchical social structures

health: a human condition measured by four components: physical, mental, social, and spiritual

hidden curriculum: the unwritten goals of schools, such as obedience to authority and conformity to cultural norms

homogamy: the tendency of people with similar characteristics to marry one another

hotelling: when companies provide employees with laptops and assign desks only on a temporary basis to whomever needs them, much like one rents a room in a hotel

household: all people who occupy the same housing unit

human agency: the ability to individually or collectively resist social pressures and provide for social change

humanizing a work setting: organizing a workplace in such a way that it develops rather than impedes human potential

hypothesis: a statement of the expected relationship between variables according to predictions from a theory

id: Freud's term for our inborn basic drives

ideology: beliefs about the way things ought to be that justify social arrangements

illegitimate opportunity structures: opportunities for crime that are woven into the texture of life

imperialism: when countries take over other countries so they can expand their markets and gain access to cheap raw materials

indentured service: a fuzzy area between contract and slavery; people whose passage to another country was paid for in exchange for labour; they paid back their transportation costs by serving their master for a specified period of time

individual discrimination: the negative treatment of one person by another on the basis of that person's perceived characteristics

individuation: a growing diversity of individual paths through the life course

in-groups: groups toward which one feels loyalty

institutional discrimination: negative treatment of a minority group that is built into a society's institutions; also called systemic discrimination

institutionalized means: approved ways of reaching cultural goals

institutionalized religion: the formal, highly structured organization, creeds, practices, and rules of conduct intended to assure doctrinal purity and aid believers in their efforts to live by a particular faith

intentional family: people who declare themselves a family and treat one another as members of the same family; originated in the late twentieth century in response to the need for intimacy not met because of distance, divorce, and death

intergenerational mobility: the change that family members make in social class from one generation to the next

internal colonialism: the policy of economically exploiting minority groups

intersectionality: the interrelationships among various inequalities

interview: direct questioning of respondents

invasion-succession cycle: the process of one group of people displacing a group whose racial-ethnic or social class characteristics differ from their own

invention: the combination of existing elements and materials to form new ones; identified by William Ogburn as the first of three processes of social change

iron law of oligarchy: Robert Michels's phrase for the tendency of formal organizations to be dominated by a small, self-perpetuating elite

job ghettoes: also known as pink ghettoes, employment areas dominated by women (and usually lower paid than areas dominated by men)

just-in-time (JIT) strategy: a way of organizing production that minimizes inventory and storage at the production site—components are produced and moved between plants on a just-in-time basis

kaizen: continuous improvement—production techniques are continuously evaluated in search of more efficient and improved methods

labelling theory: the view, developed by symbolic interactionists, that the labels people are given affect their own and others' perceptions of

them, thus channelling their behaviour into either social deviance or conformity

laissez-faire capitalism: unrestrained manufacture and trade (loosely, "leave alone" capitalism)

language: a system of symbols that can be combined in an infinite number of ways and can represent not only objects but also abstract thought

latent functions: the unintended consequences of people's actions that help keep a social system in equilibrium

lean production: employs a just-in-time strategy under which parts inventories are reduced to the amount needed at the time, reducing the demand for huge parts warehouses and large work stations

leisure: time not taken up by work or required activities such as eating, sleeping, commuting, childcare, and housework

life course analysis: an increasingly popular theoretical perspective in the field of aging. Life-course theorists consider multiple levels of analysis (micro to macro), allow for human agency, and acknowledge the longitudinal nature of life experiences

life expectancy: the number of years an average newborn can expect to live

living will: a statement signed by people in good health that clearly expresses their feelings about being kept alive on artificial life support systems

looking-glass self: a term coined by Charles Horton Cooley to refer to the process by which our self develops through internalizing others' reactions to us

macro-level analysis: an examination of large-scale patterns of society

macropolitics: the exercise of large-scale power, the government being the most common example

macrosociology: analysis of social life focusing on broad features of social structure, such as social class and the relationships of groups to one another; an approach usually used by functionalist and conflict theorists

mainstreaming: helping people become part of the mainstream of society

Malthus theorem: an observation by Thomas Malthus that although the food supply increases only arithmetically (from 1 to 2 to 3 to 4 and so on), population grows geometrically (from 2 to 4 to 8 to 16 and so forth)

manifest function: the intended consequences of people's actions designed to help some part of a social system

market: any process of buying and selling; on a more formal level, the mechanism that establishes values for the exchange of goods and services

market competition: the exchange of items between willing buyers and sellers

market force: the law of supply and demand

market restraints: laws and regulations that limit the capacity to manufacture and sell products

marriage: a group's approved mating arrangements, usually marked by a ritual of some sort

mass media: forms of communication, such as radio, newspapers, and television, directed to mass audiences

mass society: industrialized, highly bureaucratized, impersonal society

mass society theory: an explanation for participation in social movements based on the assumption that such movements offer a sense of belonging to people who have weak social ties

material culture: the material objects that distinguish a group of people, such as their art, buildings, weapons, utensils, machines, hairstyles, clothing, and jewelry

matrilineal (system of descent): a system of reckoning descent that counts only the mother's side

McDonaldization: a term denoting the increasing rationalization of the routine tasks of everyday life

means of production: the tools, factories, land, and investment capital used to produce wealth

mechanical solidarity: Durkheim's term for the unity that comes from being involved in similar occupations or activities

medicalization: the transformation of something into a matter to be treated by physicians

medicalization of social deviance: to make social deviance a medical matter, a symptom of some underlying illness that needs to be treated by physicians

medicine: one of the major social institutions that sociologists study; a society's organized ways of dealing with sickness and injury

megalopolis: an urban area consisting of at least two metropolises and their many suburbs

meritocracy: a form of social stratification in which all positions are awarded on the basis of merit

metropolis: a central city surrounded by smaller cities and their suburbs

micro-level analysis: an examination of small-scale patterns of society

micropolitics: refers to the exercise of power in everyday life

microsociology: analysis of social life focusing on social interaction; an approach usually used by symbolic interactionists

middle-range theories: explanations of human behaviour that go beyond a particular observation or research but avoid sweeping generalizations that attempt to account for everything

milling: a crowd standing or walking around as they talk excitedly about some event

minimax strategy: Richard Berk's term for the effort people make to minimize their costs and maximize their rewards

minority group: a group discriminated against on the basis of its members' physical or cultural characteristics

modernization: the process by which a *Gemeinschaft* society is transformed into a *Gesellschaft* society; the transformation of traditional societies into industrial societies

monarchy: a form of government headed by a king or queen

monolithic bias: the tendency to ignore the diversity contained within a phenomenon and to focus instead on the most general exterior features; when applied to the family, the bias results in a failure to recognize that traditional notions of the family—male breadwinner, housewife, and biological children—have been supplanted by an amazing diversity of family forms and experiences

monolithic structure: the representation of structure as homogeneous and undiversified; for example, if the family is represented as a monolithic structure, the representation ignores the complex diversity of types and forms incorporated into contemporary experiences of the family

monotheism: the belief that there is only one god

moral community: people united by their religious practices

moral panic: a fear that grips large numbers of people that some evil group or behaviour threatens the well-being of society, followed by intense hostility, sometimes violence, toward those thought responsible

mores: norms that are strictly enforced because they are thought to be essential to core values

multiculturalism (also called pluralism): a philosophy or political policy that permits or encourages ethnic variation

natural sciences: the intellectual and academic disciplines designed to comprehend, explain, and predict events in our natural environment

neocolonialism: coined by Michael Harrington, the shift after World War II where the most industrialized nations turned to international markets as a way of controlling the least industrialized nations

neoliberalism: a version of the capitalist economic system based on the realization of a 24-hour global economy, made possible by the rapid expansion of global information and telecommunications technologies

negative sanction: an expression of disapproval for breaking a norm, ranging from a mild, informal reaction such as a frown to a formal prison sentence or execution

net migration rate: the difference between the number of immigrants and emigrants per 1000 population

new social movements: social movements with a new emphasis on the world, instead of on a condition in a specific country

new technology: the emerging technologies of an era that have a significant impact on social life

noncentrist party: a political party that represents less popular ideas

nonmaterial culture: a group's ways of thinking (including its beliefs, values, and other assumptions about the world) and doing (its common patterns of behaviour, including language and other forms of interaction)

norms: the expectations or rules of behaviour that develop out of values

nuclear family: a family consisting of a husband, wife, and child(ren)

objective method (of measuring social class): a system in which people are ranked according to objective criteria such as their wealth, power, and prestige

objectivity: total neutrality

oligarchy: a form of government in which power is held by a small group of individuals; the rule of the many by the few

operational definitions: the way in which a variable in a hypothesis is measured

organic solidarity: Durkheim's term for the interdependence that results from people needing others to fulfill their jobs; solidarity based on the interdependence brought about by the division of labour

out-groups: groups toward which one feels antagonism

panic: the condition of being so fearful that one cannot function normally, and may even flee

participant observation (or fieldwork): research in which the researcher participates in a research setting while observing what is happening in that setting

patriarchy: authority vested in males; male control of a society or group; a society in which men dominate women

patrilineal (system of descent): a system of reckoning descent that counts only the father's side

peer group: a group of individuals roughly the same age linked by common interests

personal identity kit: items people use to decorate their bodies

personality disorders: the view that a personality disturbance of some sort causes an individual to violate social norms

pink ghettoes: also known as job ghettoes, employment areas dominated by women (and usually lower paid than areas dominated by men)

pluralism: the diffusion of power among many interest groups, preventing any single group from gaining control of the government

pluralistic society: a society made up of many different groups

pluralistic theory of social control: the view that society is made up of many competing groups, whose interests manage to become balanced

political socialization: the way in which young people are inculcated with beliefs, ideas, and values that embrace the civil order through the education system

polyandry: a marriage in which a woman has more than one husband polygyny: a marriage in which a man has more than one wife

population: a target group to be studied

population shrinkage: the process by which a country's population becomes smaller because its birth rate and immigration are too low to replace citizens who die and emigrate

population transfer: involuntary movement of a minority group

positive sanction: a reward or positive reaction for approved behaviour, for conformity

positivism: the application of the scientific approach to the social world

postcolonialism: theory concerned with how to understand the cultural products (print and visual media, literature, the arts, and language) coming from societies that were once colonies of Europe

postmodern society: another term for postindustrial society; its chief characteristic is the use of tools that extend the human abilities to gather and analyze information, communicate, and travel

postmodernism: analysis of contemporary social life where the use of images to convey meaning replaces social reality

power: the ability to carry out one's will, even over the resistance of others

power elite: C. Wright Mills's term for those who rule a country: the top people in the leading corporations, the most powerful generals and admirals of the armed forces, and certain elite politicians, who make the nation's major decisions

prejudice: an attitude of prejudging, usually in a negative way

prestige: respect or regard

primary group: a group characterized by intimate, long-term, face-to-face association and co-operation

primary sector: that part of the economy that extracts raw materials from the environment

primary social deviance: Edwin Lemert's term for acts of social deviance that have little effect on the self-concept

principles of scientific management: also referred to as Taylorism, scientific management sought to reduce waste and inefficiency in production by measuring every movement and regulating every step of the work process

private ownership of the means of production: the ownership of machines and factories by individuals who decide what shall be produced

proactive social movement: a social movement that promotes some social change

profane: Durkheim's term for common elements of everyday life

profession: (as opposed to a job) an occupation characterized by rigorous education, a theoretical perspective, self-regulation, authority over clients, and a professional culture that stresses service to society

proletariat: Marx's term for the exploited class, the mass of workers who do not own the means of production

propaganda: in its broad sense, the presentation of information in an attempt to influence people; in its narrow sense, one-sided information used to try to influence people

proportional representation: an electoral system in which seats in a legislature are divided according to the proportion of votes each political party receives

Protestant Ethic: Weber's term to describe the ideal of a self-denying, highly moral life, accompanied by hard work and frugality

public: a dispersed group of people who usually have an interest in the issue on which a social movement focuses; the sympathetic and hostile publics have such an interest, but a third public is either unaware of the issue or indifferent to it

public opinion: how people think about some issue

pure or basic sociology: sociological research whose only purpose is to make discoveries about life in human groups, not to make changes in those groups

qualitative or field interview: an interview in which the researcher is a participant in a conversation with the subject being interviewed

qualitative research methods: research in which emphasis is placed on observing, describing, and interpreting people's behaviour

quality circles: refer to the involvement of rank-and-file workers in detecting and correcting defects and inefficiencies in products and services

quantitative research methods: research in which emphasis is placed on precise measurement, numbers, and statistics

queer theory: an emergent theory that deliberately challenges all notions of a fixed identity; therefore, instead of viewing sex, gender, and desire as a continuum, queer theory smashes these links; gender and desire/pleasure become more "free-floating" and based on individual attraction—regardless of the sex of the other person

questionnaire: a list of questions to be asked

quiet revolution: the fundamental changes in society that occur as a result of vast numbers of women entering the work force

race: inherited physical characteristics that distinguish one group from another

racism: prejudice and discrimination on the basis of race

random sample: a sample in which everyone in the target population has the same chance of being included in the study

rapport: a feeling of trust between researchers and subjects

rationality: the acceptance of rules, efficiency, and practical results as the right way to approach human affairs

rationalization of society: a widespread acceptance of rationality and a social organization largely built around this idea

rational-legal authority: authority based on law or written rules and regulations; also called bureaucratic authority

reactive social movement: a social movement that resists some social change

redemptive social movement: a social movement that seeks to change people totally

reference groups: the groups we use as standards to evaluate ourselves

reformative social movement: a social movement that seeks to change only particular aspects of society

reformists: a category of study of feminist spirituality represented by those who advocate revealing the "liberating core" of religious teachings with female imagery and exposing and refusing to accept rituals that are clearly sexist

reincarnation: in Hinduism and Buddhism, the return of the soul after death in a different form

rejectionists: a category of study of feminist spirituality represented by those who judge the traditional teachings to be hopelessly sexist and have left it to establish a new spiritual tradition

relative deprivation theory: in this context, the belief that people join social movements on the basis of their evaluations of what they think they should have compared with what others have

reliability: the extent to which data produce consistent results

religion: according to Durkheim, beliefs and practices that separate the profane from the sacred and unite its adherents into a moral community

replication: repeating a study to test its findings

representative democracy: a form of democracy in which voters elect representatives to govern and make decisions on their behalf

reputational method (of measuring social class): a system in which people who are familiar with the reputations of others are asked to identify their social class

research method (or research design): one of seven procedures sociologists use to collect data: surveys, participant observation, qualitative interviews, secondary analysis, documents, unobtrusive measures, and experiments

reserve labour force: the unemployed; unemployed workers are thought of as being "in reserve"—capitalists take them "out of reserve" (put them back to work) during times of high production and then lay them off (put them back in reserve) when they are no longer needed

resocialization: the process of learning new norms, values, attitudes, and behaviours

resource mobilization: a theory that social movements succeed or fail on the basis of their ability to mobilize resources such as time, money, and people's skills

respondents: people who respond to a survey, either in interviews or by self-administered questionnaires

revisionists: a category of study of feminist spirituality represented by those who believe that the basic message of the major religions is liberating

revolution: armed resistance designed to overthrow a government

revolutionaries: a category of study of feminist spirituality represented by those who seek to change the established orthodoxy by importing language, images, and rituals from other traditions

riot: violent crowd behaviour aimed against people and property

risk society: in postmodern theory, a term referring to a media-created perception of society that causes Americans and Canadians to feel increasingly at risk of being victimized by crime

rituals: ceremonies or repetitive practices; in this context, religious observances or rites, often intended to evoke awe for the sacred

role extension: the incorporation of additional activities into a role

romantic love: feelings of erotic attraction accompanied by an idealization of the other

routinization of charisma: the transfer of authority from a charismatic figure to either a traditional or a rational-legal form of authority

rumour: unfounded information spread among people

sacred: Durkheim's term for things set apart or forbidden that inspire fear, awe, reverence, or deep respect

sample: the individuals intended to represent the population to be studied

sanctions: expressions of approval or disapproval given to people for upholding or violating norms

sandwich generation: people in the later middle years who find themselves caring not only for their own children but also for their aging parents

Sapir-Whorf hypothesis: Edward Sapir and Benjamin Whorf's hypothesis that language creates ways of thinking and perceiving

scapegoat: an individual or group unfairly blamed for someone else's troubles

science: the application of systematic methods to obtain knowledge and the knowledge obtained by those methods

scientific method: the use of objective, systematic observations to test theories

secondary analysis: the analysis of data already collected by other researchers

secondary group: compared with a primary group, a larger, relatively temporary, more anonymous, formal, and impersonal group based on some interest or activity, whose members are likely to interact on the basis of specific roles

secondary sector: that part of the economy that turns raw materials into manufactured goods

secondary social deviance: Edwin Lemert's term for acts of social deviance incorporated into the self-concept, around which an individual orients his or her behaviour

sect: a group larger than a cult that still feels substantial hostility from and toward society

segregation: the policy of keeping racial or ethnic groups apart

selective perception: seeing certain features of an object or situation, but remaining blind to others

self: the unique human capacity of being able to see ourselves "from the outside"; the picture we gain of how others see us

self-administered questionnaires: questionnaires filled out by respondents

self-fulfilling prophecy: Robert Merton's term for an originally false assertion that becomes true simply because it was predicted

semiperiphery: countries whose economies stagnated as a result of their dependence on trade with the core nations

sex: the biological characteristics that distinguish males and females

sex typing: the association of behaviours with one sex or the other

sexual harassment: the abuse of one's position of authority to force unwanted sexual demands on someone

shaman: the healing specialist of a preliterate tribe who attempts to control the spirits thought to cause a disease or injury; commonly called a witch doctor

sick role: a social role that excuses people from normal obligations because they are sick or injured, while at the same time expecting them to seek competent help and co-operate in getting well

significant other: an individual who significantly influences someone else's life

slavery: a system of social stratification whose essential characteristic is ownership of some people by others

social change: the alteration of culture and societies over time

social class: a large number of people with similar amounts of income and education who work at jobs roughly comparable in prestige; according to Weber, a large group of people who rank closely to one another in wealth, power, and prestige; according to Marx, one of two groups: capitalists who own the means of production or workers who sell their labour

social conservatism: a value system characterized by a belief in conventional morality and social mores and a desire to preserve them, often aggressively, through civil law and regulation; social conservatism is often linked to the economic changes associated with neoliberalism

social control: a group's formal and informal means of enforcing its norms

social deviance: the violation of rules or norms

social facts: Durkheim's term for the patterns of behaviour that characterize a social group

social groups: people who regularly and consciously interact with one another over extended periods of time

social interaction: what people do when they are in one another's presence

social location: the group memberships that people have because of their location in history and society

social mobility: movement up or down the social-class ladder

social movement: a large group of people who are organized to promote or resist social change

social movement organization: an organization developed to further the goals of a social movement

social order: a group's usual and customary social arrangements, upon which its members depend and upon which they base their lives

social placement: a function of education that funnels people into a society's various positions

social sciences: the intellectual and academic disciplines designed to understand the social world objectively by means of controlled and repeated observations

social stratification: the division of large numbers of people into layers according to their relative power, property, and prestige; applies both to nations and to people within a nation, society, or other group

socialism: an economic system characterized by the public ownership of the means of production, central planning, and the distribution of goods without a profit motive

socialization: the process by which people learn the characteristics of their group: the attitudes, values, and actions thought appropriate for them

society: a term used by sociologists to refer to a group of people who share a culture and a territory

sociological imagination: C. Wright Mills's term for a sociological vision—a way of looking at the world that allows links between the apparently private problems of the individual and important social issues

sociological perspective: an approach to understanding human behaviour that entails placing it within its broader social context

sociology: the scientific study of society and human behaviour

spirit of capitalism: Weber's term for the desire to accumulate capital as a duty—not to spend it, but as an end in itself—and to constantly reinvest it

state: a political entity that claims monopoly on the use of violence in some particular territory; commonly known as a country

status: social ranking; the position someone occupies in society or a social group

status consistency: ranking high or low on all three dimensions of social class

status inconsistency (or discrepancy): ranking high on some dimensions of social class and low on others; a contradiction or mismatch between statuses

stigma: "blemishes" that discredit a person's claim to a "normal" identity

strain theory: Robert Merton's term for the strain engendered when a society socializes large numbers of people to desire a cultural goal (such as success) but withholds from many the approved means to reach that goal; one adaptation to the strain is crime, the choice of an innovative means (one outside the approved system) to attain the cultural goal

street crime: crimes such as mugging, rape, and burglary

structural mobility: movement up or down the social-class ladder that is attributable to changes in the structure of society, not to individual efforts

structured conversation: see qualitative or field interview

structured interviews: interviews that use closed-ended questions

subculture: the values and related behaviours of a group that distinguish its members from the larger culture; a world within a world

subjective meanings: the meanings that people give their own behaviour

subjective method (of measuring social class): a system in which people are asked to state the social class to which they belong

subsistence economy: a type of economy in which human groups live off the land with little or no surplus

suburbanization: the movement from the city to the suburbs

suburbs: the communities adjacent to the political boundaries of a city

superego: Freud's term for the conscience, the internalized norms and values of our social groups

survey: the collection of data by having people answer a series of questions

sweating: historically, the term used in reference to exploitative working conditions in the garment industry, with its detailed division of labour separating the craft process (design, cutting, and marketing) from the labour-intensive tasks of sewing and finishing

symbol: something to which people attach meanings and then use to communicate with others

symbolic culture: another term for nonmaterial culture

symbolic interactionism: a theoretical perspective in which society is viewed as composed of symbols that people use to establish meaning, develop their views of the world, and communicate with one another

system of descent: how kinship is traced over generations

taboo: a norm so strong that it brings revulsion if violated

taking the role of the other: putting oneself in someone else's shoes; understanding how someone else feels and thinks and thus anticipating how that person will act

techniques of neutralization: ways of thinking or rationalizing that help people deflect society's norms

technological determinism: the view that technology determines culture, that technology takes on a life of its own and forces human behaviour to follow

technology: often defined as the applications of science, but can be conceptualized as tools (items used to accomplish tasks) and the skills or procedures necessary to make and use those tools

tertiary sector: that part of the economy that consists of service-oriented occupations

tertiary social deviance: the normalizing of behaviour considered socially deviant by mainstream society; relabelling the behaviour as non-deviant

theory: a general statement about how some parts of the world fit together and how they work; an explanation of how two or more facts are related to one another

timetables: the signals societies use to inform their members that they are old; these timetables vary around the world

tool: an object created or modified for a specific purpose

total institution: a place in which people are cut off from the rest of society and are almost totally controlled by the officials who run the place

totalitarianism: a form of government that exerts almost total control over the people

tracking: the sorting of students into different educational programs on the basis of real or perceived abilities

traditional authority: authority based on custom

traditional orientation: the idea—characteristic of tribal, peasant, and feudal societies—that the past is the best guide for the present

transformative social movement: a social movement that seeks to change society totally

triangulation: a research strategy that includes not only the comparison of different data sources, but also the use of different data-gathering techniques and methods to investigate a single phenomenon

underclass: a small group of people for whom poverty persists year after year and across generations

underemployment: the condition of having to work at a job beneath one's level of training and abilities, or of being able to find only part-time work

underground economy: exchanges of goods and services that are not reported to the government and thereby escape taxation

unitary state: a form of government in which all power resides with the central government

universal citizenship: the idea that everyone has the same basic rights by virtue of being born in a country (or by immigrating and becoming a naturalized citizen)

unobtrusive measures: various ways of observing people who do not know they are being studied

upward social mobility: movement up the social-class ladder

urban legend: a story with an ironic twist that sounds realistic but is false

urbanization: the process by which an increasing proportion of a population lives in cities

validity: the extent to which an operational definition measures what was intended

value cluster: a series of interrelated values that together form a larger whole

value contradictions: values that contradict one another; to follow the one means to come into conflict with the other

value-free: an ideal condition in which a sociologist's personal values or biases do not influence social research

values: the standards by which people define what is desirable or undesirable, good or bad, beautiful or ugly; attitudes about the way the world ought to be

variable: a factor or concept thought to be significant for human behaviour, which varies from one case to another

Verstehen: a German word used by Weber that is perhaps best understood as "to have insight into someone's situation"

virtual organizations: companies "without walls," often transcending time, space, and culture

voluntary association: a group made up of volunteers who have organized on the basis of some mutual interest

Walmartization: a term referring to profound transformations in regional and global economies through the sheer size, influence, and power of the big-box department store Wal-Mart

war: armed conflict between nations or politically distinct groups

wealth: property and income

welfare (state) capitalism: an economic system in which individuals own the means of production, but the state regulates many economic activities for the welfare of the population

white-collar crime: Edwin Sutherland's term for crimes committed by people of respectable and high social status in the course of their occupations; for example, bribery of public officials, securities violations, embezzlement, false advertising, and price-fixing

working class: those who sell their labour to the capitalist class

xenophobia: a fear of strangers

zero population growth: a demographic condition in which women bear only enough children to reproduce the population

REFERENCES

Aaron, H. J., & Harris, B. (2003). Our uncertain demographic future. In H. J. Aaron & W. G. Schwartz (Eds.), *Coping with Methuselah: The impact of molecular biology on medicine and society* (pp. 66–93). Washington, DC: Brookings Institution Press.

Aberle, D. (1966). *The Peyote religion among the Navaho.* Chicago, IL: Aldine.

Abu-Laban, S. M., & McDaniel, S. A. (2005). Beauty, status, and aging. In N. Mandell (Ed.), *Feminist issues: Race, class and sexuality* (4th ed.). Scarborough, ON: Prentice Hall Allyn and Bacon Canada.

Acker, A., & Brightwell, B. (2004). *Off our rockers and into trouble: The Raging Grannies.* Victoria, BC: TouchWood.

ACTEW. (2007). *Contingent work: employment facts from ACTEW.* Toronto: ACTEW.

Addams, J. (1981). *Twenty years at Hull-House.* New York: Signet. (Original work published 1910)

Adams, M., Walker, C., & O'Connell, P. (2011). Invisible or Involved Fathers? A Content Analysis of Representations of Parenting in Young Children's Picturebooks in the UK. *Sex Roles, 65,* 259–270.

Adorno, T. W., Frenkel-Brunswick, E., Levinson, D. J., & Sanford, R. N. (1950). *The authoritarian personality.* New York: Harper & Row.

Agliata, D., & Tantleff-Dunn, S. (2004). The impact of media exposure on males' body image. *Journal of Social and Clinical Psychology, 23*(1), 7–22.

Agrell, S. (2008, January 28). Oil industry takes its toll on domestic life. *Globe and Mail,* pp. L1, L2.

Aguirre, B. E., Quarantelli, E. L., & Mendoza, J. L. (1993). The collective behavior of fads: The characteristics, effects, and career of streaking. In R. L. Curtis, Jr. & B. E. Aguirre (Eds.), *Collective behavior and social movements* (pp. 168–182). Boston: Allyn and Bacon.

Ainsworth-Vincze, C. (2006, July 3). Values lost in translation. *Maclean's.*

Albanese, P. (2006). Small town, big benefits: The ripple effect of $7/day child care. *Canadian Review of Sociology and Anthropology, 43*(2), 125–140.

Albanese, P. (2012). The more things change . . . the more we need child care: on the fortieth anniversary of the *Report on the Royal Commission on the Status of Women.* pp. 95 to 98 in Lorne Tepperman and Angela Kalyta (eds.). *Reading sociology: Canadian perspectives* (2nd ed.) Toronto: Oxford University Press.

Alboher, M. (2008, February 28). An office space of one's own for entrepreneurs. *New York Times.* Retrieved from http://www.nytimes.com/2008/02/28/business/smallbusiness/28sbiz.html?pagewanted=all

Alderman, L. (2012, April 8). Numbers of working poor are on the rise in Europe. *New York Times (Toronto Star* ed.), p. 7.

Aldrich, N. W., Jr. (1989). *Old money: The mythology of America's upper class.* New York: Vintage Books.

Allahar, A. L., & Coté, J. E. (1998). *Richer and poorer: The structure of inequality in Canada.* Toronto: James Lorimer.

Allan, K. (2006). *Contemporary social and sociological theory.* London: Pine Forge Press.

Allard, Y. E., Wilkins, R., & Berthelot, J.-M. (2004, January). *Premature mortality in health regions with high Aboriginal populations.* Statistics Canada, Health Reports, Volume 15, Number 1, Catalogue No. 82–003.

Allport, F. (1954). *Social psychology.* Boston: Houghton Mifflin.

Alphonso, C. (2005, July 15). Schools rely on 4th "r": Raising cash for basics. *Globe and Mail,* p. A6.

Alphonso, C., & El Akkad, O. (2008, January 11). Fears of career suicide stopped educators from reporting violence. *Globe and Mail,* pp. A1, A10.

Alzheimer's Society of Toronto. (n.d.). Statistics. Retrieved from http://www.alzheimertoronto.org/ad_Statistics.htm

Ambert, A.-M. (2001). *The effect of children on parents* (2nd ed.). New York: The Haworth Press.

Ambert, A.-M. (2009). "Divorce: Facts, Causes and Consequences". 3rd Edition. *Contemporary Family Trends.* Ottawa: Vanier Institute of the Family. November. www.vifamily.ca

Ambert, A.-M. (2012). *Changing Families: Relationships in Context* (2nd Canadian ed.). Toronto: Pearson Canada.

American Sociological Association. (2011). Brief to the U.S. Supreme Court regarding *Walmart v. Dukes.* Retrieved from http://www.asanet.org/images/press/docs/pdf/Amicus_Brief_Wal-Mart_v__Dukes_et_al.pdf

Amnesty International. (2004). *Making violence against women count: Facts and figures.* Retrieved from http://web.amnesty.org/libraryindex/ENGACT770362004

Andersen, M. L. (1988). *Thinking about women: Sociological perspectives on sex and gender.* New York: Macmillan.

Anderson, E. (1978). *A place on the corner.* Chicago: University of Chicago Press.

Anderson, E. (1990). *Streetwise.* Chicago: University of Chicago Press.

Anderson, E. (2006). Streetwise. In J. M. Henslin (Ed.), *Exploring social life: Readings to accompany Essentials of Sociology* (6th ed., pp. 147–156). Boston: Allyn and Bacon.

Anderson, P. (1995, Autumn). God and the Swedish immigrants. *Sweden and America,* pp. 17–20.

Andersson, H. (2005, February 11). Born to be a slave in Niger. *BBC,* World Edition.

Angell, R. C. (1965). The sociology of human conflict. In E. B. McNeil (Ed.), *The nature of human conflict.* Englewood Cliffs, NJ: Prentice Hall.

Anschutz, D. et al. (2011). The direct effect of thin ideal focused adult television on young girls' ideal body figure. *Body Image 8,* pp. 26–33.

Appiah, K. A., & Bunzl, M. (Ed.). (2007). *Buying freedom: The ethics and economics of slave redemption.* Princeton, NJ: Princeton University Press.

Appignanesi, R., & Garratt, C. (2000). *Introducing Postmodernism.* Cambridge, MA: Icon Press.

Ariès, P. (1962). *Centuries of childhood: A social history of family life* (R. Baldick, Trans.). New York: Vintage.

Arlacchi, P. (1980). *Peasants and great estates: Society in traditional Calabria.* Cambridge, England: Cambridge University Press.

Arndt, W. F., & Gingrich, F. W. (1957). *A Greek-English lexicon of the New Testament and other early Christian literature.* Chicago: University of Chicago Press.

Arnup, K. (2005). Lesbian and gay parents. In N. Mandell & A. Duffy (Eds.), *Canadian families: Diversity, conflict and change* (pp. 176–209). Toronto: Thompson Nelson.

Artis, J. E. (2009). "Breastfeed at Your Own Risk" *Contexts.* 8(4): 28–34.

Asch, S. (1952). Effects of group pressure upon the modification and distortion of judgments. In G. Swanson, T. M. Newcomb, & E. L. Hartley (Eds.), *Readings in social psychology.* New York: Holt, Rinehart and Winston.

Ashe, A. (1992, February 27). A zero-sum game that hurts blacks. *Wall Street Journal,* p. A10.

Ashford, L. S. (2001, March). New population policies: Advancing women's health and rights. *Population Bulletin, 56*(1).

Ashford, L., & Clifton, D. (2005, February). *Women of our world 2005.* Washington, DC: Population Reference Bureau.

Atwood, M. (1972). *Surfacing.* Toronto: Doubleday

Aubin, B. (2001–2002, December 31–January 7). Where the solitudes meet. *Maclean's* (Toronto ed.), 32.

Aubrey, J. S., & Frisby, C. M. (2011). Sexual objectification in music videos: A content analysis comparing gender and genre. *Mass Communication and Society, 14,* 475–501.

Auerbach, J. D. (1990, December). Employer-supported child care as a women-responsive policy. *Journal of Family Issues, 11*(4), 384–400.

Auger, J., & Tedford-Litle, D. (2002). *The inside looking out: Competing ideas about growing old.* Halifax: Fernwood.

Aulette, J. R., & Wittner, J. (2012). *Gendered Worlds.* 2nd Edition. New York: Oxford University Press.

Ayittey, G. B. N. (1998, September 4). Black Africans are enraged at Arabs. *Wall Street Journal* (interactive ed.).

Bainbridge, W. S. (1989). Collective behavior and social movements. In R. Stark (Ed.), *Sociology* (pp. 608–640). Belmont, CA: Wadsworth.

Bajaj, V. (2012, June 17). India's poor go hungry amid plenty. *New York Times (Toronto Star* ed.), p. 1.

Baltzell, E. D. (1979). *Puritan Boston and Quaker Philadelphia.* New York: Free Press.

Baltzell, E. D., & Schneiderman, H. G. (1988, September/October). Social class in the Oval Office. *Society, 25,* 42–49.

Baluja, T. (2011, September 23). Teens ambivalent about gender equality. *Globe and Mail,* p. A3.

Barnes, F. (1995, June 14). How to rig a poll. *Wall Street Journal,* p. A14.

Barnes, H. (2001, June). A comment on Stroud and Pritchard: Child homicide, psychiatric disorder and dangerousness. *British Journal of Social Work, 31*(3).

Barnett, R., & Rivers, C. (2011). *The truth about girls and boys: Challenging toxic stereotypes about our children.* New York: Columbia University Press.

Baron, R., & Greenberg, G. (1990). *Behavior in organizations.* Boston: Allyn and Bacon.

Barry, P. (1989). "Strong Medicine: A Talk with Former Principal Henry Gradillas." *College Board Review,* Fall 1989: 2–13.

Baudrillard, J. (1983). *Simulations* (P. Foss, P. Patton, & P. Beitchman, Trans.). New York: Semiotext.

Baudrillard, J. (1993). *The transparency of evil: Essays on extreme phenomena* (J. Benedict, Trans.). London; New York: Verso.

Baudrillard, J. (1995). *The Gulf War did not take place* (P. Patton, Trans. and intro.). Bloomington: Indiana University Press.

Bauman, Z. (1994). *Intimations of postmodernity.* London: Routledge.

Baxter, J., Hewitt, B., & Haynes, M. (2008). Life course transitions and housework: Marriage, parenthood, and time on housework. *Journal of Marriage and the Family, 70*(May), 259–272.

Beagan, B. L. (2012). "Even if I don't know what I'm doing I Can make it look like I know what I'm doing": Becoming a doctor in the 1990s. pp. 64–68 in Lorne Tepperman and Angela Kalyta (eds.). *Reading sociology: Canadian perspectives* (2nd ed.). Toronto: Oxford University Press.

Beaujot, R., & Andersen, R. (2007). Time-crunch: Impact of time spent in paid and unpaid work, and its division in families. *Canadian Journal of Sociology, 32*(3), 295–315.

Beaupre, P., Dryburgh, H., & Wendt, M. (2010, June 8). Making fathers count. *Canadian Social Trends,* 25–33.

Bechard, M. (2007). Family structure by region. Statistics Canada catalogue no. 89-625-XIE. Ottawa: Minister of Industry.

Beck, R. (2011, May 7). CEOs paid more now than when economy booming. *Toronto Star,* p. B7.

Beck, U. (1992). *Risk society: Towards a new modernity.* London: Sage.

Becker, H. S. (1966). *Outsiders: Studies in the sociology of deviance.* New York: Free Press.

Becker, H. S., Geer, B., Strauss, A. L., & Hughes, E. C. (1961). *Boys in white: Student culture in medical school.* Chicago: University of Chicago Press.

Beckett, P. (1996, September 11). Even piñatas sold in Mexico seem to originate in Hollywood now. *Wall Street Journal,* p. B1.

Beeghley, L. (1996). *The structure of social stratification in the United States* (2nd ed.). Boston: Allyn and Bacon.

Belcher, J. R. (1988, Fall). Are jails replacing the mental health system for the homeless mentally ill? *Community Mental Health Journal, 24*(3), 185–195.

Belkin, L. (2008, May 17). The dinosaurs of science: More women are engineers, lab and tech workers, but they leave due to sexism. *Hamilton Spectator,* p. A13.

Bell, D. (1976). *The coming of post-industrial society: A venture in social forecasting.* Basic Books.

Bell, D. A. (1993). Remembrance of racism past: The civil rights decline. In H. Hill & J. E. Jones (Eds.), *Race in America: The struggle for equality* (pp. 73–82). Madison: University of Wisconsin Press.

Benales, C. (1973, January 1). 70 days battling starvation and freezing in the Andes: A chronicle of man's unwillingness to die. *New York Times,* p. 3.

Benford, R. D. (2007). The college sports reform movement: Reframing the "educational" industry. *The Sociological Quarterly, 48,* 1–28.

Benson, B., Meeuwisse, W., Rizos, J., Kang, J., & Bruke, C. (2011). A prospective study of concussions among National Hockey League players during regular season games: The NHL-NHLPA concussion program. *Canadian Medical Association Journal, 183*(8), 905–911.

Berger, P. L. (1963). *Invitation to sociology: A humanistic perspective.* New York: Doubleday.

Berger, P. L. (1991). *The capitalist revolution: Fifty propositions about prosperity, equality, and liberty.* New York: Basic Books.

Berk, R. A. (1974). *Collective behavior.* Dubuque, IA: Brown.

Bernard, A. (2009, February). Trends in manufacturing employment. In Statistics Canada, *Perspectives on labour and income.* Catalogue no. 75-001X (pp. 5–13). Ottawa: Statistics Canada.

Bernard, J. (1972). *The future of marriage.* New York: Bantam.

Bernard, V. W., Ottenberg, P., & Redl, F. (1971). Dehumanization: A composite psychological defense in relation to modern war. In R. Perucci & M. Pilisuk (Eds.), *The triple revolution emerging: Social problems in depth* (pp. 17–34). Boston: Little, Brown.

Berridge, C. W., & Romich, J. L. (2011). "Raising him . . . to pull his own weight": Boys' household work in single-mother households. *Journal of Family Issues, 32*(2), 157–180.

Berry, L., et al. (1999). *Canadian global almanac 2000.* Toronto: Macmillan Canada.

Bessenoff, G. R., & Del Priore, R. E. (2007). Women, weight, and age: Social comparison to magazine images across the lifespan. *Sex Roles, 56,* 215–222.

Bethune, I. (2012). Studying abroad? You'll want to read this. Retrieved from http://oncampus.macleans.ca/education/2012/02/10/studying-abroad-youll-want-to-read-this

Bianchi, S., Robinson, J., & Milkie, M. (2006). *Changing rhythms of American family life.* New York: Russell Sage Foundation.

Bibby, R. W. (2004–2005). Future families: Surveying our hopes, dreams and realities. *Transition Magazine,* 3–16.

Bibby, R. W. (2012). Why bother with organized religion? *Canadian Review of Sociology, 49*(1), 91–101.

Bielski, Z. (2012). "Who needs marriage? The joys of living alone." February 16. http://www.theglobeandmail.com/life/relationships/who-needs-marriage-the-joys-of-living-alone/article/547006/?service. Accessed May, 2012.

Bilefsky, D., & Arsu, S. (2012, May 5). In Turkey, fears of a retreat on women's rights. *New York Times.*

Billman, J. (2004). "Michelle Raises Hell: The Hottest Transgender Talent in Professional Sports is Making the Competition See Pink." *Outside Magazine,* April. Retrieved from http://outside.away.com/outside/features/200404/michelle_dumaresq.html

Bissonnette, S. (2007). *Sexy Inc.* (film). National Film Board of Canada. Retrieved from http://www.nfb.ca/film/sexy_inc/

Blackwelder, S. P. (1993). *Duality of structure in the reproduction of race, class, and gender inequality.* Paper presented at the 1993 meeting of the American Sociological Association.

Blakemore, J. E. W., & Hill, C. A. (2008). The child gender socialization scale: A measure to compare traditional and feminist parents. *Sex Roles, 58,* 192–207.

Blau, P. M., & Duncan, O. D. (1967). *The American occupational structure.* New York: John Wiley.

Blitzer, J. (2012). "Spain's Lost Generation: What Do You Do when Half Your Country's Youth is Unemployed." *The New Republic.* May 30. http://www.tnr.com. Accessed August 12, 2012.

Blee, K. (2005). Inside organized racism, on life in society: Readings to accompany *Sociology: A down to earth approach, seventh edition,* pp. 46–57.

Block, J. (2005). The politics of modern childhood: American socialisation and the crisis of individualism. In J. Goddard, S. McNamee, A. James, & A. James (Eds.), *The politics of childhood: International perspectives, contemporary developments* (pp. 32–49). London: Palgrave Macmillan.

Blow, C. M. (2011, August 14). The decade of lost children. *New York Times (Toronto Star* ed.), p. 15.

Blumer, H. (1939). Collective behavior. In R. E. Park (Ed.), *Principles of sociology* (pp. 219–288). New York: Barnes and Noble.

Blytheway, B., & Johnson, J. (2005). Cataloguing old age. In G. J. Andrews & D. R. Phillips (Eds.), *Ageing and place: Perspectives, policy and practice* (pp. 176–187). London: Routledge.

Bogaert, A. F., & McCreary, D. R. (2011). Masculinity and the distortion of self-reported height in men. *Sex Roles, 65,* 548–556.

Borcea, D. (2007, November 9). Time to rhyme: Dub poetry festival. *Hamilton Spectator,* p. A3.

Borrelli, P. (1988). The ecophilosophers. *Amicus Journal,* Spring, 30–39.

Bosman, J. (2012, March 13). After 244 years, Encyclopedia Britannica stops the presses. *New York Times.* Retrieved from http://mediadecoder.blogs.nytimes.com/2012/03/13/after-244-years-encyclopedia-britannica-stops-the-presses/?ref=global-home.

Bosworth, B. P., & Keys, B. (2004). Increased life expectancy: A global perspective. In H. J. Aaron & W. B. Schwartz (Eds.), *Coping with Methuselah: The impact of molecular biology on medicine and society* (pp. 247–283). Washington, DC: Brookings Institution Press.

Bouchard, G., & Taylor, C. (2008). *Building the future: A time for reconciliation.* Quebec: Commission de consultation sur les pratiques d'accomodement reliées aux différences culturelles.

Bourdieu, P., & Passeron, J. C. (1979). *The inheritors: French students and their relations to culture.* Chicago: University of Chicago Press.

Bourgois, P. (1994). Crack in Spanish Harlem. In J. Curtis & L. Tepperman (Eds.), *Haves and have-nots: An international reader on social inequality* (pp. 131–136). Englewood Cliffs, NJ: Prentice Hall.

Bourque, L. B. (1989). *Defining rape.* Durham, NC: Duke University Press.

Bourque, M., & St.-Amour, N. (2011). Working parents: How Quebec supports families. *Transition, 41*(4), 8–11.

Bové loses McDonald's raid appeal. (2001, March 22). *BBC News.* Retrieved from http://news.bbc.co.uk/2/hi/europe/1235827.stm

Bowles, S., & Gintis, H. (1976). *Schooling in capitalist America.* New York: Basic Books.

Boyd, N. (2000). *The beast within: Why men are violent.* Vancouver: Greystone Books.

Bradshaw, J. (2011, May 9). When a university degree just isn't enough. Retrieved from http://www.theglobeandmail.com/news/national/time-to-lead/when-a-university-degree-just-isnt-enough/article2014732/singlepage/#articlecontent.

Bragg, S., et al. (2011). Too much, too soon? Children, "sexualization" and consumer culture. *Sex Education, 11*(3), 279–291.

Brajuha, M., & Hallowell, L. (1986, January). Legal intrusion and the politics of fieldwork: The impact of the Brajuha case. *Urban Life, 14*(4), 454–478.

Brauchli, M. W. (1993, May 10). A satellite TV system is quickly moving Asia into the global village. *Wall Street Journal,* pp. A1, A8.

Braverman, H. (1974). *Labor and monopoly capital: The degradation of work in the twentieth century.* New York: Monthly Review Press.

Brean, J. (2008, February 16). Lottery winnings can sometimes be fool's gold. *National Post.* Retrieved from http://www.nationalpost.com/story-printer.html?id=314008

Brecher, J., & Costello, T. (1998). *Global Village or Global Pillage: Economic Reconstruction From the Bottom Up.* Cambridge, MA: South End Press.

Brennan, R. J. (2012, May 23). Economic Equality for Women Still Centuries Off. *Toronto Star,* p. A3.

Brennan, S., & Dauvergne, M. (2011). Police Reported Crime Statistics in Canada, 2010. Ottawa: Statistics Canada.

Brenner, J. (2000). *Women and the Politics of Class.* New York: Monthly Review Press.

Bridgwater, W. (Ed.). (1953). *The Columbia Viking desk encyclopedia.* New York: Viking Press.

Brines, J. (1994, November). Economic dependency, gender, and the division of labor at home. *American Journal of Sociology, 100*(3), 652–688.

Brockerhoff, M. P. (2000). An Urbanizing World. *Population Bulletin, 55*(3), 1–44.

Brooks, V. R. (1982). Sex differences in student dominance behavior in female and male professors' classrooms. *Sex Roles, 8*(7), 683–690.

Brown, D. (1991). *Human Universals.* New York: McGraw-Hill.

Brown, D. R., & Gary, L. E. (1988). Unemployment and psychological distress among Black American women. *Sociological Focus, 21,* 209–221.

Brown, L. (2006, December 8). Boom Lowered on Higher Education: Canada Lacks Vision, Training to Compete Globally, Federal Report Warns. *Toronto Star,* p. A4.

Brown, L. (2010, October 8). Drop-out Rate Worse for Working Students. *Toronto Star,* p. A19.

Brunvand, J. H. (1981). *The vanishing hitchhiker: American urban legends and their meanings.* New York: Norton.

Brunvand, J. H. (1984). *The choking Doberman and other new urban legends.* New York: Norton.

Brunvand, J. H. (1986). *The study of American folklore.* New York: Norton.

Bryant, C. D. (1993). Cockfighting: America's invisible sport. In J. M. Henslin (Ed.), *Down-to-earth sociology: Introductory readings* (7th ed.). New York: Free Press.

Brym, R., & St. Pierre, C. (1997). Canadian Sociology. *Contemporary Sociology, 26*(5), 543–546.

Buckley, S. (1991, June 17). Shrugging off the burden of a brainy image. *Washington Post,* p. D1.

Buechler, S. M. (1993). Beyond resource mobilization: Emerging trends in social movement theory. *Sociological Quarterly, 34*(2), 217–235.

Bueckert, D. (2003, November 11). Truck traffic sickens kids: NAFTA study points to increased air pollution at Mexican border crossing. *Hamilton Spectator,* p. A16.

Buncombe, A. (2008, March 6). India Paying Cash to Stem Abortions. *Hamilton Spectator,* p. A12.

Burgess, E. W. (1925). The growth of the city: An introduction to a research project. In R. E. Park, E. W. Burgess, & R. D. McKenzie (Eds.), *The City* (pp. 47–62). Chicago: University of Chicago Press.

Burgess, M. C. R., Stermer, S. P., & Burgess, S. R. (2007). Sex, Lies and Video Games: The Portrayal of Male and Female Characters on Video Game Covers. *Sex Roles.* 57, 419–433.

Burman, P. (1996). *Poverty's bonds: Power and agency in the social relations of welfare*. Toronto: Thompson Educational Publishing.

Burton, P., & Phipps, S. (2011). "Families, Time, and Well-being in Canada." *Canadian Public Policy*. 37(3), 395–432.

Butler, J. (1993). *Bodies That Matter: On the Discursive Limits of Sex*. New York: Routledge.

Buttel, F. H. (1987). New directions in environmental sociology. In W. R. Scott & J. F. Short, Jr. (Eds.), *Annual Review of Sociology, 13,* 465–488. Palo Alto, CA: Annual Reviews.

Callister, M. A., & Robinson, T. (2010). Content Analysis of Physical Affection Within Television Families During the 2006–2007 Season of US Children's Programming. *Journal of Children and Media.* 4(2), 155–173.

Calvo-Salguero, A., Garcia-Martinez, J. M. A., & Monteoliva, A. (2008). Differences Between and Within Genders in Gender Role Orientation According to Age and Level of Education. *Sex Roles.* 58, 535–548.

Campaign 2000. (2011). Report Card on Child and Family Poverty in Canada: Revisiting Family Security in Insecure Time. Toronto.

Canada Health Act, Annual Report (2010–2011).

Canada's prison population grew in 2006: StatsCan. (2007, November 21). *CBC News Online*. Retrieved from http://www.cbc.ca/news/canada/story/2007/11/21/stats-prisons.html

Canadian Business. (2011, October). The Rich 100. Retrieved from http://list.canadianbusiness.com/rankings/rich100/2011/Default.aspx?sp2=1&d1=a&sc1=0

Canadian Cancer Society. (2012, May 9). Canadian cancer death rate down. Retrieved from http://www.cancer.ca/Canada-wide/About%20us/Media%20centre/CW-Media%20releases/CW-2012/Canadian%20Cancer%20Statistics%201012.aspx?sc_lang=en&p=1

Canadian Council on Learning. (2006, May 31). Why is High-Quality Child Care Essential? The Link Between Quality Child Care and Early Learning. http://www.ccl-cca.ca/CCL/Reports?LessonsInLearning?20060530LinL.htm?Style=Print

Canadian Council on Learning. (2007, December). *Post-Secondary Education in Canada: Strategies for Success*. Ottawa.

Canadian Council on Learning. (2009, February). Post-Secondary Education in Canada: Meeting Our Needs? Ottawa. Retrieved from http://www.ccl-cca.ca/pdfs/PSE/2009/PSE2008_English.pdf

Canadian Council on Social Development (CCSD). (2000). *The Canadian Fact Book on Poverty*. Ottawa: CCSD.

Canadian Labour Congress. (2008a). Manufacturing Jobs Matter to Women. Fact Sheet, April 2008. Retrieved from http://canadianlabour.ca/updir/EN-manufacturing.pdf

Canadian Labour Congress. (2008b, March). Women in the Work Force: Still a Long Way from Equality. Retrieved from http://canadianlabour.ca/updir/womensequalityreportEn.pdf

Canadian Paediatric Society (Adolescent Health Committee). (2004). Dieting in adolescence. *Paediatrics & Child Health.* 9(7), 487–491.

Canadian Panel on Violence Against Women. (1993). *Changing the landscape: Ending violence—achieving equality*. Ottawa: Minister of Supply and Services.

Canadian Press. (2002, July 22). Suspensions soar in schools: Critics are alarmed at trend of punishing young for minor offences. *Toronto Star,* p. A3.

Canadian Press. (2012a, May 19). Transgender Contestant Falls Short at Miss Universe Canada. Retrieved from http://www.cbc.ca/news/canada/british-columbia/story/2012/05/19/bc-jenna-talackova-miss-universe.html

Canadian Press. (2012b, April 20). Vehicles a Bigger Danger to the Poor Than the Wealthy, Study Suggests. *Hamilton Spectator,* p. A11.

Canadian Sociology and Anthropology Association. (1995). *Code of ethics.* Montreal.

Cantril, H. (1941). *The psychology of social movements.* New York: Wiley.

CanWest News Service. (2007, October 25). More and more women are practising medicine in Canada, but a new Canadian Institute for Health Information report says male physicians still far outnumber women doctors in Canada.

Capponi, P. (1997). *Dispatches from the poverty line.* Toronto: Penguin Books.

Cardoso, F. H. (1972, July–August). Dependent capitalist development in Latin America. *New Left Review, 74,* 83–95.

Carpenter, B. (1990, September 17). Redwood radicals. *U.S. News & World Report, 109*(11), 50–51.

Carrington, T. (1993, September 20). Developed nations want poor countries to succeed on trade, but not too much. *Wall Street Journal,* p. A10.

Carroll, B., & Hackett, R. A. (2006). *Remaking Media: The Struggle to Democratize Public Communication*. London: Routledge.

Carroll, W. K. (2004). *Corporate power in a globalizing world: A study in elite social organization*. Toronto: Oxford University Press.

Cass, C., & Anderson, S. A. (2011, September 28). Most young Americans face online bullies, poll finds. *Toronto Star,* p. A16.

Castellano, M. B. (2002). Aboriginal family trends: Extended families, nuclear families and families of the heart. Vanier Institute of the Family. Retrieved from http://www.vifamily.ca/library/cft/aboriginal.html

Catalyst. (2012). Women in Management in Canada. Retrieved from http://www.catalyst.org/publication/247/women-in-management-in-canada

Cauthen, N. K., & Jasper, J. M. (1994, September). Culture, politics, and moral panics. *Sociological Forum, 9*(3), 495–503.

CBC. (2006). China's economic miracle: the high price of progress. CBC News Online. Retrieved from http://www.cbc.ca/news/background/china

CBC News. (2008a, March 6). Canada's Super-rich. Retrieved from http://www.cbc.ca/news/background/wealth/

CBC News. (2008b, February 21). Retiring Mandatory Retirement. Retrieved from http://www.cbc.ca/news/background/retirement/mandatory_retirement.html

CBC News. (2009a, September 8). Africentric school opens in Toronto. Retrieved from http://www.cbc.ca

CBC News. (2009b, October 27). Homeless have Shorter Lifespan: Study. Retrieved from http://www.cbc.ca/news/health/story/2009/10/26/homeless-mortality.html

CBC News. (2009c, October 9). Military stress injuries on the rise.

CBC News. (2011a, November 17). Toronto approves 2nd Africentric school. Retrieved from http://www.cbc.ca

CBC News. (2011b). Women's Glass Ceiling Remains. August 31. Retrieved from http://www.cbc.ca/news/business/story/2011/08/31/women-executive-conference-board.html

Central Intelligence Agency (CIA). (2009). *The World Factbook 2009*. Washington, DC: Central Intelligence Agency. Retrieved from http://www.cia.gov/library/publications/the-world-factbook/rankorder/2102rank.html

Centre for Social Justice. (2001). New UN report shows Canada low-down in poverty ranking. Toronto: Centre for Social Justice.

Chafetz, J. S. (1990). *Gender equity: An integrated theory of stability and change*. Newbury Park, CA: Sage.

Chafetz, J. S., & Dworkin, A. G. (1986). *Female revolt: Women's movements in world and historical perspective*. Totowa, NJ: Rowman & Allanheld.

Chagnon, N. A. (1977). *Yanomamo: The fierce people* (2nd ed.). New York: Holt, Rinehart and Winston.

Chambliss, W. J. (2000). *Power, Politics, and Crime*. Boulder, CO: Westview Press.

Chambliss, W. J. (2007). The Saints and the Roughnecks. In J. M. Henslin, Ed., *Down to Earth Sociology: Introductory Readings*, 14th ed. New York: Free Press. (Original work published 1973).

Chandler, D. (1995). Technological or Media Determinism. Retrieved from http://www.aber.ac.uk/media/Documents/tecdet

Chandler, T., & Fox, G. (1974). *3000 years of urban growth*. New York: Academic Press.

Chandra, V. P. (1993a). Fragmented identities: The social construction of ethnicity, 1885–1947 [Unpublished paper].

Chandra, V. P. (1993b). The present moment of the past: The metamorphosis [Unpublished paper].

Chapman, S. A. (2005). Theorizing about aging well: Constructing a narrative. *Canadian Journal of Aging, 24*(1), 9–18.

Chappell, A. T., & Lanza-Kaduce, L. (2010). Police Academy Socialization: Understanding the Lessons Learned in a Paramilitary-Bureaucratic Organization. *Journal of Comparative Ethnography, 39*(2), 187–214.

Chappell, N., Gee, E., McDonald, L., & Stones, M. (2003). *Aging in contemporary Canada*. Toronto: Prentice Hall.

Chen, S. (2012). Segregation versus Self-Determination: A Black and White Debate on Canada's First Africentric School. In Lorne Tepperman and Angela Kalyta (eds.). *Reading Sociology: Canadian Perspectives* (2nd ed., pp. 132–135). Toronto: Oxford University Press.

Chawla, R. K. (2011). "The distribution of mortgage debt in Canada." *Perspectives on Labour and Income*. Summer, 3–12.

Chawla, R. K., & Uppal, S. (2012). "Household debt in Canada." *Perspectives on Labour and Income*. Summer, 4–15.

Chen, K. (1995). "China's Women Face Obstacles in Workplace." *Wall Street Journal,* August 28, B1. B5.

Christensen, J. (2000). Africa: Dying by the numbers. Retrieved from http://www.cnn.com/SPECIALS/2000/aids/stories/overview/AIDS

Chua, A. (2011). *The Battle Hymn of the Tiger Mother*. New York: The Penguin Press.

Chui, T. (2011). "Immigrant Women." *Women in Canada: A Gender-based Statistical Report*. Ottawa: Minister of Industry. Statistics Canada, Catalogue # 89-503-X.

Chui, T., & Maheux, H. (2011). "Visible Minority Women." *Women in Canada: A Gender-based Statistical Report*. Ottawa: Minister of Industry. Statistics Canada, Catalogue # 89-503-X.

Chung, J. (2011). "Measuring voluntary interhousehold transfers in Canada." *Perspectives on Labour and Income*. 23(2): 35–44.

Chung, L. (2006, June). Education and Earnings. *Perspectives on Labour and Income*. Statistics Canada, Catalogue No. 75-001-XIE: pp. 5–12.

Church, G., Greenberg, K., & McPhedran, M. (1997). Toronto: An Urban Alternative, in Robert Geddes, ed., *Cities in Our Future: Growth and Form, Environmental Health and Social Equity*. Island Press: pp. 93–113

Clark, S. D. (1942). *The social development of Canada: An introductory study with select documents*. Toronto: University of Toronto Press.

Clark, W., Schellenberg, G. (2006). Who's Religious? *Canadian Social Trends 81*. (Summer), 2–9.

Clarke, L. H. (2001). Older women's bodies and the self: The construction of identity in later life. *Canadian Review of Sociology and Anthropology, 38*, 441–464.

Clarke, S. (2006). Theory and Practice: Psychoanalytic Sociology as Psycho-Social Studies. *Sociology*. 40, 6: 1153–1169.

Clement, W. (1975). *The Canadian corporate elite: An analysis of economic power*. Toronto: McClelland and Stewart.

Clement, W. (1977). *Continental corporate power: Economic elite linkages between Canada and the United States*. Toronto: McClelland and Stewart.

Clement, W. (1983). *Class, power and property: Essays on Canadian society*. Toronto: McClelland and Stewart.

Clement, W., & Myles, J. (1994). *Relations of ruling: Class and gender in postindustrial societies*. Montreal: McGill-Queen's University Press.

Cloward, R. A., & Ohlin, L. E. (1960). *Delinquency and opportunity: A theory of delinquent gangs*. New York: Free Press.

CNN World News. (2002, December 12). "Honor killings" rise in Pakistan. Retrieved from http://www.cnn.com

Cohen, S. (1972). *Folk Devils and Moral Panics: The Creation of the Mods and Rockers*. London: MacGibbon and Kee.

Colapinto, J. (2001). *As Nature Made Him: The Boy Who Was Raised as a Girl*. New York: Harper Collins.

Colasanti, T., Slevin, K. F., & King, N. (2006, Spring). Ageism and Feminism: From "et Cetera" to Center. *National Women's Studies Association Journal, 18*(1), 13–30.

Cole, J., & Lubman, S. (1994, January 28). Weapons merchants are going great guns in post-Cold War era. *Wall Street Journal*, pp. A1, A4.

Coleman, J. W. (1995). Politics and the abuse of power. In J. M. Henslin (Ed.), *Down to earth sociology: Introductory readings* (8th ed., pp. 442–450). New York: Free Press.

Collins, R. (1971). Functional and conflict theory of educational stratification. *American Sociological Review. 36*(6), 1002–1019.

Collins, R. (1974). *Conflict sociology: Toward an explanatory science*. New York: Academic Press.

Collins, R. (1979). *The credential society: An historical sociology of education*. New York: Academic Press.

Collins, R. (1988). *Theoretical sociology*. San Diego: Harcourt, Brace Jovanovich.

Collins, R., Chafetz, J. S., Blumberg, R. L., Coltrane, S., & Turner, J. H. (1993). Toward an integrated theory of gender stratification. *Sociological Perspectives, 36*(3), 185–216.

Community Information Centre of Metropolitan Toronto. (1997). *55 plus Ontario: A handbook on services for older adults*. Toronto: The Community Information Centre.

Compton, S. (2011). Women with activity limitations. In *Women in Canada: A gender-based statistical report*. Statistics Canada catalogue no. 89-503-X. Ottawa: Minister of Industry.

Connell, R. W. (2000). Masculinities and globalization. In M. Zinn, P. Hondagneu-Sotelo, & M. Messner (Eds.), *Gender through the prism of difference* (2nd ed., pp. 49–62). Boston: Allyn and Bacon.

Conrad, D. (2012, May 13). Nairobi's Garbage Dump Pits Pickers Against Neighbours. *Globe and Mail*. Retrieved from http://www.theglobeandmail.com/news/world/nairobis-garbage-dump-pits-pickers-against-neighbours/article2431432

Cooley, C. H. (1902). *Human nature and the social order*. New York: Scribner's.

Coontz, S. (2006). *Marriage, A History: How Love Conquered Marriage*. New York: Penguin.

Copper, B. (2001). Voices: On becoming old women. In S. Shaw and J. Lee (Eds.), *Women's Voices, Feminist Visions: Classic and Contemporary Readings* (pp. 94–97). Mountain View, California: Mayfield Publishing Company.

Cordileone, E. (2011, September 15). "Bitch sticks" target women. *Toronto Star*, p. R4.

Corsaro, W. A. (2004). *The Sociology of Childhood* (2nd ed.). Thousand Oaks, CA: Pine Forge Press.

Coser, L. A. (1977). *Masters of sociological thought: Ideas in historical and social context* (2nd ed.). New York: Harcourt Brace Jovanovich.

Courtney, K. (1995). Two sides of the environmental movement: Radical Earth First! and the Sierra Club. [Paper presented at the 1995 meetings of the American Sociological Association].

Cousins, A., & Nagpaul, H. (1970). *Urban man and society*. New York: McGraw-Hill.

Cowley, G. (1996, November 16). Attention: Aging men. *Newsweek, 66*–75.

Cowley, J. (1969). *Pioneers of Women's Liberation*. New York: Merit.

Crabb, P. B., & Marciano, D. L. (2011). Representations of Material Culture and Gender in Award-Winning Children's Books: A 20-Year Follow-up. *Journal of Research in Childhood Education. 25*: 390–398.

Crane, D. (2000, September 17). Poverty guarantees a nastier world. *Toronto Star*, p. B6.

Cribb, R. (2012, January 12). Doting dads do work-kid dance. *Toronto Star*, p. L4.

Cribb, R., & Brazao. (2007 October 20). Big-box daycare coming to Canada. *Toronto Star*. Retrieved from http://www.thestar.com/News/Canada/article/268752

Crompton, S. (2000, Winter). 100 years of . . . health. *Canadian Social Trends*, 12–17.

Crompton, S. (2011). "What's stressing the stressed? Main sources of stress among workers." *Canadian Social Trends*. 92: 44–51.

Crossen, C. (1991, November 14). *Wall Street Journal*, pp. A1, A7.

Cruikshank, M. (2003). *Learning to be Old: Gender, Culture, and Aging*. Lanham: Rowman & Littlefield Publishers, Inc.

Cumming, S., & Duffy, A. (2012). Class and gender inequality. In L. Tepperman, P. Albanese, & B. Curtis (Eds.), *Sociology: A Canadian perspective* (3rd ed., pp. 177–199). Toronto: Oxford.

Cumming, S. and Duffy. A. (2012). "Class and Status Inequality". pp. 177–199 in Lorne Tepperman, Patrizia Albanese and Jim Curtis (eds.) *Sociology: A Canadian Perspective*. 3rd Edition. Toronto: Oxford University Press.

Cunningham, G. B. (2008). Creating and Sustaining Gender Diversity in Sport Organizations. *Sex Roles*. 58, 136–145.

Currie, E. (2004). *The Road to Whatever: Middle-Class Culture and The Crisis of Adolescence*. New York: Metropolitan Books.

Curtis, B., Livingstone, D. W., & Smaller, H. (1992). *Stacking the Deck: The Streaming of Working-Class Kids in Ontario Schools*. Montreal: Our Schools/Our Selves Education Foundation.

Curtis, J., Grabb, E., & Guppy, N. (Ed.). (1999). *Social Inequality in Canada: Patterns, Problems, and Policies* (3rd ed.). Toronto: Prentice-Hall.

Curwin, E. C., & Hart, G. (1961). *Plough and pasture*. New York: Collier Books.

Cyberschool makes its debut. (1996, January). *The American Schoolboard. 183*(1), A11.

Dahl, R. A. (1961). *Who governs?* New Haven, CT: Yale University Press.

Dahl, R. A. (1982). *Dilemmas of pluralist democracy: Autonomy vs. control*. New Haven, CT: Yale University Press.

Dahrendorf, R. (1959). *Class and class conflict in industrial society*. Palo Alto, CA: Stanford University Press.

The Daily. (2006, July 31). Births 2004. http://www.statcan.ca/Daily/English.

The Daily. (2007a, December 4). 2006 Census: Immigration, citizenship, language, mobility and migration. Retrieved from http://www.statcan.ca/Daily/English/.

The Daily. (2007b, June 13). General Social Survey: Navigating family transitions. http://www.statcan.ca/Daily/English.

The Daily. (2007c, December 19). Study: Returning to work after childbirth. Retrieved from http://www.statcan.ca/Daily/English/.

The Daily. (2007d, October 29). Study: Frequency of contact between separated fathers and their children. http://www.statcan.ca/Daily/English.

The Daily. (2008a, May 1). 2006 Census: earnings, income and shelter costs. http://www.statcan.ca/Daily/English.

The Daily. (2008b, June 11). Family income and related variables: Sub-provincial data. http://www.statcan.ca/Daily/English.

The Daily. (2008c, May 5). Income of Canadians. Retrieved from http://www.statcan.ca/Daily/English.

The Daily. (2008d, February 7). Study: Participation in Sports. Retrieved from http://www.statcan.ca/Daily/English.

The Daily. (2010, March 9). Study: Projections of the diversity of the Canadian population. Retrieved from http://www.statcan.gc.ca/daily-quotidien/100309/dq100309a-eng.htm

The Daily. (2012, July 30). "Study: Lave practices of parents after birth or adoption of young children." pp. 2–3. *Statistics Canada.*

Daly, R. (2006, December 8). Woman's Extra Pay Costs Her Daycare. *Toronto Star,* p. A4.

Danesi, M. (2003). *Forever young: The "teen-aging" of modern culture.* Toronto: University of Toronto Press.

Darnell, V. (1971, May). *Qualitative-quantitative content analysis of graffiti in the public restrooms of St. Louis, Missouri, and Edwardsville, Illinois* [Master's thesis]. Edwardsville, IL: Southern Illinois University.

Daubs, K. (2012, April 6). Preschoolers assume fatter peers are mean. *Toronto Star,* pp. GT1, GT8.

Davies, S. (1999). Stubborn disparities: Explaining class inequalities in schooling. In J. Curtis, E. Grubb, and N. Guppy (Eds.), *Social Inequality in Canada: Patterns, Problems, Policies.* Toronto: Prentice-Hall.

Davies, S., & Guppy, N. (2006). *The schooled society: An introduction to the sociology of education.* Toronto: Oxford University Press.

Davis, A., Gardner, B. B., & Gardner, M. R. (1941). *Deep south: A social-anthropological study of caste and class.* Chicago: University of Chicago Press.

Davis, F. (1959, September). The cabdriver and his fare: Facets of a fleeting relationship. *American Journal of Sociology, 65,* 158–165.

Davis, K., & Moore, W. E. (1945). Some principles of stratification. *American Sociological Review, 10,* 242–249.

Davis, K., & Moore, W. E. (1953). Reply to Tumin. *American Sociological Review, 18,* 394–396.

Davis, K. (2010). Coming of Age Online: The Developmental Underpinnings of Girls' Blogs. *Journal of Adolescent Research.* 25(1), 145–171.

Davis, N. J. (1978). Prostitution: Identity, career, and legal-economic enterprise. In J. M. Henslin & E. Sagarin (Eds.), *The sociology of sex: An introductory reader* (rev. ed., pp. 195–222). New York: Schocken Books.

Davis, N. J., & Robinson, R. V. (1988, February). Class identification of men and women in the 1970s and 1980s. *American Sociological Review, 53,* 103–112. Deegan, M. J. (1988, Winter). W. E. B. du Bois

Davis, R. L. (2010). *More Perfect Union: The American Search for Marital Bliss.* Cambridge: Harvard University Press. and the women of Hull-House, 1895–1899. *American Sociologist,* 301–311.

de Jong Gierveld, J., & Havens, B. (2004). Cross-national comparisons of social isolation and loneliness: Introduction and overview. *Canadian Journal on Aging, 23*(2), 109–113.

DeKeseredy, W., & Hinch, R. (1991). *Woman Abuse: Sociological Perspectives.* Toronto: Thompson Educational Publishers.

DeMartini, J. R. (1982). Basic and applied sociological work: Divergence, convergence, or peaceful co-existence? *The Journal of Applied Behavioral Science, 18*(2), 203–215.

DeMause, L. (1975, April). Our forebears made childhood a nightmare. *Psychology Today 8*(11), 85–88.

Denzin, N. K. (1992, July–August). The suicide machine. *Society,* 7–10.

Department of Indian Affairs and Northern Development (DIAND). (2001). Basic departmental data. Retrieved from http://www.ainc-inac.gc.ca/pr/sts/bdd01/bdd01_e.pdf

Desroches, F. (1990). "Tearoom trade": A research update. *Qualitative Sociology,* Volume 31, Number 1, pp. 39–61.

de Tocqueville, A. (1955). *The old regime and the French Revolution* (S. Gilbert, Trans.). Garden City, NY: Doubleday Anchor. (Original work published 1856)

de Tocqueville, A. (1966). *Democracy in America* (J. P. Mayer & M. Lerner, Eds.). New York: Harper & Row. (Original work published 1835)

Deutsch, A. (2000, September 13). Dutch bill gives gays right to marry. *Toronto Star,* p. A13.

De Vries, B. (2010). "Friendship and Family: The Company We Keep." *Transition* (Vanier Institute of the Family). Winter: 1–4.

De Vries, B., & Johnson, C. (2002). The death of friends in later life. In R. A. Settersten, Jr., & T. J. Owens (Eds.), *New frontiers in socialization* (pp. 299–324). Amsterdam: JAI.

De Waal, F. (2005). *Our Inner Ape.* New York: Riverhead Books.

Dewan, S., & Gebeloff, R. (2012, May 26). Men Find Rewards in Jobs Dominated by Women. *New York Times.*

DeParle, J. & Tavernise, S. (2012). "In U.S. Unwed Mothers Are Now in the Majority." *New York Times (Toronto Star Edition).* March 18: 7.

de Young, M. (1989, March). The world according to NAMBLA: Accounting for deviance. *Journal of Sociology and Social Welfare, 16*(1), 111–126.

Diamond, M. (1982). Sexual identity: Monozygotic twins reared in discordant sex roles and a BBC follow-up. *Archives of Sexual Behavior, 11*(2), 181–186.

Dickson, T., & McLachlan, H. V. (1989). In search of "the spirit of capitalism": Weber's misinterpretation of Franklin. *Sociology, 23*(1), 81–89.

Dill, K. E., & Thill, K. P. (2007). Video Game Characters and the Socialization of Gender Roles: Young People's Perceptions Mirror Sexist Media Depictions. *Sex Roles 58*, 851–864.

DiManno, R. (2011, December 5). Kingston canal trial hears expert testimony on honour killing. *Toronto Star.*

Dirks, G. E. (1995). *Controversy and complexity: Canadian immigration policy during the 1980s.* Montreal: McGill-Queen's University Press.

Dobriner, W. M. (1969). *Social Structures and Systems.* Pacific Palisades, CA: Goodyear.

Domhoff, G. W. (1978). *Who really rules? New Haven and community power reexamined.* New Brunswick, NJ: Transaction.

Domhoff, G. W. (1983). *Who rules America now? A view of the '80s.* Englewood Cliffs, NJ: Prentice Hall.

Domhoff, G. W. (1990). *The power elite and the state: How policy is made in America.* Hawthorne, NY: Aldine de Gruyter.

Domhoff, G. W. (1996). *State Autonomy or Class Dominance? Case Studies on Policy Making in America.* Hawthorne, NY: Aldine de Gruyter.

Domhoff, G. W. (1997). The bohemian grove and other retreats. In J. M. Henslin (Ed.), *Down to earth sociology: Introductory readings* (9th ed., pp. 340–352). New York: Free Press.

Domhoff, G. W. (2006). *Who rules America? Power, politics, and social change* (5th ed.). New York: McGraw-Hill.

Doren, K., & Jones, C. (2000). *You Go Girl! Winning the Woman's Way.* Kansas City: Andrews McMeel Publishing.

Doucet, A. (2012). Gender Equality and Gender Differences: Parenting, Habitus, and Embodiment. pp. 107–111 in L.Tepperman and A. Kalyta (Eds.), *Reading Sociology: Canadian Perspectives* (2nd ed.). Toronto: Oxford University Press.

Douglas, A. (2011, October 12). Nurture over nature effect. *Toronto Star,* p. E9.

Douglas, A. (2012). "Dads aim for work-life balance." *Toronto Star.* May 7: E6.

Downe, P. J. (2006). Aboriginal Girls in Canada: Living Histories of Dislocation, Exploitation and Strength. In Y. Jiwani, C. Steenbergen, C. Mitchell (Eds.), *Girlhood: Redefining the Limits.* (pp. 1–14). Montreal: Black Rose.

Doyle, J. A. (1995). *The male experience* (3rd ed.). Madison, WI: WCB Brown & Benchmark Publishers.

Drolet, M. (2002). *The "who, what, when and where" of gender pay differentials.* Ottawa: Statistics Canada, Catalogue 71-584-MIE No. 4.

Drake, T. (2012). "How Much Does Raising a Child Cost?" *Canadianfinanceblog.* Accessed August 14, 2012.

Drolet, M. (2005). *Participation in postsecondary education in Canada: Has the role of parental income and education changed over the 1990s?* Ottawa: Statistics Canada, Catalogue 11F0019MIE No. 243.

Drucker, P. F. (1987, April 22). The rise and fall of the blue-collar worker. *Wall Street Journal,* p. 36.

Drucker, P. F. (1994, November). The age of social transformation. *Atlantic Monthly, 274*(5), 53+.

DuBois, S. (2011). Global 500: Walmart Stores. Retrieved from http://money.cnn.com/magazines/fortune/global500/2011/snapshots/2255.html

Du Bois, W. E. B. (1992). *Black reconstruction in America, 1860–1889.* New York: Atheneum. (Original work published 1935)

Duffy, A. (1996). Bad girls in hard times: Canadian female juvenile offenders. In G. M. O'Bireck (Ed.), *Not A Kid Anymore: Canadian Youth, Crime and Subcultures* (pp. 203–220). Toronto: Nelson Canada.

Duffy, A., Mandell, N., & Pupo, N. (1989). *Few choices: Women, work and family.* Toronto: Garamond Press.

Duffy, A., & Momirov, J. (1997). *Family violence: A Canadian introduction.* Toronto: Lorimer.

Duffy, A., & Pupo, N. (1992). *The part-time paradox: Connecting gender, work and family.* Toronto: McClelland and Stewart.

Duffy, A., & Pupo, N. (1996). *Family-friendly organizations and beyond: proposals for policy directions with women in mind.* National Forum on Family Security. Ottawa: Canada Council on Social Development.

Duffy, A. (2011). "Families in Tough Times: The Impact of Economic Crises on Canadian Families." pp. 164–210 in Mandell, Nancy and Ann Duffy eds. *Canadian Families: Diversity, Conflict and Change.* 4th Edition. Toronto: Nelson.

Dugger, C. W. (2001, April 22). Abortion in India is tipping scales sharply against girls. *New York Times.*

Duncan, G. J., Ziol-Guest, K. M., & Kalil, A. 2010. Early-childhood poverty and adult attainment, behavior, and health. *Child Development, 81*(1), 306–325.

Dunlap, R. E., & Catton, W. R., Jr. (1979). Environmental sociology. *Annual Review of Sociology, 5,* 243–273.

Dunlap, R. E., & Catton, W. R., Jr. (1983). What environmental sociologists have in common whether concerned with "built" or "natural" environments. *Sociological Inquiry, 53*(2/3), 113–135.

Dunphy, B. (2006, December 14). Rich and Poor Gap Widens. *Hamilton Spectator,* p. A14.

Durbin, S. (1995, July–August). Mexico. *Population Today,* 7.

Durkheim, E. (1933). *The division of labor in society* (G. Simpson, Trans.). New York: Free Press. (Original work published 1893)

Durkheim, E. (1938, 1958, 1964). *The rules of sociological method* (S. A. Solovay & J. H. Mueller, Trans.). New York: Free Press. (Original work published 1895)

Durkheim, E. (1965). *The elementary forms of the religious life.* New York: Free Press. (Original work published 1912)

Durkheim, E. (1966). *Suicide: A study in sociology* (J. A. Spaulding & G. Simpson, Trans.). New York: Free Press. (Original work published 1897)

Durning, A. (1990). Cradles of life. In L. W. Barnes (Ed.), *Social Problems 90/91* (pp. 231–241). Guilford, CT: Dushkin.

Dyke, D. J. (1991). *Crucified women*. Toronto: United Church.

Eckholm, E. (2002, June 21). Desire for sons drives use of prenatal scans in China. *New York Times*.

Ecklund, E. H. (2008). Religion and Spirituality Among Scientists. *Contexts* 7(1), 12–15.

The Economist. (2010, November 25). Poverty in Canada: Mean Streets. *The Economist*. Retrieved from http://www.economist.com/node/17581844/print

Eder, K. (1990). The rise of counter-culture movements against modernity: Nature as a new field of class struggle. *Theory, Culture & Society, 7*, 21–47.

Edgerton, R. B. (1992). *Sick societies: Challenging the myth of primitive harmony*. New York: Free Press.

Edwards, R. (1979). *Contested terrain: The transformation of the workplace in the twentieth century*. New York: Basic Books.

Ehrenreich, B., & English, D. (1973). *Witches, midwives, and nurses: A history of women healers*. Old Westbury, NY: Feminist Press.

Eichler, M. (1988a). *Families in Canada today: Recent changes and their policy consequences* (2nd ed.). Toronto: Gage Educational Publishing.

Eichler, M. (1988b). *Nonsexist research methods: A practical guide*. New York: Routledge.

Eichler, M. (1997). *Family shifts: Families, policies and gender equality*. Toronto: Oxford University Press.

Eisenhart, R. W. (1975, Fall). You can't hack it, little girl: A discussion of the covert psychological agenda of modern combat training. *Journal of Social Issues, 31*, 13–23.

Elkins, S. M. (1968). *Slavery: A problem in American institutional and intellectual life* (2nd ed.). Chicago: University of Chicago Press.

Elliott, P., & Mandell, N. (2001). Feminist Theories. In N. Mandell, editor. *Feminist Issues: Race, Class and Sexuality*. Toronto: Prentice Hall, pp. 23–48.

Elwell, S. (1996). Women's voices: The challenges of feminism to Judaism. In C. Wessenger (Ed.), *Religious institutions and women's leadership: New roles inside the mainstream* (pp. 331–43). Columbia, SC: University of South Carolina.

Engels, F. (1942). *The origin of the family, private property, and the state*. New York: International Publishing. (Original work published 1884)

Epstein, C. F. (1988). *Deceptive distinctions: Sex, gender, and the social order*. New Haven, CT: Yale University Press.

Epstein, C. F. (1989, January 26). Letter to the author.

Epstein, C. F. (2007, February). Great Divides: The Cultural, Cognitive and Social Bases of the Global Subordination of Women. *American Sociological Review, 72*: pp. 1–22.

Epstein, D. (2011, July 27). One Year Out: Semenya Remains a Mystery For London Olympics. *Sports Illustrated*. Retrieved from http://sportsillustrated.cnn.com/2011/writers/david_epstein/07/20/semenya/index.html

Ernst, E. G. (1988). The Baptists. In C. H. Lippy & P. W. Williams (Eds.), *Encyclopedia of the American religious experience: Studies of traditions and movements* (Vol. 1, pp. 555–577). New York: Scribners.

Escalante, J. & Dirmann, J. (1990). "The Jaime Escalante Math Program." *Journal of Negro Education, 59*(3), Summer: 407–423.

Erturk, Y. (1994). The status of Moslem women in Turkey and Saudi Arabia. In J. Curtis & L. Tepperman (Eds.), *Haves and have-nots: An international reader on social inequality* (pp. 288–293). Englewood Cliffs, NJ: Prentice Hall.

Etzioni, A. (Ed.). (1969). *The semi-professions and their organization*. New York: Free Press.

Evers, A., & Laville, J. L. (Ed.). (2004). *The Third Sector in Europe*. Northampton, Mass., Edward Elgar Publishing.

Faludi, S. (1999). *Stiffed: The betrayal of the American man*. New York: Willian Morrow & Company.

Fanon, F. (1962). *Wretched of the earth*. New York: Grove Press

Faris, R. E. L., & Dunham, W. (1939). *Mental disorders in urban areas*. Chicago: University of Chicago Press.

Farkas, G. (1996). *Human capital or cultural capital?: Ethnicity and poverty groups in an urban school district*. New York: Walter DeGruyter.

Farkas, G., Grobe, R. P., Sheehan, D., & Shuan, Y. (1990, February). Cultural resources and school success: Gender, ethnicity, and poverty groups within an urban school district. *American Sociological Review, 55*, 127–142.

Farkas, G., Sheehan, D., & Grobe, R. P. (1990, Winter). Coursework mastery and school success: Gender, ethnicity, and poverty groups within an urban school district. *American Educational Research Journal, 27*(4), 807–827.

Faulkner, R. (2008, April 11). Getting a Second Chance: More Women Than Men Go Back To Finish High School. *Hamilton Spectator*, p. A4.

Faulkner, R. (2006). "Mac Beams `Podcasts' to Potential Students." *Hamilton Spectator*, April 12: A7.

Faunce, W. A. (1981). *Problems of an industrial society* (2nd ed.). New York: McGraw-Hill.

Featherman, D. L. (1979). Opportunities are expanding. *Society, 13*, 4–11.

Featherman, D. L., & Hauser, R. M. (1978). *Opportunity and change*. New York: Academic Press.

Featherstone, L. (2004). *Selling Women Short: The Landmark Battle for Workers' Rights at Walmart*. New York: Basic Books.

Ferguson, K. E. (1984). *The Feminist Case Against Bureaucracy*. Philadelphia: Temple University Press.

Ferguson, T. (1995). *Golden Rule*. Chicago: University of Chicago.

Ferrao, V. (2010). "Paid Work" in Women in Canada: A Gender-based Statistical Report. Statistics Canada Catalogue no. 89-503-X. Ottawa: Minister of Industry.

Feshbach, M., & Friendly, A., Jr. (1992). *Ecocide in the USSR: Health and nature under siege.* New York: Basic Books.

Findlay, S. (2012, January 30). Were Shafia murders "honour killings" or domestic violence? *Toronto Star.* http://www.thestar.com/news/article/1123403--were-shafia-murders-honour-killings-or-domestic-violence

Finnie, R. (2000, September). The dynamics of poverty in Canada. *C.D. Howe Institute Commentary, 145.*

Firestone, S. (1970). *The Dialectic of Sex.* New York: Morrow.

Fisher, S. (1986). *In the patient's best interest: Women and the politics of medical decisions.* New Brunswick, NJ: Rutgers University Press.

Fishman, C. (2003, December). The Wal-Mart you don't know. *Fast Company.* Retrieved from http://pf.fastcompany.com/magazine/77/walmart.html

Fitzgerald, M. (2004, July 18). A drive-through lane to the next time zone. *New York Times,* p. BU3.

Flavelle, D. (2006, March 2). Gender Gap at the Big Table. *Hamilton Spectator,* p. A16.

Flavelle, D. (2011). "All in the family." *Toronto Star.* April 2: B6.

Fleras, A., & Elliott, J. L. (1996). *Unequal Relations: An Introduction to Race, Ethnic, and Aboriginal Dynamics in Canada* (2nd ed.). Scarborough, ON: Prentice Hall.

Flink, J. J. (1990). *The automobile age.* Cambridge, MA: MIT Press.

Foley, D. E. (1997). The great American football ritual. In J. M. Henslin (Ed.), *Down to earth sociology: Introductory readings* (9th ed., pp. 412–475). New York: Free Press.

Foley, L. A., Evancic, C., Karnik, K., King, J., & Parks, A. (1995, February). Date rape: Effects of race of assailant and victim and gender of subjects on perceptions. *Journal of Black Psychology, 21*(1), 6–18.

Fonda, F., Fultz, N., Wheeler, L., & Wray, L. (2000, November 19). *Economic and employment outcomes of obesity in middle-aged women and men.* Paper presented at Gerontological Society of America.

Fong, P. (2012, January 8). Life "impossible" on $610 a month. *Toronto Star,* p. A6.

Food and Agriculture Organization of the United Nations. (2006). World and Regional Review: Facts and Figures.

Food Banks Canada. (2011). *Hunger count: A comprehensive report on hunger and food bank use in Canada.* Retrieved from http://www.foodbankscanada.ca/HungerCount

Foote, J. (1990, February 5). Trying to take back the planet. *Newsweek, 115*(6), 24–25.

Forbes. (2012). The World's Billionaires. Retrieved from http://www.forbes.com/billionaires/#p_3_s_a0_All%20industries_Canada_All%20states

Forbes, G. B., & Frederick, D. A. (2008). The UCLA Body Project II: Breast and Body Dissatisfaction among African, Asian, European and Hispanic American College Women. *Sex Roles. 58:* 449–457.

Forbes, S. (2005). *A Natural History of Families.* Princeton: Princeton University Press.

Forcese, D. (1997). *The Canadian class structure* (4th ed.). Toronto: McGraw-Hill Ryerson.

Fost, D. (2008). They're Working on Their Own, Just Side by Side. nytimes.com. Retrieved from http://www.nytimes.com/2008/02/20/business/businessspecial2/20cowork.html?pagewanted=1&_r=1&ref=businessspecial2

Foster, R. (2008). Show and Tell: Teaching Critical Fetishism with a Bottle of Coke®. *Anthropology News,* 49:4, 38.

Fox, B. (2009). *When Couples Become Parents: The Creation of Gender in the Transition to Parenthood.* Toronto: University of Toronto Press.

Francis, D. (1986). *Controlling interest: Who owns Canada?* Toronto: Macmillan.

Frederick, D. A., Forbes, G. B., Grigorian, K. E., & Jarcho, J. M. (2007). The UCLA Body Project 1: Gender and Ethnic Differences in Self-Objectification and Body Satisfaction Among 2,206 Undergraduates. *Sex Roles.* 57: 317–327.

Frederick, J. A., & Fast, J. E. (1999, Autumn). Eldercare in Canada: Who does how much? *Canadian Social Trends, 54,* 26–30.

French, H. W. (2004, April 14). As girls "vanish," Chinese city battles tide of abortions. *New York Times.*

Frenette, M., & Zeman, K. (2007). Why Are Most University Students Women? Evidence Based on Academic Performance, Study Habits and Parental Influences. Statistics Canada catalogue no. 11F0019MIF. Ottawa: Minister of Industry.

Frenette, M., Hou, F., Morissette, R., Wannell, T., & Webber, M. (2008, May). Earnings and Incomes of Canadians Over the Past Quarter Century, 2006 Census. Statistics Canada, Catalogue 97-563-X.

Freud, S. (1930). *Civilization and its discontents.* Translated and edited by J. Strachey. New York: W.W. Norton.

Freudenburg, W. R., & Gramling, R. (1989, November). The emergence of environmental sociology: Contributions of E. Dunlap and William R. Catton, Jr. *Sociological Inquiry, 59*(4), 439–452.

Frideres, J., & Gadacz, R. (2001). *Aboriginal Peoples in Canada: Contemporary Conflicts* (6th ed.). Toronto: Prentice Hall.

Frideres, J. S. (2011). *First Nations in the Twenty-First Century.* Toronto: Oxford University Press.

Friedan, B. (1993). *The Fountain of Age.* New York: Simon and Shuster.

Friedl, E. (1990). Society and sex roles. In J. P. Spradley & McCurdy, D. W. (Eds.), *Conformity and conflict: Readings in cultural anthropology* (pp. 229–238). Glenview, IL: Scott, Foresman.

Fulcher, M., Sutfin, E. L., & Patternson, C. J. (2008). Individual Differences in Gender Development: Associations with Parental Sexual Orientation, Attitudes, and Division of Labor. *Sex Roles, 58,* 330–341.

Furtado, C. (1984). *The economic growth of Brazil: A survey of colonial to modern times. Westport, CT: Greenwood Press.*

Gabler, J., & Kaufman, J. (2006). Chess, Cheerleading, Chopin: What Gets You Into College? *Contexts, 5*(2), 45–49.

Gabriel, T. (2010, July 5). To Stop Cheats, Colleges Learn Their Trickery. *New York Times.* Assessed at http://www.nytimes.com/2010/07/06/education/06cheat.html?src=me&ref=general

Gagne, L. G. (2003). *Parental work, child-care use and young children's cognitive outcomes.* Research Paper. Statistics Canada Catalogue no. 89-594-XIE. Ottawa: Minister of Industry.

Galabuzi, G.-E. (2006). *Canada's Economic Apartheid: The Social Exclusion of Racialized Groups in the New Century.* Toronto: Canadian Scholars' Press.

Galambos, N., & Krahn, H. (2008, February). Depression and Anger Trajectories During the Transition to Adulthood. *Journal of Marriage and the Family, 70,* 15–27.

Galarneau, D., & Morissette, R. (2004, June). Immigrants: Settling for less? *Perspectives on labour and income,* pp. 5–16. Catalogue no. 75-001-XIE.

Galbraith, J. K. (1979). *The nature of mass poverty.* Cambridge, MA: Harvard University Press.

Galinsky, E. (1999). *Ask the children: What America's children really think about working parents.* New York: William Morrow and Company.

Galinsky, E., & Stein, P. J. (1990, December). The impact of human resource policies on employees: Balancing work/family life. *Journal of Family Issues, 11*(4), 368–383.

Galliher, J. F. (1991). *Deviant behavior and human rights.* Englewood Cliffs, NJ: Prentice Hall.

Gallmeier, C. P. (1988). Methodological issues in qualitative sport research: Participant observation among hockey players. *Sociological Spectrum, 8,* 213–235.

Galloway, G., & Wingrove, J. (2010, June 15). Time Crunch—All Work and No Play: Why Our Well-Being Hangs in the Balance. *Globe and Mail,* pp. A1, A6.

Galt, V. (2011, October 7). Work-Life Balance: The Impossible Dream? Globe and Mail. Retrieved from http://www.theglobeandmail.com/report-on-business/careers/top-employers/top-employers-2012/work-life-balance-the-impossible-dream/article2193165

Gans, H. J. (1962). *The urban villagers.* New York: Free Press.

Gans, H. J. (1968). *People and plans: Essays on urban problems and solutions.* New York: Basic Books.

Gans, H. J. (1970). Urbanism and suburbanism. In A. N. Cousins & H. Nagpaul (Eds.), *Urban man and society: A reader in urban ecology* (pp. 157–164). New York: Knopf.

Gans, H. J. (1991). *People, plans, and policies: Essays on poverty, racism, and other national urban problems.* New York: Columbia University Press.

Gardner, D. (2004). Getting tough with young offenders. Responding to youth crime: Do get-tough policies work? In J. V. Roberts & M. G. Grossman (Eds.), *Criminal Justice in Canada—A reader* (2nd ed.). Scarborough: Nelson/Thomson.

Garfinkel, H. (1956, March). Conditions of successful degradation ceremonies. *American Journal of Sociology, 61*(2), 420–424.

Garigue, P. (1964). French Canada: A case study in sociological analysis. *Canadian Review of Sociology.* 1(4). pp. 186–192.

Garrison, J. (2007, February 3). This Teacher is No Ordinary Joe. *Hamilton Spectator,* p. A8.

Gaszo, A. (2012). "Moral Codes of Mothering and the Introduction of Welfare-to-Work in Ontario." *Canadian Review of Sociology.* 49(1): 26–49.

Gaudet, S., Cooke, M., & Joanna, J. (2011). "Working after Childbirth: A Lifecourse Transition Analysis of Canadian Women from the 1970s to the 2000s. *Canadian Review of Sociology.* 48(2): 137-180.

Gelles, R. J., & Cornell, C. P. (1985). *Intimate violence in families.* Beverly Hills, CA: Sage Publications.

Gerin, L. (1928). *Le type économique et social des Canadiens. Milieux agricoles de traditions françaises.* Montreal: Fides.

Gerlsbeck, R. (2009, December/January). Squeezed: Canada's middle class is in financial trouble. That's in good times. What happens in a recession? *MoneySense* Magazine.

Gerson, K. (1985). *Hard choices: How women decide about work, career, and motherhood.* Berkeley: University of California Press.

Gerson, K. 2010. *The Unfinished Revolution: How a New Generation is Reshaping Family, Work and Gender in America.* New York: Oxford University Press.

Gerth, H. H., & Mills, C. W. (1958). *From Max Weber: Essays in sociology.* New York: Galaxy.

Giddens, A. (1978). *Emile Durkheim.* New York: Penguin Books.

Giddens, A. (1991). *Modernity and Self-Identity: Self and Society in the Late Modern Age.* Polity Press.

Giddens, A. 2010. *Runaway World: How Globalization is Reshaping Our Lives.* New York: Routledge.

Giele, J. Z., & Elder, G. H., Jr. (1998). Life course research: Development of a field. In J. Z. Giele & G. H. Elder, Jr. (Eds.), *Methods of life course research: Qualitative and quantitative Approaches* (pp. 5–27). Thousand Oaks: Sage Publications.

Gilbert, D. (2008). *The American Class Structure in an Age of Growing Inequality.* 7th ed. Los Angeles: Pine Forge Press.

Gilbert, D., & Kahl, J. A. (1982). *The American class structure: A new synthesis.* Homewood, IL: Dorsey Press.

Gilbert, D., & Kahl, J. A. (1993). *The American class structure: A new synthesis* (4th ed.). Homewood, IL: Dorsey Press.

Gilbert, D., & Kahl, J. A. (1998). *The American Class Structure: A New Synthesis.* 4th ed. Belmont, Calf: Wadsworth Publishing.

Gillborn, D. (1992). Citizenship, "race" and the hidden curriculum. *International Studies in the Sociology of Education, 2*(1), 57–73.

Gillborn, D. (2008). *Racism and Education: Understanding Race Inequality In Education.* New York: Routledge.

Gilleard, C. (2002, March). Aging and old age in Medieval society and the transition of modernity. *Journal of Aging and Identity, 7,* 25–41.

Gilman, C. P. (1971). *The man-made world or, our androcentric culture*. New York. (Original work published 1911)

Gilmore, J. (2010). Trends in Dropout Rates and the Labour Market Outcomes of Young Dropouts. Ottawa: Statistics Canada. Retrieved from http://www.statcan.gc.ca/pub/81-004-x/2010004/article/11339-eng.htm#b

Gitlin, T. (1997). *The twilight of common dreams: Why America is wracked by culture wars*. New York: Metropolitan Books.

Gleberzon, B., & Cutler, J. (2005, June). Age waves: Managing the transition to an older society. *CARP Action, 4.*

Glenday, D. (1989). Rich but semiperipheral: Canada's ambiguous position in the world economy. *Review: Fernand Braudel Center, 12*(2), 209–261.

Glenday, D. (1996). Mean streets and hard time: Youth unemployment and crime in Canada. In G. O'Bireck (Ed.), *Not a kid anymore: Canadian youth, crime and subcultures* (pp. 147–174). Toronto: Nelson.

Glenday, D. (1997). Lost horizons, leisure shock: Good jobs, bad jobs, uncertain future. In D. Glenday, *Good jobs, bad jobs, no jobs: The transformation of work in the 21st century* (pp. 8–34). Toronto: Harcourt Brace.

Glenday, D. (2011a). Power, compliance, resistance and creativity: Power and the differential experience of loose time in large organizations. *New Technology, Work and Employment,* Volume 26(1), pp. 29–38.

Glenday, D. (2011b). Rich but losing ground: How Canada's position in the world economy impacts jobs, social choices and life chances. In D. Glenday, A. Duffy, & N. Pupo (Eds.), *The shifting landscape of work* (pp. 15–36). Toronto: Nelson.

Glenday, D., & Duffy, A. (Ed.). (2001). *Canadian society: Meeting the challenges of the twenty-first century*. Toronto: Oxford University Press.

Glenday, D., & McMullan, J. (1970). *An historical examination into the history of the sociology of Québec.* [Paper presented to the Canadian Sociology and Anthropology Association meetings]. Newfoundland.

Glenn, S., Melis, S., & Withers, L. (2009). *Gender (in) Equality in the Labour Market: An Overview of Global Trends and Developments*. Brussels: International Trade Union Confederation. Retrieved from http://www.ituc-csi.org/IMG/pdf/GAP-09_EN.pdf

Goar, C. (2007, April 13). No way to treat a guest worker. *Toronto Star.* Retrieved from http://www.thestar.com/article/202587

Goar, C. (2012, April 13). Tories stifle a voice of social justice. *Toronto Star,* p. A19.

Godin, I., F. Kittel, Y. Coppieters, & J. Siegrist. (2005). A prospective study of cumulative job stress in relation to mental health. *BMC Public Health.* Vol. 5, no. 67.

Goelman, H., Marshall, S. K., & Ross, S., Eds. (2004). *Multiple Lenses, Multiple Images: Perspectives on the Child Across Time, Space and Disciplines*. Toronto: University of Toronto Press.

Goffman, E. (1961). *Asylums: Essays on the social situation of mental patients and other inmates.* Chicago: Aldine.

Goffman, E. (1963). *Stigma: Notes on the management of spoiled identity.* Englewood Cliffs, NJ: Prentice Hall.

Goffman, E. (1977). The arrangement between the sexes. *Theory and Society, 4,* 301–331.

Gold, R. (1952). Janitors versus tenants: A status–income dilemma. *American Journal of Sociology, 58,* 486–493.

Goleman, D. (1993, September 7). Pollsters enlist psychologists in quest for unbiased results. *New York Times,* pp. C1, C11.

Gollom, M. (2012, May 4). Vogue ban of too-thin models a "huge" step. *CBC News.* Retrieved from http://www.cbc.ca

Goode, E., & Ben-Yehuda, N. (1994). Moral panics: Culture, politics, and social construction. *Annual Review of Sociology, 20,* 149–171.

Goode, W. J. (1960, December). Encroachment, charlatanism, and the emerging profession: Psychology, sociology, and medicine. *American Sociological Review, 25*(6), 902–914.

Goodin, S., et al. (2011). "Putting on" sexiness: A content analysis of the presence of sexualizing characteristics in girls' clothing. *Sex Roles.* 65: 1–12.

Goodman, L.-A. (2008, June 12). Kim's Basking in Banff. *Hamilton Spectator,* p. Go19.

Goodwin, G. A., Horowitz, I. L., & Nardi, P. M. (1991, May). Laud Humphreys: A pioneer in the practice of social science. *Sociological Inquiry, 61,* 2, 139–147.

Gootman, E. (2012). "Down payment on a Future Family." *The New York Times (Toronto Star edition).* June 3: 9.

Goozen, S., van, H. M., Fairchild, G., Snoek, H., & Harold, G. T. (2007). The Evidence for a Neurobiological Model of Childhood Antisocial Behavior. *Psychological Bulletin, 133*(1), 149–182.

Gordon, A. (2011). "Young parents squeezed for time, money, report finds." *Toronto Star.* October 19: E9.

Gorman, C. (1997b, January 6). The disease detective. *Time,* 56–65.

Gorrie, P. (2001, June 16). Is Harris right about seniors? *Toronto Star,* p. A17.

Gorz, A. (1982). *Farewell to the working class. An essay in post-industrial socialism.* London: Pluto Press.

Gorz, A. (1985). *Paths to paradise: On the liberation from work.* London: Pluto Press.

Gracia, E., & Herrero, J. (2008, February). Is It Considered Violence? The Acceptability of Physical Punishment of Children in Europe. *Journal of Marriage and the Family, 70,* 210–217.

Graham, E. (1996, March 4). Craving closer ties, strangers come together as family. *Wall Street Journal,* pp. B1, B6.

Grant, T. (2011, November 24). Recession's disproportionate impact on aboriginals a worrisome sign. *Globe and Mail,* p. A16.

Greeley, A. M. (1964, Spring). The Protestant ethic: Time for a moratorium. *Sociological Analysis, 25,* 20–33.

Green, T. (2010). *Motherhood, Absence and Transition: When Adult Children Leave Home.* Burlington, VT: Ashgate.

Greenberg, L., & Normandin, C. (2011). Health at a Glance: Disparities in life Expectancy at Birth. Statistics Canada. Retrieved from http://www.statcan.gc.ca/pub/82-624-x/2011001/article/11427-eng.htm

Greenhouse, S. (2009). *The Big Squeeze: Tough Times for the American Worker.* New York: Anchor Books.

Greenwood, E. (1962). Attributes of a profession. In S. Nosow & W. H. Form (Eds.), *Man, work, and society: A reader in the sociology of occupations* (pp. 206–218). New York: Basic Books.

Greer, G. (1991). *The Change: Women Aging and the Menopause.* New York: Fawcet Columbine.

Gregory, A., & Milner, S. (2011). "What is 'New' about Fatherhood? The Social Construction of Fatherhood in France and the UK." *Men and Masculinities.* 14(5): 588–606.

Gregory S. P. (2005). Cross-National Correlations of Quantifiable Societal Health with Popular Religiosity and Secularism in the Prosperous Democracies A First Look. *Journal of Religion & Society,* Volume 7, pp. 1–17 ISSN 1522-5658.

Greif, M. (2010). What was the Hipster? *New York Magazine.* Retrieved from http://nymag.com/news/features/69129.

Griffin, J. H. (1961). *Black like me.* New York: New American Library.

Grisdale, M. (2007) "Transgendered Canadian Races Toward Olympic History." *NewMedia Journalism,* November 29. Retrieved from http://www.fims.uwo.ca/NewMedia2008/page13022348.aspx

Guba, E. G., & Lincoln, Y. S. (1994). Competing paradigms in qualitative research. In N. K. Denzin & Y. S. Lincoln (Eds.), *Handbook of Qualitative Research.* Thousand Oaks, CA: Sage Publications.

Guha, R. (1989, Spring). Radical American environmentalism and wilderness preservation: A third world critique. *Environmental Ethics, 11*(1), 71–83.

Guilds. (2005). *Columbia Encyclopedia* (6th ed.). New York: Columbia University Press.

Guindon, H. (1964, Summer). Social unrest, social class, and Québec's bureaucratic revolution. *Queen's Quarterly,* pp. 12–32.

Guindon, H. (1967). Two Cultures: An essay on nationalism, class, and ethnic tension. In R. H. Leach (Ed.), *Contemporary Canada.* Duke, NC: Duke University Press.

Guindon, H. (1978). The modernization of Québec and the legitimacy of the Canadian state. In D. Glenday, H. Guindon, and A. Turowetz (Eds.), *Modernization and the Canadian State* (pp. 212–246). Toronto: Macmillan.

Guindon, H. (1988). *Québec society: Tradition, modernity and nationhood.* Toronto: University of Toronto Press.

Guindon, H. (2001). Québec's social and political evolution since 1945: A view from within. In D. Glenday and A. Duffy (Eds.), *Canadian Society: Meeting the Challenges of the Twenty-First Century* (pp. 281–320). Toronto: Oxford University Press.

Haas, J. (1972). Binging: Educational control among high-steel iron workers. *American Behavioral Scientist, 16,* 27–34.

Haas, J., & Shaffir, W. (1987). *Becoming Doctors: The Adoption of a Cloak of Competence.* Greenwich, CT: JAI Press.

Haas, J., & Shaffir, W. (1993). The cloak of competence. In J. M. Henslin (Ed.), *Down to earth sociology: Introductory readings* (7th ed., pp. 432–441). New York: Free Press. (Original work published 1978).

Hall, G. S. (1904). *Adolescence: Its psychology and its relations to physiology, anthropology, sociology, sex, crime, religion, and education.* New York: Appleton.

Hall, M., Lasby, D., Ayer, S., & Gibbons, W. D. (2009). Caring Canadians, Involved Canadians: Highlights from the 2007 Canada Survey of Giving, Volunteering and Participating. Catalogue 71-542-X. Ottawa: Minister of Industry. Retrieved from http://www.givingandvolunteering.ca/files/giving/en/csgvp_highlights_2007.pdf

Hall, O. (1994). Work: The sociology of work in Canada. In A. Wipper (Ed.), *Papers in Honour of Oswald Hall.* Ottawa: Carleton University Press.

Hall, R. H. (1963, July). The concept of bureaucracy: An empirical assessment. *American Journal of Sociology, 69,* 32–40.

Hall, S. S. (1999, August 22). The bully in the mirror. *New York Times Magazine,* pp. 30–35, 58, 62, 64–65.

Halle, D. (1984). *America's working man: Work, home, and politics among blue-collar property owners.* Chicago: University of Chicago Press.

Hamermesh, D. S., & Biddle, J. E. (1994, December). Beauty and the Labor Market. *American Economic Review, 84*(5), 1174–1195.

Harder, L. (2011). "After the Nuclear Age? Some Contemporary Developments in Families and Family Law in Canada." *Contemporary Family Trends* (The Vanier Institute of the Family). June.

Hardy, K. A. (2012). Fleshy Histories: Fatness, Sex/Gender, and the Medicalized Body in the Nineteenth Century. pp. 246–250 in Lorne Tepperman and Angela Kalyta (eds.). *Reading Sociology: Canadian Perspectives* (2nd ed.). Toronto: Oxford University Press.

Hargrove, L. (2002) "Who is Michelle Dumaresq? Why is she so important?" *Pedal: Canada's Cycling Magazine.* Retrieved from http://www.pedalmag.com/index.php?module=Section&action=viewdetail&item_id=562

Harper, T. (2000, January 15). Law of the seed. *Toronto Star,* pp. L1, L3.

Harper, T. (2012, May 25). New rules redefine "suitable employment." *Toronto Star,* pp. A1, A6.

Harrington, M. (1962). *The other America: Poverty in the United States.* New York: Macmillan.

Harrington, M. (1977). *The vast majority: A journey to the world's poor.* New York: Simon & Schuster.

Harris, C., & Ullman, E. (1945). The nature of cities. *Annals of the American Academy of Political and Social Science, 242,* 7–17.

Harris, C. D. (1997). The Nature of Cities and Urban Geography in the Last half Century. *Urban Geography, 18.*

Harris, M. (1977, November 13). Why men dominate women. *New York Times Magazine,* pp. 46, 115, 117–123.

Harrison, P. (1993). *Inside the third world: The anatomy of poverty* (3rd ed.). London: Penguin Books.

Hartley, E. (1946). *Problems in prejudice.* New York: King's Crown Press.

Hartmann, H. (1976, Spring). Capitalism, Patriarchy, and Job Segregation by Sex. *Signs: Journal of Women and Culture in Society.* pp. 137–169.

Harvey, D. (1989). *The condition of postmodernity.* Oxford; New York: Blackwell.

Haub, C. (1997, April). New UN projections depict a variety of demographic futures. *Population Today, 25*(4), 1–3.

Haub, C. (2010). Did South Korea's Population Policy Work Too Well? Population Reference Bureau. Retrieved from http://www.prb.org/Articles/2010/koreafertility.aspx

Haub, C. (2011). *Population Data Sheet.* Washington, DC: Population Reference Bureau.

Haub, C., & Kent, M. (2008). *World Population Data Sheet.* Washington, DC: Population Reference Bureau.

Hauch, C. (1985). *Coping Strategies and Street Life: The Ethnography of Winnipeg's Skid Row Region,* Report No. 11, Winnipeg, Institute of Urban Studies.

Hauser, P., & Schnore, L. (Ed.). (1965). *The study of urbanization.* New York: Wiley.

Health Canada. (2010, May 10). Sex and Gender Based Analysis. Retrieved from http://www.hc-sc.gc.ca/hl-vs/gender-genre/analys/gender-sexes-eng.php

Heath, D. T. (2004). Parents' Socialization of Children in Global Perspective. In J. Macionis, N. Benokraitis, B. Ravelli (Eds.), *Seeing Ourselves: Classic, Contemporary and Cross-cultural Readings in Sociology* (pp. 102–107). Toronto: Pearson Prentice Hall.

Heesterman, W. (2005). Child Labour and Children's Rights: Policy Issues in Three Affluent Societies. In J. Goddard, S. McNamee, A. James, & A. James (Eds.), *The Politics of Childhood: International Perspectives, Contemporary Developments* (pp. 73–89). London: Palgrave Macmillan.

Hefti, A. M. (1997, September). *Globalization and migration.* European Solidarity Conference on the Philippines: Responding to Globalization, Zurich, Switzerland. Retrieved from http://www.philsol.nl/solcon/Anny-Misa.htm

Heisz, A. (2001, Autumn). Low income intensity: Urban and rural families. *Perspectives on Labour and Income, 13,* pp. 14–16.

Hellinger, D., & Judd, D. R. (1991). *The Democratic Facade.* Pacific Grove, CA: Brooks/Cole.

Hendrix, L. (1994, August). What is sexual inequality? On the definition and range of variation. *Gender and Society, 28*(3), 287–307.

Henley, N., Hamilton, M., & Thorne, B. (1985). Womanspeak and manspeak. In A. G. Sargent (Ed.), *Beyond sex roles.* St. Paul, MN: West.

Henry, F., & Tator, C. (2010). *The Colour of Democracy: Racism in Canadian Society.* 4th Edition. Toronto: Nelson.

Henslin, J. M. (1967, September). *The cab driver: An interactional analysis of an occupational culture.* Washington University Ph.D. dissertation.

Henslin, J. M. (1990). It's not a lovely place to visit, and I wouldn't want to live there. In R. G. Burgess (Ed.), *Studies in qualitative methodology, a research annual: Reflections on field experiences* (pp. 51–76). Greenwich, CT: JAI Press.

Henslin, J. M. (1993). Trust and cabbies. In J. M. Henslin (Ed.), *Down to earth sociology: Introductory readings* (7th ed., pp. 183–196). New York: Free Press.

Henslin, J. M. (1997a). Sociology and the social sciences. In J. M. Henslin (Ed.), *Down to earth sociology: Introductory readings* (9th ed., pp. 8–18). New York: Free Press.

Henslin, J. M. (1997b). The survivors of the F-227. In J. M. Henslin (Ed.), *Down to earth sociology: Introductory readings* (9th ed., pp. 237–245). New York: Free Press.

Henslin, J. M. (2005). *Sociology: A Down-to-Earth Approach* (7th ed.). Boston: Pearson.

Henslin, J. M. (2008a). *Social Problems: A Down-to-Earth Approach.* (8th ed.). Boston: Allyn and Bacon.

Henslin, J. M. (2012). *Sociology: A Down-to-Earth Approach* (11th ed.). Boston: Pearson.

Henslin, J. M., & Biggs, M. A. (1997). Behavior in pubic places: The sociology of the vaginal examination. In J. M. Henslin (Ed.), *Down to earth sociology: Introductory readings* (9th ed., pp. 203–214). New York: Free Press. (Original work published 1971 as Dramaturgical desexualization: The sociology of the vaginal examination in J. M. Henslin (Ed.), *Studies in the sociology of sex* (pp. 243–272). New York: Appleton-Century-Crofts.)

Henslin, J. M. (2012). *Sociology: A Down-to-Earth Approach.* 11th Edition. Boston: Pearson.

Hewa, S. (1993). Sociology and public policy: The debate on value-free social science. *International Journal of Sociology and Social Policy, 13*(1–2), 64–82.

Higgins, C., & Duxbury, L. (2009). Key Findings and Recommendations from The 2001 National Work-Life Conflict Study. Health Canada. Retrieved from http://www.hc-sc.gc.ca/ewh-semt/pubs/occup-travail/balancing_six-equilibre_six/index-eng.php

Higley, J., Hoffmann-Lange, U., Kadushin, C., & Moore, G. (1991, May). Elite integration in stable democracies: A reconsideration. *European Sociological Review, 7*(1), 35–53.

Hilbrecht, M., Zuzanek, J., & Mannell, R. C. (2008). Time Use, Time Pressure and Gendered Behaviour in Early and Late Adolescence. *Sex Roles, 58,* 342–357.

Hill, J. A. (2011). Endangered childhoods: how consumerism is impacting child and youth identity. *Media, Culture and Society.* 33(3), 347–362.

Hiller, H. (1996). *Canadian society: A macro analysis,* 3rd ed. Toronto: Prentice-Hall.

Hilliard, A. (1991). "Do we Have the Will to Educate All Children?" *Educational Leadership, 49,* September: 31–36.

Hippler, F. (1987). Interview in a television documentary with Bill Moyers in *Propaganda,* in the series Walk Through the 20th Century.

Ho, B., Friedland, J., Rappolt, S., & Noh, S. (2003). Caregiving for relatives with Alzheimer's disease: Feelings of Chinese-Canadian women. *Journal of Aging Studies, 17,* 301–321.

Hochschild, A. (1989). *The second shift: Working parents and the revolution at home.* New York: Viking.

Hoecker-Drysdale, Susan. (1992). *Harriet Martineau: First Woman Sociologist,* New York: Berg.

Hofstede, G. H. (1980). *Culture's consequences: International differences in work-related values.* Beverly Hills, CA: Sage Publications.

Homblin, D. J. (1973). *The first cities.* Boston: Little, Brown, Time-Life Books.

Honeycutt, K. (1995). Disgusting, pathetic, bizarrely beautiful: Representations of weight in popular culture. [Paper presented at the 1995 meetings of the American Sociological Association].

Honore, C. (2008). *Under Pressures: Rescuing Childhood From The Culture of Hyper-parenting.* Toronto: Alfred A. Knopf Canada.

Horowitz, I. L. (1966). *Three worlds of development: The theory and practice of international stratification.* New York: Oxford University Press.

Hosoda, M., Stone-Romero, E. F., & Coats, G. (2003). The effects of physical attractiveness on job-related outcomes: A meta-analysis of experimental studies. *Personnel Psychology, 56:* 431–462.

Hossfeld, K. J. (2000). Their Logic Against Them': Contradictions in Sex, Race, and Class in Silicon Valley. In Maxine Baca Zinn, Pierrette Hondagneu-Sotelo, and Michael A. Messner (Eds.), *Gender through the Prism of Difference,* 2nd ed. Boston: Allyn and Bacon: 388–400.

Hostetler, J. A. (1980). *Amish society* (3rd ed.). Baltimore: Johns Hopkins University Press.

Hostetler, A. J., Sweet, S., & Moen, P. (2007). Gendered Career Paths: A Life Course Perspective on Returning to School. *Sex Roles,* 56, 85–103.

Hoyt, H. (1939). *The structure and growth of residential neighborhoods in American cities.* Washington, DC: Federal Housing Administration.

Hoyt, H. (1971). Recent distortions of the classical models of urban structure. In L. S. Bourne (Ed.), *Internal structure of the city: Readings on space and environment* (pp. 84–96). New York: Oxford University Press.

Huber, J. (1990, February). Micro-macro links in gender stratification. *American Sociological Review, 55,* 1–10.

Huber, J., & Form, W. H. (1973). *Income and Ideology.* New York: Free Press.

Hudson, J. R. (1991). Professional sports franchise locations and city, metropolitan and regional identities. [Paper presented at the annual meetings of the American Sociological Association].

Hughes, E. C. (1943). *French Canada in transition.* Chicago: University of Chicago Press.

Human Rights Watch. (n.d.). Retrieved from http://www.hrw.org/women/

Humphreys, L. (1971). Impersonal Sex and Perceived Satisfaction. In *Studies in the Sociology Of Sex.* James Henslin eds. New York: Appleton-Century-Crofts.

Humphreys, L. (1975). *Tearoom Trade: Impersonal Sex in Public Places.* Enlarged ed. Chicago: Aldine. (Original work published 1970)

Hunt, S. (2005). *The life course: A sociological introduction.* New York: Palgrave Macmillan.

Hurst, M. (2011). "Debt and family type in Canada." *Canadian Social Trends.* April 21. Catalogue no. 11-008.

Hussain, Y. et al. (2006). Violence in the Lives of Girls in Canada: Creating Spaces of Understanding and Change. In Y. Jiwani, C. Steenbergen, C. Mitchell (Eds.), *Girlhood: Redefining the Limits* (pp. 53–69). Montreal: Black Rose.

Huws, U. (2003). *The making of the cybertariat: Virtual work in a real world.* New York: Monthly Review Press.

Hymowitz, C. (2004, November 8). Through the Glass Ceiling. *Wall Street Journal.*

Immen, W. (2008). The Latest Rage in the Office is Just That—Workers Lashing Out. *Globeandmail.com.* Retrieved from http://www.theglobeandmail.com/servlet/story/LAC.20080307.CARAGE07/BNPrint//

Immen, W. (2011, June 17). Co-Work Spaces Bring the Like-Minded Together. *Globe and Mail.* Retrieved from http://www.theglobeandmail.com/report-on-business/careers/career-advice/on-the-job/co-work-spaces-bring-the-like-minded-together/article2065882/singlepage/#articlecontentInternational Labour Organization (ILO). (2002, May 24). Press Release: *Work-related fatalities reach 2 million annually.* Retrieved from http://www.ilo.org/public/english/bureau/inf/pr/2002/23.htm

International Labour Organization. (2008). *Global Wage Report 2008/2009.* Geneva: ILO.

Inter-Parliamentary Union. (2012, March). Women in National Parliaments. Retrieved from http://www.ipu.org/wmn-e/classif.htm

Isaacson, W. (2011). *Steve Jobs.* New York: Simon & Schuster.

Iyer, N. (2002, February 28). *Working Through the Wage Gap: Report of the Task Force on Pay Equity.* Retrieved from http://www.ag.gov.bc.ca/public/working_through_the_wage_gap.pdfJackson, A. (2005). *Work and Labour in Canada: Critical Issues.* Toronto: Canadian Scholars' Press.

Jackson, A. (2010). *Work and Labour in Canada: Critical Issues* (2nd ed.). Toronto: Canadian Scholars' Press.

Jackson, E. (2011). "New trial for dad who spanked son." *Toronto Star.* September 16: A4.

Jackson, J. D. (1975). *Community & conflict: A study of French-English relations in Ontario.* Toronto: Holt, Rinehart & Winston of Canada.

Jackson, J. D., Nielsen, G. M., & Hsu, Y. (2011). *Mediated Society: A Critical Sociology of Media.* Toronto: Oxford University Press.

Jackson, S., & Scott, S. (2010). Rehabilitating Interactionism for a Feminist Sociology of Sexuality. *Sociology,* 44, 5: 811–826.

Jacobsen, T., & Adams, R. M. (1958, November 21). Salt and silt in ancient Mesopotamian agriculture. *Science*, 1251–1258.

Jaffrelot, C. (2006, April). The Impact of Affirmative Action in India: More Political Than Socioeconomic. *India Review*, 5(2), 173–189.

Jaggar, A. M. (1990). Sexual difference and sexual equality. In D. L. Rhode (Ed.), *Theoretical perspectives on sexual difference* (pp. 239–254). New Haven, CT: Yale University Press.

James, C. (2003). *Seeing Ourselves: Exploring Race, Ethnicity and Culture* (2nd ed.). Toronto: Thompson Educational Publishing.

James, C. E. (2007). Negotiating School: Marginalized Students' Participation in the Education Process. In Genevieve Fuji Johnson & Randy Enomoto, eds. *Race, Racialization, and Antiracism in Canada and Beyond*. Toronto: University of Toronto Press.

Jankowiak, W. R., & Fischer, E. F. (1992, April). A cross-cultural perspective on romantic love. *Journal of Ethnology*, 31(2), 149–155.

Jarvis, G. K., & Boldt, M. (1983). Death styles among Canada's Indians. *Social Science and Medicine*, 16, 1345–1352.

Jasper, J. M. (1991). Moral dimensions of social movements. [Paper presented at the annual meetings of the American Sociological Association].

Jasper, J. M., & Poulsen, J. D. (1995, November). Recruiting strangers and friends: Moral shocks and social networks in animal rights and anti-nuclear protests. *Social Problems*, 42(4), 493–512.

Jenish, D. (1997, November 10). *Maclean's*, 110 (45), p. 18.

Jenkins, C., & Sherman, B. (1981). *The Leisure Shock*. London: Eyre Methuen.

Jenson, J., & de Castell, S. (2011). Girls@Play. *Feminist Media Studies*. 11(2), 167–179.

Jiwani, Y. (2006). Racialized Violence And Girls and Young Women of Colour. In Y. Jiwani, C. Steenbergen, C. Mitchell (Eds.) *Girlhood: Redefining the Limits*. (pp. 70–88). Montreal: Black Rose.

Johansson, P. (1999). "Consuming the Other: The Fetish of the Western Woman in Chinese Advertising and Popular Culture." *Postcolonial Studies*, 2(3), November.

John Howard Society of Alberta. (1999). Youth crime in Canada: Public perception vs. statistical information, 1997. In J. Winterdyk & D. King (Eds.), *Diversity and justice in Canada*. Toronto: Canadian Scholars' Press.

Johne, M. (2008, January 30). Squeezed in a Generational Sandwich. *Globe and Mail*, p. E5.

Johnson, H. (1996). *Dangerous domains: Violence against women in Canada*. Toronto: Nelson Canada.

Johnson, H. (2006, October). *Measuring Violence Against Women: Statistical Trends 2006*. Statistics Canada, Catalogue No. 85-570-XIE. http://www.statcan.ca/english/research/85-570-XIE/85-570-XIE2006001.pdf

Johnson, H., & Dawson, M. (2011). *Violence Against Women in Canada: Research and Policy Perspectives*. Oxford University Press.

Johnson, J. (2002). *Getting By on the Minimum: The Lives of Working-Class Women*. New York: Routledge.

Jordan, M. (2000, May 9). Among poor villagers, female infanticide still flourishes in India. *Wall Street Journal*, pp. A1, A12.

Juergensmeyer, M. (2000). *Terror in the Mind of God: The Global Rise of Religious Violence*. Berkeley: University of California Press.

Kalish, S. (1994, March). International migration: New findings on magnitude, importance. *Population Today*, 22(3), 1–2.

Kaminski, M., & Palchikoff, K. (1997, April 14). The crisis to come. *Newsweek*, pp. 44–46.

Kanter, R. M. (1977). *Men and women of the corporation*. New York: Basic Books.

Kanter, R. M. (1983). *The change masters: Innovation and entrepreneurship in the American corporation*. New York: Simon & Schuster.

Kanter, R. M. (1997). *World class: Thriving locally in the global economy*. New York: Touchstone Books.

Kanter, R. M., Wiersema, F., & Kao, J. J. (Ed.). (1997). *Innovation: Breakthrough thinking at 3M, DuPont, GE, Pfizer, and Rubbermaid*. New York: HarperBusiness.

Kantner, J., & Revkin, A. C. (2007, April 7). Scientists Detail Climate Changes, Poles to Tropics. *New York Times*.

Karp, D. A., & Yoels, W. C. (1990). Sport and urban life. *Journal of Sport and Social Issues*, 14(2), 77–102.

Katz, A. (2005, July 16). Negative Attitudes on TV Toward Aging Affect Elderly. Global Action on Aging. http://www.globalaging.org/elderrights/us/2005/tv.htm

Keating, N., Fast, J., Frederick, J., Cranswick, K., & Perrier, C. (1999). *Eldercare in Canada: Context, content and consequences*. Ottawa: Minister of Industry.

Kelley, J., & Evans, M. D. R. (1995, April). Class and class conflict in six Western nations. *American Sociological Review*, 60, 157–178.

Kelso, W. A. (1995). *Poverty and the underclass: Changing perceptions of the poor in America*. New York: New York University Press.

Keniston, K. (1971). *Youth and dissent: The rise of a new opposition*. New York: Harcourt, Brace, Jovanovich.

Kennedy, P. (1993). *Preparing for the twenty-first century*. New York: Random House.

Kephart, W. M., & Zellner, W. W. (1994). *Extraordinary groups: An examination of unconventional life-styles* (5th ed.). New York: St. Martin's Press.

Keung, N. (2008, March 11). A Love Match? That's so last century. *Toronto Star*, pp. ID1, ID2.

Keung, N. (2012, April 2). New immigrants are the "hidden homeless." *Toronto Star*, p. GT1.

Kim, K., Paek, H. J., & Lynn, J. (2010). A Content Analysis of Smoking Fetish Videos on YouTube: Regulatory Implications for Tobacco Control. *Health Communication*, 25: 97–106.

King, R. T., Jr. (1994, October 25). Soon a chip will test blood for diseases. *Wall Street Journal*, pp. B1, B11.

Nelson, A., & Robinson, B. W. (2002). *Gender in Canada* (2nd ed.). Toronto: Prentice Hall.

Nelson, J. (2012, February 18). Elizabeth Smart marries. *Huffington Post.* Retrieved from http://www.huffingtonpost. com/2012/02/18/elizabeth-smart-marries-n-1287016.html

Nelson, R. K. (1989, November 2). Letter to the editor. *Wall Street Journal,* p. A23.

Netting, N. S. (2012). "Love and Arranged Marriage in India Today: Negotiating Adulthood." pp. 104–106 in Lorne Tepperman and Angela Kalyta eds.) *Reading Sociology: Canadian Perspectives.* 2nd Edition. Toronto: Oxford.

Newman, P. C. (1979). *The Canadian establishment* (Vol. 1). Toronto: McClelland and Stewart.

Newman, P. C. (1999). *Titans: How the new Canadian establishment seized power.* Toronto: Penguin Books Canada Ltd.

Newman, P. C. (2004). *Here Be Dragons: Telling Tales of People, Passion and Power.* Toronto: McClelland & Stewart.

Nicholson, G. (2012, April 6). Augusta in the Rough: Women, Money, Prestige. *Globe and Mail,* p. A15.

Nicolaou, N., & Shane, S. (2010). Entrepreneurship and occupational choice: Genetic and environmental influences. *Journal of Economic Behavior and Organization.* 76: 3–14.

Noack, T., & Wiik, K. (2008). Women's Choice of Surname Upon Marriage. *Journal of Marriage and the Family.* 70 (May), 507–518.

Nobelprize.org. (2012, August 28). Mother Theresa—Biography. Retrieved from http://www.nobelprize.org/nobel_prizes/peace/ laureates/1979/teresa-bio.html

Noble, D. F. (1995). *Progress without people: New technology, unemployment, and the message of resistance.* Toronto: Between the Lines.

Nomaguchi, K. (2006). Maternal Employment, Nonparental Care, Mother-Child Interactions, and Child Outcomes During Preschool Years. *Journal of Marriage and the Family.* 68 (December), pp. 1341–1369.

No More Emails, Please—Work's Over. (2011, December 28). *Hamilton Spectator,* p. A18.

Norwood, S. J., Murray, M., Nolan, A., & Bowker, A. (2011). Beautiful From the Inside Out: A School-Based Programme Designed to Increase Self-Esteem and Positive Body Image Among Preadolescents. *Canadian Journal of School Psychology.* 26(4) 263–282.

Novak, M. (1993). *Aging and society: A Canadian perspective* (2nd ed.). Toronto: Nelson Canada.

Nugent, C. (2010). "Children's Surnames, Moral Dilemmas." *Gender and Society,* 24 (4): 499-525.

O'Bireck, G. M. (1993). *Gettin' tall: Cocaine use within a subculture of Canadian professional musicians: An ethnographic inquiry.* Toronto: Canadian Scholars' Press.

O'Bireck, G. M. (Ed.). (1996). *Not a kid anymore: Canadian youth, crime and subcultures.* Toronto: Nelson Canada.

O'Brien, C. A., & Goldberg, A. (2000). Lesbians and gay men inside and outside families. In N. Mandell & A. Duffy (Eds.),

Canadian families: Diversity, conflict and change (pp. 115–145). Toronto: Harcourt Brace Canada.

O'Connell, V. (2004, May 20). Massachusetts tries to halt sale of "sweet" cigarettes. *Wall Street Journal.*

O'Donnell, V., & Wallace, S. (2011). "First Nations, Metis and Inuit Women." *Women in Canada: A Gender-based Statistical Report.* Ottawa: Minister of Industry. Statistics Canada Catalogue # 89-503-X.

OECD (Organization for Economic Cooperation and Development). (2002). Level of Educational Attainment in the Population Aged 25 to 64, OECD Countries, 2000.

OECD. (2010). *OECD Health Data 2010* (June ed.), Paris, France.

OECD. (2011a). *Divided We Stand: Why inequality keeps rising.* OECD Publishing.

OECD. (2011b). *Education at a Glance, 2011: OECD Indicators. OECD Publishing.* Retrieved from http://www.oecd.org/ dataoecd/61/2/48631582.pdf

Offen, K. (1990). Feminism and sexual difference in historical perspective. In D. L. Rhode (Ed.), *Theoretical perspectives on sexual difference* (pp. 13–20). New Haven, CT: Yale University Press.

Ogburn, W. F. (1922). *Social change with respect to culture and human nature.* New York: W. B. Huebsch. (Other editions by Viking 1927, 1938, and 1950).

Ogburn, W. F. (1961). The hypothesis of cultural lag. In T. Parsons, E. Shils, K. D. Naegele, & J. R. Pitts (Eds.), *Theories of society: Foundations of modern sociological theory* (Vol. 2, pp. 1270–1273). New York: Free Press.

Ogburn, W. F. (1964). On culture and social change: Selected papers, O. D. Duncan (Ed.) Chicago: University of Chicago Press.

Ogilvie, M. (2011, November 30). Substance use falling, teen survey reveals. *Toronto Star,* p. A3.

Ogilvie, M. (2012, April 16). Some fast foods sold to Canadians among the saltiest. *Toronto Star.*

Oliveira, M. (2012, February 25). Young, well-educated Canadians shun TV. *Toronto Star,* E4.

Oliver, P. E., & Marwell, G. (1992). Mobilizing technologies for collective action. In A. D. Morris & C. C. Mueller (Eds.), *Frontiers in social movement theory* (pp. 251–272). New Haven, CT: Yale University Press.

Olneck, M. R., & Bills, D. B. (1980). What makes Sammy run? An empirical assessment of the Bowles-Gintis correspondence theory. *American Journal of Education, 89,* 27–61.

Olsen, D. (1980). *The state elite.* Toronto: McClelland and Stewart.

Olshansky, S. J., Carnes, B., Rogers, R. G., & Smith, L. (1997, July). Infectious diseases—New and ancient threats to world health. *Population Bulletin, 52*(2), 1–51.

O'Neill, H. (1997, April 6). Strange, strange worlds. Alton Telegraph, p. A10.

Ortiz, I. (2011). Global Inequality: Beyond the Bottom Billion—A Rapid Review of Income Distribution in 141 Countries. New York: UNICEF.

Overvold, A. Z. (1988). *Surrogate Parenting.* New York: Pharos.

Palen, J. J. (1987). *The Urban World* (3rd ed.). New York: McGraw-Hill.

Pancevski, B. (2007, February 12). Imprisoned girls "may never recover." *The Australian*. Retrieved from http://www.theaustralian.news.com

Pappas, N. T., McKenry, P. C., & Skilken Catlett, B. (2004). Athlete Aggression on and Off the Ice. *Men and Masculinities*. 6(3), 291–312.

Parfit, M. (1990, April). Earth First!ers wield a mean monkey wrench. *Smithsonian, 21*(1), 184–204.

Parker-Pope, T. (2011, April 10). Fat Stigma is Now a Global Epidemic. *New York Times, Toronto Star* ed., p. 9.

Parliament of Canada. (2012). House of Commons—Members. Retrieved from http://www.parl.gc.ca/MembersOfParliament/CustomizableReports.aspx?Subject=1&Language=E

Parsons, T. (1940). An analytic approach to the theory of social stratification. *American Journal of Sociology, 45*, 841–862.

Parsons, T. (1953). Illness and the role of the physician: A sociological perspective. In C. Kluckhohn & H. A. Murray (Eds.), *Personality in nature, society, and culture* (2nd ed., pp. 609–617). New York: Knopf.

Parsons, T. (1954). The professions and social structure. In T. Parsons (Ed.), *Essays in Sociological Theory* (Rev. ed., pp. 34–49). New York: Free Press.

Pasternak, J. (2002, October). Definition of ageism. *50 Plus,* pp. 99–100.

Pearce, T. (2008, March 11). Men Twice as Likely to Get Knee Surgery. *Globe and Mail,* pp. L1, L4.

Pecoskie, T., & Buist, S. (2011, November 19). Mothers Too Soon: Groundbreaking Analysis Exposes Relationship Between Poverty and Teenage Pregnancy. *Hamilton Spectator,* pp. WR1–WR7.

Pennar, K., & Farrell, C. (1993, February 15). Notes from the underground economy. *Business Week,* pp. 98–101.

Pennington, B. (2004, October 18). Reading, writing and corporate sponsorships. *New York Times.*

Pepinsky, H. (1980). A Sociologist on Police Patrol. In *The Fieldwork Experience: Qualitative Approaches to Social Research,* ed. William, B., Shaffi, R., Robert, A., Stebbins, and Turowetz, A., pp. 223–234. New York: St. Martin's Press.

Peritz, I. (2000, February 22). Sex-change soldier hails Canada's liberal attitudes. *Globe and Mail,* pp. A1, A17.

Peritz, I. (2005, February 11). Unionized Wal-Mart employees fear second Quebec store to shut. *Globe and Mail,* p. A7.

Perkel, C. (2007, January 28). Female Profs Lag in Pay, Promotions. Retrieved from http://www.thestar.com/printArticle/175746

Perrow, C. (1991, December). A society of organizations. *Theory and Society, 20*(6), 725–762.

Persell, C. H, Catsambis, S., & Cookson, P. W., Jr. (1992). Family background, school type, and college attendance: A conjoint system of cultural capital transmission. *Journal of Research on Adolescence, 2*(1), 1–23.

Petras, J., & Veltmeyer, H. (2001). *Globalization unmasked: Imperialism in the 21st century.* Halifax: Fernwood Books.

Philp, M. (2000, June 5). Canadians enjoy long and healthy lives: But 12th-place ranking lags behind nations with more aggressive programs. *Globe and Mail.*

Picard, A. (2008, February 14). Smoking Deaths An Epidemic in India. *Globe and Mail.* p. A15.

Pier, Carol. (2007). *Discounting Rights: Wal-Mart's Violation of US Workers' Right to Freedom of Association.* New York: Human Rights Watch.

Pitt, R., & Borland, E. (2008). Bachelorhood and Men's Attitudes about Gender Roles. *Journal of Men's Studies.* 16,1, pp. 140–158.

Pizarro, M. (1998). Chicana/o power! Epistemology and methodology for social justice and empowerment in chicana/o communities. *Qualitative Studies in Education, 11*(1), 57–80.

Poisson, J. (2011a, December 26). The "genderless" baby who caused a storm of controversy in 2011. *Thestar.com.* Retrieved from http://www.thestar.com/news/article/1105515--the-genderless-baby-who-caused-a-storm-of-controversy-in-2011

Poisson, J. (2011b, May 21). Parents Keep Child's Gender Secret. *Thestar.com.* Retrieved from http://www.parentcentral.ca/parent/babiespregnancy/babies/article/995112--parents-keep-child-s-gender-secret

Polsby, N. W. (1959, December). Three problems in the analysis of community power. *American Sociological Review, 24*(6), 796–803.

Pomerantz, S. (2006). Did You See What She Was Wearing? The Power and Politics of Schoolgirl Style. In Y. Jiwani, C. Steenbergen, C. Mitchell (Eds.) *Girlhood: Redefining the Limits* (pp. 173–190). Montreal: Black Rose.

Ponting, J. R. (Ed.). (1986). *Arduous Journey: Canadian Indians and Decolonization.* Toronto: McClelland and Stewart.

Pope, H. G., Phillips, K. A., & Olivardia, R. (2000). *The Adonis Complex: The secret crisis of male body obsession.* New York: Free Press.

Porter, C. (2012, January 28). Shifting the culture of recess. *Toronto Star,* p. A12.

Porter, J. (1965). *The vertical mosaic: An analysis of social class and power in Canada.* Toronto: University of Toronto Press.

Porter, J., Porter, M., & Blishen, B. (1979). *Does money matter?* (Rev. ed.). Toronto: Macmillan.

Povoledo, E. (2012). "In Europe, a Burden for Divorced Fathers." *The New York Times (Toronto Star edition).* June 10: 2.

Powell, B. et al. *Counted Out: Same-Sex Relations and Americans' Definitions of Family.* New York: Russell Sage Foundation.

PremierLife.ca. (2011, October 26). Occupy Wall Street, Occupy Canada, Occupy London, Occupy the world. *PremierLife.ca.* Retrieved from http://www.premierlife.ca/on-campus/occupy-wall-street-occupy-canada-occupylondon-occupy-the-world/

Prentice, A. (1977). *The school promoters: Education and social class in mid-nineteenth century Upper Canada.* Toronto: McClelland and Stewart.

Priest, L. (2012, January 21). Enabling the Long-Distance House Call. *Globe and Mail,* p. A4.

Prus, R. (2007). Activities and Interdependencies in the Educational Process: An Interactionist Approach to Student Ventures in Learning. In L. Tepperman & H. Dickinson (Eds.) *Reading Sociology: Canadian Perspectives* (pp. 113–115). Don Mills: Oxford University Press.

Public Safety Canada. (2011, July 18). Bullying Prevention: Nature and Extent of Bullying in Canada.. Retrieved from http://www.publicsafety.gc.ca/res/cp/res/2008-bp-01-eng.aspx

Pupo, N. (2004, Spring). Community service: Coercion or volunteerism? *CRWS News, 29.*

Pupo, N. (2011). Walmartization and the McJob: The Jobs that Boomed in the New Economy. In N. Pupo, D. Glenday, & A. Duffy (Eds.), *The Shifting Landscape of Work* (pp.66–81). Toronto: Nelson Education Canada.

Pupo, N., & Duffy, A. (2012). Unpaid Work, Capital and Coercion. *Work Organization, Labour and Globalization.* Volume 6, Number 1, (Spring), 27–47.

Pupo, N., & Noack, A. (2010). Dialling for Service: Transforming the Public Sector Workplace in Canada. In N. Pupo & M. Thomas (Eds.), *Interrogating the New Economy: Restructuring Work in the 21st Century.* Toronto: University of Toronto Press.

Putnam, R. (2000). *Bowling Alone.* New York: Simon and Schuster.

Putney, N. M., & Bengston, V. L. (2002). Socialization and the family revisited. In R. A. Settersen, Jr., & T. J. Owens (Eds.), *New Frontiers in Socialization* (pp. 165–194). Amsterdam: JAI Press.

Quirke, L. (2012). "Keeping young minds sharp": Children's cognitive stimulation and the rise of parenting magazines, 1959–2003. pp. 368–374 in Lorne Tepperman and Angela Kalyta (eds.) *Reading Sociology: Canadian Perspectives* (2nd ed.). Toronto: Oxford University Press.

Raby, R. (2007). Polite, Well-dressed, and On Time: Secondary School Conduct Codes and the Production of Docile Citizens. In. L. Tepperman & H. Dickinson (Eds.) *Reading Sociology: Canadian Perspectives* (pp. 116–119). Don Mills: Oxford University Press.

Rathus, S., & Nevid, J. (1993). *Human Sexuality in a World of Diversity.* Boston: Allyn and Bacon.

Raymond, J.G. (1993). *Women as Wombs: Reproductive Technologies and the Battle Over Women's Freedom.* New York: HarperCollins.

Raymond, M. (2008, April). *High School Dropouts Returning to School.* Statistics Canada, Catalogue No. 81-595-MIE. Retrieved from http://www.statcan.ca/english/research/81-595-MIE/81-595-MIE2008055.pdf

Read, P. P. (1974). *Alive. The story of the Andes survivors.* Philadelphia: Lippincott.

Reed, S., & Benet, L. (1990, April 16). Ecowarrior Dave Foreman will do whatever it takes in his fight to save Mother Earth. *People Weekly, 33*(15), 113–116.

Rees, W. E. (2002, April 22). Squeezing the poor. *Toronto Star,* p. A17.

Reich, M. (1972). The economics of racism. In R. C. Edwards, M. Reich, & T. E. Weiskopf (Eds.), *The capitalist system* (pp. 313–321). Englewood Cliffs, NJ: Prentice Hall.

Reiman, J. (2001). *The Rich Get Richer and the Poor Get Prison: Ideology, Class and Criminal Justice.* Boston: Allyn and Bacon.

Reiman, J. (2004). *The Rich Get Richer and the Poor Get Prison: Ideology, Class, and Criminal Justice* (7th ed.). Boston: Allyn and Bacon.

Reinharz, S. (1997). Friends or foes: Gerontological and feminist theory. In M. Pearsall (Ed.), *The Other within Us: Feminist Explorations of Women and Aging* (pp. 73–94). Boulder, CO: Westview.

Renzetti, C. M., Curran, D. J., & Maier, S. L. (2012). *Women, Men and Society.* 6th Edition. Boston: Pearson.

Restoule, J. P. (2005). Aboriginal Identity: The Need for Historical and Contextual Perspectives. In B. Ravelli (Ed.), *Exploring Canadian Sociology* (pp. 159–168). Toronto: Pearson, Prentice Hall.

Reutter, L. I. et al. (2009). "Who do they think we are, anyway?": Perceptions and responses to poverty stigma. *Qualitative Health Research, 19*(3), 297–311.

Ribeiro, S. (2005, January 16). The costs of "Walmartization." *Znet.*

Richards, B. (1996, January 17). Doctors can diagnose illnesses long distance, to the dismay of some. *Wall Street Journal,* pp. A1, A8.

Ricks, T. E. (1994, February 14). Pentagon considers selling overseas a large part of high-tech weaponry. *Wall Street Journal,* p. A16.

Ridley, M. (2003). *The Agile Gene: How Nature Turns On Nurture.* New York: Harper Collins.

Rifkin, J. (1995). *The end of work: The decline of the global labor force and the dawn of the post-market era.* New York: Putnam.

Riley, N. E. (2004, June). China's population: New trends and challenges. *Population Bulletin, 59*(2), 3–36.

Rinehart, J. W. (2006). *The Tyranny of Work: Alienation and the Labour Process* (5th ed.). Toronto: Nelson Thomson.

Rist, R. C. (1970, August). Student social class and teacher expectations: The self-fulfilling prophecy in ghetto education. *Harvard Educational Review, 40*(3), 411–451.

Ritzer, G. (1993). *The McDonaldization of society: An investigation into the changing character of contemporary life.* Thousand Oaks, CA: Pine Forge Press.

Ritzer, G. (1998). *The McDonaldization Thesis: Explorations and Extensions.* London: Sage Publications.

Ritzer, G. (2011). *The McDonaldization of Society* (6th ed.). Thousand Oaks, CA: Sage Publications.

Robertson, I. (1987). *Sociology* (3rd ed.). New York: Worth.

Robinson, T, Callister, M., Magoffin, D., & Moore, J. (2007, August). The Portrayal of Older Characters in Disney Animated Films. *Journal of Aging Studies,* Volume 21, Number 3, 203–213.

Rodríguez, V. M. (1994, Spring). Los Angeles, USA 1992: A house divided against itself. *SSSP Newsletter,* 5–12.

Roethlisberger, F. J., & Dickson, W. J. (1939). *Management and the worker.* Cambridge, MA: Harvard University Press.

Roper, E. A., & Halloran. E. (2007). Attitudes toward Gay Men and Lesbians Among Heterosexual Male and Female Student-Athletes. *Sex Roles* 57, 919–928.

Rosaldo, M. Z. (1974). Women, culture and society: A theoretical overview. In M. Z. Rosaldo & L. Lamphere (Eds.), *Women, culture, and society.* Stanford: Stanford University Press.

Rosenthal, E. (1999, December 9). China's chic waistline: Convex to concave. *New York Times.*

Rosenthal, E. (2001). "Harsh Chinese Reality Feeds a Black Market in Women." *New York Times,* June 25.

Ross, A. (Ed.). (1999). *No sweat: Fashion, free trade, and the rights of garment workers.* New York and London: Verso.

Rossi, A. S. (1977). A biosocial perspective on parenting. *Daedalus, 106,* 1–31.

Rossi, A. S. (1984). Gender and parenthood. *American Sociological Review, 49,* 1–18.

Rotello, G. (1996, July 14). The risk in a "cure" for AIDS. *New York Times.*

Rothman, B.K. (1989). *Recreating Motherhood: Ideology and Technology in a Patriarchal Society.* New York: Norton.

Rothschild, J., & Whitt, J. A. (1986). *The cooperative workplace: Potentials and dilemmas of organizational democracy and participation.* Cambridge, England: Cambridge University Press.

Rubin, G. S. (1984). Thinking sex: Notes for a radical theory of the politics of sexuality. In Henry Abelove, Michele Aina Barale, & David M. Halperin (Eds.), *The Lesbian and Gay Studies Reader* (pp. 3–44). New York & London: Routledge.

Rubin, L. B. (1976). *Worlds of pain: Life in the working-class family.* New York: Basic Books.

Rudd, J. (2001). Dowry-Murder: An example of violence against women. *Women's Studies International Forum, 24,* pp. 513–522.

Ruggles, P. (1989, June). *Short and long term poverty in the United States: Measuring the American "underclass."* Washington, DC: Urban Institute.

Rural and Co-operatives Secretariat. (2010). Co-Operatives in Canada (2007 Data).Ottawa: Rural and Co-Operatives Secretariat. Catalogue No., A80-901/1-2007.

Rushing, W. A. (1995). *The AIDS epidemic: Social dimensions of an infectious disease.* Boulder, CO: Westview Press.

Rusli, E., Perlroth, N., & Bilton, N. (2012, May 19). The Education of Mark Zuckerberg. *New York Times.*

Russell, D. (1987, Fall). The monkeywrenchers. *Amicus Journal,* 28–42.

Samuelson, P. A., & Nordhaus, W. D. (1989). *Economics* (13th ed.). New York: McGraw-Hill.

Sanchez, L. (1994, December). Gender, labor allocations, and the psychology of entitlement within the home. *Social Forces, 13*(2), 533–553.

Sandhu, N. (2012). Petals in the Wind: *A Critical Examination of Policies Addressing Gender Inequities in India.* Critical Sociology, M.A. Program, Brock University. Unpublished major research paper.

Sang-Hun, C. (2007, December 23). Where boys were king, a shift toward baby girls. *New York Times.*

Santos, M. G. (2006). *Inside: Life Behind Bars in America.* New York: St. Martin's Griffin.

Sapir, E. (1949b). The status of linguistics as science. In D. G. Mandelbaum (Ed.), *Culture, language, and personality.* Berkeley, CA: University of California Press.

Sapir, E. (1949a). Selected writings of Edward Sapir. In D. G. Mandelbaum (Ed.), *Culture, language, and personality.* Berkeley, CA: University of California Press.

Sargent, J. D. et al. (2007). Exposure to Smoking Depictions in Movies: Its Association with Established Adolescent Smoking. *Archives of Pediatrics and Adolescent Medicine. 161*(9), 849–856.

Saturday Special. (2002, March 23). *Toronto Star,* pp. A24, 25.

Sauve, R. (2007). Family Finances… The Rest of the Story. *Transition Magazine 37,* 1 (Spring). Retrieved from http://www.vifamily.ca/library/transition/371/371.html

Sauve, R. (2011). *"The Current State of Canadian Family Finances: 2010 Report."* Family Finances. Ottawa: Vanier Institute of the Family. www.vifamily.ca

Sawatsky, J. (1980). *Men in the Shadows: The RCMP Security Service.* Toronto: Doubleday Canada.

Sawyer, R. (2001). Dire new acid rain study. *Conservation Matters, 8*(1), 23–34.

Scarce, R. (1993a, June 12–13). Rik Scarce responds: A clear-cut case of academic freedom at risk. *Daily News* (Moscow-Pullman), p. 1B.

Scarce, R. (1993b, June 15). Turnabout: Jailed for no crime at all. *Morning Tribune* (Lewiston).

Scarce, R. (1994, July). (No) trial (but) tribulations. *Journal of Contemporary Ethnography, 23*(2), 123–149.

Scott, K. (2010). "Thinking About Families: An interview with Katherine Scott, Director of Programs, Vanier Institute of the Family." *Transition.* Winter: 5-7.

Schaefer, R. T. (1989). *Sociology* (3rd ed.). New York: McGraw-Hill.

Schiller, B. (2011, June 11). Hong Kong's tale of two cities. *Toronto Star,* p. A35.

Schlosser, E. (2002). *Fast food nation: The dark side of the all-American meal.* New York: Perennial Books.

Scoffield, H. (2011, June 21). Big cities are magnet for poverty, data show. *Canadian Press.* Retrieved from http://www.thecanadianpress.com

Schooler, D., & Trinh, S. (2011). Longitudinal associations between television viewing patterns and adolescent body satisfaction. *Body Image.* 8: 34–42.

Schur, E. M. (1984). *Labeling women deviant: Gender, stigma, and social control.* New York: Random House.

Schwartz, F. N. (1989, January–February). Management women and the new facts of life. *Harvard Business Review, 89*(1), 65–76.

Schwartz, M. A. (1990). *A sociological perspective on politics.* Englewood Cliffs, NJ: Prentice Hall.

Scommegna, P. (1996, August). Teens' risk of AIDS, unintended pregnancies examined. *Population Today, 24*(8), 1–2.

Scott, E. K. (1993, August). How to stop the rapists: A question of strategy in two rape crisis centers. *Social Problems, 40*(3), 343–361.

Scott, J., & Gordon Marshall. (2005). *Oxford Dictionary of Sociology.* Oxford: Oxford University Press.

Scott-Dixon, K. (2004). *Doing IT: Women working in information technology.* Toronto: Sumach Press.

Scrivener, L. (2012, February 28). Child poverty increasingly urban. *Toronto Star,* p. A2.

Scully, D. (1990). *Understanding sexual violence: A study of convicted rapists.* Boston: Unwin Hyman.

Scully, D., & Marolla, J. (1984, June). Convicted rapists' vocabulary of motive: excuses and justifications. *Social Problems, 31*(5), 530–544.

Scully, D., & Marolla, J. (1985, February). Riding the bull at Gilley's: Convicted rapists describe the rewards of rape. *Social Problems, 32*(3), 251–263.

Seager, J. (2003). *The Penguin atlas of women in the world.* New York: Penguin Books.

Segal, N. L., Stohs, H. J., & Evans, K. (2011). Chinese twin children reared apart and reunited: First prospective study of co-twin reunions. *Adoption Quarterly, 14,* 61–78.

Selvin, M., & Goldman, A. (2007, April 10). Boomers Facing Fresh Battle at Work. *Toronto Star,* p. D16.

Service Canada. (2012). University Professors. Retrieved from http://www.servicecanada.gc.ca/eng/qc/job_futures/statistics/4121.shtml

Settersten, R. A., & Owens, T. J. (Ed.). (2002). *New frontiers in socialization: Advances in life course research.* Kidlington, Oxford: Elsevier Science Ltd.

Seubert, V. R. (September, 1991). Sociology and value neutrality: Limiting sociology to the empirical level, *American Sociologist, 2*(3/4), 210–220.

Sev'er, A. (2011). "Marriage-Go-Around: Divorce and Remarriage in Canada." pp. 243–273 in in Mandell, Nancy and Ann Duffy eds. *Canadian Families: Diversity, Conflict and Change.* 4th Edition. Toronto: Nelson.

SexualAssault.ca. (2012). Sexual Assault Statistics in Canada. Retrieved from http://www.statcan.gc.ca/daily-quotidien/110712/dq110712c-eng.htm

Sexual identity is inborn trait, according to study. (1997, March 16). *Alton Telegraph,* p. A6.

Shah, A. (2010). Women's Rights. *Global Issues.* Retrieved from http://www.globalissues.org/article/166/womens-rights#globalissues-org

Shaienks, D., Eisl-Culkin, J., & Brussiere, P. (2006, July). Follow-Up on Education and Labour Market Pathways of Young Canadians Aged 18 to 20—Results from YITS, Cycle 3. Research Paper, Statistics Canada and Human Resources and Social Development Canada, Catalogue No. 81-595-MIE, No. 045.

Shalla, V. (1997). Technology and the deskilling of work: The case of passenger agents at Air Canada. In A. Duffy, D. Glenday, & N. Pupo (Eds.), *Good jobs, bad jobs, no jobs: The transformation of work in the 21st century.* Toronto: Harcourt Brace.

Sharma, S. S. (1994). Untouchables and Brahmins in an Indian village. In J. Curtis & L. Tepperman (Eds.), *Haves and have-nots: An international reader on social inequality* (pp. 299–303). Englewood Cliffs, NJ: Prentice Hall.

Sharp, L. (1995). Steel axes for stone-age Australians. In J. M. Henslin (Ed.), *Down to earth sociology: Introductory readings* (8th ed., pp. 453–462). New York: Free Press.

Shaw, R. (2003). *The epidemic: The rot of American culture, absentee and permissive parenting and the resultant plague of joyless, selfish children.* New York: Regan Books/HarperCollins.

Shaw, S. M., & Lee, J. (2001). *Women's voices, feminist visions: Classic and contemporary readings.* Mountain View, CA: Mayfield Publishing Company.

Sheane, S. D. (2012). Putting on a good face: An examination of the emotional and aesthetic roots of presentational labour. *Economic and Industrial Democracy, 33*(1), 145–158.

Shenon, P. (1995, January 2). AIDS epidemic, late to arrive, now explodes in populous Asia. *New York Times,* pp. A1, A12.

Sherif, M., & Sherif, C. (1953). *Groups in harmony and tension.* New York: Harper & Row.

Sherman, B. (1985). *Working at Leisure.* London: Methuen.

Shibutani, T. (1966). *Improvised news: A sociological study of rumor.* Indianapolis, IN: Bobbs-Merrill.

Shields, M., & Tremblay, S. (2002). *The Health of Canada's Communities.* Ottawa: Statistics Canada, Supplement to Health Reports, 13, Catalogue 82-003.

Shields, M. (2006). Stress and depression in the employed population. Health Reports. Statistics Canada Catalogue no. 82-003. Vol. 17, no. 4.

Shigemi, J., Mino, y., Ohtsu, T., & Tsuda, T. (2002). Effects of perceived job stress on mental health: a longitudinal survey in a Japanese electronics company. *European Journal of Epidemiology.* Vol. 16, no. 4.

Shmueli, D., Prochaska, J. J., & Glantz, S. A. (2010). Effect of Smoking Scenes in Films on Immediate Smoking. *American Journal of Preventive Medicine.* 38(4), 351–358.

Silver, I. (1977, March–April). Crime and conventional wisdom. *Society, 14*(9), 15–19.

Silverman, C. (2008, March 24). Smile, Big Brother's Watching. *Globe and Mail,* p. L3.

Simkin, J. (n.d.). Harriet Martineau. Retrieved from http://www.spartacus.schoolnet.co.uk/Wmartineau.htm

Simon, J. L. (1981). *The ultimate resource.* Princeton, NJ: Princeton University Press.

Simon, J. L. (1992). Population growth is not bad for humanity. In K. Finsterbusch & G. McKenna (Eds.), *Taking sides: Clashing views on controversial social issues* (pp. 347–352). Guilford, CT: Dushkin.

Simon, J. L. (1996). *The ultimate resource 2.* Princeton, NJ: Princeton University Press.

Simon, R. (2008). The joys of parenthood reconsidered. *Contexts.* 7, 2, 40–45.

Simpson, M. (1994). *Male Impersonators: Men Performing Masculinity.* Routledge.

Sinha, K. (2011, July 9). Now, chewing tobacco outstrips smoking in India. *Times of India.* Retrieved from http://timesofindia.indiatimes.com/india/Now-chewing-tobacco-outstrips-smoking-in-India/articleshow/9157123.cms

Sinha, M. (2012). "*Family violence in Canada: A statistical profile, 2010.*" Juristat. May 22. Statistics Canada. Catalogue no. 85-002-X.

Sklair, L. (2001). *Globalization: Capitalism and its alternatives* (3rd ed.). New York: Oxford University Press.

Smith, C. S. (1995, October 9). China becomes industrial nations' most favored dump. *Wall Street Journal,* p. B1.

Smith, D. E. (1987). *The everyday world as problematic: A feminist sociology.* Boston: Northeastern University Press.

Smith, D. E. (1990). *Texts, facts and femininity: Exploring the relations of ruling.* London: Routledge.

Smith, D. E. (1999). *Writing the social: Critique, theory, and investigations.* Toronto: University of Toronto Press.

Smith, J. B., & Tirpak, D. A. (1988, October). *The potential effects of global climate change in the United States.* Washington, DC: U.S. Environmental Protection Agency.

Smith, M. (Ed.). (1990). *Breaking chains: Social movements and collective action.* New Brunswick, NJ: Transaction Publishers.

Smith, M. J., & Hightower, J. (2004). What's age got to do with it? *Education Wife Assault Newsletter on Older Woman Abuse, 13*(1). Retrieved from http://www.womanabuseprevention.com/html/ elder_abuse_newsletter.htm

Smith-Lovin, L., & Brody, C. (1989). Interruptions in group discussions: The effects of gender and group composition. *American Sociological Review, 54,* 424–435.

Snow, D. A., Zurcher, L. A., & Ekland-Olson, S. (1993). Social networks and social movements: A microstructural approach to differential recruitment. In R. L. Curtis, Jr., & B. E. Aguirre (Eds.), *Collective behavior and social movements* (pp. 323–334). Boston: Allyn and Bacon.

Snow, D. A., Zurcher, L. A., & Peters, R. (1993). Victory celebrations as theater: A dramaturgical approach to crowd behavior. In R. L. Curtis, Jr., & B. E. Aguirre (Eds.), *Collective behavior and social movements* (pp. 194–208). Boston: Allyn and Bacon.

Social Planning Toronto. (2011, September). Public System, Private Money: Fees, Fundraising and Equity in the Toronto District School Board. Toronto. Retrieved from http://socialplanningtoronto.org/wp-content/uploads/2011/09/Public-System-Private-Money-Final-Full-Report.pdf

Sokoloff, H. (2008, February 26). Grandpa says: "Push." *Globe and Mail,* pp. L1, L3.

Sontag, S. (1994). As quoted in C. K. Riessman, Women and medicalization: A new perspective. In H. D. Schwartz (Ed.), *Dominant issues in medical sociology* (3rd ed., pp. 190–211). New York: McGraw-Hill.

Sorenson, J. (2003). Everybody is a racist; it's part of human nature. In J. Blackwell, M. Smith, J. Sorenson (Eds.), *Culture of Prejudice: Arguments in Critical Social Science* (pp. 37–45). Toronto: Broadview Press.

Soron, D. (2012). Going Shopping: The Politics of Everyday Consumption. In D. Brock, R. Raby and Mark Thomas (eds.) *Power and Everyday Practices* (pp. 203–222). Toronto: Nelson Education.

Sparkes, A. C., & Smith, B. (2002). Sport, Spinal Cord Injury, Embodied Masculinities, and the Dilemmas of Narrative Identity. *Men and Masculinities.* 4(3), 258–285.

Spector, M., & Kitsuse, J. (1977). *Constructing social problems.* Menlo Park, CA: Cummings.

Spencer, M. (1996). *Foundations of modern sociology* (7th ed.). Toronto: Prentice Hall.

Spitzer, S. (1975, June). Toward a Marxian theory of deviance. *Social Problems, 22,* 608–619.

Srole, L., et al. (1978). *Mental health in the metropolis: The midtown Manhattan study.* New York: New York University Press.

Stanley, L., & Wise, S. (1993). *Breaking out again: Feminist Ontology and Epistemology* (2nd ed.). London: Routledge.

Stacey, J. (2011). *Unhitched: Love, Marriage and Family Values from West Hollywood to Western China.* New York: New York University Press.

Stapleton, J., Murphy, B., & Xing, Y. (2012). *The "working poor" in the Toronto region: Who they are, where they live and how trends are changing.* Toronto: The Metcalf Foundation. Retrieved from http://www.metcalffoundation.com

Stark, E. (1989). Friends through it all. In J. M. Henslin (Ed.), *Marriage and family in a changing society* (3rd ed., pp. 441–449). New York: Free Press.

Stark, R. (1989). *Sociology* (3rd ed.). Belmont, CA: Wadsworth.

Starna, W. A., & Watkins, R. (1991, Winter). Northern Iroquoian slavery. *Ethnohistory, 38*(1), 34–57.

Starrels, M. (1992, September). The evolution of workplace family policy research. *Journal of Family Issues, 13*(3), 259–278.

Statham, A., Miller, E. M., & Mauksch, H. O. (1988). The integration of work: Second-order analysis of qualitative research. In A. Statham, E. M. Miller, & H. O. Mauksch (Eds.), *The worth of women's work: A qualitative synthesis* (pp. 11–35). Albany, NY: State University of New York Press.

Statistical Abstract of the United States. (Published annually). Washington DC: Bureau of the Census.

Statistics Canada. (Selected years). *General Social Survey.*

Statistics Canada. (1998). *Family incomes.* Ottawa: Minister of Supply and Services, Catalogue 13-208.

Turner, R. H., & Killian, L. M. (1987). *Collective behavior* (2nd ed.). Englewood Cliffs, NJ: Prentice Hall.Udy, S. H., Jr. (1959, December). Bureaucracy and rationality in Weber's organizational theory: An empirical study. *American Sociological Review, 24,* 791–795.

Udry, J. R. (2000, June). Biological Limits of Gender Construction. *American Sociological Review, 65,* 443–457.

Ullman, E., & Harris, C. (1970). The nature of cities. In A. N. Cousins & H. Nagpaul (Eds.), *Urban man and society: A reader in urban ecology* (pp. 91–100). New York: Knopf.

UNESCO. (2011a). Global Monitoring Report: Education for All: The Hidden Crisis: Armed Conflict and Education. Retrieved from http://www.unesco.org/new/en/education/themes/leading-the-international-agenda/efareport/reports/2011-conflict and http://unesdoc.unesco.org/images/0019/001907/190743e.pdf

UNESCO. (2011b). UNESCO launches Global Partnership for Girls and Women's Education. Retrieved from http://www.unesco.org/new/en/media-services/single-view/news/unesco_launches_global_partnership_for_girls_and_womens_education

UNICEF. (2010). The children left behind: A league table of inequality in child well-being in the world's rich countries. *Innocenti Report Card 9.* Florence, Italy: UNICEF Innocenti Research Centre.

United Nations. (2001). *Human development report 2001.* New York: United Nations.

United Nations. (2003). *Human Development Report 2003.* New York: Oxford University Press.

United Nations. (2005). *Statistics and Indicators on Women and Men.* Table 3a: Life Expectancy. Retrieved from http://unstats.un.org/unsd/demographic/products/indwm/ww2005/tab3a.htm

United Nations. (2006). *Trends in total migrant stock: The 2005 revision.* Retrieved from http://esa.un.org/migration/index.asp?panel=1

United Nations. (2010). The World's Women 2010: Trends and Statistics. New York: United Nations. Retrieved from http://unstats.un.org/unsd/demographic/products/Worldswomen/WW_full%20report_color.pdf

United Nations Population Fund. (2000). *Lives together, worlds apart: Men and women in a time of change.* New York: United Nations.

United Press International Inc. (UPI). (2012, April 18). Poll: Most U.S. adults unhappy with weight. Retrieved from http://www.upi.com

University of Waterloo. (2006, June 21). UW-led research team looks at impact of child-care choices on children's development. Retrieved from http://newsrelease.uwaterloo.ca/news.php?id=4751.

Uriely, N., Ram, Y., & Malach-Pines, A. (2011). Psychoanalytic Sociology of Deviant Tourist Behavior. *Annals of Tourism Research, 38,* 3: 1051–1069.

Urquia, M. L., Frank, J. W., Glazier, R. H., & Moineddin, R. (2007, November). Birth Outcomes By Neighbourhood Income and Recent Immigration in Toronto. Statistics Canada, Health Reports, Volume 18, Number 4, Catalogue no. 82-003.

Useem, M. (1984). *The inner circle: Large corporations and the rise of business political activity in the U.S. and U.K.* New York: Oxford University Press.

Vallee, B. (2008). *The War on Women.* Toronto: Key Porter Books.

Valpy, M. (2008, April 26). Wealth Gap Exposes Fresh Labour Challenge. *Globe and Mail,* p. A14.

van Dijk, J. (2004). The role of ethnicity and religion in the social support system of older Dutch Canadians. *Canadian Journal of Aging, 23*(1), 21–34.

Van Lawick-Goodall, J. (1971). *In the shadow of man.* Boston: Houghton Mifflin.

Vanier Institute of the Family (2011a). "Families, Work and Time: Running Hard to Stand Still." *Fascinating Families.* Issue 36. http://www.vifamily.ca. Accessed June 23, 2012.

Vanier Institute of the Family (2011b). "Marriage rate continues to drop." *Fascinating Families.* Issue 40. http://www.vifamily.ca. Accessed July 16, 2012.

Vanier Institute of the Family (2011c). "Young people are still waiting for the recession to end." *Fascinating Families.* Issue 34. http://www.vifamily.ca. Accessed July 16, 2012.

Vanier Institute of the Family (2011d). "Child Abuse and Neglect." *Fascinating Families.* Issue 38. http://www.vifamily.ca. Accessed July 16, 2012.

Vanier Institute of the Family (2012a). "Blending Family Traditions." *Fascinating Families.* Issue 44. http://www.vifamily.ca. Accessed July 16, 2012.

Vanier Institute of the Family (2012b). "Trying to Conceive: Infertility in Canada." *Fascinating Families.* Issue 45. http://www.vifamily.ca. Accessed July 16, 2012.

Vann, K. (2002, March 2). Elderly murder-suicides on rise. *Toronto Star,* p. C9.

Veblen, T. (1912). *The Theory of the Leisure Class.* New York: Macmillan.

Vezina, M. (2011). "Quality of personal networks: Does living along make a difference?" *Canadian Social Trends.* November: 62–69. Catalogue no. 11-008-X.

Villanti, A., Boulay, M., & Juon, H. S. (2011). Peer, parent and media influences on adolescent smoking by developmental stage. *Addictive Behaviors.* 36: 133–136.

Vining, D. R. (2011). Sociobiology's relevance to modern society: commentary on two articles published here. *Evolution and Human Behavior.* 32: 364–347.

Violent Montreal student protest nets 17 arrests: Premier calls social disruption "unacceptable." (2012, April 20). *CBC News.*

Volti, R. (1995). *Society and technological change* (3rd ed.). New York: St. Martin's Press.

Volti, R. (2010). *Society and Technological Change* (6th ed.). New York: Worth Publishers.

Von Hoffman, N. (1970, May). Sociological snoopers. *Transaction, 7*(4), 6.

Wagley, C., & Harris, M. (1958). *Minorities in the new world.* New York: Columbia University Press.

Waldholz, M. (1991, December 2). Computer "brain" outperforms doctors in diagnosing heart attack patients. *Wall Street Journal*, p. 7B.

Waldman, P. (1995, June 12). Riots in Bahrain arouse ire of feared monarchy as the U.S. stands by. *Wall Street Journal*, pp. A1, A8.

Wallace, K. (2012, January 9). Government pensioners hit hard by meltdown. *Toronto Star*, p. A8.

Wallerstein, I. (1974). *The modern world system: Capitalist agriculture and the origins of the European world-economy in the sixteenth century.* New York: Academic Press.

Wallerstein, I. (1979). *The capitalist world-economy.* New York: Cambridge University Press.

Wallerstein, I. (1984). *The politics of the world-economy: The states, the movements, and the civilizations.* Cambridge, UK: Cambridge University Press.

Wallerstein, I. (1990). Culture as the ideological battleground of the modern world-system. In M. Featherstone (Ed.), *Global culture: Nationalism, globalization, and modernity* (pp. 31–55). London: Sage.

Wallis, M. A., & Kwok, S.-M. (Ed.). (2008). *Daily struggles: The deepening racialization and feminization of poverty in Canada.* Toronto: CSPI.

Walsh, C., Jennifer L. O., Jenny P., Lynne L., & Harriet L. M. (2011). "Elder Abuse and Oppresion: Voices of Marginalized Elders." Journal of Elder Abuse & Neglect. 23: 17–42.

Walters, J. (1990, May 18–20). Chimps in the mist. *USA Weekend*, p. 24.

Ward, L. (2002, June 14). The First Nations Governance Act. *CBC News Online.* Retrieved from http://www.cbc.ca/news/features/indian_act

Ward, O. (2012, January 19). Poverty rising in G20, says Oxfam. *Toronto Star*, p. 26.

Warner, W. L., & Hunt, P. S. (1941). *The social life of a modern community.* New Haven, CT: Yale University Press.

Warner, W. L., Hunt, P. S., Meeker, M., & Eels, K. (1949). *Social class in America.* New York: Harper.

Warr, M. (1993). Age, peers, and delinquency. *Criminology, 31*(1), 17–40.

Wartella, E., Richert, R. A., & Robb, M. B. (2010). Babies, television and videos: how did we get here? *Developmental Review.* 30: 116–127.

Watson, J. M. (1988). Outlaw motorcyclists. In J. M. Henslin (Ed.), *Down to earth sociology: Introductory readings* (5th ed., pp. 203–213). New York: Free Press.

Watters, E. (2003). *Urban tribes: A generation redefines friendship, family and commitment.* New York: Bloomsbury.

Webb, E. J., Campbell, D. T., Schwartz, R. D., & Sechrest, L. (1966). *Unobtrusive measures: Nonreactive research in the social sciences.* Chicago: Rand McNally.

Weber, M. (1946). *From Max Weber: Essays in sociology* (H. Gerth & C. Wright Mills, Trans. and Ed.). New York: Oxford University Press.

Weber, M. (1947). *The theory of social and economic organization* (A. M. Henderson & T. Parsons, Trans., T. Parsons, Ed.). Glencoe, IL: Free Press. (Original work published 1913)

Weber, M. (1958). *The Protestant ethic and the spirit of capitalism.* New York: Scribner's. (Original work published 1904–1905)

Weber, M. (1968). *Economy and society* (E. Fischoff, Trans.). New York: Bedminster Press. (Original work published 1922)

Weber, M. (1978). *Economy and society* (G. Roth & C. Wittich, Eds.). Berkeley: University of California Press. (Original work published 1922)

Weisburd, D., Wheeler, S., & Waring, E. (1991). *Crimes of the middle classes: White-collar offenders in the federal courts.* New Haven, CT: Yale University Press.

Weisskopf, M. (1992). Scientist says greenhouse effect is setting in. In Washington Post Writers Group (Eds.), *Ourselves and others: The Washington Post sociology companion* (pp. 297–298). Boston: Allyn and Bacon.

Wente, M. (2000, January 29). How David found his manhood. *Globe and Mail.*

Wente, M. (2007, January 27). The Ozzie and Harriet Gap. *Globe and Mail*, p. A25.

Wente, M. (2008, January 5). Hark! A shriek-inducing wake-up call. *Globe and Mail.* p. A19.

West, C., & Garcia, A. (1988). Conversational shift work: A study of topical transitions between women and men. *Social Problems, 35,* 551–575.

Westhead, R. (2011, October 9). Poverty a numbers game. *Toronto Star*, p. A3.

White, C. (2011, November 9). The leadership gap. *Toronto Star*, p. A23.

White, E. (2002). *Fast Girls: Teenage Tribes and The Myth of the Slut.* New York: Scribner.

White, J. A. (1991, February 13). When employees own big stake, it's a buy signal for investors. *Wall Street Journal*, pp. C1, C19.

White, J. E. (1995, July 3). Forgive us our sins. *Time,* p. 29.

White, J. M., Martin, T. F., & Bartolic, S. (2013). *Families Across the Life Course.* Toronto: Pearson.

White, N. J. (2012, May 18). Jenna Talackova, Transgendered Miss Universe Canada Contestant, Shines in Spotlight. *Toronto Star.* Retrieved from http://www.thestar.com/living/article/1181138--jenna-talackova-transgendered-miss-universe-canada-contestant-shines-in-spotlight

Whitehead, S. M., & Barrett, F. J. (Ed.). (2001). *The Masculinities Reader.* Cambridge: Polity Press.

Whorf, B. (1956). *Language, thought, and reality* (J. B. Carroll, Ed.). Cambridge, MA: MIT Press.

Whyte, W. H. (1989). *The city: Rediscovering the center.* New York: Doubleday.

Whyte, W. H. (1997). Street corner society. In J. M. Henslin (Ed.), *Down to earth sociology: Introductory readings* (9th ed., pp. 59–67). New York: Free Press.

Wilkins, R., Uppel, S., Fines, P., Senecal, S., Guimond, E., & Dion, R. (2008, January). Life Expectancy in the Inuit-Inhabited Areas of Canada, 1989 to 2003. Statistics Canada, Health Reports, Volume 19, Number 1, Catalogue no. 82-003.

Williams, C. (2010). Economic well-being. In *Women in Canada: A gender-based statistical report*. Statistics Canada catalogue no. 89-503-X. Ottawa: Minister of Industry.

Williams, J. (2004). *50 Facts that should change the world*. Duxford, Cambridge: Icon Books.

Williams, L., & Guest, M. P. (2005). Attitudes toward marriage among the urban middle-class in Vietnam, Thailand, and the Philippines. *Journal of Comparative Family Studies*. (Spring), pp. 163–188.

Willis, P. (1981). *Learning to labour: How working class kids get working class jobs*. New York: Columbia University Press.

Wilson, B., & Jette, S. (2005). Making sense of the cultural activities of Canadian youth. In N. Mandell & A. Duffy (Eds.), *Canadian families: Diversity, conflict and change* (3rd ed., pp. 64–86). Toronto: Thomson Nelson.

Wilson, S. J. (1991). *Women, families, and work*. Toronto: McGraw-Hill Ryerson.

Wilson, W. J. (1996). *When work disappears: The world of the new urban poor*. Chicago: University of Chicago Press.

Winslow, R. (1994, October 7). More doctors are adding online tools to their kits. *Wall Street Journal*, pp. B1, B4.

Winslow, R. (1995, August 18). Smoking increases heart-attack risk fivefold for people in their 30s and 40s. *Wall Street Journal*, p. B5.

Wirth, L. (1945). The problem of minority groups. In R. Linton (Ed.), *The science of man in the world crisis*. New York: Columbia University Press.

Wohl, R. R., & Strauss, A. (1958, March). Symbolic representation and the urban milieu. *American Journal of Sociology, 63*, 523–532.

Wolf, D. R. (1991). *The Rebels: A Brotherhood of Outlaw Bikers*. Toronto: University of Toronto Press.

Wolf, J. (2012). "Review of Joan B. Wolf's Is Breast Best?" *Contemporary Sociology*. 41 (2): 248–249.

Wolf, J. B. (2011). Is Breast Best? *Taking on the Breastfeeding Experts and the New High Stakes of Motherhood*. New York: New York University Press.

Womack, J. P., Jones, D. T., & Roos, D. (1991). *The machine that changed the world: The story of lean production*. New York: Harper Perrenial.

Wombs for Rent: Growth of Commercial Surrogacy. (2007, December 31). *Hamilton Spectator*, p. A6.

World Health Organization (WHO). (1946). *Constitution of the World Health Organization*. New York: World Health Organization Interim Commission.

World Health Organization. (2012, May 17). Initiative Saves Lives of Vulnerable Women and Children in the Developing World. *Globe and Mail*, p. L7.

Wright, E. O. (1985). *Class*. London: Verso.

Wrigley, J., & Dreby, J. (2006). Violent fatalities in child care. *Contexts*. 5,4, 35–40.

Xu, X. et al. (2010). Body dissatisfaction, engagement in body change behaviours and sociocultural influences on body image among Chinese adolescents. *Body Image*. 7: 156–164.

Yalnizyan, A. (2007, March). *The Rich and the Rest of Us: The Changing Face of Canada's Growing Gap*. Ottawa: Canadian Centre for Policy Alternatives.

Yalnizyan, A. (2010, December). *The Rise of Canada's Richest 1%*. Ottawa: Canadian Centre for Policy Alternatives.

Yardley, J. (2007, May 13). Faces of Abortion in China: A Young Single Woman. *New York Times*.

Yardley, J. (2010, August 21). India tries using cash bonuses to slow birthrates. *New York Times*.

Yelaja, P. (2002, May 3). Female heart attack victims less likely to be rehabilitated. *Toronto Star*, p. A17.

Yew, M. A.-T. (2012, April 25). Oops! Errant Email Accidently Fires 1,300. *Toronto Star*, p. A2.

Yinger, J. M. (1970). *The scientific study of religion*. New York: Macmillan.

Young, C. (2011). Pensions, privatization, and poverty: The gendered impact. *Canadian Journal of Women and the Law, 23*(2), 661–685.

Young, J. (1971). *The Drugtakers: The Cocial Meaning of Drug Use*. London: MacGibbon and Kee.

Young, L. E. (1995). The overlooked contributions of women to the development of American sociology: An examination of AJS articles from 1895–1926. [Paper presented at the 1995 meetings of the American Sociological Association].

York, G. (2011, November 26). When Having a Baby is a Life-or-Death Issue. *Globe and Mail*, p. A27.

Youth Criminal Justice Act: Changing the law on young criminals. (2006, June 23). *CBC News Online*. Retrieved from http://www.cbc.ca/news/background/crime/ycja.html

Zachary, G. P. (1995, November 22). Behind stocks' surge is an economy in which big U.S. firms thrive. *Wall Street Journal*, pp. A1, A5.

Zald, M. N. (1992). Looking backward to look forward: Reflections on the past and the future of the resource mobilization research program. In A. D. Morris & C. M. Mueller (Eds.), *Frontiers in social movement theory* (pp. 326–348). New Haven, CT: Yale University Press.

Zeitlin, I. M. (1990). *Ideology and the development of sociological thought* (4th ed.). Englewood Cliffs, NJ: Prentice Hall.

Zerubavel, E. (1991).The Fine Line: Making Distinctions in Everyday Life. Glencoe, IL: Free Press.

Zey, M. (1993). *Banking on fraud: Drexel, junk bonds, and buyouts*. Hawthorne, NY: Aldine de Gruyter.

Zou, H. F. (1994, July). The spirit of capitalism and long-run growth. *European Journal of Political Economy, 10*(2), 279–293.

Zuberi, D. and Ptashnick, M. (2011). "In Search of a Better Life: The Experiences of Working Poor Immigrants in Vancouver, Canada." *International Immigration. 50*, e60–e93.

Johnson, 2006, 164, 165
Johnson, C., 200
Johnson, H., 164
Johnson, J., 200
Johnson, M.M., 158
Johnson, Mark, 382
Johnston, David, 116
Jones, C., 146
Jones, Earl, 369
Jones, Jim, 336
Jordan, M., 108
Judd, D.R., 121, 273
Juon, H.S., 74

K

K'ung Fu-tsu, 335
Kadushin, C., 127
Kahl, J.A., 128, 129, 133
Kalil, A., 140
Kalish, S., 389
Kaminski, M., 354
Kanter, J., 398
Kanter, R.M., 28, 104, 227, 232
Kao, J.J., 28
Kaplan, H.R., 123
Karnik, K., 42
Karp, D.A., 396
Katz, A., 191
Katz, Jackson, 167
Kaufman, J., 83
Keating, N., 209
Kelley, Florence, 15
Kelley, J., 117
Kelly, Rick, Patti, Julie, & Michael, 94
Kelso, W.A., 130
Kemeny, A., 295
Kendall, P.L., 85
Keniston, K., 89
Kennedy, P., 102, 245
Kent, M., 385
Kent, Peter, 399
Kephart, W.M., 331
Keung, N., 137, 199, 289
Kevorkian, Jack, 352
Keys, B., 208
Kilbride, K.M., 294
Killian, L.M., 406, 408
Kim, K., 74
King, J., 42
King, N., 204
King, R.T., Jr., 423
King, William Lyon Mackenzie, 268t
Kingston, G., 148
Kinsman, G., 371
Kitsuse, J., 417
Kitsuse, J.I., 364
Klein, N., 224
Klineberg, E., 298
Knaus, W.A., 345
Knobler, S., 355
Koffler, Murray, 226
Kohn, M.L., 133
Kooistra, P.G., 179
Kopun, F., 280
Kornhauser, W., 415
Koropeckyj-Cox, T., 295

Kottak, C., 60
Krahn, H, 290
Kroc, Ray, 220
Kudielka, B.M., 356
Kuhn, Margaret, 196
Kupers, T.A., 87
Kwok, S.-M., 138

L

Lachica, E., 399
Laczko, Leslie, 56
LaDou, J., 399
LaFraniere, S., 355
Lagnado, L., 354
Lahey, K., 159
Laird, G., 131
Laker, J.A., 167
Landtman, G., 112
Lang, G.E., 417
Lang, K., 417
Langan, D., 287
Lanza-Kaduce, L., 85
Laporte, Pierre, 271
Lareau, A., 51
Larocque, S., 297
Laska, S.B., 401
Lastman, Mel, 37
Laurier, Wilfrid, 268
Laville, J.-L., 242
Laxer, J., 107
Layton, Jack, 269
Lazarsfeld, P.F., 22
Leacock, E., 150, 323
Leadlay, Alice, 210
Leadlay, Kenneth, 210
Leaper, C., 73
Leavell, S.A., 294
LeBon, Gustave, 406
Lee, D., 138
Lee, J., 204
Lee, J.-A., 294
Lee, M., 98
Leith, Rae, 163
Lemert, C., 16
Lemert, E.M., 364
Lemon, S., 355
Lenski, G, 123
Lenski, G., 390
Lenski, J., 390
LePlay, Frédéric, 13
Lerner, G., 113, 150, 152, 153
Lesage, Jean, 270, 271
Lethbridge, L., 286
Levy, M.J., Jr., 333
Lewis, K., 132
Lewis, O., 104, 142
Liebow, E., 368
Lightman, E.S., 139
Lincoln, Y.S., 178
Lind, M., 176
Lindsay, C., 209, 338
Linton, R., 53, 150
Liodakis, N., 138
Lipset, S.M., 54, 59, 263, 376
Liptak, A., 230
Lipton, M., 105

Livingstone, D.W., 315, 316, 322
Locke, John, 7
Lofland, J.F., 406, 408, 410, 411
Lombardo, A.P., 77
Lombroso, C., 361
Lorber, J., 20, 177
Lorie, A.F., 76
Lowe, G.S., 150
Lu, V., 206, 207, 317
Lubman, S., 274
Luckenbill, D.F., 363
Lundberg, O., 132
Luong, M., 136, 291
Luther, Martin, 334
Lutter, M., 123
Luxton, M, 285
Luxton, M., 161, 282
Lynn, J., 74
Lyotard, J.F., 21

M

MacArthur Foundation Research Network on an Aging Society, 207
Macdonald, B., 204
Macdonald, John A., 116f, 267, 268t
MacDonald, M., 286
MacGregor, R., 392
Mackay, C., 406
Mackay, Peter, 269
Mackenzie, Alexander, 268t
Mackenzie, H., 118, 120, 160
Mackie, M., 70, 155
MacKinnon, C.A., 162
MacKinnon, Mark, 246
MacLean, Annie Marion, 15
Maclean's, 249
MacLennan, H., 13
Magoffin, D., 191
Mahaffy, Leslie, 410
Maheux, H., 294
Mahmoud, A., 355
Mahoney, J.S., Jr., 179
Maier, S.L., 282
Mail Online, 69
Main, J.T., 113
Malach-Pines, A., 72
Mallick, H., 288
Malthus, Thomas, 383
Mamdani, M., 388
Mandela, Nelson, 263
Mandell, N., 81, 90, 154, 251, 282, 285, 293
Mander, J., 175, 423
Manji, Irshad, 332
Mannell, R.C., 76
Manning, Preston, 260
Manski, C.F., 322
Manual, K., 349
Mao, 152
Marchand, Jean, 183
Marciano, D.L., 75
Markson, E.W., 201
Markusen, E., 179
Marolla, J., 42
Marotte, B., 220
Marr, L.G., 230
Marshall, Gordon, 72

SUBJECT INDEX

Bretton Woods Agreement, 97
British Imperial Act, 113
British North America Act, 180
Brock University, 63
Buddhism, 334–335, 338
bulimia, 78
bullying, 83, 313–315
bureaucracies
  and alienation, 223
  in Canada, 270
  characteristics of, 217–220
  corporate culture, 226–229
  dysfunctions of, 221–224
  and goal displacement, 224
  ideal versus real, 220–221
  inflexibility of, 222
  management strategies, 229–235
  and organizations, 216–224
  sociological significance of, 224
  typical, 218*f*
  and women, 227
  working within, 226–229
bureaucratic authority, 262

C

Cabbagetown, 255
call systems, 60
Calvinism, 11, 216, 333
CAMI, 235
Canada
  and aging, 193–194, 194*f*, 195–196,
    200–203, 205
  birth rates, 290, 290*f*
  bureaucracy in, 270
  career opportunities in sociology, 35
  causes of death, 347*t*
  charter groups, 181–184
  child abuse, 302
  and child labour, 107
  citizenship, 188
  classifications in, 180–187
  crime in, 368
  criminal justice system, 373–374, 374*f*
  day care, 82
  demographic profile, 389*t*
  divorce rates, 295–296, 301*t*
  eating disorders, 78
  economic sectors, 249–250
  education in, 310–311
  eldercare, 209
  endangered languages in, 48
  ethnic groups, 184–187, 185*t*, 186*t*
  families, 281, 295*t*, 297–298
  feminism in, 154–155
  gender inequality in, 154–158
  and globalization, 97
  health care in, 348–349
  health in, 350–351
  homelessness in, 130
  immigration, 96, 184–187, 193, 241, 294
  incarceration in, 376
  income in, 119*f*, 119–121, 120*f*, 121*t*,
    242–243, 242*f*
  income inequality, 255
  and Kyoto Protocol, 399
  language and culture in, 180*t*

life expectancy, 131–132, 195
marriage patterns, 289
multiculturalism, 390
Native peoples, 57
and Occupy Wall Street, 412
one-parent families, 294
parliamentary system, 267
pensions, 205–207
political shift in, 260–261
political system, 266–272, 267–270
poverty, 140
poverty in, 135, 137–138, 139, 142
prime ministers, 268*t*
public policy on violence against
  women, 371–372
religion in, 81, 337–339, 338*t*
retirement rules, 206*t*
same-sex families, 296–297
as semiperipheral country, 103
and slavery, 113
social class ladder, 128*f*
sociology in, 13–14, 17
sports participation in, 84
suicide rates, 210
teen-age mothers, 291
tobacco consumption, 74
unemployment, 252*f*
urbanization in, 392
value contradictions in, 57–58
values in, 54–60
violence against women, 303
voluntarism, 225
voter turnout, 266, 266*t*
wealth in, 117–119, 118*t*
women in workforce, 251, 251*f*
work hours, 254
work in, 249–254
young adults in, 89
youth unemployment and crime, 368
Canada's Alcohol and Other Drugs Survey, 33
Canada's Association for the Fifty-Plus
  (CARP), 213
Canada Act, 180
Canada Health Act, 348, 348*t*, 349
Canada Post, 243, 244
Canadian Alliance on Mental Illness and
  Mental Health, 357
Canadian Alliance Party, 269
Canadian Association of Public Data
  Users, 32
Canadian Association of Research
  Libraries, 32
Canadian Association of Retired
  Persons, 196
Canadian Association of Small University
  Libraries, 32
Canadian Association on Gerontology, 213
Canadian Business, 258
Canadian Centre for Policy Alternatives, 426
*The Canadian Graduate Student Journal of
  Folklore and Ethnology*, 64
Canadian Institutes of Health Research—
  Institute of Aging, 213
Canadianization movement, 14
Canadian Journal of Sociology
  Online, 25, 44

The Canadian Network for the Prevention of
  Elder Abuse, 213
Canadian Organization for the Rights of
  Prostitutes, 364
Canadian Socio-economic Information
  Management System, 33
Canadian Sociological Association, 25, 43
capitalism
  changes in, 245
  consequences of, 254–255
  criticisms of, 245
  Durkheim's view of, 10
  features of, 243
  laissez-faire capitalism, 243–244
  Marx's view of, 9, 19
  new capitalism, 246
  and rationalization of society, 215–216
  and religion, 332–333
  and social class, 127
  spirit of, 11, 333
  stages of, 95*f*
  state capitalism, 243–244
  Weber's view of, 10–11
  welfare capitalism, 243–244
capitalist class, 127, 128–129
capitalist world economy, 102
careers in sociology, 23, 35
Catholicism
  in Canada, 337–338
  and capitalism, 11
  and change, 215–216
  and propaganda, 414
  in Quebec, 55, 183
  and suicide rates, 9
Centers for Disease Control and
  Prevention, 357
central tendency, 29
Centre for Research on Work and
  Society, 258
charismatic authority, 263
charismatic leader, 336
Charlottetown Accord, 271
charter groups, 181–184
Charter of Rights and Freedoms, 55, 127, 180,
  267
cheating, 324
Chicago connection, 13
child abuse, 302–303
child-bearing, 290, 298, 299
childcare, 82, 291–292, 318
child labour, 107, 303
Childless by Choice Project, 306
childless families, 295
child-rearing, 84, 133, 290–292
children. *see also* education; school
  home children, 113
  and mass media, 84
  and poverty, 140, 141
  as prey, 99
  socialization of, 81, 82, 84–85, 88–89
Children's Defense Fund, 306
Chile, 248
China
  and body image, 78
  and economic systems, 245
  and female infanticide, 108

productionist societies, 21
profane, 328
professional wrestling, 27, 52t, 63
professions, 247
profit, pursuit of, 243
profits, 51
Progressive Conservative Party, 267
Progressive Movement, 267
proletariat, 9, 19, 115
propaganda, 414
property, 115–116, 116f, 117–119.
    see also wealth
proportional representation, 271
prostitution, 364–365
Protestant Ethic, 11, 333
Protestantism
    in Canada, 338
    and capitalism, 11, 333
    and change, 215–216
    and suicide rates, 9–10
psychology, 5
Public Health Agency of Canada, 357
public opinion, 414
publics, 413f, 414
public servants, 270
pure relationship, 104
pure sociology, 22
pursuit of profit, 243

Q
qualitative analysis, 36–38
qualitative research methods, 33, 36
quality circles, 232
quality of life, 53
quantitative analysis, 36–38
quantitative research methods, 33, 36
Quebec
    and Aboriginal peoples, 181
    childcare in, 82, 291
    as distinct society, 55–56
    history of, 181–184
    parental leave, 291
    the Quiet Revolution, 13, 55, 270–271
    sociology in, 13
    and sovereignty, 270–271
    and teenage sex, 49, 49f
Quebec Act of 1774, 181
queer theory
    described, 21
    and gender, 154
    as microsociology, 22
    as theoretical perspective, 18t
questionnaires, 30–31
questions
    to research, 35
    for surveys, 30
Quiet Revolution, 13, 55, 270–271, 411
quiet revolution, 251

R
race
    and biology, 67, 172
    critical race theory, 178
    and ethnicity, 173
    and immigration, 138–139
    intergroup relations, 178–180, 178f

minority group, 173–175
myth and reality, 172–173
and postmodernism, 177
prejudice and discrimination. see
    discrimination; prejudice
racial superiority, 172–173
and social mobility, 134
in the United States, 113
and violence, 371
racial inequality. see also prejudice
conflict theory, 176–177
functionalist perspective, 176
leaned behaviour, 175
and postcolonialism, 177–178
psychological perspectives, 175–176
sociological foundation, 172–175
sociological theories of, 176–178
symbolic interactionism, 177
theoretical paradigm, 188
theories of, 175–178
radical feminist theories, 20
The Raging Grannies, 197
rain forests, 399
Ralliement des Créditistes, 267
random sample, 29
rape, 164
rapport, 31
rationality, 215
rationalization of society, 215–216
rational-legal authority, 262
reactive social movement, 411
Real Women, 19
real-world present, 21
real world versus the ideal, 42
reasonable accommodation, 13
rebellion, 367
The Rebels, 365
records, 219
redemptive social movements, 412
red tape, 221–222
reference groups, 80
reformative social movements, 412
reformists, 332
Reform Party, 269
registered Indians, 180
reincarnation, 334
rejectionists, 332
relative deprivation theory, 416
reliability, 36
religion
    beliefs, 330–331
    in Canada, 337–339, 338t
    and capitalism, 332–333
    and community, 331
    conflict theory, 331
    cults, 336
    and culture, 337
    defined, 328
    dysfunctions of, 329–330
    ecclesias, 337
    elements of, 328
    female spirituality, 331–332
    feminist theories, 331–332, 340
    functionalist perspective, 329–330
    institutionalized religion, 337
    postmodern perspective, 332, 340

rituals, 330
sects, 336–337
Sharia law, 276
and social class, 133
social-conflict paradigm, 340
and social inequality, 331
and socialization, 66, 81–82
structural functionalism, 340
and suicide rates, 9–10
symbolic interactionist perspective, 330–
    331, 340
symbols, 330
types of groups, 335–337, 335f
variations in, 337
and women, 331
world religions, 333–335, 333f
remarriage, 300–301
replaceability, 219
replication, 11, 38
representative democracy, 264, 265
representative sample, 29
reproductive technology, 163, 296
reputational method, 117
research
    analyzing results, 36–38
    and common sense, 28
    data collection, 36
    data liberation initiative, 32–33
    documents, 33
    ethics in, 38–41
    feminist methodology, 31–32
    field interview, 31–32
    fieldwork, 31
    generalizability, 31
    how not to do research, 30
    methods, choosing, 33–34, 36
    methods of, 28–34
    model of, 35–38, 36f
    participant observation, 31
    qualitative analysis, 36–38
    qualitative interview, 31–32
    qualitative methods, 33, 36
    quantitative analysis, 36–38
    quantitative methods, 33, 36
    questions for, 35
    secondary analysis, 32–33
    sharing results, 38
    structured conversation, 31–32
    surveys, 29–31
    and theory, 41–42
    topics, 28, 35
    two common strategies, 34f
    unobtrusive measures, 33
    variables, 35, 35f
research designs, 28–34, 36
reserve labour force, 176
residential schools, 319–320
resocialization, 86–87, 90
resource mobilization, 417
respondents, 30
retirement, 205–208
retreatism, 367
revisionists, 332
revolution, 261
revolutionaries, 332
Riel, Louis, 183

Taser International, 224
Taylorism, 231
teacher expectations, 323
tearooms, 41
techniques of neutralization, 364
technological determinism, 62
technology. *see also* new technology
    in the classroom, 324, 325
    and conflict theory, 248
    and control of workers, 233–234
    and culture, 60–63
    defined, 418
    gender and reproductive technology, 163
    and globalization, 106
    new technology, 60–61, 203
    reproductive technology, 296
    and seniors, 203
    and social change, 418–425
    and social class, 131
    and social inequality, 127
    and social mobility, 134–137
    and virtual organizations, 234–235
teen-age mothers, 89, 136, 291
teenagers, 49, 49f, 89
television, 75–76. *see also* mass media
terrorism, 275, 330
tertiary sector, 249
tertiary social deviance, 364
text speak, 48
theoretical paradigms
    on age discrimination, 212
    on bureaucracies, 237
    on crime and social deviance, 379
    on economics, 257
    on environment, 401f
    on family, 305
    on gender inequality, 169
    on medicine, 357
    on politics, 277
    on racial inequality, 188
    on religion, 340
    on socialization, 92
    on social stratification, 143
theoretical perspectives in sociology
    combining, 22
    conflict theory, 19
    feminist theories, 19–20, 153–154
    functional analysis, 17–19
    on gender inequality, 152–154
    major perspectives, 18t
    postmodernism, 20–21
    queer theory, 18t, 21, 22, 154
    symbolic interactionism, 17
theory, 17, 41–42
thinness, 3–4
three measures of central tendency, 29
timetables, 200
tobacco, 74–75
Toronto, 37–38
total institutions, 72, 86–87
totalitarianism, 266
tourism, 96
tracking, 315, 322–323
trade unions, 254
traditional authority, 261–262
traditional orientation, 215

traditional societies, 419t
transformative social movements, 412
transgender, 148
transnational corporations, 105–106
the trapped, 396
triangulation, 36
Trudeau, Pierre Elliott, 263
Turkey, 151
twins, 68, 148

U

underclass, 130
underemployment, 245
underground economy, 253
unemployment in Canada, 252f
unemployment rate, 14, 310
unions, 254
unitary state, 266
United States
    child poverty in, 141
    health care in, 349
    immigration in, 96
    incarceration in, 376
    power in, 272f
    religion in, 338t
    sociology in, 15–17
    unwed mothers, 291
    values in, 54
    violence against women, 303
    and weight, 78
    work hours, 254
United Way, 37
universal citizenship, 265
unobtrusive measures, 33
unwed mothers, 291
upper-middle class, 129
upward social mobility, 133
urbanization
    in Canada, 392
    city life, 394–397
    development of cities, 390–391
    global boom, 391f
    in least industrialized nations, 395
    models, 392–394, 393f
    process of, 391–392
    types of urban dwellers, 396
urban legends, 411

V

vacation, 254, 254t
validity, 36
value cluster, 59
value contradiction, 57–58
values
    Americanization of Canadian
        values, 59–60, 60t
    among Native peoples, 57
    in Canadian society, 54–60
    clash of, 59
    and culture, 51
    defined, 19
    and education, 311–313
    in Quebec, 49, 49f, 55
Vanier Institute of the Family, 306
variables, 35, 35f
Verstehen, 12

video games, 77–79
violence
    against children and youth, 302
    against the elderly, 210–211
    as entertainment, 164
    and ethnicity/race, 371
    family violence, 302–304
    feminist understanding of gender
        patterns, 165
    against gays and lesbians, 371
    and gender, 164–165
    legitimate violence, 261
    in schools, 325–326
    in sports, 359–360
    against women, 151–152, 164–165,
        303, 371
virtual organizations, 234–235
virtual present, 21
Volkswagen, 254
voluntarism, 225, 228–229
voluntary organizations, 224–226
voting, 265t, 266t

W

Walmart, 106, 121, 229–230
Walmartization, 219–220
war, 274–275, 330
The War Amps, 224
War Measures Act, 271
watchqueen, 41
wealth
    defined, 117
    income, 119f, 119–121, 120f, 121t
    lottery wins, 123
    property, 117–119
Weber, Max
    and modernity, 20
    on property, prestige, and
        power, 115–116
    on rationalization of society, 215–216
    on religion and capitalism, 332–333
    theories of, 10–11
    updated model, 128–130
    and *Verstehen*, 12
weight loss, 3–4
welfare, 137
welfare capitalism, 243–244
Western Electric Company, 34
Western perspective, 311
white-collar crime, 369–370
Whitefeather, 172
Whitehead, Mary Beth, 163
women
    and aging, 204–205
    and automobiles, 422
    and body image, 4, 204, 205
    and bureaucracies, 227
    in business, 252
    in China, 152
    early women sociolgists, 15
    and education, 310, 316
    feminism, 153–154, 248–249
    feminist theories. *see* feminist theories
    and globalization, 96–97
    and global stratification, 115
    and housework, 285–287

PHOTO CREDITS

Esther Shannon; **366** Courtesy of MADD; **369 (Top)** THE CANADIAN PRESS/Graham Hughes; **369 (Bottom)** Dick Loek / GetStock.com; **375** Corbis; **377** Fotolia/wrangler

CHAPTER 17

382 Shutterstock/jokerpro; **384** © Amoret Tanner / Alamy; **386 (Left)** Landov; **386 (Right)** James M. Henslin; **387** © Alain Le Garsmeur/ CORBIS; **390** © Sol Neelman/Corbis; **391** age fotostock / SuperStock; **394** © Image Source / Alamy; **395** © Deniscristo/ Dreamstime.com; **400** ASSOCIATED PRESS

CHAPTER 18

405 © Lentolo | Dreamstime.com; **406** The Canadian Press Images-Mario Beauregar; **407** CP PHOTO/Chuck Stoody; **410** © WizData,inc. / Alamy; **413 (Left)** Glenbow Archives NC-6-1746/ McDermid Studio; **413 (Right)** CP PHOTO/Tony Caldwell; **414** © ZUMA Press, Inc. / Alamy; **415** CP PHOTO/Adrian Wyld; **416** CP PHOTO/Shaney Komulainen; **421 (Left)** © CORBIS; **421 (Right)** Landov; **422** The Computer Museum History Center/Model photo Dennis Bourke; **423** Shizuo Kambayashi / ASSOCIATED PRESS

LITERARY CREDITS

CHAPTER 2

39 Canadian Student Survey: Next Steps: Upper-Year Canadian PSE Students' Future Plans and Debt, Canadian Alliance of Student Associations, March 2010, pg.29

CHAPTER 3

60 "The Nation's Mood," Maclean's, December 27, 2004

CHAPTER 9

206 "Mandatory retirement fades in Canada" CBC News, February 21, 2008

CHAPTER 11

241 Adapted from Carol Goar, Editorial Board, The Toronto Star www.thestar.com/ article/202587

CHAPTER 12

266 Elections Canada. Calculations and adaptation rest with the authors

CHAPTER 16

368 "From Not a Kid Anymore, Canadian Youth, Crime, and Subcultures," by G. O'Bireck, PhD. © 1996. Reprinted with the permission of Nelson, a division of Thomson Learning: www.thomsonlearning.com